Lecture Notes in Computer Science 5935

Commenced Publication in 1973
Founding and Former Series Editors:
Gerhard Goos, Juris Hartmanis, and Jan van Leeuwen

T0181166

Krishna Kant   Sriram V. Pemmaraju
Krishna M. Sivalingam   Jie Wu (Eds.)

Distributed Computing and Networking

11th International Conference, ICDCN 2010
Kolkata, India, January 3-6, 2010
Proceedings

 Springer

Volume Editors

Krishna Kant
National Science Foundation
Arlington VA 22130, USA
E-mail: krishna.kant@intel.com

Sriram V. Pemmaraju
The University of Iowa
Department of Computer Science
Iowa City, IA 52242-1419, USA
E-mail: sriram@cs.uiowa.edu

Krishna M. Sivalingam
Indian Institute of Technology (IIT)
Department of Computer Science and Engineering
Madras, Chennai 600036, India
E-mail: kristhri@gmail.com

Jie Wu
Temple University
Department of Computer and Information Science
Philadelphia, PA 119122, USA
E-mail: jiewu13@yahoo.com

Library of Congress Control Number: 2009941694

CR Subject Classification (1998): C.2, E.3, C.4, D.2.8, D.2, F.2, D.1.3, H.2.8, E.1

LNCS Sublibrary: SL 1 – Theoretical Computer Science and General Issues

ISSN   0302-9743
ISBN-10   3-642-11321-4 Springer Berlin Heidelberg New York
ISBN-13   978-3-642-11321-5 Springer Berlin Heidelberg New York

springer.com

© Springer-Verlag Berlin Heidelberg 2010
Printed in Germany

Typesetting: Camera-ready by author, data conversion by Scientific Publishing Services, Chennai, India
Printed on acid-free paper   SPIN: 12827701   06/3180   5 4 3 2 1 0

Message from the General Chairs

As General Chairs it is our pleasure to welcome you to the proceedings of ICDCN 2010, the 11th International Conference on Distributed Computing and Networking. This series of events started as the International Workshop on Distributed Computing (IWDC) in the year 2000. In view of the growing number of papers both in distributed computing and networking, and the natural synergy between the two areas, in 2006 the workshop series assumed its current name. Since then the conference has grown steadily in its reach and stature. The conference has attracted quality submissions and top speakers annually in the areas of distributed computing and networking from all over the world, thereby strengthening the connection between research in India, which has been on the rise, and the rest of the world. After a foray into Central India in the year 2009, this year the conference returned to the city of Kolkata.

ICDCN continues to be a top-class conference due to the dedicated and tireless work put in by the volunteers who organize it each year. This year again, the General Chairs were honored to work with a truly superb team who basically left us with very little to do!

A good conference is known by its technical program, and this year's program was in the able hands of a Program Committee chaired by Krishna Sivalingam and Jie Wu (Networking Track), and Krishna Kant and Sriram Pemmaraju (Distributed Computing track). There were 169 submissions, 96 to the networking track and 73 to the distributed computing track. After a rigorous review process, the committee selected 23 papers for the networking track, and 21 for the distributed computing track (16 regular, 5 short).

We would like to thank the Keynote Chair, Sajal Das, for organizing an excellent invited program. This year's keynote speakers are Prith Banerjee, Senior VP of Research, and Director HP Labs, Prabhakar Raghavan, Head of Yahoo! Labs, and Manish Gupta, Associate Director, IBM India Research Labs. The Prof. A.K. Choudhury Memorial Lecture was delivered by Sartaj Sahni, Distinguished Professor and Chair of Computer Science, University of Florida and Ashok Jhunjhunwala, the head of the Telecommunications and Computer Networks group at IIT Madras gave an invited lecture.

This year's tutorial topics included: Vehicular Communications: Standards, Protocols, Applications and Technical Challenges, by Rajeev Shorey; Informative Labeling Schemes, by Amos Korman; Middleware for Pervasive Computing, by Jiannong Cao; Secure Distributed Computing, by C. Pandurangan; Next Generation of Transportation Systems, Distributed Computing, and Data Mining, by Hillol Kargupta; Peer-to-Peer Storage Systems: Crowdsourcing the Storage Cloud, by Anwitaman Datta. We thank the Tutorial Co-chairs, Gopal Pandurangan, Violet R. Syrotiuk, and Samiran Chattopadhyaya, for their efforts in putting together this excellent tutorial program.

We would like to thank Sriram Pemmaraju who, as Publication Chair, dealt with the many details of putting the proceedings together, and the Publicity Chair, Arobinda Gupta, for doing a good job of getting the word out about the event this year. Our Industry Chairs, Sanjoy Paul and Rajeev Shorey, helped keep everyone's feet on the ground! Our congratulations to them for organizing a "cutting-edge" industry session with a set of esteemed panelists and speakers from the booming IT sector in India. This year, ICDCN also hosted a PhD Forum to encourage PhD students in India and abroad to present and discuss their research with peers in their fields. Thanks to Indranil Sengupta and Mainak Chatterjee for making this happen. Special thanks go out to the Organizing Co-chairs Devadatta Sinha, University of Calcutta, Nabendu Chaki, University of Calcutta, and Chandan Bhattacharyya, Techno India, Salt Lake, and to the Finance Chair, Sanjit Setua, University of Calcutta, for having done a marvelous job of taking care of all the nitty-gritty details of the conference organization.

The vision of the founders of this conference series, Sajal Das and Sukumar Ghosh, continues to play a key role in the Steering Committee, and we hope that under their leadership the conference will continue to grow and become one of the major international research forums in distributed computing and networking.

We thank all the authors and delegates for their participation. The success of any conference is measured by the quality of the technical presentations, the discussions that ensue, and the human networking that takes place. We expect that, given the dedication and hard work of all the organizers, the conference did not fall short on any of these measures.

January 2010   Anurag Kumar
                                                        Michel Raynal

Message from the Technical Program Chairs

Welcome to the proceedings of the 11th International Conference on Distributed Computing and Networking (ICDCN 2010). ICDCN enters its second decade as an important forum for disseminating the latest research results in distributed computing and networking.

We received 169 submissions from all over the world, including Brazil, Canada, China, France, Germany, Hong Kong, Iran, The Netherlands, Switzerland, and the USA, besides India, the host country. The submissions were carefully read and evaluated by the Program Committee, which consisted of 43 members for the Networking Track and 34 members for the Distributed Computing Track, with the additional help of external reviewers. The Program Committee selected 39 regular papers and 5 short papers for inclusion in the proceedings and presentation at the conference. The resulting technical program covers a broad swath of both distributed computing and networking. The networking track contains papers on wireless, sensor, mobile, and ad-hoc networks and on network protocols for scheduling, coverage, routing, etc., whereas the distributed computing track contains papers on fault-tolerance, security, distributed algorithms, and the theory of distributed systems.

While the technical program forms the core of the conference, this year's ICDCN was rich with many other exciting events. We were fortunate to have several distinguished scientists as keynote speakers and we had a strong tutorial program preceding the official start of the conference. In addition, we had a fabulous industry session that has the potential of strengthening research ties between academics and the industry. Finally, this year ICDCN hosted a PhD forum whose aim was to connect student researchers with peers as well as experienced researchers.

We thank all those who submitted a paper to ICDCN 2010 for their interest. We thank the Program Committee members and external reviewers for their careful reviews despite a tight schedule.

January 2010

Krishna Kant
Sriram V. Pemmaraju
Krishna M. Sivalingam
Jie Wu

Organization

ICDCN 2010 was organized by the University of Calcutta, Department of Computer Science and Engineering in collaboration with the Techno India Group, Salt Lake.

General Chairs

Michel Raynal	Institut de Recherche en Informatique et Systèmes Aléatoires (IRISA)
Anurag Kumar	Indian Institute of Science (IISc), Bangalore

Program Chairs: Networking Track

Krishna M. Sivalingam	Indian Institute of Technology (IIT) Madras
Jie Wu	Temple University

Program Chairs: Distributed Computing Track

Krishna Kant	Intel and National Science Foundation (NSF)
Sriram V. Pemmaraju	The University of Iowa

Keynote Chair

Sajal K. Das	University of Texas at Arlington and National Science Foundation (NSF)

Tutorial Chairs

Gopal Pandurangan	Purdue University
Violet R. Syrotiuk	Arizona State University
Samiran Chattopadhyaya	Jadavpur University, Kolkata, India

Publication Chair

Sriram V. Pemmaraju	The University of Iowa

Publicity Chair

Arobinda Gupta	Indian Institute of Technology, Kharagpur

Industry Chairs

Sanjoy Paul   Infosys, India
Rajeev Shorey   NIIT University, India

Finance Chair

Sanjit Setua   University of Calcutta

Organizing Committee Chairs

Devadatta Sinha   University of Calcutta
Nabendu Chaki   University of Calcutta
Chandan Bhattacharyya   Techno India, Salt Lake

Steering Committee

Pradip K. Das   Mody Institute of Technology and Science,
                                  Jaipur, India
Sajal K. Das   The University of Texas at Arlington, USA and
                                  National Science Foundation (NSF) (Co-chair)
Vijay Garg   IBM India and Univ. of Texas at Austin, USA
Sukumar Ghosh   University of Iowa, USA (Co-chair)
Anurag Kumar   Indian Institute of Science, Bangalore, India
David Peleg   Weizman Institute of Science, Israel
Michel Raynal   Institut de Recherche en Informatique et
                                  Systèmes Aléatoires (IRISA), France
Indranil Sengupta   Indian Inst. of Tech., Kharagpur, India
Bhabani Sinha   Indian Statistical Institute, Kolkata, India

Program Committee: Networking Track

Alessandro Puiatti   SUPSI-DTI, Switzerland
Anil Vullikanti   Virginia Tech (VPI), USA
Arzad Kherani   GM India Science Lab, India
Biplab Sikdar   RPI, USA
David Kotz   Dartmouth College, USA
David Simplot-Ryl   INRIA Lille, France
Deep Medhi   University of Missouri - Kansas City, USA
Deva Seetharam   IBM, India
Falko Dressler   University of Erlangen, Germany
Gaurav Raina   IIT Madras, India
Guohong Cao   Pennsylvania State University, USA

Program Committee: Distributed Computing Track

Kishore Kothapalli   IIIT Hyderabad, India
Krishnamurthy Vidyasankar   Memorial University of Newfoundland, Canada
Maria Potop-Butucaru   University Pierre and Marie Curie (Paris 6),
                                        France
Mark Tuttle   Intel, USA
Neeraj Mittal   The University of Texas at Dallas, USA
Philippas Tsigas   Chalmers University, Sweden
Pierre Fraigniaud   CNRS, France
Prasad Jayanti   Dartmouth College, USA
Rajkumar Buyya   The University of Melbourne, Australia
Roger Wattenhofer   ETH Zurich, Switzerland
Rong Zheng   University of Houston, USA
Sanjay Ranka   University of Florida, USA
Sanjoy Paul   InfoSys Technologies, India
Sebastien Tixeuil   LIP6 & INRIA Grand Large, France
Sergio Rajsbaum   UNAM, Mexico
Shlomi Dolev   Ben-Gurion University, Israel
Soma Chaudhuri   Iowa State University, USA
Stephan Eidenbenz   Los Alamos National Labs, USA
Sukumar Ghosh   The University of Iowa, USA
Tao Xie   San Diego State University, USA
Thomas Moscibroda   Microsoft Research, USA
Umakishore Ramachandran   Georgia Tech, USA
Vijay Garg   University of Texas, USA
Winston Seah   Institute for Infocomm Research, Singapore
Yehuda Afek   Tel Aviv University, Israel

Additional Referees: Networking Track

Amin Ali   James Joshi   Krishna Ramachandran
Swapnil Bhatia   Aditya Karnik   Glenn Robertson
Debojyoti Bhattacharya   R.M. Karthik   Naveen Santhapuri
Chiara Boldrini   Kim Kyunghwi   Mukundan
Swastik Brahma   Ming Li   Venkataraman
Raffaele Bruno   Qinghu Li   T. Venkatesh
Ning Cao   Tobias Limmer   S. Sree Vivek
Surendar Chandra   Changlei Liu   Guojun Wang
Saptarshi Debroy   Salahuddin Masum   Wenjing Wang
S. Sharmila Deva Selvi   Somnath Mitra   Zhenyu Yang
Juergen Eckert   Skanda Muthaiah   Eiko Yoneki
Wei Gao   Andrea Passarella   Shucheng Yu
Chase Gray   Chuan Qin
Santanu Guha   Venkatesh R.

Additional Referees: Distributed Computing Track

Yaniv Altshuler
Bharath
  Balasubramanian
Sumit Bose
Hana Chockler
Peter Chong
Jorge Cobb
Reetuparna Das
Atish Das Sarma
Sergei Frenkel
Nurit Galoz
David Hilley
Shiva Kasiviswanathan

Idit Keidar
Maleq Khan
Rajnish Kumar
Dave Lillethun
Thomas Locher
Remo Meier
Dushmanta Mohapatra
Yoram Moses
Rajarathnam Nallusamy
Danupon Nanongkai
Gal-Oz Nurit
Dmitri Perelman
Olivier Peres

Ravi Prakash
Frankel Sergey
Junsuk Shin
Benjamin Sigg
Vishak Sivakumar
Jasmin Smula
Arun Somasundara
Christian Sommer
Hwee-Pink Tan
Amitabh Trehan
Zigi Walter

Table of Contents

Keynotes

An Intelligent IT Infrastructure for the Future 1
  Prith Banerjee

Heavy Tails and Models for the Web and Social Networks 2
  Prabhakar Raghavan

Data Structures and Algorithms for Packet Forwarding and
Classification: Prof. A.K. Choudhury Memorial Lecture 3
  Sartaj Sahni

Spoken Web: A Parallel Web for the Masses: Industry Keynote 4
  Manish Gupta

India's Mobile Revolution and the Unfinished Tasks: Invited Lecture ... 5
  Ashok Jhunjhunwala

Network Protocols and Applications

Scheduling in Multi-Channel Wireless Networks 6
  Vartika Bhandari and Nitin H. Vaidya

Email Shape Analysis 18
  Paul Sroufe, Santi Phithakkitnukoon, Ram Dantu, and
  João Cangussu

Maintaining Safety in Interdomain Routing with Hierarchical
Path-Categories 30
  Jorge A. Cobb

Fault-tolerance and Security

On Communication Complexity of Secure Message Transmission in
Directed Networks 42
  Arpita Patra, Ashish Choudhary, and C. Pandu Rangan

On Composability of Reliable Unicast and Broadcast 54
  Anuj Gupta, Sandeep Hans, Kannan Srinathan, and
  C. Pandu Rangan

A Leader-Free Byzantine Consensus Algorithm 67
  Fatemeh Borran and André Schiper

Authenticated Byzantine Generals in Dual Failure Model   79
    Anuj Gupta, Prasant Gopal, Piyush Bansal, and Kannan Srinathan

Sensor Networks

Mission-Oriented k-Coverage in Mobile Wireless Sensor Networks   92
    Habib M. Ammari and Sajal K. Das

Lessons from the Sparse Sensor Network Deployment in Rural India   104
    *T.V. Prabhakar, H.S. Jamadagni, Amar Sahu, and
    R. Venkatesha Prasad*

A New Architecture for Hierarchical Sensor Networks with Mobile Data
Collectors   116
    Ataul Bari, Ying Chen, Arunita Jaekel, and Subir Bandyopadhyay

Stability Analysis of Multi-hop Routing in Sensor Networks with
Mobile Sinks   128
    Jayanthi Rao and Subir Biswas

Distributed Algorithms and Optimization

Optimizing Distributed Computing Workflows in Heterogeneous
Network Environments   142
    Yi Gu and Qishi Wu

Radio Network Distributed Algorithms in the Unknown Neighborhood
Model   155
    Bilel Derbel and El-Ghazali Talbi

Probabilistic Self-stabilizing Vertex Coloring in Unidirectional
Anonymous Networks   167
    *Samuel Bernard, Stéphane Devismes, Katy Paroux,
    Maria Potop-Butucaru, and Sébastien Tixeuil*

A Token-Based Solution to the Group Mutual l-Exclusion Problem in
Message Passing Distributed Systems (Short Paper)   178
    Abhishek Swaroop and Awadhesh Kumar Singh

Peer-to-Peer Networks and Network Tracing

The Weak Network Tracing Problem   184
    H.B. Acharya and M.G. Gouda

Poisoning the Kad Network   195
    *Thomas Locher, David Mysicka, Stefan Schmid, and
    Roger Wattenhofer*

Credit Reputation Propagation: A Strategy to Curb Free-Riding in a
Large BitTorrent Swarm   207
      Suman Paul, Subrata Nandi, and Ajit Pal

Formal Understanding of the Emergence of Superpeer Networks: A
Complex Network Approach   219
      *Bivas Mitra, Abhishek Kumar Dubey, Sujoy Ghose, and
      Niloy Ganguly*

Parallel and Distributed Systems

Parallelization of the Lanczos Algorithm on Multi-core Platforms   231
      Souvik Bhattacherjee and Abhijit Das

Supporting Malleability in Parallel Architectures with Dynamic
CPUSETs Mapping and Dynamic MPI   242
      *Márcia C. Cera, Yiannis Georgiou, Olivier Richard,
      Nicolas Maillard, and Philippe O.A. Navaux*

Impact of Object Operations and Relationships on Concurrency
Control in DOOS (Short Paper)   258
      V. Geetha and Niladhuri Sreenath

Causal Cycle Based Communication Pattern Matching (Short Paper) . . .   265
      Himadri Sekhar Paul

Wireless Networks

Channel Assignment in Virtual Cut-through Switching Based Wireless
Mesh Networks   271
      Dola Saha, Aveek Dutta, Dirk Grunwald, and Douglas Sicker

Efficient Multi-hop Broadcasting in Wireless Networks Using k-Shortest
Path Pruning   283
      Michael Q. Rieck and Subhankar Dhar

Bandwidth Provisioning in Infrastructure-Based Wireless Networks
Employing Directional Antennas   295
      *Shiva Kasiviswanathan, Bo Zhao, Sudarshan Vasudevan, and
      Bhuvan Urgaonkar*

ROTIO+: A Modified ROTIO for Nested Network Mobility   307
      Ansuman Sircar, Bhaskar Sardar, and Debashis Saha

Applications of Distributed Systems

VirtualConnection: Opportunistic Networking for Web on Demand   323
      Lateef Yusuf and Umakishore Ramachandran

Video Surveillance with PTZ Cameras: The Problem of Maximizing
Effective Monitoring Time 341
  Satyajit Banerjee, Atish Datta Chowdhury, and Subhas Kumar Ghosh

DisClus: A Distributed Clustering Technique over High Resolution
Satellite Data 353
  Sauravjyoti Sarmah and Dhruba Kumar Bhattacharyya

Performance Evaluation of a Wormhole-Routed Algorithm for Irregular
Mesh NoC Interconnect 365
  Arshin Rezazadeh, Ladan Momeni, and Mahmood Fathy

Optical, Cellular and Mobile Ad Hoc Networks

Dynamic Multipath Bandwidth Provisioning with Jitter, Throughput,
SLA Constraints in MPLS over WDM Network 376
  Palash Dey, Arkadeep Kundu, Mrinal K. Naskar,
  Amitava Mukherjee, and Mita Nasipuri

Path Protection in Translucent WDM Optical Networks 392
  Q. Rahman, Subir Bandyopadhyay, Ataul Bari, Arunita Jaekel, and
  Y.P. Aneja

Post Deployment Planning of 3G Cellular Networks through Dual
Homing of NodeBs 404
  Samir K. Sadhukhan, Swarup Mandal, Partha Bhaumik, and
  Debashis Saha

K-Directory Community: Reliable Service Discovery in MANET 420
  Vaskar Raychoudhury, Jiannong Cao, Weigang Wu, Yi Lai,
  Canfeng Chen, and Jian Ma

Theory of Distributed Systems

An Online, Derivative-Free Optimization Approach to Auto-tuning of
Computing Systems 434
  Sudheer Poojary, Ramya Raghavendra, and D. Manjunath

Consistency-Driven Probabilistic Quorum System Construction for
Improving Operation Availability 446
  Kinga Kiss Iakab, Christian Storm, and Oliver Theel

Hamiltonicity of a General OTIS Network (Short Paper) 459
  Nagendra Kumar, Rajeev Kumar, Dheeresh K. Mallick, and
  Prasanta K. Jana

Specifying Fault-Tolerance Using Split Precondition Logic
(Short Paper) 466
  Awadhesh Kumar Singh and Anup Kumar Bandyopadhyay

Network Protocols

Fast BGP Convergence Following Link/Router Failure 473
  Swapan Kumar Ray and Susmit Shannigrahi

On Using Network Tomography for Overlay Availability 485
  Umesh Bellur and Mahak Patidar

QoSBR: A Quality Based Routing Protocol for Wireless Mesh
Networks 497
  Amitangshu Pal, Sandeep Adimadhyam, and Asis Nasipuri

An ACO Based Approach for Detection of an Optimal Attack Path in
a Dynamic Environment 509
  Nirnay Ghosh, Saurav Nanda, and S.K. Ghosh

Author Index 521

An Intelligent IT Infrastructure for the Future

Prith Banerjee

HP Labs, Hewlett Packard Corporation
prith.banerjee@hp.com

Abstract. The proliferation of new modes of communication and collaboration has resulted in an explosion of digital information. To turn this challenge into an opportunity, the IT industry will have to develop novel ways to acquire, store, process, and deliver information to customers - wherever, however, and whenever they need it. An "Intelligent IT Infrastructure," which can deliver extremely high performance, adaptability and security - will be the backbone of these developments. At HP Labs, the central research arm for Hewlett Packard, we are taking a multidisciplinary approach to this problem by spanning four areas: computing, storage, networking and nanotechnology. We are working on the design of an exascale data center that will provide 1000X performance while enhancing availability, manageability and reliability and reducing the power and cooling costs. We are working on helping the transition to effective parallel and distributed computing by developing the software tools to allow application developers to harness parallelism at various levels. We are building a cloud-scale, intelligent storage system that is massively scalable, resilient to failures, self-managed and enterprise-grade. We are designing an open, programmable wired and wireless network platform that will make the introduction of new features quick, easy and cost-effective. Finally, we are making fundamental breakthroughs in nanotechnology - memristors, photonic interconnects, and sensors - that will revolutionize the way data is collected, stored and transmitted. To support the design of such an intelligent IT infrastructure, we will have to develop sophisticated system-level design automation tools that will tradeoff system-level performance, power, cost and efficiency.

K. Kant et al. (Eds.): ICDCN 2010, LNCS 5935, p. 1, 2010.
© Springer-Verlag Berlin Heidelberg 2010

Heavy Tails and Models for the Web and Social Networks

Prabhakar Raghavan

Yahoo! Labs
pragh@yahoo-inc.com

Abstract. The literature is rich with (re)discoveries of power law phenomena; this is especially true of observations of link and traffic behavior on the Web. We survey the origins of these phenomena and several (yet incomplete) attempts to model them, including our recent work on the compressibility of the Web graph and social networks. We then present a number of open problems in Web research arising from these observations.

K. Kant et al. (Eds.): ICDCN 2010, LNCS 5935, p. 2, 2010.
© Springer-Verlag Berlin Heidelberg 2010

Data Structures and Algorithms for Packet Forwarding and Classification:
Prof. A.K. Choudhury Memorial Lecture

Sartaj Sahni

Computer and Information Science and Engineering Department
University of Florida
sahni@cise.ufl.edu

Abstract. Packet forwarding and classification at Internet speed is a challenging task. We review the data structures that have been proposed for the forwarding and classification of Internet packets. Data structures for both one-dimensional and multidimensional classification as well as for static and dynamic rule tables are reviewed. Sample structures include multibit one- and two-dimensional tries and hybrid shape shifting tries. Hardware assisted solutions such as Ternary Content Addressable Memories also are reviewed.

K. Kant et al. (Eds.): ICDCN 2010, LNCS 5935, p. 3, 2010.
© Springer-Verlag Berlin Heidelberg 2010

Spoken Web: A Parallel Web for the Masses: Industry Keynote

Manish Gupta

IBM Research, India
mgupta@us.ibm.com

Abstract. In India and several other countries, the number of mobile phone sub-scribers far exceeds the number of personal computer users, and continues to grow at a much faster pace (it has already crossed the 450 million mark in India). We will present Spoken Web, an attempt to create a new world wide web, accessible over the telephone network, for the masses in these countries. The Spoken Web is based on the concepts of Hyperspeech and Hyperspeech Transfer Protocol that allow creation of "VoiceSites" and traversal of "VoiceLinks". We describe a simple voice-driven application, which allows people, without any information technology background, to create, host, and access such VoiceSites, and traverse VoiceLinks, using a voice interface over the telephone. We present our experience from pilots conducted in villages in Andhra Pradesh and Gujarat. These pilots demonstrate the ease with which a semi-literate and non-IT savvy population can create VoiceSites with locally relevant content, including schedule of education/training classes, agicultural information, and professional services, and their strong interest in accessing this information over the telephone network. We describe several outstanding challenges and opportunities in creating and using a Spoken Web for facilitating exchange of information and conducting business transactions.

K. Kant et al. (Eds.): ICDCN 2010, LNCS 5935, p. 4, 2010.
© Springer-Verlag Berlin Heidelberg 2010

India's Mobile Revolution and the Unfinished Tasks: Invited Lecture

Ashok Jhunjhunwala

IIT Madras, Chennai, India
ashok@tenet.res.in

Abstract. India has made great strides in use of Mobile telephones in recent years. Adding over 10 million phones a month, it is the fastest growing market today. The cell-phones are quickly reaching the deepest parts of the nation and serving the poorest people. The talk will examine what made this possible. It will also focus on what the unfinished telecom tasks for India are. It will examine what India is doing in terms of providing Broadband wireless connectivity to its people; what it is doing towards R&D and technology development in the county; and how it aims at building global telecom manufacturing and telecom operation companies in India.

Scheduling in Multi-Channel Wireless Networks[*]

Vartika Bhandari[**] and Nitin H. Vaidya

University of Illinois at Urbana-Champaign, USA
vartikab@acm.org, nhv@illinois.edu

Abstract. The availability of multiple orthogonal channels in a wireless network can lead to substantial performance improvement by alleviating contention and interference. However, this also gives rise to non-trivial channel coordination issues. The situation is exacerbated by variability in the achievable data-rates across channels and links. Thus, scheduling in such networks may require substantial information-exchange and lead to non-negligible overhead. This provides a strong motivation for the study of scheduling algorithms that can operate with *limited information* while still providing acceptable worst-case performance guarantees. In this paper, we make an effort in this direction by examining the scheduling implications of multiple channels and heterogeneity in channel-rates. We establish lower bounds on the performance of a class of *maximal* schedulers. We first demonstrate that when the underlying scheduling mechanism is "imperfect", the presence of multiple orthogonal channels can help alleviate the detrimental impact of the imperfect scheduler, and yield a significantly better efficiency-ratio in a wide range of network topologies. We then establish performance bounds for a scheduler that can achieve a good efficiency-ratio in the presence of channels with heterogeneous rates without requiring explicit exchange of queue-information. Our results indicate that it may be possible to achieve a desirable trade-off between performance and information.

1 Introduction

Appropriate scheduling policies are of utmost importance in achieving good throughput characteristics in a wireless network. The seminal work of Tassiulas and Ephremides yielded a *throughput-optimal* scheduler, which can schedule all "feasible" traffic flows without resulting in unbounded queues [8]. However, such an optimal scheduler is difficult to implement in practice. Hence, various imperfect scheduling strategies that trade-off throughput for simplicity have been proposed in [5,9,10,7], amongst others.

The availability of multiple orthogonal channels in a wireless network can potentially lead to substantial performance improvement by alleviating contention and interference. However, this also gives rise to non-trivial channel coordination issues. The situation is exacerbated by variability in the achievable data-rates across channels and links. Computing an optimal schedule, even in a single-channel network, is almost always intractable, due to the need for global information, as well as the computational complexity. However, imperfect schedulers requiring limited *local* information can typically be designed,

---

[*] This research was supported in part by NSF grant CNS 06-27074, US Army Research Office grant W911NF-05-1-0246, and a Vodafone Graduate Fellowship.
[**] Vartika Bhandari is now with Google Inc.

K. Kant et al. (Eds.): ICDCN 2010, LNCS 5935, pp. 6–17, 2010.
© Springer-Verlag Berlin Heidelberg 2010

which provide acceptable worst-case (and typically much better average case) performance degradation compared to the optimal. In a multi-channel network, the local information exchange required by even an imperfect scheduler can be quite prohibitive as information may be needed on a per-channel basis. For instance, Lin and Rasool [4] have described a scheduling algorithm for multi-channel multi-radio wireless networks that requires information about *per-channel* queues at all interfering links.

This provides a strong motivation for the study of scheduling algorithms that can operate with limited information, while still providing acceptable worst-case performance guarantees. In this paper, we make an effort in this direction, by examining the scheduling implications of multiple channels, and heterogeneity in channel-rates. We establish lower bounds on performance of a class of *maximal* schedulers, and describe some schedulers that require limited information-exchange between nodes. Some of the bounds presented here improve on bounds developed in past work [4].

We begin by analyzing the performance of a centralized greedy maximal scheduler. A lower bound for this scheduler was established in [4]. However, in a large variety of network topologies, the lower bound can be quite loose. Thus is particularly true for multi-channel networks with single interface nodes. We establish an alternative bound that is tighter in a range of topologies. *Our results indicate that when the underlying scheduling mechanism is imperfect, the presence of multiple orthogonal channels can help alleviate the impact of the imperfect scheduler, and yield a significantly better efficiency-ratio in a wide range of scenarios..*

We then consider the possibility of achieving efficiency-ratio comparable to the centralized greedy maximal scheduler using a simpler scheduler that works with limited information. We establish results for a class of maximal schedulers coupled with local queue-loading rules that do not require queue-information from interfering nodes.

2   Preliminaries

We consider a multi-hop wireless network. For simplicity, we largely limit our discussion to nodes equipped with a single half-duplex radio-interface capable of tuning to any one available channel at any given time. All interfaces in the network have identical capabilities, and may switch between the available channels if desired. Many of the presented results can also be used to obtain results for the case when each node is equipped with multiple interfaces; we briefly discuss this issue.

The wireless network is viewed as a directed graph, with each directed link in the graph representing an available communication link. We model interference using a *conflict* relation between links. Two links are said to conflict with each other if it is only feasible to schedule one of the links on a certain channel at any given time. The conflict relation is assumed to be symmetric. The conflict-based interference model provides a tractable approximation of reality – while it does not capture the wireless channel precisely, it is more amenable to analysis. Such conflict-based interference models have been used frequently in the past work (e.g., [11,4]).

Time is assumed to be slotted with a slot duration of 1 unit time (i.e., we use slot duration as the time unit). In each time slot, the scheduler determines which links should transmit in that time slots, as well as the channel to be used for each such transmission.

We now introduce some notation and terminology.

The network is viewed as a collection of directed links, where each link is a pair of nodes that are capable of direct communication with non-zero rate.

- L denotes the set of directed links in the network.
- C is the set of all available orthogonal channels. Thus, $|C|$ is the number of available channels.
- We say that a scheduler schedules link-channel pair (l,c) if it schedules link l for transmission on channel c.
- r_l^c denotes the rate achievable on link l by operating link l on channel c, provided that no conflicting link is also scheduled on channel c. For simplicity, we assume that $r_l^c > 0$ for all $l \in L$ and $c \in C$.[1] The rates r_l^c do not vary with time. We also define the terms: $r_{max} = \max\limits_{l \in L, c \in C} r_l^c$, and $r_{min} = \min\limits_{l \in L, c \in C} r_l^c$. When two conflicting links are scheduled simultaneously on the same channel, both achieve rate 0.
- β_s denotes the *self-skew-ratio*, defined as the minimum ratio between rates supportable over *different* channels on a *single* link. Therefore, for any two channels c and d, and any link l, we have $\frac{r_l^d}{r_l^c} \geq \beta_s$. Note that $0 < \beta_s \leq 1$.
- β_c denotes the *cross-skew-ratio*, defined as the minimum ratio between rates supportable over the *same* channel on *different* links. Therefore, for any channel c, and any two links l and l': $\frac{r_{l'}^c}{r_l^c} \geq \beta_c$. Note that $0 < \beta_c \leq 1$.

Let $r_l = \max\limits_{c \in C} r_l^c$. Let $\sigma_s = \min\limits_{l \in L} \frac{\sum\limits_{c \in C} r_l^c}{r_l}$. Note that $\sigma_s \geq 1 + \beta_s(|C| - 1)$. Moreover, in typical scenarios, σ_s will be expected to be much larger than this worst-case bound. σ_s is largest when $\beta_s = 1$, in which case $\sigma_s = |C|$.

- $b(l)$ and $e(l)$, respectively, denotes the nodes at the two endpoints of a link. In particular, link l is directed from node $b(l)$ to node $e(l)$.
- $\mathcal{E}(b(l))$ and $\mathcal{E}(e(l))$ denote the set of links incident on nodes $b(l)$ and $e(l)$, respectively. Thus, the links in $\mathcal{E}(b(l))$ and $\mathcal{E}(e(l))$ share an endpoint with link l. Since we focus on single-interface nodes, this implies that if link l is scheduled in a certain time slot, no other link in $\mathcal{E}(b(l))$ or $\mathcal{E}(e(l))$ can be scheduled at the same time. We refer to this as an *interface conflict*. Let $\mathcal{A}(l) = \mathcal{E}(b(l)) \cup \mathcal{E}(e(l))$. Note that $l \in \mathcal{A}(l)$. Links in $\mathcal{A}(l)$ are said to be *adjacent* to link l. Links that have an interface conflict with link l are those that belong to $\mathcal{E}(b(l)) \cup \mathcal{E}(e(l)) \setminus \{l\}$. Let $A_{max} = \max\limits_{l} |\mathcal{A}(l)|$.
- $\mathbf{I}(l)$ denotes the set of links that conflict with link l when scheduled on the same channel. $\mathbf{I}(l)$ may include links that also have an interface-conflict with link l. By convention, l is considered included in $\mathbf{I}(l)$. The subset of $\mathbf{I}(l)$ comprising interfering links that are not adjacent to l is denoted by $\mathbf{I}'(l)$, i.e., $\mathbf{I}'(l) = \mathbf{I}(l) \setminus \mathcal{A}(l)$. Let $I_{max} = \max\limits_{l} |\mathbf{I}'(l)|$.
- K_l denotes the maximum number of non-adjacent links in $\mathbf{I}'(l)$ that can be scheduled on a given channel simultaneously if l is not scheduled on that channel. $K_l(|C|)$

---

[1] Though we assume that $r_l^c > 0$ for all l, c, the results can be generalized very easily to handle the case where $r_l^c = 0$ for some link-channel pairs.

denotes the maximum number of non-adjacent links in $\mathbf{I}'(l)$ that can be scheduled simultaneously using any of the $|C|$ channels (without conflicts) if l is not scheduled for transmission. Note that here we exclude links that have an interface conflict with l.

- K is the largest value of K_l over all links l, i.e., $K = \max\limits_{l} K_l$. $K_{|C|}$ is the largest value of $K_l(|C|)$ over all links l, i.e., $K_{|C|} = \max\limits_{l} K_l(|C|)$. Let $I_{max} = \max\limits_{l} |\mathbf{I}'(l)|$. It is not hard to see that for *single-interface* nodes:

$$K \leq K_{|C|} \leq \min\{K|C|, I_{max}\} \tag{1}$$

We remark that the term K as used by us is similar, but not exactly the same as the term K used in [4]. In [4], K denotes the largest number of links that may be scheduled simultaneously if some link l is not scheduled, including links adjacent to l. We exclude the adjacent links in our definition of K. Throughout this text, we will refer to the quantity defined in [4] as κ instead of K.

- Let γ_l be 0 if there are no other links adjacent to l at either endpoint of l, 1 if there are other adjacent links at only one endpoint, and 2 if there are other adjacent links at both endpoints.
- γ is the largest value of γ_l over all links l, i.e., $\gamma = \max\limits_{l} \gamma_l$.
- *Load vector*: We consider single-hop traffic, i.e., any traffic that originates at a node is destined for a next-hop node, and is transmitted over the link between the two nodes. Under this assumption, all the traffic that must traverse a given link can be treated as a single flow.

  The traffic arrival process for link l is denoted by $\{\lambda(t)\}$. The arrivals in each slot t are assumed i.i.d. with average λ_l. The average load on the network is denoted by *load* vector $\overrightarrow{\lambda} = [\lambda_1, \lambda_2, ..., \lambda_{|L|}]$, where λ_l denotes the arrival rate for the flow on link l. λ_l may possibly be 0 for some links l.
- *Queues*: The packets generated by each flow are first added to a queue maintained at the source node. Depending on the algorithm, there could be a single queue for each link, or a queue for each (link, channel) pair.
- *Stability*: The system of queues in the network is said to be stable if, for all queues Q in the network, the following is true [2]:

$$\limsup_{t \to \infty} \frac{1}{t} \sum_{\tau=1}^{t} E[q(\tau)] < \infty \tag{2}$$

where $q(\tau)$ denotes the backlog in queue Q at time τ.
- *Feasible load vector*: In each time slot, the scheduler used in the network determines which links should transmit and on which channel (recall that each link is a directed link, with a transmitter and a receiver). In different time slots, the scheduler may schedule a different set of links for transmission. A load vector is said to be *feasible*, if there exists a scheduler that can schedule transmissions to achieve stability (as defined above), when using that load vector.
- *Link rate vector*: Depending on the schedule chosen in a given slot by the scheduler, each link l will have a certain transmission rate. For instance, using our notation above, if link l is scheduled to transmit on channel c, it will have rate r_l^c (we

assume that, if the scheduler schedules link l on channel c, it does not schedule another conflicting link on that channel). Thus, the *schedule* chosen for a time-slot yields a *link rate vector* for that time slot. Note that *link rate vector* specifies rate of transmission used on each link in a certain time slot. On the other hand, *load vector* specifies the rate at which traffic is generated for each link.

- *Feasible rate region*: The set of all feasible load vectors constitutes the feasible rate-region of the network, and is denoted by Λ.

- *Throughput-optimal scheduler:* A *throughput-optimal* scheduler is one that is capable of maintaining stable queues for any load vector $\overrightarrow{\lambda}$ in the interior of Λ. For simplicity of notation, we use $\overrightarrow{\lambda} \in \Lambda$ in the rest of the text to indicate a load-vector vector λ lying in the interior of a region Λ.

    From the work of [8], it is known that a scheduler that maintains a queue for each link l, and then chooses the schedule given by $\text{argmax}_{\overrightarrow{r}} \sum_l q_l r_l$, is throughput-optimal for scenarios with single-hop traffic (q_l is the backlog in link l's queue, and the maximum is taken over all possible link rate vectors $\overrightarrow{r}$). Note that q_l is a function of time, and queue-backlogs at the start of a time slot are used above for computing the schedule (or link-rate vector) for that slot.

- *Imperfect scheduler*: It is usually difficult to determine the throughput-optimal link-rate allocations, since the problem is typically computationally intractable. Hence, there has been significant recent interest in *imperfect* scheduling policies that can be implemented efficiently. In [5], cross-layer rate-control was studied for an imperfect scheduler that chooses (in each time slot) link-rate vector $\overrightarrow{s}$ such that $\sum_l q_l s_l \geq \delta \, \text{argmax}_{\overrightarrow{r}} \sum q_l r_l$, for some constant δ ($0 < \delta \leq 1$).

    It was shown [5] that any scheduler with this property can stabilize any load-vector $\overrightarrow{\lambda} \in \delta\Lambda$. Note that if a rate vector $\overrightarrow{\lambda}$ is in Λ, then the rate vector $\delta\overrightarrow{\lambda}$ is in $\delta\Lambda$. $\delta\Lambda$ is also referred to as the δ-*reduced rate-region*. If a scheduler can stabilize all $\overrightarrow{\lambda} \in \delta\Lambda$, its *efficiency-ratio* is said to be δ.

- *Maximal scheduler*: Under our assumed interference model, a schedule is said to be maximal if (a) no two links in the schedule conflict with each other, and (b) it is not possible to add any link to the schedule without creating a conflict (either conflict due to interference, or an interface-conflict).

We will also utilize the Lyapunov-drift based stability criterion from Lemma 2 of [6].

3   Scheduling in Multi-Channel Networks

As was discussed previously, throughput-optimal scheduling is often an intractable problem even in a single-channel network. However, imperfect schedulers that achieve a fraction of the stability-region can potentially be implemented in a reasonably efficient manner. Of particular interest is the class of imperfect schedulers know as *maximal schedulers*, which we defined in Section 2. The performance of maximal schedulers under various assumptions has been studied in much recent work, e.g., [10,7], with the focus largely on single-channel wireless networks. The issue of designing a distributed scheduler that approximates a maximal scheduler has been addressed in [3], etc.

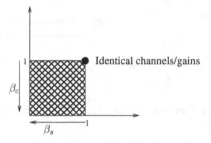

Fig. 1. 2-D visualization of channel heterogeneity

When there are multiple channels, but each node has one or few interfaces, an additional degree of complexity is added in terms of channel selection. In particular, when the link-channel rates r_l^c can be different for different links l, and channels c, the scheduling complexity is exacerbated by the fact that it is not enough to assign different channels to interfering links; for good performance, the channels must be assigned taking achievable rates into account, i.e., individual channel identities are important.

Scheduling in multi-channel multi-radio networks has been examined in [4], which argues that using a simple maximal scheduler is used in such a network could possibly lead to arbitrary degradation in efficiency-ratio (assuming arbitrary variability in rates) compared to the efficiency-ratio achieved with identical channels. A queue-loading algorithm was been proposed, in conjunction with which, a maximal scheduler can stabilize any vector in $\left(\frac{1}{\kappa+2}\right) \Lambda$, for arbitrary β_c and β_s values. This rule requires knowledge of of the length of queues at all interfering links, which can incur substantial overhead.

While variable channel gains are a real-world characteristic that cannot be ignored in designing effective protocols/algorithms, it is important that the solutions not require extensive information exchange with large overhead that offsets any performance benefit. In light of this, it is crucial to consider various points of trade-off between information and performance. In this context, the quantities β_s, β_c and σ_s defined in Section 2 prove to be useful. The quantities β_s and β_c can be viewed as two orthogonal axes for worst-case channel heterogeneity (Fig. 1). The quantity σ_s provides an aggregate (and thus averaged-out) view of heterogeneity along the β_s axis. $\beta_s = 1$ corresponds to a scenario where all channels have identical characteristics, such as bandwidth, modulation/transmission-rate, noise-levels, etc., and the link-gain is a function solely of the separation between sender and receiver. $\beta_c = 1$ corresponds to a scenario where all links have the same sender-receiver separation, and the same conditions/characteristics for any given channel, but the channels may have different characteristics, e.g., an 802.11b channel with a maximum supported data-rate of 11 Mbps, and an 802.11a channel with a maximum supported data-rate of 54 Mbps.

In this paper, we show that in a single-interface network, a simple maximal scheduler augmented with local traffic-distribution and threshold rules achieves an efficiency-ratio at least $\left(\frac{\sigma_s}{K_{|C|} + \max\{1, \gamma\} |C|}\right)$. The noteworthy features of this result are:

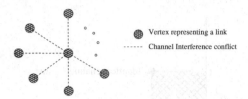

Fig. 2. Example of improved bound on efficiency ratio: link-interference topology is a star with a center link and x radial links

1. This scheduler does not require information about queues at interfering links.
2. The performance degradation (compared to the scheduler of [4]) when rates are variable, i.e., $\beta_s, \beta_c \neq 1$, is not arbitrary, and is at worst $\frac{\sigma_s}{|C|} \geq \frac{1+\beta_s(|C|-1)}{|C|} \geq \frac{1}{|C|}$. Thus, even with a purely local information based queue-loading rule, it is possible to avoid arbitrary performance degradation even in the worst case. Typically, the performance would be much better.
3. In many network scenarios, the provable lower bound of $\left(\frac{\sigma_s}{K_{|C|}+\max\{1,\gamma\}|C|} \right)$ may actually be better than $\frac{1}{\kappa+2}$. This is particularly likely to happen in networks with single-interface nodes, e.g., suppose we have three channels a,b,c with $r_l^a = 1, r_l^b = 1, r_l^c = 0.5$ for all links l. Then, in the network in Fig. 2 (where the link-interference graph is a star with x radial vertices, and there are no interface-conflicts), $K_{|C|} = x, \gamma = 0, \sigma_s = 2.5$, and we obtain a bound of $\frac{1}{0.4x+1.2}$, whereas the proved lower bound of the scheduler of [4] is $\frac{1}{x+2}$.

The multi-channel scheduling problem is further complicated if the rates r_l^c are time-varying, i.e., $r_l^c = r_l^c(t)$. However, handling such time-varying rates is beyond the scope of the results in this paper, and we address only the case where rates do not exhibit time-variation. Note that related prior work on multi-channel scheduling [4] also addresses only time-invariant rates.

4 Summary of Results

For multi-channel wireless networks with single-interface nodes, we present lower bounds on the efficiency-ratio of a class of maximal schedulers (including both centralized and distributed schedulers), which indicate that the worst-case efficiency-ratio can be higher when there are multiple channels (as compared to the single-channel case). More specifically, we show that:

– The number of links scheduled by any maximal scheduler are within at least a δ fraction of the maximum number of links activated by any feasible schedule, where:

$$\delta = \max\left\{ \frac{|C|}{K_{|C|}+\max\{1,\gamma\}|C|}, \frac{1}{\max\{1,K+\gamma\}} \right\}$$

– A centralized greedy maximal (CGM) scheduler achieves an efficiency-ratio which is at least

$\max\{\frac{\sigma_s}{K_{|C|}+\max\{1,\gamma\}|C|}, \frac{1}{\max\{1,K+\gamma\}}\}$ This constitutes an improvement over the lower bound for the CGM scheduler proved in [4]. Since $K_{|C|} \leq \min\{K|C|, I_{max}\} \leq \kappa|C|$, this new bound on efficiency-ratio can often be substantially tighter.

- We show that any maximal scheduler, in conjunction with a simple local queue-loading rule, and a threshold-based link-participation rule, achieves an efficiency-ratio of at least $\left(\frac{\sigma_s}{K_{|C|}+\max\{1,\gamma\}|C|}\right)$. This scheduler is of significant interest as it does not require information about queues at all interfering links.

Due to space constraints, proofs are omitted. Please see [1] for the proofs.

Note that the text below makes the natural assumption that two links that conflict with each other (due to interference or interface-conflict) are **not** scheduled in the same timeslot by any scheduler discussed in the rest of this paper.

5 Maximal Schedulers

We begin by presenting a result about the cardinality of the set of links scheduled by any maximal scheduler.

Theorem 1. *Let S_{opt} denote the set of links scheduled by a scheduler that seeks to maximize the number of links scheduled for transmission, and let S_{max} denote the set of links activated by any maximal scheduler. Then the following is true:*

$$|S_{max}| \geq \max\left\{\frac{|C|}{K_{|C|}+\max\{1,\gamma\}|C|}, \frac{1}{\max\{1,K+\gamma\}}\right\}|S_{opt}| \tag{3}$$

The proof is omitted due to lack of space. Please see [1].

6 Centralized Greedy Maximal Scheduler

A centralized greedy maximal (CGM) scheduler operates in the manner described below.

In each timeslot:

1. Calculate link weights $w_l^c = q_l r_l^c$ for all links l and channels c.
2. Sort the link-channel pairs (l, c) in non-increasing order of w_l^c.
3. Add the first link-channel pair in the sorted list (i.e., the one with highest weight) to the schedule for the timeslot, and remove from the list all link-channel pairs that are no longer feasible (due to either interface or interference conflicts).
4. Repeat step 3 until the list is exhausted (i.e., no more links can be added to the schedule).

In [4], it was shown that this centralized greedy maximal (CGM) scheduler can achieve an approximation-ratio which is at least $\left(\frac{1}{\kappa+2}\right)$ in a multi-channel multi-radio network, where κ is the maximum number of links conflicting with a link l that may possibly be scheduled concurrently when l is not scheduled. This bound holds for arbitrary values of β_s and β_c, and variable number of interfaces per node.

However, this bound can be quite loose in multi-channel wireless networks where each device has one or few interfaces.

In this section, we prove an improved bound on the efficiency-ratio achievable with the CGM scheduler for *single-interface* nodes. We also briefly discuss how it can be used to obtain a bound for multi-interface nodes.

Theorem 2. *Let S_{opt} denote the set of links activated by an optimal scheduler that chooses a set of link-channel pairs (l,c) for transmission such that $\sum w_l^c$ is maximized.*

Let $c^*(l)$ denote the channel assigned to link $l \in S_{opt}$ by this optimal scheduler.

Let S_g denote the set of links activated by the centralized greedy maximal (CGM) scheduler, and let $c^g(l)$ denote the channel assigned to a link $l \in S_g$.

Then:

$$\frac{\sum_{l \in S_g} w_l^{c^g(l)}}{\sum_{l \in S_{opt}} w_l^{c^*(l)}} \geq \max\left\{\frac{\sigma_s}{K_{|C|} + \max\{1,\gamma\}|C|}, \frac{1}{\max\{1,K+\gamma\}}\right\} \qquad (4)$$

The proof is omitted due to lack of space. Please see [1].

Theorem 2 leads to the following result:

Theorem 3. *The centralized greedy maximal (CGM) scheduler can stabilize the δ-reduced rate-region, where:*

$$\delta = \max\left\{\frac{\sigma_s}{K_{|C|} + \max\{1,\gamma\}|C|}, \frac{1}{\max\{1,K+\gamma\}}\right\}$$

Proof. We earlier discussed a result from [5] that any scheduler, which chooses rate-allocation $\vec{s}$ such that $\sum q_l s_l \geq \delta$ argmax $\sum q_l r_l$, can stabilize the δ-reduced rate-region. Using Theorem 2 and this result, we obtain the above result.

We remark that the above bound is independent of β_c.

6.1 Multiple Interfaces per Node

We now describe how the result can be extended to networks where each node may have more than one interface.

Given the original network *node-graph* $G = (V,E)$, construct the following transformed graph $G' = (V',E')$:

For each node $v \in V$, if v has m_v interfaces, create m_v nodes $v_1, v_2, ... v_{m_v}$ in V'. For each edge $(u,v) \in E$, where u,v have m_u, m_v interfaces respectively, create edges $(u_i,v_j), 1 \leq i \leq m_u, 1 \leq j \leq m_v$, and set $q_{(u_i,v_j)} = q_{(u,v)}$. Set the achievable channel rate appropriately for each edge in E' and each channel. For example, assuming that the channel-rate is solely a function of u,v and c, then: for each channel c, set $r^c_{(u_i,v_j)} = r^c_{(u,v)}$.

The transformed graph G' comprises only single-interface links, and thus Theorem 2 applies to it. Moreover, it is not hard to see that a schedule that maximizes $\sum q_l r_l$ in G' also maximizes $\sum q_l r_l$ in G. Thus, the efficiency-ratio from Theorem 2 for network graph G' yields an efficiency-ratio for the performance of the CGM scheduler in the multi-interface network.

We briefly touch upon how one would expect the ratio to vary as the number of interfaces at each node increases. Note that the efficiency-ratio depends on $\beta_s, |C|, K_{|C|}, \gamma$. Of these β_s and $|C|$ are always the same for both G and G'. γ is also always the same for any G' derived from a given node-graph G, as it depends only on the number of other node-links incident on either endpoint of a node-link in G (which is a property of the node topology, and not the number of interfaces each node has). However, $K_{|C|}$ might potentially increase in G' as there are many more non-adjacent interfering *links* when each interface is viewed as a distinct node. Thus, for a given number of channels $|C|$, one would expect the provable efficiency-ratio to initially decrease as we add more interfaces, and then become static.

While this may initially seem counter-intuitive, this is explained by the observation that multiple orthogonal channels yielded a better efficiency-ratio in the single-interface case since there was more spectral resource, but limited hardware (interfaces) to utilize it. Thus, the additional channels could be effectively used to alleviate the impact of sub-optimal scheduling. When the hardware is commensurate with the number of channels, the situation (compared to an optimal scheduler) increasingly starts to resemble a single-channel single-interface network.

6.2 Special Case: $|C|$ Interfaces per Node

Let us consider the special case where each node in the network has $|C|$ interfaces, and achievable rate on a link between nodes u, v and all channels $c \in C$ is solely a function of u, v and c (and not of the interfaces used). In this case, it is possible to obtain a simpler transformation. Given the original network node-graph $G = (V, E)$, construct $|C|$ copies of this graph, viz., $G_1, G_2, ..., G_{|C|}$, and view each node in each graph as having a single-interface, and each network as having access to a single channel. Then each network graph G_i can be viewed in isolation, and the throughput obtained in the original graph is the sum of the throughputs in each graph. From Theorem 2, in each graph we can show that the CGM scheduler is within $\left(\frac{1}{\max\{1, K+\gamma\}} \right)$ of the optimal. Thus, even in the overall network, the CGM scheduler is within $\left(\frac{1}{\max\{1, K+\gamma\}} \right)$ of the optimal.

7 A Rate-Proportional Maximal Multi-Channel (RPMMC) Scheduler

In this section, we describe a scheduler where a link does not require any information about queue-lengths at interfering links.

The set of all links in denoted by $\mathcal{L}$. The arrival process for link l is i.i.d. over all time-slots t, and is denoted by $\{\lambda_l(t)\}$, with $E[\lambda_l(t)] = \lambda_l$. We make no assumption about independence of arrival processes for two links l, k. However, we consider only the class of arrival processes for which $E[\lambda_l(t)\lambda_k(t)]$ is bounded, i.e., $E[\lambda_l(t)\lambda_k(t)] \leq \eta$ for all $l \in \mathcal{L}, k \in \mathcal{L}$, where η is a suitable constant.

Consider the following scheduler:

Rate-Proportional Maximal Multi-Channel (RPMMC) Scheduler
Each link maintains a queue for each channel. The length of the queue for link l and channel c at time t is denoted by $q_l^c(t)$. In time-slot t: only those link-channel pairs with $q_l^c(t) \geq r_l^c$ participate, and the scheduler computes a maximal schedule from amongst the participating links. The new arrivals during this slot, i.e., $\lambda_l(t)$ are assigned to channel-queues in proportion to the rates, i.e., $\lambda_l^c(t) = \dfrac{\lambda_l(t) r_l^c}{\sum\limits_{b \in C} r_l^b}$

Theorem 4. *The RPMMC scheduler stabilizes the queues in the network for any load-vector within the δ-reduced rate-region, where:*

$$\delta = \frac{\sigma_s}{K_{|C|} + \max\{1, \gamma\} |C|}$$

The proof is omitted due to space constraints. Please see [1].

Corollary 1. *The efficiency-ratio of the RPMMC scheduler is always at least:*

$$\left(\frac{\sigma_s}{|C|} \right) \left(\frac{1}{K + \max\{1, \gamma\}} \right)$$

Proof. The proof follows from Theorem 4 and (1).

8   Discussion

The intuition behind the RPMMC scheduler is simple: by splitting the traffic across channels in proportion to the channel-rates, each link sees the average of all channel-rates as its *effective rate*. This helps avoid worst-case scenarios where the link may end up being repeatedly scheduled on a channel that yields poor rate on that link. The algorithm is made attractive by the fact that no information about queues at interfering links is required. Furthermore we showed that the efficiency-ratio of the RPMMC scheduler is always at least $\left(\frac{\sigma_s}{|C|} \right) \left(\frac{1}{K + \max\{1, \gamma\}} \right)$. Note that $1 + \beta_s(|C| - 1) \leq \sigma_s \leq |C|$. Thus, the efficiency ratio of this algorithm does not degrade indefinitely as β_s becomes smaller. Moreover, in many practical settings, one can expect σ_s to be $\Theta(|C|)$ and the performance would be much better compared to the worst-case of $\sigma_s = 1 + \beta_s(|C| - 1)$.

9   Future Directions

The RPMMC scheduler provides motivation for further study of schedulers that work with limited information. The scheduler of Lin-Rasool [4] and the RPMMC scheduler represent two extremes of a range of possibilities, since the former uses information from all interfering links, while the latter uses no such information. Evidently, using more information can potentially allow for a better provable efficiency-ratio. However, the nature of the trade-off curve between these two extremities is not clear. For instance, an interesting question to ponder is the following: If interference extends up to M hops, but each link only has information upto $x < M$ hops, what provable bounds can be obtained? This would help quantify the extent of performance improvement achievable by increasing the information-exchange, and provide insights about suitable operating points for protocol design, since control overhead can be a concern in real-world network scenarios.

References

1. Bhandari, V.: Performance of wireless networks subject to constraints and failures. Ph.D. Thesis, UIUC (2008)
2. Georgiadis, L., Neely, M.J., Tassiulas, L.: Resource allocation and cross-layer control in wireless networks. Found. Trends Netw. 1(1), 1–144 (2006)
3. Joo, C., Shroff, N.B.: Performance of random access scheduling schemes in multi-hop wireless networks. In: Proceedings of IEEE INFOCOM, pp. 19–27 (2007)
4. Lin, X., Rasool, S.: A Distributed Joint Channel-Assignment, Scheduling and Routing Algorithm for Multi-Channel Ad-hoc Wireless Networks. In: Proceedings of IEEE INFOCOM, May 2007, pp. 1118–1126 (2007)
5. Lin, X., Shroff, N.B.: The impact of imperfect scheduling on cross-layer rate control in wireless networks. In: Proceedings of IEEE INFOCOM, pp. 1804–1814 (2005)
6. Neely, M.J., Modiano, E., Rohrs, C.E.: Dynamic power allocation and routing for time varying wireless networks. In: Proceedings of IEEE INFOCOM (2003)
7. Sharma, G., Mazumdar, R.R., Shroff, N.B.: On the complexity of scheduling in wireless networks. In: MobiCom 2006: Proceedings of the 12th annual international conference on Mobile computing and networking, pp. 227–238. ACM Press, New York (2006)
8. Tassiulas, L., Ephremides, A.: Stability properties of constrained queueing systems and scheduling policies for maximum throughput in multihop radio networks. IEEE Transactions on Automatic Control 37(12), 1936–1948 (1992)
9. Wu, X., Srikant, R.: Scheduling efficiency of distributed greedy scheduling algorithms in wireless networks. In: Proceedings of IEEE INFOCOM (2006)
10. Wu, X., Srikant, R., Perkins, J.R.: Queue-length stability of maximal greedy schedules in wireless networks. In: Workshop on Information Theory and Applications (2006)
11. Wu, X., Srikant, R., Perkins, J.R.: Scheduling efficiency of distributed greedy scheduling algorithms in wireless networks. IEEE Trans. Mob. Comput. 6(6), 595–605 (2007)

Email Shape Analysis

Paul Sroufe[1], Santi Phithakkitnukoon[1], Ram Dantu[1], and João Cangussu[2]

[1] Department of Computer Science & Engineering,
University of North Texas Denton, Texas 76203
{prs0010,santi,rdantu}@unt.edu
[2] Department of Computer Science, University of Texas at Dallas
Richardson, Texas 75083
cangussu@utdallas.edu

Abstract. Email has become an integral part of everyday life. Without a second thought we receive bills, bank statements, and sales promotions all to our inbox. Each email has hidden features that can be extracted. In this paper, we present a new mechanism to characterize an email without using content or context called Email Shape Analysis. We explore the applications of the email shape by carrying out a case study; botnet detection and two possible applications: spam filtering, and social-context based finger printing. Our in-depth analysis of botnet detection leads to very high accuracy of tracing templates and spam campaigns. However, when it comes to spam filtering we do not propose new method but rather a complementing method to the already high accuracy Bayesian spam filter. We also look at its ability to classify individual senders in personal email inbox's.

1 Introduction

The behavior of email is something that is often overlooked. Email has been with us for so long that we begin to take it for granted. However, email may yet provide new techniques for classification systems. In this paper, we introduce the concept of email shape analysis and a few of its applications. Email shape analysis is a simple yet powerful method of classifying emails without the use of conventional email analysis techniques which rely on header information, hyperlink analysis, and natural language processing. It is a method of breaking down emails into a parameterized form for use with modeling techniques. In parameterized form the email is seen as a skeleton of its text and HTML body. The skeleton is used to draw a contouring shape, which is used for email shape analysis.

One of the largest threats facing the internet privacy and security of email users is spam email. According to the NY Times in March 2009, 94% of all email is spam. Email can contain malicious code and lewd content, both of which need to be avoided by 100%. The use of a behavior based detection method will

K. Kant et al. (Eds.): ICDCN 2010, LNCS 5935, pp. 18–29, 2010.
© Springer-Verlag Berlin Heidelberg 2010

increase the accuracy and compliment current analysis methods in malicious and spam activity.

In this paper, we discuss a case study involving spam botnet detection. We also discuss the possible applications spam and ham filtering and social finger printing of senders. Recent papers presenting on this topic of botnet detection use network traffic behavior [1][2] and also domain name service blackhole listings [3], whereby botnets are discovered when they query the blackhole listings in DNS servers. By introducing shape analysis, one can further confirm the authenticity of the bot classifier.

The first application goes back to the proverbial spam question [4][5][6][7]. We look at the ability of shape analysis to correctly identify spam. In this study we are not trying to compete against the Bayesian filter, but rather compliment its decision process by offering non-content and non-context aware classification. The nature of the shape analysis classifier allows for both language independent and size independent email shape generation. This is believed to be very useful as the world becomes further integrated and spam comes in multiple languages to everyone.

In the second application, we look at the potential of email shape analysis to identify social context-based finger prints. We propose the ability to distinguish individual or group senders based on the social context. The data set for this study is one subject's personal email inbox.

The rest of the paper is organized as follows. The concept of the proposed Email Shape is described in section 2. Section 3 presents the case study email spam botnet detection. Section 4 discusses future work and their preliminary results on email spam filtering and social context-based finger print identification. Section 5 reviews some limitations of our study. Section 6 concludes the paper with a summary and an outlook on future work.

2 Email Shape

We define "shape" of an email as a shape that a human would perceive (*e.g.*, shape of a bottle). Without reading the content, shape of an email can be visualized as its contour envelope.

Email shape (e-shape) can be obtained from its "skeleton" that is simply a set of character counts for each line in the text and HTML code of email content. Let L denote the total number of lines in the email text and HTML code, and h_k denote the character count (this includes all characters and whitespace) in line k. A skeleton (H) of an email thus can be defined as follows.

$$H = \{h_1, h_2, h_3, ..., h_L\} . \tag{1}$$

Skeleton H can be treated as a random variable. Thereby the shape of an email can be derived from its skeleton by applying a Gaussian kernel density function (also known as Parzen window method) [8], which is a non-parametric approach for estimating probability density function (pdf) of a random variable and given by Eq. 2.

$$f(x) = \frac{1}{Lw} \sum_{k=1}^{L} K\left(\frac{x - h_k}{w}\right),\tag{2}$$

where $K(u)$ is the kernel function and w is the bandwidth or smoothing parameter. To select the optimal bandwidth, we use the AMISE optimal bandwidth selection based on Sheather Jones Solve-the-equation plug-in method [9]. Our kernel function is a widely used zero mean and unit variance given by Eq. 3

$$K(u) = \frac{1}{\sqrt{2\pi}} e^{-u^2/2}.\tag{3}$$

With this approach, an algorithm for finding e-shape can be constructed as shown in Alg. 1. Figure 1 illustrates the process of extracting e-shape. An example of four different e-shapes is illustrated in Fig. 2.

Algorithm 1. Email Shape
S = Email Shape(C)
Input: Email Text and HTML code (C)
Output: E-Shape (S)
1. FOR $i = 1$ to L /*L is the total number of lines in email HTML code */
2. h_i = character count of line i;
3. END FOR
4. $H = \{h_1, h_2, h_3, ..., h_L\}$; /* skeleton is extracted */
5. S =applying Gaussian kernel density function on H; /* e-shape is obtained */
6. Return S

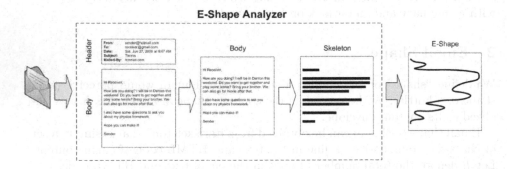

Fig. 1. Email shape analyzer

In summary, email shape is found by computing the number of character per line in an email. Almost every email has a text and HTML body. The lines are put into a file from which the Gaussian kernel density estimator smooths the rigid line graph into a normalized, smoothed graph. This graph is calculated for every email. We then performed a comparative function, called Hellinger distance, to find how closely each email shape is related.

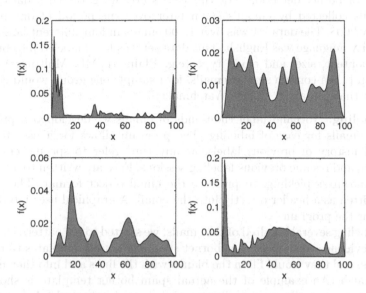

Fig. 2. An example of four different e-shapes

3   Applications of E-Shape

Our understanding of what shape analysis has to offer to the community is
only at the beginning. We present, in the paper, a case study and two future
work applications that outline some of the behaviors that shape can be used to
analyze. First, is analysis of spamming botnets by template and/or campaign
detection based on shape. By identifying similar shapes from different parts of
the globe, one could surmise that they come from a matching bot host controller.
(A bot is a compromised host that resides on the internet, usually without the
host's controller's knowledge. The term bot has negative connotation and is
usually associated with malicious behavior such as spamming, denial of service,
or phishing. A botnet is a collection of two or more bots, and sometimes on the
order of 10,000.) Second, spam filtering has become second nature to world. It
has over 99% accuracy, but what of the last less than one percent? What were
the content and context that were able to escape the filtering process? In this
application we propose that e-shape analysis can be used to get closer to the goal
of 100% spam classification. Third, e-shape analysis shows the discriminatory
power to identify individuals on a personal level. In this application we build
personal finger prints and turn our classifier over to the ham side of email.

3.1   Spam Botnet Detection

Spamming botnets are notoriously hard to pin point, often needing to use several
methods to achieve decent accuracy. Here we present another tool to use in the

assessment of botnet detection. For this case study we gathered a data set of spam emails collected by Gmail's spam filter over the period of one month, during July 2008. The data set was over 1,100 emails in four different languages. The majority language was English. This data set was hand labeled into buckets based on content, size, and email type (e.g. Plain, HTML, Multipart). Each bucket would then contain similar emails, for example one group would contain emails sent that contained "Kings Watchmaker".

Hand labeling. To hand label thousands of emails we developed a program to display emails for ease of labeling. The program allows for a user to view a recorded history of previous labels, at any time refer to specific email for comparison, and resume previous labeling sessions. Files are written to an object text file, known as pickling, to preserve the email object format. The botnet label is written as a header directly into the email. A graphical user interface is included for the program.

After labeling several hundred of the emails, we started to see patterns emerge. We found evidence to support that botnet spammer's used templates to bypass spam filters, and they would fill in the blanks with the links and info they needed to get through (An example of the actual spam botnet template is shown in Fig. 3). The spam emails are very diverse, also shown by the multiple languages. The details of our data set is listed on Table 1.

Template Discussion. In the United States over 650 million email accounts are owned by four companies: Microsoft(MSN), Yahoo, Google and AOL [10]. Google comes in a distant third to MSN and Yahoo. They are very protective of their users and to get solicited emails to them can be an expensive process. We have evidence [11][12][13] to believe botnets are using specific templates to beat out spam filters. Seen in Fig. 3, a spammer would simply need to fill in the blanks and begin his campaign. The use of randomized or individually written emails for the purpose of spamming is not feasible on any small, medium or large scale campaign. It is of note to the authors that multiple botnets could be using the same template and be classified together. A separate method will be analyzed for distinguishing them in future work.

The total number of buckets from hand labeling was 52. For analysis we discarded buckets that had less than 10-emails per. This yielded 11 buckets. The shape of the testing email was derived using Alg. 1, then classified into different botnet groups. The measure of difference in shapes between these groups was based on Hellinger distance [14] since the e-shape is built with an estimated probability density functions (pdf). By using an estimated pdf, we are able to smooth out the shape from its rigid skeleton. It also normalizes the number of lines in the email, for use of Hellinger distance. The normalization of length is what provides a size independent way to calculate shape. Looking at the template in Fig. 3, a host spammer could add another paragraph with more links and not still not drastically change the normalized e-shape of itself.

Figure 4 shows two email shapes from a Chinese botnet. Figure 4(a) is larger than Fig. 4(b) by 22 lines, a difference of 11.8%. The two shapes are considerably similar and were mapped to the same bucket by the e-shape algorithm.

```
------=_NextPart_001_2D49_73AC2523.5E4E77CE
Content-Type: text/plain
Content-Transfer-Encoding: quoted-printable

Company Name
Motto Here
=20

Dear Name,

Run the erranking resultsRun the user-friendly and technology driven Tool P=
rogram.Try the FREE 90 day trial and tart achievingoutstanding search engin=
e placement and ranking results. Run the user-friendly and technology drive=
n Optimization Tool Program.Try the FREE 90 day trial and outstanding searc=
h engine placement and ranking resultsRun t he user-friendly and technology=
 driven Optimization Tool Program. Try the FREE 90 day trial and start achi=
evingoutstanding search e ngine placement and ranking resultsRun the user-f=
riendly and techn ology driven


Sincerly,

John Smith
Manager Acounts
Company Software=20



Tel: your telephone
Fax: your fax
Web: your web site
=20


Copyright@Company Name.com
```

Fig. 3. An example of the actual spam botnet template

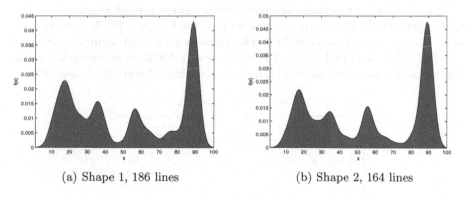

(a) Shape 1, 186 lines   (b) Shape 2, 164 lines

Fig. 4. Showing size independence of shapes from the same botnet

The signature of each botnet group was computed as the expected value (mean) of the group. We used predefined threshold level at 0.08, which found to be the optimal threshold for our study. Hellinger distance is widely used for estimating a distance (difference) between two probability measures (*e.g.*, pdf, pmf). Hellinger distance between two probability measures A and B can be computed as follows.

$$d_H^2(A,B) = \frac{1}{2}\sum_{m=1}^{M}(\sqrt{a_m}-\sqrt{b_m})^2, \qquad (4)$$

Table 1. Details of dataset for botnet detection experiment

Feature	Count
Total Emails	1,144
Email's Sizes of 1 to 100 lines	906
Email's Sizes of 101 to 200 lines	131
Email's Sizes of 201 to 300 lines	42
Email's Sizes of 301 to 400 lines	25
Email's Sizes of 401 to 500 lines	40
Emails in English	815
Emails in Chinese	270
Emails in Spanish	57
Emails in German	2

where A and B are M-tuple $\{a_1, a_2, a_3, ..., a_M\}$ and $\{b_1, b_2, b_3, ..., b_M\}$ respectively, and satisfy $a_m \geq 0, \sum_m a_m = 1, b_m \geq 0$, and $\sum_m b_m = 1$. Hellinger distance of 0 implies that $A = B$ whereas disjoint A and B yields the maximum distance of 1.

The accuracy of this data set is found from computing the number of correctly labeled emails in a bucket to the total number of emails in that bucket. A false positive indicates an email that was placed in the bucket but did not belong. A false negative would be the total number of emails, from hand labeling, that are in the rest of the buckets which belong to that bucket.

Figure 5 shows a promising accumulative accuracy rate of almost 81%. This number reflects the cumulative accuracy of all the buckets. While some buckets have a low accuracy, several of the buckets have a very good accuracy up to and including 100%, seen in Table 2. The evidence of a 100% accuracy bucket would show a positive match on an email campaign template. Accuracies below 50% are

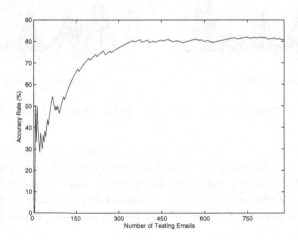

Fig. 5. A result of the botnet detection experiment based on 879 different size and language emails

Table 2. Accuracy rate of individual bucket

Bucket	Accuracy	False Negative	False Positive	Total Emails
1	41.37%	14	48	81
2	74.07%	20	20	76
3	80.95%	20	11	59
4	100%	0	0	129
5	68.75%	0	28	90
6	45.83%	0	25	67
7	100%	0	0	78
8	93.10%	14	6	81
9	88.00%	22	17	140
10	100%	0	0	118
11	100%	0	0	70

simply emails that are of similar shape. For example, bucket 6 is a mismatch of several botnet's from different languages and types of spam emails. Email shape analysis is showing good results in botnet and campaign classification, the purpose being to take context and specific content out of the classification process.

4 Future Work and Preliminary Results

In our on going work to discover and explore the full potential of e-shape analysis, we take a look at a couple of possible applications and also some preliminary analysis and results on them. Below we discuss the use of e-shape on spam filtering and on social context-based finger printing. In our finger print analysis we look at the capability of e-shape to differentiate senders from each other.

4.1 Spam Filtering

In this application of e-shape, we discuss the behavior that e-shape analysis can have on the spam filtering process. The Bayesian filter proves to be over 99% successful most all the time. However, to reach the goal of 100% further analysis is required. The Bayesian filter uses content and context to classify emails. The process could be enhanced using the method of shape analysis to "look at" if an email is spam or ham, taking content and context completely out of the equation. Surprise emails to the classifier that can't be categorized or are unique in manufacturing might make it through.

The data set used for this case study was the Trec 2007 corpus [15]. The Trec corpora are widely used in spam testing. The 2007 corpus was over 74,000 emails. However, for this study, only the first 7,500 emails were used for analysis. The corpus was approximately 67% spam and 33% ham and has been hand labeled by the Trec Team.

The method for comparison of spam versus ham was similar to that of botnet detection case study. Here we again used an unsupervised learning algorithm to classify data. We have developed a program that will take an email file in

MBOX format and calculate how many similar groups their are and classify in the same way as section 3.1. A testing email was classified to ham or spam based on the closest clustered group signature. The drawback of this process is that the buckets will need to be labeled by ham or spam, which is independent of our classifier. Once the bucket is known to be ham/spam future email's which are classified into the bucket will be labeled as such.

Preliminary results show an accumulative accuracy of about 70% for 7,500 emails. The accuracy is great considering that no content or context was even referenced. The ability for shape analysis to act as a spam filter would be recommended for use with emails that the Bayesian filter finds unsure about. Future work in that regard would be to implement shape analysis inside the Bayesian filter process.

4.2   Social Context-Based Finger Print Detection

This application is on using e-shape analysis to identify an individual's personal email finger print based on social context. We define personal fingerprint as the shape that one typically uses to contact others with. When an individual writes emails, it is believed that his shape will stay relatively the same, although length may change, the way he/she writes will not. An example of this would be an individual that creates a new line about every 40-50 characters versus a person that creates no new lines at all. It is also believed that this method can be used to reveal a user's clique's, as seen in [16]. A user will type differently to his/her boss and work mates than he/she would to their close friends. In this case study we follow the aggregate pattern of other users sending to a specific person.

For the data set, we used the top three different senders from one subject's inbox. The emails were collected over five months. Using e-shape analysis, we

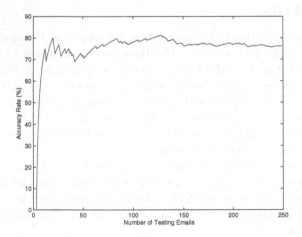

Fig. 6. A result of the social context-based individual's personal email finger print experiment based on three different individual email senders to a subject with total of about 250 emails

were able to distinguish these three senders to this subject, from unaltered emails (no thread deletion), with an accuracy of about 75% (see Fig. 6). The accuracy is considered good. Further refinement and post processing will be looked into in the future for better results. The current results now is using only the e-shape analysis.

Of the approximately 250 emails that are tested and of the three groups selected was a bi-weekly newsletter from a sales web site. The emails that came from this web site were classified with 100% accuracy and no false positives. The other two senders were from real human conversations.

This method reveals a very powerful tool in categorizing incoming emails when comparing non-human to human emails. Newsletters, advertisements, and solicitations can be moved separately by themselves to be reviewed later by a user, keeping priority emails displayed first.

5 Limitations of the Study

Currently the E-Shape analysis tool does not have a way to compliment its decision process by removing email threads and conversations. This drawback is reduced by the power of e-shape analysis, but it believed that we still yet have many abilities to unlock in this regard.

The shape analysis is a very useful tool to complement other tools as it can provide the deciding factor to many close decisions. Such is the example in spam detection where the content classifier can already achieve such a high accuracy. Some emails are short by nature, the ability for shape analysis to distinguish between others becomes limited. In the case of spam, short emails are common and the limitation impact of e-shape analysis will be mitigated to a large extent.

As mentioned earlier, and with any tool, the less information you give it, the less it can tell you. In the study of social context-based finger print detection, if a subject has a subset of friends that like to send web hyperlinks back and forth, the classifier will be unable to distinguish between users. Study of group based social awareness could be a possible application of this research.

Botnet detection is a challenging problem. There is not a singular solution to this threat, and combining the latest innovations only brings us a step closer. The purpose of E-Shape analysis for botnets is to bring the world one step closer. E-shape analysis is a tool capable of template/campaign identification to find a spamming bots before they are even able to send. Botnet identification is the next logical step of the process and can be supported with this tool.

6 Conclusion

In this paper, we present a novel concept of email shape (e-shape) and discuss three case studies using a hidden discriminatory power of e-shape. By using e-shape analysis we were able to detect botnet template/campaigns with about 81% accuracy. The botnet analysis can also be done with multiple languages and email sizes, which shows that the e-shape analysis is language and size independent. Next, we discuss the capabilities of e-shape in spam filtering. Since e-shape is neither content nor context aware, it provides a unique point of view when looking at spam emails. We used the TREC 2007 corpus to test the spam filtering capabilities of e-shape. After running 7,500 emails through the email shape detector, we had a success rate of about 70%. Lastly, we looked at social context-based finger print detection, where we analyzed a single subject's email inbox. Using three different senders, we were able to achieve an accuracy rate of over 70%.

It is important to note that while the accuracy's of our system are not "high," the system of classification is taking content and context out of the classification process. This provides a very useful tool to complement existing methods and tools that currently handle emails, such as inching the Bayesian filter closer to 100% accuracy or assisting network behavior analyzers in determining botnet relationships.

As we evolve our understanding of what e-shape analysis can offer, we plan to improve the accuracies of the existing work and release more case studies. Currently the shape analysis routine does not have any smart way of handling email conversation threads or HTML code. This is the planned next direction of our work and is believed to offer a significant increase to ham labeling accuracy.

Acknowledgment

This work is supported by the National Science Foundation under grants CNS-0627754, CNS-0619871 and CNS-0551694.

References

1. Ramachandran, A., Feamster, N.: Understanding the network-level behavior of spammers. In: SIGCOMM 2006: Proceedings of the 2006 conference on Applications, technologies, architectures, and protocols for computer communications, pp. 291–302. ACM Press, New York (2006)
2. Strayer, W.T., Lapsley, D., Walsh, R., Livadas, C.: Botnet detection based on network behavior. In: Lee, W., Wang, C., Dagon, D. (eds.) Botnet Detection: Countering the Largest Security Threat. Springer, Heidelberg (2007)
3. Ramachandran, A., Feamster, N., Dagon, D.: Detecting botnet membership with dnsbl counterintelligence. In: Lee, W., Wang, C., Dagon, D. (eds.) Botnet Detection. Advances in Information Security, vol. 36, pp. 131–142. Springer, Heidelberg (2008)
4. Sinclair, S.: Adapting bayesian statistical spam filters to the server side. J. Comput. Small Coll. 19(5), 344–346 (2004)
5. Cormack, G.V.: Email spam filtering: A systematic review. Found. Trends Inf. Retr. 1(4), 335–455 (2007)
6. Cormack, G.V., Gómez Hidalgo, J.M., Sánz, E.P.: Spam filtering for short messages. In: CIKM 2007: Proceedings of the sixteenth ACM conference on Conference on information and knowledge management, pp. 313–320. ACM Press, New York (2007)

7. Wei, C.-P., Chen, H.-C., Cheng, T.-H.: Effective spam filtering: A single-class learning and ensemble approach. Decis. Support Syst. 45(3), 491–503 (2008)
8. Parzen, E.: On Estimation of a Probability Density Function and Mode. The Annals of Mathematical Statistics 33(3), 1065–1076 (1962)
9. Sheather, S.J., Jones, M.C.: A reliable data-based bandwidth selection method for kernel density estimation. Journal of the Royal Statistical Society, Series B (53), 683–690 (1991)
10. Brownlow, M.: Email and webmail statistics (April 2008),
    http://www.email-marketing-reports.com/metrics/email-statistics.htm
11. Paul, R.: Researchers track Ron Paul spam back to Reactor botnet (December 2007), http://www.marshal8e6.com/trace/i/Template-Based-Spam,trace.996~.asp
12. Stewart, J.: Top Spam Botnets Exposed (April 2008), http://www.secureworks.com/research/threats/topbotnets/?threat=topbotnets
13. TRACElabs, Template Based Spam (May 2009), http://www.marshal8e6.com/trace/i/Template-Based-Spam,trace.996~.asp
14. Cam, L.L., Yang, G.L.: Asymptotics in Statistics: Some Basic Concepts. Springer, Heidelberg (2000)
15. Cormack, G.V., Lynam, T.R.: TREC 2007 Public Corpus (2007),
    http://plg.uwaterloo.ca/~gvcormac/treccorpus07/about.html
16. Stolfo, S.J., Hershkop, S., Hu, C.-W., Li, W.-J., Nimeskern, O., Wang, K.: Behavior-based modeling and its application to email analysis. ACM Trans. Internet Technol. 6(2), 187–221 (2006)

Maintaining Safety in Interdomain Routing with Hierarchical Path-Categories

Jorge A. Cobb

Department of Computer Science
The University of Texas at Dallas
Richardson, TX 75083-0688
cobb@utdallas.edu

Abstract. The stable-paths problem is an abstraction of the basic functionality of the Internet's BGP routing protocol. It has received considerable attention due to instabilities observed in BGP. In this abstraction, each node informs its neighboring nodes of its current path to the destination node. From the paths received from its neighbors, each node chooses the best path according to some local routing policy. However, since routing policies are chosen locally, conflicts may occur between nodes, resulting in unstable behavior. Deciding if a set of routing policies is stable is NP-hard. Thus, current solutions involve restricting routing policies to avoid instabilities, while maintaining enough flexibility for the routing policies to be useful. Recently, path-categories have been introduced. E.g., a simple system consists of a category of regular paths, and a category of backup paths. By combining path-categories into a total order (regular paths have higher priority than backup paths), it has been shown that the resulting system is stable if each category by itself is stable. In this paper, we relax the total-order of categories into a partial-order, and thus provide greater flexibility of routing choices at each node. We extend the definition of the stable-paths problem to allow such flexibility, and show that if each category is stable in itself, then the whole system is stable. In addition, we show an upper bound on the convergence time of the whole system provided each category in itself has a bounded convergence time.

1 Introduction

The Internet is an inter-connected collection of Autonomous Systems (AS'ms). To route datagrams from one AS to another, each AS learns a path to every other AS. This learning is achieved by exchanging routing information between neighboring AS'ms. In particular, each AS informs its neighbors of its current path to each destination. Therefore, each AS stores in memory the full path (i.e. sequence of AS'ms) that must be traversed to reach each destination AS. The Border Gateway Protocol (BGP) [14] is the de-facto routing protocol for sharing AS path information between neighboring AS'ms.

Our focus is the permanent failure of BGP to converge to a stable set of routes. This instability occurs for the following reason. Each AS has the freedom

K. Kant et al. (Eds.): ICDCN 2010, LNCS 5935, pp. 30–41, 2010.
© Springer-Verlag Berlin Heidelberg 2010

to implement any routing policy. I.e., each AS locally defines a preference of one path over another. These local preferences are often based on commercial relationships between AS'ms, or other factors. Given that routing policies are chosen locally, it is possible for neighboring AS'ms to have conflicting policies. It is even possible for conflicts to form a circular chain [5,15,16,10]. If so, BGP may become unstable and diverge, i.e., some AS'ms continuously alternate between different paths to the destination, never reaching a stable configuration.

Determining if a set of routing policies are stable is NP-hard [11]. Thus, current solutions for BGP instability involve restricting the routing policies so that instabilities are avoided, but still leaving enough flexibility so that the allowed routing policies are useful to Internet service providers [10,8,7].

Recently, path-categories have been introduced. A category is simply a set of paths to the destination, such that this set has been shown to be stable. Thus, if we allow BGP to operate using only the paths defined by the category, then BGP converges to a stable path for each node. A simple example may consist of two categories: regular paths and backup paths. By combining path-categories into a total order (e.g., regular paths have higher priority than backup paths), it has been shown that the resulting BGP system is stable [9].

In this paper, we relax the total-order of categories into a partial-order, and thus provide greater flexibility of routing choices at each node. We extend the definition of the stable-paths problem to allow such flexibility, and show that, if each category is stable in itself, then the whole system is stable. In addition, we show an upper bound on the convergence time of the whole system provided each category has also a bounded convergence time.

2   Stable-Path Problem and Path-Vector Protocols

2.1   AS Graphs

Griffin et. al. [10,11,13] defined an abstract model to study the divergence of BGP. It consists of a graph $G = (N, E)$, where each node in N represents an AS, and each edge in E represents a communications link between the two neighboring ASms. Although an AS is a collection of multiple routers, the behavior of all its routers is consistent. This allows an AS to be simply be represented as a single node in the model. Without loss of generality, a single destination node (i.e. AS) is assumed. We will refer to this node as *root*.

An AS path is simply a sequence of nodes. A path is said to be *rooted* if it is a simple path whose last node is the root. The objective of each node is to find a path from itself to *root* that is consistent with the path chosen by its next-hop neighbor. That is, u may chose path P, where $P = \langle u, v, w, \dots, root \rangle$, only if v currently has chosen path $\langle v, w, \dots, root \rangle$. Thus, each node stores in its memory its chosen rooted path, and it advertises this path to its neighbors.

Consider for example Figure 1(a). It contains an AS graph with five nodes: *root*, u, v, w and x. Alongside each node is a list of paths that the node is willing to take to reach the *root*. This is explained in more detail below. Figure 1(b) is similar to (a), except that the order in which paths are preferred is different.

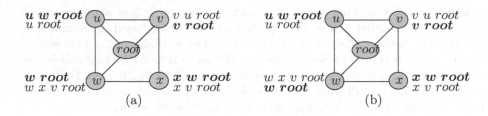

Fig. 1. SPP Instances and their solution

As mentioned earlier, each AS is free to choose from the paths offered by its neighbors according to a routing policy that is locally defined at the AS. The combined routing policy of all ASms is represented by the ranking relation $\prec$ on paths. In particular, if P and Q are paths from u to $root$, then $P \prec Q$ denotes that u prefers Q over P.

Definition 1. *Relation $\prec$ over rooted paths and the empty path $\langle\rangle$ satisfies the following.*

- $\prec$ *is transitive and irreflexive.*
- *For every node u and every pair of rooted paths P and Q originating at u,*

$$P \prec Q \vee Q \prec P$$

- *For every rooted path P,*

$$P \prec \langle\rangle \vee \langle\rangle \prec P$$

Note that if P originates at u and $P \prec \langle\rangle$, then u prefers the empty path over P, and thus, u will never choose P. In a sense, P is not allowed at u.

Consider again Figure 1. The list of allowed paths at each node is written besides it, in order of preference. E.g., u prefers path $\langle u, w, root \rangle$ over path $\langle u, root \rangle$. Figures 1(a) and 1(b) differ only in the path preference at node w.

2.2 The Stable-Paths Problem and Its Solution

Let π be a function that assigns a path to each node u. Function π must satisfy the following.

Constraint 1. *For every node u,*

- $\pi(u)$ *is either an empty path or a rooted path whose first node is u.*
- *For any two consecutive nodes v and w in $\pi(u)$, $(v, w) \in E$.*
- *If $\pi(u) \neq \langle\rangle$, then $\langle\rangle \prec \pi(u)$.*

An *instance* of the *stable paths problem* (SPP) consists of a pair $(G, \prec)$, where G is the graph representing autonomous systems and $\prec$ is the path ranking relation. A solution to an SPP instance consists of finding a path assignment π such that no node can improve the ranking of its assigned path.

Definition 2

- For any path P, P ∈ choices(u, π) iff

$$P = \langle \rangle \vee (\exists\, v,\ (u, v) \in E,\ P = \langle u, \pi(v) \rangle)$$

- For any path P, best(u, π) = P if and only if,

$$(\forall\, Q,\ Q \in choices(u, \pi),\ Q = P \vee Q \prec P)$$

Informally, $choices(u, \pi)$ contains all rooted paths originating at u that are consistent with the current paths chosen by u's neighbors. Then, $best(u, \pi)$ is the highest ranked path in the set $choices(u, \pi)$. Note that $best(u, \pi)$ may not be the highest ranking path that node u allows. It is, however, the highest ranked path among the paths available via its neighbors. E.g., in Figure 1(a), if π is denoted by the bold paths, then $best(v, \pi) = \langle v, root \rangle$. Path $\langle v, u, root \rangle$, although ranked higher, is not available, because the path assigned to u is not $\langle u, root \rangle$.

Therefore, if $\pi(u) \neq best(u, \pi)$, then node u could improve the ranking of its path if its assigned path $\pi(u)$ were equal to $best(u, \pi)$. This yields the following definition of a solution for an SPP instance. A *solution* to an SPP problem $(G, \prec)$, consists of a path assignment π, such that

$$(\forall\, u,\ \pi(u) = best(u, \pi))$$

Consider again Figure 1. Figure 1(a) has a solution, which are the paths in bold. Figure 1(b) also has the same solution. The difference between these two SPP instances will be made more apparent in the next section. Some SPP instances have more than one solution, some may have no solution.

2.3 Path-Vector Routing and Divergence

BGP attempts to find a solution to the stable-paths problem in a distributed manner. I.e., each node periodically chooses the best path from those offered by its neighbors, and then advertises this chosen path to all its neighbors. This is known as *path-vector routing*.

Since the rank of each path is chosen arbitrarily at each node, conflicting choices at neighboring nodes may prevent nodes from maintaining a stable rooted path. That is, the path chosen by some nodes will vary continuously, even though neither G nor $\prec$ changes.

Consider the SPP instance in Figure 2(a).[1] Note that each node prefers longer paths over shorter paths. E.g., u prefers the longer path $\langle u, v, root \rangle$ over the shorter path $\langle u, root \rangle$. This causes the ranking of each node to be in conflict with the ranking of its next hop to $root$. The cyclic relationship between these rankings prevents any node from obtaining a stable path to $root$. To see this, consider the following steps:

- Initially u, v, and w chose the paths $\langle u, v, root \rangle$, $\langle v, root \rangle$, and $\langle w, root \rangle$, respectively, as shown in Figure 2(b,i).

---

[1] This SPP instance is known as BAD GADGET in [10,11].

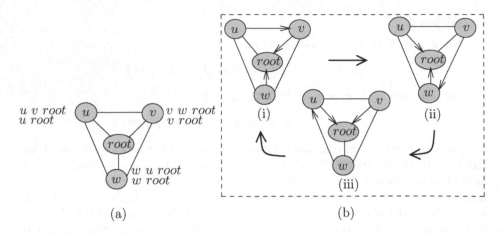

Fig. 2. Diverging SPP instance

- Node v notices that w chose path $\langle w, root \rangle$. Hence, v changes to $\langle v, w, root \rangle$. This forces u to change to $\langle u, root \rangle$ as shown in Figure 2(b,ii).
- Node w notices that u chose path $\langle u, root \rangle$. Hence, w changes to $\langle w, u, root \rangle$. This forces v to change to $\langle v, root \rangle$ as shown in Figure 2(b,iii).
- Node u notices that v chose path $\langle v, root \rangle$. Hence, u changes to $\langle u, v, root \rangle$. This forces w to change to $\langle w, root \rangle$, and the system is back to Figure 2(b,i).

Converging to a steady state is highly sensitive to the ranking of paths. In Figure 2, if the ranking of paths at u is reversed, then the system is guaranteed to reach to a steady state. As another example, consider Figure 1(b).[2] Depending on the relative order in which nodes update their rooted path, it may either converge to a steady state (i.e., a solution), or continuously diverge. Again, if the ranking of paths at w is reversed, then a steady state is always reached.

3   Solving Divergence: Related Work

From the above example, we see that, if the routing policies of BGP are not constrained, then there is no guarantee that a stable set of routes is achieved, or if such a stable set even exists. Several approaches to deal with this problem have been proposed in the literature, which we briefly overview next.

3.1   Routing Policy Analysis

One approach to ensure BGP converges is to gather the routing policies of all ASms, construct the corresponding abstract SPP instance, and then analyse it to determine if it has a solution, and if a solution will always be reached by a path-vector protocol (i.e., BGP). This approach has two problems: a) routing

---

[2] This SPP instance is known as NAUGHTY GADGET in [10,11].

policies are private to an AS, and thus, is unlikely ASms will disclose them for analysis, and more importantly, b) deciding if an SPP instance has a solution is NP-complete [11]. Actually, most interesting questions about an SPP instance, such as whether it has a single or multiple solutions, etc., are all NP-complete.

3.2 Run-Time Divergence Detection

Given that global routing-policy analysis is unlikely, various works have attempted to modify BGP in such a way that convergence is guaranteed [12][3,6][1]. These methods add additional information to each BGP message that helps routers detect whether a routing oscillation is occurring or not. If it is, nodes are prevented from taking certain paths that may recreate the oscillation. These proposals have the disadvantage of adding extra overhead to BGP, and also of providing false positives, that is, a routing oscillation may not be occurring. Thus, the network may be unnecessarily restricted from taking certain paths.

3.3 Policy Restrictions

Due to the limitations of the above methods, the main emphasis has been placed on restricting the routing policies of each AS in such a way that a stable configuration must exist and that BGP will converge to this stable configuration. These restriction on the routing policies should be flexible enough such that an AS still has significant freedom in choosing its preferred path to the destination.

The main result in restricting routing policies was the introduction of a sufficient (but not necessary) condition for an SPP instance to be stable [11], and the condition can be evaluated in polynomial time. Griffin et. al. [11] showed that if an SPP instance *does not* have a dispute wheel, then the SPP instance has all the desired properties: a unique solution (stable state), even under link failures, and a guaranteed convergence by a path-vector protocol.

A *dispute wheel* is a cyclic dependency of conflicts between nodes. The general form of a dispute wheel is shown in Figure 3. The reader is referred to [11] for a more detailed description. As a simple example, consider again the SPP instance of Figure 2(a). Note that each node has a routing policy conflict with its clockwise neighbor, that is, the order in which it prefers some paths is incompatible with its neighbor. Consider node v. It ranks paths in the following order

$\langle v, w, root \rangle$
$\langle v, root \rangle$

These same paths are ranked in opposite order at node u, that is[3]

$\langle u, v, root \rangle$
$\langle u, v, w, root \rangle$

Since each node has a conflict with its clock-wise neighbor, we have a cycle of conflicts, i.e., a dispute wheel.

---

[3] Note that $\langle u, v, w, root \rangle$ is not allowed at u, and hence, it is ranked lower than the empty path, and thus also lower than $\langle u, v, root \rangle$.

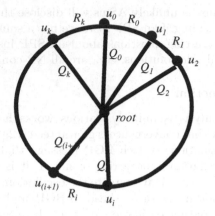

- $u_0, u_1, \dots, u_k$ are nodes (not necessarily distinct)
- R_i is a path from u_i to $u_{(i+1)}$
- Q_i is a path from u_i to $root$
- $Q_i \prec R_i \, Q_{(i+1)}$

Fig. 3. Dispute Wheel

If routing policies are designed in a manner that guarantees the lack of a dispute wheel, the resulting BGP system is stable. E.g., it has been shown that routing policies based on assigning costs to each link [11] have no dispute wheels. Also, the Internet is organized in a hierarchy of service providers and their customers. This is based on economic relationships between ASms. This "naturally occurring" routing policy has also been shown to be free of dispute wheels [7][8].

4   Totally Ordered Categories

In this paper, we consider the approach of decomposing an SPP instance in a hierarchical fashion. The firsts steps in this direction were taken by Gao, Griffin and Rexford [9], which we overview next. We present the concepts with a different notation and approach to be consistent with our results in the next section.

Definition 3. *A linear set of categories is a triple, $(G, C, \sqsubseteq)$, where*

- *G is a graph,*
- *$C \subseteq 2^{paths(G)}$ is a set, where $paths(G)$ is the set of all rooted paths in G. I.e., each element in C is a set of paths (i.e., a "category") from G.*
- *Categories are disjoint, i.e., for any $X \in C$ and $Y \in C$, $(X \neq Y) \Rightarrow (X \cap Y = \emptyset)$*
- *$\sqsubseteq$ is a total (i.e. linear) order on the elements of C.*

Definition 4. *An SPP instance $I = (G, \prec)$ is consistent with $(G, C, \sqsubseteq)$, provided:*

- *$G = \bigcup_{X \in C} X$,*
- *Let paths P and Q have the same starting node, and let them belong to different categories X and Y, respectively. If $X \sqsubseteq Y$, then $P \prec Q$.*

- *Let path P be an extension of path Q (P is obtained by extending Q with more nodes). Let $P \in X$, $Q \in Y$, where X and Y are categories ($X = Y$ is allowed). Then, $X \sqsubseteq Y$.*

Consider an SPP instance $I = (G, \prec)$ that is consistent with a linear set of categories $(G, C, \sqsubseteq)$. Assume $C = \{X, Y\}$. Let I_X be an SPP instance obtained from I by removing all nodes and edges not found in any path of X. Similarly, let $\prec_X$ be obtained from $\prec$ by eliminating all pairs of paths not included in X. Then, $I_X = (X, \prec_X)$ is an SPP instance. Similarly, I_Y is also an SPP instance. Thus, I can be decomposed into multiple SPP instances, one per category.

For example, consider a system that consists of two types of paths, regular paths and backup paths. Thus, the linear set of categories $(G, C, \sqsubseteq)$ has two categories, $C = \{X, Y\}$, where $X \sqsubseteq Y$. Category Y corresponds to the regular paths, and category X corresponds to the backup paths. The entire system, $I = (G, \prec)$, can be decomposed into two sub-instances: $I_X = (G_X, \prec_X)$, consisting of the backup paths, and $I_Y = (G_Y, \prec_Y)$ consisting of the regular paths.

Assume each sub-instance I_X is guaranteed to converge to a steady state. E.g., perhaps each I_X is designed free of dispute wheels. Then, the complete instance I will also converge. More formally, the following was shown in [9].

Theorem 1. *Let $I = (G, \prec)$ be an SPP instance that is consistent with a linear set of categories. Assume that each SPP sub-instance derived from every category is free of dispute-wheels. Then, SPP instance I is also free of dispute wheels, and thus will converge to a steady state.*

5   Partially Ordered Categories

Rather than restricting ourselves to a total order of categories, we would like to generalize the decomposition of an SPP instance into a partially-ordered set of categories. In particular, we present the following generalizations.

1. Categories form a partial order $\sqsubset$. Thus, it is possible that, for two categories X and Y, and a node u with rooted paths in both categories, u has no preference of paths in X over those in Y or vice versa. This requires changes in the manner in which an SPP instance ranks paths, and the manner in which a path-vector protocol operates.
2. We require only that each instance I_X derived from some category X be *safe*. That is, if any number of links or nodes fail in I_X, then I_X converges to a stable state. The lack of a dispute wheel is sufficient for I_X to be safe. However, as shown in [4], there are instances that are safe but have a dispute wheel. Hence, we adopt the weaker condition of safety.
3. Categories need not be path-disjoint.

Consider for example Figure 4. It consists of four categories, arranged in a partial order (denoted by the arrows). The top category consists of all paths that satisfy the customer-provider arrangement between ASms. The next two lower

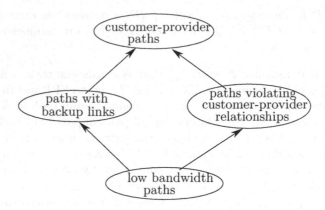

Fig. 4. Partial Order of Categories

categories correspond to paths that are taken if a node cannot find a path in the top category. The left category consists of paths that use a backup link, i.e., a link not used during regular operations, and is used only in case other paths fail. The right category consists of paths that violate the transit restrictions of customer-provider policies, but are used because the main paths are not available. Note that if a node has a path in each of the left and right categories, then the node has no preference between these two paths. Finally, the lower category consists of paths that use low-bandwidth links, and are only used as a last resort.

Given that in an SPP instance the path ranking relation $\prec$ must be a total order on rooted paths originating at the same node, a regular SPP instance cannot be consistent with a partially ordered category. We thus introduce the weaker notion of a *partially ordered SPP instance*, in which $\prec$ is allowed to be a partial order rather than a total order.

Definition 5. *A partially-ordered SPP instance $I = (G, \prec)$ is said to be consistent with a partial-order category $(G, C, \sqsubseteq)$, provided the following hold.*

- $G = \bigcup_{X \in C} X,$
- *Let paths P and Q have the same starting node, and let $P \in X$, $Q \in Y$, and $X \neq Y$. Then, if $X \sqsubseteq Y$, then $P \prec Q$.*
- *Let path P be an extension of path Q (P is obtained by extending Q with more nodes). Then, there must exist categories X and Y such that $P \in X$ and $Q \in Y$ and $(X = Y \vee X \sqsubseteq Y)$.*

We must next define what is meant by a solution of a partially-ordered SPP instance, and how it would be executed by a path-vector protocol.

Given that a path may occur in more than one category, we define the state $\pi(u)$ of a node u to be a pair, $(path, cid)$, consisting of the path currently being taken by u, and the id of the category from which u obtained this path.

Once a node chooses a path from a category, it will continue to only accept paths from this category, or from other categories ranked higher according to relation $\sqsubseteq$. The category-id allows the neighbors of node u to determine in which category u is operating on, and thus decide whether or not they should continue to use u as a next hop to the root.

To this effect, the set $choices(u, \pi)$ must be broken into two sets: local and global choices, as follows. For any path P, $P \in local\text{-}choices(u, \pi)$ iff

$$\langle\rangle \prec P \wedge (\exists\, v,\, (u, v) \in E,\, P = \langle u, \pi(v).path \rangle \wedge \pi(u).cid \sqsubseteq \pi(v).cid)$$

For any path P, $P \in global\text{-}choices(u, \pi)$ iff

$$P = \langle\rangle \vee (\exists\, v,\, (u, v) \in E,\, P = \langle u, \pi(v).path \rangle)$$

We redefine $choices(u, \pi)$ as follows.

$$choices(u, \pi) = \begin{cases} local\text{-}choices(u, \pi) & \text{if } local\text{-}choices(u, \pi) \neq \emptyset \\ global\text{-}choices(u, \pi) & \text{if } local\text{-}choices(u, \pi) = \emptyset \end{cases}$$

The definition of $best(u, \pi)$ remains as before, and also the definition of the solution of an SPP instance. The execution of a path vector protocol remains the same as before, i.e., $\pi(u).path$ is assigned $best(u, \pi)$, except that, in addition, $\pi(u).cid$ is assigned the cid of the neighbor's path.

We next present our main result. For lack of space, the proof is presented in [2].

Theorem 2. *Let $I = (G, \prec)$ be a partially ordered SPP instance that is consistent with a partially-ordered category set $(G, C, \sqsubseteq)$. Let every SPP sub-instance I_X derived from category X be safe. Then, I is safe, and the path vector protocol that implements I is also safe.*

6   Single Category-Path Per Node

Assume that, for each category X, $X \in C$, there is a bound on the time (e.g., number of execution steps) it would take for the SPP sub-instance I_X to reach a stable state. Bounds on convergence time of an SPP sub-instance can be obtained, for example, if the SPP sub-instance is based on the hierarchical relationships between customers and providers of Internet service [7][8].

In Theorem 2, we do not provide an upper bound on the convergence of the SPP instance I. Even when each sub-instance I_X has an upper bound on convergence time, an upper bound is difficult to obtain. This is because, as stated in the proof of the theorem [2], a node whose current path is in a category X may choose an entirely different category Y, take several steps, and then return to a path in category X. This affects the convergence time of category X.

In this section, to mitigate this effect, we make a simplifying assumption that allows us to prove a bound on convergence time.

Let $X_{n,1}, X_{n,2}, \ldots, X_{n,i}$ be the categories in which node n is the first node (source) of a rooted path. Then,

$$X_{n,1} \sqsubseteq X_{n,2} \sqsubseteq \cdots \sqsubseteq X_{n,i-1} \sqsubseteq X_{n,i}$$

That is, a node may only have paths along a single chain of categories in the partial order $(C, \sqsubseteq)$.

Under the above assumption, we have the following bound on convergence time.

Corollary 1. *Let $I = (G, \prec)$ be a partially ordered SPP instance that is consistent with partially-ordered category set $(G, C, \sqsubseteq)$. Let every SPP sub-instance I_X derived from category X be safe, and have an upper bound Δ on its execution time. Then, I is safe, and the path vector protocol that implements I is also safe, with a convergence time at most $\Delta \cdot depth(C, \sqsubseteq)$, where $depth(C, \sqsubseteq)$ is the length of the longest chain in the partial order $(C, \sqsubseteq)$.*

7   Concluding Remarks

In this paper, we have modified the execution model of the SPP abstraction to allow for a partial order of path categories. We have used the weakest assumption possible for each category, i.e., that the paths of the category form an SPP instance that is safe, and thus, converges to a steady state irrespective of node/link failures. We have shown that combining all the path categories into a single SPP instance results also in a safe system.

Regarding convergence time, if a bound is known for the convergence time of each category, then this bound can be applied to the combined system. We require, however, that each node only has paths along a single category chain.

Although this restriction may sound too strong, it still retains significant flexibility. Consider a path P located in category X, and let (u, v) be the first edge along P. Although P is in X, the subpath along P from v to the root does not need to be located in X, it only needs to be located at a category Y ranked higher than X. Furthermore, Y does not need to be located along the category chain of u.

In future work, we plan to investigate weaker requirements to prove upper bounds on the convergence time of the system. These, for example, may include assuming each category is free of dispute wheels, or having each node be aware of the upper bound on the running time of each category, and take advantage of this to minimize route flapping.

References

1. Ee, C.T., Ramachandran, V., Chun, B., Lakshminarayanan, K., Shenker, S.: Resolving inter-domain policy disputes. In: Proceedings of the 2007 ACM SIGCOMM Conference, Kyoto, Japan, Augustm (2007)
2. Cobb, J.A.: Maintaining Safety in Interdomain Routing with Hierarchical Path-Categories, Technical Report, Department of Computer Science, The University of Texas at Dallas
3. Cobb, J.A., Musunuri, R.: Enforcing convergence in inter-domain routing. In: Global Telecommunications Conference, IEEE GLOBECOM, pp. 1353–1358 (November 2004)

4. Feamster, N., Johari, R., Balakrishnan, H.: Implications of autonomy for the expressiveness of policy routing. In: Proceedings of the 2005 SIGCOMM Conference, October 2005, pp. 25–36 (2005)
5. Labovitz, C., Malan, G., Jahanian, F.: Internet Routing Instability. In: Proceedings of ACM SIGCOMM (September 1997)
6. Cobb, J.A., Gouda, M.G., Musunuri, R.: A Stabilizing Solution to the Stable Path Problem. In: Huang, S.-T., Herman, T. (eds.) SSS 2003. LNCS, vol. 2704, pp. 169–183. Springer, Heidelberg (2003)
7. Gao, L., Rexford, J.: Stable Internet Routing Without Global Coordination. IEEE/ACM Transactions on Networking 9(6) (December 2001)
8. Gao, L., Rexford, J.: Stable Internet Routing Without Global Coordination. In: Proc. of the ACM SIGMETRICS (June 2000)
9. Gao, L., Griffin, T.G., Rexford, J.: Inherently safe backup routing with BGP. In: IEEE INFOCOM 2001, Proceedings of Twentieth Annual Joint Conference of the IEEE Computer and Communications Societies, vol. 1, pp. 547–556 (2001)
10. Griffin, T.G., Shepherd, F.B., Wilfong, G.: Policy Disputes in Path Vector Protocols. In: Proc. of the IEEE Int'l Conf. on Net. Protocols (October 1999)
11. Griffin, T.G., Shepherd, F.B., Wilfong, G.: The Stable Paths Problem and Interdomain Routing. IEEE/ACM Tran. on Networking 10(2) (April 2002)
12. Griffin, T.G., Wilfong, G.: A Safe Path Vector Protocol. In: Proc. of the INFOCOM Conference (2000)
13. Griffin, T.G., Wilfong, G.: An Analysis of BGP Convergence Properties. In: Proc. of the ACM SIGCOMM Conf. (1999)
14. Rekhtar, Y., Li, T.: A Border Gateway Protocol. RFC1771 (1995)
15. Varadhan, K., Govindan, R., Estrin, D.: Persistent Route Oscillations in Inter-Domain Routing. Computer Networks (January 2000)
16. McPherson, D., Gill, V., Walton, D., Retana, A.: IETF RFC-3345:Border Gateway Protocol (BGP) persistent route oscillation condition (August 2002)

On Communication Complexity of Secure Message Transmission in Directed Networks

Arpita Patra*, Ashish Choudhary**, and C. Pandu Rangan***

Dept of Computer Science and Engineering
IIT Madras, Chennai India 600036
{arpitapatra10,prangan55}@gmail.com, partho_31@yahoo.co.in

Abstract. We re-visit the problem of *perfectly secure message transmission* (PSMT) in a *directed network* under the presence of a threshold adaptive Byzantine adversary, having *unbounded computing power*. Specifically, we derive the lower bounds on communication complexity of (a) two phase PSMT protocols and (b) *three or more phase* PSMT protocols in directed networks. Moreover, we show that our lower bounds are *asymptotically tight*, by designing *communication optimal* PSMT protocols in directed networks, which are first of their kind.

We re-visit the problem of *perfectly reliable message transmission* (PRMT) as well. Any PRMT protocol that sends a message containing ℓ field elements by communicating $\mathcal{O}(\ell)$ field elements, is referred as *communication optimal PRMT* or *PRMT with constant factor overhead*. Here, we characterize the class of directed networks over which *communication optimal* PRMT or PRMT *with constant factor overhead* is possible. Moreover, we design a communication optimal PRMT over a directed network that satisfies the conditions stated in our characterization.

1 Introduction

Consider the following problem: a sender **S** and a receiver **R** are part of a directed synchronous network. There are n uni-directional node disjoint paths/channels $f_1, \ldots, f_n$, which are directed from **S** to **R**, also referred as *top band*. In addition, there are u uni-directional node disjoint paths/channels $b_1, \ldots, b_u$, which are directed from **R** to **S**, also referred as *bottom band*. Each channel is abstracted as a directed edge, also called as *wire*. The wires in the top band and bottom band are mutually disjoint. Moreover, **S** and **R** do not share any information in advance. Any protocol in such a network is executed in *phases*, where phase is a communication from **S** to **R** or vice-versa. There exists a centralized adversary $\mathcal{A}_t$ having *unbounded computing power*, who controls at most t wires out of $n + u$ wires between **S** and **R** in Byzantine fashion. Thus the adversary can read and corrupt the communication through the wires under its control in

---

* Financial Support from Microsoft Research India Acknowledged.
** Financial Support from Infosys Technology India Acknowledged.
*** Work Supported by Project No. CSE/05-06/076/DITX/CPAN on Protocols for Secure Communication and Computation Sponsored by Department of Information Technology, Government of India.

any arbitrary fashion. **S** intends to communicate a message m containing ℓ field elements from a finite field $\mathbb{F}$ to **R**. The challenge is to design a protocol such that after interacting in phases as per the protocol, **R** should correctly output m, without any error, irrespective of the behaviour of $\mathcal{A}_t$. This problem is called *perfectly reliable message transmission* (PRMT)[5,4]. The problem of *perfectly secure message transmission* (PSMT)[5,4] has an additional restriction that at the end of the protocol, $\mathcal{A}_t$ should have *no* information about m what so ever.

Existing Literature. PRMT/PSMT was first introduced and studied in undirected networks by Dolev et.al in [5]. Dolev et.al abstracted the underlying undirected graph and assumed that **S** and **R** are connected by n bi-directional vertex disjoint paths, also called as *wires* and $\mathcal{A}_t$ may corrupt any t out of the n wires in Byzantine fashion. Using *wire abstraction*, Dolev et.al [5] have shown that PRMT/PSMT between **S** and **R** tolerating $\mathcal{A}_t$ is possible iff $n \geq 2t + 1$.

PRMT and PSMT in directed networks was first studied by Desmedt et.al [4]. Modelling the underlying network as a directed graph is well motivated because in practice not every communication channel admits bi-directional communication. For instance, a base-station may communicate to even a far-off hand-held device but the communication may not be possible in reverse direction. Extending the *wire abstraction* approach of Dolev et.al [5], Desmedt et.al [4] have shown that (a) PRMT tolerating $\mathcal{A}_t$ is possible iff there are at least $2t + 1$ wires in the *top band*, (b) PSMT tolerating $\mathcal{A}_t$ is possible iff there are at least $n = \max(3t - 2u + 1, 2t + 1)$ wires in the *top band*. Desmedt et.al [4] have shown the sufficiency of their characterization for PSMT by designing a PSMT protocol that requires *exponential* number of phases and has *exponential* communication complexity. Recently, PSMT protocols with constant phase and polynomial communication complexity have been proposed in [11,14], satisfying the characterization of Desmedt et.al. More recently, Patra et.al [13] have shown that *two* phase PSMT over a directed network, tolerating $\mathcal{A}_t$ is possible iff there exists $n = \max(3t - u + 1, 2t + 1)$ wires in the top band. This clearly shows that the characterization of PSMT given by Desmedt et.al [4] holds for only *three or more* phase PSMT protocols (and is not sufficient for two phase).

Motivation of Our Work and Our Contributions. A key parameter of any PRMT and PSMT protocol is its communication complexity, which is the number of field elements communicated by **S** and **R** in the protocol. Though the PSMT protocols over directed networks, reported in [11,14] are *communication efficient* (i.e. require communication complexity which is polynomial in n), they are not *communication optimal*. Over the past one decade, lot of research has been carried out to derive tight bounds on the communication complexity of PRMT/PSMT protocols in undirected networks [19,6,1]. Unfortunately, there is no complexity bounds for PRMT/PSMT protocols in directed networks. The existing bounds on the communication complexity of PRMT/PSMT in undirected networks cannot be extended to directed networks. This is because in undirected networks, there are $2t + 1$ bi-directional wires between **S** and **R**, while in directed networks, there may be different number of wires in top and bottom band. So in this paper, we derive the lower bound on the communication complexity of both two phase and *three or more* phase PSMT protocols[1]. Moreover, we show that our bounds are *asymptotically tight* by presenting polynomial time and *communication optimal* PSMT protocols which are first of their kind.

Any PRMT protocol that sends ℓ field elements, has a trivial lower bound of $\Omega(\ell)$ on its communication complexity. Thus any PRMT protocol that sends a message of ℓ field elements by communicating $\mathcal{O}(\ell)$ field elements, is referred as *communication optimal PRMT* or *PRMT with constant factor overhead*. Here, we characterize the class of directed networks over which communication optimal PRMT is possible. Moreover, we design a communication optimal PRMT over a graph that satisfies the conditions stated in our characterization.

Definitions. Our protocols work over a finite field $\mathbb{F}$ where $|\mathbb{F}| \geq (n+u)$. We use m to denote the message that **S** intends to send to **R**, where m is a sequence of $\ell \geq 1$ element(s) from $\mathbb{F}$. Any information which is sent over entire top (bottom) band is said to be *broadcast*. If some information is broadcast over at least $2t+1$ wires, then the information will be always recovered correctly at the receiving end by taking majority of the received information.

2   Preliminaries

All the protocols that we present in this paper are heavily based on the properties of Reed-Solomon (RS) encoding and decoding from coding theory [8] and the concept of pseudo-basis, an idea introduced by Kurosawa et.al [6]. We briefly recall the ideas related to them in the sequel.

Definition 1 (RS Codes [8]). *For a message block* $M = (m_1\ m_2\ \ldots\ m_k)$ *over* $\mathbb{F}$, *define* $Reed - Solomon$ *polynomial as* $P_M(x) = m_1 + m_2 x + m_3 x^2 + \ldots + m_k x^{k-1}$. *Let* $\alpha_1, \alpha_2, ..., \alpha_L, L > k$, *denote a sequence of* L *distinct and fixed elements from* $\mathbb{F}$. *Then vector* $C = (c_1\ c_2\ \ldots\ c_L)$ *where* $c_i = P_M(\alpha_i), 1 \leq i \leq L$ *is called the Reed-Solomon (RS) codeword of size* L *for the message block* M.

Given a message block $M = (m_1\ m_2\ \ldots\ m_k)$ of size k over $\mathbb{F}$, the method of computing the RS codeword C for M is called RS encoding. So we write $C = RS - ENC(M, k, L)$. Now let **A** and **B** are two specific nodes and are connected by L wires of which at most t can be under the influence of $\mathcal{A}_t$. Let **A** send the ith component of C over the ith wire. Let **B** receive C' where C and C' differs in at most t locations. Under this scenario, the error correction and detection capability of **B** in C' is given by the error correction and detection capability of RS decoding which is stated as follows:

Theorem 1 ([8,4]). *RS decoding can correct up to* c *and simultaneously detect additional* d *Byzantine errors* $(c + d \leq t)$ *in* C' *iff* $L - k \geq 2c + d$.

---

[1] Any single phase PSMT in directed network is no different from a single phase PSMT in undirected networks. Hence, from [5], any single phase PSMT in directed networks requires $n \geq 3t+1$ wires in the *top* band. Also, from [18], any single phase PSMT over $n \geq 3t+1$ wires communicates $\Omega(\frac{n\ell}{n-3t})$ field elements to securely send m containing ℓ field elements. Moreover, the bound is asymptotically tight.

2.1   Pseudo-basis and Pseudo-dimension

The current description of pseudo-basis and pseudo-dimension is from [6]. Let $\mathcal{C}$ be the set of all possible L length RS codewords over $\mathbb{F}$, which are RS encoded using polynomials of degree $k - 1$ over $\mathbb{F}$. Also we assume that the Hamming distance [8,6] of code $\mathcal{C}$ is $t + 1$ i.e. $L - (k - 1) \geq t + 1$ [6]. We may call the individual codewords in $\mathcal{C}$ as L-dimensional vectors.

Now let us return back to the settings where $\mathbf{A}$ and $\mathbf{B}$ are connected by L wires, among which t are controlled by $\mathcal{A}_t$. Let $\mathbf{A}$ sends several codewords, say γ codewords $C_1, \ldots, C_\gamma \in \mathcal{C}$ over these wires, by transmitting i^{th} component of all the codewords over i^{th} wire. Then the locations at which error occurs in these codewords are not random. This is because for all the codewords the errors always occur at the same t (or less) locations. Based on this simple and interesting observation, Kurosawa et. al. [6] introduced the concept of pseudo-basis. Let $\mathbf{B}$ receive the L length vectors $Y_1 \ldots, Y_\gamma$ such that for $i = 1, \ldots, \gamma$, $Y_i = C_i + E_i$, where $E_i = (e_{i1}, \ldots, e_{iL})$ is an error vector caused by $\mathcal{A}_t$. Notice that each E_i has at most t non-zero components. Let $support(E_i) = \{j \mid e_{ij} \neq 0\}$. Then there exist some t-subset $\{j_1, \ldots, j_t\}$ of L wires that are corrupted by $\mathcal{A}_t$ such that each error vector E_i satisfies $support(E_i) \subseteq \{j_1, \ldots, j_t\}$. This means that the space $\mathcal{E}$ spanned by $E_1, \ldots, E_\gamma$ has dimension at most t. The notion of pseudo-basis exploits this idea. Let $\mathcal{V}$ denote the L-dimensional vector space over $\mathbb{F}$. For two vectors $Y, E \in \mathcal{V}$, we write $Y = E \ mod \ \mathcal{C}$ if $Y - E \in \mathcal{C}$. Notice that for $1 \leq i \leq \gamma$, for every triplet (Y_i, C_i, E_i), $Y_i = E_i \ mod \ \mathcal{C}$ holds since $Y_i - E_i = C_i \in \mathcal{C}$.

Definition 2 (Pseudo-span [6]). *We say that $\{Y_{a_1} \ldots, Y_{a_p}\} \subset \mathcal{Y}$ pseudo-spans $\mathcal{Y}$ if each $Y_i \in \mathcal{Y}$ can be written as $Y_i = (b_1 Y_{a_1} + \ldots + b_p Y_{a_p}) \ mod \ \mathcal{C}$, for some non-zero vector $(b_1, \ldots, b_p) \in \mathbb{F}^p$.*

Definition 3 (Pseudo-dimension and pseudo-basis [6]). *Let p be the dimension of the space $\mathcal{E} = \{E_1, \ldots, E_\gamma\}$ and let $\{E_{a_1}, \ldots, E_{a_p}\} \subset \mathcal{E}$ be a basis of $\mathcal{E}$. We then say that $\mathcal{Y}$ has pseudo-dimension p and $\{Y_{a_1}, \ldots, Y_{a_p}\} \subset \mathcal{Y}$ is a pseudo-basis of $\mathcal{Y}$.*

Theorem 2 ([6]). $\mathcal{B} = \{Y_{a_1}, \ldots, Y_{a_p}\}$ *is a pseudo-basis of $\mathcal{Y}$ iff $\mathcal{B}$ is a minimal subset of $\mathcal{Y}$ which pseudo-spans $\mathcal{Y}$.*

Theorem 3 ([6]). *The pseudo-dimension of $\mathcal{Y}$ is at most t.*

Let $\mathcal{B} = \{Y_{a_1}, \ldots, Y_{a_p}\}$ be a pseudo-basis of $\mathcal{Y}$ and let $CORRUPTED = \cup_{i=1}^{p} support(E_{a_i})$. Then $CORRUPTED$ is the set of wires that the adversary $\mathcal{A}_t$ has corrupted. So,

Theorem 4 ([6]). *For each i, $support(E_i) \subseteq CORRUPTED$.*

Kurosawa et. al [6] also have provided a polynomial time algorithm which finds the pseudo-dimension p and a pseudo-basis $\mathcal{B}$ of $\mathcal{Y} = \{Y_1, \ldots, Y_\gamma\}$. We denote the algorithm as: $(p, \mathcal{B}, \mathcal{I}) = \mathbf{FindPseudo\text{-}basis}(\mathcal{Y})$. So $\mathbf{FindPseudo\text{-}basis}$ takes the set of received (by $\mathbf{B}$) vectors $\mathcal{Y}$ as input and finds the pseudo-basis $\mathcal{B} = \{Y_{a_1}, \ldots, Y_{a_p}\} \subset \mathcal{Y}$, pseudo-dimension $p = |\mathcal{B}| \leq t$ and an index set $\mathcal{I} = \{a_1, \ldots, a_p\} \subset \{1, \ldots, \gamma\}$ containing the indices of the vectors selected in $\mathcal{B}$.

2.2 Extracting Randomness

Suppose **S** and **R** agree on L random numbers $x = [x_1\ x_2\ \ldots\ x_L] \in \mathbb{F}^L$ such that $\mathcal{A}_t$ knows $L - f$ components of x, but has no information about the other f components of x. However **S** and **R** do not know which values are known to $\mathcal{A}_t$. The goal of **S** and **R** is to agree on a sequence of f elements $[y_1\ y_2\ \ldots\ y_f]$, such that $\mathcal{A}_t$ has no information about $[y_1\ y_2\ \ldots\ y_f]$. This is done by using algorithm **Algorithm EXTRAND**$_{L,f}(x)$ presented in [19].

3   PRMT with Constant Factor Overhead

In this section, we characterize the class of digraphs over which *communication optimal PRMT* protocol is possible tolerating $\mathcal{A}_t$.

Theorem 5. *Communication optimal PRMT protocol, tolerating $\mathcal{A}_t$ is possible over a digraph iff there are $n \geq 2t + 1$ wires in the top band and u wires in the bottom band where $(n - 2t) + 2u = \Omega(n)$.*

PROOF: **Sufficiency.** We design a *communication optimal* PRMT protocol **OPRMT**, which reliably sends a message m containing $\ell = \Omega(nt)$ field elements by communicating $\mathcal{O}(nt)$ field elements and terminates in three phases, provided $n = 2t + 1$ and $(n - 2t) + 2u = \Omega(n)$.

Before describing **OPRMT**, we present a special type of single phase PRMT called **SP-REL** where **S** is connected to **R** by $n \geq 2t + 1$ wires $f_1, \ldots, f_n$. **SP-REL** either sends m to **R** or it may fail because $\mathcal{A}_t$ have done corruptions exceeding some limit (but not more than t). In the later case, **R** will *only* be able to detect but cannot correct the errors to recover m. Thus **SP-REL** creates a win-win situation: if $\mathcal{A}_t$ does at most $(t - b)$ corruptions then m is recovered; else **R** detects that more than $(t - b)$ wires are corrupted. Protocol **SP-REL** is based on RS codes. Let $X = n - 2t$. We then design a *communication optimal* PRMT protocol **OPRMT** using **SP-REL** as a black-box. The proofs of the properties of **SP-REL** and **OPRMT** are available in [12].

Protocol SP-REL(m, ℓ, n, t, b): $n \geq 2t + 1, 0 \leq b \leq t$

1. **S** breaks up m into blocks $\mathbf{B_1}, \mathbf{B_2}, \ldots, \mathbf{B_z}$, each consisting of k field elements, where $k = X + b$. If ℓ is not an exact multiple of k, a default padding is used to make $\ell \bmod k = 0$.
2. For each block $\mathbf{B_i}$, **S** computes $(c_{i1}c_{i2} \ldots c_{in}) = RS - ENC(B_i, k, n)$ and sends c_{ij}, along the wire $f_j, 1 \leq j \leq n$.
3. **R** receives c'_{ij} (possibly corrupted) over f_j for $1 \leq j \leq n$ and $1 \leq i \leq z$ and applies RS decoding to each of the received n length vectors and tries to correct $t - b$ errors and simultaneously detect additional b errors.
4. If after correcting $t - b$ errors, the RS decoding algorithm does not detect additional errors in any of the z received vectors, then **R** correctly recovers $\mathbf{B_i}$, $1 \leq i \leq z$ and concatenates these blocks to recover m.
5. If $\exists e \in \{1, 2, \ldots, z\}$ such that after correcting $t - b$ errors, the decoding algorithm detects additional errors in the eth received vector, then **R** generates "ERROR" which means he has detected that more than $t - b$ faults has occurred.

Protocol OPRMT (m, ℓ, n, u, t); $|m| = \ell = (nt)$

Phase I: S to R: S executes **SP-REL**(m, ℓ, n, t, b) with $b = \min(\frac{u}{2}, \frac{t}{2})$, $n = 2t + 1$. In **SP-REL**, let $B_1^S, \ldots, B_z^S$ be the message blocks and C_i^S be the n length RS codeword corresponding to B_i^S, sent by S.

Phase II: R to S: Let R receive $C_1^R, \ldots, C_z^R$. If R recovers m after the execution of **SP-REL**, then he sends SUCCESS to S through the entire *bottom band*. Else R sends ERROR and the tuple (α, C_α^R) to S through entire *bottom band*, where R has detected more than $t - b$ faults in C_α^R.

Phase III: S to R: Let S receive SUCCESS along $u_s \geq 0$ wires and ERROR along with an tuple of the form (**index**, n **length vector**) through $u_e \geq 0$ wires. S now considers the following two cases:

- *Case 1.* $u_s \geq \frac{u}{2}$: S does nothing and terminates the protocol.
- *Case 2.* $u_e \geq \frac{u}{2}$: S checks whether it has received the same (**index**, n **length vector**) over at least $\frac{u}{2}$ wires out of the u_e wires. If not, then S does nothing and terminates the protocol. Otherwise, let S receive the same tuple (β, Γ) through at least $\frac{u}{2}$ wires out of u_e wires and do the following:
  1. Compute $\mathcal{E} = support(C_\beta^S - \Gamma)$ and the number of mismatches between C_β^S and Γ as $E = |\mathcal{E}|$.
  2. If $E \leq t - b$, then do nothing and terminate the protocol.
  3. If $E > t - b$, then consider the wires in $\mathcal{E}$ as faulty and add them to a list L_{fault}. Ignore all the wires in L_{fault} from the *top band* for further communication. For simplicity, let these be the last $|L_{fault}|$ wires in the *top* band. Re-send m by executing **SP-REL**$(m, \ell, n - |L_{fault}|, t - |L_{fault}|, |L_{fault}|)$ over the first $n - |L_{fault}|$ wires. In addition, broadcast L_{fault} to R over entire *top band*.

Message Recovery by R: If R had sent ERROR and a tuple (index, n length vector) to S during **Phase II**, then R will always correctly receive L_{fault}. Now ignoring all information received over the wires in L_{fault}, R correctly recovers m by executing the steps of **SP-REL**$(m, \ell, n - |L_{fault}|, t - |L_{fault}|, |L_{fault}|)$.

Necessity: Due to space constraints, the entire proof is available in [12].

4 Lower Bound on Communication Complexity of Two Phase PSMT

We now derive the lower bound on the communication complexity of any two phase PSMT protocol in directed networks. We then show that the bound is *asymptotically tight*. We first recall the characterization of two phase PSMT in directed networks tolerating $\mathcal{A}_t$ from [13].

Theorem 6 ([13]). *Suppose there are disjoint set of n wires in the top band and u wires in the bottom band such that $\mathcal{A}_t$ controls at most t of these $n + u$ wires. Then there exists a two phase PSMT tolerating $\mathcal{A}_t$ iff $n \geq max(3t - u + 1, 2t + 1)$.*

Now the lower bound is given by the following theorem.

Theorem 7. *Suppose there exists u wires in the bottom band and $n = \max(3t - u + 1, 2t + 1)$ wires in the top band. Then any two phase PSMT protocol which securely sends a message $m \in \mathbb{F}^\ell$ containing ℓ field elements must communicate*

(a) $\Omega\left(\frac{N\ell}{N-3t}\right)$ field elements where $0 \le u \le t$, $n \ge 3t - u + 1$ and $N = n + u \ge 3t + 1$.

(b) $\Omega\left(\frac{n\ell}{n-2t}\right)$ field elements where $u > t$ and $n \ge 2t + 1$.

PROOF (SKETCH). We first give sufficiency proof. Let $n = \max(3t - u + 1, 2t + 1)$, $u > 0, \delta = \max(u, t)$ and $N = n + u$. We design a two phase PSMT protocol **O2PSMT**, which sends a message m containing $\ell = (\delta + 1 - t)$ field elements by communicating $(N + n(\delta + 1 - t))$ field elements.

Protocol O2PSMT

Phase I: R to S: R selects a random vector $R = (r_1, \ldots, r_u)$ over $\mathbb{F}$ and sends r_j to S along wire b_j.

Phase II: S to R:

1. Let **S** receive $\overline{R}$. **S** then select a codeword C from $\mathcal{C}$ such that last u components of C is same as $\overline{R}$. This is always possible because $\delta \ge u$ and every RS codeword in $\mathcal{C}$ corresponds to a unique δ degree polynomial. Let C correspond to polynomial $F(x)$. **S** sends j^{th} component of C over wire f_j in *top band*.
2. **S** computes $\Gamma = m \oplus Z$ where $Z = \textbf{EXTRAND}_{N,\delta+1-t}(C_{(\delta+1)})$ and $C_{(\delta+1)}$ denotes the first $\delta + 1$ components of C. **S** then broadcasts the blinded message Γ over the entire *top band*.

Local Computation by R At The End of Phase II:

1. After receiving information over *top band*, **R** possesses $N = n + u$ length vector Y (by combining the values received over the top band and values sent over the bottom band) corresponding to codeword C, such that Y is different from C at most at t locations. **R** applies RS decoding algorithm on Y to recover C by correcting t errors. Once C is obtained, **R** computes Z in the same way as **S**.
2. **R** also receives Γ correctly. Now **R** recovers m by computing $m = \Gamma \oplus Z$.

In **O2PSMT**, $\mathcal{C}$ is the set of all possible RS codewords of length N, encoded using all possible polynomials of degree δ over $\mathbb{F}$, for fixed $\alpha_1, \ldots, \alpha_{n+u}$. Here α_i is associated with wire f_i for $1 \le i \le n$ and α_{n+j} is associated with b_j for $1 \le j \le u$. The hamming distance [8] between any two codeword in $\mathcal{C}$ is $N - \delta = n + u - \delta \ge 2t + 1$. For properties of protocol **O2PSMT** see [12].

The necessity proof of this theorem is heavily based on proof of Theorem 6 (for details see [12]). For part(a) of this theorem we show that for every two phase PSMT protocol sending m with $n \ge 3t - u + 1$ and $0 < u \le t$ wires in *top* and *bottom* band respectively, there exist a single phase PSMT sending m with $N = n + u$ wires (from **S** to **R**) with same communication cost. Now any single phase PSMT sending m over $N \ge 3t + 1$ wires must communicate $\Omega\left(\frac{N\ell}{N-3t}\right)$ field elements [18]. Part(b) follows from the fact that any PSMT protocol is also a PRMT protocol. Now neglecting the communication from **R** to **S**, any two phase PRMT can be reduced to single phase PRMT by following the conversion shown in [19] (see Theorem 2 of [19]). Now from [19], any single phase PRMT protocol over $n = 2t + 1$ wires has to communicate $\Omega(\frac{n\ell}{n-2t})$ field elements. $\square$

5   Lower Bounds for Three or More Phase PSMT

Recall that from [4], any three or more phase PSMT requires $n = \max(3t - 2u + 1, 2t + 1)$ wires in the *top* band to tolerate $\mathcal{A}_t$. To build our lower bound argument for three or more phase PSMT protocol, we need a few concepts from secret sharing and Maximum Distance Separable (MDS) codes.

5.1   Secret Sharing Schemes and MDS Codes

Definition 4 (x-out-of-n Secret Sharing Scheme (SSS) [17]). *An x-out-of-n Secret Sharing Scheme (SSS) is a probabilistic function $S : \mathbb{F} \to \mathbb{F}^n$ with the property that for any $M \in \mathbb{F}$ and $S(M) = (s_1, \ldots, s_n)$, no information on M can be inferred from any x elements of $(s_1, \ldots, s_n)$ and M can be recovered from any $x + 1$ elements in $(s_1, \ldots, s_n)$.*

The set of all possible $(s_1, \ldots, s_n)$ can be viewed as a code and its elements as codewords [4]. If the code is a Maximum Distance Separable (MDS) code [8,4] (e.g RS code), then it can correct c errors and simultaneously detect d additional errors iff $n - x > 2c + d$ [8,4]. An x-out-of-n SSS is called MDS x-out-of-n SSS if it is constructed from a MDS code. MDS SSSs can be constructed from any MDS codes, for example RS codes [8,9,4]. So we have the following theorem on the error correction and detection capability of MDS x-out-of-n SSS:

Theorem 8 ([8,4]). *Any MDS x-out-of-n SSS can correct c errors and detect d additional errors in a codeword iff $n - x > 2c + d$.*

5.2   The Lower Bound on Communication Complexity

We now derive the lower bound on the communication complexity of any three or more phase PSMT protocol tolerating $\mathcal{A}_t$. We first give the following definition:

Definition 5 ($(\alpha, \beta, \gamma, m, \ell)$-SSS). *Given a secret m containing ℓ field elements from $\mathbb{F}$, an $(\alpha, \beta, \gamma, m, \ell)$-SSS generates α shares of m, such that any set of β shares have full information about the secret m, while any set of γ shares have no information about the secret m with $\alpha > \beta > \gamma$.*

Theorem 9. *Suppose there exists u wires in the bottom band and $n = \max(3t - 2u+1, 2t+1)$ wires in the top band. Then any three or more phase PSMT protocol that securely sends a message m containing ℓ field elements from $\mathbb{F}$ tolerating $\mathcal{A}_t$ must communicate*

(a) $\Omega(\frac{n\ell}{n-(3t-2u)})$ field elements when $0 < u \le t$.

(b) $\Omega(\ell)$ field elements when $u > t$.

PROOF (OUTLINE): Part (a) is proved as follows: we first show that the communication complexity of any three or more phase PSMT protocol tolerating $\mathcal{A}_t$

to send a message $m \in \mathbb{F}^{\ell}$ is not less than the share complexity (sum of all the shares) of an $(n, (n - 2(t - u)), t, m, \ell)$-SSS. We then show that the share complexity of any $(n, (n - 2(t - u)), t, m, \ell)$-SSS is $\Omega(\frac{n\ell}{n-(3t-2u)})$ field elements. For complete details see [12]. Part (b) simply follows from the fact that any PSMT protocol has to at least send the message and hence $\Omega(\ell)$ field elements.   □

6   Upper Bounds for Three or More Phase PSMT

Theorem 9 has following implications: Any three or more phase PSMT protocol which wishes to send a message m containing ℓ field elements, has to communicate (i) $\Omega(\frac{n\ell}{n-(3t-2u)})$ field elements when $0 < u < \frac{t}{2}$ and $n \geq 3t - 2u + 1$, (ii) $\Omega(\frac{n\ell}{2u-t})$ field elements when $\frac{t}{2} \leq u \leq t$ and $n \geq 2t + 1$, (iii) $\Omega(\ell)$ field elements when $u > t$ and $n \geq 2t + 1$. To show that the lower bounds in (i), (ii) and (iii) are *asymptotically tight*, we present three different protocols in the sequel.

6.1   Communication Optimal PSMT with $0 < u < \frac{t}{2}$ and $n = 3t - 2u + 1$

In this section, we present a three phase communication optimal PSMT protocol called **O3PSMT**, which securely sends $\ell = n^2 u$ field elements by communicating $\mathcal{O}(n^3 u) = \mathcal{O}(n\ell)$ field elements. Informally the protocol works as follows: **S** tries to correctly establish an information theoretic secure one time pad of size $n^2 u$ with **R**. Let $\mathcal{C}$ denote the set of all RS codewords of length $n = 3t - 2u + 1$ over $\mathbb{F}$, encoded using all possible polynomials of degree t over $\mathbb{F}$, for fixed $\alpha_1, \ldots, \alpha_n$. Here α_i is associated with wire f_i. Hence the hamming distance between any two codeword is $n-t = 2t-2u+1 \geq t+1$. In protocol **O3PSMT**, **S** selects a number of random codewords from $\mathcal{C}$ and sends them across the n wires. **R** receives the codewords and finds the pseudo-basis of the received codewords. **R** then sends the pseudo-basis, pseudo-dimension and index set through the *bottom band*. We say that a pseudo-basis, pseudo-dimension and index set triple received over a wire in bottom band is **valid** iff all the codewords listed in pseudo-basis differs from the corresponding original codewords (sent by **S**) at most at t locations. Note that **S** has no knowledge on whether the original pseudo-basis generated by **R** is received by him. So **S** broadcasts all the valid triple of (pseudo basis, pseudo-dimension and index set) as received by him along with the corresponding list of corrupted wires. Now **R** correctly receives all the pseudo-basis, pseudo-dimension and index set, along with their corresponding list of corrupted wires. **R** checks whether the pseudo-basis generated by him is present in the received list of pseudo-basis. If yes then he knows the set of corrupted wires and can recover all the original codewords (sent by **S**) by neglecting the values received over those corrupted wires during first phase. Otherwise **R** learns that entire *bottom band* is corrupted and hence in the *top band* there are at most $t - u$ Byzantine faults. So **R** can correct these $t - u$ errors in each of the codeword, received during first phase and thus can recover all the original codewords. Hence in any case **S** and **R** will agree on all the codewords chosen by **S**.

Protocol O3PSMT(m, ℓ, n, u, t)

Phase I: S to R: S selects $P = n^2 u + ut = \ell + ut$ random codewords $C_1, \ldots, C_P$ from $\mathcal{C}$. Let $C_i = (c_{i1}, \ldots, c_{in})$. Also let $F_1(x), \ldots, F_P(x)$ be the t degree polynomials corresponding to the codewords. Now **S** sends j^{th} component of all the codewords along wire f_j in *top band*.

Phase II: R to S

1. Let **R** receive $Y_i = C_i + E_i$ corresponding to codeword C_i and let $\mathcal{Y} = \{Y_1, \ldots, Y_P\}$.
2. **R** invokes $(p, \mathcal{B}, \mathcal{I}) = $ **FindPseudo-basis**$(\mathcal{Y})$ to find pseudo-basis $\mathcal{B} = \{Y_{a_1}, \ldots, Y_{a_p}\} \subset \mathcal{Y}$, pseudo-dimension $p = |\mathcal{B}|$ and index set $\mathcal{I} = \{a_1, \ldots, a_p\} \subset \{1, \ldots, P\}$. **R** then broadcasts $(\mathcal{B}, p, \mathcal{I})$ through the *bottom band*.

Phase III: S to R

1. **S** may receive different triples over different wires. Let **S** receive $(\mathcal{B}^j, p^j, \mathcal{I}^j)$ over wire b_j in *bottom band*. Let $\mathcal{B}^j = \{Y_{a_1^j}^j, \ldots, Y_{a_{p^j}^j}^j\}$ and $\mathcal{I}^j = \{a_1^j, \ldots, a_{p^j}^j\}$.
2. **S** considers the triple $(\mathcal{B}^j, p^j, \mathcal{I}^j)$ as **valid** iff $p^j = |\mathcal{B}^j|$ and every n length vector listed in $\mathcal{B}^j$ is different from the corresponding original codeword at most at t locations. For every **valid** triple $(\mathcal{B}^j, p^j, \mathcal{I}^j)$, **S** finds $E_{a_1^j}^j = Y_{a_1^j}^j - C_{a_1^j} \cdots, E_{a_{p^j}^j}^j = Y_{a_{p^j}^j}^j - C_{a_{p^j}^j}$ and computes $CORRUPTED^j = \cup_{\alpha=1}^{p^j} support(E_{a_\alpha^j}^j)$.
3. **S** computes $\Lambda = \cup_j \{\mathcal{I}^j | (\mathcal{B}^j, p^j, \mathcal{I}^j)$ is a valid triple$\}$. Then **S** concatenates all the $F_i(0)$'s such $i \notin \Lambda$ and forms an information theoretic secure pad Z of length at least $n^2 u$ (since $|\Lambda| \leq ut$ and $P = n^2 u + ut$).
4. Now **S** broadcasts the following to **R**: (i) every valid triple $(\mathcal{B}^j, p^j, \mathcal{I}^j)$ and corresponding list of corrupted wires $CORRUPTED^j$ (ii) If there is no **valid** triple, then the message **"Entire Bottom band is corrupted"**, (iii) blinded message $\Gamma = Z_\ell \oplus m$ where Z_ℓ contains first ℓ elements from Z.

Local Computation by R at the End of Phase III:

1. **R** correctly receives all information sent by **S** in **Phase III** and computes Λ in same way as done by **S**.
2. If either **R** gets the message **"Entire Bottom band is corrupted"** or if **R** finds his original triple $(\mathcal{B}, p, \mathcal{I})$ is not present in the list of **valid** triples sent by **S**, then **R** does the following:
   (a) Conclude that entire *bottom band* is corrupted and hence in the top band there are at most $t - u$ faults.
   (b) Recover all $F_i(x)$ such that $i \notin \Lambda$ by applying RS decoding algorithm on Y_i and correcting $t - u$ faults.
   (c) Recover pad Z (and hence Z_ℓ) by concatenating $F_i(0)$ for all $i \notin \Lambda$ and hence the message $m = \Gamma \oplus Z_\ell$.
3. If **R** finds that his original triple $(\mathcal{B}, p, \mathcal{I})$ is present in the list of **valid** triples sent by **S** and let $(\mathcal{B}^j, p^j, \mathcal{I}^j)$ is same as $(\mathcal{B}, p, \mathcal{I})$, then **R** does following:
   (a) Identify all the wires in $CORRUPTED^j$ ($|CORRUPTED^j| \leq t$) as the corrupted wires in **Phase I**.
   (b) Ignore all information received over the wires in $CORRUPTED^j$ ($|CORRUPTED^j| \leq t$) during **Phase I**. Reconstruct all the polynomial $F_i(x)$ such that $i \notin \Lambda$ by considering the correct values on $F_i(x)$ received over remaining wires (which are at least $t + 1$) during **Phase I**.
   (c) Recover the message m in the same way as described in step 2.

But during the transmission of pseudo-basis over u wires, $\mathcal{A}_t$ can generate u distinct **valid** pseudo-basis each containing at most t disjoint codewords (this he can do by guessing with very non-zero probability). Therefore initially **S** should send sufficient number of codewords such that after removing all the ut codewords appearing in the received list of valid pseudo-basis, the remaining codewords can be used to construct an information theoretic secure pad of size n^2u. Once the pad is established, **S** uses the pad to blind the message and sends the blinded message reliably to **R**. For proof of the properties of **O3PSMT** see [12].

6.2   Communication Optimal PSMT When $\frac{t}{2} \le u \le t$ and $n \ge 2t+1$

We now outline our six phase communication optimal PSMT protocol called **O6PSMT** where $n = 2t + 1$ and $\frac{t}{2} \le u \le t$. Protocol **O6PSMT** securely sends $\ell = n^2u$ field elements by communicating $O\left(\frac{n^3u}{2u-t}\right) = O\left(\frac{n\ell}{2u-t+1}\right)$ field elements, thus *asymptotically* satisfying the lower bound given in Theorem 9. Interestingly, when $u = \frac{t}{2} + \Theta(t)$, then Protocol **O6PSMT** sends ℓ field elements securely by communicating $\mathcal{O}(\ell)$ field elements. Protocol **O6PSMT** achieves it's goal by allowing **S** and **R** to share $\frac{n^2u}{2u-t+1}$ common polynomials each of degree $2u$, such that $\mathcal{A}_t$ knows only t points on each of them. Once this is done, both **S** and **R** can generate (and agree) on an information theoretic pad of length n^2u by using **EXTRAND** algorithm. **S** can then blind the message and sends it to **R**. However, note that **S** cannot send the blinded message to **R** by sending it over the entire *top* band, as done in protocol **O3PSMT**. Because the communication complexity will then become $\mathcal{O}(n^3u)$ and hence, it will no longer satisfy the lower bound of Theorem 9. So **S** reliably sends the blinded message by using protocol **OPRMT** given in Section 3, which takes 3 phases. The rest of the protocol is similar to **O3PSMT**. For complete details see [12].

6.3   Communication Optimal PSMT When $u > t$ and $n \ge 2t+1$

If $u = t$ and $n = 2t + 1 = \Theta(t)$, then protocol **O6PSMT** securely sends $\ell = n^2u = \Theta(n^3)$ field elements by communicating $\mathcal{O}(n^3)$ field elements (for details see [12]). Hence, if $u > t$ and $n \ge 2t + 1$, then **S** and **R** can execute **O6PSMT** by considering the first $2t+1$ wires in the *top* band and first t wires in the *bottom* band. Thus, we have the following theorem:

Theorem 10. *Suppose $n \ge 2t + 1$ and $u > t$. Then there exists a six phase PSMT protocol tolerating $\mathcal{A}_t$, which securely sends ℓ ($\ell = n^3$) field elements by communicating $\mathcal{O}(\ell)$ field elements.*

7   Open Problems

It would be interesting to reduce the phase complexity of our *six phase* PSMT protocol. Also it would be interesting to design PRMT and PSMT protocols, which are communication optimal for message of any length.

References

1. Ashwinkumar, B.V., Patra, A., Choudhary, A., Srinathan, K., Pandu Rangan, C.: On tradeoff between network connectivity, phase complexity and communication complexity of reliable communication tolerating mixed adversary. In: PODC, pp. 115–124 (2008)
2. Ben-Or, M., Goldwasser, S., Wigderson, A.: Completeness theorems for non-cryptographic fault-tolerant distributed computation. In: STOC, pp. 1–10 (1988)
3. Chaum, D., Crpeau, C., Damgård, I.: Multiparty unconditionally secure protocols (extended abstract). In: STOC, pp. 11–19 (1988)
4. Desmedt, Y., Wang, Y.: Perfectly secure message transmission revisited. Cryptology ePrint Archive, Report 2002/128 (2002)
5. Dolev, D., Dwork, C., Waarts, O., Yung, M.: Perfectly secure message transmission. JACM 40(1), 17–47 (1993)
6. Kurosawa, K., Suzuki, K.: Truly efficient 2-round perfectly secure message transmission scheme. In: Smart, N.P. (ed.) EUROCRYPT 2008. LNCS, vol. 4965, pp. 324–340. Springer, Heidelberg (2008)
7. Lynch, N.A.: Distributed Algorithms. Morgan Kaufmann, San Francisco (1998)
8. MacWilliams, F.J., Sloane, N.J.A.: The Theory of Error Correcting Codes. North-Holland Publishing Company, Amsterdam (1978)
9. McEliece, R.J., Sarwate, D.V.: On sharing secrets and Reed-Solomon codes. Communications of the ACM 24(9), 583–584 (1981)
10. Menger, K.: Zur allgemeinen kurventheorie. Fundamenta Mathematicae 10, 96–115 (1927)
11. Patra, A., Choudhary, A., Pandu Rangan, C.: Constant phase efficient protocols for secure message transmission in directed networks. In: PODC, pp. 322–323 (2007)
12. Patra, A., Choudhary, A., Pandu Rangan, C.: On the communication complexity of perfectly secure message transmission in directed networks. Cryptology ePrint Archive, Report 2009/470 (2009)
13. Patra, A., Choudhary, A., Pandu Rangan, C.: Perfectly secure message transmission in directed networks revisited. In: PODC, pp. 305–328 (2009)
14. Patra, A., Shankar, B., Choudhary, A., Srinathan, K., Rangan, C.P.: Perfectly secure message transmission in directed networks tolerating threshold and non threshold adversary. In: Bao, F., Ling, S., Okamoto, T., Wang, H., Xing, C. (eds.) CANS 2007. LNCS, vol. 4856, pp. 80–101. Springer, Heidelberg (2007)
15. Pease, M., Shostak, R.E., Lamport, L.: Reaching agreement in the presence of faults. JACM 27(2), 228–234 (1980)
16. Rabin, T., Ben-Or, M.: Verifiable secret sharing and multiparty protocols with honest majority (extended abstract). In: STOC, pp. 73–85 (1989)
17. Shamir, A.: How to share a secret. Communications of the ACM 22(11), 612–613 (1979)
18. Srinathan, K.: Secure distributed communication. PhD Thesis, IIT Madras (2006)
19. Srinathan, K., Narayanan, A., Pandu Rangan, C.: Optimal perfectly secure message transmission. In: Franklin, M. (ed.) CRYPTO 2004. LNCS, vol. 3152, pp. 545–561. Springer, Heidelberg (2004)
20. Yao, A.C.: Protocols for secure computations. In: FOCS, pp. 160–164 (1982)

On Composability of Reliable Unicast and Broadcast

Anuj Gupta[1], Sandeep Hans[1], Kannan Srinathan[1], and C. Pandu Rangan[2]

[1] Center for Security, Theory and Algorithmic Research,
International Institute of Information Technology, Hyderabad - 500032, India
anujgupta@research.iiit.net
[2] Department of Computer Science, IIT Madras, India

Abstract. In the recent past composability has emerged as a key requirement for various distributed protocols. It is not enough for a protocol to be robust when it runs in isolation or in a "stand-alone" setting
but it should be robust even in an environment where several copies
of the same protocol or other protocol(s) are running simultaneously.
In this work, we investigate the composability for protocols that tolerate a bounded adversary modeled as a probabilistic polynomial time
Turing machine. We examine composability of protocols for two fundamental problems in distributed computing - reliable unicast and reliable
broadcast. We show that any composable protocol – for reliable unicast
tolerating an adversary, that corrupts up to any t nodes, requires $2t + 1$
connectivity and for reliable broadcast tolerating an adversary, that corrupts up to any t nodes, requires $n > 3t$ and $2t + 1$ connectivity.

1 Introduction

Traditionally, robustness of a protocol in a distributd environment has been analyzed with a tacit assumption that the protocol is executed in "isolation" i.e.
when an instance of the given protocol is executed, no instance of any other
protocol (including currently executed protocol) is in execution concurrently.
This is popularly known as "stand alone" execution model. However, for most
real life networks (such as LAN, Internet), a protocol is seldom executed in a
stand alone setting. Thus, the stand-alone notion of robustness is grossly inadequate for such settings. Intersestingly, it was shown that in absense of stand
alone model, protocol(s) proven to be secure in stand alone setting can become
insecure. This is popularly known as "protocol composition". Stated informally,
protocol composition refers to an environment where the participating parties
are involved in many protocol executions. In this paper we aim to investigate
composition of protocols for reliable communication.

The problem of reliable communication is one of the fundamental problems
in distributed computing. The communication can be from one node to another

K. Kant et al. (Eds.): ICDCN 2010, LNCS 5935, pp. 54–66, 2010.

(unicast), one to many (multicast), or from one to all (broadcast). Stated informally, the problem of unicast is: sender S wishes to communicate a message m to a receiver R through an arbitrary synchronous network, some of whose nodes are under the control of an adversary. It was first studied by Dolev *et al.* [1] under the setting of Byzantine adversary that can actively corrupt up to any t nodes(t-adversary) in the network. For a computationally unbounded adversary, it is well known that reliable communication between any pair of nodes is possible if and only if the network is $(2t + 1)$-connected [1,2]. In line with the observations of Dolev *et al.*[1], we completely abstract the synchronous network as a collection of κ wires connecting the sender and the receiver of which up to t wires may be Byzantine corrupt. [1] proved that such an abstraction is actually *without loss of generality* in the study of the *possibility* of reliable communication. Later, the problem was studied in several other settings [2,3,4,5,6,7,8].

The problem of reliable broadcast (Byzantine Generals Problem[BGP]) was introduced by Pease *et al.* [9,10]. The challenge is to maintain a coherent view of the world among all the honest players in spite of faulty players trying to disrupt the same. Specifically, in a BGP protocol over a point-to-point *synchronous* network of n players, the dealer starts with an input from a fixed set $V = \{0, 1\}$. At the end of the protocol (which may involve finitely many rounds of interaction), even in the presence of a t-adversary, all the honest players should output same value u. And if the dealer is honest and starts with value v, then $u = v$. There exists a rich literature on BGP. Pease *et al.* [9,10] proved that BGP tolerating a t-adversary over a completely connected synchronous network of n nodes is possible if and only if $n > 3t$. Later, studies were initiated in this problem under various settings [11,12,13,14,15,16,17,18]. An important variant of BGP is the authenticated model proposed by Pease *et al.* [9]. In this model, which we hereafter refer to as *authenticated Byzantine Generals* (ABG), the players are supplemented with "magical" powers (say a Public Key Infrastructure(PKI) and digital signatures) via which players can authenticate themselves and their messages. It is well known that in this model, tolerability against a t-adversary can be amazingly increased to as high as $n > t$. Subsequent papers on this subject include [19,20,21,22,23,24,25].

Literature has studied several notions protocol composition. We briefly define some important ones: **(i)** *Self Composition*: A protocol is said to be self composable if several executions of the same protocol run in a network, the protocol still remains robust. **(ii)** *General Composition*: The protocol needs to be robust even when it is run along with several executions of other protocols. **(iii)** *Sequential Composition* : In sequential composition, there is only one execution of a particular protocol at one point of time. **(iv)** *Parallel Composition*: In parallel composition, there can be several executions running simultaneously.

Canetti [26] introduced "universal composability" to prove the security of protocols under general composition. In general, one expects to achieve greater fault tolerance against computationally bounded adversary than against unbounded adversary. To motivate our study, we next present an example where the above intuition does not hold good.

1.1 Motivation and Our Results

For the problem of reliable unicast in the stand alone setting the "sign-flood-verify" protocol (given in Figure 1) is easily seen to tolerate a bounded adversary who can corrupt up to $t = \kappa - 1$ wires. However, when the adversary has unlimited computational powers, it is well known that perfect reliable communication protocol exists if and only if $\kappa > 2t$ [1]. We show that in the case of bounded adversary when majority of the nodes (of any vertex cut-set) in a communication network are faulty, it is impossible to design a composable protocol for reliable unicast. In the case where majority of the nodes are non-faulty, we also design a single round bit optimal composable protocol that, with an arbitrarily high probability, is reliable. Thus, we show that the stand-alone notion of robustness is not a satisfactory model and we need to examine the protocol for its composability properties.

Sign-and-Flood Protocol

The protocol assumes a PKI (Public key infrastructure) for authentication of messages. The sender wishes to send a message **m** to the receiver.

1. The sender digitally *signs* the message **m** with his private key using a well-known digital signature algorithm (say DSS); let $SIGN_S(\mathbf{m})$ denote the resultant data.
2. The sender sends $\mathbf{m}, SIGN_S(\mathbf{m})$ to the receiver along *all* the κ wires.
3. The receiver receives, say, m_i, c_i along the ith wire.
4. The receiver *verifies* the validity of the received c_i's, $1 \leq i \leq \kappa$, using the (corresponding) verification algorithm with the sender's public key. Let i^* be the minimum index such that the verification of c_{i^*} succeeded.
5. The receiver outputs the message m_{i^*} corresponding to signature c_{i^*}.

Fig. 1. A Naïve Protocol for Reliable Unicast Tolerating Bounded Adversary

Lindell *et al.* [27] initiated the study of effects of composition on fault tolerance of protocols for reliable broadcast. They proved that ABG protocols over complete graphs can be composed if and only if $n > 3t$ as compared to the bound of $n > t$ in stand alone setting. These results, in conjunction with the extant literature, imply that bounding the powers of adversary does not improve either fault tolerance for the problem of reliable communication.

Main contributions of this work are: **(i)** We present the impossibility of parallel self composable protocols for reliable unicast when the number of faults $t \geq \lceil \frac{\kappa}{2} \rceil$ even for a bounded adversary. Since this result matches the bound established in [1], we arrive at an interesting conclusion that, in the composability setting the weaker adversary does not necessary lead to higher fault tolerance. **(ii)** Our next result concerns with a single round δ-reliable protocol (A protocol is said to be δ-reliable if it succeeds to reliably transmit a message with a probability greater than $1 - \delta$). Note that the reliability of protocols tolerating bounded adversaries are based on certain assumptions on hardness of problems which are basically probabilistic in nature. In other words every such protocol may be viewed as a δ-reliable protocol for some appropriate δ corresponding to the problem. However, we have observed that these protocols are not composable, Hence a natural question is can we design an efficient composable protocol that is δ-reliable? We provide an affirmative answer. **(iii)** We give complete characterization of the graphs over which parallel composition of ABG protocols is possible. We show that ABG protocols compose in parallel over a synchronous graph G of n nodes tolerating $t - adversary$, iff $n > 3t$ and G is $2t + 1$ connected. Note that this is same as bounds for BGP over incomplete undirected graphs [13]. This shows that under composition, one need not necessarily achieve greater fault tolerance by bounding the computational powers of the adversary.

2   Our Model

We consider a set of n players, denoted by $\mathbb{P}$, communicating over a synchronous network. That is, the protocol is executed in a sequence of *rounds* where in each round, a player can perform some local computation, send new messages to all the players, receive the messages sent to him in the same round by the players (and if necessary perform some more local computation), in that order. The notion of faults in the system is captured by a virtual entity called *adversary*. During the execution, the (computationally bounded) adversary may take control of up to any t players and make them behave in any arbitrary fashion. Such an adversary is called as a t-adversary. We further assume that the communication channel between any two players is perfectly reliable and authenticated. We also assume existence of a (signature/authentication) scheme via which players authenticate themselves. This is modeled by all the players having an additional setup-tape that is generated during the preprocessing phase. Note that keys cannot be generated with in the system itself. Similar to Lindell *et al.* [27] too, we assume that the keys are generated using a trusted system and distributed to players prior to running of the protocol. No player can forge any other player's signature and the receiver can uniquely identify the sender of the message using the signature. However, the adversary can forge the signatures of all the t players under its control. We assume that players can run multiple executions of the same protocol. For the purpose of this work we work only with *stateless* composition of protocols, i.e. all honest players are oblivious of the other executions. In contrast, the adversary can coordinate between various executions, and the adversary's view at any given time includes all the messages received in all the executions.

3   Composability of Reliable Unicast

We first formally define the problem of reliable unicast.

Definition 1 (Reliable Unicast). *Given* **S** *and* **R** *over an arbitrary undirected network with κ node disjoint paths from* **S** *to* **R**. **S** *starts with a message m chosen from a finite field $\mathbb{F}$. A protocol Π is said to achieve reliable unicast if at the end of Π,* **R** *outputs m despite a t-adversary trying to prevent the same.*

3.1 Impossibility of Parallel Composability

In this section, we prove that there exist no protocol for reliable communication that is parallel composable even twice when the number of faulty wires $t \geq \lceil \frac{\kappa}{2} \rceil$.

Theorem 1. *There exists no reliable protocol under parallel self composition (for even just two executions) that can tolerate $\lceil \frac{\kappa}{2} \rceil$ or more faults.*

Proof. On the contrary let us assume that there exists a protocol Π for reliable unicast that remains reliable under parallel self composition and tolerates $\lceil \frac{\kappa}{2} \rceil$ faults. Let the sender S and the receiver R be connected by a set $W = \{w_1, w_2 \ldots w_\kappa\}$ of κ wires out of which the adversary $\mathcal{A}$ can corrupt any set of $\lceil \frac{\kappa}{2} \rceil$ wires. Let Γ_1, Γ_2 be two concurrent executions of Π between S and R. Let m_1, m_2 be the inputs to the executions Γ_1, Γ_2. W.l.o.g we can assume that Π terminates within N rounds.

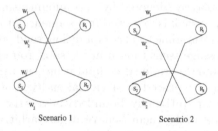

Scenario 1   Scenario 2

Fig. 2. Two indistinguishable Scenarios $\mathcal{S}_1$, $\mathcal{S}_2$

Let W_1 be the set of wires $\{w_1, w_2, \ldots, w_{\lceil \frac{\kappa}{2} \rceil}\}$. Similarly let W_2 be the set of wires $\{w_{\lceil \frac{\kappa}{2} \rceil + 1}, w_{\lceil \frac{\kappa}{2} \rceil + 2} \ldots w_\kappa\}$. Then consider the two scenarios depicted in the figure 2. The nodes S_1 and S_2 denote the sender side of the two executions Γ_1 and Γ_2, while the nodes R_1 and R_2 denote the receiver side.

Scenario $\mathcal{S}_1$

The inputs to protocol executions Γ_1 and Γ_2 are m_1, m_2 respectively. The adversary corrupts the wires W_1 and does the following.

- Swap the messages of Γ_1 and Γ_2 along the wires W_1. More formally if $msg_i(A, B, w_k)$ denotes the message sent from A to B in round i along w_k then

  - The adversary sends $msg_i(S_1, R_1, w_k)$ along wire w_k to R_2 and the message $msg_i(S_2, R_2, w_k)$ to R_1.
  - The adversary sends $msg_i(R_1, S_1, w_k)$ along wire w_k to S_2 and the message $msg_i(R_2, S_2, w_k)$ to S_1.

Scenario $\mathcal{S}_2$

The inputs to protocol executions Γ_1 and Γ_2 are m_2, m_1 respectively. The adversary corrupts the wires W_2 and does the following.

 – Swap the messages of Γ_1 and Γ_2 along the wires W_2. More formally let $msg_i(A, B, w_k)$ denotes the message sent from A to B in round i along w_k. Then for each $w_k \in W_2$,
   • The adversary sends $msg_i(S_1, R_1, w_k)$ along wire w_k to R_2 and the message $msg_i(S_2, R_2, w_k)$ to R_1.
   • The adversary sends $msg_i(R_1, S_1, w_k)$ along wire w_k to S_2 and the message $msg_i(R_2, S_2, w_k)$ to S_1.

We prove that the messages received by S and R are the same for both the scenarios. In order to prove this, we proceed by induction on the number of rounds. At the beginning of the protocol, trivially the view of the receiver is the same in both the scenarios. Let us say the view of the receiver is the same in both the scenarios is the same for the first $r - 1$ rounds. In the rth round

 – In scenario S_1, the node S_1 sends the message m_{11}, m_{12} to receiver R_1, and node S_2 sends the message m_{21}, m_{22} to node R_2. Because of adversarial strategy the receiver receives the messages m_{21}, m_{12} at node R_1 and messages m_{11}, m_{22} at node R_2.
 – In scenario S_2, the node S_1 sends the message m_{21}, m_{22} to receiver R_1, and node S_2 sends the message m_{11}, m_{12} to node R_2. The receiver receives the messages m_{21}, m_{12} at node R_1 and messages m_{11}, m_{22} at node R_2.

Thus the receiver R receives the same messages in both the scenarios. Similarly it can be seen that the messages received by S in round r in both the scenarios are the same. Hence by induction, the messages received by R is the same in both the scenarios. Thus it is impossible for the receiver to distinguish between the two scenarios. This implies that it is impossible for R to decide whether the output message for Γ_1 is m_1 or m_2. Hence no protocol for reliable unicast is parallel composable even two times when the number of faults $t \geq \lceil \frac{\kappa}{2} \rceil$. □

3.2 Sequential Composability

Theorem 2. *No r-round protocol for Reliable Message Transmission that tolerates $t \geq \lceil \frac{\kappa}{2} \rceil$ faults is sequentially composable more than $2r + 1$ times.*

Proof. The impossibility result is derived by showing that for any deterministic protocol Π r-rounds of execution of the two scenarios shown in figure 2 above can be simulated by $2r + 1$ sequential executions of Π.

Assume by contradiction that there exists a deterministic r-round protocol Π for Reliable message transmission that tolerates $t \geq \lceil \frac{\kappa}{2} \rceil$ and is sequentially composable $2r + 1$ times. The adversary can simulate one round of execution in scenario S_1 by two sequential executions of Π. For this purpose consider $2r$ sequential executions $\{\Pi_1, \Pi_2, \ldots \Pi_{2r}\}$ of Π. For each $i, 1 \leq i \leq r$ the inputs to Π_{2i-1}, Π_{2i} are m_1, m_2 respectively. Hence the *odd* executions Π_{2i-1} are used to simulate S_1, R_1 while the *even* executions Π_{2i} simulate S_2, R_2. We denote by $msg_j(A, B, w_i)$ the message sent by A to B along wire w_i in the jth round of a protocol execution. The adversary follows the following strategy to simulate Scenario S_1.

- *Execution $2k - 1$:* The adversary $\mathcal{A}$ corrupts the set of wires W_1. For each $j < k$, the adversary $\mathcal{A}$ works as follows in the jth round of Π_{2k-1}

  • On each wire $w_i \in W_1$, $\mathcal{A}$ communicates $msg_j(S_2, R_2, w_i)$ to R_1.
  • On each wire $w_i \in W_1$, $\mathcal{A}$ communicates $msg_j(R_2, S_2, w_i)$ to S_1

  Note that the for all $j < k$ the messages $msg_j(S_2, R_2, w_i), w_i \in W_1$ were obtained in the previous execution. In round k the adversary records the messages $msg_k(S_1, R_1, w_i)$ and $msg_k(R_1, S_1, w_i)$ for all $w_i \in W_1$.

- *Execution $2k$:* The adversary $\mathcal{A}$ corrupts the set of wires W_1. For each $j < k$, the adversary $\mathcal{A}$ works as follows in the jth round of Π_{2k}

  • On each wire $w_i \in W_1$, $\mathcal{A}$ communicates $msg_j(S_1, R_1, w_i)$ to R_2.
  • On each wire $w_i \in W_1$, $\mathcal{A}$ communicates $msg_j(R_1, S_1, w_i)$ to S_2.

  Note that the for all $j < k$ the messages $msg_j(S_1, R_1, w_i), w_i \in W_1$ were obtained in the previous execution. In round k the adversary records the messages $msg_k(S_2, R_2, w_i)$ and $msg_k(R_2, S_2, w_i)$ for all $w_i \in W_1$.

At the end of the round 1 of the second execution Π_2 the views of S and R is the same as the view of S_2 and R_2 at the end of round 1 in scenario $\mathcal{S}_1$. Then in the fourth sequential execution Π_4 the messages received by S and R are in the first round is the same as those received by S_2 and R_2 in round 1 of Scenario $\mathcal{S}_1$. Since Π is a deterministic protocol, the messages sent by S and R in round two of Π_4 are same as the messages sent by S_2 and R_2 in round two of Scenario $\mathcal{S}_1$. Thus even after round 2 the messages received by S and R are consistent with their views in Scenario $\mathcal{S}_1$. Using the same argument, we have that for every i, the views of S and R in Π_{2i} for the first i-rounds are identical to the views of S_2 and R_2 for the first i-rounds of Scenario $\mathcal{S}_1$. Similarly the views of S and R in Π_{2i-1} for the first i-rounds are identical to the views of S_1 and R_1.

By symmetry, it is possible for the adversary to simulate Scenario $\mathcal{S}_2$ in $2r$ sequential executions of Π. The protocol Π terminates within r rounds. Therefore after the r-rounds in Π_{2r}, S and R must terminate with output message. But it is impossible since the view of S and R at the rth round of Π_{2r} is the same as that of S_2 and R_2 after r rounds in Scenario $\mathcal{S}_1$. Hence the theorem. □

3.3   Randomized Composable Reliable Unicast for Free

We now present a single phase universally composable protocol that with a high probability reliably transmits ℓ field elements with a overall communication complexity of $O(\ell)$ field elements. We represent the block of field elements $\mathbf{M}$ that S wishes to send to R as $\mathbf{M} = [m_0\ m_1\ \ldots\ m_{\kappa(\kappa-t)}]$. In other words, a finite field $\mathbb{F}$ is so chosen that the message can be represented as a concatenation of $\kappa(\kappa - t)$ elements from $\mathbb{F}$. The protocol is given in the Figure 3 where κ is the number of wires (or more generally the number of vertex disjoint paths from the sender to the receiver) denoted as $\mathcal{W} = \{w_1, w_2, \ldots, w_\kappa\}$.

Let ϵ be a bound on the probability that the protocol does not work correctly. We require that the size of the field $\mathbb{F}$ be $\Omega(\frac{Q(\kappa)}{\epsilon})$, for some polynomial $Q(\kappa)$,

---

The Single Phase δ-Reliable Universally Composable Unicast Protocol

1. S selects $(\kappa - t)$ polynomials $p_i, 0 < i \leq (\kappa - t)$ over $\mathbb{F}$, each of degree $\kappa - 1$ with the coefficients assigned as follows: the coefficient of x^j in polynomial p_i is assigned to be $m_{i\kappa+j}$. From these $(\kappa - t)$ polynomials, S "extrapolates" another t polynomials each of degree $\kappa - 1$ by having the coefficients of x^j in all these κ polynomials (p_i's) lie on a $\kappa - t - 1$ degree polynomial.
2. S sends the polynomial p_i through w_i.
3. S chooses another κ^2 field elements at random, say $r_{ij}, 0 < i, j \leq \kappa$.
4. S sends along wire w_i, the n ordered pairs $(r_{ij}, p_j(r_{ij}))$, for all j. Let $v_{ij} = p_j(r_{ij})$.
5. Let p_i' and (r_{ij}', v_{ij}') be the values received by R. Among all the wires in $\mathcal{W}$, we say that wire w_i *contradicts* wire w_j if: $v_{ij}' \neq p_j'(r_{ij}')$.
6. Among all the wires in $\mathcal{W}$, R checks if there is a wire contradicted by at least $t + 1$ wires. All such wires are removed.
7. If there is at least one contradiction among the remaining wires, R outputs "FAILURE" and halts.
8. If there is no contradiction left, R checks whether the coefficients of x^j for the remaining polynomials (that is, after excluding those that are eliminated in the step 6) lie on a $(\kappa - t - 1)$ degree polynomial. If not, R outputs "FAILURE" and halts. If yes, R corrects the polynomials $p_i(x)$ of each corrupted wire w_i (i.e, he "corrects" those wires) using the polynomials received along the uncorrupted wires. R now knows all the polynomials $p_i(x)$.
9. R recovers **M** from the coefficients of the first $(\kappa - t)$ polynomials.

Fig. 3. An Optimal Single Phase δ-Reliable Universally Composable Unicast Protocol

but this is of course acceptable since the complexity of the protocol increases logarithmically with field size. We now discuss the correctness of the protocol. As usual, we focus only on the case wherein both the sender S and the receiver R are honest throughout the protocol. It is sufficient to prove that (a) If R does not output "FAILURE" then R always recovers the correct message **M**, and (b) There exists a suitable choice of $\mathbb{F}$ such that protocol terminates with a non-"FAILURE" output with probability $(1 - \epsilon)$, for any $\epsilon > 0$. We do exactly this in the following two lemmas. Complete proofs are given in [28].

Lemma 1. *If R does not output "FAILURE" then R always recovers the correct message* **M**.

Lemma 2. *The protocol terminates with an output that is not a "FAILURE" with high probability.*

4   Composability of Reliable Broadcast

We first formally define ABG:

Definition 2 (ABG). *A designated dealer starts with an input from a fixed set $V = \{0, 1\}$. The goal is for the players to eventually output decisions from the set V upholding the following conditions, even in the presence of a t-adversary:*

- Agreement: *All honest players decide on the same value $u \in V$.*
- Validity: *If the honest dealer starts with value $v \in V$, then $u = v$.*
- Termination: *All honest players eventually decide.*

4.1 Parallel Composition

In this section we prove that there does not exist any ABG protocol that composes in parallel even twice over a arbitrary undirected network G of n nodes, tolerating a t-adversary, if either $n \leq 3t$ or connectivity of $G \leq 2t$. Impossibility for $n \leq 3t$ follows directly from the results of Lindell *et al.* [27]. The result essentially stems from the ability of the adversary to use messages from one execution in the other parallel execution.

Though unproven, it is not difficult to see that in the stand alone setting, ABG over an arbitrary undirected network G is possible if and only if $n > t$ and G is $t + 1$ connected. The reason being: two honest players using authentication can communicate reliably if and only if there are $t + 1$ node disjoint paths between them. However, we prove that this is not sufficient when two or more executions of any ABG protocol are composed in parallel. To prove our claims, we first show that there does not exists any ABG protocol that (self)composes in parallel even twice over the network G(as shown in Figure 4) of four players $\mathbb{P} = \{A,B,C,D\}$. The proof is based upon the technique developed by Fischer *et al.* [29]. For the rest of the paper we refer to a ABG protocol Π that (self)composes under k parallel executions as Π_k.

Theorem 3. *There does not exists any Π_2 tolerating a 1-adversary over synchronous network G(Figure 4) of four players.*

Proof. Proof by contradiction. We assume there exists a protocol Π_2 over G tolerating 1-adversary. Using Π_2 we construct a well defined system and show that the system must exhibit contradictory behavior. This implies impossibility of the assumed protocol Π_2.

Using two copies of Π_2, we construct a system S (as shown in Figure 4). Formally, S is a synchronous system with a well defined output distribution for any particular input assignment. Here we donot know what system S is supposed to do. Therefore, the definition of ABG[Definition 2] does not tell us anything directly about the players' output. All we know is that S is a synchronous system and has a well defined behavior. Further, no player in S knows the complete system. Each player is aware of only his immediate neighbors.

Let E_1 and E_2 be two parallel executions of Π_2 over G. We consider three distinct scenarios α_1, α_2 and α_3 in E_1 – (i) α_1: A is the dealer and starts with input 0. Adversary corrupts B actively. (ii) α_2: C is the dealer and starts with input 0. Adversary corrupts C actively. (iii) α_3: A is the dealer and starts with input 1. Adversary corrupts B actively. Furher, Let α be an execution of S where each player starts with input value as shown in Figure 4. All the players in S are honest and follow the prescribed protocol correctly.

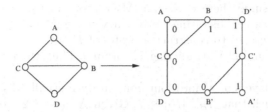

Fig. 4. Network G and system S

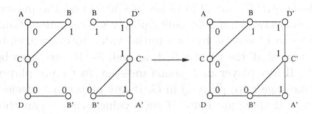

Fig. 5. Redirecting edges to make system S

Consider α from the point of view of players A, C and D. We claim[1] that whatever view A, C and D get in α, adversary can ensure that A, C and D get the same view in α_1 respectively (System S can be seen as made of two parallel executions, E_1 and E_2 of Π_2, as shown in Figure 5. Adversary corrupts B. It is easy to see that adversary can pass messages between the two parallel executions and ensure that none of A, C or D can distinguish between α, and α_1). That is, $\alpha \overset{A}{\sim} \alpha_1$, $\alpha \overset{C}{\sim} \alpha_1$, and $\alpha \overset{D}{\sim} \alpha_1$. Similarly, one can argue for $\alpha \overset{A'}{\sim} \alpha_3$, $\alpha \overset{C'}{\sim} \alpha_3$, and $\alpha \overset{D'}{\sim} \alpha_3$. Likewise, $\alpha \overset{A'}{\sim} \alpha_2$, $\alpha \overset{B'}{\sim} \alpha_2$, and $\alpha \overset{D}{\sim} \alpha_2$.

From the validity condition of ABG [Definition 2], A,C and D will eventually output 0 in α_1. Since $\alpha \overset{A}{\sim} \alpha_1$, $\alpha \overset{C}{\sim} \alpha_1$, and $\alpha \overset{D}{\sim} \alpha_1$, then A, C and D in α will also output 0 (we are able to make claims regarding player's outputs in α as views of players are same as those in α_1. Thus, by analyzing outputs in α_1, we can determine outputs in α). Similarly, one can argue that A',C' and D' in α will output 1. In α_2, since the dealer is corrupt, by the agreement condition, all honest players (A, B and D) will decide upon the same value. Then so should A', B' and D in α. But in α, D and A' have already decided upon 0 and 1 respectively. Thus, S exhibits contradictory behaviour. □

Theorem 4. *There does not exists any Π_2 tolerating a t-adversary over any undirected network $\mathcal{N}$ of n nodes if $n \leq 3t$ or $\mathcal{N}$ has $\leq 2t$ connectivity.*

Proof. The necessity of $n \leq 3t$ follows from the work of Lindell *et al.* [27]. So we focus only on the connectivity part. We prove the same via proof by

---

[1] We give only a brief sketch here. We prove the claim in [28, Lemma 3].

contradiction. Assume there exists an ABG protocol η_2, over $\mathcal{N}$, that composes in parallel twice, tolerating t-adversary when $\mathcal{N}$ has $\leq 2t$ connectivity. We show how to use η_2 to construct a protocol Π_2 over graph G(Figure 4) of four nodes A,B,C and D contradicting Theorem 3. Thus, there cannot exists any such η_2.

We partition players of $\mathcal{N}$ into four non-empty mutually disjoint subsets I_A, I_B, I_C and I_D such that $|I_B|, |I_C| \leq t$. Given $\mathcal{N}$ has $\leq 2t$ connectivity, such a partition is always possible. Note that if we remove all the nodes in I_B and I_D, then the players in I_A and I_C get disconnected. The edges in graph G can now be considered as the bundle of edges between the groups I_A, I_B, I_C and I_D in $\mathcal{N}$. Each player A,B,C and D in G keeps track of all the players in sets I_A, I_B, I_C, I_D respectively. W.l.o.g let faulty player in G simulate faulty players in $\mathcal{N}$. Each player i in G assigns its own initial value to every member of I_i and simulates the steps of all the players in I_i as well as the messages between pairs of players in I_i. If any player in I_i sends message m to any player in I_j, then player i sends message m to player j in G. If any player in I_i decides on a value v, then so does i. If there are more of such values, then i can choose any one from those values. If a player in I_i halts, then so does i.

Since η_2 is assumed to solve ABG for n players tolerating a $t-adversary$ under parallel composition, it satisfies agreement, validity and termination conditions of ABG [Definition 2]. We now show that this holds for Π_2 if it holds for η_2. For termination, let i be an honest player in G. Then i simulates at least one process in I_i, of $\mathcal{N}$. Since i is honest, then so is every process in I_i. By termination condition, every process in I_i must eventually decide. Then so should i. For validity, if all honest players of Π_2 begin with a value v, then so will all the honest players in η_2. As per validity condition, all the honest players in η_2 will decide on v. Then so will all the honest players in Π_2. For agreement, let i and j be two distinct honest players in Π_2. Each simulates all the honest players in I_i and I_j in η_2. As per agreement conditions, all honest players decide upon same value. Then all the players in I_i and I_j will decide on same vale. Then so will i and j. Thus, Π_2 composes in parallel twice and satisfies ABG [Definition 2] over G tolerating 1-adversary.   □

Theorem 5. *It is possible to design ABG Protocols that compose for any number of parallel executions over any arbitrary undirected network $\mathcal{N}$ if and only if $n > 3t$ and $\mathcal{N}$ is at least $2t + 1$ connected.*

Proof. Necessity follows from Theorem 4. For sufficiency, we observe that since $\mathcal{N}$ is atleast $2t + 1$ connected, one always simulate a complete graph [1]. Given $n > 3t$, any known ABG protocol over this complete graph works correctly and composes for any number of parallel executions. Formally, one can show that if there exists an adversary $\mathcal{A}$ that can attack one of the parallel execution and succeed when $n > 3t$ then using $\mathcal{A}$ one can contruct an adversary $\mathcal{A}'$ that is bound succeed against a stand alone execution for $n > 3t$, which violates results of Pease *et al.* [9,10]. Details in [28].   □

5 Conclusion

In this paper, contrary to the intution we concretely show that it is not always possible to achieve a higher fault tolarnce by bounding the computional powers of the adversary.

References

1. Dolev, D., Dwork, C., Waarts, O., Yung, M.: Perfectly Secure Message Transmission. JACM 40(1), 17–47 (1993)
2. Franklin, M., Wright, R.: Secure Communication in Minimal Connectivity Models. Journal of Cryptology 13(1), 9–30 (2000)
3. Sayeed, H., Abu-Amara, H.: Perfectly Secure Message Transmission in Asynchronous Networks. In: IPDPS (1995)
4. Srinathan, K., Raghavendra, P., Rangan, C.P.: On proactive perfectly secure message transmission. In: Pieprzyk, J., Ghodosi, H., Dawson, E. (eds.) ACISP 2007. LNCS, vol. 4586, Springer, Heidelberg (2007)
5. Franklin, M., Yung, M.: Secure Hypergraphs: Privacy from Partial Broadcast. In: STOC, pp. 36–44 (1995)
6. Wang, Y., Desmedt, Y.: Secure Communication in Multicast Channels: The Answer to Franklin and Wright's Question. Journal of Cryptology 14(2), 121–135 (2001)
7. Desmedt, Y.G., Wang, Y.: Perfectly secure message transmission revisited. In: Knudsen, L.R. (ed.) EUROCRYPT 2002. LNCS, vol. 2332, pp. 502–517. Springer, Heidelberg (2002)
8. Srinathan, K., Rangan, C.P.: Possibility and complexity of probabilistic reliable communications in directed networks. In: PODC (2006)
9. Pease, M., Shostak, R., Lamport, L.: Reaching agreement in the presence of faults. J. ACM 27(2), 228–234 (1980)
10. Lamport, L., Shostak, R., Pease, M.: The byzantine generals problem. ACM Trans. Program. Lang. Syst. 4(3), 382–401 (1982)
11. Fischer, M.J., Lynch, N.A., Paterson, M.S.: Impossibility of distributed consensus with one faulty process. J. ACM 32(2), 374–382 (1985)
12. Dolev, D., Dwork, C., Stockmeyer, L.: On the minimal synchronism needed for distributed consensus. J. ACM 34(1), 77–97 (1987)
13. Dolev, D.: The byzantine generals strike again. Technical report, Stanford, CA, USA (1981)
14. Fitzi, M., Maurer, U.: From partial consistency to global broadcast. In: STOC 2000, pp. 494–503 (2000)
15. Fitzi, M., Maurer, U.M.: Efficient byzantine agreement secure against general adversaries. In: International Symposium on Distributed Computing, pp. 134–148 (1998)
16. Altmann, B., Fitzi, M., Maurer, U.M.: Byzantine agreement secure against general adversaries in the dual failure model. In: International Symposium on Distributed Computing, pp. 123–137 (1999)
17. Garay, J.A.: Reaching (and Maintaining) Agreement in the Presence of Mobile Faults. In: Tel, G., Vitányi, P.M.B. (eds.) WDAG 1994. LNCS, vol. 857, pp. 253–264. Springer, Heidelberg (1994)
18. Rabin, M.O.: Randomized byzantine generals. In: FOCS, pp. 403–409 (1983)

19. Dolev, D., Strong, H.R.: Authenticated algorithms for byzantine agreement. SIAM Journal on Computing 12(4), 656–666 (1983)
20. Borcherding, M.: On the number of authenticated rounds in byzantine agreement. In: Helary, J.-M., Raynal, M. (eds.) WDAG 1995. LNCS, vol. 972, pp. 230–241. Springer, Heidelberg (1995)
21. Borcherding, M.: Partially authenticated algorithms for byzantine agreement. In: ISCA 1996, pp. 8–11 (1996)
22. Srikanth, T.K., Toueg, S.: Simulating authenticated broadcasts to derive simple fault-tolerant algorithms. Distributed Computing 2(2), 80–94 (1987)
23. Borcherding, M.: Levels of authentication in distributed agreement. In: Babaoğlu, Ö., Marzullo, K. (eds.) WDAG 1996. LNCS, vol. 1151, pp. 40–55. Springer, Heidelberg (1996)
24. Katz, J., Koo, C.Y.: On expected constant-round protocols for byzantine agreement. J. Comput. Syst. Sci. 75(2), 91–112 (2009)
25. Gong, L., Lincoln, P., Rushby, J.: Byzantine agreement with authentication: Observations and applications in tolerating hybrid and link faults (1995)
26. Canetti, R.: Universally Composable Security: A New Paradigm for Cryptographic Protocols. In: FOCS, pp. 136–145. IEEE Computer Society Press, Los Alamitos (2001), http://eprint.iacr.org/2000/067
27. Lindell, Y., Lysysanskaya, A., Rabin, T.: On the Composition of Authenticated Byzantine Agreement. In: STOC, pp. 514–523. ACM Press, New York (2002)
28. Gupta, A., Hans, S., Srinathan, K., Rangan, C.P.: On composability of reliable unicast and broadcast. Technical report, International Institute of Information Technology, Hyderabad Complete version
    http://researchweb.iiit.ac.in/~anujgupta/Work.htm
29. Fischer, M.J., Lynch, N.A., Merritt, M.: Easy impossibility proofs for distributed consensus problems. In: PODC, pp. 59–70. ACM, New York (1985)

A Leader-Free Byzantine Consensus Algorithm*

Fatemeh Borran and André Schiper

Ecole Polytechnique Fédérale de Lausanne (EPFL), Switzerland

Abstract. The paper considers the consensus problem in a partially synchronous system with Byzantine faults. It turns out that, in the partially synchronous system, all deterministic algorithms that solve consensus with Byzantine faults are leader-based. This is not the case of benign faults, which raises the following fundamental question: is it possible to design a deterministic Byzantine consensus algorithm for a partially synchronous system that is not leader-based? The paper gives a positive answer to this question, and presents a leader-free algorithm that is resilient-optimal and signature-free.

1 Introduction

In a distributed system of n processes, where each process has an initial value, Byzantine consensus is the problem of agreeing on a common value, even though some of the processes may fail in arbitrary, even malicious, ways. Consensus is related to the implementation of state machine replication, atomic broadcast, etc. It was first identified by Pease, Shostak and Lamport [1], formalized as the *interactive consistency* problem and solved in a synchronous system. An algorithm achieves interactive consistency if it allows the nonfaulty processes to come to a consistent view of the initial values of all the processes, including the faulty ones. Once interactive consistency has been achieved, the nonfaulty processes can reach consensus by applying a deterministic averaging or filtering function on the values of their view. It is shown in [1] that in a synchronous system $3t + 1$ processes are needed to solve the Byzantine consensus problem without signatures, where t is the maximum number of Byzantine processes.

Later, Fischer, Lynch and Peterson [2] proved that in an asynchronous system, no deterministic asynchronous consensus protocol can tolerate even a single crash failure. The problem can however be solved using randomization even with Byzantine faults, with at least $5t + 1$ processes, as shown by BenOr [3] and Rabin [4]. Later, Bracha [5] increased the resiliency of the randomized algorithm to $3t + 1$ using a "reliable broadcast" primitive.

In 1988, Dwork, Lynch and Stockmeyer [6], considered an asynchronous system that eventually becomes synchronous (called *partially synchronous system*). The consensus algorithms proposed in [6], for benign and for Byzantine faults, achieve safety in all executions, while guaranteeing liveness only if there exists

---

* Research funded by the Swiss National Science Foundation under grant number 200021-111701.

K. Kant et al. (Eds.): ICDCN 2010, LNCS 5935, pp. 67–78, 2010.

a period of synchrony. Recently, several papers have considered the partially synchronous system model for Byzantine consensus [7,8,9,10].

However, [10] points out a potential weakness of these Byzantine consensus algorithms, namely that they can suffer from "performance failure". According to [10], a performance failure occurs when messages are sent slowly by a Byzantine leader, but without triggering protocol timeouts, and the paper points out that the PBFT leader-based algorithm [7] is vulnerable to such an attack. Similar arguments are mentioned in [11] and in [12], where Lamport suggests the use of a virtual leader.

Interestingly, all deterministic Byzantine algorithms for non-synchronous systems are leader-based, e.g., [6,7,8,9]. Even the protocol in [10] is leader-based. However, the authors of [10] managed to make the leader-based protocol less vulnerable to performance failure attacks than PBFT [7] through a complicated mechanism that enables non-leader processes to (i) aggressively monitor the leader's performance, and (ii) compute a threshold level of acceptable performance. Note that randomized consensus algorithms such as [3,4] are not leader-based. This raises the following fundamental question: is it possible to design a deterministic Byzantine consensus algorithm for a partially synchronous system that is not leader-based? With such an algorithm, performance failure of Byzantine processes might be harmless.

One may imagine that leader-free (non-leader-based) algorithms for benign faults might be extended for Byzantine faults. A leader-free algorithm typically consists of a sequence of rounds, where in each round all processes send messages to all, and a correct process updates its value based on the values received. It is not difficult to design an algorithm based on this all-to-all communication pattern that does not violate the validity and agreement properties of consensus, even with Byzantine faults. However, termination requires that in some round r all correct processes receive exactly the same set of messages (from correct *and* from faulty processes). Let us denote this property for round r by *uniform*(r). Indeed, if *uniform*(r) holds and each correct process applies a deterministic function to the received values, the configuration becomes univalent. Can we ensure the existence of a round r in which *uniform*(r) holds?

For benign faults, it is easy to guarantee that during the synchronous period of the partially synchronous system, in every round r, all correct processes receive messages from the same set of processes. This is not the case for Byzantine faults. In round r, a Byzantine process could send a message to some correct process, and no message to some other correct process. If this happens, *uniform*(r) does not hold. Therefore one may think that with Byzantine faults the leader is needed to ensure termination, and conclude that no deterministic leader-free Byzantine consensus algorithm could exist in a partially synchronous system. In this paper, we show that this intuition is wrong.

Our new idea is the following. We started from the observation that leader-free consensus algorithms exist for the synchronous system, both for benign faults (e.g., the *FloodSet* algorithm [13]) and for Byzantine faults (e.g., the algorithm based on interactive consistency [1]). However, these algorithms violate agreement if executed during the asynchronous period of a partially synchronous system. Therefore we tried to combine these algorithms with a second algorithm that never violates agreement in an asynchronous system. This methodology turned out to be successful, and the resulting leader-free Byzantine consensus algorithm, is presented here. The algorithm requires $3t + 1$ processes and does not rely on digital signatures.

The rest of the paper is structured as follows. We define the consensus problem and our system model in Section 2. Our methodology to derive a leader-free consensus algorithm for Byzantine faults is presented in Section 3.[1] Future work is discussed in Section 4. Finally, we conclude the paper in Section 5.

2 Definitions and System Model

2.1 Byzantine Consensus

We consider a set Π of n processes, among which at most t can be Byzantine faulty. Nonfaulty processes are called correct processes. Each process has an initial value. We formally define consensus by the following properties:

- *Strong validity:* If all correct processes have the same initial value, this is the only possible decision value.
- *Agreement:* No two correct processes decide differently.
- *Termination:* All correct processes eventually decide.

2.2 System Model

We consider a partially synchronous system as defined in [6] in which processes communicate through message passing. As in [6], we consider an abstraction on top of the system model, namely a round model, defined next. Using this abstraction, rather than the raw system model, improves the clarity of the algorithms and simplifies the proofs.

There are two fault models considered with Byzantine processes: "authenticated Byzantine" faults, and "Byzantine" faults [6]. In both models a faulty process behaves arbitrarily, but in the authenticated Byzantine model messages can be signed by the sender, and it is assumed that the signature cannot be forged by any other process. No signatures are used with Byzantine faults, but the receiver of a message knows the identity of the sender.

2.3 Basic Round Model

In the round model, processing is divided into rounds of message exchange. Each round r consists of a *sending step* denoted by S_p^r (sending step of p for round r), and of a *state transition step* denoted by T_p^r. In a sending step, each process sends a message to all. A subset of the messages sent is received at the beginning of the state transition step: messages can get lost, and a message sent in round

---

[1] A simpler algorithm that uses digital signatures is proposed in [14].

r can only be received in round r. We denote by σ_p^r the message sent by p in round r, and by $\boldsymbol{\mu}_p^r$ the messages received by process p in round r ($\boldsymbol{\mu}_p^r$ is a vector of size n, where $\boldsymbol{\mu}_p^r[q]$ is the message received from q). Based on $\boldsymbol{\mu}_p^r$, process p updates its state in the state transition step.

Let *GSR* (*Global Stabilization Round*) be the smallest round, such that for all rounds $r \geq GSR$, the message sent in round r by a correct process q to a correct process p is received by p in round r. This is formally expressed by the following predicate (where $\mathcal{C}$ denotes the set of correct processes):

$$\forall r \geq GSR : \mathcal{P}_{good}(r), \text{ where } \mathcal{P}_{good}(r) \equiv \forall p, q \in \mathcal{C} : \boldsymbol{\mu}_p^r[q] = \sigma_q^r.$$

An algorithm that ensures — in a partially synchronous system — the existence of *GSR* such that $\forall r \geq GSR : \mathcal{P}_{good}(r)$, is given in [6]. Note that "$\forall r \geq GSR : \mathcal{P}_{good}(r)$" is sufficient for the termination of our algorithms, but not necessary. If the system is synchronous, the following stronger property can be ensured: $\forall r : \mathcal{P}_{good}(r)$.

3   From Synchrony to Partial Synchrony

In this section we explain our methodology to design a leader-free consensus algorithm that tolerates Byzantine faults without signatures. We start with a leader-free consensus algorithm for Byzantine faults in a synchronous system model, and then extend it to a leader-free consensus algorithm in a partially synchronous system.

3.1   Leader-Free Consensus Algorithm for a Synchronous System

One of the first consensus algorithms that tolerates Byzantine faults in synchronous systems was proposed by Pease, Shostak and Lamport [1]. It is based on an algorithm that solves the *interactive consistency* problem, which consists for each correct process p to compute a vector of values, with an element for each of the n processes, such that

- The correct processes compute exactly the same vector;
- The element of the vector corresponding to a given correct process is the initial value of that process.

The algorithm presented in [1] is not leader-based, does not require signatures, tolerates $t < n/3$ Byzantine faults, and consists of $t + 1$ rounds of exchange of messages. We briefly recall the principle of this algorithm (see Algorithm 1).

The information maintained by each process during the algorithm can be represented as a tree (called *Exponential Information Gathering (EIG)* tree in [13,15]), in which each path from the root to a leaf contains $t + 2$ nodes. Thus the height of the tree is $t + 1$. The nodes are labeled with sequences of processes' identities in the following manner. The root is labeled with the empty sequence λ ($|\lambda| = 0$). Let i be an internal node in the tree with label $\alpha = p_1 p_2 \ldots p_r$; for every $q \in \Pi$ such that $q \notin \alpha$, node i has one child labeled αq. Node i with label α will be simply called "node α".

Algorithm 1. *EIGByz* with $n > 3t$ (code of process p)

```
1: Initialization:
2:     W_p := {⟨λ, v_p⟩}                          /* v_p is the initial value of process p; val_p(λ) = v_p */

3: Round r:                                       /* 1 ≤ r ≤ t + 1 */
4:     S_p^r:
5:         send {⟨α, v⟩ ∈ W_p : |α| = r − 1 ∧ p ∉ α ∧ v ≠ ⊥} to all processes
6:     T_p^r:
7:         for all {q | ⟨α, v⟩ ∈ W_p ∧ |α| = r − 1 ∧ q ∈ Π ∧ q ∉ α} do
8:             if ⟨β, v⟩ is received from process q then
9:                 W_p := W_p ∪ {⟨βq, v⟩}                              /* val_p(βq) = v */
10:            else
11:                W_p := W_p ∪ {⟨βq, ⊥⟩}                              /* val_p(βq) = ⊥ */
12:        if r = t + 1 then
13:            for all ⟨α, v⟩ ∈ W_p from |α| = t to |α| = 1 do
14:                W_p := W_p \ ⟨α, v⟩                        /* replace val_p(α) ... */
15:                if ∃v' s.t. |⟨αq, v'⟩ ∈ W_p| ≥ n − |α| − t then
16:                    W_p := W_p ∪ ⟨α, v'⟩                   /* ... with newval_p(α) */
17:                else
18:                    W_p := W_p ∪ ⟨α, ⊥⟩                    /* ... with newval_p(α) */
19:            for all q ∈ Π do                               /* level 1 of the tree */
20:                M_p[q] := v  s.t. ⟨q, v⟩ ∈ W_p
```

Intuitively, $val_p(p_1p_2 \ldots p_r)$ (which denotes the value of node $p_1p_2 \ldots p_r$ in p's tree) represents the value v that p_r told p at round r that p_{r-1} told p_r at round $r-1$ that ... that p_1 told p_2 at round 1 that p_1's initial value is v. Each correct process p maintains the tree using a set W_p of pairs $\langle node\ label,\ node\ value \rangle$. At the beginning of round r, each process p sends the $(r-1)$th level of its tree to all processes (line 5). When p receives a message from q in format $\langle p_1p_2...p_r, v \rangle$, it adds $\langle p_1p_2...p_rq, v \rangle$ to its set W_p (line 9). If p fails to receive a message it expects from process q, p simply adds $\langle p_1p_2 \ldots p_rq, \bot \rangle$ to its set W_p (line 11).

Information gathering as described above continues for $t+1$ rounds, until the entire tree has been filled in. At this point the second stage of local computation starts. Every process p applies to each subtree a recursive data reduction function to compute a new value (lines 13 to 18). The value of the reduction function on p's subtree rooted at a node labeled α is denoted $newval_p(\alpha)$. The reduction function is defined for a node α as follows.

- If α is a leaf, its value does not change $(newval(\alpha) = val(\alpha))$;
- Otherwise, if there exists v such that $n - |\alpha| - t$ children have value v, then $newval(\alpha) = v$, else $newval(\alpha) = \bot$ (lines 16 and 18).

The reason for a quorum of size $n - |\alpha| - t$ can be explained as follows.[2] Each correct process, at the end of round $t+1$, has constructed a tree with $t+2$ levels. Any node in level $0 < k < t+1$ has $n-k$ children and a label α such that $|\alpha| = k$. If α is a label with only correct processes, then all its children except t (i.e., $n - k - t$ children) have the same value.

At the end of round $t+1$, every correct process p constructs a vector M_p of size n (corresponding to the level 1 of its tree), where $M_p[q]$ is the new value of process q (line 20). *EIGByz* ensures that:

---

[2] Since $n > 3t$, this quorum can be replaced by $\frac{n+t}{2} - |\alpha|$ (see [1]).

- The correct processes compute exactly the same vector, i.e., $\forall p, q \in \mathcal{C}$: $M_p = M_q$, and
- The element of the vector corresponding to a given correct process q is the initial value of that process, i.e., $\forall p, q \in \mathcal{C} : M_p[q] = v_q$.

Therefore, a correct process can decide by applying a deterministic function on its vector M_p. The *EIGByz* algorithm ensures the following property:

$$(\forall r, 1 \le r \le t+1 : \mathcal{P}_{good}(r)) \Rightarrow \forall p, q \in \mathcal{C} : (M_p = M_q) \wedge (|M_p| \ge |\mathcal{C}|) \quad (1)$$

where $|M_p|$ denotes the number of non-$\perp$ elements in vector M_p, and $|\mathcal{C}|$ denotes number of correct processes. The premise holds if the system is synchronous.

3.2   Extending *EIGByz* for a Partially Synchronous Model

If Algorithm 1 is executed in a partially synchronous system, it does not ensure $\forall p, q \in \mathcal{C} : (M_p = M_q) \wedge (|M_p| \ge |\mathcal{C}|)$. Therefore, it cannot ensure the agreement property of Byzantine consensus. However, following two properties hold for Algorithm 1 in synchronous as well as in asynchronous periods:

$$\forall p, q \in \mathcal{C} : M_p[q] \in \{v_q, \perp\} \quad (2)$$

$$\forall q \in \Pi \setminus \mathcal{C}, \exists v \text{ s.t. } \forall p \in \mathcal{C} : M_p[q] \in \{v, \perp\} \quad (3)$$

where v_q is the initial value of process q. The proofs are in [14].

To ensure agreement in a partially synchronous system, we need to combine Algorithm 1 with another algorithm. We show below two such algorithms: (i) a simple algorithm (Algorithm 2), which requires $n > 5t$, and (ii) a more complex algorithm with optimal resilience $n > 3t$ (Algorithm 3). In both cases, Algorithm 2 and Algorithm 3 ensure agreement, while Algorithm 1 ensures termination.

Consensus Algorithm with $n > 5t$. We start with a simple parameterized consensus algorithm (see Algorithm 2). Parametrization allows us to easily adjust the algorithm to ensure agreement for different fault models. The algorithm was first presented in [16] as *One Third Rule* algorithm ($T = E = 2n/3$) to tolerate $t < n/3$ benign faults. The parameterized version was given in [17] to tolerate "corrupted communication". Here, since we consider "Byzantine process faults" we need different values for the parameters. Note that in the context of Byzantine faults, Algorithm 2 alone does not ensure termination.

The algorithm consists of a sequence of phases ϕ, where each phase has two rounds $2\phi - 1$ and 2ϕ. Round 2ϕ is a normal round; to ensure termination, round $2\phi - 1$ will have to be simulated by Algorithm 1. Each process p has a single variable x_p, and in every round p sends x_p to all processes. Parameter T (line 7) refers to a "threshold" for updating x_p, and parameter E (line 13) refers to "enough" same values to decide.[3]

With Byzantine faults, Algorithm 2 ensures agreement with $E \ge (n + t)/2$ and $T \ge 2n - 2E + 2t$. Strong validity requires $T \ge 2t$ and $E \ge t$. Termination,

---

[3] The notation μ_p^r is introduced in Section 2.3.

Algorithm 2. Byzantine algorithm with $n > 5t$ (code of process p)

```
 1: Initialization:
 2:     x_p := v_p ∈ V                          /* v_p is the initial value of p */

 3: Round r = 2φ − 1:              /* round simulated by t + 1 micro-rounds of Algorithm 1 */
 4:     S_p^r:
 5:         send ⟨x_p⟩ to all processes
 6:     T_p^r:
 7:         if number of non-⊥ elements in μ_p^r > T then
 8:             x_p := smallest most frequent non-⊥ element in μ_p^r

 9: Round r = 2φ:
10:     S_p^r:
11:         send ⟨x_p⟩ to all processes
12:     T_p^r:
13:         if more than E elements in μ_p^r are equal to v ≠⊥ then
14:             DECIDE(v)
```

---

together with Algorithm 1, requires $n - t > T$ and $n - t > E$. Putting all together, for the case $E = T$, we get $T = E = 2(n+t)/3$ and $n > 5t$. The proofs of agreement and strong validity are in [14]. We discuss now termination. For termination, it is sufficient for Algorithm 2 to have one round $r = 2\phi - 1$ in which the following holds (where $|\boldsymbol{\mu}_p^r|$ denotes the number of non-$\bot$ elements in vector $\boldsymbol{\mu}_p^r$):

$$\forall p, q \in \mathcal{C} : (\boldsymbol{\mu}_p^r = \boldsymbol{\mu}_q^r) \wedge (|\boldsymbol{\mu}_p^r| > T) \tag{4}$$

and one round $r + 1 = 2\phi$ in which we have:

$$\forall p \in \mathcal{C} : |\boldsymbol{\mu}_p^{r+1}| > E. \tag{5}$$

If (4) holds, all correct processes set x_p to the some common value v_0 in round r (line 8), and if (5) holds all correct processes decide v_0 in round $r + 1$ (line 14).

By comparing (1) with (4) and (5), it is easy to see that Algorithm 1 ensures (4) and (5) if it is executed after GSR, and we have $|\mathcal{C}| > T$ and $|\mathcal{C}| > E$ (where $|\mathcal{C}| = n - t$). Therefore, the idea is to replace the send/receive of round $2\phi - 1$ of Algorithm 2 by the $t + 1$ micro-rounds of Algorithm 1. In other words, we simulate round $r = 2\phi - 1$ of Algorithm 2 using the $t + 1$ micro-rounds of Algorithm 1:

- Each instance of Algorithm 1 is started with $W_p = \{\langle p, x_p \rangle\}$, where x_p is defined in Algorithm 2;
- At the end of these $t + 1$ micro-rounds, the vector $\boldsymbol{M}_p$ computed by Algorithm 1 is the vector $\boldsymbol{\mu}_p$ of messages received by p in round r ($\boldsymbol{M}_p[q] = \boldsymbol{\mu}_p[q] = \bot$ means that p did not receive any message from q in round r).

Note that, the *One Third Rule* algorithm (Algorithm 2 with $T = E = 2n/3$) cannot be used with Byzantine faults because of the agreement problem. Using *EIGByz*, a Byzantine process cannot send different values to different processes in a single round, however, it can send different values to different processes in different rounds which violates agreement.

Consensus Algorithm with $n > 3t$. As Algorithm 2 requires $n > 5t$, its resilience is not optimal. Here we show a new algorithm, which uses mechanisms from several consensus algorithms, e.g., Ben-Or [3], and PBFT [7] with strong validity, and requires only $n > 3t$ (see Algorithm 3). Note that, as for Algorithm 2, Algorithm 3 ensures strong validity and agreement, but not termination. As for Algorithm 2, termination is ensured by simulating the first round of each phase ϕ of Algorithm 3 by $t + 1$ micro-round of Algorithm 1.

Algorithm 3 consists of a sequence of phases ϕ, where each phase has three rounds $(3\phi - 2, 3\phi - 1, 3\phi)$. Each process p has an estimate x_p, a vote value $vote_p$ (initially ?), a timestamp ts_p attached to $vote_p$ (initially 0), and a set $pre\text{-}vote_p$ of valid pairs $\langle vote, ts \rangle$ (initially $\emptyset$). The structure of the algorithm is as follows:

- If a correct process p receives the same estimate v in round $3\phi - 2$ from $n - t$ processes, then it accepts v as a valid vote and puts $\langle v, \phi \rangle$ in $pre\text{-}vote_p$ set. The pre-vote set is used later to detect an invalid vote.
- If a correct process p receives the same pre-vote $\langle v, \phi \rangle$ in round $3\phi - 1$ from $n - t$ processes, then it votes v (i.e., $vote_p = v$) and updates its timestamp to ϕ (i.e., $ts_p = \phi$).
- If a correct process p receives the same vote v with the same timestamp ϕ in round 3ϕ from $2t + 1$ processes, it decides v.

The algorithm guarantees that (i) two correct processes do not vote for different values in the same phase ϕ; and (ii) once $t + 1$ correct processes have the same vote v and the same timestamp ϕ, no other value can be voted in the following phases. We discuss now agreement and termination. The full proofs are in [14].

Agreement. A configuration is v-valent if (i) $\exists \phi$ such that at least $t + 1$ correct processes p have $(vote_p, ts_p) = (v, ts)$ with $ts \geq \phi$, and (ii) the other correct processes q have $(vote_q, ts_q) = (v' \neq v, ts')$ with $ts' < \phi$.

Let ϕ_0 be the smallest round in which some correct process decides v (line 26). By line 25 at least $t + 1$ correct processes p have $vote_p = v$, $ts_p = \phi_0$, and $x_p = v$ from line 20; the other correct processes q with $vote_q \neq v$ have $ts_q < \phi_0$ from line 19. Therefore the v-valent definition holds. We denote the former set by $\Pi_{=\phi_0}$, and the latter by $\Pi_{<\phi_0}$. Processes in $\Pi_{=\phi_0}$ keep $x_p = vote_p = v$ from phase ϕ_0 onward, and processes in $\Pi_{<\phi_0}$ can only update $vote_p$ to ? or v, as we explain now. This ensures agreement.

First, by lines 10 and 13, it is impossible for a correct process to have two different values with the same timestamp in its pre-vote set. By lines 27-30, in phase ϕ_0, processes in $\Pi_{<\phi_0}$ can only update $vote_p$ to ?; processes in $\Pi_{=\phi_0}$ do not update neither $vote_p$, nor x_p to some value $\neq v$. By lines 10-14, in phase $\phi_0 + 1$, correct processes can only update x_p to v and can only add $(v, \phi_0 + 1)$ to $pre\text{-}vote_p$. Therefore in round $3(\phi_0 + 1) - 1$, correct processes can only update $vote_p$ to v, i.e., only v can be decided in phase $\phi_0 + 1$. The same reasoning can be repeated for all phases after phase $\phi_0 + 1$.

Termination. We explain intuitively termination by considering the smallest phase ϕ such that $3\phi - 2 \geq GSR$. We distinguish two cases: (i) at the beginning of round $3\phi - 2$, all correct processes have $vote_p = ?$, and (ii) at the beginning of round $3\phi - 2$ at least one correct process has $vote_p \neq ?$.

Algorithm 3. Byzantine algorithm with $n > 3t$ (code of process p)

```
 1: Initialization:
 2:     x_p := v_p ∈ V                                        /* v_p is the initial value of p */
 3:     pre-vote_p := ∅
 4:     vote_p ∈ V ∪ {?}, initially ?
 5:     ts_p := 0

 6: Round r = 3φ − 2:                        /* round simulated by t + 1 micro-rounds of Algorithm 1 */
 7:     S_p^r:
 8:         send ⟨x_p, vote_p⟩ to all processes
 9:     T_p^r:
10:         if at least n − t elements in μ_p^r are equal to ⟨−, ?⟩ then
11:             x_p := smallest most frequent element ⟨x, −⟩ in μ_p^r
12:             pre-vote_p := pre-vote_p ∪ {⟨x_p, φ⟩}
13:         if at least n − t elements in μ_p^r are equal to ⟨v, −⟩ then
14:             pre-vote_p := pre-vote_p ∪ {⟨v, φ⟩}

15: Round r = 3φ − 1:
16:     S_p^r:
17:         send ⟨v | ⟨v, φ⟩ ∈ pre-vote_p⟩ to all processes
18:     T_p^r:
19:         if at least n − t elements in μ_p^r are equal to ⟨v⟩ then
20:             vote_p := v; ts_p := φ; x_p := v

21: Round r = 3φ:
22:     S_p^r:
23:         send ⟨vote_p, ts_p, pre-vote_p⟩ to all processes
24:     T_p^r:
25:         if at least 2t + 1 elements in μ_p^r are equal to ⟨v ≠ ?, φ, −⟩ then
26:             DECIDE(v)
27:         if exists ⟨v ≠ ?, ts, −⟩ in μ_p^r s.t. vote_p ≠ v and ts > ts_p then
28:             if exists t + 1 elements ⟨−, −, pre-vote⟩ in μ_p^r s.t. ⟨v, ts'⟩ ∈ pre-vote and ts' ≥ ts then
29:                 vote_p := ?; ts_p := 0; x_p := v
30:         if vote_p ≠ ? then x_p := vote_p
```

Case (i): Consider round $3\phi-2$. Since we are after *GSR*, Algorithm 1 ensures that all correct processes p receive the same set $\mu_p^{3\phi-2}$ of messages with $|\mu_p^{3\phi-2}| \geq |\mathcal{C}|$ (see formula (1)), i.e., all correct processes p set x_p to the same common value v (line 11), and add the pair $\langle v, \phi \rangle$ to *pre-vote$_p$* (line 12). It follows that, in round $3\phi - 1$, all correct processes p set *vote$_p$* to v (line 20), and all correct processes decide v in round 3ϕ (line 26).

Case (ii): This case is more complex to expose. Consider round 3ϕ, and let q be a correct process with the highest timestamp ts_q and $vote_q = v \neq ?$ at the beginning of round 3ϕ. Line 19 ensures that for any other correct process q' with $ts_{q'} = ts_q$, we have $vote_q = vote_{q'}$. Since $3\phi > GSR$, all correct processes p with $vote_p \neq v$ execute lines 27-29. Therefore, at the end of round 3ϕ all correct processes p have $x_p = v$ and $vote_p \in \{v, ?\}$, i.e., all correct processes p start round $3\phi + 1 = 3(\phi + 1) - 2$ with $x_p = v$. If the condition of line 10 holds, then the most frequent pair received is $\langle v, - \rangle$, i.e., $\langle v, \phi + 1 \rangle$ is added to *pre-vote$_p$* (line 12). The condition of line 13 necessary holds at each correct process, i.e., $\langle v, \phi + 1 \rangle$ is added to *pre-vote$_p$* (line 14). Therefore, at the end of round $3\phi + 1$, all correct processes p only have $\langle y, \phi + 1 \rangle$ with $y = v$ in *pre-vote$_p$*. It follows that, in round $3\phi + 2$, all correct processes p set *vote$_p$* to v (line 20), and all correct processes decide v in round $3\phi + 3$ (line 26).

Note that in Algorithm 3, the set $pre\text{-}vote_p$ can be bounded, based on the following observation. For instance, if $\langle v, \phi \rangle \in pre\text{-}vote_p$ and p wants to add $\langle v, \phi' \rangle$ into its pre-vote with $\phi' > \phi$, then $\langle v, \phi \rangle$ becomes obsolete.

3.3   Summary

The following table summarizes our results. The second column shows the smallest number of processes needed for each algorithm. The third and forth columns give an upper bound on number of rounds needed for a single consensus in both best and worst cases. The best case is when the system is synchronous form the beginning, i.e., $GSR = 0$. Both algorithms require n^2 messages per round.

	# processes	# rounds (best case)	# rounds (worst case)
Algorithm 2	$5t + 1$	$t + 2$	$GSR + 2(t + 2) - 1$
Algorithm 3	$3t + 1$	$t + 3$	$GSR + 2(t + 3) - 1$

3.4   Optimizations

We describe two possible optimizations that can be applied to our leader-free Byzantine consensus algorithm.

Early termination. The "early termination" optimization can be applied to Algorithm 1 (*EIGByz*). Algorithm 1 always requires $t + 1$ rounds, even in executions in which no process is faulty. With early termination, the number of rounds can be reduced in such cases.

Let f denote the actual number of faulty processes in a given execution. Moses and Waarts in [18] present an early termination version of the exponential information gathering protocol for Byzantine consensus that requires $n > 4t$ and terminates in $min\{t+1, f+2\}$ rounds. The idea is the following. Consider some node α in p's tree. Process p may know that a quorum (i.e., $n - |\alpha| - t$) of correct children of node α store the same value. When this happens, process p can already determine the value of $newval_p(\alpha)$, and can stop at the end of the next round. The paper presents another early termination protocol with optimal resiliency ($n > 3t$) that terminates in $min\{t+1, f+3\}$ rounds. These two optimizations can be applied to Algorithm 1.

One round decision. The "one round decision" optimization is relevant to Algorithm 2. One round decision means that if all correct processes start with the same initial value, and the system is synchronous from the beginning, then correct processes decide in one single round. Algorithm 2 does not achieve one round decision, because the simulation of Algorithm 1 (*EIGByz*) appears in each phase, including phase 1. To achieve one round decision, we simply skip round 1, and start Algorithm 2 with round 2. If all correct processes start with the same initial value, and $GSR = 0$, then correct processes decide in one round.

The fact that our one round decision algorithm requires "only" $n > 5t$ is not in contradiction with the result in [19], which establishes the lower bound $n = 7t+1$ for one-step decision. The reason is that we assume for fast decision a partially synchronous system with $GSR = 0$, i.e., the system is initially synchronous, while [19] considers a system that is initially asynchronous.

4 Discussion and Future Work

In a partially synchronous system the predicate $\mathcal{P}_{good}(r)$ can be ensured using the implementations given in [6]. Actually, [6] distinguishes two variant of partial synchrony: (a) one in which the communication bound Δ and the process bound Φ are *unknown*, and (b) one in which these bounds are known but hold only eventually.The implementation of the round model slightly differs depending on the partial synchrony variant that is considered. We consider here model (a), which is also the model considered in the leader-based Castro-Liskov PBFT protocol [7]. In this model a standard technique, used for example in PBFT, is to have exponentially growing timeouts. For example, in PBFT whenever the leader changes (i.e., the recovery protocol has to be executed), the timeout for the next leader is doubled. Taking this leader-based protocol as a case study, Amir et al. [10] pointed its vulnerability to performance degradation under an attack. Indeed in PBFT, f consecutive Byzantine leaders, say l_1, l_2, ..., l_f could do construct the following attack. The first leader l_1 is mute, the timeout expires, the recovery protocol is activated, and the algorithm switches to the next leader (rotating coordinator) while doubling the timeout. The same happens for leaders l_2 to l_{f-1} until l_f becomes leader. The last leader l_f sends its message as late as possible, but not too late to remain leader. If l_f remains leader forever, then the time required for any request (instance of consensus) is high.

Although PBFT does not assume a round-based model as we do in this paper, the performance failure attack is possible in the case of a leader-based protocol implemented in the round-based model, in the case the round-based model is constructed on top of a partially synchronous model of type (a). However, we believe that this is not the case for leader-free algorithms, i.e., performance failure attacks are not effective in this case. The intuition is that, once the timeout of a correct process becomes large enough to receive all messages from correct processes, Byzantine processes cannot introduce an attack that forces the correct process to double its timeout. Our future work is to validate this intuition analytically and/or experimentally, and to understand under which conditions leader-free algorithms outperform leader-based algorithms.

5 Conclusion

All previously known deterministic consensus algorithms for partially synchronous systems and Byzantine faults are leader-based. However, leader-based algorithms are vulnerable to performance degradation, which occurs when the Byzantine leader sends messages slowly, but without triggering timeouts. In the paper we have proposed a deterministic (no randomization), leader-free Byzantine consensus algorithm in a partially synchronous system. Our algorithm is resilient-optimal (it requires $3t+1$ processes) and signature-free (it doesn't rely on digital signatures). To the best of our knowledge this is the first Byzantine algorithm that satisfies all these characteristics. We have also presented optimizations for the Byzantine consensus algorithm, including one-round decision. Finally, a simpler leader-free consensus algorithm that uses digital signatures is proposed.

We have designed our algorithms using a new methodology. It consists of extending a synchronous consensus algorithm to a partially synchronous consensus algorithm using an asynchronous algorithm. The asynchronous protocol ensures safety (i.e., agreement and strong validity), while the synchronous algorithm provides liveness (i.e., termination) during periods of synchrony.

Acknowledgments. We would like to thank Martin Hutle, Nuno Santos and Olivier Rütti for their comments on an earlier version of the paper.

References

1. Pease, M., Shostak, R., Lamport, L.: Reaching agreement in the presence of faults. J. ACM 27(2), 228–234 (1980)
2. Fischer, M.J., Lynch, N.A., Paterson, M.S.: Impossibility of distributed consensus with one faulty process. JACM 32(2), 374–382 (1985)
3. Ben-Or, M.: Another advantage of free choice (extended abstract): Completely asynchronous agreement protocols. In: PODC 1983, pp. 27–30. ACM, New York (1983)
4. Rabin, M.: Randomized Byzantine generals. In: Proc. Symposium on Foundations of Computer Science, pp. 403–409 (1983)
5. Bracha, G.: An asynchronous [(n - 1)/3]-resilient consensus protocol. In: PODC 1984, pp. 154–162. ACM, New York (1984)
6. Dwork, C., Lynch, N., Stockmeyer, L.: Consensus in the presence of partial synchrony. JACM 35(2), 288–323 (1988)
7. Castro, M., Liskov, B.: Practical Byzantine fault tolerance and proactive recovery. ACM Transactions on Computer Systems (TOCS) 20(4), 398–461 (2002)
8. Martin, J.-P., Alvisi, L.: Fast Byzantine consensus. IEEE Transactions on Dependable and Secure Computing 3(3), 202–215 (2006)
9. Kotla, R., Alvisi, L., Dahlin, M., Clement, A., Wong, E.: Zyzzyva: speculative byzantine fault tolerance. SIGOPS Oper. Syst. Rev. 41(6), 45–58 (2007)
10. Amir, Y., Coan, B., Kirsch, J., Lane, J.: Byzantine replication under attack. In: DSN 2008, pp. 197–206 (2008)
11. Clement, A., Wong, E., Alvisi, L., Dahlin, M., Marchetti, M.: Making Byzantine fault tolerant systems tolerate Byzantine faults. In: NSDI 2009, Berkeley, CA, USA, pp. 153–168. USENIX Association (2009)
12. Lamport, L.: State-Machine Reconfiguration: Past, Present, and the Cloudy Future. In: DISC Workshop on Theoretical Aspects of Dynamic Distributed Systems (September 2009)
13. Lynch, N.A.: Distributed Algorithms. Morgan Kaufmann, San Francisco (1996)
14. Borran, F., Schiper, A.: A Leader-free Byzantine Consensus Algorithm. Technical report, EPFL (2009)
15. Attiya, H., Welch, J.: Distributed Computing: fundamentals, simulations, and advanced topics. John Wiley & Sons, Chichester (2004)
16. Charron-Bost, B., Schiper, A.: The Heard-Of model: computing in distributed systems with benign faults. Distributed Computing 22(1), 49–71 (2009)
17. Biely, M., Widder, J., Charron-Bost, B., Gaillard, A., Hutle, M., Schiper, A.: Tolerating corrupted communication. In: PODC 2007, pp. 244–253. ACM, New York (2007)
18. Moses, Y., Waarts, O.: Coordinated traversal: $(t + 1)$-round byzantine agreement in polynomial time. In: FOCS, pp. 246–255 (1988)
19. Song, Y.J., van Renesse, R.: Bosco: One-step byzantine asynchronous consensus. In: Taubenfeld, G. (ed.) DISC 2008. LNCS, vol. 5218, pp. 438–450. Springer, Heidelberg (2008)

Authenticated Byzantine Generals in Dual Failure Model

Anuj Gupta, Prasant Gopal, Piyush Bansal, and Kannan Srinathan

Center for Security, Theory and Algorithmic Research,
International Institute of Information Technology, Hyderabad - 500032, India
anujgupta@research.iiit.net

Abstract. Pease *et al.* introduced the problem of Byzantine Generals
(BGP) to study the effects of Byzantine faults in distributed protocols
for reliable broadcast. It is well known that BGP among n players tolerating up to t faults is (efficiently) possible iff $n > 3t$. To overcome this
severe limitation, Pease *et al.* introduced a variant of BGP, *Authenticated
Byzantine General* (ABG). Here players are supplemented with digital
signatures (or similar tools) to thwart the challenge posed by Byzantine
faults. Subsequently, they proved that with the use of authentication,
fault tolerance of protocols for reliable broadcast can be amazingly increased to $n > t$ (which is a huge improvement over the $n > 3t$).

Byzantine faults are the most generic form of faults. In a network not
all faults are always malicious. Some faulty nodes may only leak their
data while others are malicious. Motivated from this, we study the problem of ABG in (t_b, t_p)-mixed adversary model where the adversary can
corrupt up to any t_b players actively and control up to any other t_p players passively. We prove that in such a setting, ABG over a completely
connected synchronous network of n nodes tolerating a (t_b, t_p)-adversary
is possible iff $n > 2t_b + \min(t_b, t_p)$ when $t_p > 0$. Interestingly, our results
can also be seen as an attempt to unify the extant literature on BGP
and ABG.

Keywords: Reliable broadcast, Authenticated Byzantine General, Mixed
adversary.

1 Introduction

Fault tolerance of a distributed system is a highly desirable property, and has
been the subject of intensive research for many years. A fundamental problem
in the theory of distributed systems is that of designing protocols for simulating
a broadcast channel over a point to point network in the presence of faults. The
problem, introduced by Lamport *et al.* [1], is popularly known as "Byzantine
Generals problem"(BGP). Informally, the challenge is to maintain a coherent
view of the world among all the non-faulty players in spite of faulty players
trying to disrupt the same. Specifically, in a protocol for BGP over a *synchronous*
network of n players, the *General* starts with an input from a fixed set $V =
\{0, 1\}$. At the end of the protocol (which may involve finitely many rounds of

K. Kant et al. (Eds.): ICDCN 2010, LNCS 5935, pp. 79–91, 2010.
© Springer-Verlag Berlin Heidelberg 2010

interaction), even if up to any t of the n players are faulty, all non-faulty players output the same value $u \in V$ and if the General is non-faulty and starts with input $v \in V$, then $u = v$. Traditionally, the notion of faults in the network is captured via a fictitious entity called *adversary* that can choose a subset of players as "pawns". An adversary that controls up to any t of the n players is denoted by t-adversary.

The problem was first studied on an all mighty t-adversary which can corrupt upto any t of the n nodes in Byzantine fashion. These Byzantine nodes can behave arbitrarily, even colluding to bring the system down. In a completely connected synchronous network with no additional setup, classical results of [1,2] show that reliable broadcast among n parties in the presence of up to t Byzantine nodes is achievable if and only if $t < n/3$. Here a player is said to be non-faulty if and only if he faithfully executes the protocol delegated to him.

There exists a rich literature on BGP. After [1,2], studies were initiated under various settings like asynchronous networks [3], partially synchronous networks [4], incomplete networks [5], hypernetworks [6], non-threshold adversaries [7], mixed-adversaries [8], mobile adversaries [9], and probabilistic correctness [10] to name a few. An important variant of BGP is the *authenticated* model proposed by Pease *et al.* [2], which as the title of this paper suggests, is our main focus. In this model, hereafter referred as *authenticated Byzantine General* (ABG), players are supplemented with "magical" powers (say a Public Key Infrastructure (PKI) and digital signatures) using which players can authenticate themselves and their messages. It is proved that in such a model, the tolerability against a t-adversary can be amazingly increased to as high as $t < n$. Dolev and Strong [11] presented efficient protocols thereby confirming the usefulness of authentication in both possibility as well as feasibility of distributed protocols. Subsequent papers on this subject include [12,13,14,15,16,17,18].

1.1   Motivation

A large part of the literature considers the adversary to have same amount of control over all the corrupt players. However, many a times this may not be true. For example, some nodes may act in Byzantine manner while few others may atmost fail stop. In such a case modeling all the faults uniformly as Byzantine will be gross misrepresent. An elegant way to capture this is via a mixed adversary where by the adversary has varied control over different corrupt players i.e. it controls some players actively, another fraction as fail-stop. Note that the mixed adversary model not only generalizes the adversary models where only "monotype" corruption is considered but also facilitates a deeper understanding of the relationship between computability/complexity of the task at hand and the adversary's power. With respect to BGP, mixed adversary model has been considered in [19,8] to name a few. Motivated from this, we initiate the study of ABG in a setting where upto a fraction of the nodes are Byzantine and another fraction of nodes "leak" their internal state to the adversary. We model this via a (t_b, t_p)−*adversary*, where the adversary controls upto any t_b players actively and upto another t_p players passively. We strive to answer the following: *what is* *the necessary and sufficient condition(s) for simulating a broadcast channel over a completely connected point-to-point synchronous network tolerating a (t_b,t_p)-adversary ?* Note that this is same as simulating a broadcast channel for the entire gamut of adversaries between $t_b = t$, $t_p = 0$ (ABG) and $t_b = t$, $t_p = n - t$ (BGP).

2   Our Contributions and Results

The contributions of this paper are manyfold:

1. *Better definition:* As a first contribution of this work, we argue that the problem of ABG under the influence of a (t_b,t_p)-adversary requires a slight modification in the standard definition of ABG available in the extant literature. Our argument stems from the observation that a protocol that satisfies the extant definition of ABG but does not meet our definition, *fails* to simulate a broadcast channel, as originally intended. Therefore, the definition of ABG available in the extant literature is not straightaway suitable in our setting. None the less, we essentially use the same principles to define a suitably adapted and faithful definition in our setting.

2. *Complete characterization:* We give the necessary and sufficient condition(s) for designing ABG protocols tolerating a (t_b,t_p)-adversary. We prove that over a completely connected synchronous network of n nodes with $t_p > 0$, $n > 2t_b + min(t_b, t_p)$ is necessary and sufficient for existence of ABG protocols tolerating a (t_b,t_p)-adversary. For $t_p = 0$, the bound is $n > t_b$ as given by Pease *et al.* [2].

3. *Unification:* For the problem of reliable broadcast in the authenticated model (ABG), it is assumed that the adversary can forge signatures of only those players which are under its control. In contrast, the unauthenticated model (BGP), assumes no authentication tools. This can also be seen as all the players using *insecure signature schemes* and therefore the adversary can forge their signatures. With ABG tolerating a (t_b,t_p)-adversary, we initiate the study of the entire gamut of broadcasts in between, viz., an adversary that can forge signatures of up to any t_p nodes apart from controlling up to t_b nodes actively. Thus, BGP and ABG are merely two extreme points of this entire gamut. Our work gives a *characterization for the entire gamut*. Therefore, our work *unifies* the extant literature on BGP and ABG.

4. *Fault tolerance of signature schemes:* In the age of modern cryptography, it is reasonable to assume availability of Public Key Infrastructure (PKI) and digital signatures over any communication network. All known PKI and digital signature schemes are usually based on the conjectured hardness of some problems like integer factorization [20], discrete logarithms [21], permutations [22,23], lattice based problems [24,25] to name a few. Further, the proofs of the hardness of these problems seem to be beyond the reach of contemporary mathematics. Thus, it may well be the case that some of these schemes are eventually proven to be insecure.

An elegant way to deal with this is to consider the approach taken by *robust combiners* [26,27,28]. Informally, a (k, n)-robust combiner is a construction that takes n candidate protocols for a given functionality and combines them into one scheme such that even if up to any k of the n protocols are rendered incorrect during actual execution, the combined scheme is guaranteed to correctly implement the desired functionality. Note that different sets of up to k candidate protocols may fail for different executions/inputs.

In context of ABG, different players may use different signature schemes. Some of these schemes may eventually prove to be insecure. Analogous to a (k, n)-robust combiner, one will prefer to design ABG protocols that work correctly even if up to a fraction of the signature schemes are rendered insecure. We capture this by assuming that the adversary can forge signatures of up to another t_p players. Thus, t_p can also be seen as a *robustness parameter of authentication* for ABG protocols.

2.1 Organization of the Paper

In section 3 we formally introduce our model. In section 3.1 we formally define the problem statement. Section 4 gives the complete characterization of ABG tolerating a (t_b, t_p)-adversary over completely connected synchronous networks, followed by the conclusion in section 5.

3 Our Model

We consider a set of n players denoted by $\mathbb{P}$, computationally unbounded and fully connected. Communication over the network is assumed to be synchronous. That is, the protocol is executed in a sequence of *rounds* where in each round, a player can perform some local computation, send new messages to all the players, receive messages sent to him by players in the same round, (and if necessary perform some more local computation), in that order. During the execution, the adversary may take control of up to any $t_b + t_p$ players. The adversary can make t_b players to behave in any arbitrary fashion and read the internal states of upto another t_p players. W.l.o.g we assume that the adversary always uses his full power, therefore $t_b \cap t_p = \emptyset$. We further assume that the communication channel between any two players is perfectly reliable and authenticated i.e. the adversary cannot modify messages sent between non-malicious parties. We also assume existence of a signature/authentication scheme[1] where the sender signs the message to be sent. This is modeled by all parties having an additional setup-tape that is generated during the preprocessing phase.[2] Typically in such a preprocessing phase, the signature keys are generated. That is, each party gets

---

[1] In line with literature [2], we assume the authentication scheme to be secure against a computationally unbounded adversary.

[2] Note that keys cannot be generated with the system itself. It is assumed that the keys are generated using a trusted system and distributed to players prior to running of the protocol similar to [29].

its own private key, and in addition, public verification keys for all other players. No player can forge any player's signature and the receiver can uniquely identify the sender of the message from the signature. However, the adversary can forge the signature of all the (t_b+t_p) players under its control. W.l.o.g we assume that players authenticate their messages with their private key.

3.1   Problem Definition

Consider a ABG protocol wherein a player, say P_i, is passively controlled by a (t_b,t_p)-adversary. By virtue of passive corruption, the adversary can always forge messages on behalf of P_i (adversary can read his private key and use it thereafter for forging messages). In such a scenario, at the end of the ABG protocol, *is P_i required to output same value as decided upon by the honest players?* At first glance the answer may be No. The rationale being: P_i has lost his private key to the adversary, therefore, in a way P_i is helping the adversary. Thus, any correct ABG protocol need not ensure passively corrupt players (such as P_i) to output same value as honest players. However, in the sequel, we present a series of arguments to justify as to why *any valid ABG protocol tolerating a (t_b,t_p)-adversary should ensure that all passively corrupt players output same value as honest players.*

As a prelude, we remark that in the literature, a player is considered to be *faulty* if and only if he deviates from the designated protocol. Consequently, a player can be non-faulty in two ways – first the adversary is absent, (therefore) the player follows the protocol and second the adversary is present passively, (therefore) the player follows the protocol. For the rest of this paper, we refer to the former kind of non-faulty player as *honest* and the latter as *passively corrupt*. Our arguments in support of passively corrupt players are:

1. *Simulation of broadcast channel:* As highlighted in previous sections, the aim of any (valid) BGP/ABG protocol is to simulate a broadcast channel over a point to point (unreliable)network. This should also hold for ABG under the influence of a (t_b,t_p)-adversary. Now consider a physical broadcast channel, say $\mathcal{C}$, among a set of n players under the influence of (t_b,t_p)-adversary. Adversary can corrupt upto t_b players actively and upto another t_p players passively. Via $\mathcal{C}$, the General sends his input value $v \in \{0,1\}$ to all the n players. By property of $\mathcal{C}$, all the n players are guaranteed to receive value v. All honest and passively corrupt players will output v. The adversary can make all the actively corrupt players to output a value of his choice (which may be different from v). It is evident from the above scenario that for any physical broadcast channel, passively corrupt players will always decide upon the value same as honest players. Thus, any ABG protocol aiming to *truly simulate* a broadcast channel in the presence of (t_b,t_p)-adversary, *has to ensure* that all the non-faulty (honest and passively corrupt) players output the *same* value.

2. *Authentication is a means, not the end:* The objective of any (valid) BGP protocol is to simulate a broadcast channel from a designated sender to a

set of receivers. In order to facilitate this process, authentication is used as a tool in BGP protocols. Clearly, authentication is a means and broadcast is the end. In such a scenario even if the tool fails to do its job satisfactorily (as with passively corrupt players), why should the objective be altered ? In order to fulfill the original objective, all non-faulty(honest and passively corrupt) players must output same value.

3. *Ideal world/Real World:* A popular paradigm used in defining the security requirements of any task is the Ideal world/Real World simulation technique [30]. We show that in the ideal world for ABG in the presence of a (t_b, t_p)-adversary, all non-faulty players always decide on same the value. It then follows that the corresponding ABG protocol in the real world has to ensure that all non-faulty players decide on the same value.

   Consider a set of n players connected to a Trusted Third Party(TTP). The (t_b, t_p)-adversary follows its strategy. W.l.o.g let P_i be a passively corrupt player and P_j be an honest player. The General sends his value to the TTP. The TTP forwards this value to all the n players. All the non-faulty players output the value received from the TTP. Thus, in the ideal world, P_i and P_j output same value.

4. *Motivation from real life:* In order to authenticate important documents, use of physical signatures is a common practice in day-to-day life. Consider a person who forges the signature of some other person(s) for an undue benefit/advantage. It is well known that in such scenarios the law penalizes the person committing the forgery and not the victim(s) of the forgery. Analogously, for ABG under the influence of (t_b, t_p)-adversary, passively corrupt players should not be penalized for the adversary being able to forge messages on their behalf. Thus, all passively corrupt players should be part of agreement like honest players.

Based on the above discussion we now define ABG under the influence of a (t_b, t_p)-adversary. Throughout the rest of this paper we refer to it as ABG_{mix}.

Definition 1 (ABG_{mix}). *A designated General starts with an input from a fixed set $V = \{0, 1\}$. The goal is for the players to eventually output decisions from the set V upholding the following conditions, even in the presence of a (t_b, t_p)-adversary:*

- Agreement: *All non-faulty players decide on the same value $u \in V$.*
- Validity: *If the general is non-faulty and starts with the initial value $v \in V$, then $u = v$.*
- Termination: *All non-faulty players eventually decide.*

For the clarity of the reader, we reiterate certain terms that have been used extensively in the paper. A player is said to be *faulty* if and only if he deviates from the designated protocol. Consequently *non-faulty* players are ones who do not deviate from the designated protocol. A *passively corrupt* player is one who follows the designated protocol diligently, but the adversary has complete access to his internal state. An *honest* player is one who follows the designated protocol,

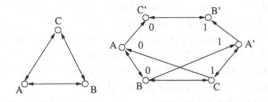

Fig. 1. Network $\mathcal{N}$ and System S

and over whom the adversary has absolutely no control. For the purpose of this paper, we refer to both *honest* and *passively corrupt* players together as non-faulty. Rest of the paper focuses on the complete characterization of ABG_{mix} over completely connected synchronous graphs.

3.2 Definitions

We now formally define some of the terms used in this paper:

Definition 2 (Adversary Structure). *An adversary structure $\mathcal{Z}$ for the player set $\mathbb{P}$ is a monotone set of subsets of $\mathbb{P}$, i.e. $\mathcal{Z} \subseteq 2^{\mathbb{P}}$, where all subsets of Z are in $\mathcal{Z}$ if $Z \in \mathcal{Z}$.*

Definition 3 (Adversary Basis). *For an adversary structure $\mathcal{Z}$, $\bar{\mathcal{Z}}$ denotes the basis of the structure, i.e. the set of the maximal sets in $\mathcal{Z}$: $\bar{\mathcal{Z}} = \{Z \in \bar{\mathcal{Z}} : \nexists Z' \in \bar{\mathcal{Z}} : Z \subset Z'\}$*

4   Complete Characterization

We first show that there does not exist any ABG_{mix} protocol over a completely connected synchronous network $\mathcal{N}$(Figure 1) of three nodes $\mathbb{P} = \{A, B, C\}$ tolerating an adversary basis $\bar{A} = \{((C), (A)), ((A), (\emptyset)), ((B, A))\}$. For the rest of this work $((x_1, \ldots, x_i),(y_1, \ldots, y_j))$ represents a single element of an adversary basis where the adversary can corrupt $x_1, \ldots, x_i$ actively and simultaneously control $y_1, \ldots, y_j$ passively.

Lemma 1. *There does not exist any protocol solving ABG_{mix} over a completely connected synchronous network $\mathcal{N}$ of three nodes $\mathbb{P} = \{A, B, C\}$ tolerating an adversary basis $\bar{A} = \{((C), (A)), ((A), (\emptyset)), ((B, A))\}$.*

Proof. Proof by contradiction. We assume there exists a protocol Π that solves ABG_{mix} over a completely connected synchronous network of three nodes $\mathbb{P} = \{A, B, C\}$ tolerating an adversary basis $\bar{A} = \{((C), (A)), ((A), (\emptyset)), ((B, A))\}$. The proof proceeds to demonstrate that there exists an input assignment for which adversary(characterized by $\bar{A}$) can ensure that non-faulty players in an execution of Π do not always have a consistent output. This contradicts our assumption of Π.

To show that $\bar{A}$ can ensure that non-faulty players do not have a consistent output, we use the technique for giving impossibility proofs, developed by Fischer *et al.* [31]. Using Π we create a protocol π'[Definition 4] in such a way that if Π exists then so does π'(Lemma 2). Using two copies of π' we construct a system S (Figure 1). We then show that S must exhibit a contradictory behavior. This implies impossibility of the assumed protocol Π.

Formally, S is a synchronous system with a well defined output distribution for every input assignment. Here we do not know what the system S does. Therefore, the definition of ABG[Definition 1] does not tell us anything directly about the players' output. All we know is that S is a synchronous system and has a well defined behavior. Further, no player in S knows the complete system. Each player in S is aware of only his immediate neighbours.

Let α_1, α_2 and α_3 be three distinct scenarios in execution of Π over $\mathcal{N}$. In α_1, A is the General starting with input 0. $\bar{A}$ corrupts C actively and controls A passively. In α_2, A is the General. $\bar{A}$ corrupts A and makes him to interact with B as if A started with input 0, and, interact with C as if A started with input 1. In α_3, A is the General starting with input 1. $\bar{A}$ corrupts B actively and controls A passively. Further, let α be an execution of L where each player starts with input value as shown in Figure 1. All the players in α are honest and follow the designated protocol correctly.

We claim that no matter for how many rounds Π executes, for any round i, whatever $view^3$ A, B get in α, $\bar{A}$ can ensure that A, B respectively get same view in α_1 i.e. $view^\alpha_{A,i} \sim view^{\alpha_1}_{A,i}$. This implies that the player A cannot ever differentiate between α_1 and α (dubbed as $\alpha_1 \overset{A}{\sim} \alpha$). Similarly, player B cannot ever differentiate between α_1 and α ($\alpha_1 \overset{B}{\sim} \alpha$). From the definition of ABG_{mix} [Definition 1], in α_1, both A, B should decide on value 0. Since $\alpha_1 \overset{A}{\sim} \alpha$ and $\alpha_1 \overset{B}{\sim} \alpha$, both A, B in α will also decide on value 0 (we are able to make claims regarding the outputs of A and B in α as their views are same as those in α_1. Thus by analyzing their outputs in α_1, we can determine there outputs in α). Similarly, $\bar{A}$ can ensure that $\alpha_3 \overset{A'}{\sim} \alpha$ and $\alpha_3 \overset{C}{\sim} \alpha$. Both A, C in α_3 should decide on value 1. Then so will both A', C in α. Similarly, we claim that $\bar{A}$ can ensure that $\alpha_2 \overset{B}{\sim} \alpha$ and $\alpha_2 \overset{C}{\sim} \alpha$. As per the definition of ABG_{mix}, B, C in α_2 should agree on same value, then so should B, C in α. But B,C have already decided upon values 0 and 1 respectively in α. This implies S must exhibit contradictory behavior. $\qquad\square$

To complete the above proof, we need to show that $\bar{A}$ can always ensure that – A, B get same view in α and α_1, B, C get same view in α and α_2 and A, C get same view in α and α_3. We prove the same in Lemma 3, 4, 5 respectively. Owing to space constraints here we only state our lemmas. Detailed proofs of these are given in [32]. We now define the protocol π'[Definition 4] and show that if Π exists then so does π'(Lemma 2).

---

[3] Informally, view of a player in an execution is all the messages it ever comes across. For a formal definition, refer to [32, Equation 2].

Definition 4 (π'). *For players $a, b \in \mathbb{P}$, any statement in Π of the kind "b sends message m to a" is replaced by "b multicasts message m to all instances of a"(i.e. a, a')[4] in π'. Similarly any statement of the kind "c sends message m to a" in Π is replaced by "c multicasts message m to all instances of a" in π'. Rest all statements in π' are same as those in Π.*

Lemma 2. *If Π exists then π' exists.*

Proof: Implied from Definition 4.   □

Lemma 3. *$\bar{A}$ can ensure $view_A^\alpha \sim view_A^{\alpha_1}$ and $view_B^\alpha \sim view_B^{\alpha_1}$*

Lemma 4. *$\bar{A}$ can ensure $view_B^\alpha \sim view_B^{\alpha_2}$ and $view_C^\alpha \sim view_C^{\alpha_2}$*

Lemma 5. *$\bar{A}$ can ensure $view_C^\alpha \sim view_C^{\alpha_3}$ and $view_{A'}^\alpha \sim view_A^{\alpha_3}$.*

Theorem 1. *There does not exist any protocol solving ABG_{mix} over a completely connected synchronous network $\mathcal{N}'$ of n nodes tolerating (t_b, t_p)-adversary if $n \leq 2t_b + min(t_b, t_p)$, for $t_p > 0$.*

Proof. Proof by contradiction. Let us assume that there exists a protocol η solving ABG_{mix} over a completely connected synchronous network $\mathcal{N}'$ of n nodes tolerating (t_b, t_p)-adversary if $n \leq 2t_b + min(t_b, t_p)$, for $t_p > 0$. We show that using η one can construct a protocol Π solving ABG_{mix} over a completely connected synchronous network $\mathcal{N}$ of three nodes $\mathbb{P} = \{A, B, C\}$ tolerating an adversary basis $\bar{A} = \{((C), (A)), ((A), (\emptyset)), ((B), A))\}$. From Lemma 1 we know that there does not exist any such Π. This contradicts our assumption of η.

We partition the n players into three mutually disjoint non-empty sets I_A, I_B and I_C such that $|I_A| \leq min(t_b, t_p)$, $|I_B| \leq t_b$ and $|I_C| \leq t_b$. Since $n \leq 2t_b + min(t_b, t_p)$, such a partitioning is always possible. The edges in $\mathcal{N}'$ can now be considered as bundle of edges between the groups I_A, I_B and I_C. Each of the three players A, B and C in Π simulate players in I_A, I_B and I_C respectively. Each player i in Π keeps track of the states of all the players in I_i. Player i assigns its input value to every member of I_i, and simulates the steps of all the players in I_i as well as the messages sent and received between pairs of players in I_i. Messages from players in I_i to players in I_j are simulated by sending same messages from player i to player j. If any player in I_i terminates then so does player i. If any player in I_i decides on value v, then so does player i.

We now prove that if η solves ABG_{mix} over $\mathcal{N}'$ tolerating (t_b, t_p)-adversary when $n \leq 2t_b + min(t_b, t_p)$, then Π solves ABG_{mix} over $\mathcal{N}$ tolerating adversary basis $\mathbb{A} = \{((C), (A)), ((A), (\emptyset)), ((B), A))\}$. Let Ψ and Ψ' be executions of η and Π respectively. W.l.o.g we let honest, passively corrupt and malicious players in Ψ to be exactly simulated by honest, passively corrupt and malicious players respectively in Ψ'. As per our assumption Ψ solves ABG_{mix}, thus satisfying Definition 1. We now show that same holds for Ψ' if it holds for Ψ. W.l.o.g in Ψ, let the general be from set I_i, then in Ψ' player i acts as the general. Note

---

[4] A and a' are independent copies of a with same authentication key.

that in Ψ if I_i is controlled actively or passively by the adversary, then so is i is Ψ'.

Let j,k ($j \neq k$) be two non-faulty players in Ψ'. j and k simulate at least one player each in Ψ. Since j and k are non-faulty, so are all players in I_j, I_k. For Ψ, all players in I_j, I_k must terminate, then so should j and k. In Ψ, all non-faulty players including all the players in I_j and I_k should decide on same value, say u, then in Ψ', j, k will also decide on u. In Ψ, if the general is non-faulty and starts with input value v, then in Ψ' too, the general will be non-faulty and starts with input value v. In such a case in ψ, all non-faulty players including all the players in I_j and I_k should have $u = v$. Then in Ψ', j, k will also have $u = v$. Clearly, ψ' also satisfies definition 1. Thus Π solves ABG_{mix} over $\mathcal{N}$ tolerating adversary basis $\mathbb{A} = \{((C),(A)),((A),(\emptyset)),((B,A))\}$.   □

We now present the main theorem of this work.

Theorem 2 (Main Theorem). ABG_{mix} is solvable iff $n > 2t_b + min(t_b, t_p)$, for $t_p > 0$.

Proof. Necessity follows from Theorem 1. For sufficiency, we present protocol solving ABG_{mix} for $n > 2t_b + min(t_b, t_p)$, $t_p > 0$. We present the protocols separately for $t_b > t_p$ and $t_b \leq t_p$.

Case of $t_b > t_p$: $n > 2t_b + min(t_b, t_p)$ reduces to $n > 2t_b + t_p$. For this we present a protocol and prove its correctness in section 4.1.

Case of $t_b \leq t_p$: $n > 2t_b + min(t_b, t_p)$ reduces to $n > 3t_b$. Here any known BGP protocol works (one such simple protocol is *EIGByz* protocol [33, page 120]). This is because for unauthenticated setting $t_p = n - t_b$. This completes the sufficiency proof. We remark that for $t_p = 0$, the result reduces to $n > t_b$ [2].   □

Remark. In general, one would expect the curve depicting the fault tolerance of ABG_{mix} to be smooth (though steep) as t_p increases from $t_p = 0$, $t_b = t$ (ABG) to $t_p = n - t$, $t_b = t$ (BGP). Contrary to the above intuition, our results unveil a striking discontinuity in the curve between $t_p = 0$ and $t_p = 1$. This is as follows – for $t_p = 0$, $t_b = t$, one gets $n > t$ as a corollary from the results of Pease *et al.* [2]. For $t_p = 1$, $t_b = t$, the bound is $n > 2t + 1$ as implied Theorem 2. Thus, $t_p = 0$ or $t_p > 0$ has an important bearing on the fault tolerance bounds of ABG_{mix}.

4.1   Protocol for $n > 2t_b + t_p$

The proposed protocol is obtained by a sequence of transformations on EIG tree [34]. A detailed discussion on the construction of EIG tree is available in [34] [33, page 108]. Our protocol *EIGPrune* is given in Figure 2. Inspite of our protocol being exponential in number of messages, we present the same for its ease of understanding.

EIGPrune Algorithm

General $\mathcal{G}$ send his value to every player. Every player assumes this value from the $\mathcal{G}$ as his input value and exchanges messages with others as per *EIGStop* protocol [33, page 103] for $t_b + t_p + 1$ rounds.

At the end of $t_b + t_p + 1$ rounds of *EIGStop* protocol, player p_i invokes **Prune**(EIG) [Definition 5]. Player p_i applies the following decision rule – take majority of the values at the first level (i.e. all the nodes with labels l such that $l \in \mathbb{P}$) of its *EIG* tree. If a majority exists, player p_i decides on that value; else, p_i decides on *default value, v_0*.

Fig. 2. *EIGPrune* algorithm

Definition 5 (Prune(EIG)). *This method that takes an EIG tree as an input and deletes subtrees say $subtree_j{}^i$ ($subtree_j{}^i$ refers to a subtree in i's EIG tree such that the subtree is rooted at node whose's label is j) of i's EIG tree as given in the sequel. For each subtree $subtree_j{}^i$, where label $j \in \mathbb{P}$, a set W_j is constructed which contains all distinct values that ever appears in $subtree_j{}^i$. If $|W_j| > 1$, $subtree_j{}^i$ is deleted and modified EIG tree is returned.*

The correctness of *EIGPrune* follows from Lemma 6 – 9. For proofs see [32].

Lemma 6. *The $subtree_j{}^i$, where j is an honest player and i is a non-faulty player, will never be deleted during* **Prune***(EIG) operation.*

Lemma 7. *After $t_b + t_p + 1$ rounds, if $subtree_j{}^i$ has more than one value then $\forall$ k, $subtree_j{}^k$ also has more than one value, there by ensuring that all $\forall$ k, $subtree_j{}^k$ are deleted $(i, j, k$ necessarily distinct), where i, k are non-faulty.*

Lemma 8. *$subtree_j{}^i$ and $subtree_j{}^k$ in the EIG trees of any two players i, k will have same values after subjecting the tree to* **Prune***(EIG), where i, k are non-faulty players.*

Lemma 9. *For $n > 2t_b + t_p$, EIGPrune algorithm solves ABG_{mix}.*

Proof. $n - (t_b + t_p)$ represents the number of honest players and according to $n > 2t_b + t_p$, $n - (t_b + t_p) > t_b$. Thus honest majority is guaranteed which vacuously implies non-faulty majority. The decision rule ensures that in case the General is non-faulty and starts with v, all non-faulty players decide on v. Further if the General is faulty, all non-faulty should agree on same value. Let i and j be any two non-faulty players. Since, decisions only occur at the end, and by previous lemma we see that $\forall i$, $subtree_j{}^i$ can have only one value which is consistent throughout all $subtree_j^i$, $\forall i \in \mathbb{P}$. This implies they have the same set of values. From the decision rule, i and j make the same decision. $\qquad \square$

5   Conclusion

The folklore has been that the use of authentication in BGP protocols reduces the Byzantine faults to fail-stop failures. Thus, the protocols designed for fail-stop faults can be quickly adapted to solve ABG. However in this paper, we show that this does not hold true in the case of ABG under the influence of mixed adversary. In a way, the problem of ABG_{mix} is between ABG and BGP. Consequentially, the protocols for ABG_{mix} use ideas from both ABG and BGP. Also, our results imply a striking discontinuity in the bounds for fault tolerance of ABG_{mix} when $t_p = 0$ and $t_p = 1$. Further, from the results of $n > 2t_b + \min(t_b, t_p)$, it appears that studying this problem over general networks will be interesting in its own right.

References

1. Lamport, L., Shostak, R., Pease, M.: The byzantine generals problem. ACM Trans. Program. Lang. Syst. 4(3), 382–401 (1982)
2. Pease, M., Shostak, R., Lamport, L.: Reaching agreement in the presence of faults. J. ACM 27(2), 228–234 (1980)
3. Fischer, M.J., Lynch, N.A., Paterson, M.S.: Impossibility of distributed consensus with one faulty process. J. ACM 32(2), 374–382 (1985)
4. Dolev, D., Dwork, C., Stockmeyer, L.: On the minimal synchronism needed for distributed consensus. J. ACM 34(1), 77–97 (1987)
5. Dolev, D.: The Byzantine Generals Strike Again. Technical report, Stanford University, Stanford, CA, USA (1981)
6. Fitzi, M., Maurer, U.: From partial consistency to global broadcast. In: STOC 2000, pp. 494–503. ACM, New York (2000)
7. Fitzi, M., Maurer, U.M.: Efficient Byzantine Agreement Secure Against General Adversaries. In: International Symposium on Distributed Computing, pp. 134–148 (1998)
8. Altmann, B., Fitzi, M., Maurer, U.M.: Byzantine agreement secure against general adversaries in the dual failure model. In: Proceedings of the 13th International Symposium on Distributed Computing, London, UK, pp. 123–137. Springer, Heidelberg (1999)
9. Garay, J.A.: Reaching (and Maintaining) Agreement in the Presence of Mobile Faults. In: Tel, G., Vitányi, P.M.B. (eds.) WDAG 1994. LNCS, vol. 857, pp. 253–264. Springer, Heidelberg (1994)
10. Rabin, M.O.: Randomized byzantine generals. In: Proc. of the 24th Annu. IEEE Symp. on Foundations of Computer Science, pp. 403–409 (1983)
11. Dolev, D., Strong, H.R.: Authenticated algorithms for byzantine agreement. SIAM Journal on Computing 12(4), 656–666 (1983)
12. Borcherding, M.: On the number of authenticated rounds in byzantine agreement. In: Helary, J.-M., Raynal, M. (eds.) WDAG 1995. LNCS, vol. 972, pp. 230–241. Springer, Heidelberg (1995)
13. Borcherding, M.: Partially authenticated algorithms for byzantine agreement. In: ISCA 1996, pp. 8–11 (1996)
14. Srikanth, T.K., Toueg, S.: Simulating authenticated broadcasts to derive simple fault-tolerant algorithms. Distributed Computing 2(2), 80–94 (1987)

15. Borcherding, M.: Levels of authentication in distributed agreement. In: Babaoğlu, Ö., Marzullo, K. (eds.) WDAG 1996. LNCS, vol. 1151, pp. 40–55. Springer, Heidelberg (1996)
16. Katz, J., Koo, C.Y.: On Expected Constant-round Protocols for Byzantine Agreement. J. Comput. Syst. Sci. 75(2), 91–112 (2009)
17. Gong, L., Lincoln, P., Rushby, J.: Byzantine agreement with authentication: Observations and applications in tolerating hybrid and link faults (1995)
18. Schmid, U., Weiss, B.: Synchronous byzantine agreement under hybrid process and link failures. Research Report 1/2004, Technische Universität Wien, Institut für Technische Informatik, Treitlstr. 1-3/182-1, 1040 Vienna, Austria (2004)
19. Garay, J.A., Perry, K.J.: A Continuum of Failure Models for Distributed Computing. In: Segall, A., Zaks, S. (eds.) WDAG 1992. LNCS, vol. 647, pp. 153–165. Springer, Heidelberg (1992)
20. Rivest, R., Shamir, A., Adleman, L.: A Method for Obtaining Digital Signatures and Public Key Cryptosystems. Communications of the ACM 21, 120–126 (1978)
21. Gamal, T.E.: A public key cryptosystem and a signature scheme based on discrete logarithms. In: CRYPTO 1985, pp. 10–18. Springer-Verlag New York, Inc., New York (1985)
22. Shamir, A.: Efficient signature schemes based on birational permutations. In: CRYPTO, pp. 1–12. Springer-Verlag New York, Inc., New York (1994)
23. Shamir, A.: Identity-based cryptosystems and signature schemes. In: CRYPTO, pp. 47–53. Springer-Verlag New York, Inc., New York (1985)
24. Gentry, C., Peikert, C., Vaikuntanathan, V.: Trapdoors for hard lattices and new cryptographic constructions. In: STOC, pp. 197–206. ACM, New York (2008)
25. Regev, O.: New lattice-based cryptographic constructions. J. ACM 51(6), 899–942 (2004)
26. Meier, R., Przydatek, B., Wullschleger, J.: Robuster combiners for oblivious transfer. In: Vadhan, S.P. (ed.) TCC 2007. LNCS, vol. 4392, pp. 404–418. Springer, Heidelberg (2007)
27. Harnik, D., Kilian, J., Naor, M., Reingold, O., Rosen, A.: On robust combiners for oblivious transfer and other primitives. In: Cramer, R. (ed.) EUROCRYPT 2005. LNCS, vol. 3494, pp. 96–113. Springer, Heidelberg (2005)
28. Meier, R., Przydatek, B.: On robust combiners for private information retrieval and other primitives. In: Dwork, C. (ed.) CRYPTO 2006. LNCS, vol. 4117, pp. 555–569. Springer, Heidelberg (2006)
29. Lindell, Y., Lysysanskaya, A., Rabin, T.: On the Composition of Authenticated Byzantine Agreement. In: STOC, pp. 514–523. ACM Press, New York (2002)
30. Canetti, R.: A unified framework for analyzing security of protocols. Electronic Colloquium on Computational Complexity (ECCC) 8(16) (2001)
31. Fischer, M.J., Lynch, N.A., Merritt, M.: Easy impossibility proofs for distributed consensus problems. In: PODC, pp. 59–70. ACM, New York (1985)
32. Gupta, A., Gopal, P., Bansal, P., Srinathan, K.: Authenticated Byzantine Generals in Dual Failure Model. Technical report, International Institute of Information Technology - Hyderabad, A complete version is http://eprint.iacr.org/2008/287
33. Lynch, N.A.: Distributed algorithms. Distributed Computing (1996)
34. Bar-Noy, A., Dolev, D., Dwork, C., Strong, H.R.: Shifting gears: changing algorithms on the fly to expedite byzantine agreement. In: PODC, pp. 42–51. ACM Press, New York (1987)

Mission-Oriented k-Coverage in Mobile Wireless Sensor Networks

Habib M. Ammari[1] and Sajal K. Das[2]

[1] Wireless Sensor and Mobile Ad-hoc Networks (WiSeMAN) Research Lab
Department of Computer Science, Hofstra University, Hempstead, NY 11549, USA
[2] Center for Research in Wireless Mobility and Networking (CReWMaN)
Department of Computer Science and Engineering, The University of Texas at Arlington,
Arlington, TX, 76019, USA
Habib.M.Ammari@hofstra.edu, das@cse.uta.edu

Abstract. The problem of sensor deployment to achieve k-coverage of a field, where every point is covered by at least k sensors, is very critical in the design of energy-efficient wireless sensor networks (WSNs). It becomes more challenging in mission-oriented WSNs, where sensors have to move in order to k-cover a *region of interest* in the field. In this paper, we consider the problem of k-coverage in mission-oriented mobile WSNs which we divide into two sub-problems, namely *sensor placement* and *sensor selection*. The sensor placement problem is to identify a subset of sensors and their locations in a region of interest so it is k-covered with a minimum number of sensors. The sensor selection problem is to determine which sensors should move to the above-computed locations in the region while minimizing the total energy consumption due to sensor mobility and communication. Simulation results show that our solution to the k-coverage problem in mission-oriented mobile WSNs outperforms an existing one in terms of the number of sensors needed to achieve k-coverage of a region of interest in the field as well as their total energy consumption.

Keywords: Mission-oriented k-coverage, placement, selection, mobility.

1 Introduction

A *wireless sensor network* (WSN) consists of a large number of tiny devices, called *sensors*. These sensors suffer from severe constraints, such as limited battery power (or *energy*), processing power, storage memory, etc., with energy being the most critical one.

In this paper, we focus on mission-oriented mobile WSNs, where the sensors are mobile, autonomous, and interact with each other to accomplish a specific mission in a region of interest in a field. In this type of network, these sensors should be continuously self-organizing so they can achieve the goals of the mission in a dynamic and collaborative manner while minimizing their energy consumption. Also, sensor mobility should be purposeful and traded off against the goals of the mission. In particular, this mobility should be energy-aware given the scarce energy of the individual sensors.

K. Kant et al. (Eds.): ICDCN 2010, LNCS 5935, pp. 92–103, 2010.

1.1 Problem Statement

In this paper, we consider the problem of k-coverage of a region of interest in a field, where each point in the region is *covered* (or *sensed*) by at least $k \geq 3$ active sensors. Precisely, we investigate the problem of mission-oriented k-coverage in mission-oriented mobile WSNs under the following requirements:

(i) *On-demand k-coverage*: A region of interest in a field should be k-covered, where $k \geq 3$, whenever needed. Consequently, a region of interest to be k-covered does not have to be the same all the time, and hence may change.

(ii) *Connectivity*: The sensors should be connected for the correct network operation.

(iii) *Mobility*: The sensors should be able to move to designated locations in a region of interest to ensure its k-coverage whenever necessary.

1.2 Contributions

Our major contributions can be summarized as follows:

(i) We propose a pseudo-random sensor placement strategy that guarantees k-coverage of a region of interest in a field by a small number of sensors. Our solution to the sensor placement problem to achieve k-coverage of a region of interest in a field is based on *Helly's Theorem* and the geometric analysis of a geometric structure, called *Reuleaux triangle*.

(ii) We propose centralized and distributed approaches that enable the sensors to move towards a region of interest and k-cover it while minimizing their mobility energy based on their closeness to the region of interest. Simulation results show that our solution to the sensor deployment problem for k-coverage in mission-oriented mobile WSNs is more energy-efficient than an existing approach in terms of the number of sensors required for k-coverage and their energy consumption.

Organization. The remainder of this paper is organized as follows. Section 2 introduces the network model while Section 3 reviews related work. Section 4 describes our sensor placement approach for mobile k-coverage and Section 5 presents our centralized and distributed protocols for mobile sensor selection. Section 6 presents simulations results of our protocols and Section 7 concludes the paper.

2 Network Model

In this section, we present our assumptions in the design of mission-oriented k-coverage protocols.

Assumption 1 (Sink Uniqueness and Location Awareness). All the sensors and the sink are aware of their locations via some localization technique [3].   •

Assumption 2 (Sensing/ Communication model). The *sensing range* of a sensor s_i is a disk of radius r, centered at ξ_i (s_i's location). Also, the *communication range* of a s_i is a disk of radius R, centered at ξ_i.   •

Assumption 3 (Homogeneity). All the sensors are *homogeneous*, i.e., have the same sensing range and the same communication range.   •

Assumption 4 (Sensor deployment). All the sensors are randomly and uniformly deployed in a field.   •

3 Related Work

In this section, we review a sample of approaches on coverage and particularly connected k-coverage in WSNs while emphasizing sensor mobility.

Recently, significant efforts have been focused on studying coverage using mobile WSNs. Liu *et al.* [7] proved that mobility of the sensors can be used to improve coverage. Wang *et al.* [14] proposed solutions to two related deployment problems in WSNs, namely sensor placement and sensor dispatch, in the presence of obstacles. Furthermore, Wang *et al.* [15] generalized their solutions to the sensor selection and dispatch problems [14] by considering multi-level coverage without obstacles. Yang and Cardei [18] dealt with the Movement-assisted Sensor Positioning (MSP) problem with a goal to increase the network lifetime. Wu and Yang [17] proposed a method, called Scan-based Movement-Assisted sensoR deploymenT (SMART), to achieve a balance state by balancing the workload of the sensors while avoiding the communication-hole problem in WSNs. Wu and Yang [16] took a step further and proposed an optimal but centralized approach based on the Hungarian method to minimize the total moving distance. Rao and Kesidis [9] investigated mobility in mission-oriented WSNs, where a sensor moves to a location so it can perform any one or all the tasks better, and hence the notion of purposeful mobility. With this type of controlled mobility, Cao *et al.* [4] proposed techniques for mobility assisted sensing and routing while considering the computation complexity, network connectivity, the energy consumption due to both mobility and communication, and the network lifetime. Wang *et al.* [11] proposed a Grid-Quorum solution that locate the closest redundant sensors with low message complexity and relocate them in a timely, efficient and balanced way using cascaded movement. Du and Lin [5] proposed an approach to improve the performance of WSNs in terms of coverage, connectivity, and routing by introducing a few mobile sensors in addition to the static ones, which constitute the majority of the sensors in the network. Wang *et al.* [13] proposed a proxy-based approach that allows the sensors to move directly to their target locations and not a zig-zag way with a goal to provide satisfactory coverage. Wang *et al.* [12] proposed a Voronoi diagram-based approach to detect coverage holes and three approaches enabling the sensors to move from densely deployed areas to sparsely deployed areas. Heo and Varshney [6] proposed distributed, energy-efficient deployment algorithms that employ a synergetic combination of cluster-structuring and a peer-to-peer deployment scheme. A comprehensive survey on node placement can be found in [20].

Unlike all previous work and except the one discussed in [15], we focus on k-coverage in mission-oriented mobile WSNs with the goal to minimize the total number of sensors necessary for k-coverage and minimize the total energy consumption due to sensor mobility and their communication. Indeed, the closest work to ours is the one proposed by Wang *et al.* [15], and hence we will compare our protocols to theirs.

4 Pseudo-random Sensor Placement for On-Demand k-Coverage

In this section, we present our pseudo-random placement strategy of the mobile sensors to k-cover a region of interest.

4.1 Ensuring k-Coverage of a Region of Interest

First, we present *Helly's Theorem* [2], a fundamental result of convexity theory.

Helly's Theorem [2]. Let E be a set of convex sets in R^n such that for $m \geq n+1$ any m sets of E have a non-empty intersection. Then, the intersection of all stes of E is non-empty.   •

Here, we want to determine the shape of this k-covered area. To this end, we present a fundamental result of convexity theory, known as *Helly's Theorem* [2], which characterizes the intersection of convex sets. We will exploit this theorem to characterize k-coverage of a field with the help of a nice geometric structure, called *Reuleaux triangle* [21]. Then, we compute the number of sensor required for k-coverage.

Lemma 1, which is a Helly's Theorem instance, characterizes the intersection of k sensing disks. Indeed, if we have $n = 2$ and $k = m$, we obtain Lemma 1.

Lemma 1 (Helly's Theorem in 2D space). Let $k \geq 3$. The intersection of k sensing disks is not empty if and only if the intersection of any three of them is not empty.   •

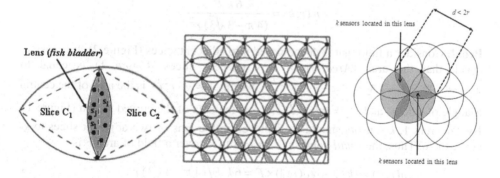

Fig. 1. Intersection of two adjacent slices

Fig. 2. Decomposing a square region into Reuleaux triangles

Fig. 3. Maximum distance between sensors in two lenses

Lemma 2 gives a *sufficient condition* for k-coverage of a field [1]. We present it here for the sake of completeness. In [1], we focused on k-coverage in static, heterogeneous WSNs.

Lemma 2 [1]. Let $k \geq 3$. A field is k-covered if any *Reuleaux triangle* region of width r (or simply *slice*) in the field contains at least k active sensors.   •

It is worth mentioning that *tiling* (i.e., covering *without* overlap) a planar field with Reuleaux triangles is impossible unless we allow overlap between them. However, it is well known that the regular triangle allows a perfect tiling of a two-dimensional space. Consider two adjacent slices that intersect in a region shaped as a *lens* (Figure 1) so that the sides of their associated regular triangles fully coincide [1]. Lemma 3 provides a characterization of k-coverage based on this notion of lens, thus improving on Lemma 2.

Lemma 3 [1]. k active sensors located in the lens of two adjacent slices in a field can k-cover both slices.

Based on Lemma 3 [1], Theorem 1 states a *tighter sufficient condition* for k-coverage of a region of interest [1].

Theorem 1 [1]. Let $k \geq 3$. A region of interest is *surely* k-covered with a small number of sensors if for any slice in the region, there is at least one adjacent slice such that their intersection (lens) has at least k active sensors.

Based on Theorem 1, Theorem 2 computes the number of sensors needed to k-cover a field of area F.

Theorem 2. Let r be the radius of the sensors' sensing disks and $k \geq 3$. The minimum number of sensors $n(r,k)$ to k-cover a field of area F is given by

$$n(r,k) = \frac{6\,k\,F}{(4\,\pi - 3\sqrt{3})\,r^2}$$

Proof. Consider a field that is decomposed into adjacent slices (Figure 2). It is easy to check that the area $\|Area(r)\|$ of two adjacent slices (Figure 1) is equal to $\| Area(r) \| = 2\,A_1 + 4\,A_2 = (4\,\pi - 3\sqrt{3})\,r^2/6$, where $A_1 = \sqrt{3}\,r^2/4$ is the area of the central triangle of side r and $A_2 = (\pi/6 - \sqrt{3}/4)\,r^2$ is the area of the curved region (Figure 1). By Theorem 1, k sensors should be deployed in the lens of two adjacent slices to k-cover them. Thus, the *small number of sensors* to k-cover a field of area F is

$$n(r,k) = (k/\| Area(r) \|) \times F = 6k\,F/(4\,\pi - 3\sqrt{3})\,r^2$$

Consider the configuration in Figure 3. To compute the minimum communication range for the network to be connected, assume all sensors are located at one of the extreme points of a lens. With a little algebra, it is easy to check that the distance between two extreme points, say p and q, of two adjacent slices is equal to $\delta(p,q) = \sqrt{3}\,r$. Thus, connectivity of k-covered WSNs requires that $R \geq \sqrt{3}\,r$.

4.2 Where Would Mobile Sensors Be Located?

In this type of WSN, there must be a node that is aware of the mission objectives of the network in the monitored field. We assume that the sink is aware of any region of interest in the field that needs to be k-covered and hence is responsible for computing the locations that should be occupied by the sensors in order to k-cover a region of interest. Also, it has been proved that the optimum location of the sink in terms of energy-efficient data gathering is the center of the field [8]. Based on Theorem 1, the sink randomly splits a region of interest into overlapping Reuleaux triangles of width r (or *slices*) such that two adjacent slices intersect in a region shaped as a *lens* (Figure 1). Thus, each region of interest to be k-covered is sliced into regular triangles of side r as shown in Figure 2. The sink exploits the result of Theorem 1 so that a region of interest is k-covered by a small number of active sensors. Hence, it identifies the necessary lenses where the active sensors should be located and broadcast this information into the network. Precisely, each lens is uniquely identified by a pair of its extreme points. Figure 3 shows the lenses that should be occupied by mobile sensors to achieve k-coverage of the region of interest.

5   Sensor Mobility for *k*-Coverage of a Region of Interest

In the previous section, we showed how the sink computes the lenses of a region of interest that should be occupied by mobile sensors to minimally k-cover the region. In this section, we describe two centralized and distributed protocols that decide which sensors move to these selected lenses while minimizing the total energy consumption due to their movement. Next, we describe both protocols in details.

5.1   Centralized Approach for Mobile Sensor Selection (CAMSEL)

In addition to slicing the region of interest and determining its lenses where sensors should be placed, the sink selects the sensors that should move to occupy these lenses. To do so, the sink needs to be aware of the current locations of all the sensors. Also, the sink has to keep track of the remaining energy of each sensor in the network. Thus, the sink is required to maintain a database for all the sensors where each entry contains a sensor's *id*, its current location, and remaining energy. This information can be gathered by the sink under the assumption that the sensors move only when they are requested by the sink. Indeed, knowing the current positions of the sensors and their closest target locations in the lenses, the sink can compute the energy consumption required to reach these target locations and update their remaining energy accordingly based on the energy model [15], [19] that will be stated in Section 6. Also, the sink can estimate the energy consumed by each sensor while monitoring a region of interest based on the energy model [15], [19].

Using this approach, the sink would be able to select a small number of sensors to fully k-cover a region of interest. Moreover, the sink would be able to minimize the total energy consumption of the sensors introduced by their mobility by choosing the sensors closer to the target region of interest to k-cover it. However, the network should guarantee that all the sensors selected by the sink to move to their target lenses receive the queries originated from the sink. For energy savings purposes, all queries are sent individually to all selected sensors. The sink will broadcast as many queries as the number of sensors necessary to k-cover a region of interest. Each query includes an *id* of a selected sensor and its target location $(x,y)_{target}$ in one of the lenses of a region of interest. Precisely, a query has the following structure: $query = <id,(x,y)_{target}>$. When a sensor receives a query, it will decide whether to forward the query toward the selected sensor based on the location of the sink and the target location $(x,y)_{target}$ in the query. Our goal is to reduce the amount of unnecessary data transmission that would flood the network to save the energy of individual sensors, thus extending the network lifetime.

5.2 Distributed Approach for Mobile Sensor Selection (DAMSEL)

In the centralized approach, the sink is supposed to be aware of the status of *all* the sensors in the network with regard to their location and energy consumption. Although our centralized approach helps obtain the best schedule in terms of energy-efficient k-coverage and minimum energy consumption due to sensor movements, it would incur delay in the sensor selection phase especially for a large network that require a huge database for maintaining the current status of all the sensors in the network. In this section, we propose a distributed approach to remedy to this shortcoming.

In this approach, the sensors will cooperate with each other to move to the region of interest to k-cover it with a small number of sensors while minimizing the energy consumption introduced by their mobility. The sink will only specify the region of interest to be k-covered, which supposed to be a square that is characterized by its center (x_0,y_0) and side length a. Thus, the sink will broadcast a *unique* query that has the following structure: $query = <(x_0,y_0),a>$. Moreover, we assume that all the sensors generate the same slicing grid of the region of interest. This means that all the sensors deterministically generate the same reference triangle whose center coincides with that of the region of interest. This would enable all the sensors to have the same set of lenses, each of which should be occupied with at least k sensors. Also, each sensor is supposed to be moving at a constant speed until it reaches its destination in the lens it selected in the region.

State Transition Diagram of DAMSEL. At any time, a sensor can be in one of the five states: WAITING, WILLING, MOVING, SENSING/COMMUNICATING, or SLEEPING. A *state transition diagram* associated with DAMSEL is shown in Figure 4. Next, we describe each of these five states of a sensor using the protocol DAMSEL:

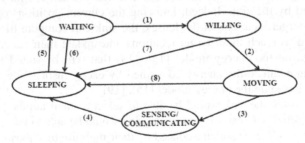

(1) k-Coverage query received
(2) Less than k WILLING_Msg received after time t_{wait}
(3) No WILLING_Msg received from another sensor closer to the target lens
(4) End of sensing and communication activity
(5) Time t_{sleep} expires
(6) Time $t_{wait-query}$ expires
(7) At least k WILLING_Msg received before time t_{wait}
(8) At least one WILLING_Msg received from another sensor closer to the target lens

Fig. 4. State diagram of DAMSEL

- *Waiting*: At the beginning of each round for mobile sensor selection, all the sensors are waiting for a query for *k*-coverage of a region of interest. Upon receipt of a *k*-coverage query from the sink, a sensor switches to the *Willing* state provided that its remaining energy would allow it to move. If a sensor does not receive any query within time $t_{waiting}$, it will switch to the *Sleeping* state.

- *Willing*: When a sensor receives a query, it computes the slicing grid for the region of interest and chooses the closest lens to which it intends to move. Then, it broadcasts a data packet, called WILLING_Msg, including its *id*, current location $(x,y)_{current}$, and target location $(x,y)_{target}$ in the selected lens in the region of interest, thus expressing its willingness to move to this lens. Precisely, this message has the following structure: WILLING_Msg = $<id,(x,y)_{current},(x,y)_{target}>$. While in the *Willing* state, if a sensor s_i receives at least *k* WILLING _Msg originated from *k* distinct sensors that are closer to the target lens than s_i, the sensor s_i will simply discard its request and selects another target lens. If after some time $t_{willing}$ a sensor finds itself unable to move to any of the first three closest lenses, it will simply give up and automatically switch to the *Sleeping* state.

- *Moving*: If after some waiting time t_{wait} the sensor that broadcasted a WILLING_Msg does not receive at least *k* MOVING_Msg originated from *k* distinct sensors that would surely move to the underlying lens, it will decide to move to its selected lens and broadcast a MOVING_Msg, thus expressing its final decision to move to this lens. While moving, if a sensor s_i receives a WILLING_Msg from another sensor s_j that is closer to the target lens than s_i, the sensor s_i will simply give up and let s_j move to this target lens. Then, the sensor s_i switches to the *Sleeping* state. This ensures that each lens is *k*-covered by the closest *k* sensors, thus avoiding wasting more energy due to sensor mobility.

- *Sensing/Communicating*: When a mobile sensor arrives at its target location in the selected lens, it will switch to the *Sensing/Communicating* state, where it would start sensing and communicating its sensed data to the sink. At the end of its sensing and communication activity in a region of interest, a sensor will move to the *Sleeping* state for a new mobile sensor selection round.

- *Sleeping*: In this state, a sensor is neither communicating with other sensors nor sensing a field, and thus its radio is turned off. However, after some time $t_{sleeping}$, it switches to the *Waiting* state to receive query messages.

5.3 How to Ensure Network Connectivity?

In this type of mission-oriented WSN, sensor mobility is necessary so any region of interest could be *k*-covered with a small number of sensors, where the degree of coverage *k* depends on the mission to be accomplished. However, this mobility may not guarantee that the network remains connected all the times. Although the sensors coordinate between themselves to *k*-cover a region of interest, there is no coordination between them with regard to their locations so they remain connected during the network operation. To alleviate this problem, the sensors select some of them, called *dMULEs*, based on their remaining energy to act as data MULEs [10] to keep the network connected. The dMULEs will transport messages on behalf of others and disseminate them to the other sensors in the network, thus enabling continuous communications between all the sensors including the sink. These messages could be either originated from the sink as queries to k-cover a region of interest or initiated from the sensors to coordinate their activity to k-cover a region of interest. These dMULEs will be used efficiently in the centralized approach for mobile sensor selection to gather information about the current locations of the sensors and inform the sink accordingly so it selects the closest ones to the region of interest to be k-covered. This helps minimize the necessary energy consumption for k-coverage due to sensor mobility.

6 Performance Evaluation

In this section, we present the simulation results of CAMSEL and DAMSEL using a high-level simulator written in the C language. We use the energy model given in [19]. Following [34], the energy required for a sensor to stay idle for 1 second is equivalent to *one unit of energy*. For fair comparison with Wang and Tseng's approach [15], we consider a square field of side length 600m and a square region of interest of side length 300m. Moreover, the *energy spent in moving* is given by $E_{mv}(d)$ $= e^{move} \times d$, where e^{move} is the energy cost for a sensor to move one unit distance, and d is the total distance traveled by a sensor [15]. As stated in [15], e^{move} is randomly selected in [0.8J, 1.2J] and the moving speed of each sensor is 1m/s. Also, the sensing range of the sensors is equal to 20m. All the simulations are repeated 100 times and the results are averaged.

Figure 5 plots the number of sensors needed to k-cover a region of interest, where r = 20m, for both CAMSEL and DAMSEL protocols. As can be seen from Figure 5a-b, CAMSEL and DAMSEL require a number of sensors for k-coverage that is close to its corresponding theoretical value computed in Theorem 2. Thus, both protocols perform well compared to the theoretical result given in Theorem 2. However, CAMSEL slightly outperforms DAMSEL as shown in Figure 6a. Indeed, with CAMSEL, the sink has a global view of the network and hence computes a small number of sensors to k-cover a region of interest, while DAMSEL helps the sensors make their decision to participate in k-coverage based on their local knowledge of their neighbors, which varies due to sensor mobility. Also, DAMSEL requires higher energy consumption than CAMSEL (Figure 6b). With DAMSEL, more sensors are willing to move to ensure k-coverage of a region of interest. Due to the distributed nature of DAMSEL, a moving sensor will not always be able to know that other sensors, which are not currently located in its neighborhood, decided to participate in k-coverage of the underlying region of interest. Figure 7a-b shows that our protocol DAMSEL outperforms the protocol Competition [15] with respect to the number of sensors required for k-coverage and the corresponding total moving energy. Indeed, our approach provides a fine analysis of k-coverage of a region of interest with a small number of sensors based on Helly's Theorem and the geometric properties of the Reuleaux triangle. In addition, the continuous collaboration between the sensors enables only a necessary number of sensors to move to a region of interest to k-cover it.

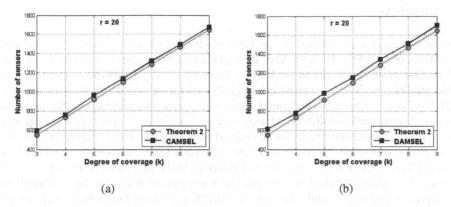

(a)   (b)

Fig. 5. CAMSEL and DAMSEL compared to the result of Theorem 2

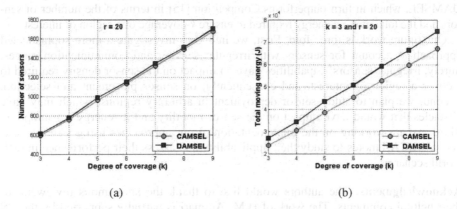

(a)   (b)

Fig. 6. CAMSEL compared to DAMSEL

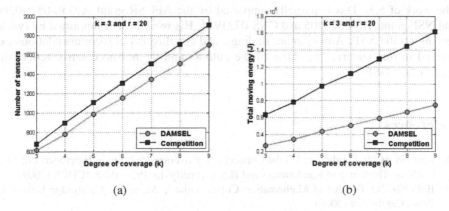

(a)   (b)

Fig. 7. DAMSEL compared to Competition

7 Conclusion

In this paper, we have studied the problem of energy-efficient k-coverage in mission-oriented mobile WSNs. First, we have shown how to achieve energy-efficient k-coverage of a region of interest based on the Helly's Theorem and the geometric properties of the Reuleaux triangle. Then, we provided a tight bound on the spatial sensor density to ensure k-coverage of a region of interest based on the above characterization. We have also proposed centralized and distributed approaches for achieving k-coverage of a region of interest using mobile sensors. In the centralized approach, the sink is responsible for slicing a region of interest into slices and designating a set of sensors to be moving to the selected lenses of that region in order to k-cover it. In the distributed approach, the sink sends only a query including the coordinates of a region of interest to be k-covered and its degree of coverage k while the sensors coordinate between themselves to ensure energy-efficient k-coverage of the region. However, to maintain network connectivity, we have used a few sensors as data MULEs. Simulation results that CAMSEL outperforms DAMSEL, which in turn outperforms Competition [15] in terms of the number of sensors and the total moving energy required to ensure k-coverage of a region of interest.

Our future work is three-fold. First, we intend to investigate a more sophisticated approach to account for sensors with irregular sensing and communication ranges. Surely, irregular sensors' capabilities have an impact on the sensor density required to k-cover a region of interest, and consequently, on sensor placement and selection. Second, we plan to study sensor deployment in arbitrary regions, which may have obstacles that would have impact on the sensor mobility and its energy consumption. Third, we are working on the implementation of our approaches using a sensor testbed of MICAZ motes to study their applicability and assess their performance in real-world scenarios.

Acknowledgments. The authors would like to thank the anonymous reviewers for their helpful comments. The work of H.M. Ammari is partially supported by the US National Science Foundation (NSF) Research Grant 0917089 and New Faculty Start-Up Research Grant from Hofstra College of Liberal Arts and Sciences Dean's Office. The work of S.K. Das is partially supported by the AFOSR grant A9550-08-1-0260 and NSF grants IIS-0326505 and CNS-0721951. His work is also supported by (while serving at) the NSF. Any opinion, findings, and conclusions or recommendations expressed in this material are those of the authors and do not necessarily reflect the views of the NSF.

References

1. Ammari, H.M., Guidici, J.: On the Connected k-Coverage Problem in Heterogeneous Sensor Nets: The Curse of Randomness and Heterogeneity. In: Proc. IEEE ICDCS (2009)
2. Bollobás, B.: The Art of Mathematics: Coffee Time in Memphis. Cambridge University Press, Cambridge (2006)
3. Bulusu, N., Heidemann, J., Estrin, D.: GPS-Less Low Cost Outdoor Localization for Very Small Devices. IEEE Personal Comm. Magazine 7(5), 28–34 (2000)

4. Cao, G., Kesidis, G., La Porta, T., Yao, B., Phoha, S.: Purposeful Mobility in Tactical Sensor Networks. In: Sensor Network Operations, Wiley-IEEE Press (2006)
5. Du, X., Lin, F.: Improving Sensor Network Performance by Deploying Mobile Sensors. In: Proc. IEEE IPCC, pp. 67–71 (2005)
6. Heo, N., Varshney, P.K.: Energy-Efficient Deployment of Intelligent Mobile Sensor Networks. IEEE TSMC – Part A: Systems and Humans 35(1), 78–92 (2005)
7. Liu, B., Brass, P., Dousse, O.: Mobility Improves Coverage of Sensor Networks. In: Proc ACM MobiHoc, pp. 308–308 (2005)
8. Luo, J., Hubaux, J.-P.: Joint Mobility and Routing for Lifetime Elongation in Wireless Sensor Networks. In: Proc. IEEE Infocom, pp. 1735–1746 (2005)
9. Rao, R., Kesidis, G.: Purposeful Mobility for Relaying and Surveillance in Mobile Ad Hoc Sensor Networks. IEEE TMC 3(3), 225–232 (2004)
10. Shah, R.C., Roy, S., Jain, S., Brunette, W.: Data MULEs: Modeling a Three-tier Architecture for Sparse Sensor Networks. In: Proc. SNPA, pp. 30–41 (2003)
11. Wang, G., Cao, G., La Porta, T., Zhang, W.: Sensor Relocation in Mobile Sensor Networks. In: Proc. IEEE Infocom, pp. 2302–2312 (2005)
12. Wang, G., Cao, G., La Porta, T.: Movement-Assisted Sensor Deployment. In: Proc. IEEE Infocom, pp. 2469–2479 (2004)
13. Wang, G., Cao, G., La Porta, T.: Proxy-Based Sensor Deployment for Mobile Sensor Networks. In: Proc. IEEE MASS, pp. 493–502 (2004)
14. Wang, Y.-C., Hu, C.-C., Tseng, Y.-C.: Efficient Placement and Dispatch of Sensors in a Wireless Sensor Network. IEEE TMC 7(2), 262–274 (2008)
15. Wang, Y.-C., Tseng, Y.-C.: Distributed Deployment Schemes for Mobile Wireless Sensor Networks to Ensure Multi-level Coverage. IEEE TPDS 19(9), 1280–1294 (2008)
16. Wu, J., Yang, S.: Optimal Movement-Assisted Sensor Deployment and Its Extensions in Wireless Sensor Networks. Simulation Modeling Practice and Theory 15, 383–399 (2007)
17. Wu, J., Yang, S.: SMART: A Scan-Based Movement-Assisted Sensor Deployment Method in Wireless Sensor Networks. In: Proc. IEEE Infocom, pp. 2313–2324 (2005)
18. Yang, S., Cardei, M.: Movement-Assisted Sensor Redeployment Scheme for Network Lifetime Increase. In: Proc. ACM MSWiM, pp. 13–20 (2007)
19. Ye, F., Zhong, G., Cheng, J., Lu, S., Zhang, L.: PEAS: A Robust Energy Conserving Protocol for Long-Lived Sensor Networks. In: Proc. IEEE ICDCS, pp. 1–10 (2003)
20. Younis, M., Akkaya, K.: Strategies and Techniques for Node Placement in Wireless Sensor Networks: A Survey. Ad Hoc Networks 6(4), 621–655 (2008)
21. http://mathworld.wolfram.com/ReuleauxTriangle.html

Lessons from the Sparse Sensor Network Deployment in Rural India

T.V. Prabhakar[1], H.S. Jamadagni[1], Amar Sahu[1], and R. Venkatesha Prasad[2]

[1] Centre for Electronics Design and Technology
Indian Institute of Science, Bangalore, India
{tvprabs,hsjam,amarsahu}@cedt.iisc.ernet.in
[2] TUDelft, The Netherlands
{r.r.venkateshaprasad}@tudelft.nl

Abstract. We discuss the key issues in the deployment of *sparse* sensor networks. The network monitors several environment parameters and is deployed in a semi-arid region for the benefit of small and marginal farmers. We begin by discussing the problems of an existing unreliable 1 sq km *sparse* network deployed in a village. The proposed solutions are implemented in a new cluster. The new cluster is a reliable 5 sq km network. Our contributions are two fold. Firstly, we describe a novel methodology to deploy a *sparse* reliable data gathering sensor network and evaluate the "safe distance" or "reliable" distance between nodes using propagation models. Secondly, we address the problem of transporting data from rural aggregation servers to urban data centres. This paper tracks our steps in deploying a sensor network in a village in India, trying to provide better diagnosis for better crop management. Keywords - Rural, Agriculture, GPRS, Sparse.

1 Introduction and Issues with the Current Network

Small and marginal farmers own about 1 to 4 hectares of land and solely depend on rainfall for irrigation. Their land is usually located at a higher elevation (2 to 25 meters) compared to the rich farm land, resulting in a high water run-off. Farming in semi-arid regions is further characterized by low rainfall, typically 500mm over 6 months. In [1] the authors explore the application of wireless sensor network technologies for the benefit of such farmers. The project site is a village named Chennakesavapura in the state of Karnataka, India. The environment parameters collected include soil moisture, temperature, pressure, and humidity. The data collected was for the purpose of crop modeling, simulation studies and explore correllation with traditional wisdom. The system was expected to provide information about the status of the standing crop by evaluating the crop stress due to water and pest attacks. By coupling this information with traditional wisdom, the objective was to improve the farming practices [2]. The advice to farmers from the system could be related to investing in purchase of water to save the crop, spraying pesticides at the right time, or adding nutrients during a specified period.

K. Kant et al. (Eds.): ICDCN 2010, LNCS 5935, pp. 104–115, 2010.

We started a pilot sensor network deployment using Mica2 motes in Chennakesavapura. The peculiarities of the terrain has farmable plots that are non-contiguous. Usually, natural features like large reserved areas, fallow patches, dried up ponds and uneven earth mounds separate them. A sensor network for such plots have to necessarily be deployed to collect localized data over a wide area, resulting in a *sparse* network. Another need for a *sparse* deployment is because small and marginal farm lands are also non-contiguous. They share borders with rich farmers who have substantial land holdings in the villages. Such a *sparse* network was discussed in [3]. The deployment was a 1 Sq km adhoc sensor network in the field and shown in Fig. 1. It shows the hybrid 2 tier network which consists of a "Sensor network - WiFi Bridge" to relay data to rural aggregation servers with a telephone link dial-up connection to transmit data to urban data centres. Cluster 1 of Fig. 1 shows that data to urban data centre is transported over 2 hops. The first hop uses 802.11 wireless link to transmit data from the remote base unit to the rural field station dial-in aggregation server. The second hop uses a telephone dial-up link to transfer data from the field station aggregation server to the CEDT Central Server. To determine the inter node distance between sensors, we conducted extensive range measurements in several outdoor terrains such as rocky, thick vegetative and plain land environments. Our experiments consisted of a pair of nodes acting as transmitter and receiver. We recorded the Received Signal Strength Indicator (RSSI) values and packet error ratios for a given distance and transmission power. The Radio Frequency(RF) range measurements show improvements with the addition of RF ground planes.

Soon after deployment, the sensor network suffered from outages due to multiple problems. We broadly classify them as: (1) outage due to sensor node's flash memory corruption and battery discharge (2) outage due to loss of connec-

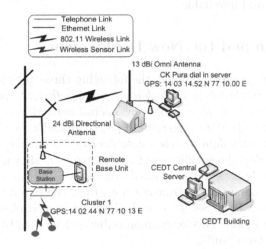

Fig. 1. Cluster1 - Existing 1 Sq-Km sensor network

tivity within the sensor network (3) outage of long distance connection due to telephone link outages, voltage fluctuations and lightning.

We found that the flash memory corruption of motes was mainly due to lightning strikes. The energy in-efficient communication software stack was responsible to bring about an outage due to battery discharge. There was need for frequent manual intervention to replace batteries;almost every week. The "Grey" areas in link connectivity were hindering a reliable sensor network. Finally, the long distance dial-up connection running for over 2 years created difficult problems. There were several instances when the telephone link & exchange were unavailable due to outages. These outages were caused due to: (a) heavy rains (b) equipment failures (c) complete discharge of large battery backup due to unavailability of grid power. The village side dial-up modems were damaged by lightening strikes 5 times till date, thus preventing connectivity to urban data centres. Often the rural aggregation server is unavailable either due to lack of grid power, or due to fluctuation in input voltage from about 90volts to about 400volts. This voltage fluctuation also affected the field aggregation units where the battery chargers were burnt due to a high voltage spike. There were 10 units destroyed in these years. Concerning the Wi-Fi based bridge design, there were several drawbacks. Firstly, our network has a long haul range of 1 km between the field bridge and the dial-in server. Signal fading and thick vegetative growth have hindered a reliable connection. Secondly, due to frequent power cuts in the village, the Wi-Fi infrastructure would power off despite large battery backup. A solar powered system was examined but had to be dismissed since it attracted human attention that resulted in node thefts. We lost about 30% of our motes. Lastly, the Wi-Fi bridge system includes many components. For instance, the RF output connection from the access point to an external antenna requires a type "N" RF connector and associated pigtail termination. Since these provide limited operations and also contribute to signal attenuation, the system with Wi-Fi is complex and unreliable.

2   Motivation and the New Deployment

Prior to the new deployment, we ask the following three questions:
1) *what is a good methodology to deploy an energy efficient* sparse *network for reliable data gathering?* 2) *How to improve overall network reliability and reduce system components?* 3) *With intermittent power available in villages, what is a good technology to relay data to urban data centres?* . Our new intervention and improved reliable deployment discussed in this paper is shown Fig. 2. Cluster2 employs a reliable link, a well evaluated communication protocol stack and a single hop GPRS connection to transmit data from the remote base unit to the urban data centre - CEDT Server. Our deployment of a wireless sensor network covers an area of 5 sq km. This heterogenous distribution has 10 sensors covering about 5 marginal farm lands.

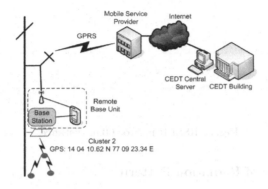

Fig. 2. Cluster2 - Improved reliable deployment

3   Related Work

Sensors monitoring small and marginal farm lands have to be deployed in a manner not to obstruct routine agricultural operations and yet participate in the network formation. Our notion of a *sparse* network is unlike existing literature and motivated differently. Most literature about *sparse* networks mention about mobile entities such as a "Mule" visiting the field periodically to collect data and thus obviating the need for a fixed network infrastructure. In [4] a three tier architecture is presented and analyzed for collecting data from the field. The paper proposes performance metrics such as latency, sensor power, data success rate, and infrastructure cost. In [5] the issue of energy efficient data collection in *sparse* networks is addressed. It proposes a protocol called "ADT" and conducts a detailed analysis. In [6] simulation results are presented indicating that controlled mobility is effective in prolonging network life time while containing the packet end-to-end delay. Rural connectivity is discussed in [7] where the focus is on applying Wi-Fi based broadband technologies for cost-effective rural communication. The paper discusses only about E-Mail and Voice mail services offered to residents in rural villages. Regarding unreliable sensor link connectivity, several literature studies [8],[9] and [10] have independently verified the existence of "grey" areas in link connectivity between nodes. In sparse networks that are being discussed in this paper, one cannot have node connectivity falling in grey regions. For this reason, sparse sensor networks fall under the category of "planned" deployments.

4   Methodology for Sparse Deployment

We propose a new methodology for sensor network deployment. We begin with the radio related issues such as connectivity, and then investigate the receiver sensitivity, data rate, and communication stack energy efficiency issues. We propose the use of GPRS for long haul data transportation.

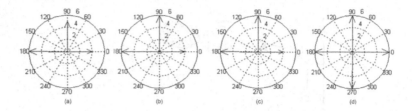

Fig. 3. RSSI Rings for 60 m distance

4.1   Knowledge of Radiation Pattern

Several studies such as [11], [12] show the existence of irregular radiation pattern
from low power and small radio using the RSSI as a measurement parameter. To
study this effect on distance, we conducted an experiment in which the transmitter was placed at the centre and four receivers were placed equidistant in all four
directions from the transmitter. Initially, the central node completes its transmission. We call this the forward transmission. The 4 reverse direction transmission
follow sequentially by the 4 nodes to study the bidirectional link reliability. An
antenna height of 1.5 meters was chosen to ensure that it was placed well above
the maximum height of the crop. Each transmitter transmits a total of 3676 packets of 34 bytes size. Data rate for these measurements was set to 38.1 kbps and
76.2 kbps. We conducted experiments for distances of 30, 60 and 90 meters. We
selected sensing and communication devices from Shockfish [13] since they offered
a communication range exceeding 1.5km for low data rates and used an ultra low
power microcontroller. The radio maps the receiver RSSI information into an integer ranging from 0 to 6 indicating a RSSI range from -85dBm up to -110dBm.
Fig. 3 shows the compass plot of received signal strength for nodes placed at four
directions from the transmitter at 60 meter distance. Fig. 3 (a), (b), (c) and (d)
correspond to 0, 5, 10 and 15 dBm power levels respectively. The Degree Of Irregularity (DOI)was found to be high at low transmission power across all distances.
Since inter node distance in our deployment is more than the measured range,
we continued the measurements to locate the effective RSSI. We found that till
100m the 15dBm transmission power level was quite effective after which the RSSI
dropped to 5 in one of the directions. Table 1 shows the recorded bit errors in all
the directions. It specifies the bit error ratio (BER) in both forward and reverse
directions. A single forward (F) and reverse (R) pair correspond to a particular
direction starting at 90°. Clearly, when the RSSI is lower than -110 dBm, the bit
errors are exceedingly high, typically in the region of $1 * 10^{-2}$, resulting in the
"unsafe" or unreliable region. The table clearly highlight that links can be highly
asymmetric for all transmission power levels.

4.2   Receiver Sensitivity

Due to higher inter node distance in sparse networks, the received signal strength
would be poor. Receivers have to set their radios to higher sensitivity levels to

Table 1. Bit Error Ratio Table

Power (dBm)	Direction	BER (60 meters)
0	90°,180°,270°,0°	$4.8*10^{-3}$(F),0(R),$1.1*10^{-4}$(F), $5.7*10^{-3}$(R),unsafe(F),unsafe(R),$2.56*10^{-5}$(F),0(R)
5	90°,180°,270°,0°	$1.6*10^{-3}$(F),$1.087*10^{-4}$(R),0(F), $1*10^{-4}$(R),unsafe(F),unsafe(R),$3.35*10^{-5}$(F),0(R)
10	90°,180°,270°,0°	0(F),0(R),0(F),0(R),unsafe(F),0(R), $5.75*10^{-5}$(F),0(R)
15	90°,180°,270°,0°	0(F),0(R),0(F),0(R),0(F),$1.97*10^{-4}$(R),0(F), 0(R)

achieve reception of weak signals. Further, the sensitivity increases as the radio data rate decreases. However, range deduced from published sensitivity or power output specifications of components is deceiving. The range specifiction often does not include the conditions of measurement. These include characteristics of the transmitting and receiving antennas, orientation, height above ground, and the performance criteria for claiming that communication was effective at that range.

To deduce the reliable or "safe distance" between a pair of nodes in a sparse network, we tested several radio propagation models and verified them with the field data results tabulated in Table 1. We performed the following steps with a 60m distance between transmitter and receiver nodes. (1) The first step is to compute the received power using equation (1), the Two Ray Ground reflection model [14].

$$P_r = P_t * G_t * G_r * h_t^2 * h_r^2/D^4 \tag{1}$$

where, P_r is the Received Power in dBm, P_t is the Transmit power in dBm, G_t is the Transmitter antenna gain in dBi, G_r is the Receiver antenna gain in dBi,h_t is the height of the transmitter antenna from the ground (in meters),h_r is the height of the receiver antenna from the ground (in meters),D is the distance between the transmitter and the receiver antenna (in meters). (2) The path loss is computed using log-normal shadowing. We apply Eq(2) and used "n", the path loss exponent for outdoor as 2 and shadowing deviation of 8.

$$PL(d)[dB] = \overline{PL}(d_0) + 10n \log(d/d_0) + X_\sigma \tag{2}$$

where, PL is the path loss expressed in dB,d_0 is the reference distance (1 metre),d is the distance between the transmitter and the receiver (in meters),n is the path loss exponent, X_σ is the shadowing deviation. (3) The link budget is computed using the equation (3). This evaluates to 65.49dB.

$$LinkBudget = P_t - P_r + G_t + G_r \tag{3}$$

4) The final step is to compute the safe distance using the equation (4). We obtained a value of 63.25m.

$$D = \sqrt{\sqrt{h_t^2 * h_r^2 * 10^{LinkBudget/10}}} \tag{4}$$

4.3   Radio Data Rate

For non real time data gathering applications, it is sufficient to support the lowest data rate with the advantage of improving the signal energy and thus improve bit error performance at the receiver. We conducted an experiment to study the effect of radio data rate on bit error performance. Measurements were made with four different power levels and two different radio data rates at 100m distance between transmitter and receiver. This distance was chosen to observe significant changes in bit error performance. Fig. 4 shows the improvement in bit errors for lower data rates. When the data rate is doubled from 38.1kbps to 76.2kbps, we typically need 3 times more transmission power to meet the target BER of $1 * 10^{-3}$.

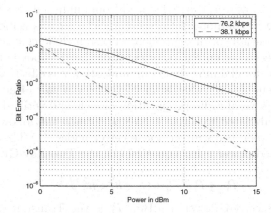

Fig. 4. Effect of Radio Data Rate on BER

4.4   Choice of MAC and Routing Protocol Stack

In sparse networks the problem of frequent link outages can affect the lifetime of the node. Since the number of nodes joining and leaving the network is fewer in number, it is appropriate to have a protocol stack intelligent enough to reduce the control plane energy consumption upon network stabilization. Additionally, there is no need for frequent routing beacons to maintain the route information in the network. For data gathering applications, The B-MAC [8] low power listen duty cycle is typically around 1% or so and thus enables increase in node life. On the other hand, synchronized protocols not only follow the classical link protocol approach but also does additional network and organization tasks. The DOZER [15] MAC-cum-Routing protocol stack uses a TDMA protocol to transfer data to the sink. Since nodes are required to be synchronized, in the event of loss of synchronization, the protocol stack is designed to be aggressive to regain synchronization. Soon after, large number of routing beacons are issued to establish the network connectivity. Thus energy consumption is significantly high to maintain node synchronization. Fig. 5 shows the periodic current pulse drawn by the

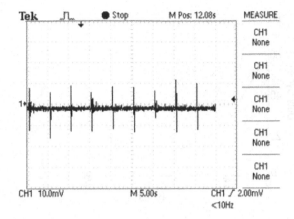

Fig. 5. Current consumption pulses by synchronized MAC based radio

radio during link disruptions. Since node synchronization is affected, nodes begin by constantly probing for neigbours to reestablish the network. Our investigations revealed that routing protocols such as the Collection Tree Protocol(CTP) protocol is inherently designed to cut down routing beacons soon after the network stabilizes. It is additionally supported by unsynchronized B-MAC protocol. An energy measurement was performed to analyze the distribution of energy between routing (control) and application (data) plane. We performed two measurements with a standard application: a) Collection Tree Protocol (CTP) with unsynchronized scheme based B-MAC b) Synchronized scheme based DOZER MAC-cum-Routing. We report here that the control plane of CTP over B-MAC consumes less energy of about 5% compared to 14% for synchronized schemes such as DOZER.

5   GPRS Measurements

In order to explore the possibility of using GPRS technologies for long haul connections, we interfaced a "GPRS - Sensor Network" bridge mamaboard from [13]. The Siemens TC65 GPRS module with flash memory for data buffering supports several power saving modes of operation.

Since GPRS technologies require sufficiently high energy for their operation, to improve energy efficiency and extend the battery backup lifetime, we set out to minimize the transmission energy overhead and thus avoid GPRS transmission on a per packet basis. We implemented a packet buffer on the mamaboard's base station flash memory and then measured the "Average On time" required to switch the GPRS module from "Power Down" mode to "GPRS Data mode" for transmitting packets of several buffer sizes. We plotted varying buffer sizes with the average on time. Fig. 6 (red line) shows the average on time for the GPRS module for packet buffer sizes of 5, 10, 20 packets. The figure also shows

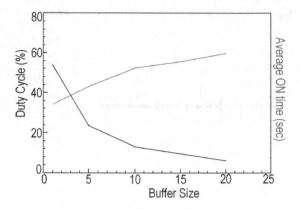

Fig. 6. TC65's Duty Cycle and Average On time

that a minimum of 38 s is required to get operational and 46 s to transmit 5 packets. We measured a peak current of 2 A as the current drawn during the transmission of 10 data packets over GPRS and then evaluated the ampere-hour(AH) requirement for packet transmission for one day to be 0.7AH/Day. By installing a 12V/24AH battery in the field, such a system should provide a life time of about 34 days from full charge until cutoff. We further investigated the impact of the average on time on the duty cycle of the TC65 module. Fig. 6(black line) shows the required duty cycle for transmitting packets of several buffer sizes. Our measurements indicate that the duty cycle varies from 23% for 5 packet buffer to 9% for 20 packet buffer. In our application, since packet latency does not significantly affect the performance, we would ideally

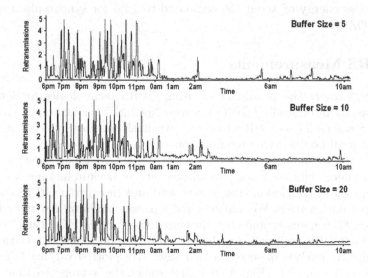

Fig. 7. GPRS retransmissions

Table 2. Average Transmission Time and Average data rate

Buffer Size	Avg. TT (buffer)	Avg. TT (1 packet)	Avg. Data Rate
5 packets	3.2 sec	0.64 sec	0.4 kbps
10 packets	3.6 sec	0.36 sec	0.71 kbps
20 packets	9.9 sec	0.49 sec	0.52 kbps

benefit with a sufficiently large packet buffer coupled with lower duty cycle for energy efficient operations. We also noticed that GPRS retransmissions was a major source of power consumption. We define "Transmission Time" as the time taken to send all the packets in the buffer over the GPRS link. We evaluated the transmission times for different buffer sizes over several hours. The sensor network fills up the buffers at a rate of 2 packets/minute. Fig. 7 shows a snap shot of the retransmission attempts for 5, 10 and 20 data packets over several hours. The average number of retransmissions from 6 pm until 7 am for the three buffer sizes was 380, 340, 370 packets respectively. Table 2 summarizes the results of our measurements carried out for several buffer sizes. We find that a buffer size of 10 is best suited for maximizing the battery lifetime of the GPRS system since the transmission time per packet is 0.36 seconds. Table 2 also shows the data rate achieved is maximum for a buffer size of 10. We found that GPRS Packet Data Channel (PDCH) is generally less frequently available from 3 pm to about 11 pm due to high voice traffic during these hours.

6   Discussions

Sparse networks can have significantly low network partitioning and node lifetime. This is because the transmit powers have to be set higher to ensure node connectivity. However, the network performs sub-optimally if nodes are deployed way beyond the suggested RIM model. Nodes can spend considarable energy to locate their neighbours and poor link qualities can bring down the life time by way of repeated packet retransmissions. Thus, RIM characterization graphs for a particular radio is one of the most important pieces of information required for deployment to ensure connectivity between any two nodes at all times. The RIM model can also be used to set the transmission power. In Fig. 3(d), 15dBm power is required to ensure reliable node connectivity, although 10dBm Fig. 3(c) would suffice, with one direction compromised. Additionally, it is useful to know the antenna direction to get the workable distance between nodes.

In our deployment we have used recharageable Nickel-Metal Hydride (Ni-MH) AA size batteries to power the sensor nodes. We are aware that these are not the best for a deployment. Lithium-Ion (Li-ion) are much superior in terms of high specific energy and power density, low self discharge, good high-temperature performance [16]. However, since these batteries require a sophisticated charging circuit and sensitive to over charge, we selected Ni-MH over Li-Ion to avoid battery explosion.

Concerning link quality, Fig. 3 and Fig. 4 together provide connectivity information and can be used to achieve the desired bit error performance at receivers. Most low power radio links are asymmetric by nature and one has to bear this in mind during deployment.

Concerning the protocol layer, while about 1.5 millijoule(mJ)of energy (for 32 bytes)is required for a packet transmission, over 2.4mJ is consumed in the event of loss of MAC level synchronization. This overhead drastically drains the battery with no useful information being transmitted from the node. On the other hand, B-MAC has no such energy overhead. Concerning routing, CTP design is based on link estimation and firmly believes that links seldom breakdown. Such guarantees can now be met if the RIM model is used during deployment. Once the network stabilizes, the number of routing beacons are reduced exponentially. While this might introduce latency in new nodes joining the network, it is not a relevant parameter for sparse networks.

Concerning GPRS data channels, the cellular operator allocation is based on capacity-on-demand principle. These resources are shared with circuit-switched data and speech users. In the GPRS measurements we conducted, considering the fixed overhead of 38 s for the module to become operational, ideally one would like to buffer maximum possible packets before switching on the GPRS radio module. However, observing Table 2 and the day long measurements, adjusting the buffer size to suite the link availability may be appropriate to reduce the transmission time and thus lower duty cycle. Another parameter that should be considered to set the buffer size is the incoming sensed data rate.

7   Summary and Conclusion

We have proposed a novel method for deploying sparse etworks. A significant amount of pre-deployment work is required before any field deployment. Several issues concerning effective radio range, transmit power, receiver sensitivity, data rate and protocol have to be first evaluated and later tested with radio propagation models to get a limit on the reliable or safe distance between nodes. The MAC-Routing discussions in the paper relate to the debate about Synchronized and Unsynchronized MAC protocols and their impact on energy requirements. In our sparse network, we show that loss of synchronization at MAC layer is a significant energy overhead. We see that CTP is appropriate because of its effective routing beacon algorithm. Designing data gathering and relaying systems in a rural setting where power availability is intermittent is extremely challenging. In this work, we explored the use of GPRS technologies for each cluster to relay data to urban data centres. In view of the extremely poor grid power availability, for battery backups to last several days, it is important to configure the power management modes coupled with the optimum duty cycle. Contrary to what is indicated in [4], with a GPRS based system, the real world indicates high data latency and low success rate.

References

1. Panchard, J., Rao, S., Prabhakar, T.V., Jamadagni, H.S., Hubaux, J.-P.: COMMON-Sense Net: Improved Water Management for Resource-Poor Farmers via Sensor Networks. In: International Conference on Information and Communication Technologies and Development, 2006. ICTD 2006 (May 2006)
2. User Requirements for marginal framers, http://commonsense.epfl.ch/COMMONSense/requirements.htm
3. Prabhakar, T.V., Rao, N.V.C., Sujay, M.S., Panchard, J., Jamadagni, H.S., Pittet, A.: Sensor Network Deployment For Agronomical Data Gathering in Semi-Arid Regions. In: 2nd International Conference on Communication Systems Software and Middleware, 2007. COMSWARE 2007 (January 2007)
4. Shah, R.C., Roy, S., Jain, S., Brunette, W.: Data MULEs: modeling a three-tier architecture for sparse sensor networks. In: Proceedings of the First IEEE 2003 IEEE International Workshop on May 11 (2003)
5. Anastasi, G., Conti, M., Monaldi, E., Passarella, A.: An Adaptive Data-transfer Protocol for Sensor Networks with Data Mules. In: IEEE International Symposium on World of Wireless, Mobile and Multimedia Networks, 2007. WoWMoM 2007, June 18-21 (2007)
6. Basagni, S., Carosi, A., Petrioli, C.: Controlled Vs. Uncontrolled Mobility in Wireless Sensor Networks: Some Performance Insights. In: IEEE 66th Vehicular Technology Conference, 2007. VTC 2007 Fall, September 30-October 3 (2007)
7. Pentland, A., Fletcher, R., Hasson, A.: DakNet: rethinking connectivity in developing nations. Computer 37(1) (January 2004)
8. Polastre, J., Hill, J., Culler, D.: Versatile Low Power Media Access for Wireless Sensor Networks. In: The Second ACM Conference on Embedded Networked Sensor Systems(SenSys) (2004)
9. Woo, A., Tong, T., Culler, D.: Taming the underlying challenges of multihop routing in sensor networks. In: Proceedings of the First ACM Conference on Embedded Networked Sensor Systems (November 2003)
10. Zhao, J., Govindan, R.: Understanding packet delivery performance in dense wireless sensor networks. In: Proceedings of the First ACM Conference on Embedded Networked Sensor Systems (November 2003)
11. Zhou, G., He, T., Krishnamurthy, S., Stankovic, J.A.: Impact of Radio Irregularity on Wireless Sensor Networks. In: The Second International conference on Mobile Systems, Applications and Services, MobiSys (2004)
12. Holland, M.M., Aures, R.G., Heinzelman, W.B.: Experimental Investigation of Radio Performance in Wireless Sensor Networks. In: The Second IEEE Workshop on Wireless Mesh Networks, WiMesh (2006)
13. Shockfish Corporation, http://www.tinynode.com/
14. Wireless Communications Principles And Practice, Theodore S Rappaport, 2nd edn
15. Burri, N., von Rickenbach, P., Wattenhofer, R.: Dozer: Ultra-Low Power Data Gathering in Sensor Networks. Information Processing in Sensor Networks(IPSN) (2007)
16. Aditya, J.P., Ferdowsi, M.: Comparison of Ni-MH and Li-Ion in Automotive Applications. IEEE Vehicle Power and Propulsion Conference(VPPC), September 3-5 (2008)

A New Architecture for Hierarchical Sensor Networks with Mobile Data Collectors*

Ataul Bari, Ying Chen, Arunita Jaekel, and Subir Bandyopadhyay

School of Computer Science, University of Windsor
401 Sunset Avenue, Windsor, ON, N9B 3P4, Canada
{bari1,chen13r,arunita,subir}@uwindsor.ca

Abstract. Hierarchical sensor networks that use higher-powered *relay nodes* as cluster heads have gained popularity in recent years. An important design problem in such networks is to determine an appropriate placement scheme for the relay nodes, in order to ensure adequate coverage and connectivity requirements with as few relay nodes as possible. Current placement techniques available in the literature typically do not consider the effects of node mobility on the placement strategy. Recently, the use of mobile data collectors (MDC) have been shown to improve network performance in a variety of sensor network applications. In this paper, we have proposed a new hierarchical architecture for heterogenous sensor networks using relay nodes, with a MDC. Our goal is to use a minimum number of relay nodes and place them optimally, such that each sensor node can send its data to at least one relay node and the trajectory of the MDC visiting the relay nodes is as short as possible. We have presented an Integer Linear Program (ILP) that jointly optimizes the above objectives for such networks. We have shown that our integrated approach can lead to significant improvements compared to the case where the problems of relay node placement and determining an optimal trajectory of the MDC are considered independently.

1   Introduction

A *sensor network* consists of tiny, low-powered and multi-functional sensor devices, operated by batteries [1]. Different models and architectures have been proposed in the literature for collecting the data from the individual sensor nodes to the *base station* [1]. In a *flat architecture*, the sensor nodes may form an ad hoc network where each sensor node uses a multi-hop path for routing its data to the base station. In two-tiered sensor networks [2], higher-powered relay nodes can be used as cluster heads to improve network performance[2] – [4]. In such a network, the sensor (relay) nodes constitute the lower (higher) tier of the network. The sensor nodes transmit their data directly to their respective cluster heads.

If a sensor node i is able to transmit data directly to a relay node j (i.e., j is located within the transmission range of i), we will say that j *covers* i. Only if j covers i, the cluster corresponding to j may *possibly* include i. Given a sensor

---

* A. Jaekel and S. Bandyopadhyay have been supported by discovery grants from the Natural Sciences and Engineering Research Council of Canada.

K. Kant et al. (Eds.): ICDCN 2010, LNCS 5935, pp. 116–127, 2010.

network, the relay nodes must be placed such that each sensor node is covered by at least one relay node. Since relay nodes are relatively expensive, it is important to ensure that the solution of the *placement problem* uses a minimum number of relay nodes. It has been shown that the placement problem, using a minimum number of relay nodes, is NP-hard [5]. The relay nodes, though provisioned with higher energy, are powered by batteries, and hence are still power constrained. Relay nodes, in general, have to handle large amounts of data. The depletion of the batteries in relay nodes is more important in determining the network *lifetime* [6]. Therefore, the design of sensor networks emphasizes the conservation of the power used by the relay nodes to prolong the network lifetime. Recently, it has been shown that the mobility of some nodes in a sensor network can be exploited to improve the network performance in a number of areas, including the coverage, the lifetime, the connectivity and fault-tolerance [7], [12] – [18].

In this paper, we are proposing a heterogenous, hierarchical wireless sensor network architecture, where the lowest tier consists of a set of sensor nodes. The middle tier consists of a number of higher powered relay nodes, each acting as a cluster head for a number of sensor nodes in the tier below. A *mobile data collector* (MDC) constitutes the upper tier. The MDC, which is not power constrained, uses a fixed trajectory to periodically visit all relay nodes and the base station. When the MDC visits a relay node, it collects data from the relay node, and when it visits the base station, it delivers all collected data to the base station. There are two advantages of the proposed architecture as follows:

- the relay nodes are relieved from the burden of "routing" data towards the base station, possibly over long distances, resulting in considerable energy savings at these nodes.
- the MDC does not need to visit each individual sensor node, as has been suggested by some researchers (e.g., [18]). This results in a significant reduction in the length of the trajectory used by the MDC and also requires less frequent visits to each node, since the buffering capabilities of the relay nodes are much higher compared to the sensor nodes.

In our model, each sensor node is assigned to exactly one cluster, generates data at a known rate, and sends the data directly to the relay node corresponding to its cluster head. The data is buffered in the relay node until the next visit by the MDC, when it is uploaded to the MDC. After uploading its data, each relay node empties its buffer, so that the buffer can be reused to collect data until the MDC visits the relay node the next time. The trajectory used by the MDC to visit each relay node plays a critically important role in the design of the network, since the length of the trajectory and the speed of the MDC determine the time interval between successive visits to any given relay node. For a given speed of the MDC, a longer trajectory means a longer time interval and hence a larger buffer size in each relay node. In other words, for a given speed of the MDC, the buffer size and hence the cost of the relay nodes is directly related to the length of the trajectory.

Both the placement problem and the minimum trajectory problem, taken separately, are known to be computationally difficult problems [2], [15]. To find the placement and the trajectory, based on a given a sensor network, it is relatively convenient to obtain the solution in two steps. In the first step, the placement problem is solved using any approach, such as those presented in [2], [11]. In the second step, the shortest trajectory problem can be solved using, for instance, any algorithm for the traveling salesman problem (TSP) [15], [18]. Here the sites to be visited are the locations of the relay nodes obtained in the first step. However, the solution to the placement problem is typically not unique. So, for the same minimum number of relay nodes to cover the sensing area, there are many possible placements of the relay nodes and the lengths of the shortest trajectories for these different placements schemes (all with the same minimum number of relay nodes) may vary significantly.

Given the locations of the nodes to be visited, a number of recent papers, (e.g., [15], [18]) have investigated how to determine the trajectory to be used by a MDC, and how to compute a schedule for visiting the nodes by the MDC. However, to the best of our knowledge, this is the first approach that jointly considers the placement of a minimum number of relay nodes that satisfies coverage requirements in the network, while determining a minimal length trajectory of the MDC. Therefore, unlike previous techniques, our approach can be used to design the middle tier network in a way that optimizes the route of the MDC as well. Based on the calculated trajectory, we can also determine the buffer capacity requirements at each relay node that would ensure the desired Quality of Service (QoS), while using the minimal resources. In this paper, we have

  i) proposed a new hierarchical architecture for heterogeneous sensor networks with MDC.
 ii) presented an Integer Linear Program (ILP) formulation to jointly solve the relay node placement and the MDC visiting schedule problems in such a way that the corresponding trajectory of the MDC is as short as possible, while ensuring that a minimal number of relay nodes are used.
iii) shown that our integrated approach can lead to significant improvements over the case where these two problems are solved in two separate steps.

The remainder of the paper is organized as follows. In Section 2, we review some related works. In Section 3, we present our network model and the ILP formulation. In Section 4 we discuss our results and conclude in Section 5.

2   Review

The problem of relay node placement in sensor networks has been widely investigated in the literature [2], [4] – [10]. In [2], a hierarchical network architecture is considered, where the entire region is divided into cells, and, after determining the optimal solutions for the placements of relay nodes for each cell, the final placement is obtained by combining these solutions. An approximation algorithm to achieve single and double connectivity of the sensor and relay nodes in a network appears in [8]. In [9], authors have proposed a two-step approximation algorithm to obtain 1-connected (in the first step) and 2-connected (in the second step, by adding extra back-up nodes to the network obtained in the first step) sensor and relay node network. In [4], authors have studied the problem of prolonging the lifetime of a sensor network with additional energy provisioning to some existing nodes and deploying relay nodes within the network. It has been shown in [5] that the problem of finding an optimal placement of relay nodes is NP-hard - even finding approximate solutions is NP-hard in some cases. Placement of relay node based on an imaginary grid has been proposed in [10].

The design of sensor networks, when some mobile entities are available, have been considered in [12] – [18]. Researchers have considered two scenarios. In scenario 1, the base station itself is termed as *mobile* since it is allowed to move. In scenario 2, there is a new entity[1] which moves through the network, gathering data as it moves and delivers the collected data to the base station at periodic intervals. Different researchers have used different terms (e.g., mobile entities, mobile base stations, mobile sinks, mobile observers, mobile nodes, mobile elements) describing these mobile units. The work of [12] has focused on prolonging the lifetime using multiple mobile base stations by an ILP formulation. In [13], multiple mobile base stations, moving in straight-line and parallel paths, have been considered where the objectives were scalability and load-balancing. In [14], an optimal data collection protocol has been proposed to extend the lifetime of the network, taking into account both the base station mobility and the multi-hop routing used. The work in [15] focussed on fault-resiliency and has proposed a scheme, based on clustering, K-means and TSP routing optimization algorithms, to solve the problem.

In a sensor network with random mobility of the MDC, the path taken by the observer is a) not repetitive, b) not determined beforehand, and c) cannot be predicted accurately. In [16], a three-tier network is considered where the mobile data collectors, lying in the middle tier, move randomly within the network, and pick-up data from the sensor nodes when the mobile nodes are within the direct communication range of the sensor nodes. In [17], a mathematical model based on queuing theory has been proposed, analyzing the performance and the trade-offs of a three-tier architecture that includes MDCs, and it has been shown that the network lifetime can be improved by exploiting the mobility of the MDCs. Partitioning Based Scheduling (PBS) is another scheduling heuristic that can be used to compute the trajectory of the MDC [18]. The objective of this approach is the reduction of data loss due to sensor buffer overflow.

3   Network Design with Mobile Data Collector

Given the locations of the sensor nodes, our objectives are to

i) use a minimum number of relay nodes, and
ii) determine the positions of the relay nodes, such that the minimum-length trajectory of the MDC visiting the relay nodes is as short as possible.

---

[1] We have called this entity a *Mobile Data Collector* in this paper.

Given a set of locations to visit, finding a minimum-length trajectory to visit all of them is a well-known problem (the Traveling Salesman Problem).

We assume that the positions of the sensor nodes are known beforehand, or can be determined (e.g., using GPS), and that the relay nodes can be placed at the locations determined by our placement strategy. The ILP formulation proposed here assumes that a set $\mathcal{R}$ of *potential* locations for the relay nodes is given as input. We have used a grid based approach [11] for generating the potential positions. However, our formulation does not depend on how $\mathcal{R}$ is generated and other approaches (such as the approach given in [2]) can easily be used. The idea used in our ILP formulation is to start with a hypothetical relay node at each of the positions specified in $\mathcal{R}$. The formulation picks as few of these relay nodes as possible so that all the design criteria mentioned above may be fulfilled.

3.1   Network Model

Let $\mathcal{S}$ be the set of n sensor nodes and $\mathcal{R}$ be the set of m potential positions of relay nodes. For convenience, we assign each node a unique label as follows:

1. for each sensor node, a label $i, m + 1 \leq i \leq m + n$,
2. for each possible location of relay node, a label $j, 1 \leq j \leq m$, and
3. the base station is labeled 0.

To simplify our description, henceforth we will use the term *relay node j* to indicate the relay node at the location corresponding to label $j \in \mathcal{R}$. As mentioned earlier, a sensor node i is said to be *covered* by relay node j, if i can transmit its data directly to j. A sensor node i may be covered by more than one relay node. Our proposed formulation designs the middle-tier relay node network such that each sensor node is assigned to exactly one cluster.

The base station and the MDC are not power and buffer constrained and, being a mobile entity, the MDC is capable of traveling to any location in the entire network. A trajectory of the MDC is defined as a path that starts from the base station, visits each relay j that is selected to be a cluster head in the middle-tier network, and comes back to the base station. We shall refer to one such trip of the MDC as a *tour*.

3.2   Notation Used

In our formulation we are given the following constants (input data):

- $\mathcal{R}$: The set of potential locations of the relay nodes.
- m: The total number of potential positions of relay nodes (i.e., $m = |\mathcal{R}|$).
- n: The total number of sensor nodes.
- i: A label identifying a sensor node $i, m + 1 \leq i \leq m + n$.
- j: A label identifying the location of a relay node $1 \leq j \leq m$.
- 0: The label of the base station.
- r_{max}: The transmission range of each sensor node.

- $d_{i,j}$: The Euclidean distance between a node i and a node j.
- C^j: The set of sensor nodes belonging to the cluster of relay node j.
- $W_1(W_2)$: A positive constant that determines the relative significance of the first (second) term of the objective function.

We also define the following variables:

- $X_{i,j}$: A binary variable defined as follows:
$$X_{i,j} = \begin{cases} 1 \text{ if the sensor node } i \text{ selects relay node } j \text{ as its cluster head,} \\ 0 \text{ otherwise.} \end{cases}$$

- Y_j: A binary variable defined as follows:
$$Y_j = \begin{cases} 1 \text{ if relay node } j \text{ is included in the middle-tier network,} \\ 0 \text{ otherwise.} \end{cases}$$

- $f_{j,k}$: A binary variable defined as follows:
$$f_{j,k} = \begin{cases} 1 \text{ if relay node } k \text{ is visited by the MDC right after visiting} \\ \quad \text{the relay node } j, \\ 0 \text{ otherwise.} \end{cases}$$

- u_j: An integer variable indicating the order of relay node j in the trajectory of the MDC.

3.3   ILP Formulation for Relay Node Placement and Trajectory Calculation

The following ILP selects a subset of $\mathcal{R}$, where each element in the selected subset will correspond to the location of a relay node in the middle-tier network so that

- the cardinality of the selected subset is minimal,
- each sensor node can send its data to at least one relay node and
- the length of the trajectory to visit all the relay nodes is minimal.

A trajectory of the MDC is determined by finding the order of visiting each of the relay nodes in the selected subset. Our objective is to jointly minimize the weighted sum of the number of relay nodes, and the total path length of the trajectory. Since our primary objective is to minimize the number of relay nodes, the first term must dominate the objective function. We do this by suitably choosing the values of W_1 and W_2.

$$\textbf{Minimize } W_1 \sum_{j=0}^{m} Y_j + W_2 \sum_{j=0}^{m} \sum_{k=0}^{m} d_{j,k} \cdot f_{j,k} \tag{1}$$

Subject to:

a) The range of transmission from a sensor node is r_{max}.

$$X_{i,j} \cdot d_{i,j} \leq r_{max} \qquad \forall i, m+1 \leq i \leq m+n, \forall j, 1 \leq j \leq m \tag{2}$$

b) If a relay node is a cluster head, it must be included in the middle-tier network.

$$Y_j \geq X_{i,j} \qquad \forall i, m+1 \leq i \leq m+n, \forall j, 1 \leq j \leq m \qquad (3)$$

c) A sensor node will transmit to exactly one relay node.

$$\sum_{j=1}^{m} X_{i,j} = 1 \qquad \forall i, m+1 \leq i \leq m+n \qquad (4)$$

d) Compute the trajectory of the MDC.

$$\sum_{k=0}^{m} f_{j,k} = Y_j \qquad \forall j, j \neq k, 0 \leq j \leq m \qquad (5)$$

$$\sum_{k=0}^{m} f_{k,j} = Y_j \qquad \forall j, j \neq k, 0 \leq j \leq m \qquad (6)$$

$$Y_0 = 1 \qquad (7)$$

$$u_0 = 0 \qquad (8)$$

$$u_j - u_k + m \cdot f_{j,k} \leq m - 1 \qquad (9)$$

Constraint (9) has to be repeated $\forall j, 0 \leq j \leq m, \forall k, 1 \leq k \leq m, j \neq k$.

$$u_j \leq m \cdot Y_j \qquad \forall j, 1 \leq j \leq m \qquad (10)$$

$$u_j \leq \sum_{k=1}^{m} Y_k \qquad \forall j, 1 \leq j \leq m \qquad (11)$$

3.4   Justification of the ILP Equations

Equation (1) is the objective function for the formulation. The function has two terms and the objective is to minimize the sum of both the terms. W_1 and W_2 are positive constants and determine the relative significance of these two terms. The first term expresses the size of the middle-tier relay node network. The objective value decreases if the number of relay nodes, selected to constitute the middle-tier network, decreases. The second term expresses the length of the trajectory of the MDC. The objective value decreases if the total path length of the trajectory decreases. Therefore, the objective function minimizes the sum of the terms such that constraints (2)–(11) are satisfied.

a) A sensor node i can transmit its data to a relay node j, only if the distance between the nodes i and j is within the transmission range, r_{max}, of the sensor node (i.e., i is covered by j).

b) If $X_{i,j} = 1$, relay node j receives data from sensor node i. In this case, j is chosen as a cluster head by i so that j must be included in the middle-tier network[2].

c) To ensure that sensor node i belongs to exactly one cluster, constraint (4) enforces that $X_{i,j} = 1$ for exactly one j.

d) Constraints (5) to (11) determine the trajectory of the MDC, i.e., the ordering in which the MDC should visit the relay nodes that are selected to be included in the middle-tier network. The idea is that, in each tour, the MDC starts from the base station, which is at index 0, visits each selected relay node j once, and returns to the base station. Constraint (5) ((6)) specifies that, if a relay node j is selected, then it has exactly one outgoing (incoming) edge. These two constraints together also ensure that the MDC does not visit a relay node j that is not selected in the middle-tier network (i.e., $Y_j = 0$). As the MDC starts and ends a round at the base station (index 0), the base station is treated as a special case. Constraint (7) specifies that the base station at index 0 is selected ($Y_0 = 1$) and constraint (8) specifies that it is the first node visited by the MDC.

Constraint (9) determines the order that is to be followed by the MDC while visiting each of the selected relay nodes. Relay nodes j and k are visited by the MDC only if both are selected (i.e., $Y_j = 1$ and $Y_k = 1$). Now, only if the relay node k is visited by the MDC right after visiting the relay node j, then $f_{j,k} = 1$, and the order of the node k is one more than the order of the node j. This is exactly what is done in constraint (9) (i.e., the constraint sets the value of $u_k = u_j + 1$). Since node 0 (the base station) is assigned order 0, the MDC visits the base station first. Then the MDC goes through all the selected relay nodes along the trajectory determined by the formulation and, finally, comes back to the base station. So, by excluding the special case of the base station (location 0), constraint (9) makes sure that the order of the relay node k is one higher than the order of relay node j, only if $f_{j,k} = 1$.

Constraint (10) ensures that no order is assigned to a relay node that is not selected. Constraint (11) sets the upper bound for the order of visit, and specifies that the last relay node visited by the MDC should be equal to the total number of relay nodes selected to be included in the middle-tier network.

3.5   Computation of the Buffer Size

To compute the buffer size of the relay nodes, we need to know i) the MDC speed, ii) the trajectory length, iii) the data communication rate by each sensor and iv) the assignment of sensor nodes to clusters. For a given speed v of the MDC and a given length l of the trajectory, as computed by our ILP, the MDC

---

[2] If relay node j is not chosen as a cluster head for any sensor node, it should not be selected. This is not specifically enforced by any constraint, but is taken care of by the objective function, which will set $Y_j = 0$, if this does not violate any of the other constraints.

visits each relay node at fixed intervals. Therefore, the buffer size of relay node j must be sufficient to store the data communicated by the sensor nodes in C^j during the interval between successive visits. Let R_j denote a continuous variable indicating the bit rate at which relay node j receives data from the sensor nodes belonging to C^j. Then the buffer of relay node j is equal to the time interval between two consecutive visits by the MDC, multiplied by the value of R_j. For a given network, the value of R_j can be computed easily by including the following constraint in our ILP formulation:

$$R_j = \sum_{i=m+1}^{m+n} b_i \cdot X_{i,j} \qquad \forall j, 1 \le j \le m \qquad (12)$$

where b_i is the data generation bit rate of sensor node i, and is given as data to the formulation. The value of b_i can be the same for all sensor nodes, or may vary from sensor to sensor. If a relay node j is selected to be included in the middle-tier and a sensor i belongs to C^j, then $X_{i,j} = 1$. Constraint (12) thus calculates the bit rate, R_j, received at relay node j, by summing the data transmitted to it by all the sensor nodes belonging to the cluster C^j. Once the formulation converges, the trajectory length, l, is known, and the time interval t, between two consecutive visits, may be computed using the formula $t = l/v$, where v is the speed of the MDC. The required minimum buffer size, $\mathcal{B}_j$, for the relay node j may be calculated easily since $\mathcal{B}_j = R_j \cdot t$. We note that, as our formulation produces a minimal length trajectory, the time interval t between two successive visits to a relay node, using this trajectory, is also minimal. This directly reduces the buffer requirements of the relay nodes.

4   Experimental Results

In this section, we present the simulation results for our joint placement and routing scheme. We have conducted different sets of simulations on a number of scenarios. In all cases, our objective is to jointly minimize the number of relay nodes required to form the middle-tier relay node network, and the length of the trajectory. We have used an experimental setup similar to [2], where the sensor nodes are randomly distributed over a $200 \times 280m^2$ area. The communication range of each sensor node is assumed to be $r_{max} = 40m$. All relay nodes are assumed to have the same initial energy of $5J$. The results are obtained using a CPLEX 9.1 solver [19].

We have simulated our scheme with varying numbers of sensor nodes in the network, ranging from $50 - 200$. For each size of the network, we randomly generated four different distributions for the locations of sensor nodes in the network. The results presented here are the averages of four runs, for each setup. As in [11], we have used a grid based approach to compute the initial potential positions of the relay nodes. We have studied three possible values of the number of potential relay node locations - 48, 88, 165. We have used the terms 48-Grid, 88-Grid and 165-Grid when discussing our results. We have selected W_1 and W_2 so that the first term always dominated the second term.

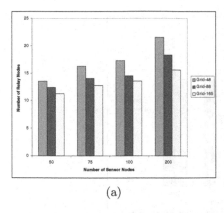 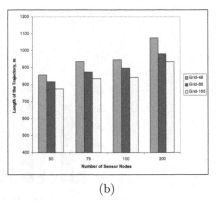

(a) (b)

Fig. 1. Variation of the (a) number of required relay nodes, (b) total length of the trajectory, using 50 - 200 sensor nodes, with various grid schemes for the potential position of relay nodes

Fig. 1(a) shows the number of relay nodes required by networks with 50 – 200 sensor nodes under various grid placement schemes. In each group, the bars are in the order 48-Grid, 88-Grid and 165-Grid, from left to right. As expected, the required number of relay nodes increases with the number of sensor nodes. Fig. 1(b) shows the total length of trajectories, as computed by our approach, on networks with 50 – 200 sensor nodes under various grid placement schemes. As shown in the figures, the quality of the solution improves by using a higher number of initial potential positions of the relay node. However, it also increases the execution time required to obtain a solution.

The objective of our next experiment was to determine the effectiveness of minimizing, jointly, the number of relay nodes and the length of the trajectory. The placement problem, has been solved by many researchers [2], [4], [11]. The idea of using an algorithm for the TSP to determine the trajectory of a MDC has been discussed in [15], [18]. We have, for comparison purposes, used a two-step approach as follows. In step 1 we determined the locations of the relay nodes using [11] and, in step 2, we used a standard TSP algorithm to determine a trajectory for the MDC. Our approach, as well as the two-step approach, minimized the number of relay nodes, so that both generated the same value. Fig. 2 shows how the average trajectory length, using our joint approach, compared to that using the two-step approach, calculated using the results of twelve different runs (four runs for each grid size) for each size of the sensor network. The amount of improvement varies with the network size, as well as with the distribution of the sensor nodes - from 9.5% for networks with a relatively large number of sensor nodes ("dense" networks) to 14% for networks with a relatively small number of sensor nodes ("sparse" networks). It is interesting to note that, in *all cases*, our approach was better than the two-step approach. Of course, it is possible that the placement problem, used alone, may place the relay nodes that results in a minimum-length trajectory but this has not happened in any situation that we considered.

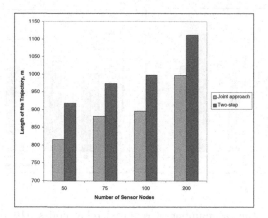

Fig. 2. Comparison of the trajectory length required by the joint approach and the two-step approach on network with different number of sensor nodes

5   Conclusions

We have proposed a hierarchical, heterogenous sensor network architecture that uses relay nodes as cluster heads. A mobile data collector or MDC periodically visits each relay node and collects the data buffered in the relay node. In this model, it is desirable to compute i) the locations of the relay nodes, which ensure coverage of all sensor nodes using a minimal number of relay nodes, and ii) a minimal length trajectory that is to be used by the MDC. In this paper, we have solved these problems jointly using an ILP formulation, with an emphasis on minimizing the number of relay nodes, while also reducing the length of the trajectory as a secondary objective. Such a reduction in the trajectory length also helps to reduce the buffer requirements for the relay nodes in the network, by reducing the time between successive visits (assuming a constant speed for the MDC). To the best of our knowledge, this is the first approach that jointly solves the relay node placement and the minimal trajectory problem on hierarchical, heterogenous sensor network. Simulation results demonstrate that our approach is suitable for practical sized networks with hundreds of sensor nodes, and has a clear advantage, in terms of total length of the trajectory, over the approaches that solve these two problems independently.

References

1. Akyildiz, I.F., Su, W., Sankarasubramaniam, Y., Cayirci, E.: Wireless sensor networks: a survey. Computer Networks 38, 393–422 (2002)
2. Tang, J., Hao, B., Sen, A.: Relay node placement in large scale wireless sensor networks. Computer Communications 29(4), 490–501 (2006)

3. Bari, A., Jaekel, A., Bandyopadhyay, S.: Integrated Clustering and Routing Strategies for Large Scale Sensor Networks. In: Akyildiz, I.F., Sivakumar, R., Ekici, E., Cavalcante de Oliveira, J., McNair, J. (eds.) NETWORKING 2007. LNCS, vol. 4479, pp. 143–154. Springer, Heidelberg (2007)
4. Hou, Y.T., Shi, Y., Sherali, H., Midkiff, S.F.: On Energy Provisioning and Relay Node Placement for Wireless Sensor Networks. IEEE Transactions on Wireless Communications 4(5), 2579–2590 (2005)
5. Suomela, J.: Computational Complexity of Relay Placement in Sensor Networks. In: Wiedermann, J., Tel, G., Pokorný, J., Bieliková, M., Štuller, J. (eds.) SOFSEM 2006. LNCS, vol. 3831, pp. 521–529. Springer, Heidelberg (2006)
6. Pan, J., Hou, Y.T., Cai, L., Shi, Y., Shen, S.X.: Topology Control for Wireless Sensor Networks. In: International Conference on Mobile Computing and Networking, pp. 286–299 (2003)
7. Bari, A., Jaekel, A.: Techniques for Exploiting Mobility in Wireless Sensor Networks. In: Handbook of Research on Mobile Business: Technical, Methodological and Social perspective, 2nd edn., pp. 445–455. IGI Global, Information Science Reference
8. Hao, B., Tang, J., Xue, G.: Fault-tolerant relay node placement in wireless sensor networks: formulation and approximation. In: HPSR, pp. 246–250 (2004)
9. Liu, H., Wan, P., Jia, W.: Fault-Tolerant Relay Node Placement in Wireless Sensor Networks. In: Wang, L. (ed.) COCOON 2005. LNCS, vol. 3595, pp. 230–239. Springer, Heidelberg (2005)
10. Bari, A., Jaekel, A., Bandyopadhyay, S.: Optimal Placement and Routing Strategies for Resilient Two-Tiered Sensor Networks. Wireless Communications and Mobile Computing 9(7), 920–937 (2009)
11. Bari, A., Jaekel, A., Bandyopadhyay, S.: Optimal Placement of Relay Nodes in Two-Tiered, Fault Tolerant Sensor Networks. In: IEEE ISCC (2007)
12. Gandham, S.R., Dawande, M., Prakash, R., Venkatesan, S.: Energy efficient schemes for wireless sensor networks with multiple mobile base stations. In: IEEE GLOBECOM, Global Telecommunication Conference, vol. 1, pp. 377–381 (2003)
13. Jea, D., Somasundara, A., Srivastava, M.: Multiple controlled mobile elements (Data Mules) for data collection in sensor networks. In: Prasanna, V.K., Iyengar, S.S., Spirakis, P.G., Welsh, M. (eds.) DCOSS 2005. LNCS, vol. 3560, pp. 244–257. Springer, Heidelberg (2005)
14. Luo, J., Hubaux, J.-P.: Joint mobility and routing for lifetime elongation in wireless sensor networks. In: IEEE INFOCOM, vol. 3, pp. 1735–1746 (2005)
15. Nakayamaa, H., Ansarib, N., Jamalipourc, A., Katoa, N.: Fault-resilient sensing in wireless sensor networks. Computer Communications 30(11-12), 2375–2384 (2007)
16. Shah, R.C., Roy, S., Jain, S., Brunette, W.: Data mules: Modeling a Three-Tier Architecture For Sparse Sensor Networks. In: IEEE Workshop on Sensor Network Protocols and Applications (2003)
17. Jain, S., Shah, R., Brunette, W., Borriello, G., Roy, S.: Exploiting Mobility for Energy Efficient Data Collection in Sensor Networks. Mobile Networks and Applications 11(3), 327–339 (2006)
18. Gu, Y., Bozdag, D., Ekici, E., Ozguner, F., Lee, C.-G.: Partitioning-Based Mobile Element Scheduling in Wireless Sensor Networks. In: IEEE Conference Sensor and Ad Hoc Communication and Network (2005)
19. ILOG CPLEX 9.1 Documentation,
    http://www.columbia.edu/~dano/resources/cplex91_man/index.html

Stability Analysis of Multi-hop Routing in Sensor Networks with Mobile Sinks

Jayanthi Rao and Subir Biswas

Electrical and Computer Engineering Department, Michigan State University
jayanthi@msu.edu, sbiswas@egr.msu.edu

Abstract. This paper presents a formulation for analyzing stability issues inherent to multi-hop routing in mobile sink based data collection systems. The paper parameterizes the extent of multi-hop routing as a hop-bound factor which is used to represent a wide spectrum of design options including single-hop with mobile sink, multi-hop with static sink, and different levels of mobile sink based multi-hop routing in between. An analytical model is developed for studying the impacts of multi-hop routing on collection delay performance. A number of thresholds are derived from the model for determining the amount of multi-hop routing that can be used for stable and efficient data collection in the context of constantly moving sinks. Finally, the system performance trends obtained from the model are validated using packet level simulations.

Keywords: Sensor network, data collection, mobile sink trajectory.

1 Introduction

Data collection using mobile sinks (MS) has been proposed [1-9] to extend the lifetime of sensor networks as sink mobility ensures that the nodes around the sink change periodically, and therefore the energy drainage due to routing is distributed more uniformly network wide. Mobile sinks can be used for both *real-time* and *non-real-time* applications. For real-time, the sink moves along its trajectory and the static sensor nodes route data to the mobile sink at its current location. In this approach, the mobile sink stays at each location for reasonably large durations before moving to the next location. As the first hop nodes of the mobile sink change over time, the burden of routing packets in the network is better distributed compared to the static sink scenario as shown in Fig. 1:a. Also, the delay incurred by data packets in the real-time scenario is in the same timescale as packet forwarding. In non-real-time data collection, a mobile sink moves along an optimal trajectory and collects data from a set of sensor nodes, commissioned as *Designated Gateways* (DG), along the trajectory. A DG collects and buffers data generated in its multi-hop neighborhood till the sink comes in contact. When each node acts as a DG, the MS collects data from every sensor using *single-hop* transmissions as shown in Fig. 1:b. Since the trajectory spans all network nodes, this scenario results in the longest possible MS trajectory. However, for a given data generation rate, the amount of data that needs to be collected from each DG is the minimum, and therefore routing-led congestions are rare. Thus,

K. Kant et al. (Eds.): ICDCN 2010, LNCS 5935, pp. 128–141, 2010.
© Springer-Verlag Berlin Heidelberg 2010

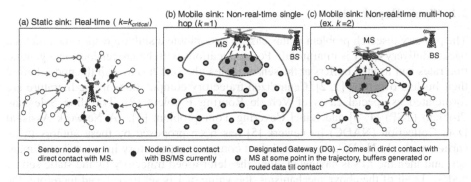

Fig. 1. a) Real-time data collection scenario with static BS; Non-real-time scenarios: b) mobile sink with single hop, and c) mobile sink with multi-hop

single-hop collection provides the other extreme of the static sink scenario illustrated in Fig. 1:a, which offers the minimum trajectory length (zero), but with high sensor energy drainage. An intermediate design approach is one in which only a subset (shown in Fig. 1:c) of the sensors are assigned as DGs, so that certain amount of *multi-hop* data collection is needed. Higher the extent of multi-hop routing, shorter the sink trajectory length. In this paper, we focus on non-real-time collection.

To quantify the extent of multi-hop routing in the above scenarios, we define a hop-bound factor k which represents the maximum number of hops that a packet is allowed to traverse from any sensor to the mobile sink. A larger k represents a larger number of sensor nodes from which data is collected and buffered in a DG before it is uploaded to the MS. With a maximum allowable round-trip time and a given MS speed, there can be a lower bound of the parameter k because reducing it further (i.e. smaller degree of multi-hop routing) may lead to round-trip travel times that are larger than the allowable limit. In addition, since the contact time of DGs with a moving mobile sink is limited, the amount of data that can be collected while the sink is moving is also limited. This can limit the amount of feasible multi-hop routing.

Specific contributions of the paper are as follows. First, a model is developed based on the hop-bound factor k to represent different data collection scenarios shown in Fig. 1. Second, this model is used as a means to study the broader impacts of multi-hop routing on data collection delay performance. The basic goal is to investigate if any arbitrary amount of multi-hop routing can be used for mobile sink deployments. In the process, a number of thresholds of k that impact stability and acceptable performance are derived from the model. Finally, the system performance trends obtained from the model are validated using a packet level simulation of a network assisted navigation and data collection framework.

2 Related Work

Since this paper deals only with mobile sink based *non-real-time* data collection, we discuss literature specifically for that mode of operation.

2.1 Single-Hop ($k = 1$)

The primary research problem in this case is to compute a sink trajectory such that the packet delivery delay is minimized. For applications with heterogeneous data generation rates and limited buffers at the sensor nodes, the sink has to visit the nodes before their buffers overflow [1, 2]. Centralized trajectory computations in the literature are formulated as special cases of Vehicle Routing Problem [2], Traveling Salesman Problem (TSP) [1, 3] and Label Covering Tour problem [4]. A Network Assisted Data Collection (NADC) framework [5] has been proposed by these authors in an earlier work. In NADC, the network first computes a trajectory in a distributed manner, and then the MS is navigated along the determined trajectory by the static sensor nodes. In all of the above mechanisms, the value of k is set to one, and therefore, the issue of stability for multi-hop routing did not arise.

2.2 Multi-hop ($k > 1$)

In multi-hop data collection, the key research problem is to jointly optimize the trajectory (includes the choice of *Designated Gateway* and the order in which they are visited) and the packet routes from the sensor nodes to the *DGs*. The paper in [6] proposes a simplified paradigm in which the sink travels along a pre-defined trajectory and nodes that come in direct contact with the sink act as the DGs. The extent of multi-hop routing here is dependent on the location of the fixed track with respect to the topology. Although this achieves better lifetime than the static-sink approach, due to the static nature of the trajectory the energy depletion is eventually experienced by the DGs or nodes along the trajectory. In [7], a joint trajectory and route optimization problem has been formulated in which for a given MS speed and a target delay deadline, a set of "rendezvous points" are chosen such that the time required to visit them meets the target delay while minimizing the energy required to route data to the rendezvous nodes. A random-walk based scheme with limited multi-hop routing was proposed in [8]. While this performs better than the single-hop version, the general concerns about coverage still remain. An extension of Network Assisted Data Collection (NADC) [5] for multi-hop routing has been presented in [9]. In this work, for a given hop-bound factor k, the network nodes first determine a set of DGs based on a distributed minimum dominating set protocol, and then the MS is navigated along the determined trajectory by the static sensor nodes. The paper also characterizes the energy-delay tradeoffs associated with the hop-bound factor k. However, the problem of dimensioning k to set the feasible amount of multi-hop routing for a maximum allowable sink round-trip time has not been explored.

3 Non-real-time Data Collection

3.1 Application Model

Consider the Mobile Sink (MS) in Fig. 1:c that repeatedly traverses a sensor field to collect data through a number of pre-selected *Designated Gateways*. The MS periodically enters the sensor field once every τ duration, which is termed as the *collection cycle*. For a given MS technology such as UAV (Unmanned Aerial Vehicle) or UGV

(Unmanned Ground Vehicle), τ is assumed to be constant, and it represents the maximum duration between the starts of two consecutive data collection trips. The time required for the MS to physically move along a trajectory and collect all data from the sensor field during each trip is referred to as the *trip collection-time* or t_{coll}. In order for the system to be stable, the quantity t_{coll} should be less than or equal to τ. After duration t_{coll}, the sink moves out of the field and re-enters at the beginning of the next *collection cycle*. Alternatively, the sink could be present in the field at all times making back-to-back trips in which case $\tau = t_{coll}$.

3.2 Practical Considerations

Trip collection-time is an important design metric from an application perspective. For energy constrained mobile sink devices, t_{coll} has to be lower than the maximum duration that the device can operate between recharging/refueling. For UAV style mobile sinks deployed in adversarial territories, the parameter t_{coll} also indicates the exposure time to hostile environments which should be minimized. Thus, with constraints on *flying time* (or *exposure time*) of a UAV (or UGV) sink, the collection framework will have to incorporate controlled multi-hop routing for reducing t_{coll}.

A mobile sink can collect data in two modes namely, *Collect-on-Move* and *Stop-on-Demand*. In *Collect-on-Move*, the sink constantly moves along its trajectory and collects data when it is within the communication range of individual DGs. In *Stop-on-Demand*, however, the sink is allowed to stop if all the data buffered in the DG cannot be collected within the contact duration while the sink is moving. Fixed wing UAVs which are incapable of stopping or hovering would need to collect data in the *Collect-on-Move* mode. On the other hand, rotary-winged UAVs and UGVs are capable of hovering/ stopping, and hence can adopt the *Stop-on-Demand* approach.

3.3 Problem Formulation

For multi-hop routing (see Fig. 1:c), the hop-bound factor k represents the maximum number of hops that a packet is allowed to travel while being routed from its originating static sensor to the MS. For a given topology, $k = 1$ indicates single hop data collection with mobile sink, and $k = k_{critical}$ indicates the minimum value of k that allows static data gathering operation shown in Fig. 1:a. The values of k between 1 and $k_{critical}$ (as shown in Fig. 1:c) can be used to achieve the desired delay or lifetime performance. MS trajectory computation with hop-bound factor k is equivalent to finding a k-constrained *minimum spanning trajectory* (MST).

We formulate the k-constrained MST discovery problem as a k-hop dominating set [10] search or a k-hop cluster formation [11] problem. The dominating nodes or the cluster-heads (referred to as *Waypoints*) represent nodes that the MS has to visit to ensure that data is collected from all network nodes using up to k hop routes. In our formulation, the first hop neighbors of the *Waypoints* act as the *Designated Gateways*. Thus, nodes send their data packets to one of the DGs using up to $k - 1$ hop routes.

One hop is incurred when the data is uploaded from a DG to the MS, resulting in a maximum of k hops for any packet. The assumptions made are as follows. First, the mobile sinks move at a constant speed. Second, the link capacities of the sensor-sensor links are sufficiently high so that the aggregated traffic never exceeds the wireless link capacity. Hence, only the limited contact time between the DGs and the MS can restrict the amount of data that can be collected.

4   Model for the Hop-Bound Factor

In this section, we develop a model for analyzing the impacts of the hop-bound k for sinks operating in the *Stop-on-Demand* mode as defined in Section 3.2. A number of modifications applicable for *Collect-on-Move* are identified afterwards.

For ease of analysis, we consider a circular network terrain with uniform and dense node distribution as shown in Fig. 2. The radius of the sensor field is R meters, density is d (nodes/m^2), C (bps) is the capacity of sink-sensor link, sensor/MS transmission range is r (m), nodal data generation rate is λ (bps) and sink speed is v (m/s). As mentioned in Section 3.3, the MS trajectory determination can be formulated as a k-hop minimum dominating set problem or k-hop clusterhead determination problem. These problems are known to be NP-hard and the determination of an optimal trajectory is beyond the scope of this paper. Our focus is specifically on the impacts of multi-hop routing in the data collection process.

The overall trajectory is split into multiple sub-trajectories of different radii as shown in Fig. 2. Each sub-trajectory is defined by the *Waypoints* that have been identified as k-hop dominating or cluster-head nodes as outlined in Section 3.3. The MS in this case first completes the outer-most sub-trajectory and then iteratively moves inward till it reaches the inner-most one. Between two successive sub-trajectories, the MS travels along the shortest distance path between the sub-trajectories. After reaching the inner-most sub-trajectory, the MS moves back to the outer-most one, and starts the next collection cycle.

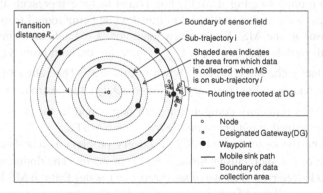

Fig. 2. Sub-trajectories and collection boundaries

The MS moves along its trajectory collecting data from the *Designated Gateways* (DG), which are chosen to be the 1-hop neighbors of the *Waypoints*. All non-DG and non-*Waypoint* nodes route their data to one of the DGs using up to k-hop routes. After the routes are set up based on criteria such as shortest-hop or minimized-energy, each DG maintains a routing tree rooted at itself, and spanning across the non-DG and non-*Waypoint* nodes. Such trees are depicted in Fig. 2.

4.1 Trajectory Length

The number of sub-trajectories can be written as $R/2kr$. The radius of the outermost sub-trajectory is $R - kr$, and adjacent sub-trajectories are mutually separated by a distance of $2kr$. Thus, the radius of the ith sub-trajectory (starting from the periphery) is $R - [kr + (i-1)2kr]$ for $i = 1$ to $R/2kr$, and the circumference is $2\pi[R - (kr(2i-1))]$. The total trajectory length L can be written as:

$$L = 2\pi \sum_{i=1}^{R/2kr} [R - (kr(2i-1))] + 2R_m \tag{1}$$

where R_m represents the total transition distance (see Fig. 2) from the outer-most to the inner-most sub-trajectory. The quantity $2R_m$ represents the cumulative distances traversed across all sub-trajectories during a complete trip.

4.2 Trip Collection-Time

For a given MS speed, with small values of d, λ and k, the contact time for each DG is likely to be sufficient to complete the data upload. However, for relatively large values of d, k or λ, the MS may need to stop at all or few DGs. Thus, depending on the specific parameters, the trip collection-time t_{coll} is determined either by the travel time of the MS, or by the total data upload time - whichever is larger. The travel time of the MS can be computed as L/v. From Eq. 1, the move time to complete all sub-trajectories is:

$$T_m = \frac{2\pi \sum_{i=1}^{R/2kr} [R - kr(2i-1)] + 2R_m}{v} = \frac{\left(\pi R^2 / 2kr\right) + 2R_m}{v} \tag{2}$$

Since the DGs are 1-hop neighbors of the *Waypoints*, a set of DGs can be seen as a cluster around a *Waypoint*. As k becomes larger, fewer *Waypoints* are required and hence, they get placed farther apart. This also increases the physical distances between the DG clusters. This implies that on certain segments of its trajectory, the MS may not be in contact with any DG. Therefore, only a fraction of the move time T_m can actually be used for data collection. Let T_p be the productive move time, which is the time during which the MS is in contact with at least one DG. T_p can be computed by multiplying the number of *Waypoints* N_w with the duration for which data can be collected when the MS is in contact with at least one DG in the vicinity of each *Waypoint*. The contact distance with at least one DG in the vicinity of a *Waypoint* can range from *2r* (when a *Waypoint* and all its DGs are collocated) to *4r* (when at least two DGs of a *Waypoint* are located on two diametrically opposite points on the circle of radius r around the *Waypoint*). Since nodes are assumed to be uniformly densely distributed, the contact period can be assumed to be symmetric around the midpoint of the contact distance range (*2r* and *4r*) leading to an average of *3r*. Therefore, T_p can be expressed as $N_w \times 3r/v$. Given that N_w can be computed as $L/(2k+1)r$, T_p can be rewritten as:

$$T_p = \frac{3L}{(2k+1)v} \tag{3}$$

Let T_u be the amount of time required to upload all the data accumulated at DGs around a *Waypoint*. If duration T_p is insufficient to collect data accumulated around a *Waypoint*, then the sink stops to collect the remaining data. So, t_{coll} is the sum of the time required to physically complete the trajectory and the stop times. Therefore, t_{coll} can be written as:

$$t_{coll} = \begin{cases} T_m & if\ (T_u \le T_p) \\ T_m + (T_u - T_p) & otherwise \end{cases} \tag{4}$$

In Eq. 4, T_m represents the portion of the trip collection-time for which the sink is moving and $(T_u - T_p)$ represents the stop duration. When the amount of data to be collected from the DGs is small $(T_u \le T_p)$, the stop component is zero. In other words the collection time is same as the sink moving time T_m. This scenario represents the *Collect-on-Move* operating mode. When $T_u > T_p$, the stop duration is non-zero, representing the *Stop-on-Demand* collection mode.

4.2.1 Stop Threshold

During each cycle τ, all generated data during the most recent collection cycle needs to be uploaded to the MS. Thus, T_u, the time required to upload the data that has been generated since the MS's previous visit, can be expressed as $(\tau \lambda n)/C$. If $T_u \le T_p$, the MS can collect all generated data without stopping at any DG. Therefore, the lowest value of k for which stops are required is referred to as the stop threshold k_{stop}. Condition for obtaining the stop threshold is:

$$\tau \lambda \pi R^2 d / C > \frac{3L}{(2k_{stop}+1)v} \tag{5}$$

Now substituting the value of L from Eq. 1 and simplifying the equation, we obtain: $c_1 k_{stop}^2 + c_2 k_{stop} + c_3 > 0$, where $c_1 = \frac{2\tau \lambda \pi R^2 dv}{3C}$, $c_2 = \frac{\tau \lambda \pi R^2 dv}{3C} - 2R_m$ and $c_3 = -\frac{\pi R^2}{2r}$

After solving the above equation for k_{stop}, the positive root is considered as the stop threshold k_{stop}. If k is larger than this *stop threshold*, the mobile sink is required to stop around one or multiple DGs in order to collect all accumulated data since its last visit. Note that there is no distinction between the stop thresholds for the *Stop-on-Demand* and *Collect-on-Move* modes.

4.2.2 Stability Threshold

As mentioned in Section 3.1, the system is stable only when the trip collection-time when $t_{coll} \leq \tau$. From Eq. 4, the condition can be written as $T_m \leq \tau$ or $T_m + (T_u - T_p) \leq \tau$ depending on the value of the stop component. In either case, as k increases, the quantities T_m and T_p decrease as seen in Eqns. 2 and 4. The lowest value of k that allows the trip collection-time to be within the collection cycle τ is referred to as the stability threshold $k_{stability}$.

Stop-on-Demand: Since in this case the stop component of the collection time is non-zero, the condition for stability is $T_m + (T_u - T_p) \leq \tau$. Substituting the values of T_m, T_p and T_u, we can write:

$$\frac{\left(\frac{\pi R^2}{2k_{stability}} r \right) + 2R_m}{v} + \frac{\lambda \tau \pi R^2 d}{C} - \frac{3\left(\frac{\pi R^2}{2k_{stability}} r + 2R_m \right)}{v(2k_{stability} + 1)} \leq \tau$$

Upon simplification, we get: $c_1 k_{stability}^2 + c_2 k_{stability} + c_3 \leq 0$, where $c_1 = 2\left(\frac{2R_m}{v} + \frac{\lambda \tau \pi R^2 d}{C} - \tau \right)$, $c_2 = \frac{\pi R^2}{rv} - \frac{6R_m}{v} + \frac{\lambda \tau \pi R^2 d}{C} - \tau$, and $c_3 = -\frac{\pi R^2}{rv}$. Similar to the stop threshold, solving this equation and choosing the positive root provides the k-threshold for stable operation.

Collect-on-Move: Since the stop component of the collection time is zero, the stability condition can be written as $T_m \leq \tau$, or $\left. \frac{\left(\frac{\pi R^2}{2rk_{stability}} \right) + 2R_m}{v} \right. \leq \tau$. Solving for $k_{stability}$, we get $k_{stability} \geq \frac{\pi R^2}{2r(v\tau - R_m)}$.

The results above indicate that certain degree of multi-hop routing can be essential in certain applications to ensure operational stability of a mobile sink in both *Stop-on-Demand* and *Collect-on-Move* modes.

4.2.3 Numerical Evaluation of the Collection Time

Using the equations derived above, we obtained the trip collection-time for a circular network terrain of radius 500m and sensor transmission range of 50m. Thus, the minimum number of hops at which static sink operation is possible is 500/50 = 10 hops (i.e. $k_{critical} = 10$). The value of the collection cycle, τ was set to 900s.

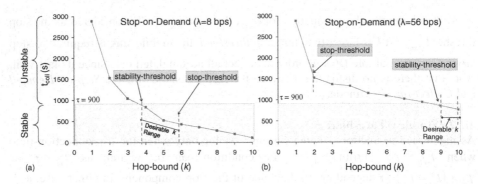

Fig. 3. Impacts of k on trip collection-time, t_{coll} in case of *Stop-on-Demand* collection

Stop-on-Demand: Fig. 3 shows the trip collection-time t_{coll} for the *Stop-on-Demand* mode with varying k. Figs 3:a and 3:b report the results for two different values of λ. For all λ, with increasing k, t_{coll} decreases monotonically, initially at a fast rate. With higher λ, it decreases at a lower rate. To understand this behavior, in Fig. 4:a we plot the quantities T_m, T_p and T_u. The move time and the productive move time T_m and T_p are dependent on k but not on λ. The upload time T_u, on the other hand, depends on λ but does not vary with k. It is evident that with increasing k, initially the quantity T_m decreases quite sharply, and then the rate of decrease reduces till k reaches $k_{critical}$, which represents the static scenario as shown in Fig. 1:a. This is because with increasing k, the sink trajectory includes fewer and fewer *Waypoints*, and hence it becomes shorter.

The quantity T_p goes down at a much faster rate because as the *Waypoints* are spread farther apart, the MS is not in contact with any DG during an increasing fraction in its trajectory. For all λ, as k increases, the t_{coll} goes down fast till the *stop threshold* k_{stop} is reached, and then at a slower rate till $k_{critical}$ is reached.

As seen in Fig. 3, t_{coll} is initially dominated by T_m, but as T_p drops below T_u (see Fig. 6), the condition $t_{coll} > T_m$ (see Eq. 4) holds. At $k = k_{critical}$, t_{coll} is the same as T_u. For $\lambda = 8$ bps case in Fig. 3:a, the values of $k < 4$ define the region of instability as the trip collection-time becomes greater than τ. For $k < 6$, the MS can collect data without stopping because $T_p > T_u$, and therefore $k_{stop} = 6$. For $k > 6$, the MS has to stop at certain DGs for stable data collection. In contrast, for $\lambda = 56$ *bps* in Fig. 3:b, $k_{stop} = 2$, and $k_{stability} = 9$. Thus, in this case k_{stop} occurs before the stability threshold. This implies that without sink stops, data collection is not feasible.

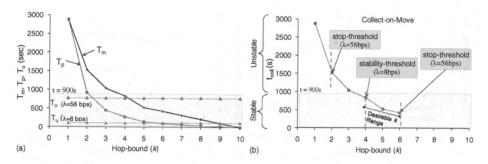

Fig. 4. a) Impacts of hop-bound k on T_m, T_p and T_u b) Collect-on-Move

Collect-on-Move: Fig. 4:b shows the impacts of varying k on trip collection-time for different data generation rates. In this case, t_{coll} is equal to the move time T_m as shown in Fig. 4:a. In Fig. 4:b, the stop threshold is identified for both scenarios $\lambda = 8$ bps and 56 bps. In this mode, the stop threshold as discussed in Section 4.2.1 defines the upper bound on the extent of multi-hop routing for stable operation. Hence, the values of k beyond k_{stop} ($k > 6$ for $\lambda = 8$ bps and $k > 2$ for $\lambda = 56$ bps) are not shown in Fig.4:b. For $\lambda = 8$ bps, the desirable range of k is $k \geq k_{stability}$ and $k < k_{stop}$. Therefore, in the case of $\lambda = 56$ bps, no value of k supports stable *Collect-on-Move* operation. This is because values of $k < 4$ lead to unacceptably long trajectories while values $k > 2$ require stops.

4.2.4 Properties of the Stop and Stability Thresholds

Stop-on-Demand: As seen in Fig. 3, the rate at which nodes generate data relative to the MS-DG contact period can impact the stop and stability thresholds. Fig. 5:a shows the trends of $k_{stability}$ and k_{stop} with increasing data rate λ. As λ increases, $k_{stability}$ increases due to higher data upload times (as seen in Fig. 3:b) which result in higher t_{coll} . Hence, in order to maintain stability, it takes a higher value of k for the trip collection-time to be lower than the collection cycle τ . This implies that as the data rate goes up, the amount of multi-hop routing required to allow stable data collection also goes up.

The stop threshold, on the other hand, experiences a downward trend with increasing λ . This is because, the value of k for which the MS has to stop and collect data decreases due to the increasing upload time. Thus, for sufficiently high data rates, even single hop data collection ($k = 1$) can require the sink to stop.

Fig. 5:b reports the impacts of sink speed on the thresholds. As the sink speed increases, the DG-MS contact times decrease, necessitating sink stops. This is why the stop threshold decreases. At the same time, since the mobile sink moves faster, T_m decreases. This effect reduces t_{coll} and enables lower values of k to achieve trip collection-times below τ , pushing the stability threshold downwards. Thus, a faster

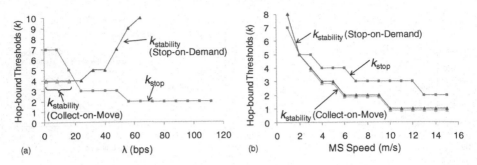

Fig. 5. Impacts of a) data rate b) sink speed on the routing thresholds

moving sink will be able to support stable collection with lower k. However, it will be more likely to need the stopping/hovering capability at a relatively lower λ.

Collect-on-Move: As mentioned in Section 4.2.3, for a *Collect-on-Move* sink, the trip-collection time is always equal to its travel time. Hence, $k_{stability}$ is insensitive to the data rate. As shown in Fig. 5, with increasing data rate, the stop threshold moves down. Since the values of k above the stop threshold are not stable, the range of k usable in this mode is restricted to $k < k_{stop}$ and $k \geq k_{stability}$. It can be observed that the range of k for stable operation continually shrinks with increasing data rate until it reaches zero. Similar to the Stop-on-Demand case, with increasing speed, the sink move time reduces and hence the $k_{stability}$ progressively goes down. k_{stop} goes down as well due to decreasing contact time with the DGs as mentioned earlier.

5   Experimental Evaluation of the Routing Thresholds

The system level performance of a network assisted data collection mechanism with mobile sink is evaluated in this section using ns2 network simulator. For the evaluation, we have used a distributed network assisted data collection mechanism [5, 9] based on the hop-bound k framework. The *Waypoints* for a given k are determined in a distributed way. In this paper, we evaluate the routing thresholds via multi-hop data collection experiments using a fixed-winged UAV style sink, moving at a constant speed of 3m/s in the *Collect-on-Move* mode. The results were obtained on a 144-node lattice network operating with IEEE 802.11 MAC protocol. For the baseline case, the data generation rate was 128 byte packet per second per node.

With this network size and the chosen wireless transmission range, k can be varied from 1 through 5 for the mobile sink scenario. The case for $k = 6$ represents the static sink scenario indicating that $k_{critical} = 6$. The trip collection-time obtained for varying k is shown in Fig. 6:a. As predicted by the model in Fig. 5, we can observe that as the hop-bound increases, t_{coll} goes down due to the reduction in trajectory length. Fig. 6:b depicts the variation of the stability threshold $k_{stability}$ with increasing collection cycle τ. Since $k_{stability}$ indicates the minimum amount of multi-hop routing that allows system stability ($t_{coll} < \tau$), as τ decreases, the amount of multi-hop routing that is required for stability goes up. In other words, higher the degree of multi-hop routing (i.e. higher k), lower the collection cycle duration that can be supported by the system.

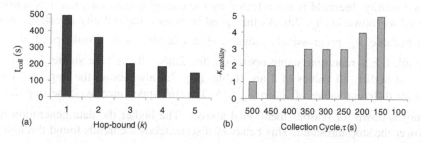

Fig. 6. Variation of (a) trip collection-time and (b) stability threshold

Now, we explore the impact of data generation rate on the thresholds. As observed in Section 4.2.4, while the stability threshold is expected to be insensitive to the data generation rate λ, the stop threshold is not. Guided by this observation, we experimentally investigate the impacts of λ on k_{stop}. In order to determine k_{stop} for different data rates, it is necessary to determine the k at which the MS-DG contact duration becomes insufficient to collect data buffered at the DGs.

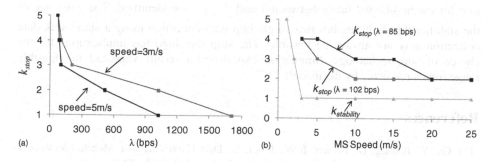

Fig. 7. Impacts of data rate and sink speed

To find that threshold value of k experimentally, it is important to identify scenarios in which the sink moves out of the range of a node when it still has packets in its wireless network interface queue. Such events happen when the DG-MS contact duration is insufficient (i.e. $k > k_{stop}$ for the given network parameters), as a result of which the interface queue starts dropping packets after the MS leaves prematurely. Stop thresholds identified using this experimental mechanism are reported in Fig. 7:a. Fig. 7:a shows the impacts of data rate (λ) and sink speed on the experimentally found stop threshold. In Fig 7:b, it can be observed that for a given sink speed, the stop threshold progressively goes down as λ increases. This behavior is in agreement with the trend of k_{stop} as found via the analytical model in Section 4 and Fig. 5. As λ increases, the amount of data buffered at the DGs increases implying that the sink would need to stop at lower values of k. For a given λ, we can also observe that the stop thresholds are lower for higher speeds. This can be attributed to the fact that increasing speed results in shorter contact durations between the MS and the DGs.

The stability threshold is not affected by the changing data rate, but it is sensitive to speed as shown in Fig. 7:b. As the speed increases, the stability threshold moves down because T_m progressively reduces. For example, with a sink speed of 1m/s, while all $k \geq 5$ represent stable operation, for 2m/s, all $k \geq 3$ are stable. For speeds 3m/s and higher, all values of k are stable. Fig. 7:b also shows the impacts of sink speed for different values of λ on k_{stop}. As the sink speed increases, the stop threshold moves down for reasons mentioned above. The higher the data generation rate, the lower the stop threshold. This behavior also matches the trends found through the analytical model in Fig. 5:b.

6 Summary and Conclusions

In this paper, we investigated the limits on the extent of multi-hop routing that can be employed in the context of mobile sink data collection. To this end, hop-bound k thresholds referred to as the stop threshold and stability threshold were derived. These thresholds are used to analyze the working of *Collect-on-Move* and *Stop-on-Demand* collection modes from a stability standpoint. As a result, the feasible region of operation for the hop-bound factor between 1 and $k_{critical}$ are identified. The existence of the stability threshold implies that single hop data collection using a static sink data collection may not always be feasible. The stop threshold has implications for the choice of sink technology. Simulation experimental results validated the feasible range trends predicted by the model.

References

[1] Gu, Y., Bozdag, D., Brewer, R.W., Ekici, E.: Data Harvesting with Mobile Elements in Wireless Sensor Networks. Computer Networks 50, 3449–3465 (2006)
[2] Somasundara, A.A., Ramamoorthy, A., Srivastava, M.B.: Mobile Element Scheduling with Dynamic Deadlines. IEEE Transaction on Mobile Computing 6, 395–410 (2007)
[3] Aioffi, W., Mateus, G., Quintao, F.: Optimization issues and algorithms for wireless sensor networks with mobile sink. In: International network optimization conference, Belgium (2007)
[4] Sugihara, R., Gupta, R.K.: Improving the Data Delivery Latency in Sensor Networks with Controlled Mobility. In: International Conference on Distributed Computing in Sensor Systems (DCOSS), Del Rey, CA (2008)
[5] Rao, J., Biswas, S.: Network Assisted Sink Navigation Protocols for Data Harvesting in Sensor Networks. In: IEEE Wireless Communications and Networking Conference (WCNC), Las Vegas (2008)

[6] Somasundara, A., Kansal, A., Jea, D., Estrin, D., Srivastava, M.B.: Controllably Mobile Infrastructure for Low Energy Embedded Networks. IEEE Transactions on Mobile Computing 5 (2006)

[7] Xing, G., Wang, T., Xei, Z., Jia, W.: Rendezvous Planning in Wireless Sensor Networks with Mobile Elements. IEEE Transactions on Mobile Computing (December 2008)

[8] Chatzigiannakis, I., Kinalis, A., Nikoletseas, S.: Sink mobility protocols for data collection in wireless sensor networks. In: ACM International Symposium on Mobility Management and Wireless Access (MOBIWAC), Spain (2006)

[9] Rao, J., Biswas, S.: Joint Routing and Navigation Protocols for Data Harvesting in sensor Networks. In: IEEE International Conference on Mobile Ad-hoc and sensor Systems (MASS), Atlanta, GA (2008)

[10] Garey, M.R., Johnson, D.S.: A guide to the Theory of NP-Completeness. W.H. Freeman, San Francisco (1979)

[11] Nocetti, F., Gonzalez, J.: Connectivity Based k-hop Clustering in Wireless Networks. Telecommunication Systems 22, 1–4 (2003)

Optimizing Distributed Computing Workflows in Heterogeneous Network Environments

Yi Gu and Qishi Wu

Department of Computer Science
University of Memphis
Memphis, TN 38152, USA
{yigu,qishiwu}@memphis.edu

Abstract. Next-generation computation-intensive applications in various science and engineering fields feature large-scale computing workflows. Supporting such computing workflows and optimizing their network performance in terms of end-to-end delay or frame rate in heterogeneous network environments are critical to the success of these distributed applications that require fast response time or smooth data flow. We formulate six linear pipeline configuration problems with different mapping objectives and network constraints, and one general workflow mapping problem. We investigate the computational complexity of these problems and design optimal or heuristic algorithms with rigorous correctness proof and performance analysis. An extensive set of optimization experiments on a large number of simulated workflows and networks illustrate the superior performance of the proposed algorithms in comparison with that of existing methods.

Keywords: Optimization, NP-complete, end-to-end delay, frame rate.

1 Introduction

Next-generation large-scale distributed applications in various science and engineering domains require the execution of computing workflows as simple as linear pipelines or as complex as directed acyclic graphs (DAGs). Mapping such distributed workflows into heterogeneous computing environments and optimizing their network performance are critical to ensuring the success of these applications and maximizing the utilization of widely dispersed system resources. We consider two types of large-scale distributed applications: interactive and streaming applications. The workflow mapping problem is to select an appropriate set of computer nodes in the computer network and assign computing modules in the workflow to those selected nodes to achieve minimum end-to-end delay (MED) for fast response in interactive applications or maximum frame rate (MFR) for smooth data flow in streaming applications.

Many optimization problems in various distributed or parallel applications face a major challenge of graph mapping or embedding that has been extensively studied in the literature [1,2,3]. Among the traditional graph mapping problems in theoretical aspects of computing, subgraph isomorphism is known to be NP-complete while the complexity of graph isomorphism still remains open. Zhu *et al.* tackled a widest path problem in overlay networks with linear capacity constraints (LCC) [4]. A graph scheduling

K. Kant et al. (Eds.): ICDCN 2010, LNCS 5935, pp. 142–154, 2010.
© Springer-Verlag Berlin Heidelberg 2010

scheme for streaming data, *Streamline*, was designed in [5] to improve the performance of graph mapping in streaming applications. Closely related to the pipeline mapping problems is the work in [6], where Benoit *et al.* presented the mapping of pipelines onto different types of network topology and connectivity. Similar mapping problems are also studied in the context of sensor networks. Sekhar *et al.* proposed an optimal algorithm for mapping subtasks onto a number of sensor nodes based on an A^* algorithm [2].

We formulate the pipeline mapping problems in heterogeneous network environments as optimization problems and categorize them into six classes with different mapping objectives and network constraints on node reuse or resource share: (i) MED with No Node Reuse (MED-NNR), (ii) MED with Contiguous Node Reuse (MED-CNR), (iii) MED with Arbitrary Node Reuse (MED-ANR), (iv) MFR with No Node Reuse or Share (MFR-NNR), (v) MFR with Contiguous Node Reuse and Share (MFR-CNR), and (vi) MFR with Arbitrary Node Reuse and Share (MFR-ANR). Here, "contiguous node reuse" means that multiple contiguous modules along the pipeline may run on the same node and "arbitrary node reuse" imposes no restriction on node reuse. We prove that MED-ANR is polynomially solvable and the rest are NP-complete. We further prove that there does not exist any λ-approximation solution to MED/MFR-NNR/CNR unless $P = NP$. We propose a set of solutions, *Efficient Linear Pipeline Configuration* (ELPC), in which an optimal solution based on *Dynamic Programming* (DP) is developed to solve MED-ANR, and a heuristic algorithm is designed for each of the rest five NP-complete problems. We also formulate the general task graph mapping with node reuse and resource share as an NP-complete optimization problem and develop a heuristic approach, *Recursive Critical Path* (RCP), which recursively selects the *Critical Path* (CP) and maps it to the computer network using a DP-based procedure. To evaluate the performance of these proposed solutions, we implement ELPC and RCP as well as other three mapping algorithms for comparison, namely *Greedy A^** [2], *Streamline* [5], and *Naive Greedy*, and conduct an extensive set of mapping experiments on simulated datasets of various sizes from small to large scales. The simulation results illustrate the performance superiority of the proposed algorithms over the existing ones.

The rest of the paper is organized as follows. We construct cost models in Section 2 and tackle pipeline and graph mapping problems in Section 3 and Section 4, respectively. Simulation-based performance evaluations are provided in Section 5.

2 Mathematical Models and Objectives

2.1 Analytical Models for Workflows and Networks

We model the workflow of a distributed application as a task graph $G_t = (V_t, E_t)$, $|V_t| = m$, where vertices represent computing modules: $w_0, w_1, \ldots, w_{m-1}$. The computing dependency between a pair of adjacent modules w_i and w_j is represented by a directed edge $e_{i,j}$ between them and the entire workflow is modeled as a DAG starting from module w_0 and ending at module w_{m-1}. Module w_j receives a data input $z_{i,j}$ from each of its preceding modules w_i and performs a predefined computing routine whose complexity is modeled as function $f_{w_j}(\cdot)$ on the total aggregated input data z_{w_j}. Once the routine completes its execution, module w_j sends a different data output $z_{j,k}$ to each of its succeeding modules w_k.

We model the computer network as an arbitrary weighted graph $G_c = (V_c, E_c)$ consisting of $|V_c| = n$ computer nodes interconnected by directed overlay network links. For simplicity, we use a normalized variable p_i to represent the overall processing power of a network node v_i. The network link $l_{i,j}$ between nodes v_i and v_j has bandwidth (BW) $b_{i,j}$ and minimum link delay (MLD) $d_{i,j}$.

When multiple modules are deployed on the same node, only those without dependency could run concurrently and share CPU resources in a fair manner, so is the case for bandwidth sharing. We specify a pair of source and destination nodes (v_s, v_d) to run modules w_0 and w_{m-1}, respectively. We also assume that module w_0 serves as a data source without any computation and module w_{m-1} performs a terminal task. We estimate the computing time of module w_i running on network node v_j to be $T_{computing}(w_i, v_j) = \frac{f_{w_i}(z_{w_i})}{p_j}$, and the transfer time of a message of size z over network link $l_{i,j}$ to be $T_{transport}(z, l_{i,j}) = \frac{z}{b_{i,j}} + d_{i,j}$. For convenience, we tabulate all the parameters of our models in Table 1.

Table 1. Parameters used in the models

Parameters	Definitions
$G_t = (V_t, E_t)$	task graph
m	number of modules in the task graph
w_i	the i-th computing workflow module
$e_{i,j}$	dependency edge from module w_i to w_j
$z_{i,j}$	data size of dependency edge $e_{i,j}$
z_{w_i}	aggregated input data size of module w_i
$f_{w_i}(\cdot)$	computational complexity of module w_i
$G_c = (V_c, E_c)$	computer network graph
n	number of nodes in the network graph
v_i	the i-th network or computer node
v_s	source node
v_d	destination node
p_i	processing power of node v_i
$l_{i,j}$	network link between nodes v_i and v_j
$b_{i,j}$	bandwidth of link $l_{i,j}$
$d_{i,j}$	minimum link delay of link $l_{i,j}$

2.2 Mapping Objective Functions

MED for interactive applications: Once a mapping scheme is determined, MED is calculated as the total time incurred on the CP, i.e. the longest path. We denote the set of contiguous modules on the CP that are allocated to the same node as a "group". A general mapping scheme divides the CP into q $(1 \leq q \leq m)$ contiguous groups g_i, $i = 0, 1, \ldots, q-1$ of modules and maps them to a network path P of not necessarily distinct q nodes, $v_{P[0]}, v_{P[1]}, \ldots, v_{P[q-1]}$ from source $v_s = v_{P[0]}$ to destination $v_d = v_{P[q-1]}$. MED can be estimated as the sum of the cost along the CP:

$$T_{MED}(\text{CP mapped to a network path } P \text{ of } q \text{ nodes}) = T_{computing} + T_{transport}$$
$$= \sum_{i=0}^{q-1} T_{g_i} + \sum_{i=0}^{q-2} T_{e(g_i, g_{i+1})} = \sum_{i=0}^{q-1} \left(\sum_{j \in g_i, j \geq 1} \frac{\alpha_{v_{P[i]}}^{w_j}}{p_{P[i]}} (f_{w_j}(z_{w_j})) \right) + \sum_{i=0}^{q-2} \left(\frac{\beta_{l_{P[i],P[i+1]}}^{e(g_i, g_{i+1})} \cdot z(g_i, g_{i+1})}{b_{P[i],P[i+1]}} + d_{P[i],P[i+1]} \right),$$
$$(1)$$

where $\alpha_{v_{P[i]}}^{w_j}$ denotes the number of modules (including w_j) running simultaneously with module w_j on node $v_{P[i]}$, and $\beta_{l_{P[i],P[i+1]}}^{e(g_i, g_{i+1})}$ denotes the total number of datasets (including $z(g_i, g_{i+1})$) transferred concurrently with dataset $z(g_i, g_{i+1})$ along edge $e(g_i, g_{i+1})$ between groups g_i and g_{i+1} over link $l_{P[i],P[i+1]}$ between nodes $v_{P[i]}$ and $v_{P[i+1]}$. Note that for NNR, $\alpha \equiv 1$ and $\beta \equiv 1$, while for CNR or ANR, we have $\alpha \geq 1$ and $\beta \geq 1$ when

CPU cycles or link bandwidths are shared by concurrent modules or data transfers. We assume that the inter-module communication cost on the same node is negligible.

MFR for streaming applications: MFR can be achieved by identifying and minimizing the time T_{BN} on a global bottleneck link or node defined as:

T_{BN}(task graph G_t mapped to computer network G_c)

$$
= \max_{\substack{w_i \in V_t, e_{j,k} \in E_t \\ v_{i'} \in V_c, l_{j',k'} \in E_c}} \left(\begin{array}{l} T_{\text{computing}}(w_i, v_{i'}), \\ T_{\text{transport}}(e_{j,k}, l_{j',k'}) \end{array} \right) = \max_{\substack{w_i \in V_t, e_{j,k} \in E_t \\ v_{i'} \in V_c, l_{j',k'} \in E_c}} \left(\begin{array}{l} \frac{\alpha_{v_{i'}}^{w_i}}{p_{i'}} f_{w_i}(z_{w_i}), \\ \frac{\beta_{l_{j',k'}}^{e_{j,k}} \cdot z_{j,k}}{b_{j',k'}} + d_{j',k'} \end{array} \right), \quad (2)
$$

where, $\alpha_{v_{i'}}^{w_i}$ denotes the number of modules (including w_i) running simultaneously with w_i on node $v_{i'}$, and $\beta_{l_{j',k'}}^{e_{j,k}}$ is the number of datasets (including $z_{j,k}$) transferred concurrently with dataset $z_{j,k}$ along edge $e_{j,k}$ over link $l_{j',k'}$ between nodes $v_{j'}$ and $v_{k'}$.

3 Linear Pipeline Optimization

We formulate and categorize the pipeline mapping problems into six classes with two mapping objectives (MED/MFR) and three network constraints (NNR/CNR/ANR). We propose a set of ELPC algorithms, in which an optimal solution is designed for MED-ANR and heuristic algorithms are proposed for the rest five NP-complete problems.

3.1 Optimal Solution to MED-ANR

We design a polynomial-time optimal algorithm based on DP for MED-ANR and provide its correctness proof. Let $T^{j-1}(v_i)$ denote the MED with the first j modules mapped to a path from the source node v_s to node v_i in the network. We have the following recursion leading to the final solution $T^{m-1}(v_d)$ in a typical 2-dimensional (2D) DP table:

$$
T^{j-1}(v_i) = \min_{j=2 \text{ to } m, v_i \in V_c} \left(\begin{array}{l} T^{j-2}(v_i) + \frac{f_{w_{j-1}}(z_{j-2,j-1})}{p_i} \\ \min_{v_u \in adj(v_i)} \left(T^{j-2}(v_u) + \frac{f_{w_{j-1}}(z_{j-2,j-1})}{p_i} + \frac{z_{j-2,j-1}}{b_{u,i}} + d_{u,i} \right) \end{array} \right), \quad (3)
$$

where $adj(v_i)$ denotes the set of preceding adjacent (or incident) neighbors of v_i, with the following base condition:

$$
T^1(v_i) \atop v_i \in V_c, \text{ and } v_i \neq v_s} = \begin{cases} \frac{f_{w_1}(z_{0,1})}{p_i} + \frac{z_{0,1}}{b_{s,i}} + d_{s,i}, & \text{if } l_{s,i} \in E_c \\ +\infty, & \text{otherwise} \end{cases} \quad (4)
$$

We have $T^0(v_s) = 0$, which indicates that module w_0 does not perform any computing on node v_s. Every cell $T^{j-1}(v_i)$ in the table represents an optimal mapping solution that maps the first j modules in the pipeline to a path between the source node v_s and node v_i in the network. In MED-ANR, each cell is calculated from the intermediate mapping results up to its adjacent nodes or itself, which are stored in its left column $T^{j-2}(\cdot)$.

Theorem 1. *The DP-based solution to MED-ANR is optimal.*

Proof. At each recursive step, there are two sub-cases, the minimum of which is chosen as the MED to fill in a new cell $T^{j-1}(v_i)$: (i) In sub-case 1, we run the new module on the same node running the last module in the previous mapping subproblem $T^{j-2}(v_i)$. In other words, the last two or more modules are mapped to the same node v_i. Therefore, we only need to add the computing time of the last module on node v_i to the previous total delay, which is represented by a horizontal incident link from its left neighbor cell in the 2D table. (ii) In sub-case 2, the new module is mapped to node v_i and the last node v_u in a previous mapping subproblem $T^{j-2}(v_u)$ is one of the neighbor nodes of node v_i, which is represented by a slanted incident link from a neighbor cell on the left column to node v_i. We calculate the end-to-end delay for all mappings using slanted incident links of node v_i and choose the minimum one, which is further compared with the one calculated in sub-case 1 using the horizontal incident link from the left neighbor cell. The minimum of these two sub-cases is selected as the MED for the partial pipeline mapping to a path between nodes v_s and v_i. Since each cell provides an optimal partial solution to a subproblem and mapping a new module does not affect the optimality of any previously computed partial solutions, this DP-based procedure provides an optimal solution to MED-ANR. The time complexity is $O(m \times |E_c|)$, where m is the number of modules in a pipeline and $|E_c|$ is the number of links in a computer network.   □

3.2 NP-Completeness of MED/MFR-NNR/CNR and MFR-ANR

We first define MED/MFR-NNR/CNR as decision problems: Given a linear computing pipeline of m modules, a directed weighted computer network G and a bound T, does there exist a mapping of the linear computing pipeline to the computer network with no or contiguous node reuse such that the end-to-end delay or bottleneck cost of the pipeline does not exceed T?

Theorem 2. *MED/MFR-NNR/CNR are NP-complete.*

Proof. We use a reduction from DISJOINT-CONNECTING-PATH (DCP) [7], which is NP-complete even when restricting to two paths in the directed graphs (2DCP) [8]. The problems clearly belong to NP: given a division of the pipeline into q groups and a path P of q nodes, we can compute the end-to-end delay or bottleneck cost in polynomial time using Eqs. 1 and 2, and check if the bound T is satisfied. We prove their NP-hardness by showing that 2DCP $\leq_p$ MED/MFR-NNR/CNR.

Consider an arbitrary instance $\mathscr{I}_1$ of 2DCP, i.e. a network graph $G = (V,E)$, $n = |V| \geq 4$ and two disjoint vertex pairs (x_1,y_1), $(x_2,y_2) \in V^2$. We ask whether G contains two mutually vertex-disjoint paths, one going from x_1 to y_1, and the other going from x_2 to y_2. We create the following instance $\mathscr{I}_2$ of our mapping problems (MED/MFR-NNR/CNR). The pipeline consists of $m = 2n+1$ modules and the computational complexity of each module w_i is $f_{w_i}(z) = 1$ for $1 \leq i \leq 2n, i \neq n$ and $f_{w_n}(z) = n^2$. In other words, only module w_n has a much higher complexity than other modules. The network consists of $|V| + 1 + (n-1)(n-2)$ nodes and $|E| + n(n-1)$ links, and is constructed as follows: starting from graph G, we add a new node t, which is connected to G with an incoming link from y_1 to t, and an outgoing link from t to x_2. We also add $0 + 1 + 2 + ... + (n-2)$ additional nodes between y_1 and t and their corresponding links to connect y_1 to t through a set of $n-1$ paths of length l (in terms of the number of nodes excluding two end nodes y_1 and t), $0 \leq l \leq n-2$, as shown in Fig. 1. Similarly, additional nodes and links are added between t and x_2 so that there exists a set of $n-1$ paths of length l, $0 \leq l \leq n-2$, between nodes t and x_2. The processing capability of each node $v_j \in V'$ in the new graph $G' = (V', E')$ is set to $p_j = 1$, except for node t, whose processing power is set to be n^2 much higher than others. All link bandwidths are set to be sufficiently high so that transport time between nodes is ignored compared to computing time. The source and destination nodes v_s and v_d are set to be x_1 and y_2, respectively. We ask if we can achieve end-to-end delay of $T_{\text{MED}} = 2n+1$ or bottleneck cost of $T_{\text{MFR}} = 1$. This instance transformation can be done in polynomial time.

We show that given a solution to $\mathscr{I}_1$, we can find a solution to $\mathscr{I}_2$ of four mapping problems. Let q_i be the length of the path from x_i to y_i (including two end nodes), $i = 1, 2$. We have $2 \leq q_i \leq n$ for both paths, and paths are disjoint. The mapping solutions are derived as follows. (i) We map the first q_1 modules starting from module w_0 one-to-one onto the q_1 nodes of the path from x_1 to y_1 with no node reuse, and thus w_0 is mapped on the source node $x_1 = v_s$ and w_{q_1-1} is mapped on node y_1. (ii) The next $n - q_1$ modules from

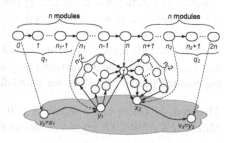

Fig. 1. Reduction from 2DCP

w_{q_1} to w_{n-1} along the pipeline are mapped one-to-one onto a path between y_1 and t (excluding two end nodes y_1 and t) of length $n - q_1$ with no node reuse; there exists such a path since $0 \leq n - q_1 \leq n - 2$. Each of the first n modules from w_0 to w_{n-1} incurs a delay of 1. (iii) We map module w_n with a complexity of n^2 to the fast node t, which also incurs a delay of $n^2/n^2 = 1$. (iv) Similar to the first n modules, the last n modules from w_{n+1} to w_{2n} are mapped on the path of length $n - q_2$ from t to x_2 (excluding two end nodes) and then on the path of length q_2 from x_2 to y_2 (including two end nodes), with no node reuse. Each of the last n modules also has a delay of 1. This mapping solution meets the requirements on no node reuse since we use the solution to $\mathscr{I}_1$: the paths from x_1 to y_1 and from x_2 to y_2 are disjointed so no node is reused. For MED problems, since each module incurs a delay of 1 and there are $2n + 1$ modules in total, the end-to-end delay of this mapping solution is $2n + 1 \leq T_{\text{MED}}$; while for MFR problems, since the delays on all modules are identical, the bottleneck cost of the entire pipeline is $1 \leq T_{\text{MFR}}$. Furthermore, the condition on contiguous node reuse is automatically satisfied by the mapping with no node reuse. Thus, we found a valid solution to $\mathscr{I}_2$ of all four mapping problems.

Reciprocally, if $\mathscr{I}_2$ has a solution, we show that $\mathscr{I}_1$ also has a solution. We prove that the mapping of $\mathscr{I}_2$ has to be of a similar form as the mapping described above (or similar but with contiguous node reuse in some instances of the problem), and thus that there exists disjoint paths $x_1 \rightarrow y_1$ and $x_2 \rightarrow y_2$. This property comes from the fact that node t must be used in the mapping. Indeed, if node t is not used to process module w_n, this module will incur a delay n^2, which is larger than the total delay bound $T_{\text{MED}} = 2n + 1$, and also becomes the bottleneck with cost larger than the bound $T_{\text{MFR}} = 1$. Since the end-to-end delay of $\mathscr{I}_2$ is less than $2n + 1$, or the bottleneck cost is less than 1, module w_n must be mapped on node t in the solution to $\mathscr{I}_2$. Note that the only way to reach node t involves using one of the $n-1$ paths going from y_1 to t. Thus, there is at least one module mapped on y_1. Let w_{n_1} be the last of these modules: $n_1 < n$, and w_{n_1+1} is not mapped on y_1. Similarly, all paths departing from t go through x_2, thus there is at least one module mapped on x_2. Let w_{n_2} be the first of these modules: $n_2 > n$, and w_{n_2-1} is not mapped on x_2. Moreover, source and destination nodes x_1 and y_2 are also used, since w_0 is mapped on x_1 and w_{2n} is mapped on y_2. Therefore, the entire mapping scheme is made up of the following three segments: (i) modules w_0 to w_{n_1} are mapped on a path between x_1 and y_1 (including two end nodes); (ii) modules w_{n_1+1} to w_{n_2-1} are mapped on a path between y_1 and x_2 (excluding two end nodes) going through t; and (iii) modules w_{n_2} to w_{2n} are mapped on a path between x_2 and y_2 (including two end nodes). Since only contiguous modules along the pipeline can be deployed on the same node, or no node reuse is performed at all in this mapping, nodes in both paths $x_1 \rightarrow y_1$ and $x_2 \rightarrow y_2$ should be distinct, and they are connected only by edges in G according to the construction of $\mathscr{I}_2$. Thus, we found disjoint paths and a solution to $\mathscr{I}_1$.   □

Theorem 3. *Given any constant* $\lambda > 0$, *there does not exist* λ-*approximation to the MED/MFR-NNR/CNR problems, unless* $P = NP$.

Proof. Given λ, assume that there exists a λ-approximation to one of the four problems. Let $\mathscr{I}_1$ be an instance of 2DCP (see proof of Theorem 2). We build the same instance $\mathscr{I}_2$ as in the previous proof, except for the speed of the fast node t and the computational complexity of module w_n, both of which are set to be λn^2 instead of n^2.

We use the λ-approximation algorithm to solve this instance $\mathscr{I}_2$ of our problem, which returns a mapping scheme of end-to-end delay or bottleneck cost T_{alg} such that $T_{alg} \leq \lambda T_{opt}$, where T_{opt} is the optimal end-to-end delay or bottleneck cost. We prove that we can solve 2DCP in polynomial time. We need to differentiate the cases of end-to-end delay and frame rate (inverse of bottleneck cost).

For MED problems: (i) If $T_{alg} > \lambda(2n+1)$, then $T_{opt} > 2n+1$ and there does not exist two disjoint paths; otherwise, we could achieve a mapping of end-to-end delay equal to $2n+1$. In this case, 2DCP has no solution. (ii) If $T_{alg} \leq \lambda(2n+1)$, we must map w_n on t; otherwise, it would incur a delay of $\lambda n^2 > \lambda(2n+1) \geq T_{alg}$, which conflicts with the condition. Hence, the mapping is similar to the one in the proof of Theorem 2, and we conclude that 2DCP has a solution.

For MFR problems: (i) If $T_{alg} > \lambda$, then $T_{opt} > 1$ and there does not exist two disjoint paths; otherwise, we could achieve a mapping of frame rate equal to 1. In this case, 2DCP has no solution. (ii) If $T_{alg} \leq \lambda$, we must map w_n on t; otherwise, it would incur a delay of $\lambda n^2 > \lambda \geq T_{alg}$, which conflicts with the condition. Hence, the mapping is similar to the one in the proof of Theorem 2. We conclude that 2DCP has a solution.

Therefore, in both cases, if 2DCP has a solution in polynomial time, then $P = NP$, hence establishing the contradiction and proving the non-approximability result.   □

The NP-completeness proof for MFR-ANR is provided in [9] based on the Widest-path with Linear Capacity Constraints (WLCC) problem, which is shown to be NP-complete in [4]. Because of the arbitrary node reuse, the non-approximability result is not directly applicable to MFR-ANR. We conjecture that MFR-ANR can be approximated, for instance by modifying classical bin-packing approximation schemes [10].

3.3   Heuristic Algorithms for NP-complete Pipeline Mapping Problems

We develop heuristic solutions by adapting the DP method for MED-ANR to the NP-complete problems with some necessary modifications. The heuristics for MED-CNR and MED-NNR are similar to that defined in Eq. 3 except that (i) in MED-CNR, we skip the cell of a neighbor node (slanted incident link) in the left column whose solution (path) involves the current node to ensure a loop-free path, and (ii) in MED-NNR, we further skip the left neighbor cell (horizontal incident link) to ensure that the current node is not reused.

For streaming applications, we use $1/T_{\mathrm{BN}}^{j-1}(v_i)$ to denote the MFR with the first j modules mapped to a path from source node v_s to node v_i in an arbitrary computer network, and have the following recursion leading to the final solution $T_{\mathrm{BN}}^{m-1}(v_d)$ in a similar 2D table:

$$
T_{\mathrm{BN}}^{j-1}(v_i) = \min_{j=2 \text{ to } m, v_i \in V_c} \left(\max \left(\begin{array}{c} T_{\mathrm{BN}}^{j-2}(v_i), \\ \dfrac{\alpha_{v_i}^{w_{j-1}} f_{w_{j-1}}(z_{j-2,j-1})}{p_i} \end{array} \right), \; \min_{v_u \in adj(v_i)} \left(\max \left(\begin{array}{c} T_{\mathrm{BN}}^{j-2}(v_u), \\ \dfrac{\alpha_{v_i}^{w_{j-1}} f_{w_{j-1}}(z_{j-2,j-1})}{p_i}, \\ \dfrac{\beta_{l_{u,i}}^{e_{j-2,j-1}} z_{j-2,j-1}}{b_{u,i}} + d_{u,i} \end{array} \right) \right) \right)
$$

(5)

with the base condition computed as:

$$
T_{\mathrm{BN}}^{1}(v_i) = \begin{cases} \max(\frac{f_{w_1}(z_{0,1})}{p_i}, \frac{z_{0,1}}{b_{s,i}} + d_{s,i}), & \forall l_{s,i} \in E_c \\ +\infty, & \text{otherwise} \end{cases}
$$

(6)

on the second column in the 2D table and we have $T_{\mathrm{BN}}^{0}(v_s) = 0$. In MFR-NNR, we have $\alpha = 1$ and $\beta = 1$. The steps for filling out the 2D table for MFR problems are similar to those for their corresponding MED problems but differ in the following aspects: at each step, we ensure that the processing power of reused nodes be equally shared and calculate the bottleneck time of the path instead of the total delay.

4   General Task Graph Optimization

In a DAG-structured task graph, modules may have multiple incoming or outgoing dependencies. The general DAG mapping problem is known to be NP-complete [3,5] even on two processors without any topology or connectivity restrictions [11]. We develop a heuristic approach using a RCP algorithm that recursively chooses the CP based on the previous round of calculation and maps it to the network using a DP procedure until a certain termination condition is met.

RCP Algorithm: We first assume the computer network to be complete with identical computer nodes and communication links and determine the initial computing and transport time cost components. Then we find the CP P_1 from w_0 to w_{m-1} in the task graph $G_t{}^1$ with initial time cost components. From this point on, we remove the assumption on resource homogeneity and connectivity completeness and map the current CP, i.e. P_1, to the real computer network using a DP-based pipeline mapping algorithm with arbitrary node reuse for MED. Those modules not located on the CP, also referred to as branch or non-critical modules, are mapped to the network using a greedy procedure. Based on the current mapping, we compute a new CP using updated time cost components in $G_t{}^i$ and calculate a new MED. The above steps are repeated until a certain condition is met. The complexity of the RCP algorithm is $O(k(m + |E_t|) \cdot |E_c|)$, where m represents the number of modules in the task graph, $|E_t|$ and $|E_c|$ denote the number of dependency edges in the task graph and communication links in the network graph, respectively, and k is the number of iterations where CPs are calculated and mapped.

Critical Path Calculation: We employ the well-known polynomial *Longest Path* (LP) algorithm to find the CP since the CP is essentially the LP in a DAG in terms of MED. The CP is selected with the nodes whose earliest start time is equal to their corresponding latest start time.

Critical Path Mapping: We adapt the pipeline mapping algorithm for MED-ANR to the CP mapping problem. The MED of a CP is calculated with partial modules on the CP mapped to a network path from the source to one node at each step, leading to the final solution that maps the entire CP to a network path reaching the destination.

Branch Modules Mapping: We design a recursive priority-based greedy algorithm to map branch modules. We first insert all critical modules into a queue Q. At each step, a module w_i is dequeued from Q and its succeeding modules are assigned to certain nodes in the following way: (i) Sort all unmapped succeeding modules $USM(w_i)$ of module w_i in a decreasing order according to their computation and communication requirements. The modules requiring more computations and communications are assigned higher priorities. (ii) Map all unmapped modules $w \in USM(w_i)$ with decreasing priorities onto either node $v(w_i)$ that runs module w_i or one of its succeeding nodes with minimum time for data transfer and module execution. (iii) Insert modules $w \in USM(w_i)$ to the end of Q. The above steps are recursively performed until Q is empty so that all modules in the task graph are assigned to the network nodes.

Table 2. Parameters of workflows and networks

Pipeline Mapping			
Problem Index	Problem Size $m, n, |E_c|$	Problem Index	Problem Size $m, n, |E_c|$
1	4, 6, 35	11	38, 47, 2200
2	6, 10, 96	12	40, 50, 22478
3	10, 15, 222	13	45, 60, 3580
4	13, 20, 396	14	50, 65, 4220
5	15, 25, 622	15	55, 70, 4890
6	19, 28, 781	16	60, 75, 5615
7	22, 31, 958	17	75, 90, 8080
8	26, 35, 1215	18	80, 100, 9996
9	30, 40, 1598	19	90, 150, 22476
10	35, 45, 2008	20	100, 200, 39990
Graph Mapping			
Problem Index	Problem Size $m, |E_t|, n, |E_c|$	Problem Index	Problem Size $m, |E_t|, n, |E_c|$
1	4, 6, 6, 35	11	38, 73, 47, 2200
2	6, 10, 10, 96	12	40, 78, 50, 2478
3	10, 18, 15, 222	13	45, 96, 60, 3580
4	13, 24, 20, 396	14	50, 102, 65, 4220
5	15, 30, 25, 622	15	55, 124, 70, 4890
6	19, 36, 28, 781	16	60, 240, 75, 5615
7	22, 44, 31, 958	17	75, 369, 90, 8080
8	26, 50, 35, 1215	18	80, 420, 100, 9996
9	30, 62, 40, 1598	19	90, 500, 150, 22496
10	35, 70, 45, 2008	20	100, 660, 200, 39990

5 Implementation and Evaluation

5.1 Implementation and Experimental Settings

For performance evaluations, we implement ELPC, RCP, and other three algorithms in comparison, namely Greedy A^*, Streamline, and Naive Greedy on the same Windows XP desktop PC equipped with a 3.0 GHz CPU and 2 Gbytes memory. We conduct an extensive set of mapping experiments for MED or MFR based on a large number of simulated computing workflows and computer networks. These simulation datasets are generated by randomly varying the following parameters of the computing workflows and computer networks within a suitably selected range of values: (i) the number of modules and the complexity of each module, (ii) the number of inter-module communications and the data size between two modules, (iii) the number of nodes and the processing power of each node, and (iv) the number of links and the BW and MLD of each link.

The topology and size of 20 simulated computing workflows and computer networks, indexed from 1 to 20, are tabulated in Table 2 for (i) pipeline mapping, where the problem size is represented by a three-tuple (m, n, E_c): m modules in the pipeline, and n nodes and $|E_c|$ links in the computer network, and (ii) graph mapping, where the problem size is represented by a four-tuple $(m, |E_t|, n, |E_c|)$: m modules and $|E_t|$ edges in the workflow or task graph, and $|n|$ nodes and $|E_c|$ links in the computer network.

5.2 Performance Evaluation for Linear Pipelines

We perform experiments on pipeline mappings under 20 different problem sizes using ELPC, Streamline, and Naive Greedy, by varying the mapping constraints, respectively.

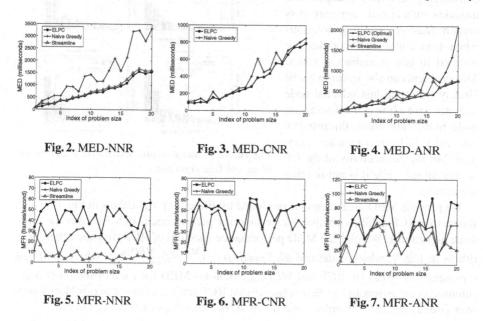

Fig. 2. MED-NNR   Fig. 3. MED-CNR   Fig. 4. MED-ANR

Fig. 5. MFR-NNR   Fig. 6. MFR-CNR   Fig. 7. MFR-ANR

The measured execution time of these algorithms varies from milliseconds for small-scale problems to seconds for large-scale ones. For a visual comparison purpose, we plot the performance measurements of MED and MFR produced by these three

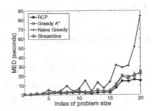

Fig. 8. MED for graph

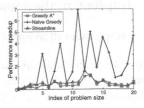

Fig. 9. RCP speedups

algorithms under three mapping constraints (NNR, CNR, and ANR) in Figs. 2, 3, 4, 5, 6, and 7, respectively. We observe that ELPC exhibits comparable or superior performances over the other two algorithms in all the cases we studied. A larger problem size with more network nodes and computing modules generally incurs a longer mapping path resulting in a longer end-to-end delay, which explains the increasing trend in Figs. 2, 3 and 4. Since the MFR is not related to the path length, the performance curves lack an obvious increasing or decreasing trend in response to varying problem sizes.

5.3 Performance Evaluation for DAG-Structured Workflows

We perform experiments of workflow mapping under 20 different problem sizes using RCP, Greedy A^*, Streamline, and Naive Greedy on a large set of simulated workflows and computer networks. Since both Greedy A^* and Streamline are designed for complete graphs without considering network topology when modules are mapped, they may miss certain feasible mapping solutions when two connected modules are mapped to two nonadjacent nodes. This problem can also occur in Naive Greedy when the last selected node does not have a link to the destination node. In RCP algorithm, this problem may arise in branch modules mapping, but the connectivity of the CP is guaranteed while it is not in other algorithms.

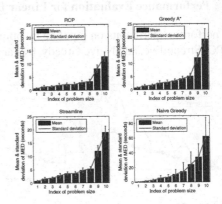

Fig. 10. Mean and standard deviation of MED performance of four algorithms

We plot the MED measurements produced by these four algorithms in Fig. 8, which shows that RCP exhibits comparable or superior performances in MED over the other three algorithms. We plot the MED performance speedup of RCP over the other algorithms in Fig. 9, which is defined as: $Speedup = \left| \frac{MED_{RCP} - MED_{other}}{MED_{RCP}} \right|$, where MED_{RCP} represents the MED for RCP and MED_{other} denotes MED for each of the other algorithms in comparison. In Fig. 9, we observe that RCP achieves one- or two-fold speedups over Greedy A^* and Streamline, and much higher speedups over Naive Greedy.

To further investigate the robustness of these mapping algorithms, we choose 10 problem sizes used in previous experiments, for each of which we randomly generate 20 problem instances and run mapping algorithms on them. We calculate and plot the mean value and standard deviation over 20 instances for each problem size in Fig. 10. Note that the value range along Y axis is from 0 to 90 seconds for Naive Greedy while it falls between 0 to 25 seconds for others. We observe that RCP achieves the best MED performance in an expected sense with the smallest standard deviation.

6   Conclusions and Future Work

We investigated the computational complexity of workflow mapping problems and designed ELPC and RCP algorithms for pipeline and graph mappings, respectively. The simulation results show that these algorithms exhibit superior performance over existing algorithms in terms of MED or MFR. The CP mapping in the current RCP algorithm is done separately without considering resource share, which may cause the mapping path to more likely fall on nodes with more resources. We will investigate more sophisticated performance models to characterize real-time computing node behaviors and estimate more accurate module execution time.

Acknowledgments

We would like to thank Anne Benoit and Yves Robert (ENS Lyon) for their help with the NP-completeness proof of the pipeline mapping problems. This research is sponsored by National Science Foundation under Grant No. CNS-0721980 and U.S. Department of Energy's Office of Science under Grant No. DE-SC0002400 with University of Memphis.

References

1. Rahman, M., Venugopal, S., Buyya, R.: A dynamic critical path algorithm for scheduling scientific workflow applications on global grids. In: Proc. of the 3rd IEEE Int. Conf. on e-Science and Grid Computing, pp. 35–42 (2007)
2. Sekhar, A., Manoj, B., Murthy, C.: A state-space search approach for optimizing reliability and cost of execution in distributed sensor networks. In: Proc. of Int. Workshop on Distributed Computing, pp. 63–74 (2005)
3. Kwok, Y., Ahmad, I.: Static scheduling algorithms for allocating directed task graphs to multiprocessors. ACM Computing Surveys 31(4), 406–471 (1999)
4. Zhu, Y., Li, B.: Overlay network with linear capacity constraints. IEEE Trans. on Parallel and Distributed Systems 19, 159–173 (2008)
5. Agarwalla, B., Ahmed, N., Hilley, D., Ramachandran, U.: Streamline: a scheduling heuristic for streaming application on the grid. In: The 13th Multimedia Computing and Networking Conf., San Jose, CA (2006)
6. Benoit, A., Robert, Y.: Mapping pipeline skeletons onto heterogeneous platforms. In: Shi, Y., van Albada, G.D., Dongarra, J., Sloot, P.M.A. (eds.) ICCS 2007. LNCS, vol. 4487, pp. 591–598. Springer, Heidelberg (2007)
7. Garey, M., Johnson, D.: Computers and Intractability: A Guide to the Theory of NP-completeness. W.H. Freeman and Company, New York (1979)

8. Fortune, S., Hopcroft, J., Wyllie, J.: The directed subgraph homeomorphism problem. Theoretical Computer Science 10, 111–121 (1980)
9. Wu, Q., Zhu, M., Gu, Y., Rao, N.: System design and algorithmic development for computational steering in distributed environments. IEEE Trans. on Parallel and Distributed Systems 99(1) (May 2009)
10. Ausiello, G., Crescenzi, P., Gambosi, G., Kann, V., Marchetti-Spaccamela, A., Protasi, M.: Complexity and Approximation. Springer, Heidelberg (1999)
11. Afrati, F., Papadimitriou, C., Papageorgiou, G.: Scheduling DAGs to minimize time and communication. In: Reif, J.H. (ed.) AWOC 1988. LNCS, vol. 319, pp. 134–138. Springer, Heidelberg (1988)

Radio Network Distributed Algorithms in the Unknown Neighborhood Model*

Bilel Derbel and El-Ghazali Talbi**

Laboratoire d'Informatique Fondamentale de Lille (LIFL)
Université des Sciences et Technologies de Lille France (USTL)
Bilel.Derbel@lifl.fr, El-ghazali.talbi@lifl.fr

Abstract. The paper deals with radio network distributed algorithms where initially no information about node degrees is available. We show that the lack of such an information affects the time complexity of existing fundamental algorithms by only a polylogarithmic factor. More precisely, given an n-node graph modeling a multi-hop radio network, we provide a $O(\log^2 n)$ time distributed algorithm that computes w.h.p., a constant approximation value of the degree of each node. We also provide a $O(\Delta \log n + \log^2 n)$ time distributed algorithm that computes w.h.p., a constant approximation value of the local maximum degree of each node, where the global maximum degree Δ of the graph is not known. Using our algorithm as a plug-and-play procedure, we show that the local maximum degree can be used instead of Δ to break the symmetry efficiently. We illustrate this claim by revisiting some fundamental algorithms that use Δ as a key parameter. First, we investigate the generic problem of simulating any point-to-point interference-free message passing algorithm in the radio network model. Then, we study the fundamental coloring problem in unit disk graphs. The obtained results show that the local maximum degree allows nodes to self-organize in a local manner and to avoid the radio interferences from being a communication bottleneck.

1 Introduction

Motivation and goals. We consider a multi-hop network of radio devices modeled by a graph. We assume that the nodes of the graph are not yet organized in any specific manner, that is, we consider a newly deployed network where no specific communication structure is available. In such a network, it is crucial that initially the nodes self-organize in some accurate manner before any tasks could be conducted. For that purpose, nodes have to communicate with their neighbors and coordinate their computations. Compared to a classical point-to-point message passing network where any two neighboring nodes are related by a direct link allowing them to communicate safely, communications between neighbors in a radio network are subject to interferences, i.e., a message sent by a node may get lost due to interferences caused by other message sending. Coping

---

* A preliminary version of this paper appeared as an inria internal research report [6].
** The two authors are supported by the Equipe Projet INRIA "DOLPHIN".

K. Kant et al. (Eds.): ICDCN 2010, LNCS 5935, pp. 155–166, 2010.
© Springer-Verlag Berlin Heidelberg 2010

with these interferences is indeed one of the major obstacles to design efficient distributed algorithms for radio networks. In this paper, we focus on what knowledge about the network is required to avoid interferences while organizing the network nodes efficiently. More specifically, we study the impact of two parameters: the degree of each node and the maximum network degree, on designing time-efficient distributed algorithms for solving basic radio network tasks. These two parameters are in fact used as crucial ingredients to compute fundamental distributed structures in many past works, e.g., node/edge coloring [10,11,5], matching [2], single-hop emulation [3], broadcasting and gossiping [7,1,4], etc. Unfortunately, nodes in a newly deployed network could even not be aware of their own neighbors. Thus, efficient algorithms working under the assumption that no knowledge about node degrees is available are more likely to be applied in a real setting. The key challenge of this paper is to provide time-efficient algorithms working under an unknown neighborhood model, i.e., a model where no information about node degrees is available.

Apart from being of a great importance in realistic settings, the unknown neighborhood model is also of a great theoretical interest. In fact, the time complexity of solving many basic tasks is tightly related to the degrees of nodes (lower and upper bounds are often functions of those degrees). To illustrate this claim, let us assume a communication model where a node can hear a message from one neighbor in a given time slot if and only if no other neighbors are being sending in that time slot. It is obvious that if a given node v has to receive one message from each of its neighbors, then the degree of v is a time lower bound. Assuming that v's neighbors know v's degree, if each neighbor (of v) transmits with a probability inversely proportional to v's degree, then we can show that the latter lower bound is almost tight. Now if we consider the problem of broadcasting a message from every node to its neighbors, then it can be shown that tuning the sending probabilities according to the maximum degree of the network leads to almost time-optimal algorithms. These observations show that a knowledge about node degree can significantly affect the most primitive network tasks. More generally, tuning the sending probability of a node according to that knowledge appears to be very helpful to avoid interferences caused by simultaneous transmissions. It is in fact a key idea to coordinate node transmissions distributively and to break the symmetry efficiently. In this work, we show how to overcome the absence of such a knowledge when thinking and designing efficient distributed algorithms: *(i)* by giving a polylogarithmic time algorithm that estimates the degree of each node and *(ii)* by showing that the maximum degree of the network is not a bottleneck parameter for computing some fundamental structures such as coloring.

The Model. We consider a classical graph based radio network model. More precisely, the network is modeled by an n-node graph $G = (V, E)$. The nodes represent a set of radio devices. There is an edge between two nodes if the two nodes are in the transmission range of one another. Nodes can communicate by sending and receiving messages. For the sake of analysis, we assume that the nodes have access to a global clock generating discrete pulses (slots). We also assume that the nodes wake up synchronously, i.e., at pulse 0 all nodes are awaken. At each pulse, a node can transmit or stay silent. A node receives a message in a given pulse iff it is silent then and precisely one of its neighbors transmits. No collision detection mechanism is available to nodes in any way.

We assume that nodes do not have any knowledge about the number of their neighbors. Nevertheless, we assume that an estimate $\tilde{n}$ on the number of nodes n in the network is known. In practice, these assumptions can be interpreted as following: nodes know that they may have between 1 and $\tilde{n}$ neighbors, but they do not know how many. As we will show, we remark that the running time of all our algorithms depends polylogarithmically on $\tilde{n}$, i.e., a rough estimate value $\tilde{n}$ of n (e.g., $\tilde{n} = n^{O(1)}$) affects the time complexity by only a constant factor. Therefore, for a sake of clarity our algorithms are described for $\tilde{n} = n$.

For every node v, we denote $\mathcal{N}(v)$ the set of v's neighbors and $d_v = |\mathcal{N}(v)|$ the degree of v. We denote $\mathcal{N}^+(v) = \mathcal{N}(v) \cup \{v\}$. The maximum degree of the network is denoted by $\Delta = \max\{d_v \mid v \in V\}$. The local maximum degree of a node v is defined by $\Delta_v = \max\{d_u \mid u \in \mathcal{N}^+(v)\}$. We say that an event occurs *with high probability* (w.h.p., for short) if the probability that the event occurs is at least $1 - 1/n^\alpha$ for a positive constant α which can be made arbitrarily large by setting the corresponding parameters to large enough values.

Contributions and Outline. Our first contribution (Section 2) is a $O(\log^2 n)$ time distributed algorithm that computes w.h.p., a constant approximation value of the degree of each node. The idea of the algorithm is based on the claim that if the nodes transmit with the same probability p then the probability that a given node v hears a message from its neighbors is maximized for $p = 1/d_v$. Thus, to decide on an estimate value of its degree, a node v changes its sending probability periodically and tries to detect the sending probability for which it hears the most often messages from its neighbors.

Our second contribution (Section 3) is a $O(\Delta \log n + \log^2 n)$ time distributed algorithm that computes w.h.p., a constant approximation value $\widetilde{\Delta_v}$ of the local maximum degree Δ_v of every node v. The idea of the algorithm is based on the claim that if all the neighbors of a given node v send with the same probability $p = 1/d_v$ then w.h.p., node v hears a message from each neighbor during a $O(d_v \log n)$ time period. Thus, by combining this claim with our first algorithm, we are able to coordinate the nodes (by periodically varying their sending probabilities) so that every node can communicate its approximate degree to neighbors having a lower degree.

The third result of the paper (Section 4) is more general in the sense that it allows us to overcome the lack of information about the (global) maximum degree Δ. Our analysis reveals that fundamental tasks using the knowledge of Δ as a key assumption can still be scheduled efficiently when such a knowledge is not available. We illustrate this claim for three fundamental problems: (i) the SRS (Single Round Simulation) problem [1] which consists in simulating the rounds of a synchronous point-to-point message passing algorithm into the radio network model, (ii) the classical node coloring problem [10,11] which consists in coloring the nodes such that every two neighbors have distinct colors (iii) a variant of the maximum matching problem [5] which consists in computing a set of distance-2 pairwise disjoint edges. We revised these three problems under the assumption that no information about node degrees is available and we show that using an approximate value of the local maximum degree of each node is sufficient to obtain essentially the same time complexity.

2 From Scratch Approximation of Node Degrees

2.1 Description of the Algorithm

Algorithm INITNETWORK (Fig. 1) works in $\log n$ phases. At each phase i, every node transmits with a decreasing probability $p_i = p_{i-1}/2$ for $k = \Theta(\log n)$ rounds. At each phase, each node counts the number of times it hears a message (variable c_i). If that number exceeds a threshold $\widetilde{\beta} \, k$ then the node decides that its degree is order of $1/p_i$. Roughly speaking, we will show that if all the neighbors of a node v are sending with the same probability p_i, then w.h.p., the number of times node v hears a message is roughly order of k when p_i is roughly order of $1/d_v$. Thus, by varying geometrically the sending probability at each phase from $1/2$ to $1/n$, each node is likely to experience a phase where it hears order of k messages, and can decide on an approximate value of its degree.

In order to obtain the w.h.p. correctness property of our algorithm, the precise value of $\widetilde{\beta}$ and k are to be fixed later in the analysis.

Input: An n-node graph G, an integer $k = \Theta(\log n)$, and a small constant $\widetilde{\beta}$.
Output: A constant approximate value $\widetilde{d_v}$ of d_v.

1 **for** $i = 1$ **to** $\log n$ **do**
2      $c_i := 0$; $p_i := 1/2^i$;
3   **for** $j = 1$ **to** k **do**
4   v sends a 'ping' message with probability p_i;
5   **if** v hears a 'ping' message **then** $c_i := c_i + 1$;
6   **if** $c_i \geq \widetilde{\beta} \, k$ **then** $\widetilde{d_v} := 2^i$;

Fig. 1. Algorithm INITNETWORK; code for a node v

2.2 Analysis

Fact 1 (e.g., [10,11]). $\forall x \geq 1$ and $|t| \leq x$, $e^t \left(1 - \dfrac{t^2}{x}\right) \leq \left(1 + \dfrac{t}{x}\right)^x \leq e^t$.

Fact 2 (Chernoff and Hoeffding's Inequalities, e.g., [9]). Let $X_1, \cdots, X_k$ be k independent Bernoulli trials, $\mathbb{P}(X_i = 1) = p = 1 - \mathbb{P}(X_i = 0)$. Let $X = \sum_{i=1}^{k} X_i$, and $\mathbb{E}(X) = \mu$. For any ϵ and ϵ' verifying $0 < \epsilon < 1$ and $\epsilon' > 0$, we have: $\mathbb{P}(X < (1 - \epsilon)\mu) < e^{-\mu \epsilon^2 / 2}$ and $\mathbb{P}(X - \mu \geq k\epsilon') \leq e^{-2k\epsilon'^2}$.

Let $c_i(v)$ be the value of counter c_i of node v at the end of a given phase i.

Lemma 1. *Given a node $v \in V$, we have $\mathbb{E}(c_i(v)) = k \cdot d_v \cdot p_i \cdot (1 - p_i)^{d_v}$.*

Proof. Due to lack of space, this proof is omitted (see [6]).   □

Lemma 2. *There exist positive constants $\nu, \beta, \epsilon > 0$ such that: (1) For any node v and phase i such that $i - 1 \leq \log d_v \leq i$, $\mathbb{E}(c_i(v)) \geq \beta \cdot k$, and (2) For any node v and phase $i \notin [\log(d_v) - 2, \log(d_v) + 4]$, $\mathbb{E}(c_i(v)) \leq ((1 - \epsilon)\beta - \nu) \cdot k$.*

Proof. Due to lack of space, this proof is omitted (see [6]).   □

In the following, we set $\widetilde{\beta} = (1 - \epsilon)\beta$ in algorithm INITNETWORK where ϵ and β are the constants from the previous lemma. We also set $k = \alpha \cdot \max\left\{ \beta/2\varepsilon^2, 1/(2\nu^2) \right\} \cdot \log n$, where $\alpha \geq 1$ is any constant. We say that a node decides on the value of $\widetilde{d_v}$ at phase i if the condition $c_i \geq \widetilde{\beta}k$ is true.

Lemma 3. *Given a node v and a phase i verifying $i \in [\log(d_v), \log(d_v) + 1]$, v decides on the value of $\widetilde{d_v}$ at phase i with probability at least $1 - 1/n^\alpha$.*

Proof. At phase $i \in [\log(d_v), \log(d_v) + 1]$, we have $1/p_{i-1} \leq d_v \leq 1/p_i$. Thus, using the Chernoff's inequality, we have:

$$\mathbb{P}\left(c_i(v) < (1 - \varepsilon)\mathbb{E}(c_i(v))\right) \leq_{\text{Fact 2}} \exp\left(-\frac{\varepsilon^2}{2} \cdot \mathbb{E}(c_i(v))\right)$$
$$\leq_{\text{Lemma 2}} \exp\left(-\frac{\varepsilon^2}{2} \cdot \beta \cdot k\right) \leq \frac{1}{n^\alpha}$$

Now, using Lemma 2, for $i \in [\log(d_v), \log(d_v) + 1]$, we have $\mathbb{E}(c_i(v)) \geq \beta k$. Thus $\mathbb{P}\left(c_i(v) < (1 - \varepsilon)\beta k\right) = \mathbb{P}\left(c_i(v) < \widetilde{\beta}k\right) \leq 1/n^\alpha$, and the lemma is proved.   □

In the next lemma, we prove that w.h.p., a node v does not decide on the value of $\widetilde{d_v}$ at a phase not in the range of $\log d_v$, i.e., w.h.p., the condition $c_i(v) \geq \widetilde{\beta}k$ does not hold for i not order of $\log d_v$.

Lemma 4. *Given a node v and a phase i verifying $i \notin [\log(d_v) - 2, \log(d_v) + 4]$, v does not decide on the value of $\widetilde{d_v}$ at phase i with probability at least $1 - 1/n^\alpha$.*

Proof. Take a phase $i \notin [\log(d_v) - 2, \log(d_v) + 4]$. By Lemma 2, we have $\mathbb{E}(c_i(v)) \leq (\widetilde{\beta} - \nu)k$. Thus, using the Hoeffding's inequality, we have

$$\mathbb{P}\left(c_i(v) \geq \widetilde{\beta}k\right) = \mathbb{P}\left(c_i(v) - \mathbb{E}(c_i(v)) \geq \left(\widetilde{\beta} - \frac{\mathbb{E}(c_i(v))}{k}\right)k\right)$$
$$\leq_{\text{Fact 2}} \exp\left(-2k\left(\widetilde{\beta} - \frac{\mathbb{E}(c_i(v))}{k}\right)^2\right)$$
$$\leq_{\text{Lemma 2}} \exp\left(-2k\nu^2\right) \leq \frac{1}{n^\alpha}$$ □

Theorem 1. *In $O(\log^2 n)$ time, algorithm* INITNETWORK *outputs w.h.p., a constant approximation value of the degree of any node.*

Proof. The running time is straightforward. Using the two previous lemmas, a node v decides *only* at a phase i verifying $i \in [\log(d_v) - 2, \log(d_v) + 4]$ with probability at least $(1 - 1/n^\alpha)^k$. Thus all nodes decide on such a phase with probability at least :

$$\prod_{v \in V}\left(1 - \frac{1}{n^\alpha}\right)^k = \left(1 - \frac{1}{n^\alpha}\right)^{k \cdot n} \geq_{\text{Fact 1}} 1 - \frac{1}{n^{\alpha-2}}$$

The last inequality holds for a sufficiently large constant α and $k = \Theta(\log n)$. □

3 An Algorithm for Computing the Local Maximum Degree

The idea of algorithm LOCALMAXDEGREE (Fig. 2) is to coordinate the sending probabilities so that each node can successfully send its approximate degree to neighbors having lower degrees. Given a node v, the crucial observation is that if all its neighbors are sending with probability $1/d_v$, then within $O(d_v \log n)$ time, v will receive a message from each neighbor (w.h.p.). The main difficulty is that a neighbor u of v does not know the degree of v. Thus, neighbor u cannot set its sending probability to the required value. Moreover, node u may have other neighbors with different degrees. Thus, node u should change its sending probability according to those neighbors. The key idea of our algorithm is to decrease geometrically the sending probability p_i each $\Theta((1/p_i)\log n)$ time period, from $p_i = 1/2$ until reaching $p_i = \Theta(1/d_v)$. Thus, at a phase i, nodes having a degree order of $1/p_i$ can hear a message from neighbors having larger degrees. Note that nodes with low degree will finish their while loop early.

Theorem 2. *In $O(\Delta \log n + \log^2 n)$ time, algorithm* LOCALMAXDEGREE *outputs, w.h.p., a constant approximation of the local maximum degree of any node.*

Input: An n-node graph G and a parameter $k = \Theta(\log n)$.
Output: A constant approximate value $\widetilde{\Delta_v}$ of Δ_v.
1 Run algorithm INITNETWORK and compute $\widetilde{d_v}$;
2 $\widetilde{\Delta_v} := \widetilde{d_v}$; $i := 0$;
3 **while** $i \leq \Theta(\log(\widetilde{d_v}))$ **do**
4     $i := i + 1$; $p_i := 1/2^i$;
5   **for** $j = 1$ **to** k/p_i **do**
6   v sends message "$\widetilde{d_v}$" with probability p_i;
7   **if** v *hears a message* "$\widetilde{d_w}$" *from node* w *and* $\widetilde{d_w} > \widetilde{\Delta_v}$ **then** $\widetilde{\Delta_v} := \widetilde{d_w}$;

Fig. 2. Algorithm LOCALMAXDEGREE; code for a node v

Proof. Let us consider a phase i and a node v verifying $d_v = \Theta(1/p_i)$. Assuming that algorithm INITNETWORK outputs the estimate value of the degree of each node, and from the initialization step (line 2) of algorithm LOCALMAXDEGREE, the condition of the while loop is still true for all nodes having degree at least order of $1/p_i$, i.e., neighbors of v with higher degree are still active at phase i.

Let u be a neighbor of v with degree at least order of $\Theta(1/p_i)$. We denote "$(u \longrightarrow v)^{(j,i)}$" the event "node v hears a message from neighbor u at a given iteration j of the for loop of phase i" and "$(u \longrightarrow v)^{(*,i)}$" the event "node v hears a message from neighbor u at phase i". Thus, we have that:

$$\mathbb{P}\left((u \longrightarrow v)^{(j,i)}\right) \geq p_i(1-p_i)^{d_v} \tag{1}$$

$$\implies \quad \mathbb{P}\left((u \longrightarrow v)^{(j,i)}\right) \geq_{\text{Fact 1}} p_i \cdot e^{-p_i d_v} \cdot \left(1 - d_v p_i^2\right)$$

$$= \Theta(\frac{1}{d_v}) \cdot e^{-\Theta(1)} \cdot \left(1 - \Theta(\frac{1}{d_v})\right)$$

$$= \Theta(\frac{1}{d_v})$$

Thus,

$$\mathbb{P}\left(\neg(u \longrightarrow v)^{(*,i)}\right) \leq \left(1 - \Theta\left(\frac{1}{d_v}\right)\right)^{\frac{k}{p_i}} \leq \left(1 - \Theta\left(\frac{1}{d_v}\right)\right)^{\Theta(kd_v)} \leq e^{-\Theta(k)}$$

Thus, the probability that nodes having degree $\Theta(1/p_i)$ do not receive a message from their neighbors with larger degree can be upper bounded as following:

$$\sum_{v \in V, d_v = \Theta(1/p_i)} \sum_{u \in \mathcal{N}(v), d_u > d_v} \leq n \cdot \Theta(\frac{1}{p_i}) \cdot e^{-\Theta(k)} \leq \frac{1}{n^{\Theta(1)}}$$

The last inequality holds for well chosen $k = \Theta(\log n)$. Thus, w.h.p., every node with degree order of $1/p_i$ receives a message from each of its neighbors having a larger degree. We remark that we have implicitly assumed that for a node v with a degree order of $1/p_i$, there exist some neighbors having larger degree (up to a constant). If this is not true, then from the initialization step in line 2, node v will decide that its local maximum degree is its own degree. Since the value $\widetilde{d_u}$ sent by a node u is w.h.p. a constant approximation of u's degree, a simple verification shows that w.h.p., all nodes with a degree order of $1/p_i$ succeeds computing their local maximum degree at phase i. This allows us to easily conclude that at the end of the algorithm, w.h.p., for every node v, $\widetilde{\Delta_v} = \Theta(\Delta_v)$.

Since $\widetilde{d_v} \leq \Theta(\Delta)$ for every node v, the time complexity is at most:

$$O(\log^2 n) + \sum_{i=1}^{\Theta(\log \Delta)} \frac{k}{p_i} = O(\log^2 n) + k \cdot \sum_{i=1}^{\Theta(\log \Delta)} 2^i$$

$$= O(\log^2 n + \log n \cdot 2^{\log \Delta})$$

$$= O(\log^2 n + \Delta \log n) \qquad \square$$

4   Applications

4.1   On Simulating the Message Passing Model

The first application of the previous algorithms is on simulating the standard synchronous point-to-point message passing model on the graph-based radio model. This problem was first studied in [1]. Paraphrasing the introduction in [1], that study was motivated by the fact that "whenever a type of communication mode emerges, new algorithms have to be developed for it for all standard network operations. Thus, simulation procedures could help to convert algorithms designed for networks with the same topology but different means of communication to algorithms for the new communication mode. In particular, since designing algorithms for radio networks from scratch turns to be a hard task, the simulation of algorithms for standard message-passing systems may prove to be a plausible approach". This motivation is still of interest since, compared to the advances gained by the research community in the classical message passing model, solving efficiently distributed tasks in a radio network model is still open for many fundamental problems.

The work in [1] concentrated on round-by-round simulations where a separate phase of radio transmission is dedicated to simulate each *single round* of the original algorithm: in a single round of the original algorithm, it is assumed that each node can send a message to each neighbor. A general primitive called single-round simulation (SRS) as a building block is provided. The goal of this primitive is to ensure that every message passed by the original algorithm will be effectively transmitted (and received) during the simulation. We refer to this as the SRS problem. For the *general* message passing model where a node can send a *different* message to its neighbors at each pulse, a randomized distributed SRS algorithm with running time $O(\Delta^2 \log n)$ was given. For the so-called *uniform* message passing model where a node sends the *same* message to its neighbors at each pulse, the authors gave a randomized distributed SRS algorithm with $O(\Delta \log n)$ running time. The SRS algorithms in [1] use Δ as a key parameter to schedule the sending probability of each node. Thus, these algorithms are impracticable in the unknown neighborhood model. By using our algorithms to compute an approximation of the local maximum degree of each node, and by locally using the computed value instead of Δ, we can prove the following:

Theorem 3. *In the unknown neighborhood model, the nodes of any n-node graph can be initialized in $O(\Delta \log n + \log^2 n)$ time so that the SRS problem can be solved w.h.p., for the uniform (resp. general) message passing model in $O(\Delta \log n)$ (resp. $O(\Delta^2 \log n)$) time.*

Proof. First we consider a uniform point-to-point message passing algorithm $\mathcal{A}$. For now let us assume that d_v and Δ_v are known for each node v. Consider a round of $\mathcal{A}$. To solve the SRS problem: each node v must send a message M_v to all its neighbors during that round (the message must be received by each neighbor). Consider the following SRS algorithm: each node v transmits message M_v with probability $1/\Delta_v$ for r_v rounds (r_v is to be fixed later).

Given a node v, let $(u \longrightarrow v)$ denote the event "v hears the message M_u in a single transmission round". Let $(u \longrightarrow v)^*$ denote the event "v hears the message M_u during the r_v transmission rounds". Thus, we have:

$$\mathbb{P}\left((u \longrightarrow v)\right) = \frac{1}{\Delta_u} \cdot \prod_{w \in \mathcal{N}^+(v) \setminus \{u\}} \left(1 - \frac{1}{\Delta_w}\right)$$

Using the fact that $\forall w \in \mathcal{N}^+(v), \Delta_w \geq d_v$, we obtain

$$\mathbb{P}\left((u \longrightarrow v)\right) \geq \frac{1}{\Delta_u} \cdot \left(1 - \frac{1}{d_v}\right)^{d_v} \geq \Theta\left(\frac{1}{\Delta_u}\right)$$

$$\implies \quad \mathbb{P}\left(\neg(u \longrightarrow v)^*\right) \leq \left(1 - \frac{1}{\Theta(\Delta_u)}\right)^{r_u} \leq \exp\left(-\Theta\left(\frac{r_u}{\Delta_u}\right)\right)$$

Hence, the probability that node u fails sending M_u to at least one neighbor v satisfies

$$\mathbb{P}\left(\neg(u \longrightarrow v)^*, v \in \mathcal{N}(u)\right) \leq \sum_{v \in \mathcal{N}(u)} \mathbb{P}\left(\neg(u \longrightarrow v)^*\right) \leq d_u \cdot \exp\left(-\Theta\left(\frac{r_u}{\Delta_u}\right)\right)$$

Thus by choosing $r_u = \Theta\left(\Delta_u \cdot \log(d_u \cdot n)\right)$, node u succeeds sending M_u to all its neighbors with probability at least $1 - 1/n^{\Theta(1)}$. Thus, the SRS algorithm succeeds for all nodes with probability at least $(1 - 1/n^{\Theta(1)})^n \geq 1 - 1/n^{\Theta(1)}$. Note that the constant hidden in the Θ notation when fixing r_u is to be tuned carefully to obtain the w.h.p., property. In particular, a constant approximation value of Δ_u and d_u affects r_u by only a constant. Since algorithm LOCALMAXDEGREE succeeds for all nodes w.h.p., it is not difficult to conclude that w.h.p., the SRS algorithm is successful for all nodes. Here, let us remark that the SRS algorithm has the nice property that sparse nodes are not penalized by dense regions, i.e., a node u terminates a SRS within $r_u = O(\Delta_u \log n)$ time.

Now, let us consider the *general* point-to-point message passing model, i.e., at each round of the original algorithm, a node v can send a different message to each neighbor (at most d_v messages each round). It is easy to see that the previous SRS algorithm can be easily extended to this general case: each node v applies the previous SRS procedure each $O(\Delta_v \log n)$ time period for each of the d_v messages to be delivered. It is not difficult to prove that w.h.p., the messages are received within $O(d_v \cdot \Delta_v \log n)$. However, this is not sufficient to guarantee the correctness of the SRS algorithm since a message sent from node u to node v can be received by another neighbor w of u. By concatenating nodes identifiers to messages, a node receiving a message can easily know if the message was for him. If unique identifiers are not available, then each node selects randomly an identifier from the $\{1, \cdots, n^{O(1)}\}$. Hence, it is easy to show that each node picks a unique identifier w.h.p. Then, each node sends its identifier to its neighbors using the uniform SRS procedure. Thus, w.h.p., in $O(\Delta \log n)$ time, each node can learn the identifiers of its neighbors. $\qquad\square$

Remark 1. In the correctness proof of algorithm LOCALMAXDEGREE (Theorem 2), we used the fact that nodes having a degree smaller than order of p_i at a phase i have already finished computing their local maximum degree and so they are silent, i.e., only nodes having a degree larger than order of p_i remain active and can transmit. This assumption is no longer true if the nodes begin running the simulation process described in Theorem 3 after terminating algorithm LOCALMAXDEGREE. However, in our SRS procedure, each node v transmits with probability order of Δ_v. Thus, Equation 1 in the proof of Theorem 2 still holds when replacing p_i by $\Theta(p_i)$. The other inequalities given in Theorem 2 are then affected by only a constant and Theorem 2 still holds w.h.p.

Corollary 1. *Given a uniform (resp. general) point-to-point message passing algorithm $\mathcal{A}$ running on an n-node graph G in τ time ($\tau = n^{O(1)}$), there exists a distributed algorithm that simulates w.h.p., $\mathcal{A}$ in the unknown neighborhood radio model in $O(\Delta \log n \cdot \tau + \log^2 n)$ time (resp. $O(\Delta^2 \log n \cdot \tau + \log^2 n)$ time).*

Corollary 2. *Consider a point-to-point message passing algorithm $\mathcal{A}$ running on an n-node graph G in τ time ($\tau = n^{O(1)}$). Assume that at each round of algorithm $\mathcal{A}$, each node sends the same message to a bounded number of neighbors and another message to the remaining neighbors. Then, there exists a distributed algorithm that simulates w.h.p., algorithm $\mathcal{A}$ in the unknown neighborhood radio model in $O(\Delta \log n \cdot \tau + \log^2 n)$ time.*

Consider for instance the *local broadcasting* problem where each node has to broadcast a message to its neighbors. Using the previous results it is straightforward that this problem can be solved w.h.p., in $O(\Delta \log n + \log^2 n)$ time. This could be for instance compared with a randomized $O(\Delta \log^3 n)$ time protocol for the same problem in the SINR (Signal-to-Interference-plus-Noise-Ratio) radio model (not the graph based model) given recently in [8].

4.2 On Computing a Coloring in Unit Disk Graphs

Node and edge coloring are one of the most important and fundamental tasks in distributed radio networks. In fact, coloring can be considered as a basic tool to initially organize unstructured wireless ad hoc and sensor networks. This is well-motivated for instance by associating different colors with different time-slots in a time-division multiple access (TDMA) scheme. In the following paragraphs, we revised some coloring related problems in the unknown neighborhood model.

Node coloring. A correct node coloring is an assignment of a color to each node in the graph, such that any two adjacent nodes have different colors. In [10,11], the authors provide an algorithm that produces w.h.p., a correct coloring with $O(\Delta)$ colors in $O(\Delta \log n)$ time for unit disk graphs. That algorithm requires that Δ is known to all nodes. In the conclusion of [10,11], it was asked whether we can get rid of Δ. Using our algorithms, we answer that question in the positive:

Proposition 1. *In the unknown neighborhood model, there exists a distributed algorithm that produces w.h.p., a $O(\Delta)$ node coloring within $O(\Delta \log n + \log^2 n)$ time on any n-node unit disk graph.*

Proof (Sketch). Due to lack of space, we only give the very general guidelines to prove the proposition. More specifically, we run the coloring algorithm of [10,11] by using the approximated local maximum degree for each node instead of parameter Δ. By carefully redefining the constants used in [10,11] according to our approximation factor, the reasoning used in [10,11] can still be proved to hold w.h.p. In particular, we use some arguments from Remark 1 to ensure that the coloring process from [10,11] does not interfere with the initialization step. □

One should however note that, at the same time and independently of our result [6], Schneider and Wattenhofer [12] came up with a new $O(\Delta + \log^2 n)$ time algorithm for Δ-coloring without knowledge of Δ.

Partial strong edge coloring. A correct edge coloring is an assignment of a color to each edge in the graph, such that any two adjacent edges have a different color. One can find many variants of the edge coloring problem. In particular, in [5], the authors considered the problem of computing a strong (or a distance-2) edge coloring, that is the problem of assigning distinct colors to any pair of edges between which there is a path of length at most two. The algorithms described there are based on computing an approximate maximum strong matching by an algorithm originally described in [2]. Computing a strong maximum matching consists in computing a set, with maximum cardinality, of edges mutually at distance at least 2. In [5], it is proved that a $O(1)$-approximate solution to the strong maximum matching can be computed in $O(\rho \log n)$ time for unit disk graphs[1], where ρ denotes the time it takes to compute the *active degree* of each node. Following the same terminology than in [5], a node is said to be *active* in a given round if it decides to transmit. Then, the active degree of a node is the number of its neighbors that are active in the current round. Using our algorithms, we can show that $\rho = O(\log^2 n)$. Thus, we obtain the following:

Proposition 2. *In the unknown neighborhood model, there exists a distributed algorithm that produces w.h.p., a $O(1)$-approximate strong matching in $O(\log^3 n)$ time on any n-node unit disk graph.*

5   Conclusion

In this paper, we have shown that computing in the unknown neighborhood model is up to a polylogarithmic factor similar to computing in the known neighborhood model. We have also shown that, for some distributed tasks, computing the local maximum degree of each node is sufficient to overcome the need to know the global parameter Δ. Many open issues can however be investigated. For instance, although the correctness of our algorithms was proved analytically, it would be nice to give an experimental analysis and/or to study the impact

---

[1] In [5], it is also assumed that a node can hear collisions which is actually stronger than the assumptions of our model.

of changing the values the constants used in our algorithms through simulation. Another interesting field of research is to derive new algorithms which are both time and *energy* efficient and to extend our algorithms to non graph based models and/or to multi-channel radio networks.

References

1. Alon, N., Bar-Noy, A., Linial, N., Peleg, D.: On the complexity of radio communication. In: 21st annual ACM Symposium on Theory of computing (STOC 1989), pp. 274–285. ACM, New York (1989)
2. Balakrishnan, H., Barrett, C.L., Anil Kumar, V.S., Marathe, M.V., Thite, S.: The distance-2 matching problem and its relationship to the mac-layer capacity of ad hoc wireless networks. IEEE Journal on Selected Areas in Communications 22(6), 1069–1079 (2004)
3. Bar-Yehuda, R., Goldreich, O., Itai, A.: Efficient emulation of single-hop radio network with collision detection on multi-hop radio network with no collision detection. In: Bermond, J.-C., Raynal, M. (eds.) WDAG 1989. LNCS, vol. 392, pp. 24–32. Springer, Heidelberg (1989)
4. Bar-Yehuda, R., Israeli, A., Itai, A.: Multiple communication in multi-hop radio networks. In: 8th ACM Symposium on Principles of distributed computing (PODC 1989), pp. 329–338 (1989)
5. Barrett, C.L., Kumar, V.S.A., Marathe, M.V., Thite, S., Istrate, G.: Strong edge coloring for channel assignment in wireless radio networks. In: 4th annual IEEE international conference on Pervasive Computing and Communications Workshops (PERCOMW 2006), Washington, DC, USA, p. 106. IEEE Computer Society Press, Los Alamitos (2006)
6. Derbel, B., Talbi, E.-G.: Radio network distributed algorithms in the unknown neighborhood model. In: Technical Report HAL, inria-00292155, RR-6581 (June 2008), http://hal.inria.fr
7. Gasieniec, L., Peleg, D., Xin, Q.: Faster communication in known topology radio networks. In: 24th symposium on principles of distributed computing (PODC 2005), pp. 129–137. ACM, New York (2005)
8. Goussevskaia, O., Moscibroda, T., Wattenhofer, R.: Local Broadcasting in the Physical Interference Model. In: International Workshop on Foundations of Mobile Computing (DialM-POMC), Toronto, Canada, August 2008, pp. 35–44 (2008)
9. Mitzenmacher, M., Upfal, E.: Probability and Computing, Randomized Algorithms and probabilistic analysis. Cambridge University Press, Cambridge (2005)
10. Moscibroda, T., Wattenhofer, R.: Coloring Unstructured Radio Networks. In: 17th ACM Symposium on Parallelism in Algorithms and Architectures (SPAA 2005), July 2005, pp. 39–48 (2005)
11. Moscibroda, T., Wattenhofer, R.: Coloring unstructured radio networks. Distributed Computing 21(4), 271–284 (2008)
12. Schneider, J., Wattenhofer, R.: Coloring unstructured wireless multi-hop networks. In: 28th Symposium on Principles of Distributed Computing (PODC 2009), pp. 210–219 (2009)

Probabilistic Self-stabilizing Vertex Coloring in Unidirectional Anonymous Networks

Samuel Bernard[1], Stéphane Devismes[2], Katy Paroux[3],
Maria Potop-Butucaru[1], and Sébastien Tixeuil[1]

[1] Université Pierre et Marie Curie - Paris 6
[2] Université Grenoble I
[3] INRIA Bretagne Atlantique

Abstract. A distributed algorithm is self-stabilizing if after faults and attacks hit the system and place it in some arbitrary global state, the system recovers from this catastrophic situation without external intervention in finite time. Unidirectional networks preclude many common techniques in self-stabilization from being used, such as preserving local predicates. The focus of this work is on the classical vertex coloring problem, that is a basic building block for many resource allocation problems arising in wireless sensor networks.

In this paper, we investigate the gain in complexity that can be obtained through randomization. We present a probabilistically self-stabilizing algorithm that uses k states per process, where k is a parameter of the algorithm. When $k = \Delta + 1$, the algorithm recovers in expected $O(\Delta n)$ actions. When k may grow arbitrarily, the algorithm recovers in expected $O(n)$ actions in total. Thus, our algorithm can be made optimal with respect to space or time complexity. Our case study hints that randomization could help filling the complexity gap between bidirectionnal and unidirectionnal networks.

Keywords: Wireless sensor networks, distributed algorithms, self-stabilization, unidirectional anonymous networks, lower and upper bounds, coloring problem, randomization.

1 Introduction

Wireless sensor networks are already used in a variety of fields, like home appliances, irrigation, medicine, monitoring, real-time control systems, military defense applications, etc. Recent advances in hardware design and manufacturing, computing and storage capabilities of the sensing devices themselves, have made it practically possible to envision very large size sensor networks comprising hundreds of thousands or even millions of autonomous sensor nodes. The scalability requirements of future wireless sensor networks drives new problems to application designers. For example, it becomes unrealistic to ensure human maintainance of such networks, to assume unique identifiers will be available, or to expect every sensor node to have exactly the same communication capabilities as its neighbors. Moreover, when sensor networks are deployed in unattended environments, it is likely that faults and attacks will hit the system.

K. Kant et al. (Eds.): ICDCN 2010, LNCS 5935, pp. 167–177, 2010.

One of the most versatile technique to ensure forward recovery of distributed systems is that of *self-stabilization* [6,7]. A distributed algorithm is self-stabilizing if after faults and attacks hit the system and place it in some arbitrary global state, the system recovers from this catastrophic situation without external (*e.g.* human) intervention in finite time. Self-stabilization makes no hypotheses about the extent or the nature of the faults and attacks that may harm the system, yet may induce some overhead (*e.g.* memory, time) when there are no faults, compared to a classical (*i.e.* non-stabilizing) solution. Computing space and time bounds for particular problems in a self-stabilizing setting is thus crucial to evaluate the impact of adding forward recovery properties to the system.

The vast majority of self-stabilizing solutions in the literature [7] considers *bidirectional* communications capabilities, *i.e.* if a process u is able to send information to another process v, then v is always able to send information back to u. This assumption is valid in many cases, but cannot capture the fact that asymmetric situations may occur, *e.g.* in wireless sensor networks, it is possible that u is able to send information to v yet v cannot send any information back to u (u may have a wider range antenna than v). Asymmetric situations, that we denote in the following under the term of *unidirectional* networks, preclude many common techniques in self-stabilization from being used, such as preserving local predicates (a process u may take an action that violates a predicate involving its outgoing neighbors without u knowing it, since u cannot get any input from them).

Related works. Investigating the possibility of self-stabilization in unidirectional networks such as those resulting from wireless communication medium was recently emphasized in several papers [1,3,4,5,8,9,10][1]. In particular, [4] shows that in the simple case of acyclic unidirectional networks, nearly any recursive function can be computed anonymously in a self-stabilizing way. Computing global tasks in a general topology requires either unique identifiers [1,3,8] or distinguished processes [5,9,10].

The paper most related to our work [2] studies *deterministic* solutions to the self-stabilizing vertex coloring problem in *unidirectional networks*. To satisfy the vertex coloring specification in unidirectional networks, an algorithm must ensure that no two neighboring nodes (*i.e.* two nodes u and v such that either u can send information to v, or v can send information to u, but not necessarily both) have identical colors. When deterministic solutions are considered, [2] proves a lower bound of n states per process (where n is the network size) and a recovery time of at least $n(n-1)/2$ actions in total (and thus $\Omega(n)$ actions per process). [2] also presents a deterministic algorithm for vertex coloring with matching upper bounds that performs in arbitrary graphs.

Those high lower bounds results contrast with the many low upper bounds existing in the litterature about *bidirectional* networks. Indeed, both deterministic and probabilistic solutions to the vertex coloring problem [11,13] in bidirectional networks require only a number of states that is proportional to the network

---

[1] We do consider here the overwhelming number of contributions that assume a unidirectional ring shaped network, please refer to [7] for additional references.

maximum degree Δ, and the number of actions per process in order to recover is $O(\Delta)$ (in the case of a deterministic algorithm) or expected $O(1)$ (in the case of a probabilistic one). Moreover, since the length of the chain of causality after a correcting action is executed is only one, strict Byzantine containement can be achieved [14].

Our contribution. In this paper, we investigate the possibility of lowering complexity results for the vertex coloring problem in *unidirectional networks* by means of randomization. We first observe that at least $\Delta + 1$ states per process and a recovery time of $\Omega(n)$ actions in total (and thus $\Omega(1)$ actions per process) are required. We present a probabilistically self-stabilizing algorithm for vertex coloring that uses k states per process, where k is a parameter of the algorithm. When $k = \Delta + 1$ (*i.e.* when the number of used colors is optimal), the algorithm recovers in expected $O(\Delta n)$ actions in total. When k may grow arbitrarily, the algorithm recovers in expected $O(n)$ actions in total (*i.e.* an optimal – constant – number of actions per node). Thus, our algorithm can be made optimal with respect to space or time complexity. This results solves the open question of [2] with respect to the computing power of probabilistic protocols. Our results are particularly well suited to dynamic wireless sensor networks as we make no hypothesis about the availability of unique identifiers for the various nodes, *i.e.* the participants are completely *anonymous*.

Outline. The remaining of the paper is organized as follows: Section 2 presents the programming model and problem specification, while Section 3 presents our randomized solution to the problem. Section 4 gives some concluding remarks and open questions.

2   Model

Distributed Program model. A distributed program consists of a set V of n processes which may not have unique identifiers. Therefore, processes will be referred in the following as anonymous. A process maintains a set of variables that it can read or update, that define its *state*. Each variable ranges over a fixed domain of values. We use small case letters to denote singleton variables, and capital ones to denote sets. A process contains a set of *constants* that it can read but not update. A binary relation E is defined over distinct processes such that $(i, j) \in E$ if and only if j can read the variables maintained by i; i is a *predecessor* of j, and j is a *successor* of i. The set of predecessors (resp. successors) of i is denoted by $P.i$ (resp. $S.i$), and the union of predecessors and successors of i is denoted by $N.i$, the *neighbors* of i. In some case, we are interested in the iterated notions of those sets, *e.g.* $S.i^0 = i$, $S.i^1 = S.i$, ..., $S.i^k = \cup_{j \in S.i} S.j^{k-1}$. The values $\delta_{in}.i$, $\delta_{out}.i$, and $\delta.i$ denote respectively $|P.i|$, $|S.i|$, and $|N.i|$; Δ_{in}, Δ_{out}, and Δ denote the maximum possible values of $\delta_{in}.i$, $\delta_{out}.i$, and $\delta.i$ over all processes in V.

An action has the form $\langle name \rangle : \langle guard \rangle \longrightarrow \langle command \rangle$. A *guard* is a Boolean predicate over the variables of the process and its communication neighbors. A *command* is a sequence of statements assigning new values to the variables of the process. We refer to a variable v and an action a of process i as $v.i$ and $a.i$ respectively. A *parameter* is used to define a set of actions as one parameterized action.

A *configuration* of the distributed program is the assignment of a value to every variable of each process from its corresponding domain. Each process contains a set of actions referred in the following as *algorithm*. In the following we consider that processes are *uniform*. That is, all the processes contain the exact same set of actions. An action is *enabled* in some configuration if its guard is **true** in this configuration. A *computation* is a maximal sequence of configurations such that for each configuration γ_i, the next configuration γ_{i+1} is obtained by executing the command of at least one action that is enabled in γ_i. Maximality of a computation means that the computation is infinite or it eventually reaches in a terminal configuration where none of the actions are enabled. *silent.*

A *scheduler* is a predicate on computations, that is, a scheduler is a set of possible computations, such that every computation in this set satisfies the scheduler predicate. The *unfair distributed* scheduler, that we use in the sequel, corresponds to predicate **true** (that is, all computations are allowed).

A configuration *conforms* to a predicate if this predicate is **true** in this configuration; otherwise the configuration *violates* the predicate. By this definition every configuration conforms to predicate **true** and none conforms to **false**. Let R and S be predicates over the configurations of the program. Predicate R is *closed* with respect to the program actions if every configuration of the computation that starts in a configuration conforming to R also conforms to R. Predicate R *converges* to S if R and S are closed and any computation starting from a configuration conforming to R contains a configuration conforming to S. The program *deterministically stabilizes* to R if and only if **true** converges to R. The program *probabilistically stabilizes* to R if and only if **true** converges to R with probability 1.

Problem specification. Consider a set of colors ranging from 0 to $k - 1$, for some integer $k \geq 1$. Each process i defines a function *color.i* that takes as input the states of i and its predecessors, and outputs a value in $\{0, \ldots, k - 1\}$. The *unidirectional vertex coloring* predicate is satisfied if and only if for every $(i, j) \in E$, $color.i \neq color.j$.

3   Probabilistic Self-stabilizing Unidirectional Coloring

We first observe two lower bounds that hold for any kind of program that is self-stabilizing or probabilistically self-stabilizing for the unidirectional coloring specification:

1. *The minimal number of states per process is* $\Delta + 1$. Consider a bidirectional clique network (that is $(\Delta + 1)$-sized), and assume the output of the coloring protocol is now fixed (that is, the network is vertex colored). Suppose that only Δ states per process are used, then at least two processes i and j have

the same state, and have the same view of their predecessors. As a result $color.i = color.j$, and i and j being neighbors, the unidirectional coloring predicate does not hold in this terminal configuration.

2. *The minimal number of moves overall is $\Omega(n)$.* Consider a unidirectional chain of processes which are all initially in the same state. For every process but one, the color is identical to that of its predecessor. Since a change of state may only resolve two conflicts (that of the moving node and that of its successor), a number of overall moves at least equal to $\lfloor n/2 \rfloor$ is required, thus $\Omega(n)$ moves.

The algorithm presented as Algorithm 1 can be informally described as follows. If a process has the same color as one of its predecessors then it chooses a new color in the set of available colors (*i.e.* the set of colors that are not already used by any of its predecessors), or retains its current color.

The algorithm is only slightly different from its classical self-stabilizing *bidirectional* counterpart [11] by the fact that a node may retain its own color (the random color is always changed in [11]). This is due to the fact that some particular networks could drive the classical probabilistic protocol into a deterministic behavior. The example presented in Figure 1.*a* depicts an execution of a two nodes network such that boths nodes are both predecessor and successor of one another. With our definition, each node has $\delta.i = 1$, and thus only two colors are available for each of them. If node may not reuse their own color, then they must choose a different one. Only one such color is available, and unfortunately this color is the same for both of them. As a result, when both nodes start with the same color 0, and are always scheduled for execution simultaneously, they both choose the same (different form 0) color 1. The argument can then be repeated to induce an infinite loop that never stabilizes. Such a scenario may not happen with our scheme, since there always exists a positive probability that even if selected simultaneously, two neighboring such node choose different colors (see execution in Figure 1.*b*).

The colors are chosen in a set of size k, where k is a parameter of the algorithm, using uniform probability $1/k$. In the following, we show that Algorithm 1 is probabilistically self-stabilizing for the unidirectional coloring problem if $k > \Delta$. To reach that goal we proceed in two steps: first we show that any terminal configuration satisfies the unidirectional coloring predicate (Lemma 1); secondly, we show that the expected number of steps to reach a terminal configuration starting from an arbitrary one is bounded (Lemma 6).

Lemma 1. *Any terminal configuration satisfies the unidirectional coloring predicate.*

Proof. In a terminal configuration, every process i satisfies $\forall j \in P.i, c.i \neq c.j$ and $\forall j \in S.i, c.i \neq c.j$. Hence, in a terminal configuration, every process i has a color that is different from those of its neighbors, which proves the lemma.

Definition 1 (Conflict). *Let p be a process and γ a configuration. The tuple (p,γ) is called a* conflict *if and only if there exists $q \in P.p$ (the predecessors of p) such that $c.q = c.p$ in γ.*

Algorithm 1. A uniform probabilistic coloring algorithm for general unidirectional networks

process i
const
    k : integer
    $P.i$: set of predecessors of i
    $C.i$: set of colors of nodes in $P.i$
parameter
    p : node in $P.i$
var
    $c.i$: color of node i
function
    random(S : set of colors) : color
        // returns a color in S chosen with uniform probability
action
    $p \in P.i,\ c.i = c.p \rightarrow$
        $c.i := \text{random}\,((\{0,\ldots,k-1\} \setminus C.i) \cup \{c.i\})$

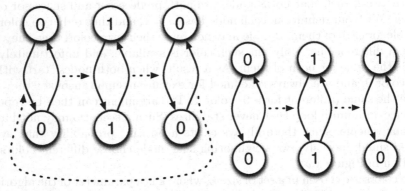

(a) Degenerate deterministic execution   (b) Still probabilistic execution

Fig. 1. Executions of coloring process in degenerate networks

Lemma 2. *Assume* $k > \Delta$. *The number* X_1 *of conflicts created by the color change of Process* p *is equal to a sum of* $\alpha.p$ *Bernoulli random variables with common parameter* $\beta.p$, *where* $\alpha.p = \delta.p - \delta_{in}.p$ *and*

$$\beta.p = \frac{1}{k - |C.p|} \leqslant \frac{1}{k - \delta_{in}.p}. \tag{1}$$

Proof. The idea of the proof is illustrated in Figure 2 for $k = 5$, $\delta.p = 4$, and $\delta_{in}.p = 1 = |C.p|$, where process p is denoted in dark gray. The random variable X_1 is the sum of 3 Bernoulli random variables [12] with common parameter $1/4$.

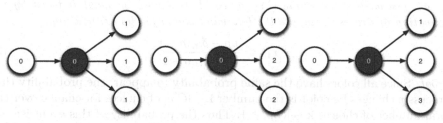

(a) A case where p may create 0 or 3 conflicts   (b) A case where p may create at most 2 conflicts   (c) A case where p may create at most 1 conflict

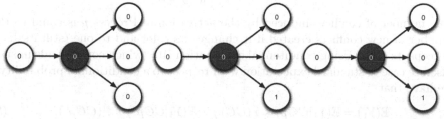

(d) A case where p may not create any conflict   (e) A case where p may create 0 or 2 conflicts   (f) A case where p may create at most 1 conflict

Fig. 2. Illustrating the number of conflicts with color change, for $k = 5$, $\delta.p = 4$, and $\delta_{in}.p = 1$

When a process p actually changes its color, this new color is chosen in a set of $k - |C.p|$ colors which contains at least $k - \delta_{in}.p$ colors. That is, there are k colors and it cannot choose a color chosen by one of its predecessors, therefore $|C.p|$ colors are removed from the set of possible choices, which means that at most $\delta_{in}.p$ colors are removed.

Let q be a successor of p which is not a predecessor of p. After p changes its color, p and q are in conflict if and only if p chooses the color of q. The probability that p chooses the color of q is equal to one over the number of choices for the color of p: $1/(k - |C.p|)$.

Since the number of successors of p not in the set of predecessors of p is $\delta.p - \delta_{in}.p$, the number of conflicts created by p is a sum of $\alpha.p$ Bernoulli random variables taking value one with probability $1/(k - |C.p|)$, where $\alpha.p = \delta.p - \delta_{in}.p$. Since these Bernoulli random variables are in general not independent, one cannot expect their sum to follow the binomial law. However, their dependence does *not* impact the expectation of their sum.

Lemma 3. *Assume $k > \Delta$. The probability of the event CCp that the Process p does change its color is equal to:*

$$\mathbb{P}(CCp) = \frac{k - |C.p|}{k - |C.p| + 1}. \tag{2}$$

As a consequence, the number Y_1 of conflicts (same or new) induced by the activation of Process p admits the following bound for its expectation:

$$\mathbb{E}(Y_1) \leqslant \frac{\delta.p - \delta_{in}.p + 1}{k - \delta_{in}.p + 1}. \tag{3}$$

Proof. Since all colors have the same probability to appear, the probability that Process p changes its color is the number $k - |C.p|$ of choices for change over the total number of choices $k - |C.p| + 1$. Thus the probability of this event is:

$$\mathbb{P}(CCp) = \frac{k - |C.p|}{k - |C.p| + 1}. \tag{4}$$

The number of conflicts induced by the activation of Process p is equal to the number of new conflicts created if it changes its color and to one (still itself) if it keeps its color. Using conditonnal expectation [16] (which corresponds in such discrete case to standard expectation with respect to a conditionnal probability), we have that

$$\mathbb{E}(Y_1) = \mathbb{E}(Y_1|CCp) \times \mathbb{P}(CCp) + \mathbb{E}(Y_1|CCp^c) \times \mathbb{P}(CCp^c), \tag{5}$$

where CCp^c denotes the complementary of the event CCp. Thus we obtain

$$\mathbb{E}(Y_1) = \mathbb{E}(X_1) \times \mathbb{P}(CCp) + 1 \times \mathbb{P}(CCp^c), \tag{6}$$

where X_1 has the same meaning as in Lemma 2, and thanks to lemma 2 we obtain

$$\mathbb{E}(Y_1) = \frac{\delta.p - \delta_{in}.p + 1}{k - |C.p| + 1} \leqslant \frac{\delta.p - \delta_{in}.p + 1}{k - \delta_{in}.p + 1}. \tag{7}$$

Lemma 4. *Assume $k > \Delta$. The expected number of conflicts induced by an activation of Process p is less than or equal to:*

$$M = \frac{\Delta}{k} < 1. \tag{8}$$

Proof. Observe that for all $p \in V, \Delta \geqslant \delta.p$, therefore for all $p \in V$,

$$\frac{\delta.p - \delta_{in}.p + 1}{k - \delta_{in}.p + 1} \leqslant \frac{\Delta - \delta_{in}.p + 1}{k - \delta_{in}.p + 1}. \tag{9}$$

In order to find an upper bound for this value, let the function f be

$$f : x \in [1, \Delta] \mapsto \frac{\Delta - x + 1}{k - x + 1}. \tag{10}$$

Its derivative exists and is equal to

$$f'(x) = \frac{\Delta - k}{(k - x + 1)^2}. \tag{11}$$

By hypothesis, we have that $k > \Delta$, so $f'(x) < 0$ for all $x \in [1, \Delta]$ and f is decreasing. Therefore, $f(x)$ is maximal when $x = 1$, which leads to

$$\frac{\delta.p - \delta_{in}.p + 1}{k - \delta_{in}.p + 1} \leqslant \frac{\Delta - \delta_{in}.p + 1}{k - \delta_{in}.p + 1} \leqslant \frac{\Delta}{k}. \tag{12}$$

Lemma 5. *Assume* k > Δ. *Let* (p, γ) *be a conflict. The expected number of steps necessary to solve this conflict is less than:*

$$\frac{1}{1 - M} = \frac{k}{k - \Delta}. \tag{13}$$

Proof. The expected number of conflicts created by a single process is given by Lemma 4. Let us explain how we deal with the second stage when resolving conflicts, then any further stage follows by induction. Our idea is to introduce the following probabilistic tool. We consider a branching tree which is a generalisation of a Galton-Watson tree [15], where the number of offsprings are dependant random variables. As previously mentioned, this dependency does not matter when computing the expectation.

Recall that Y_1 is the number of conflicts induced by an activation of a Process p. We will denote by Y_2 the number of conflicts created at the second stage. As observed above,

- either process p changes its color and then the number Y_2 of conflicts induced by the activation of the associated Y_1 Processes is equal to a sum of Y_1 random variables T_q where q is a successor of p not in the set of predecessors of p and in conflict with p;
- or process p keeps its color, and $Y_1 = 1$, the number Y_2 of conflicts created will be equal in law to Y_1.

In the first case, each T_q has the same behaviour as $Y_1 = T_p$ (with different parameters) and is independant from Y_1. Then we have the following:

$$\mathbb{E}(Y_2) \leqslant \mathbb{E}\left(\sum_{j=1}^{Y_1} T_{q_j}\right) = \sum_{y=1}^{\alpha.p}\left(\mathbb{E}(\sum_{j=1}^{y} T_{q_j})\mathbb{P}(Y_1 = y)\right)$$

$$\leqslant \sum_{y=1}^{\alpha.p}\left(y[\max_q \mathbb{E}(T_q)]\mathbb{P}(Y_1 = y)\right) = \mathbb{E}(Y_1)\, M \leqslant M^2.$$

By induction, the expected number of conflicts $\mathbb{E}(Y_\ell)$ created at stage ℓ is less than

$$\mathbb{E}(Y_1)\, M^{\ell-1} \leqslant M^\ell.$$

Since $M < 1$, we have a convergent geometric series. Thus the expected total number of conflicts is less than $1/(1 - M)$.

Lemma 6. *Assume* k > Δ. *Starting from an arbitrary configuration, the expected number of color changes to reach a configuration verifying the unidirectional coloring predicate is less than or equal to:*

$$\frac{n\,k}{k - \Delta}. \tag{14}$$

Proof. In the worst case the number of initial conflicts is n. Then the proof is a direct consequence of Lemma 5.

Theorem 1. *Algorithm 1 is a probabilistic self-stabilizing solution for the unidirectional coloring when* k $> \Delta$.

Proof. The proof is a direct consequence of Lemmas 1 and 6.

Notice that with a minimal number of colors (*i.e.*, k $= \Delta + 1$), the expected number of steps to reach a terminal configuration starting from an arbitrary configuration is less than $n(\Delta+1)$. Moreover, when the number of colors increases (*i.e.*, k $\rightarrow \infty$), the expected number of steps to reach a terminal configuration starting from an arbitrary configuration converges to n.

4   Conclusion

We investigated the intrinsic complexity of performing local tasks in unidirectional anonymous networks in a self-stabilizing setting. Contrary to "classical" bidirectional networks, local vertex coloring now induces global complexity (n states per process at least, n moves per process at least) for *deterministic* solutions. By contrast, we presented asymptotically optimal solutions for the *probabilistic* case (that actually match the bounds obtained for bidirectional networks). This work raises several important open questions:

1. Our probabilistic solution can be tuned to be optimal in space (and is then with a Δ multiplicative penalty in time), or optimal in time, but not both. However, our lower bounds do not preclude the existence of probabilistic solutions that are optimal for both complexity measures.
2. Our lower bound on the number of colors is generic (it should hold for graphs of any shape), while the *chromatic number* of a graph denote the actual number of colors that are needed to color a particular graph. It is worth investigating whether our protocol can color particular graphs with a lower number of colors.

References

1. Afek, Y., Bremler-Barr, A.: Self-stabilizing unidirectional network algorithms by power supply. Chicago J. Theor. Comput. Sci. (1998)
2. Bernard, S., Devismes, S., Potop-Butucaru, M.G., Tixeuil, S.: Optimal deterministic self-stabilizing vertex coloring in unidirectional anonymous networks. In: Proceedings of the IEEE International Conference on Parallel and Distributed Processing Systems (IPDPS 2009), Rome, Italy, May 2009. IEEE Press, Los Alamitos (2009)
3. Cobb, J.A., Gouda, M.G.: Stabilization of routing in directed networks. In: Datta, A.K., Herman, T. (eds.) WSS 2001. LNCS, vol. 2194, pp. 51–66. Springer, Heidelberg (2001)
4. Das, S.K., Datta, A.K., Tixeuil, S.: Self-stabilizing algorithms in dag structured networks. Parallel Processing Letters 9(4), 563–574 (1999)
5. Delaët, S., Ducourthial, B., Tixeuil, S.: Self-stabilization with r-operators revisited. Journal of Aerospace Computing, Information, and Communication (2006)

6. Dijkstra, E.W.: Self-stabilizing systems in spite of distributed control. Commun. ACM 17(11), 643–644 (1974)
7. Dolev, S.: Self-stabilization. MIT Press, Cambridge (2000)
8. Dolev, S., Schiller, E.: Self-stabilizing group communication in directed networks. Acta Inf. 40(9), 609–636 (2004)
9. Ducourthial, B., Tixeuil, S.: Self-stabilization with r-operators. Distributed Computing 14(3), 147–162 (2001)
10. Ducourthial, B., Tixeuil, S.: Self-stabilization with path algebra. Theoretical Computer Science 293(1), 219–236 (2003); Extended abstract in Sirocco 2000
11. Gradinariu, M., Tixeuil, S.: Self-stabilizing vertex coloring of arbitrary graphs. In: International Conference on Principles of Distributed Systems (OPODIS 2000), Paris, France, December 2000, pp. 55–70 (2000)
12. Hald, A.: A history of probability and statistics and their applications before 1750. Wiley Series in Probability and Mathematical Statistics: Probability and Mathematical Statistics, p. 586. John Wiley & Sons Inc., New York (1990) (A Wiley-Interscience Publication)
13. Mitton, N., Fleury, E., Guérin-Lassous, I., Séricola, B., Tixeuil, S.: On fast randomized colorings in sensor networks. In: Proceedings of ICPADS 2006, pp. 31–38. IEEE Computer Society Press, Los Alamitos (2006)
14. Nesterenko, M., Arora, A.: Tolerance to unbounded byzantine faults. In: 21st Symposium on Reliable Distributed Systems (SRDS 2002), p. 22. IEEE Computer Society Press, Los Alamitos (2002)
15. Norris, J.R.: Markov chains. Cambridge Series in Statistical and Probabilistic Mathematics, vol. 2. Cambridge University Press, Cambridge (1998); Reprint of 1997 original
16. Ross, S.M.: Introduction to probability models, 7th edn. Harcourt/Academic Press, Burlington (2000)

A Token-Based Solution to the Group Mutual l-Exclusion Problem in Message Passing Distributed Systems

(Short Paper)

Abhishek Swaroop[1] and Awadhesh Kumar Singh[2]

[1] Department of Computer Sc. and Engineering, G.P.M. College of Engineering,
G.T. Karnal Road, Delhi, India-110036
abhi_pul@yahoo.co.in
[2] Department of Computer Engineering, National Institute of Technology,
Kurukshetra, Haryana, India-136119
aksinreck@rediffmail.com

Abstract. The Group Mutual l-Exclusion (GMLE) problem is an interesting combination of two widely studied generalizations of the classical mutual exclusion problem namely, k-exclusion and group mutual exclusion (GME). In GMLE, up to l sessions can be held simultaneously. In the present exposition, we propose a token-based algorithm to the GMLE problem. To the best of our knowledge, this is the first token-based algorithm for the GMLE problem. The proposed algorithm satisfies all properties necessary for a GMLE algorithm.

Keywords: Concurrency, Token, Mutual exclusion, Request set.

1 Introduction

The Group Mutual-l Exclusion problem (GMLE) is a variant of the group mutual exclusion (GME) problem [2]. The GMLE problem was introduced and solved for the shared memory model by Vidyasankar [1]. Later on, Jiang [3] proposed a solution to the GMLE problem using k-write-read coteries. In GMLE problem, up to l groups (resources) can be accessed simultaneously and a process interested in any one of these l groups may enter in critical section (CS). However, a process interested in a group, other than these l groups, must wait. Any solution to the GMLE problem must satisfy safety, freedom from starvation, and l-deadlock avoidance properties [1].

In the present exposition, we propose a token-based solution to the GMLE problem, called DRS_GMLE, henceforth. The proposed solution is the first token-based solution for the GMLE problem. The number of available rooms at any point of time is indicated by a variable contained by the token. DRS_GMLE uses the concept of dynamic request sets [4] and the captain-follower approach [5].

We assume a fully connected, asynchronous distributed system, consisting of n processes. The processes are numbered from 1 to n. The communication channels are reliable and FIFO. We assume that T is the maximum message propagation delay.

2 Working of DRS_GMLE

The data structures used and pseudo code of DRS_GMLE are given in appendix A and appendix B respectively. Below, we present an overview of working of DRS_GMLE.

K. Kant et al. (Eds.): ICDCN 2010, LNCS 5935, pp. 178–183, 2010.
© Springer-Verlag Berlin Heidelberg 2010

A process may remain in one of the following states: (i) N-Not requesting (ii) R-Requesting (iii) EC-Executing in CS as captain (iv) HI-Holding idle token (v) EF-Executing in CS as follower (vi) WTT-Waiting $2T$ time before transferring TOKEN to new captain (vii) HS- not in CS but holding TOKEN as followers are in CS.

There are four possibilities for a requesting process, say P_i. (i) P_i is not holding the TOKEN. P_i forwards its request to all processes in its request set, and waits for the TOKEN or ALLOW message. (ii) P_i is in state HS. If the token queue is not empty the request is added in the token queue. However, if the token queue is empty and there exists a compatible room, P_i changes its state to EC and enters CS. On the other hand, if the token queue is empty, no compatible room exists, and a free room is available then P_i enters CS as captain. Otherwise, the request is added in the token queue. (iii) P_i is in state HI. P_i initiates a new session by occupying a room and enters in CS as captain. (iv) P_i is in state WTT. The request is added in the token queue.

On receiving a request from P_j, P_i discards the stale requests. Otherwise, P_i takes action according to its state. (i) P_i is in state R and $j \notin RS_i$. It adds j in its request set and forwards P_i's request to P_j. (ii) P_i is executing in CS as captain. P_i tries to find an open room compatible with P_j's request. On successfully finding a compatible room, it adds P_j in the list of followers for the room and sends an ALLOW message to P_j. However, if no room, compatible with P_j's request exists and an empty room is available, P_i opens a new room, adds P_j in the follower's list of the room, and sends an ALLOW message. Nevertheless, if no room is compatible with g and no free room is available, the request is added in the token queue. (iii) P_i is in state HI. It transfers the TOKEN to P_j. (iv) P_i is in state HS. If the token queue is empty, P_i tries to find a room compatible with P_j's request. If a compatible room exists, P_j is added in its list of followers, and P_i sends an ALLLOW message to P_j. Otherwise, it checks whether a free room is available. If so, it changes state to WTT, informs all followers that P_j will be next captain, and sends TOKEN to P_j after $2T$ time. However, if token queue is not empty or no free/compatible room is available, request is added in the token queue.

The captain waits for $2T$ time units, before transferring the TOKEN, so that the followers, which are still in CS, may receive the information about the new captain. If a follower has already sent COMPLETE message to the current captain before receiving INFORM message, the message will reach the current captain before transferring the TOKEN to the new captain.

Upon receiving ALLOW message, P_i enters CS as follower. P_i sends a COMPLETE message to captain on exiting from CS.

When process P_i receives a COMPLETE message from P_j for room t_x, it may be in any one of the following four states. (a) P_i is in state R. It adds P_j in $rec\_comp_i[t_x]$. (b) P_i is in state EC. It removes P_j from follower's list of room t_x and checks, if all followers have come out of room t_x. If so, it increments t_ra and changes the data structures associated with room t_x accordingly. Further, if token queue is not empty and t_x is not the room occupied by P_i, it opens room t_x by selecting the group at the front of the token queue and sends ALLOW message to all processes requesting this group. (c) P_i is in state WTT. P_i removes P_j from corresponding followers list. (d) P_i is in state HS. It removes P_j from the followers list of room t_x. If there is no pending request in the token queue, and all rooms are empty, P_i sets its state to HI. However, if queue is empty or all rooms are occupied, P_i holds the token in state HS. On the other hand, if there are pending requests and some rooms are free, P_i selects process at the front of the token queue as the next captain and group requested by it as the next group, informs followers in CS about next captain, and sends TOKEN to next captain after $2T$ time.

Upon receiving the TOKEN, process P_i removes those processes from the corresponding follower's lists from which it received the COMPLETE message before receiving the TOKEN. Subsequently, it modifies the data structures related to the rooms accordingly. P_i sends an ALLOW message to all processes having pending requests compatible with any of the open rooms. Further, if some rooms are free and there are still pending requests in the token queue, P_i selects groups from token queue, opens rooms using selected groups, and invites the processes to join these rooms.

On exiting CS, captain P_i checks whether all followers of room occupied by it, have exited. If so, it increments t_ra and modifies data structures accordingly. Now, there are three possibilities. (i) All rooms are empty and there is no pending request. P_i holds the TOKEN in state HI. (ii) The token queue is empty or there is no empty room. P_i holds the TOKEN in state HS. (iii) There are some empty rooms and pending requests too. P_i sets its state to WTT, adds all possible token holders in its request set, selects next captain and next group, and informs all followers, which are still in CS, about new captain. P_i transfers TOKEN to the new captain after $2T$ time.

3   Correctness of DRS_GMLE

Theorem 1. The total number of groups being accessed by the processes in CS at any point of time is less than or equal to l.

Proof. DRS_GMLE ensures that all the processes, occupying a particular room, use the same group. The variable t_ra initialized to l, denotes the number of free rooms available. The value of t_ra is decremented on opening a room and a room is not opened until $t\_ra > 0$. Hence, at most l groups can be accessed simultaneously.

Lemma 1. If P_i and P_j are two processes then *either* $P_j \in RS_i$ *or* $P_i \in RS_j$.

Proof. Initially, the condition is true as the request set of P_1 is empty and the request set of any other processes P_i contains all other processes except P_i. It can be proved by induction on events changing request sets that the condition remains true.

Lemma 2. The request of P_i will eventually reach the TOKEN holding process.

Proof. The proof is obvious from lemma 1 and working of DRS_GMLE.

Theorem 2. The request of a process P_i for group g will eventually be serviced.

Proof. Let us assume the contrary. An arbitrary process P_i is starving. Thus, P_i could receive neither TOKEN nor ALLOW message. Now, there are two possible cases. (i) The request of P_i could not reach the token holding process (captain). (ii) P_i is forced to wait indefinitely in the token queue. However, from lemma 2, first possibility can not occur. Thus, only case (ii) is possible. Since, the token queue is an FCFS queue; therefore, P_i will be waiting indefinitely in the token queue, if the token queue is not moving. In other words, the process at the front of the token queue is forced to wait indefinitely. This is only possible, if the captain is not able to transfer the TOKEN to the front element of the token queue. This can happen if either (a) the captain is executing in CS indefinitely or (b) the captain is not executing in CS and all rooms are occupied with the followers and the captain is waiting indefinitely for their exit. However, since a process may remain in CS only for a finite time and the captain holding the token in state HS, stops permitting new processes in the presence of a conflicting request, none of the above two operations namely, (a) and (b) can continue for infinitely long time. Therefore, initial assumption is wrong and the theorem holds.

Theorem 3. DRS_GMLE satisfies the *l*-deadlock avoidance property.

Proof. The variable t_ra associated with the token ensures that not more than l groups can be accessed simultaneously by the processes in CS. Moreover, if there are less than l open rooms and the token holding process receives a request for a new group, it immediately opens a new room and sends permission to the requesting process. Hence, the *l*-deadlock avoidance property is satisfied in DRS_GMLE.

4   Performance of DRS_GMLE

The message complexity, maximum concurrency, light load waiting time and heavy load synchronization delay of DRS_GMLE are $O(n)$, n, $2T$, and $4T$ respectively. The simulation experiments were conducted in order to evaluate the performance of DRS_GMLE. The major results have been presented in figure 1.

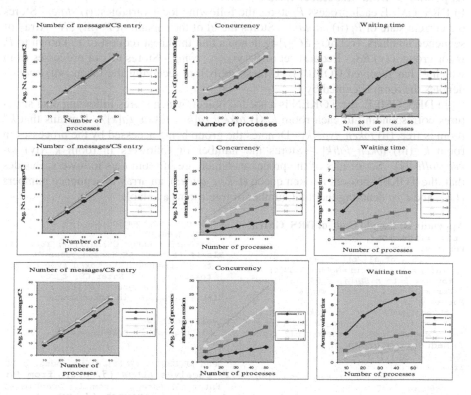

Fig. 1. Performance comparison of DRS_GMLE

5 Conclusions

In this paper, we proposed a token-based algorithm (DRS_GMLE) to solve the GMLE problem in message passing systems. DRS_GMLE satisfies the necessary requirements for GMLE problem, namely safety, starvation freedom, and l- deadlock avoidance. In DRS_GMLE, the total number of rooms can be increased or decreased easily by changing the value of a variable.

References

1. Vidyasankar, K.: A Simple Group Mutual-l Exclusion Algorithm. Information Processing Letters 85(2), 79–85 (2003)
2. Joung, Y.J.: Asynchronous Group Mutual Exclusion (extended abstract). In: 17th annual ACM Symposium on Principles of Distributed Computing, pp. 51–60 (1998)
3. Jiang, J.R.: A Distributed Group k-Exclusion Algorithm using k-Write-Read Coteries. In: International Computer Symposium 2004, pp. 1346–1351 (2004)
4. Chang, Y.I., Singhal, M., Liu, T.: A Dynamic Token-Based Mutual Exclusion Algorithm. In: 14th International Phoneix Conference on Computer and Comm., pp. 240–246 (1991)
5. Swaroop, A., Singh, A.K.: A Token-Based Fair Algorithm for Group Mutual Exclusion in Distributed Systems. Journal of Computer Science 3(10), 829–835 (2007)

Appendix A: Data Structures Used
In DRS_GMLE each process P_i stores the following local variables: (i) $state_i$ - Stores the current state of P_i (ii) $captain_i$ - Stores the id of the captain of P_i (iii) SN_i- Array of sequence numbers. (iv) SG_i- $SG_i[j]=g$ denotes that the latest request of P_j known to P_i is for group g (v) RS_i - Request set of P_i (vi) rec_comp_i - Stores id's of processes from which P_i has received COMPLETE message before receiving the token (vii) $room_i$ - denotes the room occupied by P_i

In DRS_GMLE, the TOKEN is a special object, which stores following data structures corresponding to each room k. (i) $token\_ra[k]$ - $token\_ra[k] = 1$ means that k^{th} room is free. (ii) $token\_type[k]$ - Denotes the group being accessed by the processes in room k. (iii) $token\_fol[k]$ - Stores the number of followers in room k. (iv) $token\_follist[k]$ - Set of id's of the processes which are in room k as followers. Besides that, the TOKEN possess a token queue ($token\_queue$), an array of sequence numbers (LN), and t_ra denoting the total number of free rooms available.

Appendix B: Pseudo Code of DRS_GMLE

```
Initialization:
For i =1 to n
  RSᵢ = id's of all other processes;
  stateᵢ = N; captainᵢ=NULL;    LN[i] = 0
  For j = 1 to n SNᵢ[j] = 0; SGᵢ[j] = " "
  For k= 0 to l-1 rec_compᵢ[k] = " "
For k= 0 to l-1
  token_type[k] = " ";  token_ra[k]=1
  token_fol[k]= 0;token_follist[k]= " "
token_queue= ∅;RSᵢ=∅; stateᵢ= HI; t_ra=l
Pᵢ Requesting group g:
SNᵢ[i]++; SGᵢ[i]=g
If (stateᵢ=HI)
  t₁=get_freeroom( ); token_type[t₁]=g;
  token_ra[t₁]=0
  roomᵢ=t₁; LN[i]++; stateᵢ=EC; Enter CS
Elseif (stateᵢ=HS)
```

```
If((t₂=get_comproom(g ))!= -1) &&
  (token_queue=∅)
  stateᵢ=EC; enter CS;LN[i]++; roomᵢ=t₂
Elseif (t_ra>0) && (token_queue=∅)
  t₁=get_freeroom( ); token_type[t₁]=g;
  token_ra[t₁]=0; Enter CS; t_ra--
  roomᵢ=t₁; stateᵢ=EC; LN[i]++ ;
Else add request in token_queue

Elseif (stateᵢ=WTT)
  Add request in token_queue
Else
  stateᵢ=R
  Send REQUEST(i,SNᵢ[i],g) to nodes in RSᵢ
Pᵢ receives ALLOW (j, g,tₖ) from Pⱼ:
  Enter CS;stateᵢ=EF;roomᵢ=tₖ; captainᵢ=j
Pᵢ receives REQUEST (j ,RN, g)
If (RN>SNᵢ[j])
```

```
SNᵢ[j]=RN; SGᵢ[j]=g
Switch (stateᵢ)
Case R:

 If  j∉RSᵢ

  Append j in RSᵢ;
  Forward Pᵢ's request to Pⱼ
 Case EC:
  If((t₂=get_comproom(g))!= -1)
    LN[j]++; token_fol[t₂]++
    Append j in token_follist[t₂]
    Send ALLOW (i,g,t₂) to Pⱼ
  Elseif((t₁=get_freeroom())!= -1)
    t-ra--; token_ra[t₁]=0
    token_follist[t₁]=j; LN[j]++
    token_type[t₁]=g;token_fol[t₁]=1;
    Send ALLOW (i,g,t₁) to Pⱼ
  Else append request in token_queue
Case HI:
  Append j in RSᵢ;t₁=get_freeroom();
  token_fol[t₁]=0; token_type[t₁]=g;
  token_follist[t₁]=∅;t_ra--;
  token_ra[t₁]=0;
  Send TOKEN (t₁, g, token_queue,
  LN,token_fol, token_follist,
  token_type, token_ra, t_ra) to Pⱼ
Case WTT: If ( j∉RSᵢ ) add j in RSᵢ
     Append request in token_queue
Case HS:
  If ((t₂=get_comproom(g))!= -1) &&
  (token_queue=∅)
  token_fol[t₂]++; LN[j]++;
  Append j in token_follist[t₂]
  Send ALLOW (i,g,t₂) to Pⱼ
  Elseif ((t₁=get_freeroom( )) != -1)
   stateᵢ=WTT;Call sel_nextcoord(t₁)
  Else append request in token_queue
Case N/EF:

 If ( j∉RSᵢ ) Append j in RSᵢ

Pᵢ exits from CS:
If (stateᵢ=EF)
  Send COMPLETE (i,roomᵢ) to captainᵢ
  stateᵢ=N; captainᵢ=NULL;
Else
  tₓ = roomᵢ;
  If (token_fol[tₓ]==0)
  t_ra++;token_ra[tₓ]=1;
  token_type[tₓ]=" "
If(t_ra=1) && (token_queue=∅)
  stateᵢ=HI
Elseif ((t_ra=0)||(token_queue=∅))
  stateᵢ=HS
Else
  t₁=get_freeroom( );stateᵢ=WTT ;
  Call sel_nextcoord( t₁)
Pᵢ receives COMPLETE (j,tₓ):
If (stateᵢ=R) Append j in rec_compᵢ[tₓ]
Elseif (stateᵢ=EC)
  token_fol[tₓ]--;
  Remove j from token_follist[tₓ]
  If (token_fol[tₓ]=0) && (tₓ!=roomᵢ)
  t_ra++;token_type[tₓ]= " ";
  token_ra[tₓ]=1
  If (token_queue≠ ∅)
   Let gₖ is the group at the front
   of token_queue;Send ALLOW (i, gₖ,
   tₓ) to processes in token queue
   requesting gₖ; remove these from
```

```
token_queue; Update LN, token.fol
and token_follist; t_ra--;
token_ra[tₓ]=0; token_type[tₓ]=gₖ
Elseif (stateᵢ=HS)
  token_fol[tₓ]--;
  Remove j from token_follist[tₓ]
  If (token_fol[tₓ]=0)
  t_ra++; token_type[tₓ]= " ";
  token_ra[tₓ]=1
  If (t_ra=1) && (token_queue=∅)
    stateᵢ=HI
  Elseif (t_ra=0) || (token_queue=∅)
    stateᵢ=HS
  Else
    t₁=get_freeroom( ); stateᵢ=WTT ;
    Call sel_nextcoord(t₁)
  Else
   Remove j from token_follist[tₓ];
   token_fol[tₓ]--
Pᵢ receives TOKEN(tₓ, g, token_queue,
LN,token_fol, token_follist,
token_type,token_ra,t_ra):
token_ra[tₓ]=0; t_ra--; roomᵢ=tₓ
token_type[tₓ]=g; stateᵢ=EC;Enter CS;
Remove Pᵢ's request from token_queue
Update token_queue; LN[i]++
Foreach room t₁
  Foreach x in rec_compᵢ[t₁]
   Remove x from token_follist[t₁];
   token_fol[t₁]--;
   If (token_fol[t₁]==0)
   t_ra++;token_ra[t₁]=1;
   token_type[t₁]=" "
Foreach room tᵧ
  Foreach process x in token_queue
   If x requesting group token_type[tᵧ]
    Send ALLOW(i,token_type[tᵧ],tᵧ) to x
    Remove x's request from token_queue
    token_fol[tᵧ]++; LN[x]++
    Append x in token_follist[tᵧ];
Foreach room t₁ except tₓ
  If (token_ra[t₁]=1)&& (token_queue=∅)
  Let gₖ is group at front of to-
  ken_queue; t_ra--; token_ra[t₁]=0;
  token_type[t₁]=gₖ;Send ALLOW (i,gₖ,
  t₁) to nodes in token_queue
  requesting for gₖ;  Remove these
  from token_queue;Append them in
  token_follist[t₁]; increment
  token_fol[t₁] and LN accordingly
Pᵢ receives INFORM from Pⱼ
If (captainᵢ!=NULL) captainᵢ=j
Sel_nextcoord(tₓ)
```
Append all possible token holders in
RSᵢ; Select the process at the front of
token_queue as next_ c and its group as
next_g; Inform followers still in CS
about new captain next_c; Forward TOKEN
(tₓ, next_g , token_queue, LN,
token_fol, token_follist, token_type,
token_ra,t_ra) to next_c after 2T time
```
get_freeroom( )
```
If (a room tₓ is free) return (tₓ)
Else return (-1)
```
get_comproom(g)
```
If (room tₓ with token_type[tₓ]=g is
available) return (tₓ) Else return (-1)

The Weak Network Tracing Problem

H.B. Acharya[1] and M.G. Gouda[1,2]

[1] The University of Texas at Austin, USA
[2] The National Science Foundation, USA
{acharya,gouda}@cs.utexas.edu

Abstract. Computing the topology of a network in the Internet is a problem that has attracted considerable research interest. The usual method is to employ Traceroute, which produces sequences of nodes that occur along the routes from one node (source) to another (destination). In every trace thus produced, a node occurs by either its unique identifier, or by the anonymous identifier $"*"$. We have earlier proved that there exists no algorithm that can take a set of traces produced by running Traceroute on network N and compute one topology which is guaranteed to be the topology of N. This paper proves a much stronger result: no algorithm can produce a small set of topologies that is guaranteed to contain the topology of N, as the size of the solution set is exponentially large. This result holds even when every edge occurs in a trace, all the unique identifiers of all the nodes are known, and the number of nodes that are irregular (anonymous in some traces) is given. On the basis of this strong result, we suggest that efforts to exactly reconstruct network topology should focus on special cases where the solution set is small.

1 Introduction

A wide variety of networked applications can be optimized for performance using information about the underlying network, i.e. the topology of the actual connectivity graph showing the paths along which packets are routed. One example of such an approach is P4P [11], which enables P2P networks to optimize traffic within each ISP and reduce cross-ISP traffic. Considerable research has been devoted to the problem of reconstructing the topology of a network in the Internet [9].

The usual mechanism for generating the topology of a network is by the use of Traceroute [5]. Traceroute is executed on a node, called the source, by specifying the address of a destination node. This execution produces a sequence of identifiers, called a *trace*, corresponding to the route taken by packets traveling from the source to the destination. A trace set T is generated by repeatedly executing Traceroute over a network N, varying the *terminal* nodes, i.e. the source and destination.

In theory, given that T contains traces covering every node and every edge, it is possible to reconstruct the network exactly. However, in practice, there arise problems: incomplete coverage, anonymity (nodes may refuse to state their unique identifiers), and aliasing (nodes may have multiple unique identifiers).

K. Kant et al. (Eds.): ICDCN 2010, LNCS 5935, pp. 184–194, 2010.

The situation is further complicated by load balancing, which may cause incorrect traces; tools such as Paris Traceroute [10] attempt to correct this problem.

This paper deals with the node anonymity problem. An anonymous node in a trace may or may not be identical to any other anonymous or named node. Consequently, there may be multiple topologies for the computed network, all of which can generate the observed trace set. Previous work, as discussed in Section 5, employs heuristics to compute a topology with a "small" number of anonymous nodes. We consider the extreme case where no nodes are consistently anonymous; a node may be anonymous in some trace, but there exists at least one trace in trace set T where it states its unique identifier. Such nodes are called *irregular* nodes. In our earlier paper [1] we have proved that even in this special case, given a trace set it is not in general possible to compute a unique network topology, or even a constant number of network topologies. This paper proves a much stronger negative result: there is no general algorithm that takes as input a trace set and computes a solution set (of all possible network topologies) of polynomial size. This result is true even if m, the number of anonymous nodes, is known a priori; the size of the solution set is worst-case exponential in m. Further, we show that the result holds even under multiple strong assumptions (stable and symmetric routing, unique identifiers, and complete coverage). This proves that the problem remains intractable to the strongest known network tracing techniques, such as Paris Traceroute and inference of missing links [8].

In the next section, we formally define terms such as network, trace and trace set, so as to be able to develop our mathematical treatment of the problem.

2   Networks, Traces and Network Tracing

In this section, we present formal definitions of the terms used in the paper. We also explain why we assume several strong conditions. Finally, we provide a formal statement of the problem studied.

2.1   Term Definitions

A network N is a connected graph where nodes have unique identifiers. Nodes are either *regular* or *irregular*, and either *terminal* or *non-terminal*. (These terms are used below.)

A *trace* is a sequence of node identifiers.

A trace t is said to be *generable from* a network N iff the following four conditions are satisfied:

(a) t represents a simple path in N.
(b) The first and last identifiers in t are the unique identifiers of terminal nodes in N.
(c) Each regular node "a"in N appears as "a" in t.
(d) Each irregular node "$a/*$"in N appears as either "a" or "$*_i$" in t, where i is a unique integer in t.

A *trace set* T is *generable from* a network N iff the following five conditions are satisfied:

1. Every trace in T is generable from N.
2. For every pair of terminal nodes x, y in N, T has at least one trace between x and y.
3. Every edge in N occurs in at least one trace in T.
4. The unique identifier of every node in N occurs in at least one trace in T.
5. T is *consistent*: for every two distinct nodes x and y, exactly the same nodes must occur between x and y in every trace in T where both x and y occur.

These conditions, and our reasons for assuming them, are discussed in detail below.

2.2 Generable Trace Sets

The five conditions, that we impose on a trace set T to be generable from a network N, may appear too strong. However, as we illustrate below, if any one of these conditions is not satisfied by a trace set T, then trace set T becomes generable from an exponentially large number of networks.

As an example, we exhibit a trace set T_1 that is generable from any one of $m!$ networks when Condition 5 is not satisfied by T_1, but Conditions 1 through 4 are.

$$T_1 = \{(a, b_1, d), (a, b_2, d), \ldots (a, b_m, d),$$
$$(a, *_1, c_1, d), (a, *_2, c_2, d), \ldots (a, *_m, c_m, d)\}$$

The terminal nodes are a and d, while the nodes $b_1, ..b_m$ and $c_1, ..c_m$ are non-terminal nodes. As a and d appear with their unique identifiers in every trace, they are definitely regular nodes.

It is straightforward to show that the trace set T_1 can be generated from every member of the family of networks shown in Figure 1. This family consists of $m!$ networks, since $\{b_{i1}, b_{i2}, .., b_{im}\} = \{b_1, b_2, .., b_m\}$ but there are $m!$ permutations that satisfy this condition.

Note that there is no way to decide which unique identifier corresponds to any of the anonymous identifiers $*_1, *_2 .. *_m$. If we only assume that there are no loops in a route, then each of the anonymous nodes may still correspond to several unique identifiers. For example, $*_1$ may correspond to any one of the identifiers $b_1, b_2..b_m$; $*_2$ may correspond to any of the remaining identifiers, and so on. Hence the number of topologies is $m!$.

Our results are negative, and bound the power of any algorithm to take as input a trace set generable from network N and compute the topology of N. In order to show that we do not depend on conditions like inconsistent routing, which may or may not be true, we assume the worst case, develop our theory assuming that all these conditions are met, and prove that our results are still valid.

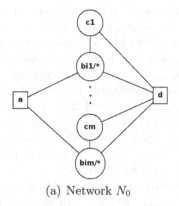

(a) Network N_0

Fig. 1. A family of topologies for T_1

2.3   The Weak Network Tracing Problem

We can now state a formal definition of the problem studied in this paper.

The *weak network tracing problem* can be stated as follows: "Design an algorithm that takes as input a trace set T, that is generable from a network, and produces a small set $S = \{N_1, .., N_k\}$ of networks such that T is generable from each network in this set and not from any network outside this set." We have previously proved [2] that the cardinality of S is not bounded by a constant. The current paper proves that the problem is indeed unsolvable - the size of the solution set S is, in general, exponential in the number of irregular nodes (and therefore not small). (From this, it is trivial to see that the original network tracing problem, which is similar to the weak problem but requires that the solution set S have exactly one network, is unsolvable.)

3   The Impossibility of Weak Network Tracing

In this section, we begin by considering the special case of a network with exactly one irregular node, and show how to construct a pathological trace set. This construction is then extended to show how the number of possible network topologies grows with the number of irregular nodes. The formal analysis, proving that the solution set is exponential in size for this trace set, is given in Section 4. (Note that we count all topologies which only differ in which nodes are marked as irregular, as a single topology.)

3.1   Weak Tracing with One Irregular Node

Consider the simplest possible trace with an anonymous node, $(a, *_1, b)$. This trace cannot be the only trace in a trace set generable from any network, because by consistent routing neither a nor b lie on the path connecting a and b, so the unique identifier of at least one node - $*_1$ - is unknown. This violates condition 4 (from Section 2).

We add two new traces (a, x_1, y_1) and (b, x_1, y_1). This introduces the new node y_1 and identifies $*_1$ to be x_1, as it is the only node one hop from a (and also the only node one hop from b). Note that it was essential to add two new traces rather than one, as y_1 is a new terminal, and so by condition 2 there is at least one trace connecting y_1 to every other terminal - a and b.

We can repeat this step an arbitrarily large number of times, adding the new traces (a, x_i, y_i) and (b, x_i, y_i) for $i = 1, 2..k$. In order to satisfy Condition 2, we also add the traces (y_i, y_j) for all $i \neq j$. For brevity, we name the whole operation (adding the two traces, and adding traces to maintain a completely connected graph among the y_i) 'Op1'. Note that k, the number of times we choose to execute Op1, is a positive integer.

For any value of k, the trace set is generable from a network; further, given $k > 1$, it is not possible to state which x_i corresponds to $*_1$.

All the topologies generated thus far are identical, only differing in the placement of the irregular node. (For the case where $k = 3$, this topology is shown in network N_1 of Figure 2. In the figure, we show $*_1 = x_1$.) Now we take the critical step : we replace

(a, x_1, y_1) with $(a, *_1, y_1)$,
and (b, x_1, y_1) with $(b, *_1, y_1)$.

This step will be referred to as 'Op2'.

The trace set is no longer generable from a network, as Condition 4 (all identifiers must occur in a trace set) is now violated. We replace

$(a, *_1, b)$ with (a, x_1, b),

so the trace set is generable from a network again. This step is called 'Op3'.

The importance of this change is that, now, we no longer know which node connects y_1 to a or b. Setting $*_1 = x_i$ produces a different topology for every i. (The different topologies are not even necessarily isomorphic.) Note that we could have selected any one x_i (instead of x_1) and interchanged its place with $*_1$ in the trace set; the results would have been the same.

As an example, we present the special case when $k = 3$ in Figure 2. The trace set

$$T_2 = \{(a, x_1, b), (a, *_1, y_1), (a, x_2, y_2), (a, x_3, y_3),$$
$$(b, *_2, y_1), (b, x_2, y_2), (b, x_3, y_3),$$
$$(y_1, y_2), (y_1, y_3), (y_2, y_3)\}$$

is generable from any of the three networks N_1, N_2 and N_3 in the figure. Note that all these networks have exactly one irregular node; hence, even if the number of irregular nodes is known, it does not help to distinguish between them.

3.2 Weak Tracing in a General Network

We now extend the previous construction to the case of a general network with $m > 0$ irregular nodes.

First, we observe that simply repeating the previous construction and allowing the presence of m irregular nodes will result in the same number of topologies

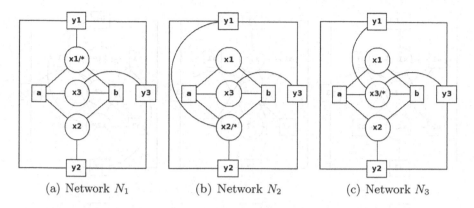

(a) Network N_1 (b) Network N_2 (c) Network N_3

Fig. 2. Networks generable from T_2

as allowing only one. The reason is that, in our trace set, the only traces with
the identifier x_i are (a_i, x_i, y_i) and (b_i, x_i, y_i). Both these traces identify which
x-node y_i is connected to. When we apply Op2 to replace the identifier x_i with
an anonymous identifier, the resultant trace set is no longer generable from a
network. To make the trace set generable from a network again, we must apply
Op3 after Op2, and specify a path (a, x_i, b). Unfortunately, we cannot apply
Op3 more than once; once we specify a path (a, x_1, b), Condition 5 - consistent
routing - prevents us from specifying any other path (a, x_i, b) where $i \neq 1$. Hence
we cannot replace any other x_i with an anonymous identifier.

In order to overcome this problem, we introduce more a and b nodes. We
rename the original terminals a and b to a_1 and b_1, and add new pairs of terminals
a_2 and b_2 , .., a_m and b_m. Each of these terminals is connected to x_1 .. x_k, i.e.
the exact same connections as the original a and b. To achieve this in the trace
set, we add the traces (a_i, x_i, b_i) and (a_i, x_i, y_i) for all i.

To satisfy Condition 2, which states that there must exist at least one trace
between every pair of terminals, there must also be traces connecting every a_i
to a_j and b_j, $j \neq i$. There are many ways we can write such traces; for this
construction,we simply add the traces (a_i, x_1, a_j) and (a_i, x_1, b_j) for all values of
i and j. We call the entire operation involved in adding one new pair of terminals
'Op4', so Op4 is executed m times.

We can now perform Op2 multiple times, choosing a node x_i every time. In
each execution, we replace all traces $(\Box, x_i, y_i)$ with $(\Box, *_j, y_i)$ where $\Box$ is any
identifier. Note that we no longer need to explicitly perform Op3. The reason is
that, in this construction, we have already added traces of the form (a_i, x_i, b_i).
Even though the traces (a_i, x_i, y_i) and b_i, x_i, y_i are lost, the remaining trace
(a_i, x_i, b_i) contains the identifier x_i. As all five conditions are still satisfied, the
trace set remains generable from a network after Op2 is executed.

Note that there are two upper bounds on the number of times that Op2 can
be executed - k, the number of nodes x_i, and m, the number of irregular nodes.
As our goal is to demonstrate the existence of a trace set that is generable

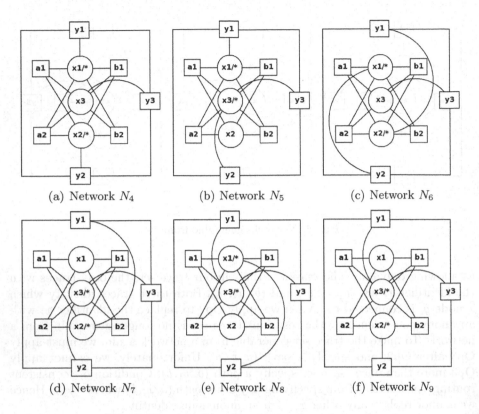

(a) Network N_4 (b) Network N_5 (c) Network N_6

(d) Network N_7 (e) Network N_8 (f) Network N_9

Fig. 3. Networks from T_3 with two irregular nodes

from each of an exponential number of topologies, we are free to specify any (satisfiable) conditions for this set. We now add the condition that $m \leq k$. In our construction, we may choose any m of the k available x_i-nodes as irregular nodes, so there are $\binom{k}{m}$ distinct trace sets that can be constructed by our method.

We now present as an example a trace set generated with the parameters $m = 2, k = 3$. For our example, the x_i identifiers that we replace with anonymous identifiers are x_1 and x_2. The trace set

$$T_3 = \{(a_1, x_1, b_1), (a_1, x_1, a_2), (a_1, *_1, y_1), (a_1, *_2, y_2), (a_1, x_3, y_3), (a_1, x_1, b_2)$$
$$(a_2, x_1, b_1), (a_2, x_2, b_2), (a_2, *_3, y_1), (a_2, *_4, y_2), (a_2, x_3, y_3)$$
$$(b_1, *_5, y_1), (b_1, x_1, b_2), (b_1, *_6, y_2), (b_1, x_3, y_3),$$
$$(b_2, *_7, y_1), (b_2, *_8, y_2), (b_2, x_3, y_3),$$
$$(y_1, y_2), (y_1, y_3), (y_2, y_3)\}$$

is generable from any of the networks N_4, N_5, N_6, N_7, N_8, and N_9 in Figure 3. Note that all these networks have exactly two irregular nodes. If the number of irregular nodes was not known, the networks N_{10}, N_{11} and N_{12} in Figure 4 would also be members of the solution set.

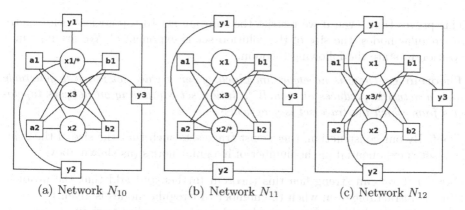

(a) Network N_{10} (b) Network N_{11} (c) Network N_{12}

Fig. 4. Networks from T_3 with one irregular node

4   Size of the Solution Set

In this section, we use the trace set constructed in Section 3 and derive a formal proof that the number of candidate topologies computed from any such trace set is exponential.

Multiple topologies are possible because, for m of the y_i nodes, the only available information is that they are known to be connected to some irregular node. It is not possible to determine exactly which x_i-nodes they are connected to.

By construction, there are k x_i-nodes.

If the number of irregular nodes is not known, then from the trace set, for each of m y_i-nodes there are k possible x_i-nodes to choose to connect to, and the total number of valid topologies is at least k^m. (The number is actually larger because there is no reason to assume that each y_i-node connects to exactly one x_i-node. For example, given the traces $(a_5, *_i, y_8)$ and $(b_5, *_j, y_8)$, we do not know that $*_i = *_j$. However, if we consider only the cases when every y_i-node connects to exactly one x_i-node, we see there are k^m cases. As this is the size of a subset of the solution set, k^m is a lower bound on the number of topologies, and is clearly exponential.)

Now we deal with the case when the number of irregular nodes in a topology is exactly m. In this case, when a y_i-node "chooses" which x_i-node to connect to, it cannot choose an x_i-node that has already been chosen by another y_i-node. Hence the number of topologies is

$$^k P_m = \frac{k!}{(k-m)!}$$

Hence the number of possible topologies is

$$\frac{k!}{(k-m)!} = (k-m+1).(k-m+2)..(k)$$

$$\geq 1.2..m$$

$$= m!$$

$$\geq 2^{m-1}$$

This proves that, even if we restrict the solution set to topologies with exactly m irregular nodes, the size of the solution set is exponential. We are now in a position to state the following theorem.

Theorem 1. *There is no algorithm which, given a trace set which is generable from a network, produces an "small" solution set containing all network topologies from which the trace set is generable.*

Proof. By our construction, there exist trace sets such that the size of the solution set is exponential in the number of irregular nodes (as shown above).

(Note that we can strengthen this theorem further and add that the problem remains intractable even when the number of irregular nodes is given.)
We will now show how these results relate to our earlier work in [2].

We express k is terms of m and n, where n is the total number of nodes. Observe that in the construction, we start with two unique identifiers(a and b), remove two identifiers (again a and b), and add new identifiers by executing Op2 (k times) and Op4(m times). Also note that each execution of Op2 or Op4 adds two new identifiers, and as each node has exactly one unique identifier, the number of unique identifiers is also n.

Using the notation $\#(a_i)$ to represent the number of a_i nodes etc. we have

$$\#(a_i) = \#(b_i) = k$$
$$\#(x_i) = \#(m_i) = m$$
$$\Rightarrow k + k + m + m = n$$
$$\Rightarrow k = \frac{n - 2m}{2}$$

We can now state the following theorem:

Theorem 2. *Given a trace set generable from a network, and known to have exactly one irregular node, the size of the solution set (ie. the number of network topologies that the trace set is generable from) is linear in the number of unique identifiers.*

Proof. We substitute $m = 1$ into the equations derived above. The size of the solution set is given by

$$\frac{k!}{(k-1)!} = k$$
$$= \frac{n - 2m}{2}$$
$$= \frac{n - 2}{2}$$

which is clearly $O(n)$.

This is obviously a stronger version of Theorem 7 in [2], which states that the size of the solution set is not upper-bounded by any constant.

5   Related Work

Anonymous router resolution is an established problem in topology mapping studies. Unfortunately, many authors simply avoid dealing with the problem. For example, in [5], the authors stop traces as soon as they encounter an anonymous router. In [4], authors handle anonymous routers by replacing them either with arcs connecting known routers, or with random fresh unique identifiers. It is trivial to see that both approaches produce inaccurate maps. The "sandwich" approach used in [3], merges a chain of anonymous nodes, "sandwiched" between the same pair of known nodes, with each other - thereby losing resolution.

The theoretical study of the router resolution problem was started by Yao et al., who formulate it as an optimization problem [12]. Their goal is to build the smallest possible topology by combining anonymous nodes with each other under two constraints : trace preservation and distance preservation. They prove that the optimum topology inference under these conditions is NP-complete, then propose an $O(n^5)$ heuristic.

All further study of the problem has been based on heuristics. Jin et al. propose two approaches in [9]. The first, an ISOMAP based dimensionality reduction approach, uses link delays or node connectivity as attributes in the dimensionality reduction process. This is an $O(n^3)$ algorithm. (Their approach has been attacked as they ignore the difficulty of estimating individual link delays from round trip delays in path traces [6].) The second, a simple $O(n^2)$ neighbor matching heuristic, suffers from accuracy problems: it has high rates of both false positives and false negatives. Gunes et al. propose their own heuristics in [7], and show performance strictly better than $O(n^3)$ for five heuristics they apply in succession.

In our work, we try to return to a rigorous theoretical approach, and identify a problem complementary to that studied by Yao; in their study, the authors assume that all anonymous nodes must remain consistently anonymous, while in [1] we explore what happens if no nodes are truly anonymous, only irregular. In [2], we show that the (strong) network tracing problem is unsolvable in the general case, but provide special cases of networks, such as trees and odd rings, where it becomes solvable. We also begin our study of the weak network tracing problem. This paper reports our results from studying weak network tracing, strengthens our earlier results, and proves (by counterexample) that there exists no general algorithm to produce a complete but "small" solution set.

6   Conclusion

This paper concludes our study of the general weak network tracing problem, and proves that no solution exists. On this basis, we suggest that research in network tracing focus on special cases that are known to be tractable; for instance, trees and odd rings. We anticipate the scope for a rich body of future work that studies which topologies are tractable to compute from their trace sets. Further, as our theory is developed under strong constraints such as complete coverage and consistent routing, it would be interesting to study whether these topologies remain easy to compute as these constraints are relaxed.

As our work is graph-theoretic in nature and does not make use of any domain-specific information, we anticipate that it may also be of interest in other problem domains. For example, in social networks which allow an observer to see that A and B are friends-of-friends but not who their mutual friend is, the mutual friend is an irregular node. In such a case, we can use the results in this paper to state that, in general, plotting the social network from "chains of friends" (traces) is a provably hard problem.

References

1. Acharya, H.B., Gouda, M.G.: Brief announcement: The theory of network tracing. In: Principles of Distributed Computing (May 2009) (Accepted)
2. Acharya, H.B., Gouda, M.G.: The theory of network tracing. In: 11th International Symposium on Stabilization, Safety, and Security of Distributed Systems (June 2009) (Submitted for review)
3. Bilir, S., Sarac, K., Korkmaz, T.: Intersection characteristics of end-to-end internet paths and trees. In: 13th IEEE International Conference on Network Protocols, pp. 378–390 (November 2005)
4. Broido, A., Claffy, K.C.: Internet topology: connectivity of ip graphs. Scalability and Traffic Control in IP Networks 4526(1), 172–187 (2001)
5. Cheswick, B., Burch, H., Branigan, S.: Mapping and visualizing the internet. In: Proceedings of the USENIX Annual Technical Conference, pp. 1–12. USENIX Association, Berkeley (2000)
6. Feldman, D., Shavitt, Y.: Automatic large scale generation of internet pop level maps. In: IEEE Global Telecommunications Conference (GLOBECOM), December 4, pp. 1–6 (2008)
7. Gunes, M., Sarac, K.: Resolving anonymous routers in internet topology measurement studies. In: INFOCOM 2008. The 27th Conference on Computer Communications. IEEE, pp. 1076–1084 (April 2008)
8. Gunes, M.H., Sarac, K.: Inferring subnets in router-level topology collection studies. In: Proceedings of the 7th ACM SIGCOMM conference on Internet measurement, pp. 203–208. ACM Press, New York (2007)
9. Jin, X., Yiu, W.-P.K., Chan, S.-H.G., Wang, Y.: Network topology inference based on end-to-end measurements. IEEE Journal on Selected Areas in Communications 24(12), 2182–2195 (2006)
10. Viger, F., Augustin, B., Cuvellier, X., Magnien, C., Latapy, M., Friedman, T., Teixeira, R.: Detection, understanding, and prevention of traceroute measurement artifacts. Computer Networks 52(5), 998–1018 (2008)
11. Xie, H., Yang, Y.R., Krishnamurthy, A., Liu, Y.G., Silberschatz, A.: P4p: provider portal for applications. SIGCOMM Computer Communications Review 38(4), 351–362 (2008)
12. Yao, B., Viswanathan, R., Chang, F., Waddington, D.: Topology inference in the presence of anonymous routers. In: Twenty-Second Annual Joint Conference of the IEEE Computer and Communications Societies. IEEE, March-3 April 2003, vol. 1, pp. 353–363 (2003)

Poisoning the Kad Network*

Thomas Locher[1], David Mysicka[1], Stefan Schmid[2], and Roger Wattenhofer[1]

[1] Computer Engineering and Networks Laboratory (TIK), ETH Zurich, Zurich, Switzerland
{lochert,wattenhofer}@tik.ee.ethz.ch, dmysicka@ethz.ch
[2] Deutsche Telekom Laboratories, TU Berlin, Berlin, Germany
stefan@net.t-labs.tu-berlin.de

Abstract. Since the demise of the Overnet network, the Kad network has become not only the most popular but also the only widely used peer-to-peer system based on a distributed hash table. It is likely that its user base will continue to grow in numbers over the next few years as, unlike the eDonkey network, it does not depend on central servers, which increases scalability and reliability. Moreover, the Kad network is more efficient than unstructured systems such as Gnutella. However, we show that today's Kad network can be attacked in several ways by carrying out several (well-known) attacks on the Kad network. The presented attacks could be used either to hamper the correct functioning of the network itself, to censor contents, or to harm other entities in the Internet not participating in the Kad network such as ordinary web servers. While there are simple heuristics to reduce the impact of some of the attacks, we believe that the presented attacks cannot be thwarted easily in any fully decentralized peer-to-peer system without some kind of a centralized certification and verification authority.

1 Introduction

Peer-to-peer (p2p) computing is one of the most intriguing new networking paradigms of the last decade. Not only do structured p2p systems, which typically implement a distributed hash table (DHT), possess crucial advantages over centralized systems for applications such as reliable data dissemination, structured p2p systems may also play a pivotal role in the challenging endeavor to redesign the Internet due to their valued properties such as small routing tables, fault tolerance, and scalability.

In this paper, we question whether the p2p approach is mature enough to step outside of its "comfort zone" of file sharing and related applications. In particular, not much is known about the ability of DHTs to meet critical security requirements (as those required nowadays, e.g., for domain name servers) and its ability to withstand attacks. To this end, as a case study, we evaluate the feasibility of various attacks in the Kad network, as it is currently the most widely deployed p2p system based on a DHT with more than a million simultaneous users [15].

Our study reveals that while the Kad network functions reliably under normal operation, today's Kad network has several critical vulnerabilities, despite ongoing efforts on

---

* Research in part supported by the Swiss National Science Foundation (SNF).

K. Kant et al. (Eds.): ICDCN 2010, LNCS 5935, pp. 195–206, 2010.

the developers' part to prevent fraudulent and destructive use. This paper describes several protocol exploits that prevent peers from accessing particular files in the system. In order to obstruct access to specific files, file requests can be hijacked, and subsequently, arbitrary information can be returned instead of the actual data. Alternatively, we show that publishing peers can be overwhelmed with bogus information such that pointers to the original files can no longer be accessed. Moreover, it is even possible to *eclipse* certain peers, i.e., to fill up their routing tables with information about malicious peers, which can subsequently intercept all messages. Additionally, we briefly discuss how our network poisoning attacks can also be used to harm machines outside the Kad network, e.g. web servers, by tricking the peers into performing a Kad-steered distributed denial of service (DDoS) attack. It is virtually impossible to determine the true culprit in this scenario, as the peer initiating the attack does not take part in the attack, which makes this kind of attack appealing to malicious peers.

All our attacks have been tested on the real Kad network using a modified C++ eMule client. Already with three attackers, virtually no peer in the system was able to find content associated with any given keyword for several hours, which demonstrates that with moderate computational resources access to any targeted content can be undermined easily.

The remainder of this paper is organized as follows. The basic functionality of Kad is described in Section 2. We present and evaluate our attacks in Section 3. Section 4 briefly discusses crucial implications of the attacks and points out the difficulty of finding effective countermeasures. After reviewing related literature in Section 5, the paper concludes in Section 6.

2   eMule and Kad

The Kad network is a DHT-based p2p network that implements the *Kademlia protocol* [10]. Access to the Kad network is provided through the *eMule*[1] client, which can also connect to the server-based *eDonkey*[2] network.

Each peer in the Kad network has a 128-bit identifier (ID) which is normally created by a random generator. This ID is stored at the peer even after it has left the network and is re-used once the peer returns. Routing in the network is performed using these identifiers and the XOR metric, which defines the distance between two identifiers as the bitwise exclusive or (XOR) of these identifiers interpreted as an integer. For all $i \in [0, 127]$, every peer stores the addresses of a few other peers whose distance to its own ID is between 2^i and 2^{i+1}, resulting in a connected network whose diameter is logarithmically bounded in the number of peers. For each of these *contacts* in the routing table, a Kad ID, an IP address, and a port is stored.

The publish and retrieval mechanisms work roughly as follows. Each keyword, i.e., a word in a file name, and the file itself, are hashed, and information about the keywords, its associated file, and the address of the owner is published in the network, i.e., this information is stored at the peers in the DHT whose identifers are closest to the respective hash values. More specifically, in Kad, information is replicated ten times in a

---

[1] See http://www.emule-project.net/
[2] See http://en.wikipedia.org/wiki/EDonkey_network/

zone where peers agree in the first 8 bits with the published key. Usually, this so-called *tolerance zone* contains several thousand peers. While most of the peers are very close to the key, this is not always the case, e.g., due to churn and also for keys that are very popular and published by many different peers.

If a peer wants to download a file with a certain name (a particular sequence of keywords), it first queries the peer whose identifier is closest to the hash of the *first* of the specified keywords, and this peer returns the information of all files whose file names contain all the given keywords, and also the corresponding file hashes. The requesting peer p_1 can then download the desired file by querying the peer p_2 whose identifier is closest to the file hash, as p_2 keeps track of all the peers in the network that actually own a copy of the file.

3   Attacks

This section presents three different attacks which limit the Kad network's participants access to a given file f. In a *node insertion attack*, an attacking peer seeks to attract search requests for f, which are answered with bogus information. Alternatively, access to f can be denied by filling up the index tables of other peers publishing information about f (*publish attack*). Finally, we describe how an attacker can *eclipse* an arbitrary peer: By controlling all the peer's incoming and outgoing traffic, the attacker can prevent a peer from either publishing information about f or from accessing it.

3.1   Node Insertion Attack

By performing a *node insertion attack*, it is possible to corrupt the network by spreading polluted information, e.g., about the list of sources, keywords, or comments. We have implemented the attacks for *keywords*, that is, a search for the attacked keyword will not give the correct results, but instead arbitrary data chosen by the attacker is returned.

For this attack to work, we have to ensure that the search requests for the specific keyword are routed to the attacking peer rather than to the peers storing the original information. This can be achieved as follows. In the Kad network, a peer normally creates its ID using a random number generator; however, any alternative mechanism will work as well, as there is no verification of a peer's ID. In our modified eMule client, it is possible to select the peer's Kad ID manually. Thus, an attacker can choose its ID such that it matches the hash value of the targeted keyword. Consequently, the peer will become the node closest to this ID and will receive most of the corresponding search requests. The nodes storing the correct files typically have a larger distance to the keyword's ID than the attacker, as the probability for a peer to have a random ID that perfectly matches the 128-bit keyword ID is negligible.

In order to guarantee that peers looking for a certain keyword only receive faked results, the attacker must provide enough result tuples, as the eMule client terminates the search after having gathered 300 tuples. The attacker further has to include the keywords received from a peer in the filenames, otherwise the replies are not accepted. In our attacks, we use filenames that contain a unique number, the message "File removed from Kad!", and the keywords. Unique file hashes are needed such that the 300 tuples are not displayed as one tuple in eMule's search window.

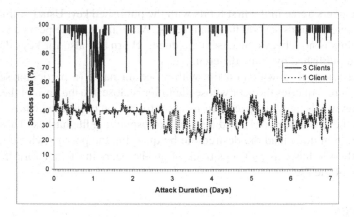

Fig. 1. Percentage of successfully hijacked keyword requests in a node insertion attack for 1 and 3 attackers during a time period of one week

We frequently observed that eMule sends search requests not only to the closest peer, even though this peer provided enough answers. This can be explained by the delay caused when transmitting the 300 search results from the closest peer. eMule will send another request to the second closest peer before all of the results are received from the closest one. This of course may harm the effectiveness of the attack, and hence it is beneficial to gain control over the second, third, etc. closest IDs as well by means of additional attackers. These attackers behave exactly the same way: All requests are answered by supplying 300 faked tuples.

Figure 1 depicts the traces obtained during two week-long node insertion attacks performed using our modified eMule client on the keyword "Simpsons." Note that this attack influences all queries in the entire Kad network not only for the search term "Simpsons", but also all other queries starting with the term "Simpsons" such as "Simpsons Movie" or "Simpsons Soundtrack" etc. are affected automatically.

In the first trace, only one attacker whose ID exactly matches the hash of the keyword infiltrated the network. We used another client to search for the term "Simpsons" once a minute and examined the returned results. Since a single attacker is not sufficient, as mentioned before, the attack is moderately successful in that only approximately 40% of the returned results originated from the attacker. What is more, every single query returned at least some results that are not faked. Further experiments showed that using two attackers instead of one does not increase the success rate substantially, but three attackers is already enough to hijack virtually all requests. The second trace shows the success rate of the node insertion attack using three attackers. On average, more than 95% of all returned tuples were faked, and every batch of tuples contained at least some bogus data created by the attackers. The plot shows that there are sudden drops of the success rate once in a while. An explanation for this behavior is that peers join and leave the network at a high rate, resulting in inaccurate routing tables. Consequently, a lookup request can be routed to a peer that still stores results for this request and does not know about our attacking peers yet.

The attack was repeated at other times using different keywords. All our other experiment resulted in a similar picture and confirmed our findings made with the "Simpsons" keyword. Our attacking peers received roughly 8 requests per minute from other peers in the network during the experiments. As expected, the peer having the closest ID received the most requests at a rate of roughly 4 requests per minute.

3.2 Publish Attack

In contrast to the node insertion attack, which forces the search requests to be routed to the attacker, the publish attack directly attacks the peers closest to the ID of the attacked keyword, comment, or source entry. The index tables stored by the peers in the Kad network have a limited length; for instance, the keyword table can store up to 50,000 entries for a specific ID. Moreover, a peer will never return more than 300 result tuples per request, giving priority to the latest additions to the index table. This makes it possible to replace the original information by filling up the tables of the corresponding peers with poisoned entries. Thus, an attacker seeks to publish a large amount of information on these peers. Once the index tables of the attacked peers are full, they will not accept any other publish requests by other peers anymore. Therefore, the attacked peers will only return our poisoned entries instead of the original information. Since every entry has an expiration time (24 hours for keyword and comment entries, and 5 hours for source entries), the clients have to be re-attacked periodically in order to achieve a constant fraction of poisoned entries. In addition, an attacker has to take into consideration the newly joining peers in the network; if they have an ID close to the one attacked, their tables also have to be filled.

We have implemented the publish attack for keyword entries as well, again by modifying the original eMule application. An existing timer method is used to run the attack every 10 minutes. In the first phase, the 12 peers closest to the targeted ID are located using eMule's search mechanism. In each run, only peers are selected that have not been attacked before or that need to be re-attacked due to the expiration of the poisoned entries. In the second phase, all the peers found in the first phase are attacked, beginning with the closest peer found. In order to guarantee a full cache list, 50,000 poisoned entries are sent divided into 250 packets containing 200 entries each. In order to prevent overloading the attacked client, the sending rate was limited to 5 packets per second. Every entry consists of a unique hash value and filename as in the node insertion attack. Since these entries ought to match all search requests containing the attacked keyword, it is necessary to include all additional relevant keywords (e.g. song titles for an interpreter, year and language for a film title) in the filename; otherwise, all the lookups with additional keywords would not receive the poisoned entries, because not all the keywords are included. In the node insertion attack, this problem does not occur as the additional keywords are obtained from every search request and can directly be appended to the filename to match the request. The success of each run is measured with the load value sent in every response to a publish packet. This value should increase with every poisoned packet sent, from a starting level of about 10 - 20% to 100% when the attack is finished.

In comparison to the node insertion attack, it is clearly harder to maintain a high success rate using the publish attack, due to the permanent arrivals of new peers and

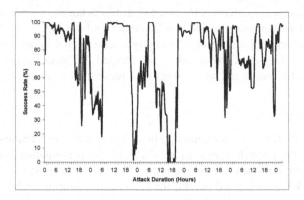

Fig. 2. Percentage of faked replies received in a publish attack for the keyword "Simpsons" during a time period of 5 days. Sometimes, the success rate drops but then recovers again quickly.

the need to re-attack the peers periodically. While the node insertion attack yields constantly high rates, this is not true for the publish attack. Figure 2 plots the success rate of an attack on the keyword "Simpsons" over a period of 5 days. While the attack works fairly well on average, at a success rate of roughly 80%, the success rate periodically drops and remains low for a certain time period before it recovers again.

Overall, the success rate is much lower than in the case of a node insertion attack, although performing a publish attack is much more expensive. Again, repeating the attack at other times using different keywords results in a similar pattern. The reason for this peculiar behavior is that the peers responsible for the targeted IDs that are online during the phase where the success rate is low refuse to accept our publish messages. In fact, these peers do not even reply to publish messages, even though they can be contacted, otherwise we could not receive any lookup results from them. As this behavior is not in accord with the protocol implemented in the real eMule client, we suspect that modified versions of the original client cause this effect. What clients are used is hard to determine as they do not directly provide this information. Thus, the use of modified clients appears to be another reason why the node insertion attack is superior to the publish attack. In order to improve the success rate, a more sophisticated implementation could be used where the attack is split up into two concurrent processes. The first one would permanently search for new peers with an ID close to the one attacked and pass them to the second process which would then attack these peers simultaneously. This would minimize the time during which peers can respond with original data. As this improvement would not solve the problem of uncooperative peers, it was not implemented.

3.3 Eclipse Attack

Instead of poisoning the network to keep peers from obtaining certain information, we can also attack the requesting peers directly and keep them from sending requests into the Kad network. In the eclipse attack, the attacker takes over the targeted peer's routing table such that it is unable to communicate with any other peer in the Kad network except the attacker. As the attacker simulates the whole Kad network for that peer, it can manipulate the attacked peer in arbitrary ways, e.g., it can specify what results are returned for any lookup, or modify comments for any file. The peer's requests can also be directed back into the Kad network, but modified arbitrarily.

Typically, the contacts in the Kad routing table are not uniformly distributed over the whole ID space. Rather, most of the contacts are located around the peer's ID to maintain short lookup paths when searching for other peers in the Kad network (cf. [10]). The attacker takes advantage of the fact that there are relatively few contacts in most parts of the ID space. Concretely, we inject faked peer entries into these parts of the routing table to achieve a dominating position. Subsequently, the faked peers are selected for almost all requests. If we set the IP address of all those faked entries to the address of our attacking peer, we receive most requests of the attacked peer and can process them as desired. We make use of the fact that the standard eMule client accepts multiple neighbors of the same IP address.

Our measurements showed that a peer running eMule for an extended period of time has up to 900 contacts in its routing table. As the maximum number of contacts is 6,310, there is plenty of space in the routing table for faked entries. In order to inject faked entries the *Hello Request* message is used, which is normally utilized during connection set up to check whether known peers are still alive. As a side-effect of this message, the sender of the message is added to the receiver's routing table. After enough entries are injected, the attacking peer has to process the requests from all those entries in order to keep them in the routing table of the attacked node.

We implemented the eclipse attack in a stand-alone application and ported all necessary parts from the source code of eMule. The application maintains a list that holds all faked entries sent to the attacked peer. This is necessary, because every new entry in the routing table is validated by sending a hello request. This request has to be answered

Table 1. Percentage of faked replies received during 10 runs of the eclipse attack. Each run r was measured 15 minutes with an interval of one minute.

Minute	r_1	r_2	r_3	r_4	r_5	r_6	r_7	r_8	r_9	r_{10}	$\bar{r}$
1.	0	0	0	0	0	0	0	0	0	0	0
2.	0	0	0	0	0	0	0	0	0	0	0
3.	0	0	0	0	0	0	0	0	0	0	0
4.	0	0	0	81	0	0	78	0	0	0	15.9
5.	72	100	100	65	23	100	81	81	100	65	78.7
6.	78	100	90	72	85	100	78	72	100	81	85.6
7.	81	82	100	81	78	81	100	78	100	100	88.1
8.	65	100	100	100	81	100	100	68	81	100	89.5
9.	58	100	100	95	100	100	100	89	100	100	94.2
10.	78	100	100	100	100	100	98	100	100	100	97.6
11.	100	100	100	100	100	100	100	100	100	100	100
12.	100	100	100	100	100	100	100	100	100	100	100
13.	100	100	100	100	100	100	100	100	100	100	100
14.	100	100	100	100	100	100	100	100	100	100	100
15.	100	100	100	100	100	100	100	100	100	100	100

with the same ID as we have chosen when injecting the entry. In order to differentiate between the entries, we assign a new port to every faked entry and maintain a data structure to store this information. The other part of our application processes the requests of the attacked peer. If it asks for new peers close to a specific ID, we reply with new faked peers that match this ID, or are very close to it, to guarantee the success of the attack. If the peer asks for stored information we deliver poisoned results, as in the two attacks discussed before.

Table 1 shows the results of 10 repeated eclipse attacks under the same conditions. To measure the success rate of the attacks, we periodically ran searches on the attacked peer and counted the number of poisoned results. As the success rate virtually always reaches 100% within minutes, we can conclude that the attack works well, especially if the attack is focused on a single keyword, but it is naturally limited to merely a single attacked peer. The other two attacks are clearly preferable if an attacker aims at hiding content from *all* peers.

4 Discussion

The preceding section has presented three different attacks that can be used to keep peers from acquiring the requested information. Naturally, these attacks can also be combined in order to increase the chances of a successful attack. However, these poisoning attacks cannot only be used for this purpose. Rather, they can serve an attacker as basic building blocks to pursue completely different aims.

We will now briefly illustrate how they can be used for another attack. The resources of the Kad network's peers and our attacks can be used to drive a *distributed denial of service attack* (DDoS) against any machine internal or external to the Kad network as follows: A node insertion attack is performed in order to occupy some popular keywords. Let μ be the machine (e.g., a server) to be attacked. We inform all requesters that μ contains the desired files. Consequently, all requests are directed to the attacked machine. Of course, the resulting load on μ is not larger than on the machine performing the node insertion. However, the advantage of this attack is that the attacking machine *remains hidden*; moreover, it is generally harder to counter a distributed DoS attack than a normal DoS attack as the requests originate from different (and valid) IP addresses. Also the Publish Attack can be used for the DDoS attack if we advertise wrong IP bindings of keywords. This has the additional advantage that the attack induces more load on the attacked machine than on the attacker, as the different Kad peers are directed to the attacked machine directly. Note that DDoS attacks using a p2p system such as Kad are particularly nasty as the peers store information about sources for a long period of time, implying that such an attack could last several days with steadily changing peers involuntarily performing the attack.

As all the described attacks can be performed easily and have a large impact, it is mandatory to derive and implement counteractive measures. In order to overcome the node insertion attack it must be guaranteed that choosing specific IDs is infeasible. A straightforward approach, which is often described in literature (and which is used, e.g., by the Azureus BitTorrent client), is to bind the ID directly to the peers' IP addresses, e.g., by hashing the IP address. However, there are several reasons why real-world p2p systems do not adhere to this simple rule. First, multiple peers may share the same IP address, for example, peers in a local area network behind a NAT router are typically addressed using the same public IP address. These peers would all have the same peer identifier. Second, IP addresses are often given out dynamically and the assignment of addresses may change. In case of an ID-IP binding, this implies that peers have to rebuild their routing tables when reconnecting to the network with a new IP. Additionally, all the credits gathered by uploading data would be lost irretrievably because the peer ID changed and hence the peer cannot be recognized by other peers anymore. It seems that some of these problems can be solved easily and the IP address can still be incorporated into the ID, e.g., by hashing the IP address and a randomly chosen bit string to solve the NAT problem, or by using a different, randomly chosen ID for the credit system, together with a public and private key pair to protect it against misuse.[3] Hashing the IP address and a user-generated bit string is preferable to including the port as this would require a static assignment of ports, and switching ports would also lead to a new ID. However, the crucial observation is that creating such a binding is not sufficient to avert the attack in general, as long as the ID includes a user-generated part. Assuming that a hash function such as SHA-1 is used, an attacker can try out millions of bit string in a short period of time in order to generate an ID that is closest to the targeted keyword even in a network containing more than a million peers. These observations indicate that some form of peer authentication is required, which is hard to achieve without the use of a centralized verification service. As part of the strength of the network is its completely decentralized structure, relying on servers does not seem to be an acceptable solution.

A simple heuristic to render the Kad network more resilient to publish and eclipse attacks is to limit the amount of information a peer accepts from the same IP address, i.e., a peer does not allow that its entire contact list is filled by peers using the same IP address. This is also a critical solution as several peers behind a NAT may indeed have the same public IP address. What is more, an attacker with several IP addresses at its disposal can circumvent this security measure.

A crucial observation is that many of the discussed vulnerabilities do not only pertain to the Kad network, such attacks can be launched against any fully decentralized system that does not incorporate strong verification mechanisms. We believe that in recent literature, some promising approaches have been proposed, especially the work on join-leave attacks [13] by Scheideler, who studies how to spread peers over a virtual ID space $[0, 1)$ in a robust way. In [4], Awerbuch and Scheideler proposed a robust distributed (round-robin) random number generator. Interestingly, while constructing a single random number is difficult, it turns out that a *set of random numbers* can be generated by a group of peers in a scalable manner that is resilient to a constant fraction of adversarial peers. Unlike the verifiable secret sharing algorithm described in [2], their solution cannot fail if the initiating peer does not behave correctly, and a peer cannot rerun the protocol sufficiently many times until an ID is generated that falls into a desired range. This is certainly a desirable property to overcome the node insertion attacks described in this paper. However, important questions remain open, for instance, how to handle concurrent rejoin operations, or how to cope with ongoing DoS attacks.

---

[3] In fact, Kad already uses public and private keys to authenticate peers whenever a new session starts.

5   Related Work

Peer-to-peer networks have become the most popular medium for bulk data dissemination, and a large fraction of today's Internet traffic is due to p2p file sharing.[4] The immense computational resources of p2p networks are also attractive to attackers, and there is already a large body of literature on the subject [5,20].[5] Reasons to attack a p2p system can be manifold: For example, a peer may seek to perform a more or less passive "rational attack" [12] to be able to benefit from the system without contributing any resources itself (see, e.g., the *BitThief* BitTorrent client [9]).

While such selfishness can threaten a peer-to-peer system, which essentially relies on the participants' contributions, there are more malicious attacks seeking to harm the system directly. An attacker may, for example, strive to partition the system or to eclipse individual nodes. The eclipse attack [14], as also described in this work, can be used by a set of malicious peers to position themselves around a given peer in the network such that the peer's contact list consists only of the colluding peers. In a *Sybil attack* [7], a single entity creates multiple entities of itself in order to gain control over a certain fraction of the system. Such an attack can undermine redundancy mechanisms and is hard to counter in a completely decentralized environment. Attackers may also exploit a peer-to-peer system to efficiently spread a *worm* [21]. Furthermore, the resources of a p2p system may also be used to attack *any* machine connected to the Internet regardless of whether it is part of the peer-to-peer network or not. A *denial of service attack* can be launched in various p2p systems, e.g., Gnutella [1], Overnet [11], and BitTorrent [6]. During this attack, information about the victim, i.e., the targeted machine in the attack, is spread in the system. The victim is falsely declared as an owner of popular content, causing other peers searching for this content to contact the victim repeatedly. In BitTorrent, tracker information can be faked which leads peers to believe that the victim is a tracker for the desired content [6]. In the Kad network, DoS attacks can be launched by means of a redirection attack where a queried peer, the attacker, will return a response containing the address of the victim [19]. As mentioned before, the attacks presented in this work can also be used to launch a DoS attack.

The work closest in spirit to ours is the study of *index poisoning attacks* in FastTrack and Overnet [8]. Their index poisoning attack is akin to our publish attack where bogus information is pushed aggressively to the nodes responsible for the desired keywords. However, while this attack is also quite successful, it is not as effective in the Kad network as it is in FastTrack and Overnet. We showed that a different, even simpler poisoning attack is feasible and more effective. Moreover, our study of attacks in the Kad network is not limited to content poisoning and index poisoning, but also considers the eclipse attack to prevent peers from accessing a specific file. It is also worth pointing out that, in comparison to Kad, it is generally easier to perform attacks on Overnet, as it, e.g., does not check whether the sender of a publish message provided its own IP address as the owner of the file, and no cryptography is used for authentication.

While we believe that there are methods to contain the potential damage caused by such attacks to a certain extent, it is known that some sort of logically centralized entity

---

[4] See http://www.cachelogic.com/research/

[5] See also http://www.prolexic.com/news/20070514-alert.php/

is required to thwart attacks such as the Sybil attack [7]. There is also some interesting theoretical work on how to identify and exclude large sets of colluding peers [3]. However, the described techniques cannot be used to counter our attacks as we require only a very small number of attackers close to a given ID, which is not sufficient to raise suspicion. For a more thorough discussion of possible countermeasures against attacks in p2p networks, the reader is referred to the corresponding literature (e.g., [5]).

Finally, the *Kad network* itself has been the subject of various works. Stutzbach et al. [17] describe implementation details of Kad in eMule, and [18] presents crawling results on the behavior of Kad peers. Steiner et al. [15] collected an extensive, interesting set of data about the Kad network by crawling the network during several weeks. For example, they found that different classes of participating peers exist inside the network. Finally, [16] initiated the study of Sybil attacks in Kad. The authors propose to tie the possibility of obtaining a Kad ID to the possession of a cell phone number. Their solution therefore requires a centralized entity.

6 Conclusion

Structured peer-to-peer systems are likely to gain importance in the near future. This is mainly due to the fact that structured p2p networks have many desirable properties whose usefulness goes far beyond efficient file sharing. Driven by these properties, the use of DHTs or similar structured networks has been proposed as the foundation of the "future Internet" in order to overcome the deficiencies of today's Internet.

This paper has provided evidence that the Kad network, which is currently the only widely deployed p2p network based on a DHT, can be attacked with a small amount of computing resources such that access to popular files is denied. It is clear that such attacks could significantly lower the throughput of the entire system as the sought-after files are no longer found, and that this imposed censorship would frustrate the users. Moreover, the possibility of leveraging the immense computational resources of the entire system to attack arbitrary machines constitutes a serious threat. We argue that the presented attacks can basically be launched in any peer-to-peer system that does not incorporate sound peer authentication mechanisms.

We have discussed different approaches to overcome these vulnerabilities. While there are both practical and theoretical schemes that seem to improve the robustness, more research is needed how to apply them optimally "in the wild".

References

1. Athanasopoulos, E., Anagnostakis, K.G., Markatos, E.P.: Misusing Unstructured P2P Systems to Perform DoS Attacks: The Network That Never Forgets. In: Zhou, J., Yung, M., Bao, F. (eds.) ACNS 2006. LNCS, vol. 3989, pp. 130–145. Springer, Heidelberg (2006)
2. Awerbuch, B., Scheideler, C.: Towards a Scalable and Robust DHT. In: Proc. SPAA (2006)
3. Awerbuch, B., Scheideler, C.: Towards Scalable and Robust Overlay Networks. In: Proc. 6th Int. Workshop on Peer-to-Peer Systems, IPTPS (2007)
4. Baruch, A., Christian, S.: Robust Random Number Generation for Peer-to-Peer Systems. Theor. Comput. Sci. 410(6-7), 453–466 (2009)

5. Castro, M., Druschel, P., Ganesh, A., Rowstron, A., Wallach, D.S.: Secure Routing for Structured Peer-to-Peer Overlay Networks. In: Proc. OSDI (2002)
6. El Defrawy, K., Gjoka, M., Markopoulou, A.: BotTorrent: Misusing BitTorrent to Launch DDoS Attacks. In: Proc. 3rd Workshop on Steps to Reducing Unwanted Traffic on the Internet, SRUTI (2007)
7. Douceur, J.R.: The sybil attack. In: Druschel, P., Kaashoek, M.F., Rowstron, A. (eds.) IPTPS 2002. LNCS, vol. 2429, p. 251. Springer, Heidelberg (2002)
8. Liang, J., Naoumov, N., Ross, K.W.: The Index Poisoning Attack in P2P File Sharing Systems. In: Proc. INFOCOM (2006)
9. Locher, T., Moor, P., Schmid, S., Wattenhofer, R.: Free Riding in BitTorrent is Cheap. In: Proc. HotNets (2006)
10. Maymounkov, P., Mazières, D.: A Peer-to-Peer Information System Based on the XOR Metric. In: Druschel, P., Kaashoek, M.F., Rowstron, A. (eds.) IPTPS 2002. LNCS, vol. 2429. Springer, Heidelberg (2002)
11. Naoumov, N., Ross, K.: Exploiting P2P Systems for DDoS Attacks. In: Proc. 1st International Conference on Scalable Information Systems, INFOSCALE (2006)
12. Nielson, S.J., Crosby, S.A., Wallach, D.S.: A taxonomy of rational attacks. In: Castro, M., van Renesse, R. (eds.) IPTPS 2005. LNCS, vol. 3640, pp. 36–46. Springer, Heidelberg (2005)
13. Christian, S.: How to Spread Adversarial Nodes?: Rotate!. In: Proc. STOC (2005)
14. Singh, A., Ngan, T.-W.J., Druschel, P., Wallach, D.S.: Eclipse Attacks on Overlay Networks: Threats and Defenses. In: Proc. INFOCOM (2006)
15. Steiner, M., Biersack, E.W., Ennajjary, T.: Actively Monitoring Peers in the KAD. In: Proc. 6th Int. Workshop on Peer-to-Peer Systems, IPTPS (2007)
16. Steiner, M., En-Najjary, T., Biersack, E.W.: Exploiting KAD: Possible Uses and Misuses. SIGCOMM Comput. Commun. Rev. 37(5), 65–70 (2007)
17. Stutzbach, D., Rejaie, R.: Improving Lookup Performance over a Widely-Deployed DHT. In: Proc. INFOCOM (2006)
18. Stutzbach, D., Rejaie, R.: Understanding Churn in Peer-to-Peer Networks. In: Proc. 6th Internet Measurement Conference, IMC (2006)
19. Sun, X., Torres, R., Rao, S.: Preventing DDoS Attacks with P2P Systems through Robust Membership Management. Technical Report TR-ECE-07-13, Purdue University (2007)
20. Wallach, D.S.: A Survey of Peer-to-Peer Security Issues. In: International Symposium on Software Security (2002)
21. Zhou, L., Zhang, L., McSherry, F., Immorlica, N., Costa, M., Chien, S.: A first look at peer-to-peer worms: Threats and defenses. In: Castro, M., van Renesse, R. (eds.) IPTPS 2005. LNCS, vol. 3640, pp. 24–35. Springer, Heidelberg (2005)

Credit Reputation Propagation: A Strategy to Curb Free-Riding in a Large BitTorrent Swarm

Suman Paul[1], Subrata Nandi[2], and Ajit Pal[3]

[1] Department of Electronics & Electrical Communication Engineering,
Indian Institute of Technology Kharagpur, West Bengal - 721302, India
[2] Department of Computer Science & Engineering,
National Institute of Technology Durgapur, West Bengal - 721309, India
[3] Department of Computer Science & Engineering,
Indian Institute of Technology Kharagpur, West Bengal - 721302, India

Abstract. BitTorrent ensures cooperation among peers through its in-built collaborative mechanisms, however due to lack of proper incentives, significant amount of free riding is observed in it. Though in the existing literature, there exists some strategies to prevent free-riding, however, in case of large swarm sizes, it can be shown that they fail to stop free riding attempts effectively. To overcome this limitation, this paper presents a novel approach based on propagating the knowledge about the existence of possible free riders in the form of reputation among the peers within the swarm. It is shown, how a possible free riding attempt on a peer is reported to others and how this knowledge is utilized in deciding whether to upload to a particular peer or not within a BitTorrent swarm. Simulation results demonstrate how the proposed strategy effectively punishes free riders even in large swarm sizes.

1 Introduction

Peer-to-Peer (P2P) networks such as Gnutella, Napster, KaZaA and BitTorrent have risen in popularity and have become quite popular in recent times. Content distribution through these networks has emerged as a considerable portion [6] of Internet traffic within a few years. In order to ensure the growth and success of these networks, it is necessary to study two important properties viz., scalability and robustness, and overcome the existing shortcomings. BitTorrent is one of the most popular peer-to-peer content distribution protocols. The scalability properties of BitTorrent and its ability to handle flash crowds has resulted in its widespread usage. In June 2004, BitTorrent constituted 53% of all P2P traffic [7]. In 2006, 18% of all broadband traffic was due to BitTorrent [8].

Users who attempt to benefit from the resources of others without offering their own resources in exchange are termed *free-riders*. BitTorrent is based on collaborative contribution from its user. However, it is possible to exploit the incentive mechanism and not contribute to the network against the true spirit of P2P. Since a P2P network depends on the users for the specification of its quality of service (QoS), hence free-riding is detrimental to the performance of such a

K. Kant et al. (Eds.): ICDCN 2010, LNCS 5935, pp. 207–218, 2010.

network. Jun et. al. [4] showed that through minor modifications, a free-rider can achieve the same file download completion time as a contributor in BitTorrent. Sirivianos et al. [10] showed that by obtaining a larger than normal view of the BitTorrent *swarm*, a client can increase its chances of discovering seeds and of getting unchoked by leechers. Free riding is also present in P2P systems other than BitTorrent. In 2000, a measurement study of the Gnutella file-sharing network [9] found that approximately 70% of peers provide no files and that the top 1% of the peers are responsible for 37% of the total files shared. Similar patterns have been observed in subsequent studies of Napster and Gnutella networks [11]. In 2005, [12] found free-riders have increased to 85% of all Gnutella users.

Related Work: Several studies found that the incentive mechanism of BitTorrent is not enough to deter free-riding. Bharambe et al. [13] found that in some cases some peers upload as much as 6.26 times the amount they themselves download which represents considerable unfairness. Qiu and Srikant [14] presented a fluid model for BitTorrent-like networks and found that *optimistic unchoking* can induce free riding. Several modifications have been proposed to the original Bit Torrent protocol in order to make it more robust. Li et al. [3] proposed a mechanism by which *seeds*, i.e., nodes that have a complete copy of a file, service downloaders based on their current uploading rate. However, since the number of seeds is very few as compared to the number of leechers in case of large swarms, hence free riders cannot be punished effectively as they can still exploit leechers. Jun et al. [4] proposed an incentive mechanism in which peer would tolerate only a certain amount of deficit between the downloaded and the upload amount. This sort of strategy is equivalent to maintaining credit for the number of file pieces uploaded or downloaded for each peer in the system and is henceforth referred to as the Credit Based System(CBS). However, on analysis it is found that the modification proposed by Jun et al. effectively punishes free riders only when the swarm size is small.

Motivation and Objective: Consider as an example the following scenario: the tracker log of the 1.77GB Linux Redhat 9 distribution shows a flash crowd of more than 50,000 peers initiating a download in the first 5 days [5]. In such huge swarm sizes free riders can easily complete a download even if they get a single file piece from each peer. Later in section 3, we demonstrate that the existing CBS [4] strategy fails to work under such scenarios. Hence, it is essential that leechers communicate the knowledge of free riders among themselves to control the free-riding problem. The major contribution of this paper in dealing with the problem of free riding in large swarms is proposing a mechanism in which peers propagate the knowledge of free riders among themselves in the form of reputation earned according to the willingness to upload and take this information into account while deciding whether to upload to a peer.

The rest of the paper is organized as follows. Section 2 discusses in brief the BitTorrent protocol. Section 3 discusses the limitations of the Credit Based System in terms of handling free riding in large swarms while Section 4 describes the Credit Reputation Propagation Strategy and the metrics we use to evaluate the performance of the system. The results of the simulations have been presented and analyzed in Section 5. Finally, we conclude in section 5 by identifying the possible set of parameters using which the performance of BitTorrent can be improved.

2   Basics of BitTorrent

In this section we outline the key aspects of the basic BitTorrent protocol and explain why it is unable to stop or discourage free riding. BitTorrent is a protocol for distributing files[1]. In BitTorrent, files are split up into chunks (typically 256 KB) which are called pieces. A peer can download different pieces of a file from multiple peers at the same time while uploading in a similar fashion. There are three components in the system: trackers, seeds and leechers. The tracker for a file is the central server which keeps track of all the peers currently in the system and helps peers in finding each other. A seed is a peer with a complete copy of the file while leechers are those that are at various stages of completion of the download.

A peer that wants to download a file first connects to the tracker of the file. The tracker then returns a random list of peers that have the file. The downloader then establishes a connection to these other peers and finds out what pieces reside in each of the other peers. A downloader then requests pieces which it does not have from all the peers to which it is connected. BitTorrent follows the *rarest first policy* under which a peer first downloads the pieces that are most rare in its own peer set. Each peer uploads to only a fixed number of peer(unchoking) at a given time who are selected according to the download rate from them. Each peer tries to maximize its download rate by requesting pieces from peers with high upload rates. In order to allow each peer to explore the downloading rates available from other peers, BitTorrent uses *optimistic choking* [1]. Under this, each peer randomly selects a fifth peer from which it receives a downloading request and uploads to it. In case of BitTorrent seeds, they favor unchoking of the fastest downloaders regardless of their contribution to the network. So, the more is the number of seeds, the more it is conducive for free riders. Also, in a large swarm, a non compliant client can connect to more number of peers than the standard to increase its chances of becoming optimistically unchoked. However, the underlying challenge is to find a tradeoff between incentive and punishment as both compete against each other. Incorporating more incentives would make it fast while making it easier for users to free ride whereas imposing more punishments would lead to more number of compliant peers being penalized. Hence it is important to find an optimum balance between the two.

In the next section we outline the limitations of the Credit Based System as the size of the swarm increases.

3   Limitations of the Credit Based System

Jun et. al.[4] proposed the credit based system(CBS) in which a peer would only upload a definite number of chunks more than what it downloads from a particular peer. In other words, they proposed that if a peer uploads u pieces and downloads d pieces, the deficit $u\text{-}d$, called the nice factor, can be used to decide whether to maintain a link or not. In order to be altruistic and in order to enable other peers to bootstrap, a peer would always take the first initiative to upload a predecided number of piece called the 'nice factor'. However this credit based system is highly dependent on the size of the swarm as well as the size of the file being downloaded. If the size of the file is small and the number of leechers available in the swarm is large, free riders can exploit the tit-for-tat mechanism as well as CBS by downloading a few pieces of the file from each leecher as allowed by the nice factor. The large size of the swarm ensures that there are always leechers available to the free riders to download pieces of the file. Hence the free riders cannot be appropriately penalized by the existing system as even the availability of a single piece from each peer would be enough to complete a download. The simulation results attached provide further proof to this theory.

We quantify the effectiveness of the CRPS modification proposed by us in terms of the following metrics:

Mean download times: One of our main aims in proposing a modification to the BitTorrent protocol is to reduce the download times experienced by the leechers. Also in order to discourage free riding in the network we wish to punish free riders such that they experience download times that are higher from the leechers.

Difference in the download times: The only way of measuring the amount of punishment meted out to a free rider is to compare its download time with the mean download time of leechers. Our objective is always to maximize this difference. The more the difference in the download times of the leechers and free riders, the more effective we can term CRPS. However, at the same time we should keep in our mind that although the difference in the mean download times may be high, the download times of the leechers should not be too high in comparison to the CBS or the standard BitTorrent protocol as in such cases the modification proposed would be unrealistic.

Experiment: We plot the download completion times of leechers and free riders in a BitTorrent system and that of a Credit Based System. Fig 1(a) shows the download completion times of a BitTorrent swarm in our simulator. In Fig 1(a) the peer numbered 0 on the X axis is the seed while the peers numbered 1-25 and 26-50 are, respectively, the leechers and free riders. It can be seen from Fig 1(a) that there is no significant difference in the download times of the leechers and the free riders. So the free riders are able to achieve as much as the leechers while conserving precious upload bandwidth. Hence the incentive to upload which the original BitTorrent protocol was designed for is defeated.

In all our experiments, the seed is available to the leechers and free riders throughout the duration of the experiment. We vary the number of leechers as well as free riders is orders to simulate different situations. The simulations can be divided broadly into two types, one in which the size of the swarm is small and where we show the performance of our simulator for the BitTorrent

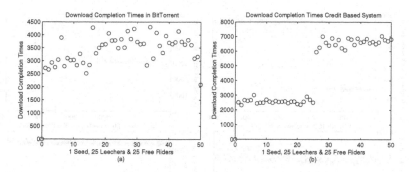

Fig. 1. (a) Download times taken by a BitTorrent swarm consisting of 25 leechers, 25 free riders and 1 seed (b) Download times taken in CBS for 25 leechers, 25 free riders and 1 seed in BitTorrent

protocol and CBS modification. The second type is the one in which the size of the swarm is large in comparison to the number of file pieces, where we show the failure of the CBS and highlight the success of CRPS in appropriately punishing free riders.

Fig 1(b) shows the download completion times for a swarm consisting of 1 seed, 25 leechers and 25 free riders under the credit based system proposed by Jun et. al. for a file having 132 pieces. It shows that CBS effectively discourages free riding because the download times experienced by the free riders is considerably high as compared to leechers. However, in this case the size of the swarm is small in comparison to the number of file pieces required to be downloaded. However, as mentioned earlier, this situation changes completely as the size of the swarm increases.

Experiment: We now analyze the case when the size of the swarm is large compared to the number of file pieces to be downloaded. We simulate a case where there are 500 leechers and free riders in the swarm. When the number of leechers is less, i.e., the population is dominated by the free riders as in the scatter plots of Figs 2(a) and 2(b), we find that CBS successfully penalizes the free riders. However it can be seen that the difference in the download time decreases significantly as the number of leechers is increased, indicating that the penalty faced by the free riders is quite less. In the case of Figs 2(c) and 2(d) where the the number of leechers has increased to 50% or more, we find that CBS has been rendered completely useless as there is either very little or no difference in the download times of the leechers and the free riders. The situation can be explained as follows. In CBS, every peer can download at least one file piece from every other peer before having to upload file pieces. If the size of the swarm is large, a free rider has enough number of leechers at its disposal to download file pieces for the entire file before having to contact the peers for a second time. Hence the need arises for a mechanism where a peer can report its information on free riders so that this exploitation can be prevented.

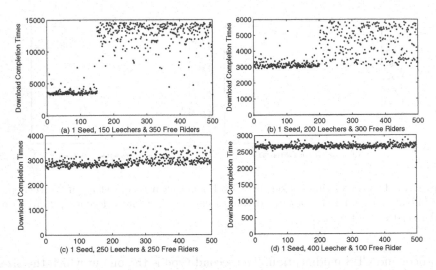

Fig. 2. Limitation of the CBS system in effectively penalizing free riders for a large swarm with varying leecher and free rider ratio and 132 file pieces

4   The Credit Reputation Propagation Strategy(CRPS)

Our aim is to make free riding more difficult and appropriately punish free riders even in large swarms by imposing additional restrictions over and above the BitTorrent protocol as well as the credit based modification. We propose to implement a *Credit Reputation Propagation Strategy* where every *free riding attempt* by a peer is reported to a predecided fraction of the swarm. A *free riding attempt* may be defined as a effort by peer, already under the nice factor deficit with another peer, to request another piece of the file. This free riding effort of a peer is reported to other peers by the peer to which the request has been made. All the peers in the CRPS modification of the BitTorrent protocol maintain a list of *free riding scores* of other peers in the swarm. Whenever a peer receives information about a free riding attempt from any of its neighbors, it increments this score. Also, whenever after downloading a file piece, a peer finds that the provider of the file piece has its free riding score above a particular threshold, it informs the predecided fraction of peers in the swam about this gesture. The receivers of this message respond to this by decrementing the free riding score of the peer. In this way a leecher, which might have been reported as a free rider by several of its neighbors in the swarm, can have its free riding score reduced in order to decrease its chances of being penalized in the future. Once the score crosses the *Upload Threshold*, it is blocked by all leechers in the swarm. Thus we have devised a policy of assigning every user a free riding score which other peers would use to decide whether or not to upload to a particular peer. As suggested in [4], a peer would upload only a certain number of chunks more than what it downloads from a particular peer as per the nice factor after which it is choked. Moreover, in our mechanism we additionally report the event of a peer being

Algorithm 1. CRPS Procedure

Peer A requests a piece from Peer B

 1: **if** (Pieces uploaded to A)-(Pieces downloaded from A) > *Credit Threshold* **then**
 2:     Update/Increment Free Riding Score of A in B's record
 3:     Randomly select $x\%$ peers from the swarm
 4:     Report A's free riding attempt to these peers
 5: **else**
 6:     **if** Free riding score of A < *Upload Threshold* **then**
 7:         Upload requested file piece to A
 8:         Increment pieces uploaded to A in B's record
 9:         Increment pieces download from B in A's record
10:     **end if**
11: **end if**

On receipt of a free riding attempt information of A from B
  C increments Free Riding Score of A in its record

---

choked due to non-compliance of the uploading policy by incrementing the *free riding score* and transmitting it to others in the swarm. This score is used by all peers in order to decide whether to upload to a particular peer or not. In the case of this score crossing a predefined threshold for a particular peer, it will be blocked by all the peers in that particular swarm. This policy would further deter free-riding. The details procedure is outlined in Algorithm 1. We verify this by comprehensive simulation test on our discrete simulator.

4.1   Critical Issues of the Strategy

The performance of the CRPS modification depends severely on the parameters discussed below.

Upload Threshold selection: The amount of strictness imposed on the network is defined by this parameter. A low threshold for the free riding score would mean that a very strict policy is being followed towards free riders. Also this would lead to more compliant peers being punished as well. The frequency of the scores is a random distribution and hence can be approximated by separate Gaussian distributions for leechers and free riders as shown in Fig 3. The point at which both these curves intersect gives us a possible Upload Threshold. An upload threshold lesser than this would mean that although free riders are punished very strictly, more numbers of leechers end up being penalized as well. An upload threshold beyond this point means that more importance is attached to leechers completing their downloads rather than punishing free riders.

Credit Threshold: This parameter is equivalent to the number of file pieces a peer is able to download before it has to start uploading or face being reported for free riding behavior. A strict credit limit policy would encourage more tit-for-tat

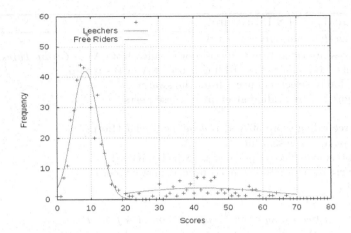

Fig. 3. Estimation of Upload Threshold using Gaussian function for 100% propagation

behavior. However, the overhead on the network in order to report free riding to others would also increase.

Fraction of peers score is reported: This parameters specifies the eagerness of the network in reporting free riding as well as the amount of overhead it can tolerate to report these events. A cent percent value of this fraction would result in free riders getting blocked more quickly while incurring a high overhead.

Score Updating Rule: Every peer maintains a score for other peers in the network. Whenever a free riding attempt is reported, this score is updated by other peers. The updating is done on a linear scale, i.e. the score is either incremented or decremented according to whether a free riding attempt or a piece uploading event was reported.

4.2   Metrics

In order to take into account both the incentive and punishment aspects while deciding the Upload Threshold, we use the metric:

$$M = \alpha \frac{[T_{leecher}]_{BTP}}{[T_{leecher}]_{CRPS}} + (1-\alpha)\frac{[T_{FR}-T_{leecher}]_{CRPS}}{[T_{FR}-T_{leecher}]_{Ideal}}, 0 < \alpha \le 1 \qquad (1)$$

where, $[T_{leecher}]_{BTP}$ denotes the mean download time taken by the leechers in the standard BitTorrent protocol. $[T_{leecher}]_{CRPS}$ denotes the mean download time taken by the leechers in the modified Credit Reputation Propagation Strategy. $[T_{FR}-T_{leecher}]_{CRPS}$ denotes the difference in the mean download times of the leechers and the free riders in the modified Credit Reputation Propagation Strategy and $[T_{FR}-T_{leecher}]_{ideal}$ denotes the difference in the mean download times of the leechers and the free riders in the ideal case of a Credit Based

System in which every leecher knows every free rider in the system and hence never uploads any file pieces to them, and α denotes the weights we attach to the two separate fractions, i.e., the time taken to download by the leechers and the difference in the download times of the leechers and the free riders.

It can be seen that the two fractions in the metric M represent two different aspects of optimization of the system, one in which we would like to bring the download times of the leechers in the modified CRPS as close to the original BitTorrent protocol as possible while the other represents the importance we attach to meting out as much penalty as compared to the ideal situation as possible. We try to strike a balance in between the two as required by us by changing α. Our aim is always to maximize the value of the metric M which would represent the optimum value for the adjustable parameters.

5   Experimental Results

We adopt a simulation-based approach to explore the aspects of BitTorrent and to analyze the performance of the proposed modification. Our simulator models the BitTorrent mechanisms viz., local rarest first, tit-for-tat, etc. as well as peer block exchanges. We do not model packet delays or data loss in the simulation. Also we assume that the upload/download bandwidth of a peer is the same for all the peers and is equally shared by all the connections. Each of these leechers and free riders leave the network as soon as they have a full copy of the file. The number of concurrent upload transfers is limited to 5 which includes optimistic unchoke.

We use this simple simulation model to analyze the time taken by the peers to download a complete copy of the file and whether our methodology is efficient in reducing the download time of the leechers by blocking the free riders. We try to analyze the difference in the download completion times of the leechers and free riders. Also we try to find out how this is affected by the size of the swarm and if an equilibrium point can be reached between the fraction of the swarm to whom the free riding score is transmitted to the size of the swarm.

In the Credit Reputation Propagation Strategy, whenever a peer requests for a second piece for a straight consecutive time, the event is reported to a section or all of the other peers of the swarm in order that they take into account the free riding attempts on other peers in addition to their own. We use a parameter termed as the *free riding score* to keep a track of free riding attempts. A member of the swarm keeps such scores of other peers who have tried to free ride or have been reported about by others. The score is incremented on a linear scale everytime someone attempts to free ride on itself or others. Also since some of the leechers may also get penalized in the process because of the unavailability of resources or the lack of opportunity to upload, we set a lower threshold beyond which a peer uploads, it would be reported to others. Hence everytime a peer with a score above the lower threshold uploads, others would decrement its free riding score such that it is not uselessly penalized. If we can devise a threshold for the free riding score which if a peer crosses, it would never be unchoked by other leechers, we can effectively deter free riding.

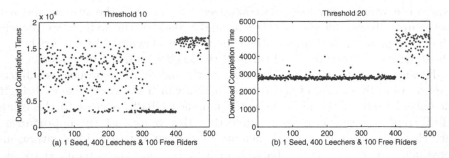

Fig. 4. Download completion times for threshold = 10, 15 and 20, for 50% propagation in CRPS

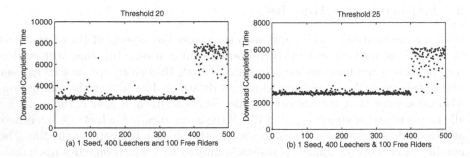

Fig. 5. Download completion times for threshold = 20 and 25, for 80% propagation in CRPS

Experiment: We plot the download completion times for different thresholds and different percentages of propagation. Figures 4, 5 and 6 show the increase in the difference in the download times of the leechers and the free riders. We see in Figures 4(a), 5(a) and 6(a) that if we set a threshold close to the mean download time of leechers then the number of leechers penalized is quite significant whereas the difference in the download time of the leechers and free riders is very impressive. However, if a high number of leechers are penalized, it shows that even compliant peers are being punished. Figures 4(b), 5(b) and 6(b) show that as we increase the threshold score the difference in the download times of the leechers and the free riders decreases while a compliant peer is only occasionally punished. Hence a trade off has to be found in order to set the threshold.

Experiment: We plot the metric values for different percentages of propagation and different threshold values. Fig. 7, as expected, shows that if we do not take into account the time of completion of download for the peers, then setting as low a threshold limit as possible would give the best value for the metric M. It can be seen from Fig. 7(a) that a clear maxima exists for the metric M for α = 50%, where we attach equal significance to the mean time of completion of

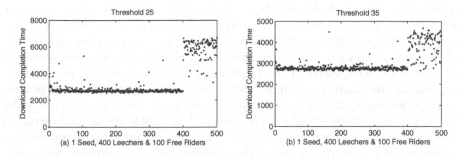

Fig. 6. Download completion times for threshold = 25, 30 and 35, for 100% propagation in CRPS

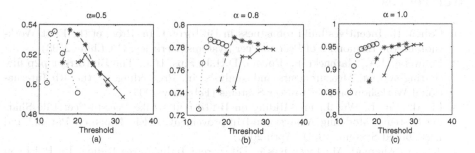

Fig. 7. Comparison of the values of the metric M for different values of α and propagation.(o-50%, *-80% and x-100%)

download for leechers and the mean difference in the download time of leechers and free riders. Fig. 7(c) again shows that if we ignore the difference in the download times of leechers and free riders then setting a higher threshold would give a good value of the metric M as in that case download times for everyone would decrease.

6   Conclusion

In this paper, we present the Credit Reputation Propagation Strategy which effectively penalizes free riding attempts even in large BitTorrent swarms. The novelty of our proposal is that, peers take extra initiative of propagating the credit scores which essentially discourages free riding even in a large swarm, thus overcomes the limitation of existing proposals. We explore the effect of propagation of the reputation to different fraction of peers in the swarm which may induce some overhead to the system. A metric has been defined that combines the average download times as well as the difference in the download times of leechers and free riders to evaluate the overall performance of the system. The effect of the upload threshold, which is a critical design parameter of our strategy has been studied throughly. For example, our metric suggests that in case equal weightage is given to incentive and punishment i.e. when $\alpha = 0.5$, then both 80% propagation with threshold 18 and 50% propagation with threshold 13, leads to optimum network performance. Further it is observed across all values of α i.e. irrespective of the weightage given to incentive or punishment, propagating information to almost half of the swarm population can provide a ood performance, implying an acceptable overhead. We observed that under CRPS, the free riders are effectively punished as visible in form of increased download completion times as compared to leechers. As future work, we propose studies aimed at analytic modeling the performance of the system taking into account the actual overhead incurred due to reputation propagation.

References

1. Cohen, B.: Incentives build robustness in BitTorrent. In: Proc. of the First Workshop on the Economics of Peer-to-Peer Systems, Berkeley, CA (June 2003)
2. Pouwelse, J.A., Garbacki, P., Epema, D.H.J., Sips, H.J.: The BitTorrent p2p file-sharing system: Measurements and analysis. In: Proceedings of the 4th International Workshop on Peer-to-Peer Systems (February 2005)
3. Li, M., Yu, J., Wu, J.: Free-Riding on BitTorrent - Like Peer-to-Peer File Sharing Systems: Modeling Analysis and Improvement. IEEE Trans. on Parallel and Distributed Systems 19(4) (April 2008)
4. Jun, S., Ahamad, M.: Incentives in BitTorrent Induce Free Riding. In: P2PEcon (August 2005)
5. Izal, M., Urvoy-Keller, G., Biersack, E.W., Felber, P.A., Al Hamra, A., Garc s-Erice, L.: Dissecting BitTorrent: Five Months in a Torrent's Lifetime. In: Passive and Active Measurement Workshop 2004, France (April 2004)
6. Karagiannis, T., et al.: Is P2Pdying or just hiding? In: Proc. of Globecom 2004, Dallas, TX, November 29-December 3 (2004)
7. Parker, A.: The true picture of peer-to-peer filesharing (2004), http://www.cachelogic.com
8. Ellis, L.: BitTorrent Swarms Have a Deadly Bite on Broadband Nets. Multichannel News (May 2006)
9. Adar, E., Huberman, B.A.: Free riding on Gnutella. First Monday 5(10) (2000)
10. Sirivianos, M., et al.: Free-riding in BitTorrent networks with the large view exploit. In: International Workshop on Peer-to-Peer Systems (2007)
11. Saroiu, S., Gummadi, P.K., Gribble, S.D.: A Measurement Study of Peer-to-Peer File Sharing Systems. In: Proc. of Multimedia Computing and Networking (MMCN) 2002, San Jose, CA, USA (January 2002)
12. Hughes, D., Coulson, G., Walkerdine, J.: Free Riding on Gnutella Revisited: The Bell Tolls? IEEE Distributed Systems Online 6(6) (2005)
13. Bharambe, A.R., Herley, C., Padmanabhan, V.N.: Analysing snd Improving Bit-Torrent Performance., Tech. Report MSR-TR-2005-03, Microsoft Research (2005)
14. Qiu, D., Srikant, R.: Modeling and Performance Analysis of BitTorrent-Like-Peer-to-Peer Networks. In: Proc. ACM SIGCOMM 2004 (August 2004)

Formal Understanding of the Emergence of Superpeer Networks: A Complex Network Approach

Bivas Mitra, Abhishek Kumar Dubey, Sujoy Ghose, and Niloy Ganguly

Department of Computer Science and Engineering
Indian Institute of Technology, Kharagpur, India
{bivasm,abhish,sujoy,niloy}@cse.iitkgp.ernet.in

Abstract. In this paper, we develop a formal framework which explains the emergence of superpeer networks on execution of the bootstrapping protocols by incoming nodes. Bootstrapping protocols exploit physical properties of the online peers like resource content, processing power, storage space etc as well as takes the finiteness of bandwidth of each online peer into consideration. With the help of rate equations, we show that application of these protocols results in the emergence of superpeer nodes in the network - the exact degree distribution is evaluated. We validate the framework developed in this paper through extensive simulation. Interestingly, our analysis reveals that increase in the amount of resource and the number of resourceful nodes in the network do not always help to increase the fraction of superpeer nodes. The impact of the frequent departure of the peers on the topology of the emerging network is also evaluated. As an application study, we show that our framework can explain the topological configuration of commercial Gnutella networks.

Keywords: Superpeer networks, degree distribution, bootstrapping protocols, rate equation, preferential attachment.

1 Introduction

Currently superpeer networks have proved to be the most influencing peer-to-peer topology and form the underlying architecture of various commercial peer-to-peer (p2p) based systems like KaZaA, Gnutella, Skype etc [1]. The constituent nodes in these networks maintain a two layer overlay topology where the top layer consists of the high speed superpeers and the bottom layer consists of the ordinary peers [2]. Superpeer network is formed mainly as a result of the bootstrapping or joining protocol followed by incoming peers. The bootstrapping protocol selects some online peers (nodes) that are already part of the network and sends connection requests to them [3]. It becomes quite evident that connecting to a 'good' node containing large amount of shared resources, processing power, storage space improves the performance of search and other regular p2p activities. An incoming peer joining commercial peer-to-peer networks like Gnutella collects the list of 'good' hosts from the GWebCache which

K. Kant et al. (Eds.): ICDCN 2010, LNCS 5935, pp. 219–230, 2010.
© Springer-Verlag Berlin Heidelberg 2010

is a distributed repository for maintaining the information of 'good' online nodes in the network [3]. The superpeer networks emerged following these bootstrapping protocols exhibit two regimes or 'bimodality' in their degree distribution; one regime consists of the large number of low degree peer nodes and another one consists of the small number of high degree superpeers [4]. The emergence of bimodal network due to the bootstrapping of peers is an *interesting* observation. This is not obvious why bootstrapping of nodes leads to the emergence of bimodal network, hardly there is any explanation found in the literature. [5,6,7] have shown the emergence of scale free networks as a result of the preferential attachment of incoming nodes with the 'good' existing nodes[1]. In line with that, one can reasonably expect that the additional constraint of finiteness of bandwidth present in computer networks may lead to power law distribution with an exponential cutoff degree. However, we observe that the superpeer networks follow bimodal degree distribution that sharply deviates from the power law behavior of scale free networks [2,4].

In this paper, we develop a theoretical framework to explain the appearance of superpeer networks due to the execution of servents like limewire, mutella etc [3,8]. In order to develop the framework, we model the bootstrapping protocols by the node attachment rule where the probability of joining of an incoming peer to an online node is proportional to the 'goodness' of the online node. 'Goodness' of a peer can be characterized by the *node property* (later quantified as node weight) like amount of resource, processing power, storage space etc that a particular peer possesses. Beyond this, we identify that in p2p networks, bandwidth of a node is finite and restricts its maximum degree (*cutoff degree*). A node, after reaching its maximum degree, rejects any further connection requests from incoming peers. Our framework shows that the interplay of finite bandwidth with node property plays key role in the emergence of bimodal network. The outline of the paper is as follows. In section 2, we state and model the bootstrapping protocol followed by peer servents. Section 3 proposes a formal framework considering that all peers join the network with fixed cutoff degree. In section 4, we generalize the theory for the case where different peers join the network with variable cutoff degrees. In section 5, we report the change in the superpeer topology due to the frequent departure of the online nodes, termed as peer churn. In light of the developed framework, an empirical analysis of the global nature of the Gnutella 0.6 network is provided in section 6. Section 7 concludes the paper.

2   Bootstrapping Protocol

In this section, we illustrate and model the bootstrapping protocol that is executed by different servent programs. Servents like limewire and gnucleus maintain a list of resourceful hosts and give priority to them during connection initiation [3]. We

---

[1] The 'goodness' of a node has focused both towards link property (such as degree centrality) and node property (such as 'fitness') [7].

model the bootstrapping protocols through node attachment rules where probability of attachment of the incoming peer to an online node is proportional to the node property (weight) of the online node. The generalized bootstrapping protocol is mentioned next. The cutoff degree $k_c(i)$ is same for all peers i in the analysis of section 3 while it is varied in section 4.

> **Input**: Nodes, where each node i comes with individual node weight w_i
> and a maximum cutoff degree $k_c(i)$
> **Output**: Network emerged due to joining of the nodes
> **foreach** *Incoming node i* **do**
>   Node i preferentially chooses m' $(m' > m)$ online nodes based on their weights
>   **while** *m online nodes are not connected with i* **do**
> j = select an online node
>   The node i sends the connection request to j
>   **if** *degree(j)$< k_c(j)$* **then**
>   Node i connects with node j
>   **end**
>   **else**
>   Node j rejects the connection request
>   **end**
>   **end**
> **end**

3 Development of Analytical Framework: Peers Joining with Fixed Cutoff Degree

In this section, we develop a network growth formalism in order to explain the emergence of superpeer networks. We assume that each incoming peer joins the network at a timestep n with some node weight and connects to m online nodes in the network following the bootstrapping protocol. The minimum and maximum weight of a node in the network can be w_{min} and w_{max} respectively. The probability that an incoming peer has weight w_i is f_{w_i} and all the nodes have some fixed cutoff degree k_c. Any node upon reaching the degree k_c rejects any further connection request from the incoming peer.

We introduce the term set_{w_i} to denote the set of nodes in the network with weight w_i. Initially we intend to compute p_{k,w_i}, the fraction of k degree nodes in set_{w_i}. This can be computed by observing the shift in the number of k degree nodes to $k+1$ degree nodes as well as $k-1$ degree nodes to k degree node due to the attachment of a new node at time step n. Let the fraction of nodes in set_{w_i} having degree k at some timestep n be p_{k,n,w_i}, then the total number of k degree nodes in set_{w_i} before addition of a new node is $nf_{w_i}p_{k,n,w_i}$ and after addition of the node becomes $(n+1)f_{w_i}p_{k,n+1,w_i}$. Hence the change in the number of k degree nodes in set_{w_i} becomes

$$\Delta n_{k,w_i} = (n+1)f_{w_i}p_{k,n+1,w_i} - nf_{w_i}p_{k,n,w_i} \tag{1}$$

We formulate rate equations [5] depicting these changes for some arbitrary set_{w_i}. By solving those rate equations, we calculate p_{k,w_i} and subsequently the degree distribution p_k (fraction of nodes having degree k) of the entire network.

Methodology
The probability that an online node i will receive an incoming link is proportional to the node weight w_i and can be depicted as

$$A_{w_i} = \frac{w_i f_{w_i} \beta_i}{\sum_{i'=min}^{max} w_{i'} f_{w_{i'}} \beta_{i'}} \qquad degree(i) < k_c \qquad (2)$$
$$= 0 \qquad degree(i) \geq k_c$$

where $\beta_i = 1 - p_{k_c,w_i}$ (p_{k_c,w_i} is the fraction of nodes in set_{w_i} that reached the cutoff degree k_c hence stopped accepting new links) implies the fraction of nodes in set_{w_i} capable of accepting new links from the incoming peer. The numerator of Eq. (2) represents the total amount of weight of nodes in set_{w_i} that are allowed to take incoming links. The denominator normalizes the fraction by the total amount of weight of all the nodes in the network that are allowed to take incoming links.

The addition of a new node of degree m at timestep $n+1$ changes the total number of k degree nodes in set_{w_i}. Since all the nodes in the set_{w_i} contain equal weight w_i, the chance of getting a new link for the nodes having degree k depends upon its fraction present in the set at that timestep and can be expressed as $\frac{p_{k,n,w_i}}{1-p_{k_c,w_i}}$. The denominator takes care of the fact that the nodes, that have reached the cutoff degree k_c do not participate in the formation of new link. Due to the addition of a new node of degree m in the network, some k degree nodes in set_{w_i} acquire a new link and become degree $k+1$. So the amount of decrease in the number of nodes of degree k, ($m \leq k < k_c$) in set_{w_i} due to this outflux is

$$\delta_{k \to (k+1)} = \frac{p_{k,n,w_i}}{1 - p_{k_c,w_i}} \times A_{w_i} m \qquad (3)$$

Similarly a fraction of nodes having degree $k-1$, get a new link and move to the degree k.

We now write the rate equations in order to formulate the change in the number of k degree nodes in an individual set_{w_i} due to the attachment of a new node of degree m. Three pertinent degree ranges $k = m$, $m < k < k_c$ and $k = k_c$ are taken into consideration.

Rate equation for $k = m$
Since the probability of joining of a node having weight w_i in the network is f_{w_i}, the joining of one new node of degree m on average increases f_{w_i} fraction of m degree nodes in the set_{w_i}. Hence net change in the number of nodes having degree $k = m$ can be expressed as

$$\Delta n_{m,w_i} = f_{w_i} - \frac{p_{m,n,w_i}}{1 - p_{k_c,w_i}} \times A_{w_i} m \qquad (4)$$

Similarly **Rate equation for** $m < k < k_c$

$$\Delta n_{k,w_i} = \left(\frac{p_{k-1,n,w_i} - p_{k,n,w_i}}{1 - p_{k_c,w_i}} \right) \times A_{w_i} m \tag{5}$$

and **Rate equation for** $k = k_c$.

Since the nodes having degree k_c are not allowed to take any incoming links, only nodes are accumulated at degree $k = k_c$. Hence

$$\Delta n_{k,w_i} = \frac{p_{k-1,n,w_i}}{1 - p_{k_c,w_i}} \times A_{w_i} m \tag{6}$$

Computing degree distribution

Solving those rate equations, we obtain the degree distribution of the entire network. Assuming $\alpha_i = 1 + \frac{\sum_j w_j f_{w_j} \beta_j}{w_i m}$ and at stationary condition $p_{k,n+1,w_i} = p_{k,n,w_i} = p_{k,w_i}$ [5], we get

$$p_k = \sum_{i=min}^{max} p_{k,w_i} f_{w_i} = \begin{cases} \sum_{i=min}^{max} \frac{\alpha_i - 1}{\alpha_i} f_{w_i} & \text{if } k = m \\ \sum_{i=min}^{max} \frac{\alpha_i - 1}{\alpha_i^{k-m+1}} f_{w_i} & \text{if } m < k < k_c \\ \sum_{i=min}^{max} \frac{1}{\alpha_i^{k_c-m}} f_{w_i} & \text{if } k = k_c \end{cases} \tag{7}$$

Note that Eq. (7) is an open form equation. The iterative substitution method applied on p_{k_c,w_i} obtained from Eq. (7) yields the solution of β_i that is subsequently used to compute α_i.

Emergence of superpeer nodes

A closer look at the equations reveals that two modes appear in the degree distribution, one in the region k close to m, another at $k = k_c$. **Conditions: a.** In order to show the appearance of spike or mode at $k = k_c$, we have to satisfy the condition $p_{k_c} > p_{k_c-1}$ and $p_{k_c} > p_{k_c+1}$. **b.** In order to show the modal behavior in the region k close to m, we have to satisfy the condition $p_k < p_{k-1}$ for $m < k < k_c$. This also confirms that no other spikes have emerged in the network.

Fulfilling condition a: First of all, we show that the fraction of nodes having degree k_c, p_{k_c} is greater than p_{k_c-1}. From Eq. (6), we find that

$$\frac{p_{k_c}}{p_{k_c-1}} \approx \sum_{i=min}^{max} f_{w_i} \frac{p_{k_c,w_i}}{p_{k_c-1,w_i}} = m \frac{\sum_i w_i f_{w_i}}{\sum_i w_i f_{w_i} \beta_i} > m$$

as $0 < \beta_i < 1$. Since, $m \geq 1$, $\frac{p_{k_c}}{p_{k_c-1}} > 1$ subsequently $p_{k_c} > p_{k_c-1}$. Secondly, the definition of the bootstrapping model gives $p_k = 0$ for $k > k_c$. Hence, we conclude the presence of a spike at degree k_c.

Fulfilling condition b: We find for $m < k < k_c$, the probability p_k continuously decreases. This can be understood from Eq. (5) of the set_{w_i}

$$\frac{p_{k,w_i}}{p_{k-1,w_i}} = \frac{1}{\alpha_i} < 1$$

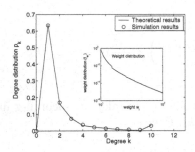
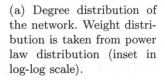
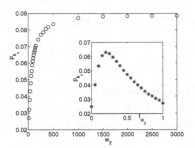

(a) Degree distribution of the network. Weight distribution is taken from power law distribution (inset in log-log scale).

(b) The figure shows the change in p_{k_c} due to change in w_2 and f_{w_2} for the bimodal weight distribution (simulation results).

Fig. 1. Fig. 1(a) represents the degree distribution of the network emerged following bootstrapping protocol with fixed cutoff degree $k_c = 10$ and $m = 1$. The nodes join the network with weights taken from the power law distribution ($\gamma = 2.5$). Inset of Fig. 1(b) indicates the presence of optimum f_{w_2} (i.e. $f^*_{w_2}$) at which p_{k_c} becomes maximum.

Hence for the entire network, $p_k < p_{k-1}$. These two observations confirm the presence of two distinct modes in the bimodal degree distribution and direct to the emergence of high degree superpeer nodes at degree k_c.

3.1   Simulation Results

We validate the theoretically obtained degree distribution (Eq. (7)) by simulating the emergence of the network (Fig. 1(a)). In these simulations, we follow the exactly same procedure and assumptions that we have taken for the theoretical modeling. The stochastic simulation set up is as follows. During bootstrapping, each node joins the network with some weight ($10 \leq w \leq 100$) taken from a power law distribution ($f_w \sim w^{-\gamma}$) [9]. The total number of nodes in the system is considered to be 5000 and we perform 500 individual realizations and plot the average of them. Fig. 1(a) shows that the agreement between the theoretical and simulation results is exact which validates the correctness of the theoretical model. The figure also produces the evidence of the emergence of two distinct regions in the degree distribution - the peer and superpeer regions; the accumulation of the superpeer nodes occurs at degree $k_c = 10$. In the following, we investigate the influence of different parameters on the amount of superpeers in the network (p_{k_c}). In order to gain more insights, we consider a simple bimodal weight distribution where nodes join with two weights w_1 (low) and w_2 (high) with individual fractions f_{w_1} (high) and f_{w_2} (low) respectively.

3.2 Impact of Node Weight w_2 on p_{k_c}

In order to examine the impact of node weight, we perform the simulation with $w_1 = 10$ and $f_{w_1} = 0.8$. The node weight w_2 is varied from 10 to 3000 and we observe how it affects p_{k_c} (at $k_c=10$). It can be observed from Fig. 1(b) that initial increase in w_2 rapidly increases the fraction of superpeer nodes in the network. However, after a certain threshold, the p_{k_c} stabilizes and further increase in weight does not increase p_{k_c}. Mathematically from Eq. (7), as $w_2 \to \infty$, p_{k_c} becomes

$$\lim_{w_2 \to \infty} p_{k_c} = f_{w_2} \prod_{j=m}^{k_c-1} \frac{j}{(j + \frac{2}{m} f_{w_2} m_2 \beta_2)} \tag{8}$$

and converges to some finite value. Hence, we conclude that after some threshold limit, increase in the node weight does not increase the amount of superpeers in the network.

3.3 Impact of Fraction of High Weight Nodes (f_{w_2}) on p_{k_c}

In order to observe the impact of f_{w_2} on p_{k_c}, we simulate the bootstrapping protocol with two weights $w_1 = 10$ and $w_2 = 100$ and gradually increase the f_{w_2} (i.e. decrease f_{w_1}). Common intuition is that, increase in f_{w_2} in the network should increase p_{k_c} (number of superpeers) as well. However, inset of Fig. 1(b) shows that the initial increase in f_{w_2} increases p_{k_c}. But after reaching some maximum value ($p_{k_c}^*$), p_{k_c} decreases.

4 Development of Analytical Framework: Peers Joining with Variable Cutoff Degrees

In reality, nodes join the network with various bandwidth connections like ISDN, ADSL, leased line etc. Subsequently the cutoff degree of individual nodes becomes different from one another. For simplicity, we can assume that there is a fixed number of discrete cutoff degrees each representing a type of connection. We therefore generalize the bootstrapping in the following way. We assume that the probabilities that a node j joins the network with cutoff degree $k_c(j)$ and weight w_j are $q_{k_c(j)}$ and f_{w_j} respectively ($q_{k_c(j)}$ and f_{w_j} are independent). Suppose the minimum and maximum cutoff degrees are $k_c(min)$ and $k_c(max)$ respectively. Similar to section 3, the probability that an online node of weight w_i (i.e. in set_{w_i}) receives a new link from the incoming peer

$$\widehat{A}_{w_i} = \frac{w_i f_{w_i} \widehat{\beta}_i}{\sum_{i=min}^{max} w_i f_{w_i} \widehat{\beta}_i} \tag{9}$$

where

$$\widehat{\beta}_i = 1 - \sum_{k=k_c(min)}^{k_c(max)} p_{k,w_i}(1 - S_{k,w_i}) \tag{10}$$

implies the fraction of nodes in set_{w_i} capable of accepting new links from the incoming peer. Here S_{k,w_i} is the fraction of k degree nodes in set_{w_i} whose cutoff degree is greater than k and hence are still capable of taking incoming connections. We calculate the exact expression for S_{k,w_i} later in this section.

Similar to the fixed cutoff, we formulate the rate equations to characterize joining of an incoming node of degree m. Based on the behavior of S_{k,w_i}, the formulation of rate equations and subsequently the computation of degree distribution is done in two parts; nodes with degree $m \leq k < k_c(min)$ in part A and nodes with degree $k_c(min) \leq k \leq k_c(max)$ in part B.

Part A : Dynamics analysis for $m \leq k < k_c(min)$
In this case, S_{k,w_i} becomes trivially 1, hence the rate equations for $m \leq k < k_c(min)$ are similar to the Eqs. (4) and (5). Therefore, we calculate p_{k,w_i} from Eq. (7).

Part B : Dynamics analysis for $k_c(min) \leq k \leq k_c(max)$
An important difference between part B with part A is that, at each k ($k_c(min) \leq k \leq k_c(max)$), a fraction of nodes reaches their cutoff degree and stops taking links from the incoming nodes. So the calculation of S_{k,w_i} becomes nontrivial and their values take a major role in formulating the rate equations. We start our analysis with the nodes having smallest cutoff degree $k = k_c(min)$.

Calculation for $k = k_c(min)$
We defined earlier that S_{k,w_i} is the fraction of nodes having degree $k = k_c(min)$ in the set_{w_i} that have not reached their cutoff and still capable of taking incoming links. Hence similar to Eq. (3), $\frac{p_{k,w_i}}{\widehat{\beta}_i} \widehat{A}_{w_i} m S_{k,w_i}$ number of nodes can move from degree $k_c(min)$ to $k_c(min) + 1$ and hence leave the $k_c(min)$ set. On the other hand, the mean number of nodes with degree $k - 1$ that accepts new link and moves to degree k can be calculated from Eq. (3). The net change in the number of nodes having degree k (for $k = k_c(min)$) due to the attachment of a new node

$$\Delta n_{k,w_i} = \frac{(p_{k-1,w_i} - p_{k,w_i} S_{k,w_i})}{\widehat{\beta}_i} \times \widehat{A}_{w_i} m \qquad (11)$$

Calculation of S_{k,w_i} for $k = k_c(min)$
The mean number of nodes of degree $(k - 1)$ that acquires the new links from the incoming node and moves from the degree $(k - 1)$ to degree k is $\widehat{\delta}_{(k-1) \to k} = \frac{p_{k-1,w_i}}{\widehat{\beta}_i} \widehat{A}_{w_i} m$. As q_k is the probability that a node joins the network with cutoff degree $k = k_c(min)$, hence $\widehat{\delta}_{(k-1) \to k} \times \frac{q_k}{\sum_{k'=k}^{k_c(max)} q_{k'}}$ specifies the number of nodes that moves from degree $(k - 1)$ to k and also reaches their maximum degree $k = k_c(min)$. If the fraction of k degree nodes in set_{w_i} is p_{k,w_i}, then the fraction of nodes reaching the cutoff degree k can be normalized as

$$1 - S_{k,w_i} = \frac{\frac{p_{k-1,w_i}}{\widehat{\beta}_i} \widehat{A}_{w_i} m q_k^*}{p_{k,w_i}} \Rightarrow S_{k,w_i} = 1 - \frac{\frac{p_{k-1,w_i}}{\widehat{\beta}_i} \widehat{A}_{w_i} m q_k^*}{p_{k,w_i}} \qquad (12)$$

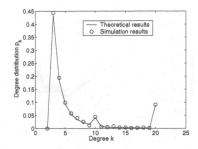

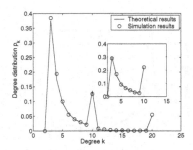

(a) Degree distribution of the emerging network in case 1.

(b) Degree distribution of the emerging network in case 2 and case 3 (inset).

Fig. 2. Case 1: fractions of nodes joined with cutoff degrees $3, 10$ and 20 are $0.5, 0.1$ and 0.4 respectively. Case 2: fractions of nodes joined with cutoff degrees $3, 10$ and 20 are $0.5, 0.3$ and 0.2 respectively. Inset in Fig 2(b) shows case 3 where 50% nodes joined with cutoff 3 and rest 50% joined with cutoff 10.

where $q_k^* = \frac{q_k}{\sum_{k'=k}^{k_c(max)} q_{k'}}$. Substituting the value of S_{k,w_i} in Eq. (11) and rearranging p_{k,w_i}, we get

$$p_{k,w_i} = \frac{p_{k-1,w_i}}{\widehat{\alpha}_i}\left(1 + \frac{f_{w_i}q_k^*}{\widehat{\alpha}_i - 1}\right) \tag{13}$$

where $\widehat{\alpha}_i = 1 + \frac{\sum w_j f_{w_j} \widehat{\beta}_j}{w_i m}$.

Continuing the calculations for $k_c(min) < k \le k_c(max)$, we obtain the generalized equation

$$p_{k,w_i} = \frac{1}{\widehat{\alpha}_i}\left(1 + \frac{f_{w_i}q_k^*}{\widehat{\alpha}_i - 1}\right)\left(p_{k-1,w_i} + \sum_{j=1}^{k-k_c(min)}(-1)^j \prod_{t=1}^{j} \frac{p_{k-j-1,w_i}f_{w_i}}{(\widehat{\alpha}_i - 1)}q_{k-t}^*\right) \tag{14}$$

The degree distribution of the entire network p_k is calculated by summing up p_{k,w_i} over all w_i's, i.e. $p_k = \sum_{i'=min}^{max} p_{k,w_{i'}} f_{w_{i'}}$.

4.1 Simulation Results

In order to validate our framework, we simulate the bootstrapping protocol where nodes join with variable cutoff degrees (Fig. 2(a)). We consider that the weight distribution (f_w) of the incoming nodes follows power law distribution (with $\gamma = 2.5$) [9] and the nodes can have 3 different cutoff degrees $3, 10$ and 20. At the time of joining, each node establishes connections with 3 online nodes in the network i.e. $m = 3$. We assume that the 50% of nodes join through dial up connection having cutoff degree 3. Rest 10% of nodes join (say) through ISDN connection with cutoff degree 10 and 40% (say) through leased line connection with cutoff

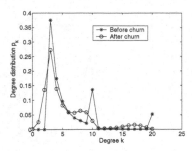
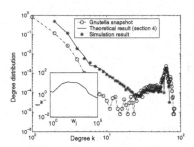

(a) Degree distribution before and after churn in
Fig 2(b).The total percentage of nodes removed in
peer churn is 21%.

(b) Degree distribution of
Gnutella network taken
from the topological snapshot [12]. The inset shows
the weight distribution of
the incoming nodes [13].

Fig. 3. Fig 3(a) shows the effect of peer churn on the network emerged in Fig 2(b).
Fig. 3(b) illustrates the comparative study between the real world Gnutella networks [12], our theoretical model and simulation results.

degree 20. We assume that all the nodes having degree ≥ 10 can be considered
as superpeer nodes. The total number of nodes in the simulation system is 5000
and we perform 500 realizations. Fig. 2(a) shows that the agreement between
the theoretical model (Eq. (14)) and simulation is exact.

Measuring the amount of superpeers in the network
The Fig. 2(a) shows that in case 1, total amount of superpeer nodes (i.e. degree
≥ 10) in the network is 0.1472. On the other hand, if the fractions of nodes
joined with cutoff degrees 3, 10 and 20 are 0.5, 0.3 and 0.2 respectively (Fig. 2(b),
referred as case 2), the amount of superpeers in the network becomes 0.2158. If
50% of nodes joins with cutoff 3 and rest 50% joins with a cutoff 10, the total
amount of superpeers in the network becomes 0.2761 (inset of Fig. 2(b), referred
as case 3). Hence our results show that instead of joining the network through
multiple high bandwidth connections, using a single bandwidth is optimal for
the emergence of highest amount of superpeers in the network.

5   Impact of Peer Churn on the Topology of the Emerging Network

In this section, we calculate the degree distribution of the emerging network in
face of peer churn [10]. In [11], we developed a theory to calculate the degree
distribution of the deformed network after removal of a fraction of nodes along
with their adjacent links. Mathematically, if the initial degree distribution of the
network is p_k and the probability of removal of a node having degree k is f_k,

then the degree distribution of the deformed network after node removal can be
expressed as

$$p'_k = \sum_{q=k}^{\infty} \binom{q}{k} \phi^{q-k}(1-\phi)^k p_q^s \tag{15}$$

where in large scale networks, $\phi = \frac{\sum_{i=0}^{\infty} i \, p_i f_i}{\sum_{k=0}^{\infty} k \, p_k}$ and $p_q^s = \frac{(1-f_q)p_q}{1-\sum_{i=0}^{\infty} p_i f_i}$. We model
the peer churn as the removal of nodes from the network. In p2p networks, it has
been observed that peers having higher connectivity (e.g. superpeers) are more
stable in the network than the peers having lower connectivity. Hence in peer
churn, it is quite realistic to assume that the probability of removal of a node
is inversely proportional to the degree of that node i.e. $f_k = \frac{1}{k}$. We substitute
this f_k and initial degree distribution p_k (obtained from Eq. (14)) in Eq. (15)
to calculate the degree distribution of the emerging network after peer churn.
Fig. 3(a) shows the change in the network topology due to peer churn in the
network which has emerged in Fig. 2(b). The Fig. 3(a) shows that even in face
of such heavy churn, the bimodality in the degree distribution is still maintained.
However, the disappearance of old modes and emergence of new modes in the
degree distribution is an interesting observation.

6   Case Study with Gnutella Network

We simulate Gnutella network following the snapshot obtained from the Multimedia & Internetworking Research Group, University of Oregon, USA [12].
The snapshot is collected by the research group during September 2004 and the
size of the network simulated from the snapshot is of $1,31,869$ nodes. In order
to check whether the degree distribution of Gnutella can be explained through
the developed framework, we theoretically compute the degree distribution of
the emerging network (from section 4) by taking the weights from the weight
distribution of the inset of Fig. 3(b) [13]. During connection initiation, most
of the servents initially connect to multiple online peers [3] therefore we keep
$m = 2$. The probability $q_{k_c(j)}$ of joining of a node j with cutoff degree $k_c(j)$ is adjusted accordingly to fit the calculated degree distribution close to the Gnutella
network.

   As can be seen from Fig. 3(b), our theoretical model can mimic the degree
distribution of Gnutella network with reasonable accuracy, however there are
some deviations. The possible reason is, due to the finite size of the web cache,
the GWebCache is totally populated by the high degree nodes in the network.
Henceforth, the peers having low degree do not receive any connection from the
incoming node. Thus most of the low degree peer nodes remain with the low
degree and subsequently the amount of low degree nodes in Gnutella network
becomes lower than theoretically calculated value.

7   Conclusion and Discussion

In this paper, we have used rate equations to develop a formalism for calculating
the degree distribution of superpeer networks. We have modeled the commercial

bootstrapping protocol that follow preferential attachment policy to join online peer based upon its processing power, storage space etc. The available bandwidth also plays an important role in modeling the protocol. The results presented in this paper show that the interplay of finite bandwidth with node property plays key role in the emergence of superpeer network. Our formalism shows certain interesting phenomena like (a.) resource of a machine can be exploited only upto a point and putting many high resource machines in the network can in fact be detrimental towards emergence of superpeer nodes. (b.) Joining of the resourceful nodes through single high bandwidth line (like leased line) increases the amount of superpeers in the network than joining through multiple bandwidth lines (like ISDN, ADSL, leased line etc). In summary, we claim that the analytical framework as well as the interesting findings of this paper will provide a useful toolbox for design engineers to impart various desirable properties to superpeer networks.

References

1. Pyun, Y.J., Reeves, D.S.: Constructing a Balanced, log(N)-Diameter Super-peer Topology. In: Proceedings of the 4th International Conference on Peer-to-Peer Computing, Zurich, Switzerland (August 2004)
2. Yang, B., Garcua-Molina, H.: Designing a Super-Peer Networks. In: Proceedings of the International Conference on Data Engineering, Los Alamitos, CA (March 2003)
3. Karbhari, P., Ammar, M.H., Dhamdhere, A., Raj, H., Riley, G.F., Zegura, E.W.: Bootstrapping in Gnutella: A measurement study. In: Barakat, C., Pratt, I. (eds.) PAM 2004. LNCS, vol. 3015, pp. 22–32. Springer, Heidelberg (2004)
4. Mitra, B., Peruani, F., Ghose, S., Ganguly, N.: Analyzing the Vulnerability of the Superpeer Networks Against Attack. ACM CCS, Alexandria, USA (2007)
5. Barabasi, A.L., Albert, R.: Emergence Of Scaling In Random Networks. Science 286, 509–512 (1999)
6. Krapivsky, P.L., Redner, S.: Organization of Growing Random Networks. Physical Review E 63, 066123 (2001)
7. Bianconi, G., Barabasi, A.L.: Competition and Multiscaling in Evolving Networks. Europhys. Lett. 54, 436 (2001)
8. Gnutella Protocol Specification v0.4 (2007), http://www.limewire.com
9. Ronga, L., Burnett, I.: Dynamic Resource Adaptation in a Heterogeneous Peer-to-Peer Environment. In: Second IEEE Consumer Communications and Networking Conference, Las Vegas, USA, January 2005, pp. 416–420 (2005)
10. Mitra, B., Peruani, F., Ghose, S., Ganguly, N.: Brief Announcement: Measuring Robustness of Superpeer Topologies. In: Proceedings of the ACM PODC, Portland, USA (2007)
11. Mitra, B., Ganguly, N., Ghose, S., Peruani, F.: Generalized Theory for Node Disruption in Finite-size Complex Networks. Physical Review E 78, 026115 (2008)
12. Gnutella sanpshpt (2004), http://mirage.cs.uoregon.edu/P2P/info.cgi
13. Saroiu, P., Gummadi, K., Gribble, S.D.: A Measurement Study of Peer-to-Peer File Sharing Systems. In: Proceedings of Multimedia Computing and Networking, San Jose, California, USA (January 2002)

Parallelization of the Lanczos Algorithm on Multi-core Platforms

Souvik Bhattacherjee and Abhijit Das

Department of Computer Science & Engineering
Indian Institute of Technology, Kharagpur
India 721302
{souvikb,abhij}@cse.iitkgp.ernet.in

Abstract. In this paper, we report our parallel implementations of the Lanczos sparse linear system solving algorithm over large prime fields, on a multi-core platform. We employ several load-balancing methods suited to these platforms. We have carried out process-level and thread-level parallel implementations under two different arithmetic libraries, and the best speedup obtained is 6.57 on eight cores. To the best of our knowledge, no implementation of the Lanczos algorithm on a multi-core platform is ever reported in the literature. Moreover, we seem to have achieved significantly larger speedup compared to all previously reported implementations of this algorithm.

Keywords: Sparse linear system, Lanczos algorithm, modular arithmetic, prime field, multi-core machine, parallelization, load balancing.

1 Introduction

The discrete logarithm problem over finite fields serves as the basis of several cryptographic primitives. For example, the Diffie-Hellman key-agreement protocol, the ElGamal public-key cryptosystem and the digital signature algorithm (DSA) [1] rely on the difficulty of solving the discrete logarithm problem, for their security. The fastest known algorithms for solving the discrete logarithm problem require the solution of large sparse linear systems over finite rings. As the size of the system of equations increases, standard Gaussian elimination becomes impractical. Some alternative methods prove to be computationally more attractive than Gaussian elimination, particularly for large and sparse linear systems. Efficient implementations of these iterative system solvers are quite challenging, and the linear-algebra phase often turns out to be the practical bottleneck in the context of solving the discrete logarithm problem. The Lanczos method [2,3,4,5] and the Wiedemann method [6,7,8] are two iterative system solvers that outperform Gaussian elimination for large sparse linear systems. In this paper, we concentrate upon solving linear systems modulo primes q using the Lanczos algorithm.

The sieving part of standard discrete-logarithm algorithms turns out to be massively parallelizable. On the contrary, the system-solving part offers some

K. Kant et al. (Eds.): ICDCN 2010, LNCS 5935, pp. 231–241, 2010.

resistance to massive parallelization. The main focus of this paper is the establishment of good parallelization potentials of the Lanczos system solver, at least for a limited number of processing elements.

Published results pertaining to parallelizing the Lanczos algorithm are either abstract in nature [9], or focused towards systems over $\mathbf{GF}(2)$ [10]. The best speedup is obtained by [10] and is about 6. The parallel Lanczos implementation over large prime fields, reported by [11], achieves a modest speedup of about 4.5 on 8 processors and a speedup of about 9 on 32 processors. A common feature of all these implementations is that they have been carried out in distributed environments.

In this paper, we report our parallel implementation of the Lanczos algorithm over large finite fields in multi-core shared-memory architectures. We perform both thread-level parallelism using Pthreads and OpenMP [12] and process-level parallelism using shared memory and semaphores. Our process-level implementations outperform our thread-level implementations in terms of scalability. Using novel load-balancing ideas, we have been able to achieve a speedup of 6.57 on 8 cores.

The rest of the paper is organized as follows. In Section 2, we briefly describe the standard Lanczos algorithm. Implementation details of the sequential Lanczos algorithm are presented in Section 3. In Section 4, we describe our parallel implementations with emphasis on load-balancing strategies and issues involved in thread-level and process-level parallelism. The experimental results are presented in Section 5. We conclude the paper in Section 6 after highlighting some directions for future research.

2   The Lanczos Algorithm

We are given an $m \times n$ matrix B over a prime field $\mathbf{GF}(q)$ with $m > n$ to represent the linear system

$$B\boldsymbol{x} \equiv \boldsymbol{u} \ (\text{mod } q). \tag{1}$$

We assume that the equations are consistent and $\boldsymbol{u}$ is in the column space of B. The computation of discrete logarithms requires the solution $\boldsymbol{x}$ to be unique, that is, the matrix B to be of full column rank. Since the system is overdetermined, this requirement is ensured with a high probability. The Lanczos algorithm is classically applicable to systems of the form

$$A\boldsymbol{x} = \boldsymbol{b}, \tag{2}$$

where A is a symmetric, positive-definite matrix over the field of real numbers. In order to adapt this algorithm to the case of finite fields, we transform Eqn.(1) to Eqn.(2) by letting

$$A = B^t B, \tag{3}$$

$$\boldsymbol{b} = B^t \boldsymbol{u}, \tag{4}$$

where B^t denotes the transpose of B. Now, A is a symmetric matrix, but the requirement of positive definiteness makes no sense in a setting of finite fields. The algorithm continues to work if we instead require that $w_i^t A w_i \neq 0$ for $w_i \neq 0$. If the modulus q is large, this condition is satisfied with a very high probability. A solution of Eqn.(1) is definitely a solution of Eqn.(2). The converse too is expected with a high probability.

The standard Lanczos algorithm solves Eqn.(2) by starting with the initializations: $w_0 = b$, $v_1 = A w_0$, $w_1 = v_1 - w_0(v_1^t A w_0)/(w_0^t A w_0)$, $a_0 = (w_0^t w_0)/(w_0^t A w_0)$, $x_0 = a_0 w_0$. Subsequently, for $i = 1, 2, 3, \ldots$, the steps in Algorithm 1 are repeated until $w_i^t A w_i = 0$, which is equivalent to the condition $w_i = 0$ (with high probability). When this condition is satisfied, the vector x_{i-1} is a solution to Eqn.(2).

Algorithm 1. An iteration in the Lanczos Algorithm

1: $v_{i+1} = A w_i$

2: $w_{i+1} = v_{i+1} - \dfrac{w_i(v_{i+1}^t A w_i)}{(w_i^t A w_i)} - \dfrac{w_{i-1}(v_{i+1}^t A w_{i-1})}{(w_{i-1}^t A w_{i-1})}$

3: $a_i = \dfrac{(w_i^t b)}{(w_i^t A w_i)}$

4: $x_i = x_{i-1} + a_i w_{i-1}$

For more details on the Lanczos algorithm, we refer the reader to [5].

3   Sequential Implementation

In this section, we describe our sequential implementation of the standard Lanczos algorithm, modulo a large prime q. This sequential implementation is parallelized later. Systems of linear equations were available to us from an implementation of the linear sieve method [13]. Larger systems were generated randomly in accordance with the statistics followed by the entries in the linear-sieve matrices.

3.1   Representing the Matrix B

Due to the nature of the sieving algorithm, the coefficients of the system of equations have very small positive or negative magnitudes. For the current set of matrices, we have the coefficients $\in [-2, c]$, where $c \leq 50$. Most of these coefficients are ± 1. Each such coefficient can be stored as a signed single-precision (32-bit) integer.

Matrices generated by the sieve algorithms are necessarily very sparse. In our case, each row contains only $O(\log q)$ non-zero entries. We store the matrix in a compressed row storage (CRS) format, where each row is represented by an array of coefficient-column index pairs (val, col_ind) for the non-zero entries only. We concatenate the arrays for different rows into a single one-dimensional array, and use a separate array row_ptr to mark the start indices of the rows in the concatenated (*val, col_ind*) array. If there are N non-zero entries in the matrix, then the concatenated array of (*val, col_ind*) pairs requires a storage proportional to N. The array *row_ptr* demands a size of $m + 1$ for pointing to the start indices of the rows. As an example, the CRS format of the matrix

$$B = \begin{bmatrix} 10 & 0 & 0 & 0 & -2 \\ 3 & 9 & 0 & 0 & 0 \\ 0 & 7 & 8 & 7 & 0 \\ 3 & 0 & 8 & 0 & 5 \\ 0 & 8 & 0 & -1 & 0 \\ 0 & 4 & 0 & 0 & 2 \end{bmatrix}$$

is shown in Fig. 1. We assume that array indexing starts from 1.

Fig. 1. The Compressed Row Storage format of B

$$\begin{array}{l|c|c|c|c|c|c|c|c|c|c|c|c|c} val & 10 & 3 & 3 & 9 & 7 & 8 & 4 & 8 & 8 & 7 & -1 & -2 & 5 & 2 \\ \hline row\_ind & 1 & 2 & 4 & 2 & 3 & 5 & 6 & 3 & 4 & 3 & 5 & 1 & 4 & 6 \end{array} \qquad col\_ptr\;\boxed{1\,4\,8\,10\,12\,15}$$

Fig. 2. The Compressed Column Storage format of B

We apply the Lanczos method on the modified matrix $A = B^t B$. Since A is expected to be significantly less sparse than B, we do not compute A explicitly. We instead store both B and B^t. The multiplication $A\boldsymbol{w}_i$ is computed as $B^t(B\boldsymbol{w}_i)$. The CRS format of storage of B is not suitable during the outer multiplication. We need B^t in the CRS format, or equivalently B in the compressed column storage (CCS) format, as illustrated in Fig. 2. Although this leads to duplicate storage for the same matrix, the resulting overhead in the running time turns out to be negligible, and the extra space requirement tolerable.

3.2 The Structure of the Matrix B

The most time-consuming step in the Lanczos iteration is the matrix-vector multiplication $A\boldsymbol{w}_i = B^t(B\boldsymbol{w}_i)$. Optimizing strategies to speed up this operation call for an investigation of the structure of the matrix B. As we see later, this structure also has important bearings on load balancing.

The n columns of B are composed of two blocks. The first t columns of B correspond to small primes in the factor base (see the linear-sieve algorithm [13]). The remaining columns of B correspond to the $2M + 1$ variables arising out of the sieving interval. For $1 \leq i \leq t$, the i-th column heuristically contains about m/p_i non-zero entries, where p_i is the i-th prime. For small values of i, these columns are, therefore, rather dense. The last $2M + 1$ entries in each row contain exactly two non-zero entries which are -1. The two -1 values may happen to coincide, resulting in a single non-zero entry of -2, but this event has a very low probability and is ignored in our subsequent discussion. Each of the last $2M + 1$ columns contains $2m/n$ non-zero entries on an average. For $m \leq 2n$, this value is ≤ 4.

About three-fourth of the non-zero entries of B are $+1$. Most of the remaining non-zero entries are -1. While multiplying a vector by B or B^t, one gives special attention to the matrix entries ± 1. In a typical sum of the form $\sum_r b_r w_{ir}$ with non-zero entries b_r of B and entries w_{ir} of the vector $\boldsymbol{w}_i$, the addition of the product $b_r w_{ir}$ is replaced by the addition of w_{ir} if $b_r = 1$ or by the subtraction of w_{ir} if $b_r = -1$. Moreover, if we *know* beforehand a particular value of b_r (like $b_r = -1$ in the last $2M + 1$ rows of B^t), a multi-way branching based upon the value of b_r may be replaced by a single unconditional operation (like subtraction for $b_r = -1$). Finally, as pointed out in [11], a good strategy to speed up the matrix-vector multiplication is to perform the modulo q reduction after the entire expression $\sum_r b_r w_{ir}$ is evaluated. Since b_r are single-precision integers and w_{ir} are general elements of $\mathbf{GF}(q)$, the word size of $\sum_r b_r w_{ir}$ is only slightly larger than that of q, even when there are many terms in the sum (like during multiplication by the first row of B^t).

During the matrix-vector multiplication operation, when a particular row of B or B^t is to be multiplied by a vector, only those vector entries which correspond to the indices of the non-zero matrix entries are needed for multiplication. Since B is a sparse matrix, these indices are usually widely apart. This, in turn, indicates that almost every multiplication of a matrix entry by a vector entry encounters a page fault while accessing the vector entry. The effect of these page faults is more pronounced in a parallel implementation, where multiple processes or threads vie for shared L2 cache memory. This problem can be solved by rearranging the rows and columns of B so as to bring the non-zero entries as close to each other as possible. For linear-sieve matrices, the $m \times (2M + 1)$ block of the entries with value -1 readily yields to such rearrangement possibilities. Our experience suggests that it is possible to bring the -1 values close to each other for over 50% of the occurrences.

It is important to comment here that although the above optimization tricks are applied to matrices generated from the linear-sieve method, they apply identically to matrices generated by other sieving algorithms. The cubic-sieve method [13] generates matrices with the only exception that exactly three (instead of two) non-zero entries of -1 are present in the last $2M + 1$ columns in each row. Matrices generated by the number-field-sieve method [14] do not contain the block of -1's. They instead contain two copies of the block resembling the first t columns of linear-sieve matrices. One of these blocks corresponds to small rational primes and has small positive entries, whereas the other block corresponds to small complex primes and has small negative entries. In any case, most of the non-zero entries of the matrices are ± 1.

4   Parallel Implementation

We now elaborate our efforts to parallelize the Lanczos iteration given as
Algorithm 1. The different iterations of the Lanczos loop are inherently sequential, that is, no iteration may start before the previous iteration completes. We
instead parallelize each iteration separately. More precisely, each of the following operations is individually parallelized: matrix-vector product, vector-vector
product, scalar-vector product, vector-vector addition and subtraction, and vector copy.

4.1   Load Balancing

Suppose that each basic operation is distributed to run in parallel in P processors. In order to avoid long waits during synchronization, each parallelization
step must involve careful load balancing among the P processors. For most of the
operations just mentioned, an equitable load distribution is straightforward. For
example, each addition, subtraction or multiplication operation on two (dense)
vectors of size n is most equitably distributed if each processor handles exactly
n/P entries of the operand vectors.

Non-trivial efforts are needed by the matrix-vector product $v_{i+1} = B^t(Bw_i)$.
This operation is actually carried out as two matrix-vector products:

    a. $z = Bw_i$
    b. $v_{i+1} = B^t z$

The first of these products involves multiplication of the vector w_i by the rows
of B. The rows of B do not show significant variations among one another, in
terms of both the number of non-zero entries and the values of these entries. As
a result, it suffices to distribute an equal number m/P of rows to each processor.
For small values of P (like $P \leq 8$), the number m/P is large enough to absorb
small statistical variations among the different rows.

The second product involves multiplication of z by the columns of B. There
exist marked variations among the different columns of B, in terms of both the
count of non-zero entries and the values of these entries. A blind distribution
of n/P columns of B to each processor leads to very serious load imbalance
among the processors. The implementation of [10] starts with the distribution
of an equal number of columns to each processor. It subsequently interchanges
columns among the processors until each processor gets an approximately equal
share of non-zero entries. In the end, this strategy achieves both an equal number
of columns and an equal number of non-zero entries, for each processor.

Since we work in a shared-memory architecture, data transmission delays are
not of concern to us, so we drop the requirement of equality in the number of
columns across different processors. Second, we consider the fact that an equality
in the number of non-zero entries is not a good measure of the actual load, since
our implementation handles the three types of non-zero values of a matrix entry
(1, -1 and anything else) differently. We assign appropriate weights to these
three types of entries, based upon the time needed to perform the respective

arithmetic operations by the underlying multiple-precision integer library. A scheme that worked well for our implementations is to assign a weight of 1.0 to each matrix entry $+1$, a weight of 1.2 to each matrix entry -1, and a weight of 1.5 to a non-zero entry other than ± 1.

Such a system of assigning a fixed weight to each non-zero value, although justifiable and capable of producing nearly optimal solutions, looks somewhat heuristic and can be improved upon. The trouble is we do not explicitly consider the dependence of the timing of an arithmetic operation on the values of its operands. For example, each non-zero entry of B other than ± 1 involves a multiplication, the running time of which may depend on the value of the matrix entry. Moreover, the value of the accumulating sum also plays a role in the timing. An exact characterization of this dependence appears well beyond the control of a programmer, because several factors (including the implementation of the multiple-precision library, the effects of the compiler, the instruction set of the processor) play potentially important roles in this connection.

In view of this, we suggest the following strategy. We actually record the timing against each non-zero entry of B, when B^t is multiplied by a vector z. This vector z may be chosen randomly from $\mathbf{GF}(q)^m$. Another strategy is to run a few iterations of the Lanczos loop itself and record the element-wise timings during the product $B^t z$. (For a few initial iterations, the vector w_i remains sparse, so timing data for, say, the first ten iterations may be discarded.) Data obtained from a reasonable number of multiplications $B^t z$ is averaged to assign a *true* weight to each non-zero entry of B.

The weight of a column is the sum of the weights of its non-zero entries. We distribute columns to P processors in such a way that each processor receives an equal share of the total load. To each processor, we first assign a chunk from the first t columns. The resulting load imbalance is later repaired by distributing chunks from the remaining $2M+1$ columns. In a linear-sieve matrix, $2M+1 \gg t$ (for example, $t = 7,000$ and $2M+1 = 60,001$ for the matrix we have from [13]). Moreover, each of the last $2M + 1$ columns is rather low-weight. As a result, a fine load balancing among the processors is easy to achieve.

4.2 Load Balancing in Parallel

A limitation of the above load-balancing scheme is that the timing figures are measured by a sequential version of the code. However, we apply these timing data in a parallel environment which may be quite different from a sequential environment. This means that operations that are equitably distributed according to sequential timing data may lead to improper load balancing. We solve this problem by measuring the timings from runs of the matrix-vector multiplication in parallel. We start with a crude load-balancing scheme in which the columns of B are alternately distributed to the processes/threads. Unfortunately, a practical implementation of this strategy did not yield better performance in our experiments. Nonetheless, we mention this strategy here with the hope that it may prove to be useful in related settings.

4.3   Thread-Level vs. Process-Level Parallelism

We carried out our implementations on an eight-core machine using thread-level parallelism (TLP) provided by Pthreads and OpenMP, and process-level parallelism (PLP) involving shared memory and semaphores. The Lanczos algorithm was initially programmed using functions from the GMP [15] library, prefixed with mpz. These functions allocate dynamic memory to output operands, giving rise to heap contention. Assigning each thread its own heap, as can be achieved by the Hoard memory allocator [16], eliminated the problem. As an alternative approach, we considered the fast, low-level mpn routines provided by GMP. Unlike mpz, the mpn functions do not allocate memory to its output operands and assume that an appropriate amount of memory is already allocated to each output operand. Before starting the Lanczos loop, we allocated memory to all loop variables. This made fast GMP routines usable even in a thread-level implementation, without costly waits arising out of heap contention.

We also investigated an alternative implementation of the Lanczos algorithm, using both TLP and PLP. A proprietary library CCrypto was used for this implementation. This library was written and optimized for 32-bit architectures. With some efforts, it could be ported to 64-bit architectures, but absence of platform-specific optimization tricks resulted in a library somewhat slower than GMP. Since our primary focus was to investigate the parallelization possibilities of the Lanczos algorithm, we continued to work with the slow library. Indeed, the highest speedup figures were obtained by PLP under the CCrypto library.

5   Experimental Results

The computations were carried out on an Intel® Xeon® E5410 dual-socket quad-core Linux server. The eight processors run at a clock speed of 2.33 GHz and support 64-bit computations. The machine has 8 GBytes of main memory and a shared L2 cache of size 24 MBytes across 8 cores. One of the linear systems (q-149) used in testing the algorithm was obtained by the linear-sieve method. Larger systems were generated imitating the distribution of elements in the q-149 matrix. Here, we report our implementation on a $1,600,000 \times 2,200,000$ system (q-512) modulo a 512-bit prime. The thread-level parallelism was obtained separately using Pthreads and OpenMP version 4.3.2. We also exploited process-level parallelism under low-level shared-memory and semaphore constructs. All these implementations used GMP version 4.3.1, for multi-precision computations. The CCrypto library, on the other hand, was used in conjunction with Pthreads (TLP) and also with shared memory and semaphores (PLP).

Fig. 3 shows the process-level and the thread-level speedups for the system q-512, obtained as a function of the number of cores, by GMP and CCrypto. We obtained a maximum speedup of 6.57 using a combination of PLP and CCrypto, whereas a maximum speedup of 5.11 was registered using a combination of PLP and GMP. For the thread-level implementations, the maximum speedup obtained was 4.51 with GMP and 5.96 with CCrypto. From Fig. 3(b), we notice that the speedup figures obtained by Pthreads and OpenMP were

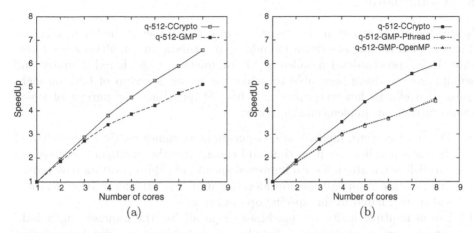

Fig. 3. Speedup: (a) Process-level parallelism   (b) Thread-level parallelism

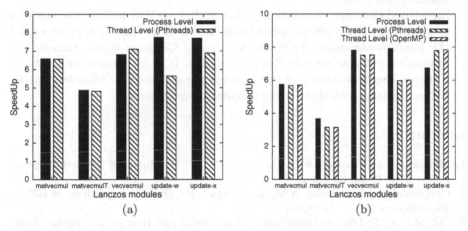

Fig. 4. Speedup obtained by individual modules of Lanczos   (a) CCrypto   (b) GMP

almost identical. However, it remains unexplained why thread-level implementations consistently exhibit somewhat poorer performance than the corresponding process-level implementations.

Fig. 4 shows the speedup values achieved by the major modules of the Lanczos loop. In these figures, `matvecmul` stands for multiplication by B, `matvecmulT` denotes multiplication by B^t, and `vecvecmul` stands for the average over the three products $v_{i+1}^t v_{i+1}$, $v_{i+1}^t v_i$, $w_i^t v_{i+1}$. Finally, `update-w` stands for the computation of w_{i+1} (Step 2 of Algorithm 1) without the vector-vector products, and `update-x` represents the computation of x_i (Steps 3 and 4 of Algorithm 1). It is evident from Fig. 4 that the matrix-vector products (particularly the multiplication by B^t) constitute the practical bottleneck in the parallelization of the Lanczos algorithm.

6   Conclusion

In this paper, we report an aggressive attempt to parallelize the Lanczos sparse linear system solving algorithm modulo large primes, on a multi-core architecture. Using process-level parallelism in conjunction with shared memory and semaphores, we have been able to achieve a record speedup of 6.57 on eight cores. Our efforts, however, open up a host of questions, the pursuit of which would further our implementation study.

a) The matrix-vector multiplication operation consumes nearly three-fourth of the total parallel execution time and constitutes the practical bottleneck in parallelization attempts. An improved speedup in this operation may reduce the absolute running time considerably, and this calls for further research endeavor tailored to this specific operation only.

b) Use of multiple multi-core machines to parallelize the Lanczos solver indicates a new combination of distributed and shared-memory computation and may lead to more positive results in favor of the parallelizability of the Lanczos algorithm.

c) Structured Gaussian elimination [4] is a technique that reduces the size of a sparse matrix and is often applied before invoking a sparse system solver like the Lanczos algorithm. Typically, structured Gaussian elimination results in smaller but considerably denser matrices. It is an interesting study to compare the performance of the Lanczos algorithm on a (relatively) dense reduced matrix with that on the original sparse matrix.

References

1. Menezes, A.J., Vanstone, S.A., Oorschot, P.C.V.: Handbook of Applied Cryptography. CRC Press, Inc., Boca Raton (1996)
2. Coppersmith, D., Odlyzko, A.M., Schroeppel, R.: Discrete logarithms in GF(p). Algorithmica 1(1), 1–15 (1986)
3. Odlyzko, A.M.: Discrete logarithms in finite fields and their cryptographic significance. In: Beth, T., Cot, N., Ingemarsson, I. (eds.) EUROCRYPT 1984. LNCS, vol. 209, pp. 224–314. Springer, Heidelberg (1985)
4. LaMacchia, B.A., Odlyzko, A.M.: Solving large sparse linear systems over finite fields. In: Menezes, A., Vanstone, S.A. (eds.) CRYPTO 1990. LNCS, vol. 537, pp. 109–133. Springer, Heidelberg (1991)
5. Montgomery, P.L.: A block Lanczos algorithm for finding dependencies over GF(2). In: Guillou, L.C., Quisquater, J.-J. (eds.) EUROCRYPT 1995. LNCS, vol. 921, pp. 106–120. Springer, Heidelberg (1995)
6. Wiedemann, D.H.: Solving sparse linear equations over finite fields. IEEE Transactions on Information Theory 32, 54–62 (1986)
7. Penninga, O.: Finding column dependencies in sparse systems over F_2 by block Wiedemann. Master's thesis, Centrum voor Wiskunde en Informatica, Amsterdam, The Netherlands (1998)
8. Dumas, J.G., Villard, G.: Computing the rank of large sparse matrices over finite fields. Computer Algebra in Scientific Computing CASC, Technische Universität München, Germany (2002)

9. Yang, L.T., Brent, R.P.: The parallel improved Lanczos method for integer factorization over finite fields for public key cryptosystems. In: ICPP Workshops, pp. 106–114 (2001)
10. Hwang, W., Kim, D.: Load balanced block Lanczos algorithm over GF(2) for factorization of large keys. In: Robert, Y., Parashar, M., Badrinath, R., Prasanna, V.K. (eds.) HiPC 2006. LNCS, vol. 4297, pp. 375–386. Springer, Heidelberg (2006)
11. Page, D.: Parallel solution of sparse linear systems defined over GF(p). Technical Report CSTR-05-003, University of Bristol (2004)
12. OpenMP: The OpenMP API Specification for Parallel Programming, http://www.openmp.org/
13. Das, A., Veni Madhavan, C.E.: On the cubic sieve method for computing discrete logarithms over prime fields. International Journal of Computer Mathematics 82, 1481–1495 (2005)
14. Weber, D.: Computing discrete logarithms with the general number field sieve. In: Cohen, H. (ed.) ANTS 1996. LNCS, vol. 1122, pp. 337–361. Springer, Heidelberg (1996)
15. GNU: The GNU MP Bignum Library, http://gmplib.org/
16. Berger, E.D., McKinley, K.S., Blumofe, R.D., Wilson, P.R.: Hoard: A scalable memory allocator for multithreaded applications. In: ASPLOS, pp. 117–128 (2000)

Supporting Malleability in Parallel Architectures with Dynamic CPUSETs Mapping and Dynamic MPI

Márcia C. Cera[1], Yiannis Georgiou[2], Olivier Richard[2], Nicolas Maillard[1], and Philippe O.A. Navaux[1]

[1] Universidade Federal do Rio Grande do Sul, Brazil
{marcia.cera,nicolas,navaux}@inf.ufrgs.br
[2] Laboratoire d'Informatique de Grenoble, France
{Yiannis.Georgiou,Olivier.Richard}@imag.fr

Abstract. Current parallel architectures take advantage of new hardware evolution, like the use of multicore machines in clusters and grids. The availability of such resources may also be dynamic. Therefore, some kind of adaptation is required by the applications and the resource manager to perform a good resource utilization. Malleable applications can provide a certain flexibility, adapting themselves on-the-fly, according to variations in the amount of available resources. However, to enable the execution of this kind of applications, some support from the resource manager is required, thus introducing important complexities like special allocation and scheduling policies. Under this context, we investigate some techniques to provide malleable behavior on MPI applications and the impact of this support upon a resource manager. Our study deals with two approaches to obtain malleability: dynamic CPUSETs mapping and dynamic MPI, using the OAR resource manager. The validation experiments were conducted upon Grid5000 platform. The testbed associates the charge of real workload traces and the execution of MPI benchmarks. Our results show that a dynamic approach using malleable jobs can lead to almost 25% of improvement in the resources utilization, when compared to a non-dynamic approach. Furthermore, the complexity of the malleability support, for the resource manager, seems to be overlapped by the improvement reached.

1 Introduction

Nowadays, a widely used trend for clusters of computers is to be composed by multicore machines. Furthermore, today's parallel architectures eventually include some dynamicity or flexibility in their resource availability. One example is the shared utilization of multicore machines. As applications have different execution times, the cores availability change dynamically. In such dynamic scenario, achieving a good resource utilization is a challenge. This paper studies alternatives to improve the resources utilization of current parallel architectures. Our motivations concern about *Quality of Service advantages* - better resources are used, faster work is executed and more users can be satisfied; *idle cycles minimization or elimination* - improvement of resources utilization can reduce idle cycles and conserve energy.

Improving resource utilization is directly related to the resource management and allocation. Resource management systems (RMS) are responsible to schedule jobs upon

K. Kant et al. (Eds.): ICDCN 2010, LNCS 5935, pp. 242–257, 2010.

the available resources and also to launch and monitor them. According to Feitelson and Rudolph [1], jobs can be: rigid, moldable, malleable or evolving. We are specially interested in malleable jobs because they can adapt themselves to resources with dynamic availability, and thus provide a better utilization of the current parallel architectures resources. However, malleable jobs demand a special treatment, with more complex allocation and scheduling policies. Thus, we investigate the complexity of treating malleable jobs and compare it with the gain/improvements of resources utilization.

The contribution of this paper is twofold: To study two different approaches that provide malleability to MPI jobs; To experiment those techniques upon a flexible resource management system in order to measure the advantages and the difficulties to support malleable jobs.

Our study uses two approaches to provide malleability: dynamic CPUSETs mapping and dynamic MPI. The first one is well-adapted to multicore machines and allows any parallel job to exploit malleability, through a fine control and manipulation of the available cores. The second approach uses a dynamic MPI application, able to adapt itself to the available cluster nodes. Note that, dynamic MPI means that applications are developed to be malleable employing MPI-2 dynamic process creation and fault tolerance mechanisms.

The impact of the support of these two malleability approaches upon resource managers, is evaluated considering a specific flexible RMS called OAR [2]. The experiments were performed upon Grid5000 platform using real workload traces of a known supercomputer. Our goal is to make a close analysis of the malleable application behavior in a scenario near to the real one. The results obtained show that cluster utilization can be improved in almost 25% using both of malleability approaches, when compared with a non-malleable approach. Furthermore, the advantages obtained by a possible integration of malleable jobs upon a resource manager seem to outperform the complexities of their support.

The remainder of this paper is organized as follows. Section 2 introduces the definitions and related works about job malleability and its support in today's resource managers. After that, Section 3 describes the two approaches to provide malleable behavior and the reasons of choosing them. Explanations about experimenting applications and their results, with CPUSETs mapping and dynamic MPI, are shown in Section 4. Finally, Section 5 describes our concluding remarks and the future work perspectives.

2 Related Works and Definitions

In the context of resource managers or job schedulers, parallel applications are represented as jobs, which have a running time t and a number of processors p. Feitelson and Rudolph [1] proposed four jobs classes based on the parameter p and the resource manager support. *Rigid* jobs require a fixed p, specified by the users, for a certain t time. In *moldable*, the resource manager choose p at start time from a range of choices given by the users. The job adapts to p that will not change at execution time. In *evolving*, p may change on-the-fly as job demand, which must be satisfied to avoid crashes. In *malleable*, p may also change on-the-fly, but the changes are required by the resource manager. In other words, malleable jobs are able to adapt themselves to changes in resources availability.

There are relevant theoretical results describing requirements, execution scheme and algorithms to efficiently schedule malleable applications [3]. Moreover, there is a growing interest to offer malleability in practice, because it can improve both resource utilization and response time [1,4,5,6,7]. Furthermore, a good approach towards the support of malleable jobs can be achieved by a co-design of runtime-system and programming environment [1]. This assertion can be observed in some practice malleability initiatives like PCM and Dynaco. PCM (Process Checkpointing and Migration) [8,9,10] uses migration to implement split and merge operations reconfiguring application according to resources availability. PCM demands an instrumentation of MPI code, using its API and specifying which data structures are involved in malleable operations. It interacts with a specific framework, IOS (Internet Operating System), performing like a resource manager, which is composed by an agents network to profile informations about resources and applications.

In the same way, Dynaco [11] enables MPI applications to spawn new processes when resources become available or stop them when resources are announced to disappear. To provide malleable features, Dynaco must know the adaptive decision procedures, a description of problems in the planning of adaptation, and the implementation of adaptive actions. Also, the programmer must include *points* on its source code identifying safe states to perform adaptive actions ensuring application correctness. Dynaco has its own resource manager, Koala, providing data and processor co-allocation, resource monitoring and fault tolerance.

Excluding initiatives with their own systems to provide resource management like the previously introduced, and according to our up-to-date knowledge, there is no existing implementation of malleable jobs support upon a generic resource manager since it is a rather complicated task. Nevertheless, some previous work have studied specific prototypes for the direct support of malleable jobs [7,6] with different constraints. For instance, Utrera et al. [6] proposes: a virtual malleability combining moldability (to decide the number of processes at start time), folding (to make the jobs malleable) and Co-Scheduling (to share resources). It uses Co-Scheduling to share processors after a job folding and migration to use the new processors after a job expansion. Our work also explores a similar folding technique, with dynamic CPUSETs mapping in multi-core machines.

In [7], an Application Parallelism Manager (APM) provides dynamic online scheduling with malleable jobs upon shared memory architectures (SMP). The approach combined the advantages of time and space sharing scheduling. It achieved a 100% system utilization and a direct response time. Nevertheless the system was not directly adaptable to distributed-memory machines with message-passing and this work, as far as we know, has not evolved in a real implementation of the prototype.

We try to investigate the requirements of malleable jobs considering a generic resource management system, OAR [2]. It is an open source Resource Management System, which has evolved towards a certain 'versatility'. OAR provides a robust solution, used as a production system in various cases (Grid5000 [12], Ciment[1]). Moreover, due to its open architectural choices, based upon high level components (Database and Perl/Ruby Programming Languages), it can be easily extended to integrate new features

---

[1] https://ciment.ujf-grenoble.fr/cigri

and treat research issues. In our context, we exploit the capabilities of *Best Effort* jobs, also presented on [13]. They are defined as jobs with minimum priority, able to harness the idle resources of a cluster, but they will be directly killed when the resources are required. The idea of *Best Effort* jobs is comparable with the notion of 'cycle stealing' initiated by Condor [14] and the High Throughput Computing approach.

3 Supporting Malleability with Dynamic CPUSETs Mapping and Dynamic MPI

Based on issues highlighted in Section 2, we study the use of malleability to improve the utilization of current parallel architectures. Through our experiences, we evaluate the resources utilization and the overhead to support malleability on MPI applications. Under our context, the resources dynamicity is represented by their availability. In other words, once it is possible identify the unused resources (*i.e.* the idle ones), they can be used in low priority executions. Such set of unused resources will be change on-the-fly according new jobs arrives or old ones finishes characterizing its dynamicity.

Dynamic CPUSETs mapping and dynamic MPI were the approaches selected by us to provide malleability. As we explain later they have different levels of complexity. Our goal is to experiment those techniques upon a resource management system, in order to be able to value the advantages and the complexities of their support. We therefore constructed a prototype using features of OAR resource management system. OAR modularity and flexibility permitted us to integrate the above techniques without actually implementing them on its core.

The module that we developed aside OAR is based on two notions: the *Best Effort* job type as described in Section 2 and a resource discovery command, which provides the current and near-future available resources. To provide malleability using OAR we consider that a malleable job is constructed by a rigid and a *Best Effort* part. The rigid part stays always intact so that it can guarantee the job completeness. In the same time, the *Best Effort* part is responsible for the flexibility of the job. Hence, using the resource discovery command, which informs the application for the variations on the resources availability, we come to two scenarios: *Best Effort* jobs can be either *killed* meaning malleable job shrinking or further *submitted*, allowing malleable job growing. This prototype based on bash scripts is transparent to the user and does not request special care about the two parts of the OAR malleable job, in any of the two proposed malleability techniques.

3.1 Dynamic CPUSETs Mapping Requirements

CPUSETs[2] are lightweight objects in the Linux kernel that enable users to partition their multiprocessor machine by creating execution areas. CPUSETs are used by the resource management systems to provide CPU execution affinity and cleaner process deletion when the job is finished.

Dynamic CPUSETs mapping technique is the on-the-fly manipulation of the amount of cores per node allocated to an application. This technique is simple and well-adapted

---

[2] http://www.bullopensource.org/cpuset/

to multicore machines. CPUSETs mapping allows expanding or folding of the application upon the same node. In more detail, if we have multiple processes of a MPI application executing upon a multicore node, then those processes can be executed upon one or more cores of the same node. CPUSETs mapping is a system level technique and it is transparent to the application. It can provide a level of malleability upon any MPI application and it is completely independent of the application source code. The only restriction is that the malleability is performed separately upon each node, which means that multiple processes have to be initiated upon at least one core of a node. Furthermore to take full advantage of the malleability possibilities, the number of processes started upon a node should be equal or larger than the number of cores per node. For instance, a 16 processes MPI application should be ideally initiated upon 4 nodes of a 4 cores-per-node cluster or upon 2 nodes of a 8 cores-per-node cluster.

In the context of CPUSETs mapping technique, the specific OAR malleability prototype, defines the rigid part of a malleable job to occupy one core of each participating node. This feature comes from the CPUSETs restriction explained above. When more cores of the same nodes become available, then *Best Effort* jobs are further submitted. In the same time the CPUSETs mapping technique performs the expanding operation so that the application processes that were sharing a core migrate to the newly available cores. In the opposite case, when an external rigid job asks for resources, some *Best Effort* jobs need to be killed. In this case, the CPUSETs mapping technique performs a folding of processes on the fewer remaining cores, and the demanded cores are given to the arriving rigid job. Therefore, malleability is achieved by the use of *Best Effort* jobs and the CPUSETs folding and expanding of processes. Figure 1 presents some scenarios, showing the different stages for only one of the participating nodes of the cluster.

It seems that besides the restrictions, this system level approach can actually provide malleability without complicating the function of OAR resource manager. Nevertheless, there are issues that have to be taken into account. The overhead of the expanding or folding operation upon the application has to be measured. Furthermore, since our context concerns cluster of shared memory architectures, it will be interesting to see how two different MPI applications running upon different cores on the same node, would perform during the expanding and folding phases.

3.2 Dynamic MPI Requirements

Dynamic MPI applications have malleable behavior since they perform growing and shrinking operations adapting themselves to variations in the availability of the resources. In growing, some application workload is destined to new resources through MPI processes spawning, which is a feature of the MPI-2 norm (MPI_Comm_spawn and correlated primitives) [15]. In shrinking, processes running on resources announced as unavailable must be safely finalized and some procedure is required to prevent application crash. We adopted a simple one: tasks executing in processes being shrunk are identified and will be restarted in the future. It is not optimal, but ensures application results correctness.

The malleability operations, growing and shrinking, are handled by a library called *lib-dynamicMPI*. This library interact with the OAR to receive information about

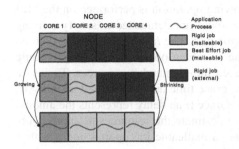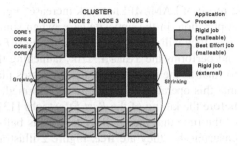

Fig. 1. Behavior of CPUSETs mapping technique upon one of the participating nodes

Fig. 2. Dynamic MPI application performing growing and shrinking upon 4 participating nodes

variations in the amount of resources available to dynamic MPI applications. According to these informations, *lib-dynamicMPI* launches the appropriate malleable action enabling the adaptation of the application to the availability of the resources, and thus the library is like a bridge between MPI applications and resource manager. As part of the growing operation, the *lib-dynamicMPI* ensures that spawning processes will be placed into the new resources. The library intercepts the MPI_Comm_spawn calls and set the physical location of the new processes according to the informations provided by the OAR. This feature is an evolution of our previous work, in which the destination of the dynamic processes was decided following one of two policies: Round-Robin (standard) and workload-based (to chose the less overloaded resource) [16], without interactions with a resource manager.

In the experiments of this paper, *lib-dynamicMPI* and dynamic MPI application are implemented with LAM/MPI[3] distribution. This MPI distribution offers a stable implementation of dynamic process creation and ways to manage dynamic resources. This last feature is provided by two commands: lamgrow to increase and lamshrink to decrease the amount of nodes available in LAM/MPI network (LAM/MPI applications run up a known set of resources, which begins by lamboot before application starting time and ends by lamhalt after application execution). Note that LAM/MPI enables the management of nodes, which can be composed by many cores, but cannot manage isolated cores. The lamgrow and lamshrink commands will always be called by *lib-dynamicMPI* when some change is announced by OAR. Once there are changes in LAM/MPI network, the malleable applications perform the appropriate operation - growing or shrinking.

As previously explained, in our experiments, a malleable job is composed by rigid and *Best Effort* parts. In the context of dynamic MPI, the rigid part is composed by the minimum unit manageable in LAM/MPI, *i.e.* one node. The *Best Effort* part is as large as the amount of resources available, which is determined by the resource discovery command. The malleable application begins by taking into account the initial amount of resources available, *i.e.*, the initial size of the malleable job. When a *Best Effort* job is further submitted, *lib-dynamicMPI* is notified and launches the lamgrow. As

---

[3] http://www.lam-mpi.org/

a result of LAM/MPI network increase, a growing operation is performed on the MPI application. In the opposite case, when some nodes are demanded to satisfy arriving jobs, they will be requested from the *Best Effort* part. The *lib-dynamicMPI* is notified and performs the `lamshrink`, launching the shrinking operation and the procedure to finalize the execution of the processes placed into demanded resources. To ensure that this operation will be safely performed, a grace time delay is applied upon OAR, before the killing of the *Best Effort* jobs [13]. Grace time delay represents the amount of the time that the OAR system waits before destinate the resources to another job, ensuring that they are free. Figure 2 illustrates a malleable job upon 4 nodes with 4 cores performing growing and shrinking operations.

4 Experimental Evaluation

This section presents results using resources from Grid5000 platform [12]. The experiments were performed upon a cluster (IBM System x3455) composed by DualCPU-DualCore AMD Opteron 2218 (2.6 GHz/2 MB L2 cache/800 MHz) and 4GB memory per node with Gigabit Ethernet.

We chose two applications to investigate the malleable jobs requirements. For CPUSETs mapping technique we used the NAS benchmarks [17], which are widely used to evaluate the performance of parallel supercomputers. We will present results of BT (Block Tridiagonal Solver) and CG (Conjugate Gradient) class C benchmarks with their MPI3.3 implementation[4]. Although our approach is applicable to the entire set of NAS applications, we chose the results of two of them to details in this paper for space reasons.

In dynamic MPI tests, we used a malleable implementation of the Mandelbrot fractal *i.e.* a Mandelbrot able to grow or shrink, during the execution time, according the resource availability. Although Mandelbrot problem does not require malleable features to be solved, we adopted a well-known MPI application to become malleable through *lib-dynamicMPI*. The malleable Mandelbrot starts with a master that will spawn workers (one by core available), manager tasks and store the results. Workers receive tasks, execute them, return results and wait for more tasks. Mandelbrot is able to identify resources changes and launch the malleable operations. In growing, new workers are spawned upon resources that become available, and in shrinking workers inform to master which are the executing tasks and then finalize their execution.

Two series of experiments were chosen to test malleability through the above 2 techniques. The first operates through increasing or decreasing of resources, without using the resource manager. In this way, we can evaluate the malleability impact in applications performance without considering the issues related to the resource manager. The results of these experiments are presented in Sections 4.1 and 4.2.

The second series of experiments evaluates the OAR resource manager support to malleable jobs. Our testbed is based on workload trace injection, to provide the typical rigid jobs of the cluster, along with a demo that submits one malleable job at a time. In such initial work we do not deal with multiple malleable jobs which initiate more complex scheduling issues (equipartitioning, etc). We measure the overall resources

---

[4] http://www.nas.nasa.gov/Resources/Software/npb_changes.html

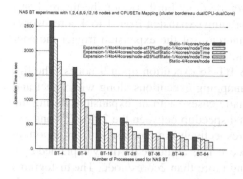

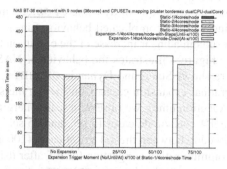

Fig. 3. NAS BT-(4,9,16,25,36,49,64) behavior with Static and Dynamic CPUSETs mapping operations with direct expansion from 1 to 4 cores

Fig. 4. NAS BT-36 behavior with Static and Dynamic CPUSETs mapping operation with gradual and direct expansion from 1 to 4 cores

utilization and the impact of malleability upon the rigid workload. In more detail, the experiments are based on real workload traces from DAS2 grid platform [18], which represent the workload of twelve month (year 2003) on 5 clusters. A specific cluster and time range is selected from these traces, to charge Grid5000 resources. Malleable applications will operate using the idle resources, *i.e.* the resources that were not charged from normal workload injection. In this way, the dynamic events are guided by resource availability as can be seen in Section 4.3.

4.1 Malleability on Multicore Nodes with Dynamic CPUSETs Mapping

In this series of experiments we evaluate the impact of the CPUSETs mapping technique upon NAS benchmarks. In Figure 3 we present the results of NAS BT application performing static and dynamic CPUSETs mapping. In each case the 'Static-1/4cores/node' box implies the use of 1 core per participating node that is the minimum folding of processes that can be applied. On the other hand, 'Static-4/4cores/node' box implies the use of 4 cores per node, which represents the maximum expansion of processes that can be made upon a dualCPU/dualCore architecture. For instance, in the case of BT-36 we use 9 nodes with 4 processes running upon each node: 4 processes on 1 core for the Static-1/4 case and 1 process on 1 core for the Static 4/4 case. The 3 boxes between the above 'Static-1/4' and 'Static-4/4' instances represent different dynamic instances using the dynamic CPUSETs mapping approach. All 3 instances imply the use of 1 core per participating node at the beginning of the execution performing a dynamic CPUSETs expansion to use 4 cores after specific time intervals. The expansion trigger moment is placed on the 25%, 50% and 75% of the 'Static-1/4cores/node' execution time of each BT.

It is interesting to see the speedup between the Static cases of '1/4' and '4/4' cores/ node among each different BT. We observe that this speedup becomes more important as the number of BT processes go smaller. In the case of BT-4 the speedup from the use of 4/4 cores/node to 1/4 is 1597 sec. which means 61,5% of the 1/4 cores/node time. Whereas the relevant speedup of BT-25 is 350 sec. or 53,8% of the 1/4 time, and to

BT-64 is 100 sec. or 33,3% of the 1/4 cores/node time. Furthermore, the figure shows that the technique of dynamic CPUSETs mapping expansion from 1 to 4 cores works fine without complicated behavior. Linear increase of the expansion trigger moment results in a linear increase of the execution time.

Figure 4 illustrates the behavior of NAS BT-36 execution upon 9 nodes. The figure shows Static and Dynamic CPUSETs mapping executions along with direct and gradual expansion cases. Considering the static cases (with no expansions during the execution time), we observe a really marginal speedup between the 2/4 to 3/4 and 3/4 to 4/4 cores/node cases (5 sec. and 25 sec. respectively) in contrast with an important speedup between the 1/4 to 2/4 cases (200 sec.). This could be partially explained by a communication congestion for BT after using more than 2cores/node. The histograms representing the dynamic CPUSETs direct and gradual expansions, show us that gradual expansions result in faster execution times. Indeed for each case of the gradual expansion, we perform 3 expansions: 1/4 to 2/4, 2/4 to 3/4 and 3/4 to 4/4 cores/node until a specific instant. On the opposite case of direct expansion we perform only one: from 1/4 to 4/4 cores/node at the above same instant. Thus, after this same instant, both cases are using 4/4 cores/node. The difference is that in the first one there has already taken place 3 expansions whereas in the second one only 1 expansion. For BT benchmark, the results show that it is better to perform gradual small expansions whenever resources are free, in contrast of waiting multiple free resources and perform one bigger direct expansion. Moreover, these results show that the overhead of the expansion process, is marginal, when trading-off with the gain of using the one or more new cores.

Figure 5 illustrates the experiments of 3 different cases of BT upon different number of nodes. In more detail we try to measure the impact of the use of different number of nodes - with one process per core - on their execution time. For every different BT, we experiment with the ideal case of using equal number of nodes with processes (BT-16,36,64 with 16,36 and 64 nodes respectively) along with the case of using equal number of processes with cores (BT-16,36,64 with 4,9 and 16 nodes respectively). It seems that it is always faster to use more nodes. This can be explained by the fact that processes do not share communication links and memory. Nevertheless, this speedup is not very significant implying that, for BT application, the second case is more interesting to use. This is because, we can also perform malleability operations with dynamic CPUSETs mapping techniques. Hence, although we have a worst performance we can achieve better overall resources utilization.

Figure 6 presents static and dynamic cases in a Dedicated (DM) or Shared Memory (SM) context of BT-64 and CG-64 benchmarks. Concerning the Static and Dedicated memory cases of BT-64 and CG-64 we can observe that the only important speedup is between the use of 1/4 to 2/4 cores/node for BT-64, whereas for all the rest the performance is quite the same. In the shared memory context, all performances decreased as expected because the benchmarks were sharing memory and communication links. Nevertheless, BT-64 presented an important sensitivity to resources dynamism. This can be observed by the fact that we have a significant performance degradation for BT-64 when it uses 1 core and CG-64 uses 3 cores of the same node; and by the fact that the performance is upgraded for BT-64 when the above roles are inversed. Finally it seems that a dynamic on-the-fly expansion with CPUSETs mapping technique, using

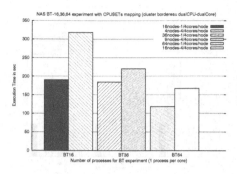

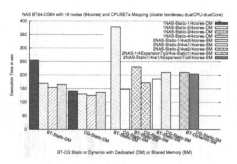

Fig. 5. NAS (BT-16,36,64) behavior with 1 process per core, different number of nodes and Static CPUSETs mapping operations

Fig. 6. NAS BT-64 and CG-64 behavior, with Shared Memory and Static/Dynamic CPUSETs mapping operations

from 1 to 3 cores/node, achieves a good performance as compared to the Static cases with shared memory. On the same time the degradation of CG-64 performance is small when BT-64 is expanding.

In the second series of our experiments we will be using BT and CG in a shared memory context. According to those last results, where BT presents more sensitivity in resources dynamism than CG, we decided to implicate BT with malleability whereas CG will represent the rigid applications. We have conducted experiments using all different NAS benchmarks and the CPUSETs Mapping technique was validated in all cases. Nevertheless, different performances were observed. Future extended versions of this work will include these experiments.

The figures of this section show the results obtained when performing only expanding operations. Nevertheless, our experiments indicated that the behavior is similar when performing folding operations. Due to lack of space, they were omitted. An in-depth analysis of the memory contention in a CPUSETs mapping context is currently under study and will be discussed and quantified in future works.

4.2 Malleability on a Cluster with Dynamic MPI

In the experiments of this section, we used the maximum of 64 cores, coming from 16 nodes (dualCPU/dualcore per node). Figures 7 and 8, show the execution time of the dynamic MPI application performing growing and shrinking operations respectively. In the growing, the application begins with the amount of cores shown in x axis (representing 25%, 50% and 75% of the total number of cores) and grows until 64 cores. In shrinking, it starts with 64 and shrinks until the x values of cores. We made two experiments: *(i)* a dynamic event is performed **at** a time limit, and *(ii)* dynamic events are gradually performed **until** a time limit. Time limit is defined as 25%, 50% or 75% of the parallel reference time. Reference time is always the execution time with the initial number of cores, *i.e.*, x to growing and 64 to shrinking.

Let p_r be the number of cores on which a reference time t_r has been measured. Thus, the parallel reference application performs $W = t_r \times p_r$ operations. The application is progressively run on more than p_r cores:

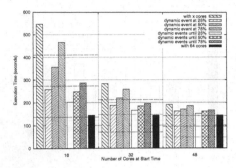 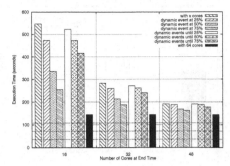

Fig. 7. Growing in dynamic MPI application: execution time *vs.* number of cores at starting time

Fig. 8. Shrinking in dynamic MPI application: execution time *vs.* number of cores at ending time

- In the first experiment (dynamic events at a time limit) it is run during $\alpha t_r (0 \leq \alpha \leq 1)$ seconds on p_r cores, and then on p cores;
- In the second experiment (dynamic events until a time limit) it is run during αt_r $(0 \leq \alpha \leq 1)$ seconds on a gradual increasing or decreasing number of cores, until reaching p cores. Then it is run until completion, without anymore changes. The number of cores increases or decreases at regular timesteps of c units. In fact, $c = 4$, since the `lamgrow` command only enables to add a whole node (2 CPUs with 2 cores) to LAM/MPI network. The number of gradual timesteps is therefore $\frac{p-p_r}{c}$, and each one lasts $\delta = \frac{\alpha t_r}{\frac{p-p_r}{c}}$ sec.

Ideal speedup in the first experiment. The execution on p_r cores has duration αt_r. At this point, $(1 - \alpha)W$ operations remain to be performed, by p cores. Ideally, this second phase runs in time $(1 - \alpha)W/p$. Therefore, the total parallel time in this case is $t_p = \alpha t_r + (1 - \alpha)t_r p_r/p$, and the speedup t_r/t_p is:

$$S = \frac{1}{\frac{p_r}{p}(1 - \alpha) + \alpha} \tag{1}$$

Ideal speedup in the second experiment. As in the previous case, the number of operations performed during the first αt_r seconds, can be computed, to obtain the parallel time of the second part of the execution on p cores. At the ith timestep $(i = 0...\frac{p-p_r}{c} - 1)$, the program is run with $p_r + ci$ cores in time δ sec. Therefore, the number of operations n_i that are executed is $\delta(p_r + ci)$. When all the p cores are available (*i.e.* at time αt_r), $\sum_{i=0}^{(p-p_r)/c-1} n_i$ operations have been run, leaving $W - \sum_{i=0}^{(p-p_r)/c-1} n_i$ to be run by p cores. Thus, the second phase has duration:

$$\frac{t_r p_r - \sum_{i=0}^{(p-p_r)/c-1} \delta(p_r + ci)}{p}, \tag{2}$$

and the total execution time in this second experiment is therefore:

$$t_p = \alpha t_r + \frac{t_r p_r - \sum_{i=0}^{(p-p_r)/c-1} \delta(p_r + ci)}{p}. \tag{3}$$

Besides,

$$\sum_{i=0}^{(p-p_r)/c-1} \delta(p_r + ci) = \delta p_r \frac{p - p_r}{c} + c\delta \sum_{i=0}^{\frac{p-p_r}{c}-1} i = \delta p_r \frac{p - p_r}{c} + c\delta \frac{(\frac{p-p_r}{c} - 1)\frac{p-p_r}{c}}{2}.$$

(4)

And since $\delta = \frac{\alpha t_r}{\frac{p-p_r}{c}}$, the latter equation yields:

$$\sum_{i=0}^{(p-p_r)/c-1} \delta(p_r + ci) = \alpha t_r p_r + \frac{\alpha t_r}{2}(p - p_r - c).$$

(5)

Therefore, the total parallel time in this case is:

$$t_p = \alpha t_r + \frac{t_r p_r - \alpha p_r t_r - \frac{\alpha t_r}{2}(p - p_r - c)}{p} = \frac{t_r}{2p}(2p_r + \alpha(p - p_r + c)).$$

(6)

And the parallel speedup t_r/t_p is:

$$S = \frac{2p}{2p_r + \alpha(p - p_r + c)}.$$

(7)

Table 1. Speedup of the dynamic MPI application

	Growing						Shrinking				
p_r	p	α	S	$S(eq.1)$	S	$S(eq.7)$	p_r	p	α	S	$S(eq.1)$	S	$S(eq.7)$
		0.25	2.12	2.29	2.70	2.84			0.25	0.30	0.31	0.28	0.27
16	64	0.50	1.53	1.60	2.20	2.21	64	16	0.50	0.43	0.40	0.30	0.30
		0.75	1.17	1.23	1.91	1.80			0.75	0.57	0.57	0.35	0.34
		0.25	1.51	1.60	1.71	1.75			0.25	0.55	0.57	0.53	0.53
32	64	0.50	1.29	1.33	1.54	1.56	64	32	0.50	0.68	0.67	0.55	0.56
		0.75	1.09	1.14	1.45	1.41			0.75	0.77	0.80	0.60	0.60
		0.25	1.18	1.23	1.26	1.27			0.25	0.77	0.80	0.76	0.77
48	64	0.50	1.12	1.14	1.18	1.21	64	48	0.50	0.86	0.86	0.77	0.79
		0.75	1.03	1.07	1.15	1.15			0.75	0.89	0.92	0.81	0.81

Table 1 shows the speedups, in which S is the speedup in practice (t_r/t_p), $S(eq.1)$ is the ideal speedup to the first experiment using the Equation 1, and $S(eq.7)$ to the second one using the Equation 7. In growing, practical speedups are slightly lower than the ideal ones, representing the overhead to perform the spawning of new processes. As Lepère et al. [3] the standard behavior in on-the-fly resources addition is that such addition cannot increases the application execution time. In the Table 1, we observe that growing speedups are always greater than 1, meaning that the new cores could improve application performance decreasing its execution time as expected. In shrinking, all speedups values are lower than 1, as the exclusion of nodes decreases the performance. In this case, practical speedup is quite similar to the theoretical one and the variations become from the execution of the procedures to avoid application crash. Summing up, the speedups show that our dynamic MPI application is able to perform upon resources with a dynamic availability.

4.3   Improving Resource Utilization Using Malleability

The second series of experiments, aims at the evaluation of the two malleability techniques upon the OAR resource manager. Experiments for both approaches, follow the same guidelines as explained in Section 4. A workload of 5 hours 'slice' of DAS2 workload with 40% of cluster utilization is injected into OAR. This workload charges the resources, representing the normal workload of the cluster. At same time one malleable job per time is submitted and will run upon the free resources, *i.e.* those that are not used by the normal workload.

The main differences of the experiments, for the two different malleability techniques, lay upon the type of application executed and on the way the malleable job is submitted on each case. For the CPUSETs mapping approach we execute BT benchmarks for the malleable job and CG benchmarks for the static workload jobs, so that we can observe the impact on resources utilization in a shared memory context. The malleable job is submitted to OAR in accordance to the guidelines of Section 3.1. This means that one core per participating node has to be occupied by the rigid part of the malleable job. Since the time of one NAS BT execution is rather small, especially with big number of processes, we decided that the malleable job will have to execute 8 NAS BT applications in a row. At the same time, CG benchmarks are continuously executed during the normal jobs allocation, as noted in the workload trace file. The number of processes for each NAS execution during the experiment is chosen according to the number of current free resources.

In the experiments of the Dynamic MPI case, the malleable job implies the execution of Mandelbrot benchmark. The normal workload jobs (from DAS2 workload traces) are empty 'sleep' jobs, just occupying the resources for a specific time. Since the malleability is performed using whole nodes, there was no need to perform real application executions with the normal workload jobs. As explained on subsection 3.2, the malleable job is submitted to OAR, by occupying only one whole node in the rigid part of the malleable job and the *Best Effort* part is as large as the amount of remaining resources.

The dynamic executions of both techniques are compared with non-dynamic experiments running the same applications. In more details, the malleable jobs submission is substituted by moldable-besteffort jobs submission. As moldable-besteffort job, we define a moldable job that starts its execution upon all free cluster resources and remains without changes until its execution ending. This means that if more resources become available they will be not used by the moldable-besteffort job and when some resources are demanded to supply arriving jobs, it will be immediately killed, like a *Best Effort* job.

Since the experimental results figures are very similar for both malleability approaches, we include only the figures featuring the support of CPUSETs mapping technique upon OAR. Figures 9 and 10 show the results of malleable and moldable-besteffort jobs respectively. It is interesting to observe the gain upon the cluster resources utilization to the dynamic context, presented in Figure 9, as compared to the non-dynamic case in Figure 10. The white vertical lines of Figure 9 until 5500 sec., represent the release of *Best Effort* jobs resources. This happens, when one group of 8 BT executions are finished until the next malleable job begins and new *Best Effort* jobs occupy the free resources. Also, at starting time the malleable job begins, only with the

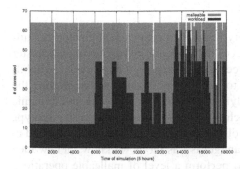
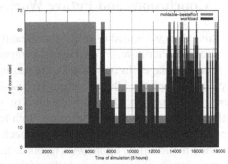

Fig. 9. Malleable job executing BT application upon the free resources of the normal workload

Fig. 10. Moldable-besteffort job executing BT application upon the free resources of the normal workload

rigid part (*i.e.* only one core) and immediately expands using the other available cores in the *Best Effort* part of the malleable job. After 5500 sec. the execution of malleable jobs start to be influenced by jobs from the workload (normal jobs). In that way, the white lines (empty spaces) also mean that the application did not have enough time to grow itself, before a new normal job arrived.

In terms of resources utilisation, since the normal workload makes use of 40% of cluster resources, this leaves a total 60% of free resources. Moldable-besteffort jobs use a 32% of the idle resources arriving at 72% of total cluster resources used. On the other hand, in the dynamic context of malleability approaches, the use of idle resources reach 57% arriving at 97% of overall cluster utilisation. Hence, an improvement of almost **25%** of resources utilization is achieved when the dynamic approaches are compared with the non-dynamic one. Furthermore, we observed the number of jobs executed during the 5 hours of experimentation. In the dynamic context, we obtained 8 successfully 'Terminated' malleable jobs, compared to 4 'Terminated' and 5 in 'Error State', for the non-dynamic one. The impact of the response time, for the normal workload, was also measured. The results have shown 8 sec. of average response time in the non-dynamic context, compared to 81 sec. of average response time in the dynamic CPUSETs mapping technique and 44 sec. in the Dynamic MPI technique. The big response time of the dynamic CPUSETs mapping technique, is explained by the allocation of one core per node by the rigid part of the malleable job. This limits the number of free resources for jobs coming from the normal workload. The response time for Dynamic MPI approach, is explained by the 40 sec. grace time delay to the MPI malleable application. This grace time was added to OAR for the shrinking operations, as presented on Section 3.2.

Although our initial experiments consider only one workload trace and one malleable job at a time, they enabled the verification of a significant improvement in resource utilization brought by the employment of the malleable jobs when compared to a non-dynamic approach. In other words, we reach our experiments goal, which was verify if the efforts to enable malleable jobs upon OAR would be outperformed by the gain reached in resource utilization. Future works will include experiments with different workload traces and multiple malleable jobs.

5 Conclusions and Future Works

In this paper we aimed to employ malleability features to provide better resources utilization. Furthermore, we analyzed the impact of the malleability support upon a cluster resource manager. In our context, the resources dynamicity is guide by their availability, *i.e.*, unused (or idle) resources are used to perform malleable jobs, improving the resource utilization. Our study focused on dynamic CPUSETs mapping and dynamic MPI as ways to provide malleability. Both techniques were implemented as a prototype upon OAR resource manager. The approach of dynamic CPUSETs mapping applied to provide malleability, upon OAR resource manager is - as far as we know - a new idea in the area. It is an interesting alternative to perform a level of malleable operations efficiently, which does not require changes in the application source code. On the other hand, some constraints must be respected: *i.e.* always start processes upon at least one core of all participating nodes and have as much processes as the maximum amount of cores that can be available. We also identified that besides CPUSETs mapping technique, a good memory management is essential to memory-bound applications. In the future, we wish to improve our CPUSETs study considering memory issues, by increasing the range of applications which perform well using this technique.

The implementation of MPI-2 features in current MPI distributions, gives the means to develop malleable applications. The impact of malleability upon MPI applications, is outperformed by the gain upon resources utilization. On the other hand, the applications should be notified with the resources availability. Such information is provided to the MPI applications from the OAR. Moreover, we believe that some support to resources dynamism from MPI distributions is required by malleable applications, as provided in LAM/MPI by `lamgrow` and `lamshrink`. Our future work will aim to the *lib-dynamicMPI* independence from MPI distribution. We also consider to increase the range of programs, to study the malleability upon non-bag-of-tasks applications. Finally, some improvements upon communication between OAR and *lib-dynamicMPI*, have to be made.

The study of the two malleability approaches - dynamic CPUSETs mapping which is in system level and dynamic MPI application which is in application level - upon a resource manager is another important contribution of this paper. We identified both approaches requirements and their support by an OAR module and we tried to relate their impact on complexity and gain. We concluded that the complexity is outperformed by the gain. This conclusion, based on tests - using a real workload injected in OAR - proved that malleable jobs as compared to a non-malleable approach, enable an almost 25% greater resource utilization.

Acknowledgements

The authors would like to thank CAPES, Bull OpenSource and MESCAL project for supporting this research. Furthermore, we thank Grid5000 for their experimental platform.

References

1. Feitelson, D.G., Rudolph, L.: Toward convergence in job schedulers for parallel supercomputers. In: Job Scheduling Strategies for Parallel Processing, pp. 1–26. Springer, Heidelberg (1996)
2. Capit, N., Costa, G.D., Georgiou, Y., Huard, G., Martin, C., Mounié, G., Neyron, P., Richard, O.: A batch scheduler with high level components. In: 5th Int. Symposium on Cluster Computing and the Grid, Cardiff, UK, pp. 776–783. IEEE, Los Alamitos (2005)
3. Lepère, R., Trystram, D., Woeginger, G.J.: Approximation algorithms for scheduling malleable tasks under precedence constraints. International Journal of Foundations of Computer Science 13(4), 613–627 (2002)
4. Kalé, L.V., Kumar, S., DeSouza, J.: A malleable-job system for timeshared parallel machines. In: 2nd Int. Symposium on Cluster Computing and the Grid, Washington, USA, pp. 230–238. IEEE, Los Alamitos (2002)
5. Hungershöfer, J.: On the combined scheduling of malleable and rigid jobs. In: 16th Symposium on Computer Architecture and High Performance Computing (SBAC-PAD), pp. 206–213 (2004)
6. Utrera, G., Corbalán, J., Labarta, J.: Implementing malleability on MPI jobs. In: 13th Int. Conference on Parallel Architectures and Compilation Techniques, pp. 215–224. IEEE, Los Alamitos (2004)
7. Hungershöfer, J., Achim Streit, J.M.W.: Efficient resource management for malleable applications. Technical Report TR-003-01, Paderborn Center for Parallel Computing (2001)
8. El Maghraoui, K., Desell, T.J., Szymanski, B.K., Varela, C.A.: Malleable iterative mpi applications. Concurrency and Computation: Practice and Experience 21(3), 393–413 (2009)
9. Maghraoui, K.E., Desell, T.J., Szymanski, B.K., Varela, C.A.: Dynamic malleability in iterative MPI applications. In: 7th Int. Symposium on Cluster Computing and the Grid, pp. 591–598. IEEE, Los Alamitos (2007)
10. Desell, T., Maghraoui, K.E., Varela, C.A.: Malleable applications for scalable high performance computing. Cluster Computing 10(3), 323–337 (2007)
11. Buisson, J., Sonmez, O., Mohamed, H., Epema, D.: Scheduling malleable applications in multicluster systems. In: Int. Conference on Cluster Computing, pp. 372–381. IEEE, Los Alamitos (2007)
12. Bolze, R., Cappello, F., Caron, E., Dayd, M., Desprez, F., Jeannot, E., Jgou, Y., Lantri, S., Leduc, J., Melab, N., Mornet, G., Namyst, R., Primet, P., Quetier, B., Richard, O., Talbi, I.G., Ira, T.: Grid 5000: a large scale and highly reconfigurable experimental grid testbed. Int. Journal of High Performance Computing Applications 20(4), 481–494 (2006)
13. Georgiou, Y., Richard, O., Capit, N.: Evaluations of the lightweight grid cigri upon the grid 5000 platform. In: Third IEEE International Conference on e-Science and Grid Computing, Washington, DC, USA, pp. 279–286. IEEE Computer Society, Los Alamitos (2007)
14. Litzkow, M., Livny, M., Mutka, M.: Condor - a hunter of idle workstations. In: Proceedings of the 8th International Conference of Distributed Computing Systems (1988)
15. Gropp, W., Lusk, E., Thakur, R.: Using MPI-2 Advanced Features of the Message-Passing Interface. The MIT Press, Cambridge (1999)
16. Cera, M.C., Pezzi, G.P., Mathias, E.N., Maillard, N., Navaux, P.O.A.: Improving the dynamic creation of processes in MPI-2. In: Mohr, B., Träff, J.L., Worringen, J., Dongarra, J. (eds.) PVM/MPI 2006. LNCS, vol. 4192, pp. 247–255. Springer, Heidelberg (2006)
17. Bailey, D., Harris, T., Saphir, W., Wijngaart, R.V.D., Woo, A., Yarrow, M.: The nas parallel benchmarks 2.0. Technical Report NAS-95-020, NASA Ames Research Center (1995)
18. Li, H., Groep, D.L., Wolters, L.: Workload characteristics of a multi-cluster supercomputer. In: Feitelson, D.G., Rudolph, L., Schwiegelshohn, U. (eds.) JSSPP 2004. LNCS, vol. 3277, pp. 176–193. Springer, Heidelberg (2005)

Impact of Object Operations and Relationships on Concurrency Control in DOOS

(Short Paper)

V. Geetha and Niladhuri Sreenath

Pondicherry Engineering College, Puducherry 605014, India
{vgeetha,nsreenath}@pec.edu

Abstract. The objective of this paper is to analyze the impact of object operations and relationships in concurrency control (CC)using multi granular locking model in Distributed object oriented system. The types and properties of object operations and relationships have been used to propose the lock types and granularity size. The sub types and properties of object relationships like inheritance, aggregation have been used to propose an enhanced compatibility matrix given in [KIM1] and [LEE1].

1   Introduction

Distributed System(DS) is a collection of sites that allow sharing of resources to other nodes as and when requested. The data resources are usually modeled as databases in distributed systems. The characteristics desirable in DS like higher quality, flexibility, scalability and locational transparency are provided by object oriented concepts and hence the distributed relational databases are modeled as OODBMS.

In [GRAY1][GRAY2], a multi granular lock model has been proposed for RDBMS. This has been extended for OODBMS by defining compatibility matrix supporting object relationships like inheritance and aggregation in [GARZA1], for concurrency control in ORION, a popular implementation of OODBMS. This compatibility matrix was inadequate to support shared composition and supported only bottom up assembly of existing objects. These drawbacks were overcome in [KIM1] by defining separate locking modes for shared and exclusive composition. They had the drawback of poor concurrency for composite objects and there were no specific locking modes to support schema changes. 14 separate locking modes for schemas, classes and instances have been proposed in [LEE1].The possibility of semantic lock models for DOOS is given in [ROES1], but in this also it was not discussed in detail.

The implementation of concurrency control mechanisms in data store layer eliminates the possibility of using primitive data resources like files which lack in such concurrency control mechanisms. Hence Distributed Object Oriented Systems (DOOS) become the obvious solution. The distributed systems have evolved as DOOS by blending the goodness of client/server model and OO paradigm.

In DOOS, the clients have to make requests for objects rather than procedures. The operations implemented in the object will access the required data resources

K. Kant et al. (Eds.): ICDCN 2010, LNCS 5935, pp. 258–264, 2010.

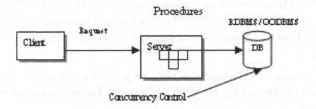

Fig. 1. Concurrency Control at Database Tier in Distributed System

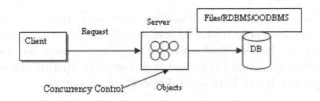

Fig. 2. Concurrency Control at at Server Tier in DOOS

copied into the data members of the object.The mapping of distributed objects on persistent storage models like files, RDBMS, OODBMS is suggested in [DAN1]. As objects are the only means to satisfy client requests in DOOS, it will be more appropriate to define concurrency control mechanisms for objects in server tier. This will help to support all types of persistent storages. Fig 1 and 2 shows the architecture of DS and DOOS with shifting of concurrency control mechanisms to higher abstraction. Since the client requests in DOOS is of the format (ObjectID. operation), this has to be converted into appropriate lock type and granule size. This paper analyses the classification of object operations and relationships to assign the type of locks. The locks are defined for various operations based on their types and properties for each object relationship separately. The hierarchy of granules in DOOS is also defined. The compatibility matrix defined in [LEE1] for OODBMS is extended for adaption in DOOS.

Chapter 2 introduces basic concepts of OOP. Chapter 3 is dedicated to definition of lock types, hierarchy of granules and compatibility matrix for DOOS. Chapter 4 concludes the paper.

2   Review of Object Oriented Concepts

2.1   Types and Properties of Object Operations

The client requests are satisfied by executing the operations defined in the object. These operations need to operate on the data to satisfy the request. Depending on the type of operation, the Read or Write operations can be ascertained. Then concurrency control mechanisms can be defined whenever there are R-W and W-W conflicts.The object operations are classified into 3 types in [DIRK1][DIRK2]:

Query operation: It returns some information about the object being queried. It does not change the objects state. There are four main query operation types:- Get operation, Boolean Query operation, Comparison operation, Conversion operation.

Mutation operation: It changes the objects state (mutates it). There are three main mutation operation types: - Set operation, Initialization operation, Command operation.

Helper operations: It performs some support task for the calling object. There are two types of helper operations: - Factory operation and Assertion operation.

Apart from having types, operations also have properties. Properties specify whether the operation is primitive or composed, whether it is available for overriding through subclasses (*Hook operation*), or it is a mere wrapper around a more complicated operation (*Template operation*). An operation has exactly one operation type, but it can have several operation properties.

3   Concurrency Control in DOOS

3.1   Conflict Problems in DOOS

The conflict issues in OODB due to concurrency is addressed in [LEE1]. They may be adapted for DOOS with some changes.

1. *Runtime-Runtime conflict:* When objects of both base and inherited sub classes try to access the same data concurrently, it will lead to inconsistency. Similarly, when two composite objects with shared component object are concurrently accessed, it will also lead to inconsistency.

2. *Runtime-Design time conflict:* When a transaction tries to access an object or all the objects of a class for execution, while another transaction access the same class to modify its behaviour, it will lead to Runtime Design time conflict.

3. *Design time-Design time conflict:* This happens specifically in classes related by inheritance. The behaviour of base class is inherited in sub class. Any attempt to modify both base and sub classes simultaneously may lead to inconsistency.

In this paper only Runtime - Runtime conflicts for inheritance and aggregation in DOOS are addressed.

3.2   Hierarchy of Lock Granules in OODS

Multi granular lock model is needed to enhance the concurrency. It allows the choice of data from coarse grain to fine grain as needed for the particular request.Coarse grains reduce the number of locks but increases concurrency control. Fine grains increase the number of locks, but granularity level must be chosen. Fig.3. shows hierarchy of lock granules in DOOS.

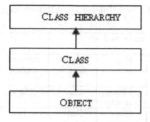

Fig. 3. Hierarchy of Lock Granules in OODS

3.3   Types of Locks Based on Operation Types for Inheritance

The following types of lock modes for coarse and fine granules for inheritance are defined in [GRAY1]. Instance objects can have only S and X locks. The class objects can be locked in S, X, IS, IX and SIX modes. Table 1 defines the locks based on the types of object operations. The types of locks are also based on the class level or object level instance. If it is a class level operation, then class hierarchy is set by intention locks and classes are set by S or X locks. If it is an instance operation, then class is set by intention locks and objects with S or X locks. The operation types or properties can be identified using doc tools like Javadoc, doc++. The objects are accessible only after their creation. Their accessibility ceases after destruction. Table 2 defines the lockable granules for various operations based on their properties. By combining the types and properties of operations, the lock type and lockable granule size can be deduced.

3.4   Compatibility Matrix for Inheritance

The compatibility matrix defines the compatibility of current lock mode with requested lock mode. The inheritance is classified as exclusive inheritance or shared inheritance. The inheritance types namely single inheritance, multilevel

Table 1. Type of Lock based on Operation Types for inheritance

GRANULARITY METHOD TYPES		Class/Instance	Class hierarchy / Class
Query method		S	IS
Mutation method	Set / Initialization method	X	IX
	Command method	S & X	SIX
Helper method	Factory method	X	IX
	Assertion method	S	IS

Table 2. Granularity of Lock based on Object Operations in inheritance

Method properties	Instance method				Class method			
Method types	Primitive method	Composed method	Hook method	Template method	Primitive method	Composed method	Hook method	Template method
Query method	Object	Object	Class hierarchy	Class	Class	Class	Class hierarchy	Class
Mutation method	Object	Object	Class hierarchy	Class	Class	Class	Class hierarchy	Class
Helper method (factory method)	-	Object	Class hierarchy	Object	-	Class	Class hierarchy	Class

Table 3. Revised Compatibility Matrix for granularity locking for Inheritance

Current mode   Requested mode ⟶

	IS	ISCS	IX	IXCS	S	SIX	SIXCS	X
IS	Y	Y	Y	Y	Y	Y	Y	N
ISCS	Y	Y	Y	Y	Y	Y	Y	N
IX	Y	Y	Y	Y	N	N	N	N
ISCS	Y	Y	Y	Y	N	N	N	N
S	Y	Y	N	N	Y	N	N	N
SIX	Y	Y	N	N	N	N	N	N
SIXCS	Y	Y	N	N	N	N	N	N
X	N	N	N	N	N	N	N	N

inheritance and multiple inheritance allow exclusive inheritance of a parent class to one or more child classes. But in hierarchical inheritance, several sub classes are inherited from the same parent class or the parent is shared by many siblings. If the compatibility matrix specified in [KIM1] is extended for this shared inheritance, then concurrency will be lowered. At any time only one sub class is allowed to lock the parent class. Hence separate intention lock modes must be defined to increase concurrency. So three more locking modes ISCS (Intention Shared Class Shared), IXCS (Intention Exclusive Class Shared) and SIXCS (Shared Intention Exclusive Class Shared) can be defined. These locking modes appended to the compatibility matrix in [KIM1] is in table 3. If the multi granular locks in [LEE1] is used, then point (h) of instance locking model in [LEE1] must be extended to class locking model for shared inheritance also.

3.5   Types of Locks Based on Operation Types for Composition

When a client requests a composite object, its class must be set intention lock and the component objects that constitute the composite object must also be set intention object lock. These intention locks, while locking the particular object that constitute the composite objects, lets other objects of the same class to

Table 4. Type of Lock based on Operation Types for Composition

METHOD TYPES		ROOT OBJECT	ROOT CLASS	EXCLUSIVE COMPONENT CLASS	SHARED COMPONENT CLASS
QUERY METHOD		S	IS	ISO	ISOS
MUTATION METHOD	SET METHOD / INITIALIZATION METHOD	X	IX	IXO	IXOS
	COMMAND	S/X	SIX	SIXO	SIXOS
HELPER METHOD	FACTORY METHOD	AS PER CREATION AND DELETION RULE BASD ON DEPENDENT / INDEPENDENT COMPOSITION			
	ASSERTION METHOD	S	IS	ISO	ISOS

Table 5. Granularity of locks for Composite Objects

CLASS TYPE	GRANULARITY OF LOCKS
PRIMITIVE CLASS	Component object
NON PRIMITIVE CLASS	Object hierarchy

Table 6. Compatibility Matrix for Inheritance and Composition

Current mode   Requested mode

	IS	ISCS	IX	IXCS	S	SIX	SIXCS	X	ISO	IXO	SIXO	ISOS	IXOS	SIXOS
IS	Y	Y	Y	Y	Y	Y	Y	N	Y	N	N	Y	N	N
ISCS	Y	Y	Y	Y	Y	Y	Y	N	Y	N	N	Y	N	N
IX	Y	Y	Y	Y	N	N	N	N	N	N	N	N	N	N
ISCS	Y	Y	Y	Y	N	N	N	N	N	N	N	N	N	N
S	Y	Y	N	N	Y	N	N	N	Y	N	N	Y	N	N
SIX	Y	Y	N	N	N	N	N	N	N	N	N	N	N	N
SIXCS	Y	Y	N	N	N	N	N	N	N	N	N	N	N	N
X	N	N	N	N	N	N	N	N	N	N	N	N	N	N
ISO	Y	Y	N	N	Y	N	N	N	Y	Y	Y	Y	Y	Y
IXO	N	N	N	N	N	N	N	N	Y	Y	N	Y	Y	N
SIXO	N	N	N	N	N	N	N	N	Y	N	N	Y	N	N
ISOS	Y	Y	N	N	Y	N	N	N	Y	Y	Y	Y	N	N
IXOS	N	N	N	N	N	N	N	N	Y	Y	N	N	N	N
SIXOS	N	N	N	N	N	N	N	N	Y	N	N	N	N	N

be used by other clients. This improves concurrency. Composition may have exclusive or shared reference [GARZ1]. Table 4 and 5 gives the types of locks based on operation types for composition and their granularity.The compatibility matrix in Table 6 defines the semantics of all lock modes.

4   Conclusion

The benefits of CC technique in DOOS are: 1. The shift of CC technique to server tier supports use of legacy files.2. The lock types and granularity for both inheritance and composition have been proposed. The system will translate the transaction in the form of ObjectID.Operation into its equivalent lock requests for the resources needed. It also helps to identify the implicit resources to be locked to maintain the consistency of the system. Efforts can be taken to improve the system by:- 1. Further refinement of the compatibility matrix to enhance concurrency control. 2. New compatibility matrix may be provided from the usage of various combinations of class relationships.

References

[GRAY1]   Gray, J.N., Lorie, R.A., Putzolu, G.R., Traiger, L.I.: Granularity of locks and degrees of consistency in shared database. In: Nijssen, G.M. (ed.) Modeling in Database management system, pp. 393–491. Elsevier, North Holland (1978)

[GARZ1]   Garza, J.F., Kim, W.: Transaction management in an object oriented database system. In: Proc. ACM SIGMOD Intl conference (1987)

[KIM1]   Kim, W., Bertino, E., Garza, J.F.: Composite Objects revisited. Object oriented Programming, systems, Languages and Applications, 327–340 (1990)

[LEE1]   Lee, S.Y., Liou, R.L.: A Multi- Granularity Locking model for concurrency control in Object Oriented Database Systems. IEEE Transactions on Knowledge and Data Engineering 8(1) (February 1996)

[DAN1]   Daniels, J., Cook, S.: Strategies for sharing objects in distributed systems. JOOP 5(8), 27–36 (1993)

[GRAY2]   Gray, J.N.: Notes on Data Base Operating Systems, IBM Research Report RJ2188, IBM Research, SanJose, Calif (1978)

[DIRK1]   Riehle, D., Berczuk, S.P.: Types of Member Functions, Report (June 2000)

[DIRK2]   Riehle, D., Berczuk, S.P.: Properties of Member Functions, Report (October 2000)

[ROES1]   Roesler, M., Buckard, W.A.: Deadlock Resolution and Semantic lock models for Object Oriented Distributed Systems. ACM SIGMOD Record 17(3), 351–369 (1988)

Causal Cycle Based Communication Pattern Matching

(Short Paper)

Himadri Sekhar Paul

Interra Systems India (P) Ltd.,
Sector-V, Salt Lake,
Kolkata - 700091
himadrip@cal.interrasystems.com

Abstract. A distributed system employing checkpoint and rollback-recovery as a fault tolerance mechanism, suffers from overhead attributed by the technique. Authors in [4] proposes a technique to automatically identify a checkpoint and recovery protocol based on a pre-estimated database of overhead measures. The technique depends on computation of similarity between a pair of communication patterns. The computation involves first partitioning both the communication patterns into small pieces or *splices*. A pair of splices, one taken from each of the two communication patterns in question, are then compared to compute a similarity measure. Splicing a communication pattern is an important step in the method since it bears heavy significance for later steps in the computation. This paper introduces a new method for splicing. Experimental results show that the technique yields better similarity measure values in comparison to results reported in [4].

1 Introduction

Fault tolerance is an important issue in distributed systems, and checkpoint and rollback-recovery is a cost effective technique to address the issue. A variety of checkpoint and recovery protocols have been proposed for distributed systems [2]. However, there are some overheads associated with all these protocols. For a distributed system hosting long running applications, performance of a checkpoint and recovery protocol is an important issue because it directly affects the overall throughput of the system. The overheads depend on various system and application characteristics, like network speed, stable storage latency, checkpoint size, fault distributed, etc. [5]. Since the performance of a checkpoint and recovery protocol depends on the application characteristic, like communication pattern, the choice of a protocol may change with the application hosted in the system. In [4] the authors proposed an automated method to dynamically identify a checkpoint and recovery protocol which is likely to affect better throughput in the system. The method utilizes an archive of performance values of different checkpoint and recovery protocols under different application and system conditions. The method proposes to determine the parameters from the system and the application and then choose the checkpoint and recovery

K. Kant et al. (Eds.): ICDCN 2010, LNCS 5935, pp. 265–270, 2010.

protocol from the achieve which corresponds to the best performance measure for these parameters.

Comparing parameters, except communication pattern, are trivial. The first step in the computation of similarity between a pair of communication patterns, is to partition both the communication patterns into *splices*. The next step is to find a similarity measure between a pair of splices, one taken from each of the communication patterns. This step will generate a series of similarity values, which are then combined into a single measure. This measure is then declared as the similarity measure for the pair of communication patterns.

The results published in [4] indicate that in many cases where the two communication patterns are same, the similarity measure obtained by the technique implies some difference between them. In this paper we propose a splicing technique based on causal information present in the communication patterns. Experimental results based on the proposed splicing technique show more accurate similarity measure values when the patterns are same.

Section 2 presents some definitions required for presentation of our work and also discusses the related works. Section 3 we present our motivation behind this work and in section 4 we describe the algorithm for causal cycle based splicing. Experimental results are presented and discussed upon in section 5. Section 6 presents some concluding remarks.

2   Background

In this section, first we present some definitions which are related to our work. Then we describe the basic communication pattern matching technique proposed in [4] which serves as the basis of this paper.

Definitions. *An event e_1 is said to have happened before another event e_2 or, e_2 causally depends of e_1 (denoted as $e_1 \succ e_2$), iff (1) e_1 and e_2 are the events in the same process and e_1 occurred before e_2 or, (2) e_1 and e_2 are the events in different processes and e_1 is the send event of a message m and e_2 is the receive event of m or, (3) there is an event e', such that $e_1 \succ e'$ and $e' \succ e_2$ [1].*

A causal path is an ordered set of events in a distributed system, where each event happened before on all other preceding events in the set [3].

A causal cycle is a causal path, where the first event and the last event in the path belong to the same process.

This paper is based on the work reported in [4] which is briefly presented in the following section.

2.1   Related Work

A wide variety of checkpoint and recovery protocols for distributed system has been proposed in literature [2]. Authors in [4] proposed a technique to dynamically determine a checkpoint and recovery protocol best suited for the current application running in the system. The technique proposes to use a database of performance measures under different checkpoint and recovery protocols and, system and application parameters. Let us say $\mathbf{D} \subset (P_1 \times P_2 \times \cdots \times P_n \times C \times R)$ be a performance database, where P_i is the domain for the value of the ith parameter, C is the set of checkpoint and recovery protocols, and R is domain of the performance value of the protocols in C. The outline of determining a checkpoint and recovery protocol is as follows:

1. Capture the parameter values while an application is running as $(d_1, d_2, \ldots d_n)$, where $d_i \in P_i$. Some of the parameters, which are related to the application and hence are dynamic, need to be captured while the application is running. The other parameters can be pre-determined for the system.
2. Choose a set of entries $\mathbf{P} = \{(p_1, p_2, \ldots p_n, c, r) : \forall_{i=0}^{n}(|p_i - d_i| < \phi)\} \subset \mathbf{D}$, where ϕ is small.
3. Choose a protocol c' such that c' is associated with r' and r' is the maximum value among all performance values in all records in $\mathbf{P}$.

The domains of all the parameters, except the communication pattern, are numbers and therefore comparing them is trivial. A communication pattern is essentially a directed graph with embedded temporal information. Comparing a pair graphs is a computationally challenging problem. Moreover, the complexity of the problem is compounded by the fact that the same application running in the same distributed environment, may generate two different communication patterns in two different runs due to non-deterministic external influences like, communication latency and failure, etc. Therefore the object of interest is not to identify the *same* communication patterns, but the *similar* ones.

Author es in [4] converts a communication pattern into a weighted, directed graph by removing all temporal information. The similarity between a pair of communication patterns is then computed as the graph similarity measure of the two resulting graphs. Such a model has the capability to tolerate temporal differences in communication patterns. *Splicing* is used to retain and control temporal information in the similarity computation.

Splicing is nothing but a method of annotating the communication pattern with boundaries. A splice is a region in the communication pattern which falls within two consecutive splice boundaries. Splices determine how closely the method examines the communication patterns. Splicing should not be too fine such that spurious messages corrupt the similarity measure. Also splicing should not be too coarse that all the temporal information is lost. In [4] authors proposed three different methods of splicing which are based on time or number of messages. The results reported therein use time-based splicing technique. The following section presents our motivation for a new splicing technique.

3   Motivation of Our Work

The objective of communication pattern matching is to generate a high value of similarity measure when the pair of communication patterns are similar. For very

Table 1. Comparison of Communication Pattern similarity measures

	J	Mat	GS	Tree3	Tree4	Ring	RAND1
Results in [4]	1.000000	1.000000	**0.488950**	**0.828558**	**0.879312**	**0.998479**	1.000000
Our Result	1.000000	1.000000	**1.000000**	**1.000000**	**1.000000**	**1.000000**	1.000000

dissimilar communication patterns it should generate a low value. Communication pattern similarity measure is nothing but statistical mean of the similarity values of the series the splice pairs generated from them. Therefore, when the communication patterns are similar, all the splice pairs should also be similar.

The splicing algorithm first splices one of the communication patterns and then splices the other one such that the similarity measure can be maximized. The problem is computationally costly and heuristics based on some characteristic of the communication pattern are applied. The splicing methods proposed in [4] uses characteristics like time or message count. These techniques are vulnerable to message delivery latency, duplicate messages, computation latency, etc.

Row 1 of table 1 shows an excerpt of similarity measures reported in [4]. The table shows similarity values of 7 different communication patterns compared with itself. Three of the communication patterns are captured from the three different scientific applications namely, Jacobi's algorithm for solution of a set of simultaneous equations (J), large matrix multiplication (Mat), and Gram-Schmidth algorithm for vector normalization (GS). The communication patterns namely, Tree3, Tree4, Ring, and RAND1 are generated synthetically. In Tree3 and Tree4 the nodes are placed in a tree topology with degree 3 and 4 respectively and in Ring the nodes are placed in a ring topology. RAND1 a randomly generated communication pattern. The results show that in some cases when the same communication pattern is compared with itself, the method failed to identify them as the same pattern. Those cases are marked in bold face.

Splicing technique which exploits the interdependency of the messages should produce better result. Causal dependency is one such tool. In this paper we propose a splicing technique based on causal relation among messages.

4   Causal Cycle Based Splicing

The underlying idea of the proposed splicing technique is to incorporate some knowledge of the communication which can be modeled as causal dependency. The basic assumption is that if a node sends a message, it will trigger a chain of send events in the system, which are causally related. Also that when a node initiates a communication, it is likely to expect some result back from the system. This can be modeled as a causal cycle. The basic idea of splicing in this case is to splice along the causal cycle boundaries.

The splicing algorithm is described in figure 1. The method identifies a message from the communication pattern, marks the message as dependency of the receiver on the sender in a dependency graph, and then checks whether this new

Causal Cycle based Splicing of Communication Pattern

Input: C: A communication pattern
Output: M: A communication pattern with splice boundaries.

1. Let s be the first send event of any of an arbitrary process in C.
2. Initialize: Create an empty directed graph G with n nodes, n is the number of processes in C.
3. Let r be the receive event corresponding to the send event s.
4. Add an edge $P_s \rightarrow P_r$ in G, where P_s contains the event s and P_r contains r.
5. Invoke $IsCausalCycle(G, P_s, P_r)$ to check if the message $s \rightarrow r$ creates a causal cycle.
   > If no causal cycle found, Goto 6
   > Otherwise, (causal cycle found)
   >> i. Insert splice boundary up to the events seen in C.
   >> ii. Goto 1
6. Let s be the next send event in C for P_r.
7. Goto 3

FUNCTION: IsCausalCycle

Input: G: A communication pattern, P_s: sender, P_r: receiver
Output: True if a causal cycle in found for message send from P_s to P_r, otherwise false.

1. for each process P in G
   (a) if $(P \rightarrow sender \in G)$ return true
   (b) if $(IsCausalCycle(G, P, P_r))$ return true
2. return false

Fig. 1. Causal Cycle based Splicing Algorithm

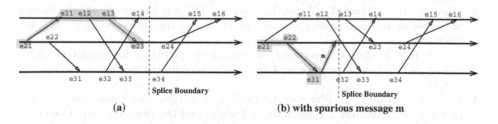

(a)   (b) with spurious message m

Fig. 2. Causal cycle based splicing

dependency creates a causal cycle, since the first message marked in the dependency graph. Once we detect a causal cycle, a splice boundary is generated in the pattern. Figure 2(a) shows splices generated by the splicing technique.

The technique is tolerant to spurious messages unless such spurious messages generate spurious causal cycles. For example, in figure 2(b) the spurious message m generates a spurious causal cycle and therefore a different splice. When the second pattern is being spliced for a given splice of the first pattern, a set of possible splice boundaries are detected within a certain windows in the pattern, and the splice boundary is chosen where the similarity measure for the splice pair is maximum. This technique filters out spurious causal cycles as in figure 2(b).

In the next section we discuss the experimental results using the causal cycle based splicing.

5   Result and Discussions

We have followed the same experimental setup as discussed in section 2.1. Row 2 of table 1 shows similarity values of the same set of 7 communication patterns compared with itself. The entries in row 2 of table 1, marked as bold, show similarity values as 1 which implies that the communication patterns compared are exactly same, in contrast to the results in row 1. The results indicate that the method can now identify a pair of patterns as same when they actually are.

6   Conclusion

In this paper, we have proposed a new communication pattern splicing method which is based on causal information present in communication patterns. The method is used as a part of the communication pattern comparison scheme proposed in [4]. Experimental results show improvement in detection of same patterns in comparison to splicing methods proposed in [4].

References

1. Lamport, L.: Time, clocks, and the ordering of events in a distributed system. Communications of the ACM 21(7), 558–565 (1978)
2. Elnozahy, E.N., Alvisi, L., Wang, Y., Johnson, D.B.: A survey of rollbak-recovery protocols in message-passing sytems. ACM Computing Surveys 34(3), 375–408 (2002)
3. Netzer, R.H.B., Xu, J.: Necessary and sufficient conditions for consistent global snapshots. IEEE Transactions on Parallel and Distributed Systems 6(2), 165–169 (1995)
4. Paul, H.S., Gupta, A., Sharma, A.: Finding a suitable checkpoint and recovery protocol for a distributed application. J. Parallel and Distributed Computing 66(5), 732–749 (2006)
5. Paul, H.S., Gupta, A., Badrinath, R.: Performance comparison of checkpoint and recovery protocols. Concurrency and Computation: Practice and Experience 15(15), 1363–1386 (2003)

Channel Assignment in Virtual Cut-through Switching Based Wireless Mesh Networks

Dola Saha, Aveek Dutta, Dirk Grunwald, and Douglas Sicker

University of Colorado
Boulder, CO 80309–0430 USA

Abstract. Conventional wireless networks employ a contention based channel access mechanism, which not only imposes high latency but also reduces goodput of the network. Lack of interference estimation algorithms over the entire network results in unpredictable collision, packet loss and retransmissions. Advances in multicarrier modulation techniques enable us to group subcarriers into orthogonal subchannels and treat them separately as information carriers. While this provides an increased number of non-interfering channels, intelligent utilization of the given spectrum is also required. In this paper, a solution for decreasing latency in mesh networks has been proposed by aptly incorporating a virtual cut-through switching technique to route packets in the network. To alleviate the impact of interference on packet reception, we also propose a fast pair-wise interference detection scheme, which is used for channel allocation. The cumulative performance of the proposed protocol shows improvement over existing Wi-Fi based mesh networks that provide a motivating platform for future protocol developments using this technique.

1 Introduction

Orthogonal Frequency Division Multiplexing (OFDM) is a multicarrier modulation scheme that has the ability to transmit data in closely spaced multiple carriers that do not interfere with each other. Using OFDM as the basic technology, Orthogonal Frequency Division Multiple Access (OFDMA) has been developed as a multi-user channel access mechanism that combines a subset of the available subcarriers into a subchannel, which then can be used for multiple access techniques. Orthogonal subchannels can be utilized for simultaneous transmission and reception by any node equipped with two antennas, one for transmission and the other for reception, provided the transmission and reception subchannels do not overlap. Such an approach minimizes the latency of each packet, and thus motivates the investigation of intelligent allocation of subchannels to nodes for simultaneous transmission and reception.

This paper focuses on utilization of OFDMA for concurrent transmission and reception such that each node in a wireless network has a property to relay packets "on the fly" while it is still receiving a part of the packet. To efficiently relay packets to non-interfering subchannels, we propose a centralized channel allocation mechanism, which utilizes the information of link and possible interference. The link information is gathered by transmitting a known training sequence. The interference information is also generated by scheduling two transmissions at the same time, and detecting the

K. Kant et al. (Eds.): ICDCN 2010, LNCS 5935, pp. 271–282, 2010.
© Springer-Verlag Berlin Heidelberg 2010

actual interference. Then, this link and interference information is converted to an edge-coloring problem of graph theory, where only chosen routes are considered for channel assignment.

We evaluate our protocol through simulations and experiment with a varied set of topologies to show improvement in various parameters. We also propose a FPGA based prototype hardware platform which is capable of relaying packets from one subchannel to another. Our evaluation suggests that with correct detection of possible interference in the network and proper utilization of this information for channel allocation algorithms leads to encouraging performance enhancements for wireless networks.

2   Related Work

Inter-nodal processing delay plays an important role in determining the overall performance of the network. Researchers have made constant efforts to decrease this latency to improve the network throughput. Ram Ramanathan [1] proposes to bypass the inadequacies of the conventional IP stack to support Wireless Mesh Networks by using virtual cut-through circuit switching thus reducing the overhead of four-way handshaking. Mctasney et al. [2, 3] introduce wireless wormhole switching to minimize the processing delay in each node by aptly incorporating the idea of virtual channels in flit-based wormhole switching techniques [4] in multi-computer networks. Our proposed protocol has lower latency than abovementioned methods, and we compare them in more details in §3.2.

To efficiently utilize the potential of wireless virtual cut-through switching, we need to define resource allocation mechanisms. Ramanathan [5] proposes to unify the scheme of channel assignment in varied architectures into a generalized graph coloring method, which we utilize to assign subchannels to the relay nodes in our network. However, these techniques are developed for platforms not capable of simultaneous transmission and reception as a relay.

Interference in the wireless medium is a key contributor to packet loss, higher latency, retransmissions and control overheads. For a practical virtual cut-through switching without any MAC layer acknowledgment, we need good knowledge of the source of interference. Most of the previous work in this domain [6–8] is based on interference estimation rather than actual measurement. In this paper, we propose to measure and detect the possible interference before channel assignment, which enhances the overall performance of the network.

3   Wireless Virtual Cut-through Switching

3.1   Physical Layer Architecture

Utilizing the OFDMA technique, a node is expected to simultaneously transmit data packets generated at its own application layer, receive data packets that are destined to its application layer and also forward or relay data packets from one subchannel to another. To perform these tasks simultaneously, a node is equipped with two antennas, one for transmission and another for reception. The node initially receives the signal from the receiver antenna, performs Fast Fourier Transform (FFT) to convert the time domain signal to frequency domain. The signal is then passed through the equalizer block to compensate for any phase or amplitude errors introduced as it passes through the channel. Next, the signal is passed through the channel switch block, which is set by the channel assignment algorithm to switch the frequency to a different subchannel. Finally, the signal is converted back to time domain by the Inverse Fast Fourier Transform (IFFT) block and transmitted by the transmitter antenna. If the relaying node has packets to transmit, it has to be fed into the IFFT block at the same time as the switched, relayed signal, but at a different subchannel. However, if the channel switch block does not know the number of the subchannel to relay, then the complete packet is received, decoded and forwarded to MAC layer of the relaying node.

3.2   Comparison with Concurrent Technologies

Figure 1 shows approximate latency incurred in four systems, IEEE 802.11, flit-based relay, Time Division Multiplexing(TDMA) and virtual cut-through switching. It has to be noted, that IEEE 802.11 has a half duplex radio, and so there is no overlapping transmissions. Also, there is significant amount of gap in between the packets due to back-off algorithms. When we move from IEEE 802.11 to flit-based systems, which has a full-duplex radio, we have to divide the whole bandwidth into three to overlap the transmissions for all the three hops. Hence, the transmission time of any packet is increased three times. If T is the time required to transmit a packet using full bandwidth, then the time required to transmit the same packet in one-third of the bandwidth is $3T$. The processing delay is added in each of the flits, which increases as we opt for smaller flit size. Time Division Multiple Access can be utilized to minimize the flit overhead,

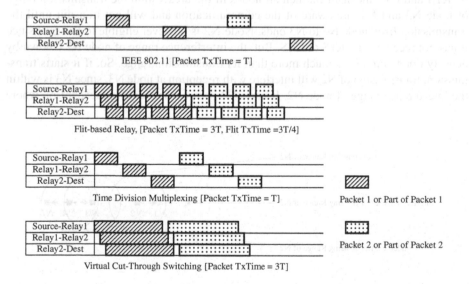

Fig. 1. Comparison of Latency of Packets - X Axis showing time

where the whole packet is transmitted all at once, using the complete bandwidth, but the transmissions shall not overlap in time, which will cause interference. The virtual cut through switching utilizes partial bandwidth for transmission in each hop and switches to a different part of the bandwidth in the next hop. It has an advantage of transmitting a complete packet all together, and hence the processing delay is incorporated once in the packet. The latency clearly shows that using wireless virtual cut-through switching, a packet is transferred to destination in minimum time.

There are a few assumptions in the physical layer, which we expect that with advancement of research and technologies, will be feasible in the near future. Our primary assumption is that all the nodes are time synchronized with a precision of less than a microsecond, such that all the OFDM symbols at any receiver overlap in time. We only consider co-channel interference, and no adjacent-channel interference, which may occur at the relay due to close spacing of the transmitting and receiving subcarriers. Research on various interference cancellation techniques [9, 10] may lead to reduction of co-channel interference in our cut-through switching.

4   Receiver and Interference Detection at Physical Layer

4.1   Challenges of Interference Detection

The existing wireless networks aim to minimize interference and thus collision by either transmitting control packets like RTS and CTS and thus reserving the transmission medium, or by sensing the channel. We show that none of these techniques are appropriate for proper estimation of interference in the wireless channel. Figure 2 shows a simple network of five nodes. Consider that there is an ongoing communication from node N4 to node N3. If we consider that nodes N3 and N4 have negotiated transmissions by RTS and CTS mechanism, then all nodes in the area within the transmission range of node N3 and N4, are aware of the communication and will not transmit until the transmission from node N4 to N3 ends. Node N2 is however eligible to transmit since it has not received any RTS or CTS. But, the interference range of node N2 (shown by densely dotted circle), is much more than its transmission range. So, if it starts transmission, transmission of N2 will interfere with reception at node N3, since N3 is within the interference range of node N2. If node N2 uses carrier sensing mechanism, where

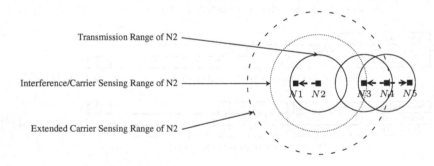

Fig. 2. Challenges of Interference Detection

the carrier sensing range equals the interference range, N2 will still not be able to sense the signal from node N4, which is outside the interference range of N2. If the sensing range of N2 is extended to include node N4, shown in loosely dotted circle, N2 will actually sense the signal transmitted from node N4 and will wait to avoid interference. However, if the transmission from node N4 is not meant for node N3, but for node N5, then there will be no interference at node N5. But, increasing the sensing range will lead to unnecessary backoff and underutilization of the wireless media.

4.2   Link Detection

In this section, we propose a link detection scheme, which is utilized later in routing and channel assignment. The link detection scheme is similar to any "hello-packet" transmission scheme to detect the reception; but instead of transmitting packets, we transmit a series of known sequences of duration of one OFDM symbol. The symbol duration, denoted by S, is $4\mu s$ in IEEE 802.11a [11], and hence the overhead of link detection is extremely low compared to packet transmission techniques. We utilize the existence of time synchronized network to schedule each node's transmission in each time slot of duration of one OFDM symbol. All other nodes except for the transmitter waits in receive mode and if the sequence is received correctly, the node recognizes the existence of the link $l_{i,j}$, where node n_i is the transmitter and node n_j is the receiver. However, for precise estimation of existing links, this procedure has to be done repeatedly for X times, $X > 1$. This procedure has to be performed periodically in a mobile environment to gather the neighborhood information. However, it has to be noted that the link detection scheme considers asymmetric links, and so if $l_{i,j}$ is a valid link, that does not necessarily mean $l_{j,i}$ is also a valid link in the network.

4.3   Interference Detection

In this section, we propose an interference detection scheme, which is utilized in the channel assignment algorithm to allocate interference-free subchannels to flows for routing packets. We exploit the existence of time synchronous nodes to schedule a pair of nodes to transmit at each time slot. As described in 4.2, we use known sequences of OFDM symbol duration to be transmitted by the transmitters. All other nodes wait in receiving mode to receive the sequence. A receiver can (a) possibly receive the sequence without any interference, (b) may receive a garbled signal due to interference, or (c) may not receive any signal at all. We consider that in the first case, one of the transmitters is close enough to the receiver such that there is no interference from the other one and the link information already exists from the link detection phase. In the second scenario, there exists an interference, and the receiver node, n_k, recognizes the interference $intf_{i,j,k}$, which indicates that when nodes n_i and n_j transmit at the same time in same channel, they interfere at node n_k. In the last scenario, the transmitters are far away and do not interfere at node n_k. To eliminate any false detection, this procedure has to be done repeatedly X times, $X > 1$. This procedure has to be performed periodically in a mobile environment to gather the neighborhood information.

4.4 Overhead

In this section, we discuss the overhead incurred in the link detection and interference detection scheme proposed in sections 4.2 and 4.3. The total time to detect all links in a network of N nodes is given by $(N \times X \times S)$. The total time increases linearly as the number of nodes in the network increases. The total time to detect all possible interference in a network of N nodes is given by $\left[\frac{n \times (n-1)}{2} \times X \times S \right] \mu s$. The total time increases as a square of the nodes as the number of nodes in the network increases. In a 100 node scenario with $X = 2$, link detection and interference detection times are $0.8 ms$ and $40 ms$, respectively. But with approximate knowledge of geographic location, we can simultaneously scheduling multiple pairs for transmitters that are far away to essentially reduce the overhead.

5 Interference-Aware Channel Assignment

In this section, we propose the centralized channel assignment algorithm which takes advantage of the knowledge of existing link and interference information, and incorporates that into an edge coloring problem to allocate subchannels to links. Firstly, we assign subchannels to the links only where there is a possibility of packet exchange. We consider that the flows are predefined and we choose a shortest path from source to destination for each flow. So, the links that appear in the route are the only possible sites for packet exchange. By restricting the subchannel assignment only to the routes, we minimize the degree of complexity of the channel assignment problem. We also enhance the spectrum utilization by not assigning subchannels to any unused links.

Let us consider that N is the set of all nodes in the network, and n_i denotes the i-th node in the network. L is the set of all valid links $l_{t,r}$ in the network, where $l_{t,r}$ denotes a link from node n_t to n_r. In other words, if node n_t transmits, then node n_r receives the packet correctly in absence of any interference. R is the set of all links that is a part of any route defined by the shortest path routing. Hence, $R \subseteq L$. I is the set of interference, consisting of $int f_{t_1,t_2,r}$, which indicates that when nodes n_{t_1} and n_{t_2} transmit at the same time, then the signals interfere at the node n_r.

Vertex Selection for Graph Coloring Problem. We are interested in assigning subchannels to the links in the set R. Hence, we choose all the links $l_{t,r} \in R$ as the vertices in graph coloring problem. If a link has multiple occurrences in the set R, we incorporate all the occurrences as different vertices of the graph. Hence, the total number of vertices in the graph equals $|R|$.

Edge Selection for Graph Coloring Problem. After selecting the vertices, we connect them with edges only where the vertices in the graph cannot be assigned the same color, or in other words, the links in the network cannot be assigned the same subchannel. With this notion in mind, we incorporate three procedures for edge inclusion.

Common Node: Select an edge between the vertices l_{t_1,r_1} and l_{t_2,r_2}, if there exists a common transmitter or receiver in between these two links. This ensures that a relay node does not transmit and receive in the same subchannel to avoid interference at its reception. By assigning an edge between common transmitters (for example, l_{t_i,r_1} and l_{t_i,r_2}) we ensure that separate subchannels are assigned to cater different flows handled by the same node n_t. Due to similar reasons, we assign an edge between common receivers. Mathematically, an edge is chosen if, $\forall l_{t_1,r_1}, l_{t_2,r_2} \in R[$ if $(n_{t_1} = n_{t_2})$ or $(n_{t_1} = n_{r_2})$ or $(n_{r_1} = n_{t_2})$ or $(n_{r_1} = n_{r_2})]$. The algorithm for this procedure is shown in line 6 of algorithm 1.

Link: If there exists a link between a transmitter and a receiver in the chosen routes, then they cannot be allocated the same subchannel, as the transmission from the transmitter will interfere with the reception at the receiver. This idea is incorporated to select another set of edges for the graph coloring problem. Mathematically, an edge is chosen if, $\forall l_{t_1,r_1}, l_{t_2,r_2} \in R[$ if $(l_{t_1,r_2} \in L)$ or $(l_{t_2,r_1} \in L)]$. The algorithm for this procedure is shown in line 9 of algorithm 1.

Interference: Finally, we incorporate the edges between interfering links. From section 4.3, we are aware of the interference sites, and already generated set I of interference. Hence, we examine all the links in the set R in pairs, and choose an edge, if there exists an interference at any one of the two receivers when both the transmitters in the paired link transmit at the same time. Mathematically, an edge is chosen if, $\forall l_{t_1,r_1}, l_{t_2,r_2} \in R[$ if $(int f_{t_1,t_2,r_1} \in I)$ or $(int f_{t_1,t_2,r_2} \in I)]$. The algorithm for this procedure is shown in line 12 of algorithm 1.

Algorithm 1. Selecting Edges to Generate Graph

```
 1: for all l_{t_1,r_1} ∈ R do
 2:     for all l_{t_2,r_2} ∈ R do
 3:         if l_{t_1,r_1} = l_{t_2,r_2} then
 4:             continue;
 5:         end if
 6:         if t_1 = t_2 or t_1 = r_2 or r_1 = t_2 or r_1 = r_2 then
 7:             Add Edge between l_{t_1,r_1} and l_{t_2,r_2}
 8:         end if
 9:         if l_{t_1,r_2} ∈ L or l_{t_2,r_1} ∈ L then
10:             Add Edge between l_{t_1,r_1} and l_{t_2,r_2}
11:         end if
12:         if int f_{t_1,t_2,r_1} ∈ I or int f_{t_1,t_2,r_2} ∈ I then
13:             Add Edge between l_{t_1,r_1} and l_{t_2,r_2}
14:         end if
15:     end for
16: end for
```

Graph Coloring. Once the vertices and edges are selected for graph coloring problem, we use Progressive Minimum Neighbors First (PMNF) algorithm [5] to color the vertices of the graph. The graph coloring results in assignment of colors to the vertices in the graph, or assignment of subchannels to the links. The total number of subchannels required equals the total number of colors required for coloring. So, we divide the complete bandwidth of 48 subcarriers by the number of subchannels required to get the width of each subchannel. If 48 is not divisible by the number of subchannels, (for example 10), we utilize subcarriers upto the multiple of number of subchannels less than the total number of subcarriers (in this case 40). Although the bandwidth remains partially unutilized, we argue that this is required for fair allocation of bandwidth per flow.

6   Hardware Implementation

To demonstrate the proposed physical layer routing we implemented a prototype using a software defined radio platform. The SDR involves an OFDM transceiver, the design and implementation of which has been detailed in [12, 13]. The platform is capable of transmitting and receiving generic 802.11a/g packets as described in physical layer specification [14]. The OFDM transceiver components consist of a custom radio front-end responsible for up/down conversion to/from the $2.4GHz$ ISM band and a Xilinx ExtremeDSP development kit IV manufactured from Nallatech, containing Virtex-IV FPGA.

The OFDM receiver has been customized to be able to decode the information bits from a certain set of subcarriers, called subchannels. To make the transmission frequency agile, the $20MHz$ channel is split into two subchannels, subchannel #1 has subcarriers −26 to −1 and subchannel #2 has subcarriers 1 to 26. This type of full duplex transceiver requires the use of two sets of radio front-ends. Using the receiver and the transmitter as a pipeline with negligible turnaround time between the receive and transmit mode, latency in multihop mesh networks can be significantly reduced. The pipeline is used to switch incoming packets on-the-fly onto another subchannel.

The spectrum of the incoming signal and the operation of the switch is shown in Fig.3. The top figure shows the incoming signal having data on all subcarriers. The second one shows that only information contained in subchannel #2 has been separated and equalized. This signal is fed to the frequency switch and switched over to

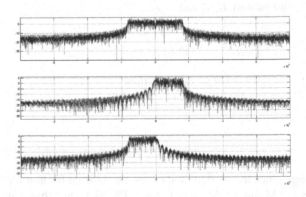

Fig. 3. Input and Output Spectrum for Switch

subchannel #1 as shown in the third figure, followed by transmission by the transmitter front-end.

7 Performance Evaluation

To evaluate the performance of the proposed protocol, we performed simulations using QualNet [15] network simulator and compared the performance with conventional IEEE 802.11a based MAC protocol. Our protocol is referred to as 'relay', while IEEE 802.11a based MAC protocol is refereed to as '802.11' throughout rest of the section. We implement OFDMA based transceiver in QualNet, operating at $2.4GHz$. The link detection and interference detection has also been implemented with $X = 10$, such that 10 OFDM symbols were used to transmit and detect any link or interference. In order to make the simulation similar to the hardware under development [12, 13], we incorporated the processing delay at three stages: a) *Transmission Delay* equals to $11\mu s$, b) *Delay at Relay* equals to $18\mu s$, and c) *Reception Delay* equals to $15\mu s$,. Table 1 shows the parameters used for simulation. We evaluate the protocol in random scenario, varying the number of flows, and varying the number of nodes.

Performance Evaluation with Increasing Number of Flows. We increment the number of flows and evaluate the performance of our protocol, as shown in figure 4. Average throughput and PDR decreases, while end-to-end delay increases, as the number of flows increase in the network. This is due to more number of simultaneous transmission being scheduled at the same time to accommodate the increasing number of flows. In all the cases, 'relay' performs better than '802.11'. Also, we observe that the jitter shown in performance is much more noticeable in '802.11' than in 'relay'. The aggregate throughput of the network is however improved at least 1.21 times up to 1.83 times in 'relay' over '802.11'.

Performance Evaluation with Increasing Number of Nodes. We increment the number of nodes, keeping the node density constant and evaluate the performance of the proposed protocol as shown in figure 5. Average throughput and PDR decreases, while

Table 1. Simulation Parameters

Seeds	10
Packet Size	1024bytes
Simulation Time	120secs
Pathloss Model	Two-Ray
Application Layer	CBR
Transport Layer	UDP
Mobility	None
Topology	Random
CBR Packet Injection Interval	615μs

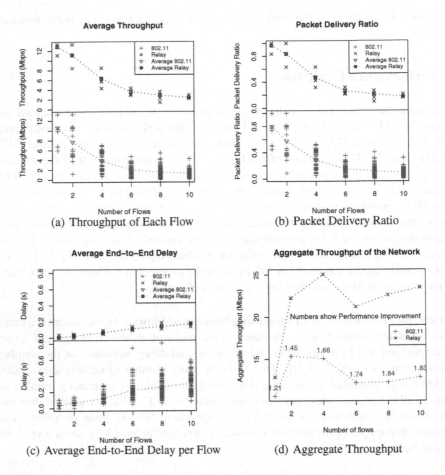

(a) Throughput of Each Flow

(b) Packet Delivery Ratio

(c) Average End-to-End Delay per Flow

(d) Aggregate Throughput

Fig. 4. Performance Improvement in Random Scenario with increasing number of Simultaneous Flows

end-to-end delay increases, as the number of nodes increase in the network. As the number of nodes increases, with node density being constant, the total area also increases, which indicates that the average hops for random source destination pair also increases. Performance decreases due to more number of simultaneous communications in both '802.11' and 'relay'. In all the cases, 'relay' performs better than '802.11'. Also, we observe that the jitter shown in performance is more in '802.11' than in 'relay'. The aggregate throughput of the network is however improved at least 1.62 times up to 2.93 times in 'relay' over '802.11'. The performance improvement is dependent on the topology, node density, number of flows and many other topological parameters, but on an average in most of the cases, we observe a two-fold improvement in overall performance of the network.

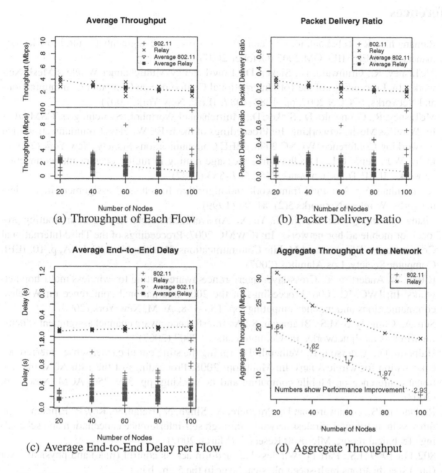

(a) Throughput of Each Flow

(b) Packet Delivery Ratio

(c) Average End-to-End Delay per Flow

(d) Aggregate Throughput

Fig. 5. Performance Improvement in Random Scenario with increasing number of Nodes

8   Conclusion

In this paper, we investigate the challenges of interference detection in wireless networks and propose a solution for this. We also incorporate this detection information in a centralized channel assignment algorithm, that collects the information from all the nodes and processes the information centrally. Although much work remains to be done, this paper shows the potential of effective interference detection scheme and its use in channel assignment in virtual cut-through switching based wireless networks. The performance is improved with respect to increased average throughput, packet delivery ratio and end-to-end delay. The aggregate throughput of the network increases up to three times compared to the conventional IEEE 802.11 based MAC protocol. Based on our overall evaluation, we believe that the virtual cut-through switching based physical layer can offer significant performance improvements in wireless multihop networks.

References

[1] Ramanathan, R., Tchakountio, F.: Channel access over path segments for ultra low latency manets. In: IEEE MILCOM 2007 (October 2007)

[2] McTasney, R., Grunwald, D., Sicker, D.: Low-Latency Multichannel Wireless Mesh Networks. In: Proceedings of the 16th International Conference on Computer Communications and Networks, ICCCN 2007, pp. 1082–1087. IEEE, New York (2007)

[3] McTasney, R., Grunwald, D., Sicker, D.: Multichannel Wormhole Switching vs. CSMA/CA for Wireless Mesh Networking. In: Proceedings of the IEEE Wireless Communications and Networking Conference, WCNC 2008. IEEE Communications Society, New York (2008)

[4] Dally, W.J., Seitz, C.L.: Deadlock-free message routing in multiprocessor interconnection networks. IEEE Trans. Comput. 36(5), 547–553 (1987)

[5] Ramanathan, R.: A unified framework and algorithm for channel assignment in wireless networks. Wireless Networks 5(2), 81–94 (1999)

[6] Zhang, X., Liu, Q., Shi, D., Liu, Y., Yu, X.: An average link interference-aware routing protocol for mobile ad hoc networks. In: ICWMC 2007: Proceedings of the Third International Conference on Wireless and Mobile Communications, Washington, DC, USA, p. 10. IEEE Computer Society, Los Alamitos (2007)

[7] ElBatt, T., Andersen, T.: Cross-layer interference-aware routing for wireless multi-hop networks. In: IWCMC 2006: Proceedings of the 2006 international conference on Wireless communications and mobile computing, pp. 153–158. ACM, New York (2006)

[8] Sen, A., Ganguly, S.M.S., Bhatnagar, S.: An interference-aware channel assignment scheme for wireless mesh networks. In: Communications 2007 (2007)

[9] Halperin, D., Anderson, T., Wetherall, D.: Taking the sting out of carrier sense: interference cancellation for wireless lans. In: MobiCom 2008: Proceedings of the 14th ACM international conference on Mobile computing and networking, pp. 339–350. ACM, New York (2008)

[10] Radunovic, B., Gunawardena, D., Proutiere, A., Singh, N., Balan, V., Key, P.: Efficiency and fairness in distributed wireless networks through self-interference cancellation and scheduling. Technical report, Microsoft Research (March 2009)

[11] 802.11a 1999, I.S.: Part 11: Wireless lan medium access control (mac) and physical layer (phy) specifications high-speed physical layer in the 5 ghz band

[12] Fifield, J., Kasemir, P., Grunwald, D., Sicker, D.: Experiences with a platform for frequency-agile techniques. In: DYSPAN 2007 (2007)

[13] Dutta, A., Fifield, J., Schelle, G., Grunwald, D., Sicker, D.: An intelligent physical layer for cognitive radio networks. In: WICON 2008: Proceedings of the 4th international conference on Wireless internet (2008)

[14] 802.11-1999, I.S.: Part 11: Wireless lan medium access control (mac) and physical layer (phy) specifications

[15] Technologies, S.N.: QualNet network simulator, version 4.0

Efficient Multi-hop Broadcasting in Wireless Networks Using k-Shortest Path Pruning

Michael Q. Rieck[1] and Subhankar Dhar[2]

[1] Drake University
mrieck@drake.edu
[2] San José State University
dhar_s@cob.sjsu.edu

Abstract. In this paper, we proposed a multi-hop wireless broadcast method called k-Shortest Path Pruning (k-SPP). It is based on the Dominant Pruning method of Lim and Kim, and improves upon it in the context of certain routing protocols, such as Zone Routing Protocol. In our approach, every node must know about its k-hop neighborhood, for some constant $k \geq 3$. Experimental results demonstrate that our technique requires fewer transmissions than Dominant Pruning broadcasting.

1 Introduction

Broadcasting a message to all the nodes of a network is often used in wireless ad hoc networks for route discovery and a variety of communication services. It can also be useful at the application level. Various popular routing protocols such as Ad Hoc On-demand Distance Vector routing (AODV) use broadcasting to establish and maintain routes. The routing protocols generally require each node to learn about its local neighborhood, out to some distance, usually just one or two hops. Some protocols though, of particular interest to us, require a distance of at least three hops.

The basic assumption is made here that each node that forwards the message does so by means of a single transmissions to all of its one-hop neighbors. Each of these receives the message, and then might or might not also forward the message. In the simplest approach, each node that has just received the message, and has not yet forwarded it, automatically forwards it to its one-hop neighbors. This is referred to as "blind flooding." Since every node ends up transmitting the message, this technique, though simple, is costly in terms of transmissions. In fact, every node receives the message from each of its one-hop neighbors. Hence, there are lots of redundant transmissions. In order to make routing efficient, several researchers have proposed protocols that require less transmissions and overhead ([2], [8], [9], [10], [13]).

The Dominant Pruning (DP) algorithm of Lim and Kim [13] substantially reduces the number of transmissions used to broadcast a message in a multi-hop wireless network. This approach requires that each node maintains awareness not only of its one-hop neighbors, but also its two-hop neighbors. However, a number of routing protocols ([1], [3], [12], [14], [16], [17], [19]) demand that each node acquire even

K. Kant et al. (Eds.): ICDCN 2010, LNCS 5935, pp. 283–294, 2010.
© Springer-Verlag Berlin Heidelberg 2010

more information. In order for these protocols to perform, the nodes must exchange "hello" messages until each gains an awareness of all of the nodes within a certain distance (number of hops) of itself, and also the links between these. Assuming this distance is greater than two, then it is possible to improve on the DP algorithm by means of a method that we call k-Shortest Path Pruning (k-SPP). This name was chosen because the algorithm strives to produce a broadcast tree whose paths from the root node (message source) is as short as possible.

In both DP and k-SPP, this broadcast tree is a spanning tree such that the root and the internal nodes are the only nodes that forward the message. Each does so by transmitting to all of its one-hop neighbors simultaneously. In the extreme case where each node has an awareness of the entire network (as is the case in some proactive routing protocols), the k-SPP broadcast tree would actually just be the tree used for breadth-first graph traversal (or Dijkstra's algorithm). Thus the paths from the root are indeed shortest paths connecting the root to other nodes. But when each node's view is restricted to its own locality, out to some given distance, then the broadcast tree that results from k-SPP is merely an approximation of the breadth-first tree. The paths from the root are guaranteed to be locally as short as possible, but this property cannot be assured globally.

Our contribution in this paper can be summarized as follows. We adapt Dominant Pruning and improve upon it in the context of certain routing protocols, such as Zone Routing Protocol [14]. In our approach, every node has an awareness of the nodes in its vicinity, out to at least three hops. Our method, called k-Shortest Path Pruning (k-SPP), requires fewer transmissions than Dominant Pruning. The advantage of this technique is more efficient broadcasting involving guaranteed local shortest path routing.

2   Related Work

2.1   Dominant Pruning and Other Broadcast Methods

In order to make flooding more efficient, several modified flooding techniques have been proposed to overcome the redundancy of transmissions. The problem of building a minimum cost flooding problem tree (MCFT) can be reduced to the Minimum Connected Dominating Set (MCDS) problem, which is NP-complete problem. This has been shown by Lim and Kim [13]. Recall that a subset D of nodes of a graph G is a dominating set if every node not in D is adjacent to at least one node in D. The Minimum Connected Dominating Set (MCDS) problem means finding a smallest dominating set D whose induced subgraph is connected. Since MCDS is NP complete problem, several approximation algorithms have been proposed in this regard [5].

Lim and Kim [13] proposed two flooding methods: Self-Pruning and Dominant Pruning (DP). In Self-Pruning, each node shares its list of adjacent nodes, with these adjacent nodes. This is done via periodic "hello" messages. Also, Self-Pruning requires fewer transmissions than blind flooding. On the other hand, Dominant Pruning requires the additional information about nodes that are two hops away, and consequently, outperforms Self-Pruning by further reducing the number of transmissions. Spohn and Garcia-Luna-Aceves [15] proposed Enhanced Dominant Pruning (EDP) for route discovery and integrated this with AODV. They showed that this approach performs better than standard AODV.

Mosko et al [10], combined dominating-set broadcast distribution with AODV RREQ process and proposed three heuristics. They showed that there is significant savings in RREQ traffic while maintaining the same or better latency and delivery ratio. Hoque et al [8] developed a broadcast algorithm for ad-hoc networks called Enhanced Partial Dominant Pruning (EPDP) that greatly reduces redundant transmissions. In [2], the authors proposed a limited flooding scheme that utilizes the clusterheads of each cluster. In particular, the Neighbors Dependent Cluster Algorithm is an on-demand clustering algorithm which can provide better, more stable and robust structures than existing clustering algorithms like Lowest-ID and Highest-Connectivity Cluster Algorithm.

2.2 Zone Routing and Related Routing Protocols

Z. J. Haas introduced the Zone Routing Protocol in [6]. It is a hybrid routing protocol (both proactive and reactive) that uses more than one-hop neighborhood information. A "zone" around a node consists of its k-hop neighborhood ($k \geq 2$). ZRP consists of a proactive routing protocol known as Intra-zone Routing Protocol (IARP), that is used for routing within a zone and a reactive routing protocol known as Inter-zone Routing Protocol (IERP) that is used for routing between different zones, respectively. A route to a destination within the local zone can be established from the proactively cached routing table of the source by IARP, therefore, if the source and destination is in the same zone, the packet can be delivered immediately. To send a packet from one zone to the other, route discovery happens reactively. Further developments along these lines can be found in [7], [11], [19].

The MaxMin scheme for clustering nodes in a wireless ad hoc network is described in [1]. The authors prove that finding a minimum k-hop dominating set is NP-complete. They use the nodes selected in this set to divide the graph into a set of clusters. They define unique IDs for each node and select a node into the dominating set if it has the highest ID in a k neighborhood. They describe a distributed way of finding the dominating nodes by flooding the node ID information for k rounds to all the neighbors of the node. Further, they do another k rounds of flooding to determine the clusters dominated by each node selected in the dominating set. This algorithm is constant-time.

B. Liang and Z. J. Haas [12] use a distributed greedy algorithm to produce a k-dominating set. To do so, they reduce the problem of finding this set to a special case of the Set Covering Problem, a well-known NP-complete problem. However, each node in their method needs to maintain an awareness of its local $2k$-hop neighborhood [12]. M. Q. Rieck, S. Dhar et al [3], [16], [17] also developed routing protocols based on k-dominating sets and algorithms for obtaining such sets, with a special focus on shortest path routing.

In [18], Y. Wu and Y. Li proposed a novel distributed algorithm LDA with low message complexity to construct a k-connected m-dominating set for positive integers k and m whose size is guaranteed to be within a small constant factor of the optimal solution when the maximum node degree is a constant. They also propose a centralized algorithm ICGA with a constant performance ratio to construct a km-CDS.

In [4], F. Dai and J. Wu proposed three localized protocols that construct a k-connected k-dominating set (k-CDS) as a virtual backbone of wireless networks. Two protocols are extensions of existing CDS algorithms. The third scheme is a generic paradigm, which enables many existing virtual backbone formation algorithms to produce a k-CDS with high probability. Experimental results show that these protocols can select a small k-CDS with relatively low overhead.

The authors of [9] proposed a clustering scheme that considers various factors. As a solution of minimum k-hop dominating set, their scheme generates small number of clusters to reduce the backbone changes and inter-cluster maintenance overhead. The new metric, intra-connection degree is introduced to evaluate better cluster candidate for joining so that the mobile nodes can stay longer. This metric also serves as an intra-connectivity and intra-communication reliability measurement. Moreover, they utilize the cluster stretching mechanism to reduce the leaving rate which affects higher cluster-based protocols. Finally, performance results are carefully studied by comprehensive simulation in wide-scale networks.

3 k-Shortest Path Pruning Algorithm

3.1   Preliminaries

In our previous work on k-dominating sets ([3], [16], [17]) we assumed that each node maintains an awareness of all the other nodes within $k+1$ hops of itself (for some positive integer k), and the links between these, except for links connecting two nodes that are both a distance $k + 1$ from the given node. We refer to this subgraph as the "extended k-local view" of the given node. Each node must make $k + 1$ transmissions to set this up. We will continue working in this context, but with the focus on shortest path pruning, and refer to this as "k-SPP."

As with our earlier work, it is important to understand when the notion of distance between two nodes, y and z, in the extended k-local view of another node x, is guaranteed to agree with the distance between y and z in the network graph as a whole. A basic fact in this regard [3, Theorem 2] (slightly altered) states that this is so, provided that the distance from y to x plus the distance from x to z does not exceed $k+1$. Whenever distances in an extended k-local view are considered in the k-SPP algorithm, as described below, the reader should observe that the theorem applies. As a result, it is never necessary to distinguish between distances measured in the extended k-local view, versus corresponding distances in the network graph. They are the same. We will let $d(y, z)$ denote the distance from y to z.

3.2   Basic Description of Dominant Pruning

k-SPP proceeds along a strategy motivated by and quite similar to DP. Let us briefly review DP. When a node w forwards a broadcast message, it does so to all of its one-hop neighbors, using a single transmission. When one of these neighbors x receives the message, it is obliged to check the message header to see whether or not its own ID is among the IDs in the "forward list," located in the header. If this is the case, then this node becomes obliged to also forward the message to all of its one-hop neighbors, after appropriately changing the forward list. k-SPP follows this same strategy as well, and only differs from DP in so far as how the forward list is chosen.

Still considering DP, x decides which nodes to put in the forward list, as follows. A set U is first determined. This consists of two-hop neighbors of x that are not adjacent to w, nor to any node in the received forward list. Then an algorithm such as the greedy algorithm is used to select a small set F of one-hop neighbors of x with the property that every member of U is adjacent to some member of F. The IDs of the members of F then constitute the forward list when x transmits the message.

3.3   Basic Description of k-SPP

We turn now to the k-SPP algorithm. We provide here a rough description of the algorithm, inviting the reader to examine the pseudocode below for further details. Here we'll assume the message has already propagated a distance of at least k from the source, for simplicity. In the pseudocode, this assumption will be dropped. Besides the forward list, the k-SPP algorithm requires that the message header also contain a list, called the "history list," containing the IDs of the k most recent nodes along the forwarding path leading to x. This list ends with w, which transmitted the message to x. In this way, the tail of the message path is remembered, as message forwarding progresses.

When x receives the message from w, the k-SPP algorithm proceeds in a manner similar to the DP algorithm. However, a different set of two-hop neighbors is selected in place of the set U, resulting in a different set of one-hop neighbors in place of the set F. We will let D denote the new set of two-hop neighbors, the one used in the k-SPP algorithm. A two-hop neighbor z of x might be included in D if it would be included in U (so $D \subseteq U$), and if the node y that is $k - 1$ hops before x in the history list is such that $d(y, z) = k + 1$. It is automatic that $d(y, x) = k - 1$. Since $d(x, z) = 2$, [3, Theorem 2] applies, and x lies along a shortest path connecting y to z.

However, x is also in a position to see any other node x' in the forward list from w, and to determine if z is also a two-hop neighbor of x', and would be part of the D set for x'. (The node x knows that $d(y, z) = k + 1$ and that $d(y, x') = k - 1$. It can check to see if $d(x', z) = 2$.) If such an x' exists, and if the ID for x' is greater than that of x (an arbitrary ordering of the nodes), then x will *not* include z in its D set, reasoning that x' (or a similar node) will include z in its D set. This further reduces redundancy in message forwarding.

Once the set D has been determined, a set T of one-hop neighbors of x is selected to "cover" the set D, in much the same way that F covers U in the DP algorithm. However, we here take a more restrictive view of what it means for a one-hop neighbor v of x to cover a two-hop neighbor z of x. Let u denote the first node in the history list, so u precedes x by k hops along the path. It is required that $d(u, v) = k + 1$. It is automatic that $d(u, x) = k$, and of course $d(x, v) = 1$. So x lies along a shortest path connecting u and v. Once the set T has been selected, the IDs of the members of T constitute the forward list when x transmits the message. Of course, the history list portion of the message header also needs to be updated appropriately.

Both the DP and k-SPP algorithms are intended to execute in an asynchronous distributed manner, although synchronized versions are considered too in Sect. 4. In practice, it is too expensive to synchronize the network nodes or to exchange overhead messages to simulate synchronization. Depending on the order in which the nodes forward the message, it occasionally becomes necessary for a node that has already forwarded the message to forward it again upon receiving it again along a different path.

We assume that the message header also contains the usual "hop count" that indicates the length of the forwarding path thus far. When a node receives the message more than once, it must check this hop count. If the hop count for the most recently received copy of the message is less than or equal to the hop counts for all previous received copies of the message, then it is possible that the message needs to be forwarded again, based on the newly received copy. A new forward list would need to be determined, but some two-hop neighbors could be omitted if they would not result in new future forwarding paths for the message. If the resulting forward list is empty, and if the current node has previously transmitted the message, then there is no reason for it to retransmit the message. In our simulations, we discovered that retransmissions were fairly common, but do not contribute substantially to the total number of transmissions, proportionally speaking.

3.4 A Generalization

The work of Lim and Kim [13] does not discuss the possibility that a given node might receive the message from multiple neighbors before possibly forwarding the message itself. We however wish to admit this possibility, as a generalization. In this more general setting, suppose that x recently received the message from a subset W of its one-hop neighbors, with each of these forwarded messages containing the ID for x in its header. The node x would then identify all of its two-hop neighbors that are not adjacent to any member of W, nor any of the nodes in the forward lists received by x. Let U now denote this set of two-hop neighbors. The DP algorithm proceeds as before by selecting a small set F of one-hop neighbors of x such that every member of U is adjacent to some member of F.

We now switch the discussion to a similar generalization of k-SPP. Let x, W and U continue to be as above. We require that the history list part of the message header contain a list of the IDs of all the nodes that preceded x by no more than k hops, along *some* forwarding path leading to x. When x receives the message from the nodes in W, it computes the sets D and T in a manner that is a straightforward adaptation of the original approach. Here though, u and y might be any nodes that are k and $k-1$ (respectively) hops in the past, as long as they are selected to be adjacent.

3.5   An Example

Figure 1 shows an example of using the above generalization of the k-SPP algorithm when $k = 3$. Therefore, each node has an extended 3-local view that includes all nodes out to a distance 4. The network in this example has 36 nodes and 57 (bidirectional) links. Some of the links are represented by dashed line segments. Other links, ones that play a more active role in this example, have either an arrow or pair of arrows in place of a dashed line segment. The broadcast message originates with node 13.

This example was produced during the simulations explained in Sect. 4, and was less efficient than average, but demonstrates well what can happen. At any moment, one of the nodes that has already received the message and which sees that it must forward it, is chosen at random to transmit next. Thus the nodes transmit one at a time.

Node 13 begins executing the algorithm. It determines that its two-hop neighbors can be covered by two of its one-hop neighbors, namely 2 and 25. As would be the case for DP, these two nodes constitute the forward list when 13 transmits the message. Later, when 0 receives the message from 25, and begins determining its

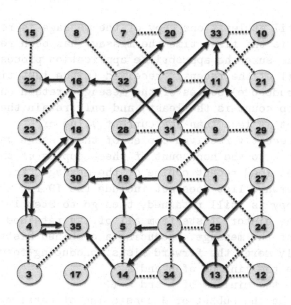

Fig. 1. Example of 3-SPP

own forward list, it observes that its two-hop neighbor 29 will receive the message when 27 transmits (since 0 and 27 are both in the forward list from 25), and so 0 ignores 29. However, even if 27 had not been part of the forward list that 0 received, 0 would still have omitted 29 from its D set because 0 can see that the distance from 13 to 29 is 3 hops, not 4 hops. Thus 0 does not lie along a shortest path connecting 13 to 29.

In our simulation, node 35 received the message from 4 prior to receiving it again, from 14. As a result, upon receiving the message the second time, 35 realizes that the message has just arrived (from 14) along a shorter path. Thus, it is obliged to forward the message back to 4, and thence to 26, and so on. This is unfortunate. However, in practice, it could be possible to use time delays (or other mechanism) to time the transmissions in an roughly synchronous manner, minimizing the likelihood that a node would receive the message first along a path that is substantially longer than the node's true distance from the root node. Again, the example here was particularly inefficient, compared to the average for similar random graphs.

3.6 Pseudocode

We here provide pseudocode for the (generalized) k-SPP algorithm. Each node x maintains an integer variable h that remembers the shortest forwarding path seen so far, from the root node (source) to x. Actually, h would depend on x and the particular message being broadcast. We are only focused on one broadcast message though. Initially, h is ∞, except for the root node's h, which is set to 0. Each node x repeats the following pseudocode, as necessary.

```
1.   Wait until at least one copy of the message is received by x.
2.   If this is the first time the message has been received by x,
     then make sure the appropriate application processes it.
3.   Among all of the recently received (since last time through
     this pseudocode) copies of the message, retain only those
     whose hop count is the least, and only retain these if this
     hop count is less than the current value of h.
4.   If any recently received copies of the message were retained,
     then set h to the hop count of these copies of the message.
5.   Among retained recent copies of the message, throw away any
     whose forward list does not include the ID for x.
6.   If no copy is still retained, then go to Step 19.
7.   Merge the history lists from all of the retained recent
     copies of the message, producing a combined history list H.
8.   Similarly merge the forward lists, producing forward list F.
9.   Let p be the minimum of h and k.
10.  Let q be the minimum of h and k-1.
11.  Let S_p be the subset of H consisting of entries from p hops
     in the past.
```

12. Let S_q be the subset of H consisting of entries from q hops in the past.
13. Let C be the set of one-hop neighbors v of x for which some element u in S_p satisfies d(u,v) = p+1.
14. Let U be the set of two-hop neighbors of x that are not adjacent to any member of the intersection of F and H.
15. Let D be the subset of U consisting of nodes z for which some element y in S_q satisfies d(y,z) = q+2.
16. Consider the bipartite graph whose vertex sets are C and D, with and edge connecting v in C to z in D if and only if there exists u in S_p and y in S_q such that d(u,y) = p-q, d(u,v) = p+1 and d(y,z) = q+2.
17. Use the greedy algorithm to select a small subset T of C such that each element of D is adjacent (in the bipartite graph) to some element of T.
18. If T is nonempty or if x has not already transmitted the message, then proceed as follows:
18a. Prepare to transmit the message by substituting the new forward list T into the message header.
18b. Update the message history list, using H. Entries get moved one hop further into the past, but entries that are k hops in past, get dropped. x becomes the only node one hop in past.
18c. x now transmits the message to all of its one-hop neighbors.
19. Halt. (However, if the same message is received again later, then begin the algorithm anew, without resetting h.)

4   Performance Evaluation

4.1   Methodology

3-SPP and 4-SPP were tested against DP. In doing so, random graphs were generated as follows. We used N^2 nodes (N = 6, 7, 8, 9, 10, 11 or 12) arranged to form an N-by-N grid. Nodes whose horizontal and vertical coordinates each differed by at most one, in absolute value, were potentially adjacent. The decision whether to actually make them adjacent (by including a link) was made randomly, with a probability of one-half. (The example in Fig. 1 in the previous section was obtained in this manner.) We feel that the resulting random graphs were reasonable approximations to true ad hoc networks, and substantially easier to check by hand than random geometric graphs. This allowed us to gain a high degree of confidence in our C++ code and resulting data. The C++ code is available from the first author upon request.

For each value of N, we ran tests on 2000 randomly generated graphs, and averaged the results. We ran each of DP, 3-SPP, 4-SPP and ∞-SPP, in a "synchronous" and "asynchronous" mode. ∞-SPP suggests of course that each node maintains a complete awareness of the entire network, resulting in forwarding paths that are truly as short as possible.

In the synchronous mode, we simulated the behavior of the network under the supposition of definite time units such that whenever a node received the message during a given time unit, and assuming that it was then obliged to forward the message, it did so during the next time unit. This is probably an unrealistic assumption though, and would require too much coordination among the nodes.

In the asynchronous mode, for simplicity, we assumed that no two nodes transmit at exactly the same time. We arranged for the nodes to transmit one at a time, in a randomly selected order. However, we made certain restrictions concerning this. At any given moment, we maintained a list of nodes that had received the message and had became obliged to forward it. We also remembered the number of hops that each copy of the message followed to reach each of these nodes. When it was time to select a node to transmit the message, one of these nodes was selected at random, but in such a way that nodes receiving messages with smaller hop counts were more likely to be selected over nodes receiving messages with larger hop counts.

4.2   Experimental Results

Figure 2 shows the results of our experiments. There was no appreciable difference between running DP synchronously versus asynchronously. For ∞-SPP, it makes absolutely no difference whether synchronous or asynchronous mode is used. Therefore, we provide only one plot in our chart for each of DP and ∞-SPP. The vertical component of the chart shows the percentage of nodes that were required to transmit the broadcast message. Of course, the horizontal component reflects the value of N (6, 7, ..., 12).

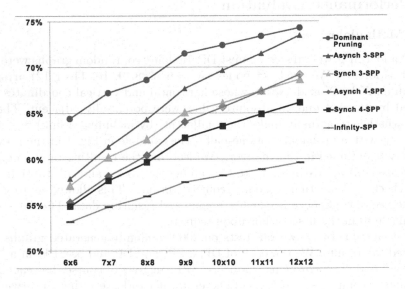

Fig. 2. Experimental Results

Plots for 3-SPP and 4-SPP, in both synchronous and asynchronous modes, are also provided. In the asynchronous cases, occasionally some nodes needed to transmit more than once, and hence contributed an extra amount to the transmission count in our results.

The results for ∞-SPP can be thought of as an idillic but possibly unrealistic goal. While k-SPP, for $k = 3$ or 4, cannot be expected to achieve this goal, they do manage to get much closer to it than does DP, at least when the network is not too large.

5 Conclusion

In this paper, we have improved an existing broadcasting technique, Dominant Pruning (DP), with a new method called k-Shortest Path Pruning (k-SPP). Both DP and k-SPP require only some of the network nodes to forward a broadcast message, while the remaining nodes simply receive it. Each time a node forwards the message, it does so via a single transmission to all of its one-hop neighbors, using a message header that contains information to steer future message forwarding.

Our experimental results show that k-SPP outperforms DP in terms of the number of transmissions. It does however require that each node be aware of its vicinity, out to at least three hops. The algorithm is more complicate, as well. However, the energy savings owing to far fewer transmissions would justify using k-SPP in place of DP in many contexts.

The extent to which message forwarding can be approximately coordinated can have a substantial effect on the performance of k-SPP. Ideally, all nodes that receive the message after the same number of hops, and which must then forward it, do so at exactly the same time. Our synchronized experiments make this unrealistic assumption. However, even though exact synchronization may be impractical, the use of approximately synchronized clocks would yield behavior closer to our synchronized, rather than our asynchronous, test results. We plan to explore this possibility more fully in future work.

References

1. Amis, A.D., Prakash, R., Vuong, T.H.P., Huynh, D.T.: Max-Min D-Cluster Formation in Wireless Ad Hoc Networks. In: Proc. IEEE Conf. Computer Comm. (INFOCOM), vol. 1, pp. 32–41 (2000)
2. Chiang, T.-C., Wu, P.-Y., Huang, Y.-M.: A Limited Flooding Scheme for Mobile Ad Hoc Networks. In: IEEE Int. Conf. Wireless and Mobile Computing, Networking and Communications (WiMob), vol. 3, pp. 473–478 (2005)
3. Dhar, S., Rieck, M.Q., Pai, S., Kim, E.-J.: Distributed Routing Schemes for Ad Hoc Networks Using d-SPR Sets. Microprocessors and Microsystems 28(8), 427–437 (2004)
4. Dai, F., Wu, J.: On Constructing k-Connected k-Dominating Set in Wireless Network. In: IEEE 19th Int. Conf. Parallel and Distributed Processing (2005)

5. Guha, S., Khuller, S.: Approximation Algorithms for Connected Dominating Sets. Algorithmica 20(4), 374–387 (1998)
6. Haas, Z.J.: A New Routing Protocol for the Reconfigurable Wireless Networks. In: IEEE 6th Int. Conf. Universal Personal Communications, vol. 2, pp. 562–566 (1997)
7. Haas, Z.J., Pearlman, M.R.: The Performance of a New Routing Protocol for the Recongurable Wireless Networks. In: IEEE Int. Conf. Communication (ICC 1998), vol. 1, pp. 156–160 (1998)
8. Hoque, M.E., Rahman, F., Kundu, S.K., Rahman, A.: Enhanced Partial Dominant Pruning (EPDP) Based Broadcasting in Ad Hoc Wireless Networks. In: Int. Symp. Performance Evaluation of Computer and Telecommunication Systems, SPECTS, pp. 143–150 (2008)
9. Mai, K.T., Shin, D., Choo, H.: Connectivity-based Clustering with Stretching Technique in MANETs. In: Proc. 3rd Int. Conf. Ubiquitous Information Management and Communication (ICUIMC), pp. 200–206 (2009)
10. Mosko, M., Garcia-Luna-Aceves, J.J., Perkins, C.E.: Distribution of Route Requests using Dominating-set Neighbor Elimination in an On-demand Routing Protocol. In: Proc. IEEE Global Telecommunications Conference (GLOBECOM), vol. 2, pp. 1018–1022 (2003)
11. Koyama, A., Honma, Y., Arai, J., Barolli, L.: An Enhanced Zone-based Routing Protocol for Mobile Ad-hoc Networks Based on Route Reliability. In: 20th Int. Conf. Advanced Information Networking and Applications, vol. 1, pp. 18–20 (2006)
12. Liang, B., Haas, Z.J.: Virtual Backbone Generation and Maintenance in Ad hoc Network Mobility Management. In: Proc. 19th Ann. Joint Conf. IEEE Computer and Comm. Soc (INFOCOM), pp. 1293–1302 (2000)
13. Lim, H., Kim, C.: Flooding in Wireless Ad Hoc Networks. Computer Communications Journal 24(3-4), 353–363 (2001)
14. Pearlman, M.R., Haas, Z.J.: Determining the Optimal Configuration for the Zone Routing Protocol. IEEE J. Selected Areas in Communications 17(8), 1395–1414 (1999)
15. Spohn, M.A., Garcia-Luna-Aceves, J.J.: Enhanced Dominant Pruning Applied to the Route Discovery Process of On-demand Routing Protocols. In: Proc. 12th IEEE Int. Conf. Computer Communications and Networks, pp. 497–502 (2003)
16. Rieck, M.Q., Dhar, S.: Hierarchical Routing in Sensor Networks using k-dominating Sets. In: Proc. 7th Int. Wksp. Distributed Computing (IWDC), pp. 306–317 (2005)
17. Rieck, M.Q., Pai, S., Dhar, S.: Distributed Routing Algorithms for Multi-hop Ad Hoc Networks Using d-hop Connected d-Dominating Sets. Computer Networks 47(6), 785–799 (2005)
18. Wu, Y., Li, Y.: Construction Algorithms for k-Connected m-Dominating Sets in Wireless Sensor Networks. In: Proc. 9th ACM Int. Symp. Mobile Ad Hoc Networking and Computing (MobiHoc), pp. 83–90 (2008)
19. Yang, C.-C., Tseng, L.-P.: Fisheye Zone Routing Protocol for Mobile Ad hoc Networks. In: 2nd IEEE Consumer Communications and Networking Conf. (CCNC), pp. 1–6 (2005)

Bandwidth Provisioning in Infrastructure-Based Wireless Networks Employing Directional Antennas

Shiva Kasiviswanathan[1], Bo Zhao[2], Sudarshan Vasudevan[3],
and Bhuvan Urgaonkar[2]

[1] Los Alamos National Laboratory
kasivisw@gmail.com
[2] Pennsylvania State University
{bzhao,bhuvan}@cse.psu.edu
[3] University of Massachusetts Amherst
svasu@cs.umass.edu

Abstract. Motivated by the widespread proliferation of wireless networks employing directional antennas, we study the problem of provisioning bandwidth in such networks. Given a set of subscribers and one or more access points possessing directional antennas, we formalize the problem of orienting these antennas in two fundamental settings: (i) subscriber-centric, where the objective is to fairly allocate bandwidth among the subscribers and (ii) provider-centric, where the objective is to maximize the revenue generated by satisfying the bandwidth requirements of subscribers.

For both the problems, we first design algorithms for a network with only one access point working under the assumption that the number of antennas does not exceed the number of non-interfering channels. Using the well-regarded lexicographic max-min fair allocation as the objective for a subscriber-centric network, we present an optimum dynamic programming algorithm. For a provider-centric network, the allocation problem turns out to be NP-hard. We present a greedy heuristic based algorithm that guarantees almost half of the optimum revenue. We later enhance both these algorithms to operate in more general networks with multiple access points and no restrictions on the relative numbers of antennas and channels. A simulation-based evaluation using OPNET demonstrates the efficacy of our approaches and provides us further in insights into these problems.

1   Introduction

There has been a growing interest in the use of directional antennas in communication networks [1,2]. Unlike omni-directional antennas, which transmit in all directions simultaneously, directional antennas can transmit in a particular direction over a smaller area. For the same amount of power, directional antennas provide longer range and greater spatial re-use in comparison with omni-directional antennas. Several studies point out that directional antennas have

K. Kant et al. (Eds.): ICDCN 2010, LNCS 5935, pp. 295–306, 2010.

the potential to improve the capacity of wireless networks [3,4]. Furthermore, there have been several recent efforts [5] to build low-cost steerable directional antennas. It can therefore be imagined that directional antennas will be widely used in a variety of wireless networks. However, directional antennas introduce some unique challenges in the design and operation of wireless networks. In particular, unlike networks with omni-directional antennas, such networks require mechanisms for orienting the antenna.

Our focus in this paper is on bandwidth allocation[1] in infrastructure-based wireless networks such as cellular networks and IEEE 802.11 WLANs. In these networks, wireless nodes (called subscribers) affiliate themselves with *base stations* (also called *access points (APs)* in this paper), each of which typically has a high-speed connection to the rest of the network. We assume that each subscriber can be only assigned to one antenna (and correspondingly, a single channel). A directional antenna can only provide connectivity to a subscriber if it geometrically covers it. The bandwidth allocated to a subscriber depends on the number of other subscribers covered by a directional antenna. For example, if a directional antenna on an AP transmits on a channel with bandwidth b and covers n subscribers sharing the bandwidth equally, each subscriber receives a bandwidth of b/n. We are interested in algorithms for orienting the antennas and assigning them to the subscribers such that the resulting allocation of bandwidth to the subscribers has some desirable properties (such as those concerning fairness or efficiency of allocation; we describe two concrete examples below.)

There have been several proposals to handle the challenges introduced by the usage of directional antennas in the context of neighbor discovery [6], medium access control [7,8], and routing [1] in multi-hop wireless networks. Whereas existing research has experimentally demonstrated the performance benefits offered by using multi-radio access points (APs) equipped with *omni-directional* antennas [9], bandwidth allocation with directional antennas has not been studied. As we will see in this paper, the problem becomes significantly more challenging with directional antennas.

We consider two fundamental bandwidth allocation problems in this paper. In both the settings, we are given: (i) the locations of a set of wireless subscribers, and (ii) the locations of the APs present in the network. Each AP is equipped with one or more directional antennas. Each antenna has an associated bandwidth that is to be shared among all the subscribers associated with that antenna.

In the first problem formulation, which we call the *subscriber-centric provisioning*, the goal of the network is to choose an assignment of subscribers to the antennas that ensures a max-min fair distribution [10] of bandwidth among the affiliated subscribers. Max-min fairness is a simple, well-recognized egalitarian objective that has gained wide acceptance for defining fairness in both wired and wireless networks [10,11]. This formulation captures the bandwidth provisioning problem that arises in a network where subscribers are homogeneous and do not pay differently for the service received. As an example, consider an AP providing

---

[1] We use the term *bandwidth* as synonymous with *data rate*, unless otherwise specified.

network connectivity to users in offices and university buildings. Given the locations of these wireless users and assuming uniformity in how the quality of their network connectivity translates into their productivity, it would be desirable for the AP to align its antennas in order to achieve equal allocations of bandwidth among the subscribers.

The second formulation we consider is called the *provider-centric provisioning*. Unlike the subscriber-centric problem, each subscriber specifies a bandwidth requirement to the network provider. If a subscriber's requirement can be satisfied, it pays the provider a cost proportional to the requirement. A subscriber does not pay the provider if its requirement is not satisfied. The goal of the provider is to choose orientations of the antennas and assignment of subscribers to the antennas such that the network provider's revenue is maximized. This formulation captures scenarios where the subscribers are independent entities, each interested in the quality of its own network connectivity and willing to pay for receiving it.

Both these problems are related to geometric covering problems, where we have a set of points in a two-dimensional plane and we want to cover them with the minimum possible number of objects of some shape [12,13]. The shapes of objects correspond to the patterns of directional antennas. Similar to [3,2,6], we model a directional antenna as a circular sector centered at the AP. In a recent paper [14], the authors considered the problem of minimizing the number of directional antennas for satisfying all customer demands. Although, the revenue maximization problem considered in this paper is related to the problem considered in [14], it requires fundamentally different algorithmic ideas and techniques.

We make the following key contributions in this paper.

① We start by considering the restricted version of the problems where we have a single AP and number of antennas on the AP does not exceed the number of non-interfering channels (we refer to this set of restrictions as *RestAntChan*). Under these restrictions we,

   a) Develop a dynamic programming algorithm that achieves an optimum max-min fair allocation for the subscriber-centric model.

   b) Show that revenue-maximization for the provider-centric model is NP-hard. We develop a greedy algorithm that guarantees close to half of the optimal revenue in the worst case and runs in time linear in number of subscribers.

② Building upon the algorithms above, we devise heuristics for bandwidth allocation in networks with multiple APs and without any restrictions on the relative numbers of antennas per AP.

③ We evaluate our algorithms by conducting an extensive simulation study using the OPNET [15] simulator, both in a single-AP and the more general multiple AP settings. Our simulations show that our algorithms achieve near-optimal allocations over a range of parameter settings.

Due to space limitations, we exclude most of the proofs and the experimental results. All omitted details appear in the full version [16].

2 Network Model and Problem Definitions

We begin this section by describing the wireless network model assumed in our research. Next, we formally define the two bandwidth provisioning problems that we study in this paper. For sake of simplicity we define the model and problems with respect to a single AP. The definitions naturally generalize to the case of multiple APs.

2.1 Background and Network Model

We consider a wireless network consisting of one AP with m directional antennas, each capable of being steered in a direction chosen by the AP. Each antenna has a bandwidth of b bits/second, a transmission range of R meters, and a span of ρ degrees. Each antenna has to be associated with one of the available channels. The network has n wireless subscribers whose locations are fixed and are known to the AP. All subscribers are assumed to be at most R meters away from the AP.

We will deal with points in radial coordinates and with circular orderings. The origin of our coordinate system lies at the AP. A point (θ, r) is equivalent to a Cartesian point $(r \times \sin\theta, r \times \cos\theta)$. Equality of angles is understood modulo 2π, i.e., $\alpha = \beta$ means that for a certain integer j we have $\alpha = \beta + 2j\pi$. We denote the set of n subscribers by $U = \{1, \ldots, n\}$ and the location of subscriber i by (θ_i, r_i). A directional antenna is characterized by four parameters. The first three parameters, namely range R, bandwidth b, and range ρ, have already been introduced. The fourth parameter denotes the *direction* that the AP steers the antenna in, denoted by the radial angle α in our coordinate system. A directional antenna with parameters (R, b, ρ, α) can provide connectivity to subscribers with radial coordinates (θ, r) such that $\alpha \leq \theta \leq \alpha + \rho$ and $r \leq R$; we say that the antenna can *cover* these subscribers. Henceforth, we assume the bandwidth of each antenna to be 1 bandwidth unit (1 bandwidth unit = b bits/second); all variables denoting bandwidth are assumed to be scaled appropriately. For subscriber i, we define the set of its *right neighbors* $Nbr_{right}(i)$ and the set of its *left neighbors* $Nbr_{left}(i)$ as follows.

$$Nbr_{right}(i) = \{j \in U : \ \theta_j = \theta_i + \beta \text{ with } 0 \leq \beta \leq \rho\}$$
$$Nbr_{left}(i) = \{j \in U : \ \theta_j = \theta_i - \beta \text{ with } 0 \leq \beta \leq \rho\}$$

$Nbr_{right}(i)$ consists of all subscribers whose angular separation from i is at most ρ in the counter-clockwise direction and $Nbr_{left}(i)$ represents the same in the clockwise direction.

2.2 Subscriber-Centric Provisioning

The first setting that we consider is a wireless network where the network provider is expected to provide max-min fair bandwidth allocation when provisioning its subscribers. We call the problem of achieving a max-min fair bandwidth allocation as the subscriber-centric provisioning.

We begin by formally defining the notion of max-min fairness. It is defined via a type of equilibrium. Given two k-tuples, $X = (x_1, \ldots, x_k)$ and $Y = (y_1, \ldots, y_k)$, each in non-decreasing order, we say that X lexicographically dominates Y if $X = Y$, or there exists some index p such that $x_p > y_p$ and $x_q = y_q$ for all $q < p$. If X lexicographically dominates Y, we also say that X is *as fair as* Y. A *bandwidth allocation vector* is a n-tuple denoting the allocation of bandwidth to the n subscribers. A solution F to a subscriber-centric instance consists of a disjoint collection of m sets $S_1, \ldots, S_m \subseteq U$ such that each set can be covered by one antenna, and an allocation vector $B(F) = (b_1, \ldots, b_n)$ such that, for $j \in \{1, \ldots, m\}$, a) $\sum_{i \in S_j} b_i \leq 1$ and b) $\bigcup_j S_j = U$. Here, the set S_j represents the subscribers *assigned* to antenna j (meaning the AP would provide connectivity to the subscribers in S_j using the antenna j) and b_i denotes the bandwidth that the subscriber i gets in the allocation. Finally, $\forall i, j$, we require that the antennas covering S_i and S_j be associated with different channels if the sectors corresponding to the antennas intersect. Max-min fairness enforces the following *max-min equilibrium* condition on the allocation vector: For any collection of sets $\{S_1, \ldots, S_m\}$ and allocation vector $B(F)$, the vector $B(F)$ must be the fairest allocation.

2.3 Provider-Centric Provisioning

A fundamentally different provisioning problem arises in networks where the subscribers are interested only in the quality of their own network connectivity. The subscribers are, therefore, willing to pay the provider for the network bandwidth. We assume that the revenue obtained from a subscriber i is $\Lambda \cdot d_i$ if its requirement d_i is satisfied (Λ is a network-wide constant), and 0 otherwise. Here, $d_i \in [0, 1]$ (due to normalization of the antenna bandwidth mentioned above). The objective of the provisioning is to determine a bandwidth allocation that maximizes the revenue that the provider can generate from the subscribers. We assume that in such a provider-centric provisioning problem, each subscriber has a bandwidth requirement $d_i > 0$. For a set of subscribers S, define *weight* $d(S)$ as $\sum_{i \in S} d_i$. A set of subscribers S is said to be *valid* iff a) $d(S) \leq 1$ and b) S can be covered with a single antenna. A solution to a provider-centric instance consists of valid disjoint sets of subscribers $S_1, \ldots, S_m$. Again, $\forall i, j$, we require that the antennas covering S_i and S_j be associated with different channels if the sectors corresponding to the antennas intersect. The objective of maximizing revenue in this case is the same as maximizing the sum of weights. That is, we want valid sets $S_1, \ldots, S_m$ maximizing $\sum_{i=1}^{m} d(S_i)$. This problem is NP-hard. The NP-hardness follows from a simple reduction from a variant of classical "bin packing" problem.

2.4 Notations

Recall from Section 2.1 that $Nbr_{left}(i)$ denotes the set of all subscribers whose angular separation from i is at most ρ in the counter-clockwise direction and

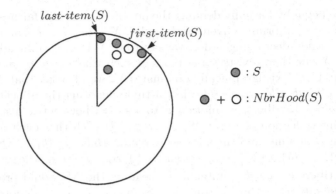

Fig. 1. The subscribers denoted by the shaded circles are part of set S. The $NbrHood(S)$ contains all subscribers between $first\text{-}item(S)$ and $last\text{-}item(S)$.

$Nbr_{right}(i)$ represents the same in the clockwise direction. Without loss of generality, we assume that the direction θ_i of a subscriber i with respect to the AP is different for each $i \in U$.

To capture spatial closeness of subscribers, we define a directed graph (which is a simple directed cycle) (U, E). To define this graph consider the unit radius circle centered at the origin and passing though the set of radial coordinates $(1, \theta_1), (1, \theta_2), \ldots, (1, \theta_n)$. Now we walk along the circle in counter-clockwise direction and add an edge directed (i, j) to E if the point $(1, \theta_j)$ is encountered immediately after $(1, \theta_i)$. Additionally, we say that subscribers i and j are *contiguous*. We define the function *successor* as follows: for an element (i, j) of E, $successor(i) = j$. We use $path(a, b)$ to denote the set of subscribers in the path from a to b in this graph.

Also, we define for any set of subscribers S a *neighborhood* $NbrHood(S)$ as follows: $NbrHood(S) = Nbr_{left}(a) \cap Nbr_{right}(b)$, if there exist $a, b \in S$ such that $S \subseteq Nbr_{left}(a) \cap Nbr_{right}(b)$. Intuitively, for a set S, its neighborhood $NbrHood(S)$ contains all the subscribers lying geographically between the first and last subscribers in S in an ordering of the members of S in the counter-clockwise direction. $NbrHood(S)$ is defined for a set S iff any two subscribers in S are within ρ of each other. For set S, we define $first\text{-}item(S)$ as the subscriber j such that for some subscriber k we have $NbrHood(S) = Nbr_{left}(j) \cap Nbr_{right}(k)$. The subscriber k is defined as $last\text{-}item(S)$. See Figure 1.

3 Subscriber-Centric Bandwidth Provisioning

In this section, we describe a dynamic programming formulation that provides a max-min fair allocation in a network with a single AP possessing fewer antennas (m) than the number of non-interfering channels (i.e., under the restrictions of *RestAntChan*). The general idea is to show the existence of a solution in which the allocations are restricted to a very special form. In turn, the best solution in that special form can be found using dynamic programming. We start with any optimal solution and show that it can be transformed into another solution which has this special form. Note that this transformation is an existential proof (non-algorithmic) and the algorithm itself is described in the next subsection.

Let $\mathcal{F}$ denote any optimal solution with ordered sets $O_1, \ldots, O_m$, so that (U, E) has a simple path with the subsequence $first\text{-}item(O_1)$, $first\text{-}item(O_2)$, $\ldots$, $first\text{-}item(O_m)$ and $NbrHood(O_1)$ is not a subset of $NbrHood(O_i)$ for any $i \in \{2, \ldots, m\}$. We now establish some properties of the sets in the optimal solution. Let $B_j(\mathcal{F})$ be the bandwidth vector for subscribers associated with antenna j. The following lemma notes the simple fact that in the solution $\mathcal{F}$ if $|O_j| = c$, then $B_j(\mathcal{F}) = (\frac{1}{c}, \ldots, \frac{1}{c})$.

Lemma 1. *Let $\mathcal{F}$ be any optimal solution of a subscriber-centric instance with sets $O_1, \ldots, O_m$. For any set O_j with $|O_j| = c$, $B_j(\mathcal{F}) = \left(\frac{1}{c}, \ldots, \frac{1}{c}\right)$.*

As a consequence of the above lemma, we have the following max-min equilibrium condition: when all the antennas are omni-directional ($\rho = 360$), the fairest allocation vector allocates a bandwidth of m/n to each subscriber.

A set S of subscribers is said to be a *feasible* set if: (i) all the subscribers in S are contiguous, i.e., there exists $a, b \in U$ such that $path(a, b) = S$, and (ii) $NbrHood(S)$ is defined. We reassign subscribers in $O_1, \ldots, O_m$ to create a new solution $\mathcal{F}'$ with sets $S_1, \ldots, S_m$ such that $|O_j| = |S_j|$ and S_j is feasible. Note that since the cardinality of every set remains the fairness is not affected (from Lemma 1).

The process of replacing each O_j with S_j is described in the algorithm RE-PLACE (Figure 2).The algorithm replaces subscriber sets that cover geographically overlapping areas into sets that cover non-overlapping areas. For doing the re-assignment we define the following notation:

```
x ← 0
y ← first-item(O₁)
S₀ ← ∅
D ← |Overlap(O₁)|
do forever
    if D ≥ 1
        D ← D − 1
        Sₓ ← Sₓ ∪ {y}
        y ← successor(y)
    else
        if x = m
            terminate the loop
        x ← x + 1
        Sₓ ← ∅
        D ← |Oₓ|
```

Fig. 2. Algorithm REPLACE

$$overlap(O_j, O_k) = \begin{cases} \varnothing \text{ if } first\text{-}item(O_j) \notin NbrHood(O_k) \quad \text{or} \quad j = k; \\ NbrHood(O_j) \cap O_k \text{ otherwise.} \end{cases}$$

$$Overlap(O_j) = \bigcup_{O_k \in \mathcal{F}} overlap(O_j, O_k).$$

Recall that all the subscribers in $NbrHood(O_j)$ (neighborhood of O_j) are within angular distance ρ from each other. $NbrHood(O_j)$ includes all the members of O_j and possibly members of other sets. $Overlap(O_j)$ represents these other members within the neighborhood of O_j. In particular, $overlap(O_j, O_k)$ represents members of O_k that are within the neighborhood of O_j. The following lemma proves the existence of solution $\mathcal{F}'$.

Lemma 2. *Any solution $\mathcal{F}$ for a subscriber-centric instance with sets $O_1, \ldots, O_m$ can be replaced with a solution $\mathcal{F}'$ with sets $S_1, \ldots, S_m$ such that for all $1 \le j \le m$ (i) $|S_j| = |O_j|$, (ii) subscribers in S_j are contiguous, and (iii) $NbrHood(S_j)$ is defined.*

3.1 Dynamic Programming Formulation

From Lemma 2, we know that we can convert any optimal solution $\mathcal{F}$ into a new optimal solution $\mathcal{F}'$ in which all sets in are feasible. We now show that, the solution $\mathcal{F}'$, i.e., sets $S_1, \ldots, S_m$ can be found using dynamic programming.

For every $a, b \in U$ the dynamic programming considers allocating exactly k ($\le m$) antennas to subscribers in $path(a, b)$, a sub-problem whose optimal solution is denoted by $M[a, b, k]$. Intuitively, $M[a, b, k]$ denotes the optimal bandwidth allocation vector obtained by allocating k antennas to cover all the nodes in $path(a, b)$. Remember that $path(a, b)$ defines a set of subscribers in the path between a and b in (U, E).

Recursive Formula in Dynamic Programming: Let ϕ be a special symbol, indicating that no feasible solution exists for the sub-problem. For any $a, b \in U$, $M[a, b, k]$ is set as

$$\text{LMAX}_c \left\{ M[a, c, k-1] \circ \left(\underbrace{\frac{1}{|path(d,b)|}, \ldots, \frac{1}{|path(d,b)|}}_{\text{total of } |path(d,b)| \text{ times}} \right) \right\}$$

if there exists $c \in path(a, b)$, $(c, d) \in E$, and $d \in path(a, b)$ such that $M[a, c, k-1]$ is not assigned ϕ, and $NbrHood(path(d, b))$ is defined. Here, "$\circ$" denotes concatenation of vectors. The operator LMAX_c defines lexicographically the biggest vector over the range of c (all vectors are sorted in non-decreasing order before applying this). If these conditions are not met, $M[a, b, k]$ is assigned ϕ, i.e., $path(a, b)$ cannot be covered with k antennas. For the base case we have $M[a, a, p] = (1)$, where $1 \le p \le m$. Also $M[a, b, 1]$ equals

$$\underbrace{\left(\frac{1}{|path(a,b)|}, \cdots, \frac{1}{|path(a,b)|} \right)}_{\text{total of } |path(a,b)| \text{ times}}$$

if $NbrHood(path(a,b))$ is defined, otherwise it is set to ϕ.

The correctness of the dynamic programming is straightforward (as for every $path(a,b)$ and every possible number of antennas that could be assigned to $path(a,b)$ we try all possible contiguous allocations, therefore finding $\mathcal{F}'$). The number of entries in the table M is of $O(n^2 m)$ each of which can be computed in $O(n^2)$ time. We conclude this section with the following.

Theorem 1. *The above algorithm finds the optimum solution for the subscriber-centric provisioning problem (under the restrictions of RestAntChan) in $O(n^4 m)$ time.*

4   Provider-Centric Bandwidth Provisioning

As in the previous section, we consider a network with a single AP possessing fewer antennas (m) than the number of non-interfering channels (i.e., under the restrictions of *RestAntChan*). We describe a simple algorithm achieving ≈ 2-approximation for this restricted version of provider-centric provisioning. More precisely, we show that the revenue our algorithm generates is (almost) at least half of the revenue achievable by any optimal algorithm.

The algorithm GREEDY specified in Figure 3 packs all the subscribers in U into valid sets (defined in Section 2.3). To enable the packing, we construct an

```
j ← 1
i ← t
D ← ∅
first-item(S₁) ← i
while i ≤ n
    if dᵢ + d(Sⱼ) ≤ 1 and
            Sⱼ ∪ {i} ⊆ Nbr_left(first-item(Sⱼ))
        Sⱼ ← Sⱼ ∪ {i}
        i ← successor(i)
    else
        D ← D ∪ d(Sⱼ)
        j ← j + 1
        first-item(Sⱼ) ← i
D ← D ∪ d(Sⱼ)
output the sum of m largest entries in D
```

Fig. 3. Algorithm GREEDY. $\mathcal{D}$ is a set of values, each denoting the revenue associated with a subscriber set.

ordered list L from the set of subscribers U. The list L starts with a subscriber t satisfying

$$d(Nbr_{right}(t)) = \min\{d(Nbr_{right}(i)) : i \in U\}.$$

Two subscribers i, j are consecutive in L if $(i, j) \in E$, where E is the edges of the graph constructed in Section 2.4. We start greedy packing from the lowest unpacked subscriber (in the list L) and close an antenna for packing purposes if either the antenna cannot accommodate an subscriber or if it reaches its maximum range (ρ). Therefore all the sets constructed by GREEDY are valid.

The running time of the algorithm GREEDY is linear in the number of subscribers. We conclude this section with the following theorem. The constant of proportionality arising in the theorem is what relates the revenue to subscriber requirement in the statement of the provider-centric provisioning (see Section 2.3).

Theorem 2. *There exists a linear time algorithm for the problem of provider-centric provisioning (under the restrictions of* RestAntChan*) which produces a revenue which is at least half of the optimal revenue minus* $\Lambda/2$.

5 Practical Considerations

In this section, we attempt to relax two restrictions imposed on the bandwidth provisioning problems so far: (i) the restriction that number of antennas on an AP does not exceed the number of non-interfering channels, and (ii) the presence of only one AP in the network. We find these problems to be significantly less amenable to a theoretical study similar to that presented in the previous sections. We develop heuristics that build upon the algorithms developed for the restricted models. We use the OPNET [15] network simulator version 12.0 to evaluate our algorithms. The evaluation methodology and results are presented in [16].

5.1 Channel Assignment

In practice, wireless networks divide available bandwidthinto (possibly overlapping) channels. For example, in 802.11 networks there are 11 overlapping channels. Only 3 channels (say channels 1, 6, and 11) can be considered non-interfering. Consider a single AP network where the number of antennas exceeds the number of available non-interfering channels. (An example could be a single AP employing 802.11b and possessing 4 directional antennas.) At least two antennas would have to share the same channel in such a network. This has two important design implications that we must consider.

- Bandwidth Sharing: All antennas using the same channel share the aggregate bandwidth available to the channel.
- Interference: Orienting multiple antennas using the same channel such that the regions covered by them overlap may cause unacceptable degradation of signal quality and throughput.

Theoretical properties. These phenomena change the nature of our allocation problems. In particular, instead of treating each antenna as capable of sustaining a data rate of b bits/sec, *we must treat each non-interfering channel as the entity with a data rate of b*; all antennas using this channel must share the data rate b amongst them. We suspect that the subscriber-centric problem continues to be easy (i.e., not NP-hard). The provider-centric problem however continues to be NP-hard.

Heuristics. Let $C_1, C_2, \ldots$ denote the channels. Let $A_1, A_2, \ldots$ denote the antennas. Our heuristic for subscriber-centric provisioning, SUB-HEUR, works as follows. SUB-HEUR first derives antenna orientations and assignments of subscribers to antennas given by the dynamic programming based algorithm presented in Section 3.1. It then associates a channel to each antenna in a round-robin fashion (antennas A_1 gets C_1; A_2 gets C_2, etc.) Whenever multiple antennas covering intersecting sectors get associated with the same channel (this can happen in regions of high subscriber density), SUB-HEUR replaces these with a single antenna. It enlarges the angular span of this antenna to cover the total area covered by the antennas being replaced.

Our heuristic for provider-centric provisioning, PROV-HEUR, operates in a similar manner. It first derives antenna orientations and assignments of subscribers to antennas given by the approximation algorithm GREEDY (Section 4). It then associates channels with the antennas using the round-robin scheme described for SUB-HEUR. Whenever multiple antennas covering intersecting sectors get associated with the same channel PROV-HEUR replaces these with a single antenna. It then considers the set of subscribers covered by the antennas being replaced in a decreasing order of their data rate requirements (and hence in a decreasing order of the revenue they would generate.) The subset whose requirements can be met by one antenna are retained; the rest are discarded (meaning not assigned to any antenna.) Finally, PROV-HEUR enlarges the angular span of this antenna to cover all the retained subscribers.

5.2   Multiple Access Points

The chief difficulty when allocating bandwidth in a network with multiple APs arises when dealing with a subscriber that can potentially be covered by more than one APs. For such subscribers, we need to decide association with which AP would best serve the objective of the network provider.

Theoretical properties. The hardness of the subscriber-centric problem in a network with multiple APs (with or without the restriction *RestAntChan*) is open. The provider-centric problem clearly is NP-hard (since it was NP-hard even with one AP). However, unlike for the single AP case, we do not yet have an algorithm with provable approximation ratio.

Heuristics. Each AP first determines antenna orientations and subscriber assignments *independently* using the heuristics developed above. For sets of antennas with intersecting sectors, the heuristics then attempt to modify the association of channels to antennas. The heuristic for subscriber-centric allocation operates by attempting to equally divide subscribers in intersecting areas among available antennas. The heuristic for provider-centric allocation attempts to include subscribers with highest revenue and drops subscribers that can not be accommodated. Remaining antennas using the same channel and covering intersecting sectors are merged and their angular spans adjusted appropriately.

References

1. Choudhury, R., Yang, X., Ramanathan, R., Vaidya, N.: Using directional antennas for medium access control in ad hoc networks. In: Proceedings of the ACM MOBICOM 2002, pp. 59–70 (2002)
2. Ramanathan, R.: On the performance of beamforming antennas. In: Proceedings of the ACM MobiHoc 2001, pp. 95–105 (2001)
3. Yi, S., Pei, Y., Kalyanaraman, S.: On the capacity improvement of ad hoc wireless networks using directional antennas. In: Proceedings of the ACM MobiHoc 2003, pp. 108–116 (2003)
4. Peraki, C., Servetto, S.: On the maximum stable throughput problem in random networks with directional antennas. In: Proceedings of the ACM MobiHoc 2003, pp. 76–87 (2003)
5. Kuga, Y., Cha, J., Ritcey, J.A., Kajiya, J.: Mechanically steerable antennas using dielectric phase shifters. In: Proceedings of the IEEE- APS and URSI, pp. 161–164 (2004)
6. Vasudevan, S., Kurose, J., Towsley, D.: On neighbor discovery in wireless networks with directional antennas. In: Proceedings of the IEEE INFOCOM 2005, pp. 590–600 (2005)
7. Nasipuri, A., Ye, S., You, J., Hiromoto, R.: A MAC protocol for mobile ad hoc networks using directional antennas. In: Proceedings of the IEEE WCNC 2000, pp. 1214–1219 (2000)
8. Bao, L., Garcia-Luna-Aceves, J.: Transmission scheduling in ad hoc networks with directional antennas. In: Proceedings of the ACM MOBICOM 2002, pp. 48–58 (2002)
9. Zhu, J., Roy, S.: 802.11 mesh networks with two-radio access points. In: Proceedings of the IEEE ICC 2005, pp. 3609–3615 (2005)
10. Bertsekas, D., Gallager, R.: Data Networks. Prentice-Hall, Englewood Cliffs (1987)
11. Huang, X.L., Bensaou, B.: On max-min fairness and scheduling in wireless ad-hoc networks: analytical framework and implementation. In: Proceedings of the ACM MobiHoc 2001, pp. 221–231. ACM, New York (2001)
12. Brönnimann, H., Goodrich, M.T.: Almost optimal set covers in finite vc-dimension. Discrete & Computational Geometry 14(4), 463–479 (1995)
13. Clarkson, K.L., Varadarajan, K.R.: Improved approximation algorithms for geometric set cover. In: Proceedings of the ACM SoCG 2005, pp. 135–141 (2005)
14. Berman, P., Jeong, J., Kasiviswanathan, S.P., Urgaonkar, B.: Packing to angles and sectors. In: Proceedings of the ACM SPAA 2007, pp. 171–180 (2007)
15. OPNET: Opnet modeler version 12.0, 2007 (2007), http://www.opnet.com
16. Zhao, B., Kasiviswanathan, S., Vasudevan, S., Urgaonkar, B.: Bandwidth provisioning in infrastructure-based wireless networks employing directional antennas. Technical Report CSE-07-008, Pennsylvania State University, http://csl.cse.psu.edu/?q=node/108

ROTIO+: A Modified ROTIO for Nested Network Mobility

Ansuman Sircar[1], Bhaskar Sardar[1], and Debashis Saha[2]

[1] IT Dept, Jadavpur University, Kolkata
ansuman.sircar@tcs.com, bhaskargit@yahoo.co.in
[2] MIS Group, IIMC, Kolkata
ds@iimcal.ac.in

Abstract. The NEMO Basic Support (NBS) protocol ensures session continuity for all nodes in a moving network by maintaining a tunnel between Mobile Router (MR) and its Home Agent (HA). The NBS protocol, however, suffers from sub-optimality problem in routing, which gets amplified as the level of nesting increases [4]. The ROTIO [5] is a route optimization scheme for nested NEMO that restricts the number of tunnels to two thereby alleviating the pinball routing problem to a great extent. In this paper, we propose ROTIO+, a simple but practical extension of ROTIO scheme, to further reduce the number of tunnels to one in nested NEMO. In ROTIO+ scheme, the MR uses two binding updates (BUs): one to its HA and the other to the Top Level Mobile Router (TLMR). In the BU to its HA, it provides both the Care of Address (CoA) and Home Address (HoA) of the TLMR. Under normal circumstances, the HA routes all packets for the MR to the CoA of the TLMR. When the QoS decreases beyond a threshold i.e. the TLMR is changing the point of attachment, the HA sends the packet to the HoA of the TLMR. Thus, the scheme limits the number of visits to HA to one for a nested network and also has a fall back scheme when the TLMR changes point of attachment. The results show that it is an effective solution for route optimisation problem in nested NEMO.

Keywords: NEMO Basic Support protocol, MIPv6, Route optimization, ROTIO, Nested NEMO.

1 Introduction

The proliferation of mobile computing devices such as Mobile Telephones, Personal Digital Assistants (PDAs) and Laptop computers has created the need for continuous Internet connectivity through IP layer. In a vehicle, a group of such mobile computing devices move together as a unit, forming a moving network. This is popularly known as Network Mobility (NEMO) [1]. A simple example is being that of a person carrying a PDA and a Laptop while travelling in a car. Managing the mobility of such devices, known as Mobile Hosts (MHs), is possible using Mobile IP (MIP) (e.g. Mobile IPv6 (MIPv6) [2]) protocols. However, this would require all MHs to be MIP capable and be able to process a storm of control packets to perform MIP functions. Moreover, all MHs within a moving network may not be sophisticated enough to run such

K. Kant et al. (Eds.): ICDCN 2010, LNCS 5935, pp. 307–322, 2010.

mobility support protocol. These problems are addressed by the NEMO working group with the Internet Engineering Task Force (IETF).

In NEMO, a network segment or subnet can move and attach to arbitrary points in the routing infrastructure. This moving network can only be accessed via specific gateways called Mobile Routers (MR) that manage its movement. To ensure session continuity for all nodes in the moving network, the IETF proposed the NEMO Basic Support Protocol (NBS) [3]. In the NBS protocol, each MR has a Home Agent (HA) where it resides when it is not moving. Since the MR is a part of the home network, the mobile network has a Home Address (HoA) belonging to the set of addresses assigned to the home network. This HoA remains assigned to the MR even when it is away. When the MR is attached to a foreign network, the MR acquires an address from the visited network, called the Care of Address (CoA). The connectivity with the MR is established through a bi-directional tunnel between the MR and its HA, known as MRHA tunnel, using the bind between the HoA and the CoA. This tunnel is set up when the MR sends a successful Binding Update (BU) to its HA, informing the HA of its current point of attachment. All communications to the moving networking has to be routed through the HA of the MR via the MRHA tunnel to reach the foreign network (i.e. the CoA) where the MR is currently residing. Thus, the MR can provide accessibilities to its own Mobile Network Nodes (MNNs), which are attached to its ingress interface that has its own network prefix.

In order to provide Internet connectivity, a MR can either connect to an Access Router (AR) or to another MR, which in turn is connected to Internet. This property of MR, whereby it attaches to other MRs, results in formation of a nested NEMO. In a real life scenario, this can be envisioned as a Personal Area Network (PAN) accessing Internet via MR of a car on a ship, which in turn contains a mobile network of larger scale with its own MR as show in Figure 1. This nested network of MRs is a simple

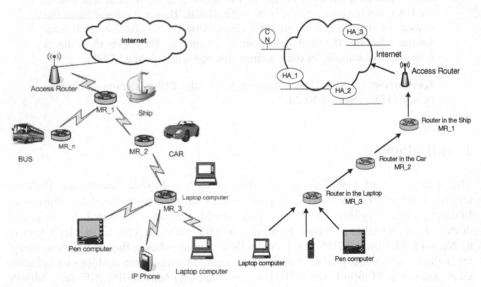

Fig. 1. On Board Vehicular Network   **Fig. 2.** Nested Mobile Network

nesting but can vary in complexity. Initially MR_1, MR_2 and MR_3 are attached to their own home network. Note that HA_n is the HA of MR_n. Suppose that a Local Fixed Node (LFN) is connected to MR_3's ingress interface. After MR_1 moves to a foreign link (MR_1 is attached to the AR), MR_2 is connected to MR_1. Then, MR_3 with the LFN is connected to MR_2. The situation will look like as given in Figure 2. Here, MR_1 is the Top Level Mobile Router (TLMR) of the Nested Mobile Network and is the gateway to the whole Nested Mobile Network. Now, according to NBS protocol, all the MRs will establish a MRHA tunnel with their respective HAs. When a Correspondent Node (CN) sends a packet to the LFN in the nested network, the current NBS protocol requires the packet to visit the HAs of all the MRs. This has been pictorially depicted in Figure 3. As can be seen from Figure 3, this method of routing is inefficient and also results in increase of the packet size due to the encapsulations at each HA.

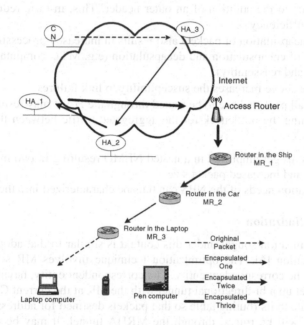

Fig. 3. Packet Routing in NBS

As the degree of nesting increases, the packets destined for an LFN in a Nested NEMO will suffer more and more inefficient routing [4]. This is the so-called pinball routing problem, which, in turn, also introduces a number of inefficiencies in the routing mechanism. We discuss about these inefficiencies in Section II.

The route optimization using tree information option (ROTIO) [5] restricts the number of tunnels to two, thereby, alleviating the pinball routing problem to a great extent. This paper proposes ROTIO+, a modification of ROTIO, which improvises upon the ROTIO and restricts the number of tunnels to one while maintaining the basic advantages of the ROTIO.

The rest of this paper is organized as follows. Section 2 introduces sub-optimality in the NEMO Route optimization. In Section 3, we describe ROTIO+. Section 4 evaluates ROTIO+ vis-à-vis the performance indicators. Section V concludes the paper.

2 Sub Optimality in NBS

According to NBS protocol, in nested NEMO, the data packets must go through multiple HAs and results in several encapsulations. The sub-optimal effects due to several MRHA tunnels are the following [4].

- The NBS protocol results longer route leading to increased delay.
- The encapsulation of packets in the MRHA tunnel results in increase packet size due to the addition of an outer header. This, in turn, reduces the bandwidth efficiency.
- The encapsulation of packets also results in increased processing delay at the points of encapsulation and decapsulation (e.g. MTU computation, fragmentation and reassembly).
- All the above increases the susceptibility to link failures.
- Since all packets have to be routed through the HA it may result in home link becoming the bottleneck for the aggregated traffic between the corresponding nodes.

All these problems get amplified in a nested NEMO resulting in two major problems: pinball routing and increased packet size

The optimization needs of the NBS can thus be characterized into the following.

1) NEMO Optimization

The route optimization sought under this context is similar to that adopted by MIPv6 Route Optimization [6]. The optimization technique involves MR sending binding information to the correspondent entity. The correspondent entity, having received the BU, can then set up a bi-directional tunnel with the MR at the current CoA of the MR, and inject a route to its routing table so that packets destined for address in the mobile network prefix will be routed through the MRHA tunnel. It may be noted that, the correspondent entity can be a CN or a correspondent router. In case of correspondent router, the route optimization process terminates at the correspondent router and assumption that the correspondent router is located closer to the correspondent node than the home network. The examples of this approach are Optimized Route Cache [7] protocol and Path Control Header Protocol [8]. Figure 4 gives a generalised concept of this type of optimization.

2) Nested NEMO Optimization

The nested NEMO amplifies the inefficiencies of the NBS protocol. So, the solutions look for addressing the pinball routing by decreasing the number of visits to the HAs and reducing the number of tunnels. The other inefficiencies linked with nested

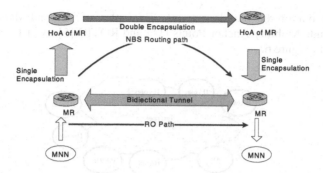

Fig. 4. NEMO Optimization

NEMO are related to these two attributes and solution for these in turn reduces the other efficiencies: decreasing the number of HAs and decreasing the number of encapsulations. Examples of the routing optimization schemes under this scenario are Reverse Routing Header [9] and Access Router Option [10]. The bypassing of HAs is shown in Figure 5.

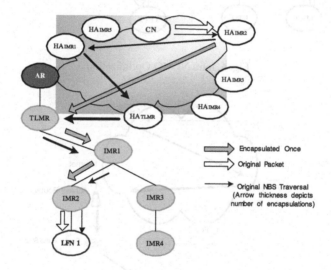

Fig. 5. Nested NEMO Optimization

3) Intra NEMO Optimization

The Intra NEMO routing is about a situation when the two corresponding MNNs are within the same nested network. The NBS requires a packet sent from one MNN to the other to leave the network, visit the HA of each MR before reaching other MNN. This apart from increasing the packet size and transmission delay also results in disruption of service when the gateway to the Internet, i.e. TLMR, gets disconnected. The solution seeks routing mechanism that would allow traffic between two MNNs nested within the same mobile network to follow a direct path between them without being routed out of the mobile network. Examples of intra NEMO optimization schemes include Mobility Anchor Points [11] and ROTIO [5]. A pictorial representation is given in Figure 6.

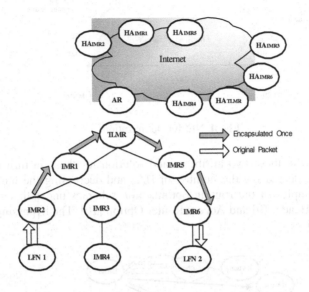

Fig. 6. Intra NEMO Optimization

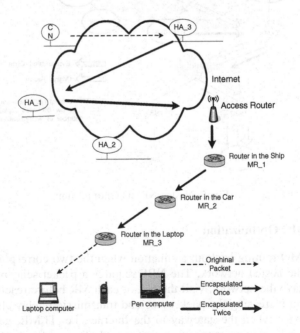

Fig. 7. Route Optimization in ROTIO

3   ROTIO+

The ROTIO [5] is based on the Tree Information Option (TIO). In the ROTIO scheme, each MR in the nested NEMO sends two BUs: one to its HA and other to the TLMR. The former BU contains the TLMR's home address while the latter contains routing information between the issuing MR and the TLMR. This alleviates the pinball routing problem significantly. Now, a packet from a CN only needs to visit two transit nodes, regardless of the degree of nesting. This is shown in Figure 7. The ROTIO is also extended to perform routing between two MNNs inside the same nested network more efficiently and to substantially reduce the disruption time when a mobile network hands off. The ROTIO+ scheme improves on ROTIO scheme and limits the number of tunnels to one. Simultaneously, it also retains the advantages of ROTIO, which includes facilitation of Intra-NEMO routing.

3.1 Design Considerations

The major considerations for the ROTIO+ scheme are the following:

1. The nested NEMO as has been visualized will be in a vehicular network. In the example given in Figure 1, the router of the ship will function as the TLMR, which keeps changing its CoA. All other routers will be part of the subnet that TLMR will carry with it
2. Most of the movements of the Intermediate MR (IMR) will happen within the subnet of the TLMR.
3. The IMR will move out of the TLMR subnet only when the mobile device moves out of the vehicular network. In such scenarios, it will get attached to a different MR or directly to the access router.
4. The frequency of TLMR changing its point of attachment will be far greater than the IMR attaching itself to a different MR outside the subnet of the TLMR.
5. The HAs will be able to maintain two routing addresses for MR, one being the primary (CoA of TLMR) and the other being the fail over (HoA of TLMR). It would be able to run additional algorithm for sending data packets to the alternate address (HoA of TLMR) during handoff.

3.2 ROTIO+

The Basic ROTIO proposes to extend the TIO and call it as xTIO (extended TIO). The xTIO sub-option will contain the CoAs of the MRs in a Nested NEMO. Additionally, xTIO is appended to each BU message so as to inform an MR of all its ancestor MRs. In the scheme, Router Advertisement (RA) messages contain the xTIO. The TLMR forms an RA message with its HoA in the TreeID field and each MR appends its CoA using the xTIO sub-option as the RA is propagated through the tree. Figure 8 shows the TIO format in an RA message.

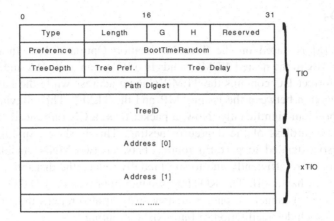

Fig. 8. TIO and xTIO Option

Determining TLMR: When an MR receives a RA message without the xTIO option it is the TLMR, otherwise it is an IMR.

RA Messages: The TLMR propagates RA messages to the IMRs along with the TIO option where the HoA of the TLMR is given in the TreeID field. The IMRs then append their CoA into the xTIO option and propagates the RA message downwards. Thus, by listening the RA message the IMRs can maintain an IMR list that stores the list of CoAs of all ancestor MRs.

BU: The ROTIO has two kinds of BUs: a local BU and a normal BU.

Normal BU: It is sent to the MR's HA. TLMR will send its CoA to its HA and IMR will send HoA of TLMR to its HA.

Local BU: It is sent by the IMR to TLMR containing the xTIO option that lets the TLMR learn the topology of the Nested Mobile Network.

In ROTIO+, we modify the RA messages and the normal BU IMR that is sent to the HA.

RA Messages: The TLMR and IMR will continue to use the TIO and xTIO option in the RA messages to MRs down the tree. However, the first address field after the TreeID will contain the CoA of the TLMR. The CoA of IMRs will follow the CoA of the TLMR.

BU: The IMRs will send two BUs to HA in the same message. The first one being the primary routing address which will be the CoA of the TLMR and the second one being the alternate routing address which will be HoA of the TLMR.

3.3 Routing in ROTIO+

RA and Tree Discovery: When an MR joins a tree it determines the point of attachment based on the TIO given in the RA message from the routers it is able to reach. The identifier of the tree is the HoA of the TLMR that is present in the TreeID. The xTIO in RA propagated down the tree, contains the CoA of the ancestor MRs. The IMRs store the list of CoAs of the ancestor MRs.

BU: There will be two BUs as proposed in ROTIO+. The local BU will be sent to TLMR and the normal BU to the HA of the MR. The TLMR will only send a normal BU message to its HA. This is illustrated in Figure 9.

BU by TLMR: TLMR also sends a BU to its HA which is the normal BU. Each time the tree changes its point of attachment; the BU message will be sent only by the TLMR to it's HA with the current CoA. IMRs will not send any BU if their position with respect to the TLMR remains unchanged.

BU by IMR: Each time an IMR receives RA message, it evaluates if it is optimally connected to the tree. Also, it matches the CoA of the TLMR in the RA with what it had stored earlier. If there is difference then it sends a BU to its HA.

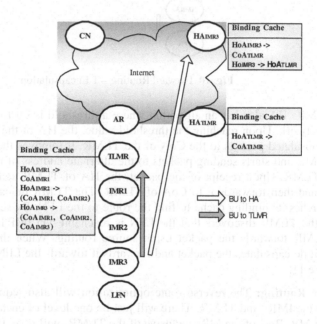

Fig. 9. BU in ROTIO+

Forward Route Optimization: Figure 10 illustrates the forward route optimisation in ROTIO+. A packet sent from the CN toward the LFN is routed to the closest MR's HA. Since IMR3's HA already has the binding information that IMR3 is located below the TLMR, the packet is encapsulated and sent to the CoA of the TLMR. After receiving the packet, the TLMR searches its binding cache to find the route to the LFN. By searching the binding cache, the TLMR discovers that the LFN is reachable via IMR1, IMR2 and IMR3. The TLMR forwards the packet using source routing. When the packet arrives at IMR3 it decapsulates the packet and forwards it towards the LFN.

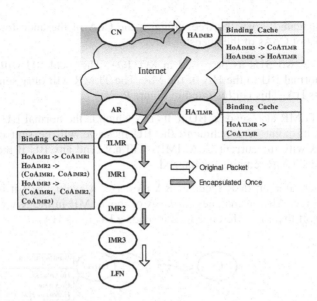

Fig. 10. Forward Routing – 1 Encapsulation

The MRs HA also has an algorithm where a threshold is set for packet loss (QoS) in the network. Upon reaching the threshold value, the HA of the IMR stops sending the encapsulated packets to the CoA of the TLMR. It removes the entry for the CoA of the IMR and starts sending packets to the alternate address of the TLMR i.e. HoA of the TLMR. Upon receipt of the packet, the HA of TLMR again encapsulates the packet and then forwards it to CoA of TLMR. The TLMR de-capsulates the packet and searches its binding cache to find the route to the LFN. By searching the binding cache, the TLMR discovers that the LFN is reachable via IMR1, IMR2 and IMR3. The TLMR forwards the packet using source routing. When the packet arrives at IMR3, it de-capsulates the packet and forwards it towards the LFN. This is illustrated in Figure 11.

Reverse Routing: The reverse route optimization will also require some modifications in the IMRs and TLMR. There will just be one level of encapsulation at the immediate MR. Rest of the MRs inclusive of the TLMR, will relay the packet up till the access router. The encapsulation in the immediate MR is preventing ingress filtering at the HA of the IMR. This is illustrated in Figure 12.

4   Evaluation of ROTIO+

The ROTIO+ is evaluated for efficient routing based on the reduction in sub-optimality, packet size, overall network load, and signalling overhead. The other features of importance to be evaluated are location Privacy and security. Location privacy, mobility transparency, and security are similar to that of ROTIO. A tabular representation of performance evaluation of ROTIO+ vis-à-vis some of the proposed routing optimization schemes is given in Table 1.

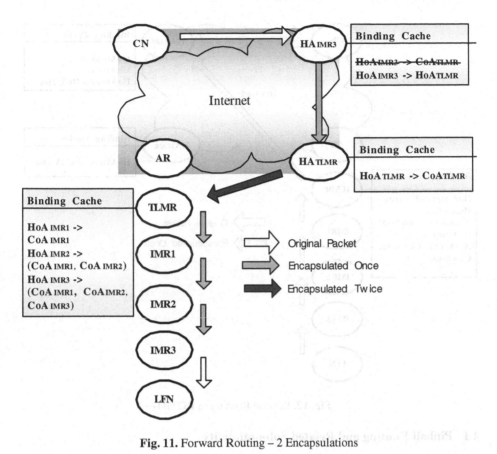

Fig. 11. Forward Routing – 2 Encapsulations

Table 1. Comparison between Route Optimization Protocols

RO Criteria	NBS	ARO	RBU+	RRH	NPI	HMIP-RO	ROTIO	ROTIO+
End-to-End Route Optimization	Poor	Good	Moderate	Good	Good	Moderate	Moderate+	Good
Location Privacy	Strong	Weak	Weak	Weak	Weak	Strong	Strong	Strong
Intra-NEMO route optimization	Poor	Poor	Moderate	Poor	Poor	Moderate	Good	Good
Handoff disruption	Moderate	Poor	Poor	Poor	Poor	Moderate	Good	Moderate+
Packet Overhead	Heavy	Light	Light	Heavy	Light	Light	Moderate	Light
Processing overhead	Light	Moderate	Moderate	Moderate	Moderate	Heavy	Moderate	Light

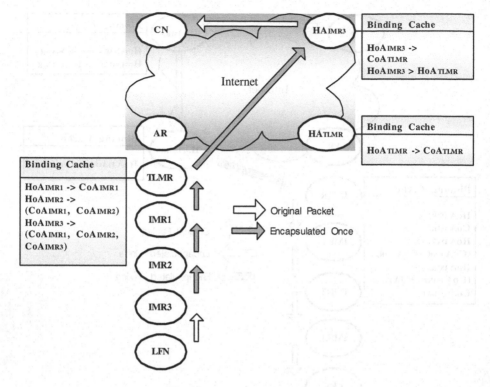

Fig. 12. Reverse Routing in ROTIO+

4.1 Pinball Routing and Related Sub-optimality

The ROTIO+ requires just one encapsulation for routing the packet. When the TLMR changes its point of attachment it acquires a new CoA, the number encapsulation will be two for a limited time period i.e. till the IMR sends a BU based on the updated RA message received from the TLMR. So, it effectively limits the number of MRHA tunnels and visits to the HA to one for most part of the routing. As the number of encapsulation is limited the packet size only increases by one outer header (i.e. by 20 bytes). The chance of packet fragmentation and susceptibility to link failure gets reduced. The processing delay due to packet encapsulation and decapsulation also gets minimized.

Encapsulation results in an addition of an IP header of size 20 bytes. So, in NBS the packet size after encapsulation for all nesting levels is $[(20+k)+20*(n+1)]$ bytes, where $20+k$ is the size of the original IP packet and n is the level of nesting. In ROTIO, the number of encapsulation is two irrespective of number of nesting levels. So, in ROTIO, the packet size after encapsulations is $[(20+k)+20*2]$. In ROTIO+ the maximum number of encapsulation is one irrespective of nesting levels. So, in ROTIO+, the packet size after encapsulation is $[(20+k)+20]$. Let us assume that the original IP packet is of 1400 bytes, MTU for the end-to-end path is 1500 bytes. The effect of encapsulations on IP packet is shown in Figure 13. We can see that as the level of nesting increases, the packet size increases in NBS protocol and after four encapsulations the IP packet needs to be fragmented. But, in ROTIO and ROTIO+, the packet size is constant. We can see that the packet size after encapsulations is smaller in ROTIO+ than ROTIO.

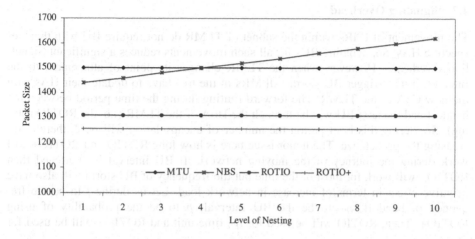

Fig. 13. Impact of Nesting on Packet Size

The advantage of using ROTIO+ over ROTIO becomes much clear if we consider the overall network load due to encapsulations. The additional headers actually amplify the overall network load. Let us consider that the size of an IP packet is 1400 bytes including header. We consider the number of packets generated per second to/from the moving network and compute the total load generated by the optimization schemes. Figure 14 shows the difference in network load generated by ROTIO+ and

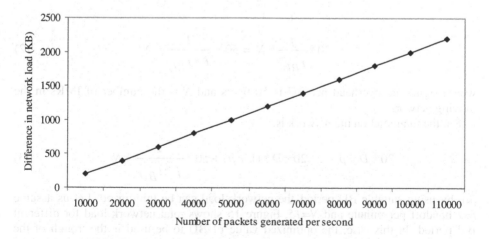

Fig. 14. Effect on Network Load Due to Encapsulations

ROTIO. It can be seen that ROTIO+ is more efficient than ROTIO in reducing network load, e.g. if 100000 packets are generated per second, then ROTIO+ reduces 2.0 MB network load than ROTIO.

4.2 Signaling Overhead

The movement of IMRs within the subnet of TLMR do not require BU with their respective HAs. So, avoiding BUs for all such movements reduces a significant Signalling Overhead. However, when the TLMR changes its point of attachment to the Internet, it may trigger BU storm. All MRs in the tree have to update their HAs with the new CoA of the TLMR. The forward routing during the time period between the handoff and the next BU will be through the HoA of the TLMR (i.e. the ROTIO routing). So, during this brief period the number of encapsulation will be 2, thereby increasing the packet size. The major issue here is how long ROTIO and ROTIO+ will work during the journey of the moving network. If BU interval is shortened then ROTIO+ will work for most of the time but the frequency of BU storm will also have negative effect in terms of increase in network load. Let us define f to be the frequency of handoff, t_{BU} to be the BU Interval, p to be the probability of using ROTIO+. Then, ROTIO will be used for t_{BU} time unit and ROTIO+ will be used for $\frac{1}{f} - t_{BU}$ time unit. So, the probability of using the ROTIO+ is:

$$p = \frac{\frac{1}{f} - t_{BU}}{\frac{1}{f}} = 1 - f * t_{BU} \qquad (1)$$

The network load due to data packets is $20*D*p + 2*20*D*(1-p)$, where D is the total number of data packets generated. The network load due to BU is:

$$50 * \frac{\frac{1}{f}}{t_{BU}} * N = 50 * \frac{1}{f * t_{BU}} * N \qquad (2)$$

where signalling overhead per BU is 50 bytes and N is the number of IMRs in the moving network.

So, the total load on the network is:

$$20 * D * p + 2 * 20 * D * (1 - p) + 50 * \frac{1}{f * t_{BU}} * N \qquad (3)$$

So, by using suitable BU period, the network load can be minimized. Let us assume $f=1$ handoff per minute and $N=15$. Figure 15 shows total network load for different BU period. In this case, the optimized value of BU to be used is the trough of the graph i.e. for $D=3000$ packets per minute $t_{BU}=7$ second, for $D=3500$ packets per minute $t_{BU}=6$ second.

4.3 Delay During Handoff

The ROTIO+ scheme also supports the seamless handoff. The handoffs are initially handled by the TLMR. It sends BU to its HA for every change in its attachment to Internet. The IMRs will send BU after receipt of RA from the TLMR. Till the new CoA of the TLMR is received by the HA for IMR, the routing is continued through the HA of the TLMR.

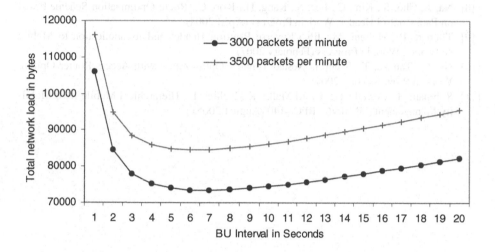

Fig. 15. Optimizing BU Interval

5 Conclusions

In this paper, we have proposed ROTIO+, a route optimization solution for nested NEMO. It retains the basic advantages of ROTIO like intra NEMO optimization while reducing the number of tunnels required to one. The signaling needs for RA and BUs are also judiciously used so as to avoid BU Storms and unwanted signaling overhead. The session continuity during hand-offs is effectively maintained and optimized route post hand-off is restored at the shortest possible time. Thus, ROTIO+ proves to be an effective solution for route optimization problem in nested NEMO. Our future work includes implementing ROTIO+ and comparing its performance with ROTIO.

References

[1] Ernst, T.: Network Mobility Support Goals and Requirements, RFC 4886 (July 2007)
[2] Johnson, D., Perkins, C., Arkko, J.: Mobility Support in IPv6, RFC 3775 (June 2004)
[3] Devarapalli, V., Wakikawa, R., Petrescu, A., Thubert P.: Network Mobility (NEMO) Basic Support Protocol, RFC 3963 (January 2005)

[4] Ng, C., Thubert, P., Watari, M., Zhao, F.: Network Mobility Route Optimization Problem Statement, RFC 4888 (July 2007)

[5] Cho, H., Kwon, T., Choi, Y.: Route Optimization Using Tree Information Option for Nested Mobile Networks. IEEE JSAC 24(9), 1717–1724 (2006)

[6] Vogt, C., Arkko, J.: A Taxonomy and Analysis of Enhancements to Mobile IPv6 Route Optimization, RFC 4651 (February 2007)

[7] Wakikawa, R., Watari, M.: Optimized Route Cache Protocol (ORC), Work in Progress (November 2004)

[8] Na, J., Cho, S., Kim, C., Lee, S., Kang, H., Koo, C.: Route Optimization Scheme based on Path Control Header, Work in Progress (April 2004)

[9] Thubert, P., Molteni, M.: IPv6 Reverse Routing Header and its application to Mobile Networks, Work in Progress (February 2007)

[10] Ng, C., Tanaka, T.: Securing Nested Tunnels Optimization with Access Router Option, Work in Progress (July 2004)

[11] Soliman, H., Castelluccia, C., El Malki, K., Bellier, L.: Hierarchical Mobile IPv6 Mobility Management (HMIPv6), RFC 4140 (August 2005)

VirtualConnection: Opportunistic Networking for Web on Demand

Lateef Yusuf and Umakishore Ramachandran

Georgia Institute of Technology
{imlateef,rama}@cc.gatech.edu

Abstract. Social networks such as Facebook and Secondlife are popular. Wireless devices abound from affluent countries to developing countries. Social networks need wide area Internet support. Wireless interfaces offer ad hoc networking capability, without the need for infrastructure support. Web on Demand (WoD) aims to bridge the gap between ad hoc social networks (people in close proximity with shared interests) and ad hoc networking. A key requirement for WoD is transparent connection management. This paper makes three contributions: First, an abstraction called VirtualConnection for transparent connection creation and migration, with socket-like API; second, an implementation on iPAQs (Windows Mobile) as a user level library, and proof of efficacy of using this abstraction for realizing WoD; third, evaluations to establish the performance of this abstraction. In particular, we show the performance degradation due to virtualizing the connection is negligible.

Keywords: Connection virtualization, connection management, communication library, opportunistic networking, ad-hoc networks.

1 Introduction

A young school boy is helping an old blind lady cross the street in a busy city street in India. The Good Samaritan driver in a pickup truck notices the stranded car with a flat tire on the shoulder of a U.S. highway and pulls up behind the car to help fix the flat. A local farmer in a Kenyan village train station overhears two foreign visitors discussing the possibility of bad weather ruining their vacation plans. He gives them his expert opinion on the weather based on experience and offers them useful travel tips.

All of the above are simple social examples of people weaving their own *ad hoc* local human web and offering or obtaining service from others: the old lady in the Indian city did not call the Red Cross; the stranded driver on the US highway did not call AAA; the foreigners in Kenya did not turn to The Weather Channel. How can we realize the electronic equivalence of such Web on Demand?

From affluent countries to the third world, mobile devices are becoming more prevalent. They are equipped with multiple network interfaces that could allow such devices in close proximity to communicate directly with one another. Social networking is becoming very popular and trendy allowing friends and family to stay connected. However, currently social networks as we know it (such as Facebook, Secondlife) require infrastructure support in the form of wide area Internet.

K. Kant et al. (Eds.): ICDCN 2010, LNCS 5935, pp. 323–340, 2010.

In this paper, we focus on a more restricted form of *ad hoc social network*, very much akin to the human social networks that we mentioned earlier.

Today, personal wireless devices (mostly in the form of cellphones) have penetrated deep into the societal fabric. Africa is reported to have the fastest growth rate for cellphone subscribers, and by one estimate [16] over 80% of the world's population has access to some form of a mobile wireless device. Given that most users, even in the third world, may have access to devices with wireless connectivity; could mobile wireless devices in close proximity form a web of their own and serve the needs of an ad hoc social network? This is the vision behind *Web on Demand (WoD)*. WoD complements the World Wide Web and leverages it when it is available. The most important aspect of WoD is that it democratizes personalized local access to services with a global reach. Specifically, our goal is service provision on wireless devices without reliance on infrastructure support. The vision behind web on demand is to bridge the gap between ad hoc social networks and *ad hoc* wireless networking.

A key requirement and feature of WoD is automatic and adaptive connection management among interacting devices. These devices typically have multiple network interfaces with different characteristics of power, bandwidth and range. Multiple applications also have heterogeneous requirements on bandwidth, time-sensitivity and quality of service. Examples of these network interfaces include Wi-Fi adapters for wireless networks, Cellular (GSM or CDMA) interface for wide area access, and Bluetooth, ZigBee [24] and IrDA for personal area networks. A number of applications including web browsing, video streaming and file sharing are now available for use with these devices. A connection management layer could exploit commonalities among devices in WoD and present a virtual interface for interaction and data exchange. Such data dissemination is inherently peer-to-peer in nature: a mobile node may download varying file types such as an image, audio clip or streaming video from a peer and vice versa. Therefore, it is important to guarantee the stable and efficient transmission of information even in circumstances when a particular network interface may become unavailable, such as when users leave and enter a mobile hotspot for example.

The focus of this paper is to present the design and evaluation of a connection virtualization framework for use in realizing WoD. We provide a middleware stack for opportunistic networking among the heterogeneous interfaces that may be present on each device. The architecture virtualizes the connection between two ad hoc peers and automatically chooses a physical connection based on metrics such as power and delay, transparent to the application.

VirtualConnection is a system to hide the complexity and heterogeneity of these network devices while at the same time supporting the communication requirements of these applications.

The main goal of VirtualConnection is to provide middleware for adaptive management of connections. Based on prevailing context and by a fine-tuned switching mechanism, we can choose the appropriate wireless interface in an adaptive fashion without degrading the performance of the requests made by applications. The architecture is based on the maintenance of a *virtual socket*, a socket interface for client-server applications. Applications register data transfer requests with a virtual socket which transparently manages the network interfaces, by selecting the best interface for a particular data transfer request and transparently switching among interfaces when necessary.

VirtualConnection identifies the factors affecting the quality of a connection, including the data rate, power consumption of application, available battery, network transmission range supported by each adapter and the time-sensitivity of the data requests. It uses these factors to determine whether there is a new best connection available to use. The system requires little or no modification to existing application logic and so can be easily adopted. The middleware sits on top of the transport layer in the networking stack and handles the automatic connection and transfer of data between heterogeneous network interfaces; thereby freeing the programmer from the burden of having to self-manage those interfaces.

While there is previous work on opportunistic networking, few of them have focused on providing system support for abstraction of heterogeneous network devices in ad hoc scenarios. Delay Tolerant Networks (such as Haggle [9, 10]) support opportunistic networking between devices but focus on message ferrying and relay rather than ad hoc connections. Ad hoc overlay networks, MANETs and mesh networks (such as PeopleNet [6] and Mob [15]) provide targeted services such as bandwidth aggregation and information queries. Also a number of projects and applications use Bluetooth and uPnP to allow devices (cellphones, PDAs, GPS receivers, digital cameras, etc.) to be "discovered" and form a personal area network (PAN) for exchanging information. These are standalone solutions that typically use one of the network interfaces rather than a connection abstraction. Rocks [12], Tesla [20], Dharma [21], and Host Mobility Manager [22] provide abstraction for end-to-end connectivity management using multiple network interfaces to resume network connections during failures and disconnections. They do not however provide a mechanism for periodic selection of optimal network interfaces, nor do they support multi-hop data transfers through heterogeneous interfaces. VirtualConnection also incorporates recent results from works such as Coolspots [1] and Breadcrumbs [2] on energy management.

Via the VirtualConnection abstraction, the paper makes the following contributions:

- An architecture for providing adaptive connectivity to applications in the presence of heterogeneous network interfaces. The connection management supports transparent migration across the network interfaces whenever necessary.
- A system design and implementation of VirtualConnection as a user level library providing API calls that mimic the standard socket API to applications.
- An experimental evaluation of VirtualConnection using a WoD prototype that confirms the efficacy of the system design. Specifically, we show that the performance degradation of VirtualConnection is negligible.

Sections 2 and 3 describe the system architecture and connection management for our system. Sections 4 and 5 present VirtualConnection implementation details and results, respectively. Section 6 presents related work. Finally, Section 7 concludes the paper with future work.

2 System Architecture

The VirtualConnection architecture is designed to facilitate communication among participants of a WoD. VirtualConnection supports both single-hop and multi-hop transfer modes. In single-hop mode, there is a point to point connection between entities in a WoD while multi-hop mode allows forwarding of messages among entities in a WoD. Multiple VirtualConnections in a single participant allow the participant to simultaneously connect with other members of WoD through peered connections. For example in a single-hop VirtualConnection mode, taking advantage of the multiple interfaces available to it, peer A may be using Wi-Fi to download a file from peer B, while simultaneously running a chat with peer C using Bluetooth (Figure 1-(a)).

On the other hand, in a multi-hop VirtualConnection mode, even though Peer A and Peer C have no common adapter they can use for communication, they can relay their traffic through Peer B, which has the ability to communicate with both of them (Figure 1-(b)). This scenario will only occur if Peer B explicitly chooses to allow packet forwarding. Peer A can relay traffic through Peer B's Wi-Fi adapter, which in turn passes the requested data to Peer C using the Bluetooth adapter Peer B shares with Peer C. This multi-hop configuration illustrates one of the major advantages of cooperation among participating entities in a typical WoD.

The VirtualConnection abstraction is designed to guarantee connectivity during the lifecycle of a particular peer connection. The lifecycle of a connection can be divided into the following stages:

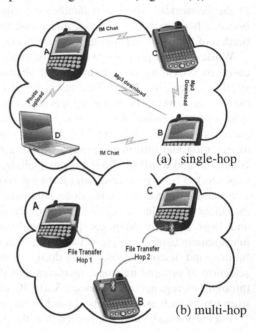

(a) single-hop

(b) multi-hop

Fig. 1. WoD Prototypes

- *Connection Initiation*: This happens at the beginning when an application requests a connection with a peer. It includes the discovery of adapters on both peers, the selection of the adapter to use and the establishment of a control socket to monitor the progress of the connection.
- *Connection Maintenance*: Immediately after the connection has been established, the virtual connection enters maintenance mode. This requires an evaluation of the connection using the required metrics. If there is a better interface for communication, the connection can be migrated to the new interface. Also, when there is a disconnection from one interface, the connection will be automatically switched to any available interface. Any pending data is sent after the migration is completed, thereby avoiding data loss. If no interface is available to do the switching, the connection will be suspended and the application will be notified.
- *Connection Teardown*: This involves closing the virtual socket by closing all physical sockets involved in the connection. The network adapter can be disconnected to save power if there is no application requesting a connection.

VirtualConnection uses a simple abstraction of a *virtual socket* to manage each connection request. A virtual socket is the logical link that manages the sending and receiving of data packets between two peer endpoints. Each virtual socket can communicate with an endpoint of different transport types including TCP, UDP or Bluetooth. The virtual socket is responsible for receiving and delivering data to the applications. The virtual socket keeps logical

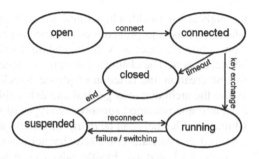

Fig. 2. State Diagram of VirtualConnection

send and receive buffers that correspond to those of the underlying transport protocols supported on the physical interfaces. The operations supported by the virtual socket are:

- **open(p, t, r):** opens a new connection with a given peer p, using a transport t; r is a Boolean measure of the time-sensitivity of the packets which can be true (real-time) or false (normal); p must include an initial address and address type to connect to.
- **send(d, c, p):** sends c bytes from buffer d to the peer p.
- **receive (d, c, p):** receives c bytes from peer p into buffer d.
- **close():** closes the virtual socket and removes the application from the application list.

The benefit of this API design is to resemble the native socket API as much as possible without supporting the full-range of the native socket API methods. The eventual goal of VirtualConnection is to use virtual socket to replace native socket calls by implementing a system-wide hook that traps operating system socket calls and extends them with virtual socket calls (similar to the Exokernel [19] approach). The WoD library will be interposed between the application code and the operating system. It will export the operating system socket API to applications and transparently use the WoD library in ordinary applications. This will allow the execution of existing applications without any modification to the application code.

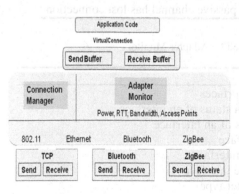

Fig. 3. System Architecture

Figure 3 illustrates the architecture of the proposed system. The core modules in the architecture are the Connection Manager and the adapter monitor. The Connection Manager is responsible for adaptive network management. It creates a virtual socket on connection start and maintains the virtual socket throughout the lifetime of the connection. It is responsible for switching between adapters when there is a better option for the connection.

The new connection option may be cheaper because it saves power and has a better throughput. If a real-time transport is requested, the Connection Manager uses the highest-bandwidth adapter and does not attempt to switch the connection between adapters. This is to prevent performance degradation because of switching costs. The Connection Manager uses the logical abstraction of a *channel* to manage connections between peers. The channel is the pipe between two virtual sockets and is responsible for the creation and deletion of physical sockets supported by the different adapters. While the architecture is general and extensible to any number of protocol stacks, the current implementation supports two types of system sockets by the channel: TCP and Bluetooth. Channels can be *active* or *passive* depending on whether they are currently involved in data transfers. Each channel has two background threads that continually estimate RTT and bandwidth values used in evaluation of the current connection between any two peer endpoints. Therefore, a single virtual socket may have multiple underlying channels corresponding to the identical types of physical sockets available between two given peers. Table 1 lists some of the events the Connection Manager generates during the lifetime of a specific connection.

The Adapter Monitor gathers statistics about the state of each adapter on the peer including type of adapter (Wireless 802.11, PPP, Ethernet, Bluetooth, ZigBee), current address of the adapter (IP address, Bluetooth address, ZigBee address), state of the adapter (On, Off, Connected, Disconnected, Sleeping, Transmitting, Idle), speed of the adapter, current throughput of the adapter, estimated bandwidth capability, battery level (0-100) of the mobile device and access points available at the adapter (Table 2). Adapter Monitor opens a connection between the two peers and transmits a random amount of data to estimate end-to-end throughput and bandwidth [2], [4]. The throughput is expressed in terms of the RTT of the data transfer.

Table 1. Events raised by the Connection Manager

Event Type	Meaning
CONN_NEW	A new connection has been established
CONN_OFF	The active channel has lost connection
CONN_ON	The active channel has resumed connection
CONN_SWITCH	A new active channel is proposed for the connection
CONT_DEL	One or more control socket has been removed
CONT_CHG	One or more passive channel has lost connection

Table 2. Messages reported by Adapter Monitor

Message Type	Description
INT_LIST	List of current interfaces
INT_STATUS	Active connection status of an interface
INT_OPSTATUS	Operational status of an interface
INT_SPEED	Speed of an interface
INT_BANDWIDTH	Bandwidth of an interface
ACTIVE_INT	Request the active interface
INT_TYPE	Request the adapter type
INT_PWR	Power consumption of adapter as a ratio of lowest adapter

3 Connection Management

In this section, we introduce the finer details of adaptive connection management. We begin by providing a step-by-step elaboration of the activities, events and messages that are exchanged between peers during connection establishment and maintenance (Sections 3.1 and 3.2). We then describe how VirtualConnection determines the appropriate adapter to use for a given connection (Section 3.3). We conclude with a detailed description of connection establishment when VirtualConnection runs multi-hop mode (Section 3.4).

3.1 Connection Negotiation

Table 3 lists the different message types exchanged between peers during the lifetime of a connection. After an application invokes an open() call, a number of things happens under the cover. VirtualConnection retrieves the list of adapters (using the INT_LIST request message shown in Table 2) and their network information including the INT_TYPE, INT_BANDWIDTH, INT_STATUS, and INT_OPSTATUS) from the adapter monitor. It connects to the initial address of the peer, passed through the open() call. VirtualConnection then attempts to establish a virtual socket with the desired peer by performing the following steps:

Table 3. Messages exchanged by VirtualConnection

Message Type	Description
ADAPTERSLIST	List of network adapters
CIPHER	Connection ID
BUFFERSIZE	Peer Receive Buffer Size
COMMONADAPTERS	List of identical types of adapters
NETADDRESS	Active channel network address
SWITCHADDRESS	Begin Connection Switching

1. *Determine common adapters*: It exchanges the adapters' list (ADAPTER-SLIST message) with the peer using the specified address and determines the identical types of adapters between the two lists (COMMONADAPTERS message).
2. *Establish the control sockets*: It creates a control socket for each and every common adapter between the two peers. The control socket is used to detect data connection failure and for the initial estimation of RTT and the bandwidth of the adapters. A UDP socket is used for IP-based adapters while a Bluetooth socket is used for Bluetooth adapters.
3. *Create a virtual socket*: It chooses the best network adapter and creates a virtual socket. The virtual socket is bound to the address of the chosen adapter.
4. *Exchange buffer size*: The peers exchange the size of their TCP receives buffer sizes (BUFFERSIZE message).

5. *Exchange network address*: The peers exchange the network address of the chosen adapters (NETADDRESS message).

6. *Creates connection cipher*: VirtualConnection establishes an encrypted identifier for the connection and then performs a key exchange for later authentication (CIPHER message).

Subsequent data transfer requests with calls to send() and receive() use the chosen adapter until an improved connection is available. When an application sends data, VirtualConnection keeps a copy of the data in an in-flight buffer similar to that specified in Rocks [12]. It increments the count of bytes sent when an application sends data and increments the size of bytes received when an application receives data. The size of the in-flight buffer is the sum of the size of its socket send buffer and the size of the peer's socket receive buffer. It uses a simple sliding window protocol to discard older data whenever new data arrives. Incurring an additional copy for virtualizing the physical connection is necessary to avoid data loss during migration from one physical adapter to another. We show that this additional copy has little impact on the actual performance measured with VirtualConnection (see Section 5.2).

3.2 Connection Migration and Switching

When the Connection Manager raises the CONN_OFF or the CONN_SWITCH event (see Table 1), the virtual socket initiates the switching procedure. It creates a new physical socket at the new chosen adapter and then performs the following steps:

1. *Suspend all I/O calls:* It blocks all I/O operations (send(), receive()) until switching is completed

2. *Send a switch connection message*: it sends a message (SWITCHADDRESS) to the peer notifying a connection switch and the network address to be used for further communication. The message is sent through the control sockets of all common adapters determined at the initiation of the connection.

3. *Authenticate*: The peers authenticate by exchanging the connection cipher created during the execution of an open() call.

4. *Close existing socket:* It closes the previous physical socket and binds the virtual socket to the newly-created socket.

5. *Send in-flight data*: VirtualConnection retransmits any data that is pending in the in-flight buffer. It determines the amount of in-flight data it needs to resend by comparing the number of bytes that were received by the peer to the number of bytes it sent. This ensures no data is lost as a result of the switching process.

To handle failures, VirtualConnection implements the switching procedure on a CONN_OFF event differently from that of a CONN_SWITCH event. On a CONN_SWITCH event, VirtualConnection maintains a timeout for each stage of the switching procedure. The timeout corresponds to twice the average time measured for each stage of the switching procedure. It then aborts the switching procedure if the timeout expires and immediately tries to use the existing active channel for communication. However, no timeout is used in the case of a CONN_OFF event since there is no existing connection which can be used to process data transfers and the goal in that case is to try to reestablish connection as soon as feasible.

It should be noted that the application is completely unaware of this physical adapter switching; once the switching is complete, normal operation resumes using the new interface.

3.3 Determining the Optimal Connection

The Connection Manager retrieves metrics from the adapter monitor such as the state of the adapter, bandwidth, throughput, and battery level. Each metric has an assigned weight which is used to calculate the cost of connection with that adapter. The adapter with the lowest connection cost is chosen for a given connection. Since there has been extensive work on battery and power management, the current VirtualConnection architecture simply uses the results in [1] and [3] to reduce power degradation. CoolSpots [1] explores many policies for switching between Wi-Fi and Bluetooth adapters in order to enhance battery life. We adopt the "cap-static" policy which performs best among a range of data transfer benchmarks. The cap-static policy recommends a switching period of 250ms. Therefore, the evaluation of adapters to determine whether there is a "cheaper" adapter occurs every 250ms in our implementation as well, and switching is performed when two consecutive evaluations suggests a better connection. The evaluation requires retrieving metrics from the adapter monitor such as the state of the adapter (connected, disconnected) and the current power level. Adapter Monitor returns INT_LIST sorted by INT_OPSTATUS, then by INT_BANDWIDTH, and then by INT_PWR. When the measured power level is below 20% [3], the connection prompts a switch to the cheapest power adapter available (in the case of Wi-Fi and Bluetooth, the connection is switched to Bluetooth).

3.4 Multi-hop Configuration

VirtualConnection can run in one of two modes: *single-hop* and *multi-hop*. The multi-hop mode allows packet forwarding in situations which may otherwise be impossible as seen in Figure 1-(b). Even though Peer A and Peer C have no common adapter they can use for communication, they can relay their traffic through Peer B, which has the ability to communicate with both of them. This scenario will only occur if Peer B explicitly chooses to allow packet forwarding. Peer A can relay traffic through Peer B Wi-Fi adapter, which in turn passes the requested data to Peer C using the Bluetooth adapter Peer B shares with Peer C. This multi-hop configuration illustrates one of the major advantages of cooperation among participating entities in a typical WoD.

VirtualConnection uses a modification of the Ad-hoc On-demand Distance Vector (AODV) [23] protocol to support multi-hop application-layer routing. For the example in Figure 1-(b), when Peer B intends to communicate with a Peer C whose route is not known, it broadcasts a Route Request packet (RREQ). Each RREQ contains an ID, sequence numbers, hop count, source and destination node addresses, source and destination address type, and control flags (Table 4). The RREQ is sent through all the available network interfaces Peer A shares with Peer B, which then propagates the RREQ to Peer C. When the RREQ reaches Peer C, a Route Reply packet (RREP) is generated and forwarded along the RREQ route back to Peer A. Each RREP contains destination sequence numbers; route lifetime, hop count, source and destination node

Table 4. VirtualConnection RREQ Header

RREQ			
type	flags	Recvd	hopcnt

Destination Address
Destination Address Type
Destination Sequence Number
Source Address
Source Address Type
Source Sequence Number

addresses, source and destination address type, and control flags. To avoid broadcast storms, intermediate nodes, such as Peer B, simply drop duplicate RREQ.

The multi-hop multi-radio connection configuration can be divided into the following stages:

1. *Routing Initiation*: VirtualConnection attempts to make a connection to the destination address of the peer through each of its network interfaces. After a timeout and number of retries, multi-hop routing is enabled. Otherwise, if any of the direct connections is successful, direct routing is used.

2. *Route Discovery*: VirtualConnection tries to locate a possible route to the destination through the following steps:
   - The source node initiates the discovery by broadcasting an RREQ packet through all interfaces.
   - If any of the intermediate nodes has a valid route for the destination in its cache, the node will send an RREP to the source node. Otherwise, if the intermediate node does not know of such a route, it again broadcasts the RREQ through all of its network interfaces.
   - Any duplicated RREQ from the same sender and same sequence number is simply discarded.
   - When an RREQ reaches the destination node, it adds the route to its cache. It then generates an RREP which it sends through the Reverse Route back to the source. The destination responds to every new RREQ that it receives.
   - Upon receiving an RREP, the source adds the route to its cache. It then attempts to connect to the destination node.

3. *Data Transfer:* Once a valid route is discovered and a connection is established, VirtualConnection begins processing data request to and from the source node to the destination.

4   Implementation

In this section we describe the salient implementation details of VirtualConnection. The implementation described here is written in C# 3.0. The system is a user library that exposes the API calls described in Section 2. We assume that the initial endpoints (IP Address, Bluetooth Address) of a peer requesting a new connection are known at the start of a connection. The implementation shares a single adapter monitor among all connections and a unique connection manager for each individual connection. The adapter monitor is a singleton class that is instantiated by the first connection request. The adapter monitor uses a background thread that monitors the status of all the adapters and raises one of three possible events: connected, disconnected, operational. Using the singleton class and raising events allow multiple applications to share the same adapter monitor, saving on system resources. The per-VirtualConnection Connection Manager subscribes to the adapter monitor events and initiates adapter switching or connection migration when any of the events are raised. The implementation uses the .NET *XmlSerializer* class to serialize messages, lists and objects used by the VirtualConnection.

4.1 Interface Detection

The OpenNETCF framework *OpenNETCF.Net.NetworkInformation.NetInterface* class supplies most of the needed statistics used by VirtualConnection. The list of all interfaces is retrieved using the *NetInterface.GetAllNetworkInterfaces()* function call. The class also supplies the speed, connection status, and operational status of the NetworkInterface among other properties. The Bluetooth radio's statistics are retrieved using the *InTheHand.Net.Bluetooth.BluetoothRadio* class. The RTT of the network interface is estimated using a simple ping packet. The bandwidth estimation involves downloading a random size byte array from the peer. Each interface address is represented by two fields: address data (a byte array), and address type (an enumeration).

4.2 Connection Switching

On an open() VirtualConnection API call, the Connection Manager retrieves the list of adapters from the adapter monitor (the INT_LIST message), exchanges the list with the peer at the address supplied at open() and then creates a new virtual socket to handle all data transfer requests on this new connection. It determines common adapter types and records their known addresses. The Connection Manager also creates a channel for each identical type of adapter (Figure 4). Each channel then creates a control socket that is used for exchanging control information; switch

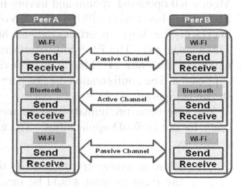

Fig. 4. VirtualConnection

connection messages, connection cipher and adapter address changes. After the creation of the channels, the Connection Manager creates a globally unique identifier (GUID) which serves as the connection cipher. The GUID is then exchanged between the two peers and kept in a connection list, which is an array of existing connections. It selects an active channel and binds the channel to the virtual socket. Any invocation of send() and receive() uses the underlying system socket currently assigned to the active channel.

4.3 Routing

The windows kernel selects the default outgoing network interface for IP packets. However, an application can bind a local socket to a specific network interface. After selecting the adapter used by the active channel, VirtualConnection binds the local socket to the address of the adapter. Data is then routed through the adapter to the destination. The multi-hop configuration uses a routing table that contains the destination address, next-hop and the network interface to use. In multi-hop mode, the Connection Manager initially tries a direct connection to the peer on an open() API call. If attempt fails, RREQ packets are then broadcasted to nodes in order to discover a path to the peer. If no path is found after a configurable timeout, an error status is reported. The Bluetooth RFCOMM protocol is used for data transfers over Bluetooth and TCP/IP is used for data transfers over Wi-Fi. They are both reliable transport protocols that do not require additional management for data loss.

5 Evaluation

We have implemented VirtualConnection prototype on Windows Mobile 6, as a user-level library. The implementation is developed using the .Net Compact Framework 3.5, the OpenNETCF Smart Development Library 2.2 and the Bluetooth library from IntheHand.Net using the C# programming language. The Bluetooth implementation currently supports the Microsoft Bluetooth stack. The Wi-Fi adapters are programmatically configured to ad hoc mode. The prototype WoD consists of three mobile devices and one laptop as shown in Figure 1. We use three windows mobile devices (two HP iPAQ *111 Classic Handheld,* and one HP iPAQ *hw6940*), running Windows Mobile 6.0 operating system and having both Wi-Fi and Bluetooth network devices. Each iPAQ has a with 1200 mAh, 3.7 Volt battery. The laptop has an inbuilt Wi-Fi interface. The Wi-Fi interfaces are all 802.11b devices with a raw maximum of 11Mb/s data rate. The Bluetooth interfaces are all Bluetooth 2.0 devices with a raw maximum data rate of 2Mb/s. Each device runs a download application or a chat application. The configuration creates peer wise connections between the members as shown in Figure 1.

We have done preliminary performance evaluation of our VirtualConnection library for use in WoD applications. The experiments we report below fall into three categories:

1. Micro measurements to quantify the set up cost of VirtualConnection and relate them to what would be incurred on a native protocol stack (Wi-Fi or Bluetooth). The micro measurement also includes connection migration cost when an adapter switch is required/desired.
2. Data transfer measurements to quantify the latency and throughput using VirtualConnection and relate them to corresponding results using Wi-Fi and Bluetooth.
3. Automatic connection switching measurements to show the VirtualConnection at work in switching among available interfaces, which is reflected in the observed latency for data transfer.

5.1 Connection and Switching Costs

We have measured the delay for establishing a connection between each peer wise connection in the WoD prototype. The experiments are repeated 100 times and the average values are recorded as shown in Table 5. We compare the values with that of using only a plain Bluetooth implementation and a plain Wi-Fi implementation.

The overhead incurred by VirtualConnection for connection setup is less than 600ms. It involves delay due to exchange of adapters' lists, chosen channel address and the connection cipher. The experiments show that VirtualConnection does not incur significant startup penalty. The overhead is minimal and acceptable for the additional functionalities provided by VirtualConnection for the intended scenarios where WoD would be deployed.

Table 5. Connection Costs

Setup Stage	Costs(milliseconds)
Socket Initiation	0.54
Adapters List Exchange	392.1
Transfer Adapter Determination	188.7
Connection ID	0.69
Control Sockets Establishment	2.68
Connection Establishment	7.5
Total Setup	585.6

Table 6 shows the switching costs incurred in switching between Wi-Fi and Bluetooth.

Most of the overhead incurred is due to synchronizing the two peers to agree on a new underlying adapter to use. Once the new socket has been established, the connection time is almost equal to that incurred for establishing a bare TCP or Bluetooth socket. The switching event takes about 600 ms to detect since the Connection Manager evaluates the connection every 250 ms and recommends switching after two consecutive positive evaluations. The automatic switching time is less than 200 ms and is considerably less than the delay that would be incurred for a manual migration of the connection between the peers for example.

Table 6. Switching Costs

Switching Stage	Costs (milliseconds)
Switch Message	3.28
New Channel Creation	96.13
Connection Reestablishment	7.51
Switch Message	3.28

5.2 Throughput and Latency

We have measured the average throughput and latency of downloading a 20 MB file between two iPAQs in the WoD prototype: iPAQ A and iPAQ B. The first set of experiments measured the performance of VirtualConnection using a single adapter by disabling one of the adapters on both iPAQs. The results are shown in Figure 5. The throughput and latency values compare favorably with the results of native implementation of the same experiments on 802.11 and Bluetooth network interfaces. This is because the main cost incurred by VirtualConnection is the copying costs of maintaining an in-flight data buffer. The latency overhead is very small (an average of about 7.4ms for a 20MB file, less than 0.2% of native implementation) and imperceptible at the application level. The throughput is also close to measured values from native implementation.

To demonstrate the switching between the two adapters, the connections start with a Bluetooth connection and an mp3 file (20MB) is downloaded by iPAQ A from iPAQ B. During the transfer, iPAQ B is gradually moved away from iPAQ A until the Bluetooth connection becomes unavailable and the system automatically switches to Wi-Fi (about 9 meters). Then iPAQ B is moved back to iPAQ A until the connection switches back to Bluetooth. The graph (Figure 6) shows how the observed latency change as the VirtualConnection switches back and forth between the two interfaces. Incidentally, these numbers, respectively correspond to the latency numbers recorded in the previous latency experiment with either Wi-Fi or Bluetooth (compare Figure 5-(b) and Figure 6).

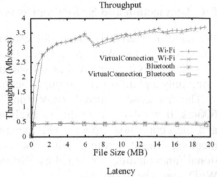

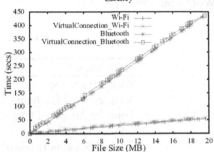

Fig. 5. Average throughput and latency of VirtualConnection over Wi-Fi, Bluetooth

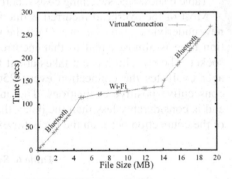

Fig. 6. Average latency using Virtual-Connection with connection switching

Figure 7 shows that the mean throughput in the WoD is very close to that obtained from native implementations. To calculate the mean throughput, we establish up to ten different simultaneous file transfers among peers in the WoD prototype.

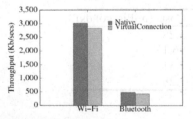

Fig. 7. Mean throughput in WoD prototype. The mean is computed from ten simultaneous file transfers among peers in the WoD prototype

5.3 Resource Usage

We measured the average battery level when a peer wise connection is run for as long as fifteen hours. The current battery level is determined with the *PowerBatteryStrength* function in the *Microsoft.WindowsMobile.Status.SystemState* class. To reduce energy wastage, the Adapter Monitor actively measures the channel capacity of just the top two adapters. As an additional optimization when the client device has low battery power (about 20% remaining), the adapter monitor discontinues active bandwidth estimation and only monitors the connection and operational status of the adapters. The results show that additional power costs incurred by Virtual-Connection over the native implementation is minimal. The overhead is due to the extra power consumption for bandwidth estimation and additional power incurred by the control sockets. In actual usage, Virtual-Connection enhances battery lifetime since the cheapest power adapter (Bluetooth in this case) is preferred whenever possible. We demonstrate energy savings (about 67%) of VirtualConnection by measuring the battery level during a switching experiment similar to that explained in Section 5.2 but with a 1.5 GB file (Figure 8).

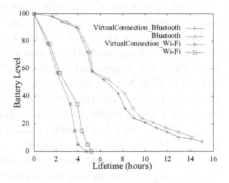

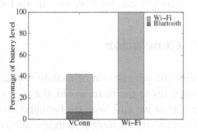

Fig. 8. Battery Lifetime of iPAQ 111 running VirtualConnection. The top figure compares the energy usage of VirtualConnection to that of the native implementations. The bottom figure illustrates energy savings using Virtual-Connection with connection switching.

6 Related Work

There is a number of works that use heterogeneous wireless interfaces for data transfer. Many of these works are aimed towards energy efficiency by using another interface to complement Wi-Fi and save power (examples include Coolspots [1], and Wake-on-wireless [2]), while our work targets abstracting the heterogeneous interfaces to provide transparent connectivity in ad hoc scenarios. Projects such as Breadcrumbs [2] and Context-for-wireless [7], and Blue-Fi [25] allow the use of multiple network adapters for communication but focus on prediction algorithms to determine when to use the cheapest network adapters in terms of power savings. They require geo-location using GPS, cell IDs or Bluetooth access points and the use of the system by a mobile user along a predictable path. VirtualConnection is complementary to such systems, and can be leveraged by these systems to abstract their connection management.

Rocks [12], Tesla [20], Dharma [21], and Host Mobility Manager [22] allow connectivity management in mobile hosts but are focused on IP-based session management in client-server applications as an extension for Mobile IP.

Some other works (such as [13, 14, 17, 18]) focus on the cooperation between Wi-Fi and Cellular networks to improve performance in multiple radio scenarios. Our work does not require the cooperation between adapters and is an application layer solution. MultiNet [8] considers connecting a single Wi-Fi card to multiple access points to increase the capacity of the device and saving on energy. Our work is focused on using multiple adapters to connect to multiple access points.

Another set of related work includes opportunistic networking approaches such as Haggle [10, 11], and ad hoc networks such as PeopleNet [6] and Mob [15]. They are focused on delay tolerant networking and wide area social services, respectively. Our work is targeted towards ad hoc networks where the members are co-located and can exist as a standalone web or interact with other webs.

7 Conclusion

With the penetration of mobile wireless devices in the societal fabric from the affluent countries to the third world, there is a huge opportunity to use these devices for realizing what we call Web on Demand - a bridge between social networks and the wireless connectivity of mobile wireless devices. A key enabler for WoD is connection transparency so that the WoD can be realized with whatever connectivity is currently available and best suited for serving the need of the WoD. We have proposed an abstraction called VirtualConnection that does precisely this. It provides automatic pair-wise selection of the network interface based on quality of service and other parameters that are specifiable from the application level for the set of devices that need to form a WoD.

This paper makes several contributions. First it presents an architecture for realizing the VirtualConnection abstraction. The architecture is general and can accommodate any number and types of network interfaces. The connection management part of the architecture does three things: automatically selects the network interface given the needs of an application; continually monitors the interfaces to detect changes (such as disconnection, power usage, etc.); and triggers switching from one interface to another transparent to the application. Second, we have implemented the abstraction as a user level library providing API calls that mimic standard socket interface. The implementation runs on Windows Mobile 6 and currently supports two network interfaces, namely, 802.11 and Bluetooth. We have shown the efficacy of using this library by implementing a prototype WoD supporting two applications: file download and chat. Third, we have conducted preliminary evaluations to show that the performance of VirtualConnection is close to native implementation of sockets. The evaluations include costs involved in connection set up, switching interfaces, latency and throughput measurements for file transfer, and the automatic interface switching by the VirtualConnection. We are currently investigating appropriate mechanisms for extending the regular socket library of native operating systems with VirtualConnection (similar to efforts such Exokernel [19]) for allowing its use without requiring any change to the applications.

This paper only addresses the connection management aspect of the WoD vision. There are a number of problems that need to be addressed including name management for a number of WoDs a given device may want to participate in (based on interests), isolation and protection guarantees between such WoDs, etc. These issues are complementary to the transparent connection management problem that is at the heart of realizing the WoD vision, and represent possible future directions of our research.

References

1. Pering, T., Agarwal, Y., Gupta, R., Want, R.: CoolSpots: Reducing the Power Consumption of Wireless Mobile Devices with Multiple Radio Interfaces. In: Proceedings of the Annual ACM/USENIX International Conference on Mobile Systems, Applications and Services, pp. 220–232 (2006)
2. Nicholson, A., Noble, B.: BreadCrumbs: Forecasting Mobile Connectivity. In: Proceedings of the 14th Annual ACM International Conference on Mobile Computing and Networking (2008)
3. Ravi, N., Scott, J., Iftode, L.: Context-aware Battery Management for Mobile Phones. In: PerCom 2008: Proceedings of the 6th Annual IEEE International Conference on Pervasive Computing and Communications, Dallas, TX (March 2008)
4. Prasad, R., Murray, M., Dovrolis, C., Claffy, K.: Bandwidth Estimation: Metrics, Measurement Techniques, and Tools. IEEE Network (June 2003)
5. Andersen, D., Bansal, D., Curtis, D., Seshan, S., Balakrishnan, H.: System Support for Bandwidth Management and Content Adaptation in Internet Applications. In: Proc. Symposium on Operating Systems Design and Implementation (October 2000)
6. Motani, M., Srinivasan, V., Nuggehalli, P.S.: PeopleNet: Engineering a Wireless Virtual Social Network. In: Proceedings of the 11th annual International conference on Mobile Computing and Networking, pp. 243–257 (2005)
7. Rahmati, A., Zhong, L.: Context-for-wireless: Context-sensitive Energy Efficient Wireless Data Transfer. In: Proceedings of the 5th International Conference on Mobile Systems, Applications and Services, pp. 165–178 (2007)
8. Chandra, R., Bahl, P., Bahl, P.: MultiNet: Connecting to Multiple IEEE 802.11 Networks Using a Single Wireless Card. In: Proceedings of the 23rd Annual Joint Conference of the IEEE Computer and Communications Societies (INFOCOM), Hong Kong, China, March 2004, pp. 882–893 (2004)
9. Leguay, J., Lindgren, A., Scott, J., Friedman, T., Crowcroft, J.: Opportunistic Content Distribution in an Urban Setting. In: Proceedings of the 2006 SIGCOMM workshop on Challenged Networks, pp. 205–212 (2006)
10. Haggle, http://www.haggleproject.org/index.php/Main_Page
11. Scott, J., Hui, P., Crowcroft, J., Diot, C.: Haggle: A Networking Architecture Designed Around Mobile Users. In: Third Annual IFIP Conference on Wireless On-demand Network Systems and Services (WONS 2006), Les Menuires, France (January 2006)
12. Zandy, V., Miller, B.: Reliable Network Connections. In: Proceedings of the Eighth ACM International Conference on Mobile Computing and Networking, Atlanta, GA, September 2002, pp. 95–106 (2002)
13. Salkintzis, A.K., Fors, C., Pazhyannur, R.: WLAN-GPRS Integration for Next-Generation Mobile Data Networks. IEEE Wireless Communications 9 (5), 112–124

14. Buddhikot, M.M., Chandranmenon, G., Han, S., Lee, Y.W., Miller, S.: Design and Implementation of WLAN/CDMA2000 Interworking Architecture. IEEE Communications 91(2000)
15. Chakravorty, R., Agarwal, S., Banerjee, S., Pratt, I.: Mob: a Mobile Bazaar for Wide-area Wireless. In: Proceedings of the 11th Annual International Conference on Mobile Computing and Networking, pp. 228–242 (2005)
16. Universal access – how mobile can bring communications to all (2005)
17. Bharghavan, V.: Challenges and Solutions to Adaptive Computing and Seamless Mobility over Heterogeneous Wireless Networks. Int. Journal on Wireless Personal Communications 4(2), 217–256
18. Hsieh, H.Y., Kim, K.H., Sivakumar, R.: An End to End Approach for Transparent Mobility across Heterogeneous Wireless Networks. Mobile Networks and Applications 9(4), 363–378 (2004)
19. Engler, D., Kaashoek, F., O'Toole, J.: Exokernel: An Operating System Architecture for Application-Level Resource Management. In: Proc. 15th SOSP, Copper Mountain, CO, December 1995, pp. 251–266 (1995)
20. Salz, J., Snoeren, A.C., Balakrishnan, H.: TESLA: A Transparent, Extensible Session Layer Architecture for End-to-End Network Services. In: Proc. of the Fourth USENIX Symposium on Internet Technologies and Systems (USITS) (March 2003)
21. Mao, Y., Knutsson, B., Lu, H., Smith, J.: DHARMA: Distributed Home Agent for Robust Mobile Access. In: Proceedings of the IEEE Infocom 2005 Conference, Miami (March 2005)
22. Peddemors, A., Zandbelt, H., Bargh, M.: A Mechanism for Host Mobility Management supporting Application Awareness. In: Proceedings of the Second International Conference on Mobile Systems, Applications, and Services (MobiSys 2004) (June 2004)
23. Perkins, C., Royer, E.M., Das, S.: Ad hoc On-Demand Distance Vector (AODV) Routing. IETF RFC 3561 (2003)
24. ZigBee Alliance, http://www.zigbee.org/
25. Ananthanarayanan, G., Stoica, I.: Blue-Fi: Enhancing Wi-Fi Performance using Bluetooth Signals. In: Proceedings of the Seventh International Conference on Mobile Systems, Applications, and Services (MobiSys 2009) (2009)

Video Surveillance with PTZ Cameras: The Problem of Maximizing Effective Monitoring Time

Satyajit Banerjee, Atish Datta Chowdhury, and Subhas Kumar Ghosh

Honeywell Technology Solutions,
151/1, Doraisanipalya, Bannerghatta Road, Bangalore 560076, India
{satyajit.banerjee,atish.chowdhury,subhas.kumar}@honeywell.com

Abstract. The effectiveness of the surveillance (monitoring a set of mobile targets with a set of cameras) depends on the resolution of the monitored images and the duration for which the targets are monitored. PTZ cameras are a natural choice to maintain a desired level of resolution for mobile targets. Maintaining resolution by controlling the camera parameters above a desired threshold value, however, implies that the field of regard of a camera cannot be arbitrarily broadened to include multiple targets. Camera for each target needs to be judiciously chosen to ensure monitoring for prolonged time interval. In this paper we propose a metric viz. average effective monitoring time (AEMT), towards capturing the effectiveness of video based surveillance. To achieve enhanced AEMT, we formulate an optimization problem in terms of associating cameras with the targets based on an appropriate weight function and design an efficient distributed algorithm. Simulation results show that our approach contributes significantly towards improving AEMT.

1 Introduction

Monitoring a set of mobile targets with a set of cameras is one of the most important tasks of large scale video surveillance. With advancements in embedded technology and affordability of smart PTZ cameras, it naturally becomes attractive to build large surveillance networks with many inexpensive smart cameras, more so for their ever-growing wireless connectivity (and hence reduced deployment costs) [1]. While video surveillance may have some deterrence value and is useful as digital evidence, a significant benefit of monitoring lies in the manual/automated analysis of the captured video, either on-line or as part of forensic investigations[1]. In this sense, the effectiveness of video surveillance directly depends on the quality of analysis and hence increases with improvements in the resolution of the captured images and the duration for which the targets are monitored (e.g. [2] specifies such resolution requirements for optimal human examination and permanent storage of image).

This makes it necessary to set a minimum threshold of resolution which needs to be maintained while monitoring targets (Henceforth in this paper *monitoring*

K. Kant et al. (Eds.): ICDCN 2010, LNCS 5935, pp. 341–352, 2010.
© Springer-Verlag Berlin Heidelberg 2010

a target would imply observing it with a minimum threshold of resolution, unless explicitly mentioned otherwise). PTZ cameras are a natural choice for controlling the camera parameters so as to maintain a desired level of resolution with on-camera control loops that allow them to *lock on* to a moving target.

Maintaining a resolution above a desired threshold value, however, implies that the field of regard of a camera cannot be arbitrarily broadened to include multiple targets. This can adversely affect the collective duration for which the targets are monitored. This is because, as the number of targets increases, a fixed number of cameras may not be able to simultaneously monitor all of them with the desired resolution. Furthermore, there can be obstacles occluding the view of a camera inside its field of regard and thus camera for each target needs to be judiciously chosen to ensure monitoring for prolonged time interval.

In absence of other specific surveillance objectives (e.g. looking out for a well-known target) and assuming that one applies the best possible image analysis techniques, it follows therefore that the extent to which the targets are monitored can be looked at as a measure of effectiveness of video surveillance (with a fixed number of PTZ cameras). In this paper we formalize this observation and propose a metric viz. Average Effective Monitoring Time (AEMT), towards capturing the effectiveness of video based surveillance. A precise definition of AEMT is provided in section-2.

The rest of the paper is organized as follows. In section-2 we formally define the proposed metric (viz. AEMT) and motivate the need for a carefully planned camera-target association. In section-3 we formulate an optimization problem in terms of associating cameras with targets based on an appropriate weight function, towards improving AEMT. Subsequently in section-4 we consider a distributed solution for a large autonomous video surveillance network of PTZ cameras and in particular, design an efficient distributed algorithm towards solving the optimization problem. In section-6 we present results on the effectiveness of our algorithm through simulation. Finally in section-7 we discuss the contribution of our work in the light of related work and conclude.

2   Average Effective Monitoring Time

Our objective is to monitor a set of mobile targets by a set of PTZ cameras while maintaining resolution above a desired threshold. Once assigned a target, a smart camera is assumed to be able to locally control its PTZ parameters in order to monitor the target within its field of regard. The cameras are assumed to be equipped with the necessary video analysis software [3] and on-camera control algorithms to achieve this. Since the targets are mobile, it may not be possible for a PTZ camera to lock on to multiple targets without sacrificing the level of resolution especially when the targets end up having divergent tracks. Hence we consider assigning one camera to monitor at most one target. On the other hand, a new camera-target association incurs some initial monitoring penalty. This is because, typically a few initial frames are required by a camera to *learn* about the new target and its background before it can start to perform video motion analysis and monitor the target. Assume that, during a surveillance period, a target t is continuously monitored by some camera(s) over *mutually disjoint* time intervals $\{[\tau_{i1}, \tau_{i2}]\}_{1 \leq i \leq k}$. Such time intervals can possibly be of varying lengths. We provide the formal definition of AEMT below.

Definition 1. *The effective monitoring time (EMT) for the target t is defined as* $\sum_{1 \leq i \leq k}(\tau_{i2} - \tau_{i1} - l_i)$, *where l_i is the time spent on initial learning during the ith time interval.*

Definition 2. *The average effective monitoring (AEMT) of a set of targets T over the entire surveillance period is defined as* $\sum_{1 \leq i \leq |T|} emt_i / |T|$, *where emt_i is the EMT of target t_i. In the sequel, we normalize AEMT by the total surveillance period and measure it in percentage.*

Thus AEMT reflects the duration of effective monitoring of the targets, on an average, during the entire surveillance period. It also takes into account the lack of monitoring during the learning phase whenever a fresh camera target association is encountered. Given a fixed number of cameras, assigning *multiple cameras to the same target* increases the possibility of some targets not being monitored at all, as illustrated in Figure-1(a). The situation worsens as the number of targets increases. In effect, this decreases the AEMT of the surveillance solution. Hence, we consider a 1-1 assignment of cameras to targets for the duration of surveillance. We alternately refer to this assignment as a camera-target association.

3   Optimization Problem

For mobile targets, a camera-target association which is effective at a given instance of time might become stale at a later instance. Thus a core component of a solution towards improving AEMT would be a 1-1 camera-target assignment procedure, invoked at regular intervals, so as to ensure effective monitoring of targets throughout the surveillance period. In this section we explain the formulation of an optimization problem for the periodic camera-target assignments.

It follows from the Definition-1 that EMT of a target decreases when the target goes un-monitored for some time. Furthermore, its EMT can also decrease as a result of penalty incurred due to frequent camera switches (this can decrease the value of EMT even if the target is continuously monitored, although by different cameras). Both of these can reduce the overall AEMT (Definition-2). Our objective function towards improving AEMT, therefore, attempts to reduce target misses *and* camera switches.

We represent the targets and the cameras as a *bipartite graph* (we use standard graph theoretic terminologies which can be found in [4]) $G = (T \cup C, E, w)$, where T is the set of targets at a given point in time, and C is the set of cameras. Vertices of this graph are elements in $T \cup C$, and set of edges of this graph are defined as $E = \{\{t, c\} : t \in T, c \in C$ and t is in the field of regard of $c\}$. Finally, $w(t, c)$ is an edge weight induced on a target t by a camera c. Intuitively, in order to reduce camera switches, we use an appropriate *weight function* to

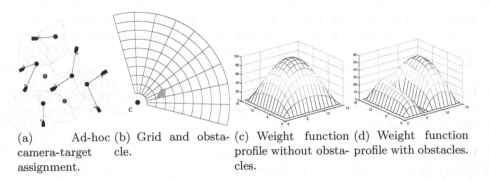

(a)   Ad-hoc (b) Grid and obsta- (c) Weight function (d) Weight function
camera-target   cle.   profile without obsta- profile with obstacles.
assignment.   cles.

Fig. 1. Weight function

prolong camera-target associations. Observe that a 1-1 assignment of cameras to targets now corresponds to a *matching* on this bipartite graph G. To reduce target misses, we consider a variant of *maximum cardinality matching* in G.

3.1   Weight Function

Our weight function has two additive components. The first component represents the expected duration of time for which a target can be effectively monitored by a given camera. This favors camera-target pairs with potential to form long-term associations. The second component is an additive weight applied to *existing* camera-target associations. This biases the weight function against new camera-target associations up to a certain extent.

In absence of obstacles, it is straight forward to design a weight function that reflects the expected duration of a camera-target association. Assuming uniform probability of a target's motion in either direction, it can be designed in terms of the target's position within the field of regard of the camera. I.e. it can simply have a maximum value at the center and uniformly decrease to a minimum value at the edges. However, in presence of obstacles, this approach will not work - since a target may be rendered invisible to a camera while being well within its field of regard. Moreover, a weight function which is appropriate in the presence of obstacles should also reduce to the above simple function when no obstacles are present.

Towards designing our weight function, we assume a 2-D movement model for the targets and estimate the expected number of steps executed by a target before it either goes out of the field of regard of a camera or is rendered invisible by some obstacle. We assume that a camera knows the position and geometry of each of the obstacles in its field of regard. We approximate the position of a target to its nearest grid point (as shown in Figure-1(b)) and assume that they move only along the grid points following a Brownian motion as follows: in each step, a target moves one step along one of the four possible directions or stays stationary with uniform probability ($\frac{1}{5}$). A target is made to disappear once it reaches a point (henceforth, *blind points*) which is either outside the field of regard of the camera or not visible by the camera due to obstacles. We define our weight function using the following notations, where N is the number of grid points:

- Normalized adjacency matrix $A = [a_{ij}]_{N \times N}$, where $a_{ij} = \frac{1}{5}$ if i is one of the neighbors of j or j itself and j is not a blind point, $a_{ij} = 0$, otherwise.
- Probability vector at step s, $P^s = [p_i^s]_{N \times 1}$, where p_i^s is the probability of the target being present in the ith grid point after s steps.
- Blind points represented as $B = [b_i]_{N \times 1}$, where b_i is equal to 1 if it is a blind point, zero otherwise.

Note that, $P^0 = [p_i^0]_{N \times 1}$, where $p_i^0 = 1$, if the target is initially at grid point i, zero otherwise. After s steps, the resultant probability vector is given by $P^s = A.P^{s-1}$ and thus $P^s = A^s.P^0$. The probability that the target hits a blind point (for the first time) after s steps is given by $P^s.B^T$ (B^T is the transpose of the vector B), and thus the expected number of steps for the target to hit a blind point is given by $\sum_s s.P^s.B^T$. Here, the value of the expression $\sum_s t.P^s.B^T$ can be approximated by a finite summation followed by truncation, i.e. $\lfloor \sum_{1 \le s \le s^*} s.P^s.B^T \rfloor$ where s^* terms need to be added to cater to the application specific accuracy requirement, and we designate it as the weight induced on the grid point i. Figure-1(c) and Figure-1(d) show weight values computed at every grid point with and without obstacles respectively corresponding to the 2-D grid and obstacle layout in Figure-1(b). The value of the extra positive weight (bonus) accorded to *existing* camera-target associations is decided based on the duration of the initial learning phase and will generally vary from one surveillance application to other. Formally, given B, the blind points in the field of regard of a camera c and P^0 capturing the initial position of t,

Definition 3. $w(t,c) = \lfloor \sum_{1 \le s \le s^*} s.A^s.P^0.B^T \rfloor + w_0.asgn(c,t)$ *where* $asgn(t,c)$ $= 1$ *if c and t currently form a camera-target association, zero otherwise.*

Note that, $w(t,c)$ always returns a bounded integer, between say, $w_{\min}$ and $w_{\max}$.

3.2 Matching Objective

A matching in G is defined as a set edges $M \subseteq E$, such that no two edges in M share a common vertex. Since our objective is to have a 1-1 camera-target association, we only consider matching in G. A maximum cardinality matching in G is a matching with maximum number of edges. Therefore to reduce target misses, we need to consider maximum cardinality matching in G. However, the graph G is edge-weighted according to the weight function in Section-3.1. Combining that with the requirement of maximum cardinality, we need to choose a matching which has maximum weight (according to our weight function) amongst the set of maximum cardinality matching. Such a matching is called maximum weight maximum cardinality matching (MWMCM).

It may be noted that, our weight function always returns a bounded integer, In particular, edge weights of G are bounded below and above respectively by some integers $w_{\min}$ and $w_{\max}$. In [5], it is shown that finding an MWMCM on bounded integer weighted graphs reduces to finding MWM on the same graph with transformed weights. Using this, we recast our optimization problem of finding an MWMCM in G as follows:

Problem 1. Find an MWM in $G_\lambda \triangleq (T \cup C, E, w_\lambda)$, where $w_\lambda(e) = \lambda w(e) + (1 - \lambda)$ and $0 < \lambda < 2/(((|T| + |C| - 2)w_{\max} - (|T| + |C|)w_{\min} + 2)$.

4   Distributed Autonomous Surveillance

As the number of cameras in surveillance network increases it becomes difficult for manual analysis across a large number of cameras. This difficulty naturally extends to the problem of improving AEMT and drives the need for automated surveillance solutions for camera-target assignments.

In situations where the surveillance video data is streamed on-line from all the cameras to a central server for analysis, it is natural to solve the optimization problem-1 centrally as well. However a centralized surveillance solution may not be scalable for large surveillance networks for the following reasons: (i) adding cameras may add significant engineering costs (including provisioning for the increased demand on throughput) (ii) the central server will continue to be a single point of failure.

Thus, it is attractive to think of the monitoring functionality to be pushed towards the edge of the autonomous surveillance networks. Such a surveillance solution depends on the cooperation and communication amongst the smart cameras - and is hence *distributed*. It is *autonomous* in the sense that it is intended to minimize the manual intervention in general and eliminate human decision making in choosing the best camera target associations - in particular. A distributed autonomous solution obviates the need of collating/analyzing the monitored data at a central point, enabling it to scale better. Indeed, smart cameras enable distributed autonomous surveillance by providing capabilities of local (on-camera) video analysis. The on-camera computational resources are currently sufficient for running reasonable video detection algorithms[3] and with the advancement of embedded technologies, it may be possible to run more sophisticated video analysis algorithms on them. There remains of course the issue of storing the surveillance records for forensic purposes which we assume will be done separately by lazily collecting the data across all cameras, say, once every few hours, depending on the capacity of their local storages. The cameras are assumed to be uniformly calibrated to a global coordinate system, and have identical capabilities. They are assumed to form a wireless mesh network with knowledge of their immediate neighbors and the total number of cameras in the surveillance network. The cameras are assumed to be aware of the obstacles in their respective fields of regard and those of their neighbors. They are also expected to be equipped with an on-camera control mechanism that allows them to control their PTZ parameters in order to lock on to a given target at an appropriate level of resolution. Finally, each smart camera is expected to have sufficient support for video motion analysis.

In Step 1 of the assignment algorithm, viz. initialization, each camera c obtains information of all the targets that are available in its field of regard and exchanges this information with all its one hop neighbors. It then computes the weights of the edges in G induced on each of these targets by itself and each of the neighbors. In step 2, the cameras run a distributed algorithm to compute an optimal camera-target assignment. At the end of it, they are assumed to complete the (re)assignment by exchanging the information about possible changes in the assigned targets. Note that results like [6] can be used to design topology transparent scheduling strategies in order to ensure a fast enough exchange. Following this, in step 3 they monitor the assigned targets for the duration of the period by locking-on to the respective targets, analyzing them, and optionally raising an alarm on suspicion. Given the mobility of the targets, the goodness of an assignment may reduce over time. Hence the camera-target (re) assignment needs to be *periodically*. Accordingly, steps 1 - 3 are repeated, based on the choice of the period, over the entire duration of surveillance.

In the next subsection we present a distributed algorithm of constant round complexity corresponding to step 2 above, for computing the camera-target (re)assignments.

4.1   Distributed Camera-Target Assignment

We consider the classical synchronous distributed model of computation. In particular, we model our wireless surveillance network as a connected undirected graph $S = (C, L)$, where C ($|C| = n$) is a set of wireless PTZ cameras and L is the set of communication links. A pair of cameras share a communication link if and only if they are within the communication range (R_c) of each other. Our objective is to compute a maximum weight matching on the bipartite graph G_λ as defined in optimization problem-1, using the underlying network graph S. It follows from the finiteness of the field of regard of a camera that the maximum distance between a camera and target corresponding to an edge in G is bounded. We denote this as the sensing range (R_s).

Since the targets are mobile and the edge-weights of the induced bipartite graph depend on their positions, our distributed algorithm needs to terminate fast. Hence it is desirable to have an algorithm with low round complexity while possibly sacrificing the *approximation factor* of the computed matching. A ρ-approximate MWM solution ($0 < \rho < 1$) is a matching M such that the weight of M is at least ρ times that of the maximum weight matching.

A distributed greedy algorithm for finding 1/2-approximate maximum weight matching on a graph is presented in [7] which eventually uses the notion of *locally heaviest edge* as defined in [8]. If we extend the idea of [7] to find a maximum weight matching on the induced bipartite graph it will guarantee 1/2-approximation but the algorithm may run for n rounds in the worst case, as illustrated next. Here we characterize the combinatorial structure that is responsible for the worst case behavior in the greedy algorithm and use some novel techniques to overcome it, thereby obtaining a $(1/2 - \delta)$ approximation matching in *constant* rounds.

We assume that the communication range (R_c) is at least twice of the sensing range (R_s), *i.e.*, $R_c \geq 2R_s$. In the rest of the paper, we say $(w_1, n_1) > (w_2, n_2)$ (where w_1, w_2, n_1, n_2 are integers) if either $w_1 > w_2$ or $w_1 = w_2 \wedge n_1 > n_2$. We use the notaion w_{ij} to denote the weight induced on target t_i by camera c_j.

A simple greedy algorithm will include each edge $\{t, c\}$ in the matching set if its weight is more than every edge incident either on t or c and then delete all the other edges incident on t or c from the bipartite graph G. So in the worst case, a sequence of the form $(t_1, c_1, \ldots t_l, c_l)$ satisfying $(w_{kk-1}, k-1) > (w_{kk}, k)$ for $2 \leq k \leq l$ and $(w_{kk}, k) > (w_{k+1k}, k+1)$ for $1 \leq k \leq l-1$ will make the algorithm terminate only after n rounds, since in every round exactly one matching edge will be formed from left to right of the sequence. For example, if the input bipartite graph is as in Figure-2(a), the above algorithm will choose the edges, exactly one in each round, in the order $\{t_1, c_1\}, \{t_2, c_2\}, \{t_3, c_3\}$. Thus consuming $n = 3$ rounds. Bounding the integer weights does not improve the situation because even if each pair of camera and target in the sequence has the same weight, they will still be ordered by their indices. We design our algorithm such that *multiple* edges can be selected from such a sequence in each round thereby making the round complexity sub-linear. In particular for a pair of edges $\{t_k, c_k\}$, $\{t_{k+1}, c_k\}$, $(w_{kk}, k) > (w_{k+1k}, k+1)$ featuring in such a sequence, our algorithm permits choosing $\{t_{k+1}, c_k\}$, in the presence of $\{t_k, c_k\}$, unless $\epsilon w_{kk} \geq w_{k+1k}$ for some given $0 < \epsilon < 1$. This reduces the upper bound on the worst case length of the *chain of dependencies* in such sequences and thus brings down the worst case round complexity of the algorithm (vide Lemma-1 in the Section-5). Given $\epsilon = 1/2$, on the input graph as in Figure-2(a), our algorithm will choose $\{t_1, c_1\}$ and $\{t_3, c_2\}$ in the very first round and then terminate. While reducing the number of rounds in the worst case, the algorithm also ensures bounded approximation (vide Lemma-2 in the Section-5).

Our algorithm (presented as Algorithm-1) returns, in *constant rounds*, a $(1/2-\delta)$-approximate MWM in G when the value of the tunable is set $\epsilon = 1 - 2\delta$. Refer

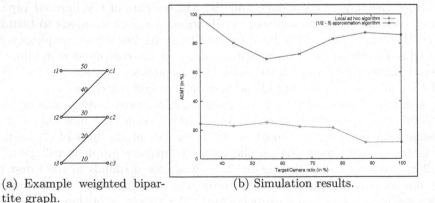

(a) Example weighted bipar-   (b) Simulation results.
tite graph.

Fig. 2. Example graph and simulation results

to the Section-5 for the proof of correctness and performance analysis of the algorithm.

```
/*** Initialization ***/
1: Compute weight (using definition-3 and transforming it following optimization problem 1) and then
   transforming the weight as in Section-3.2) induced on each target in the field of regard of c_j by itself and
   each of its 1-hop neighbors.
/*** Main algorithm ***/
2: while c_j is yet to be resolved do
      Let t_a be the target (if any) having maximum (non-zero) weight amongst all the targets for which c_j is
      the best camera and t_b the best target (if any) for camera c_j. (Note that, t_a and t_b can be identical.)
      if (∃t_a such that w_aj > εw_bj) then
          Select (t_a, c_j) as a matching edge and inform its 1-hop neighbors about the newly formed
          matching pair and stop participating any more.
      end
      For each information obtained on some newly formed matching pair of camera-target from the 1-hop
      neighbors, discard both the camera and target from the subsequent contention.
   end
```

Algorithm 1. Synchronous $(\frac{1}{2} - \delta)$-approximation MWM algorithm for camera c_j

5 Analysis of the Algorithm

During the Initialization phase of Algorithm-1 each camera c receives information from all the one-neighbor and their targets. Since we assume $R_c \geq 2R_s$, it implies that if a target t is visible to c and some camera c' then c and c' are one-hop neighbors. Hence, we observe the following:

Observation 1. *Consistency: For camera c, let T_c be a set of targets defined as $T_c = \{t : t \text{ is visible to } c\}$ and the set of cameras C_{T_c} defined as $C_{T_c} = \{c' : \exists t \in T_c \text{ such that } t \text{ is visible to } c'\}$. Each camera c collects full information of T_c and C_{T_c} during the initialization phase of Algorithm-1.*

Whenever $\{t_i, c_j\}$ is selected as a matching edge in some round, there can not be any other $\{t_i, c_{j'}\}$ that simultaneously gets selected, because (w_{ij}, j) is the unique best option for the target t_i. Again, at any given round for a given camera c_j only one such edge $\{t_i, c_j\}$ is selected. Thus in a given round, no non-matching results. Since a selected edge $\{t_i, c_j\}$ is removed from the graph for subsequent rounds, Algorithm-1 guarantees a matching solution. Hence, the following observation holds:

Observation 2. *Safety: Algorithm-1 guarantees matching in every round.*

We capture the performance of the proposed algorithm is the following lemmas.

Lemma 1. *The approximation factor guaranteed by Algorithm-1 is $\epsilon/2$.*

Proof. At any point of the Algorithm-1, when an edge $\{t_i, c_j\}$ is selected as a matching edge, it rules out at most two other camera-target edges from the *optimum set*, say $\{t_{i'}, c_j\}$ and $\{t_i, c_{j'}\}$. Now, $w_{ij} \geq w_{ij'}$ and $w_{ij} > \epsilon w_{i'j}$, otherwise $\{t_i, c_j\}$ could not have been selected in the presence of either $\{t_i, c_{j'}\}$ or $\{t_{i'}, c_j\}$. Therefore, $2w_{ij} > w_{ij'} + \epsilon w_{i'j}$ i.e. $2w_{ij} > \epsilon(w_{ij'} + w_{i'j})$. Summing up the weights of all the matching edges (forming a *maximal* set) resulted by Algorithm-1 it follows that the weight of the output matching is at least $\epsilon/2$ times the weight of the maximum weight matching.

Thus to achieve an approximation factor of $1/2 - \delta$ ($0 < \delta < 1/2$), the value of ϵ needs to be chosen as $\epsilon = 1 - 2\delta$.

Lemma 2. *Algorithm-1 terminates within $R = \log(\frac{w_{\max}}{w_{\min}})/\log(\frac{1}{\epsilon}) + 1$ rounds.*

Proof. Suppose, by contradiction, there exists some unresolved camera c_0 after $R = \log(\frac{w_{\max}}{w_{\min}})/\log(\frac{1}{\epsilon}) + 1$ rounds. This implies that at the beginning of Rth round (alternatively at the end of the $R - 1$ rounds) *exists* some target t_1 and some camera c_1 such that $\epsilon w_{11} \geq w_{10}$. Here, t_1 happens to be the best target for c_0 but not vice versa. Similarly, existence of c_1 after $R - 1$ rounds implies $\exists$ some target t_2 and some camera c_2 such that $\epsilon w_{22} \geq w_{21}$ and also $w_{21} \geq w_{11}$. Hence there an alternate sequence of cameras and targets $(c_R, t_R \ldots t_1, c_0)$ such that $\epsilon w_{(i+1)(i+1)} \geq w_{(i+1)i}$ and $w_{(i+1)i} \geq w_{ii}$ for $0 \leq i < R$. Hence it follows that $\epsilon^R w_{RR} \geq w_{10}$, i.e. $w_{RR}/w_{10} \geq 1/\epsilon^R$. Using $R = \log(\frac{w_{\max}}{w_{\min}})/\log(\frac{1}{\epsilon}) + 1$, it implies that the ratio of the weight of two camera-target pairs is greater than or equal to $1/\epsilon^{\log(\frac{w_{\max}}{w_{\min}})/\log(\frac{1}{\epsilon}) + 2} = w_{\max}/(\epsilon w_{\min})$, where $\epsilon < 1$. This is a contradiction, since the value of the ratio can be at most $w_{\max}/w_{\min}$.

Thus, for given $w_{\min}$, $w_{\max}$ and δ the Algorithm-1 runs for $\mathcal{O}(1)$ rounds in the worst case. Hence, Lemma-1 and Lemma-2 together imply the following theorem.

Theorem 1. *Algorithm-1, when run for $\epsilon = 1 - 2\delta$, guarantees $(1/2 - \delta)$ approximation factor in constant rounds.*

6   Simulation Results

We simulated our algorithm over a surveillance region having arbitrary camera deployments with possible overlaps in the fields of regard. The surveillance region was simulated to have obstacles with arbitrary geometry parameterized by their 2D location, range and orientation. Cameras and obstacles were placed independently. Subsequently, targets were placed in the surveillance region with random initial location and some initial assignment with the cameras. In order to model the network of cameras and wireless communication between them we used network simulator *ns2*.

According to our chosen motion model, targets follow the Brownian movement as described in the Section-3.1. We considered 9 cameras charged with monitoring $3, 4, \ldots, 9$ targets. The simulation was carried out for 100 independent scenario each consisting of 20 assignment-monitoring cycle. The weights of camera-target assignments were normalized to a scale between 1 and 100 with bonus weight 10 if applicable.

We contrasted the performance of our algorithm (Algorithm-1) empirically with a *local ad hoc* approach where each camera locks on to its best possible target based on local information only. Note that, such an approach may not result 1-1 association. The relative performance is presented in Fig-2(b) which clearly demonstrates that our approach based on ($\frac{1}{2} - \delta$)-approximation algorithm significantly outperforms the local greedy based approach.

7   Previous Results and Conclusion

Distributed surveillance using active camera networks is one of the important research areas in computer vision. Issues of tracking multiple objects with multiple video cameras have been studied extensively in past from various perspective. A large body of such works are concerned with development of image processing algorithms for detecting objects of interest reliably and/or for analyzing their activities [1].

In recent years deployment of autonomous camera surveillance systems for practical and academic purposes have increased significantly [9]. Autonomous camera surveillance systems are required to operate with limited human intervention in a changing environment and behave efficiently, even when uncertain or limited knowledge about the environment is available. Undoubtedly, in such situation a higher level planning and coordination becomes important. Closest to our work from this aspect is view planning of cameras[10].

Another important direction of work considers optimal camera selection problem for effective resource utilization, where objective function mostly includes minimizing measurement error. Ercan et. al. presented in [11] a camera selection problem for localizing single target. Isler et. al. in [12] considered the focus of attention problem (**FOA**). Given n targets, $2n$ sensors, and a cost function $c\,(i,j,k)$ indicating cost of tracking target k with sensor i and j. The cost $c\,(i,j,k)$ is assumed to be the expected error associated with position estimate obtained by fusing the information obtained from sensor i and j for target k. The selection problem in this case is to obtain an assignment: a set of n triples such that each target is tracked by two sensors, and no sensor is used to track more than one target, while cost is minimized.

As stated earlier we solve a weighted matching problem (in a distributed setup). Several works exists on computing matching in sequential setup (e.g. [13]) or in distributed setup (e.g. [14]) However, it is important to note that we design a distributed algorithm in which network graph and the graph for which matching is computed are essentially different.

Along with camera-target assignment and monitoring, in practice, there needs to be solutions for *identifying* individual targets. New targets may appear anytime, which need to be picked up by appropriate sensors (cameras). A *target* may not be limited to an individual object - but may represent a group of objects that move in spatial proximity. Furthermore, such a group can break up, leading to the creation of new targets. Along the same lines, multiple individual targets may coalesce to form a group, thereby reducing the number of targets. The smart cameras are assumed to have enough video processing smarts in future, so as to be able to progressively support these scenarios. Another important related functionality required for the whole surveillance cycle is target *rediscovery under occlusions* - i.e. identifying lost targets (which went into the blind zones of the cameras) and making them available for next assignment, when then resurface. We assume that target rediscovery can be performed by existing state of the art (e.g. [15]).

References

1. Bramberger, M., Doblander, A., Maier, A., Rinner, B., Schwabach, H.: Distributed embedded smart cameras for surveillance applications. Computer 39(2), 68 (2006)
2. Information technology - Face Recognition Format for Data Interchange, ANSI INCITS 385-2004 (2004)
3. Hampapur, A., Brown, L., Connell, J., Ekin, A., Haas, N., Lu, M., Merkl, H., Pankanti, S.: Smart video surveillance: exploring the concept of multiscale spatiotemporal tracking. Signal Processing Magazine, IEEE 22(2), 38–51 (2005)
4. Bondy, J.A., Murty, U.S.R.: Graph Theory. Graduate Texts in Mathematics, vol. 244. Springer, Heidelberg (2008)
5. Banerjee, S., DattaChowdhury, A., Ghosh, S.K.: Efficient algorithms for variants of weighted matching and assignment problems. Mathematics in Computer Science 1(4), 673–688 (2008)
6. Chu, W., Colbourn, C.J., Syrotiuk, V.R.: The effects of synchronization on topology-transparent scheduling. Wirel. Netw. 12(6), 681–690 (2006)
7. Hoepman, J.H.: Simple distributed weighted matchings. CoRR cs.DC/0410047 (2004)
8. Preis, R.: Linear time 1/2-approximation algorithm for maximum weighted matching in general graphs
9. Wanqing, L., Igor, K., Serge, L., Chaminda, W.: A prototype of autonomous intelligent surveillance cameras. In: AVSS 2006: Proceedings of the IEEE International Conference on Video and Signal Based Surveillance, Washington, DC, USA, p. 101. IEEE Computer Society Press, Los Alamitos (2006)
10. Karuppiah, D., Grupen, R., Hanson, A., Riseman, E.: Smart resource reconfiguration by exploiting dynamics in perceptual tasks. In: IEEE/RSJ International Conference on Intelligent Robots and Systems, 2005 (IROS 2005), pp. 1513–1519 (2005)
11. Ercan, A.O., Yang, D.B., Gamal, A.E., Guibas, L.J.: Optimal placement and selection of camera network nodes for target localization. In: Gibbons, P.B., Abdelzaher, T., Aspnes, J., Rao, R. (eds.) DCOSS 2006. LNCS, vol. 4026, pp. 389–404. Springer, Heidelberg (2006)
12. Isler, V., Spletzer, J., Khanna, S., Taylor, C.J.: Target tracking with distributed sensors: The focus of attention problem. Computer Vision and Image Understanding Journal 1-2, 225–247 (2005); Special Issue on Attention and Performance in Computer Vision
13. Pettie, S., Sanders, P.: A simpler linear time $2/3 - \epsilon$ approximation for maximum weight matching. Inf. Process. Lett. 91(6), 271–276 (2004)
14. Lotker, Z., Patt-Shamir, B., Rosen, A.: Distributed approximate matching. In: PODC 2007: Proceedings of the twenty-sixth annual ACM symposium on Principles of distributed computing, pp. 167–174. ACM Press, New York (2007)
15. Pan, J., Hu, B.: Robust occlusion handling in object tracking. In: IEEE Conference on Computer Vision and Pattern Recognition, CVPR 2007, pp. 1–8 (2007)

DisClus: A Distributed Clustering Technique over High Resolution Satellite Data

Sauravjyoti Sarmah and Dhruba Kumar Bhattacharyya

Dept. of Comp Sc & Engg., Tezpur University*, Napaam 784 028, India
{sjs,dkb}@tezu.ernet.in

Abstract. This paper presents a distributed Grid-Density based Satellite data Clustering technique, $DisClus^1$, which can detect clusters of arbitrary shapes and sizes over high resolution, multi-spectral satellite datasets. Quality of the clusters is further enhanced by incorporating a partitioning based method for the reassignment of the border pixels to the most relevant clusters. Experimental results are presented to establish the superiority of the technique in terms of scale-up, speedup as well as cluster quality.

Keywords: Clustering, grid, density, satellite image, high resolution.

1 Introduction

Clustering conserves the homogeneous property within a cluster i.e., data points within a cluster are more similar than the data points belonging to different clusters [1]. A high resolution satellite image is a remotely sensed image of the earth's surface which is a collection of huge amount of information in terms of number of pixels where each pixel in the image represents an area on the earth's surface. Multi-spectral images are the main type of images acquired by remote sensing. This technology is originally developed for space-based imaging which can capture light of frequencies beyond the visible range of light, such as infrared, which helps to extract additional information that the human eye fails to capture with its receptors for red, green and blue. A multi-spectral satellite image is a digital image comprising of multiple bands where each band represents a particular wavelength of light. Clustering a multi-spectral satellite image is a process of discovering a finite number of non-overlapping regions or clusters in an image data space. Remotely sensed satellite images mainly consists of objects (regions) such as vegetation, water bodies, concrete structures, open spaces, habitation, clouds etc. which are separated due to their different reflectance characteristics, leading to wide variety of clusters of different sizes, shapes and densities.

Major clustering techniques have been classified into partitioning, hierarchical, density-based, grid-based and model-based. Among these techniques,

---

* The department is funded by DRS Phase-I under SAP of UGC.
[1] This work is funded by ISRO under RESPOND scheme.

K. Kant et al. (Eds.): ICDCN 2010, LNCS 5935, pp. 353–364, 2010.

the density-based approach is known for its capability of discovering arbitrary shaped clusters of good quality even in noisy datasets [2], [3], [4] and [5]. Grid-based clustering approach is famous for its fast processing time especially for large datasets. Among the popular grid based clustering techniques, STING [6], CLIQUE [7] and pMAFIA [8] are examples. DGDCT [9] is a distributed grid-density based clustering technique which can detect multi-density and embedded clusters over large spatial data. Parallel and distributed computing is expected to relieve current clustering methods from the sequential bottleneck, providing the ability to scale massive datasets and improving the response time. The parallel k-means algorithm [10], PDBSCAN [11], DBDC [12], P-AutoClass [13] are among some of the parallel and distributed algorithms. K-means [14] and ISODATA [15] are two popular algorithms widely used for detecting clusters in satellite images. Other clustering techniques for multi-spectral satellite images are: EM (Expectation and Maximization) based [16], symmetry measure based [17], FCM based [18] and GA based [19], [20], [21].

Based on our selected survey and experimental analysis, it has been observed that handling large scale data is a challenging task. To discover clusters of varying shapes and sizes effectively over massive spatial datasets is a difficult task. To address these challenges, this paper presents a distributed grid-density based clustering algorithm ($DisClus$) based on $SCLUST$ [22] which can detect clusters over high resolution satellite datasets qualitatively. Further, the post processing phase helps in smoothening the bordering regions of clusters. The method was tested over satellite datasets and the results have been found to be satisfactory.

2   The SCLUST Algorithm

In $SCLUST$ [22], each pixel data is considered as a point in the space and is represented with 5 dimensions: (x, y, h, s, i), where x and y are the pixel's coordinates, h the hue, s the saturation and i the intensity of the pixel. The image data space is divided into grid cells and the grid cells whose HSI values w.r.t. the neighboring cells are similar are merged. This process continues until no more cells can be merged and a rough cluster is obtained. After obtaining the set of rough clusters, the border cells in the rough clusters are found out and clustering proceeds at the pixel level using a partitioning algorithm to obtain the finer clustering of the dataset.

Clustering process starts with dividing the data space into a set of non-overlapping grid cells and maps the pixels to each cell. It then calculates the number of pixels in each grid cell, $cell\_density$, and converts the RGB values of each pixel to its corresponding HSI values. The algorithm uses the cell information ($cell\_density$) of the grid structure and clusters the data points according to their surrounding cells. The clustering process is divided into two steps. In the first step, the rough clusters present in the image space are obtained and the second step deals with smoothening of the cluster borders to obtain quality cluster.

Step 1: Rough Clustering: In this phase, the maximum occurring hue value in the data space is found out and the grid cell with maximum pixels having this hue value becomes the seed for cluster expansion. The difference of the HSI values of the remaining pixels with this seed is calculated. If the difference value is less than some threshold θ, then that corresponding pixels difference value becomes 1 else 0. The image is thus converted into a 0-1 matrix. The *population count* (number of 1^s in each grid cell) of each grid cell is computed and based on it the corresponding population-object-ratio calculated. The clustering process now starts with the grid-cell having the highest *population_object_ratio* value POR (POR = *population count/cell_density*). The remaining cells are then clustered iteratively in order of their POR values, thereby building new clusters or merging with existing clusters. The cells adjacent to a cluster can only be merged. A neighbor search is conducted, starting at the highest POR value grid-cell and by inspecting the adjacent cells. If a neighbor cell Q is found which satisfies the density confidence condition of a cell w.r.t. current cell P, i.e. $\mid POR_P - POR_Q \geq \alpha \mid$, then Q is merged with P and the search proceeds recursively with this neighbor cell. Here, α is a user input. This search is similar to a graph traversal where the nodes represent the cells and an edge between two nodes exists if the respective cells are adjacent and satisfies the confidence condition of a cell. The process of cell merging stops when no more cells satisfy the confidence condition of a cell. The process then starts the next cluster formation from the set of unclassified cells with the pixel having the maximum hue pixel. The process continues recursively merging neighboring cells that satisfy the confidence condition of a cell. This process of merging cells and selecting seeds is repeated until all the useful cells have been classified. The classified cells represent the rough clusters and finally the pixels receive the *cluster_id* of the respective cells. When no more expansion is possible, the method checks for unclassified grid cells having hue values similar to that in the most recently formed cluster. Cluster expansion starts as before with these cells and tagged with the same cluster id as the recently formed cluster. This process continues iteratively until no more grid cells satisfy the given condition. The method then restarts with the next maximum occurring hue from the unclassified grid cells. When no more cluster expansion is possible the method is terminated. Thus, we obtained all the clusters present in the image data. After obtaining the rough clusters, we concentrate on smoothing the boundaries of the clusters. Figure 1 shows the result of clustering for an example image. The rough clusters as shown in Fig. 1b obtained are grainy in nature which is a drawback of a grid based algorithm. To obtain clusters with smooth borders, the border cells are identified and re-clustered using a partitioning based approach and the result is shown in Fig. 1c.

Step 2: Cluster Border Smoothening: In this step, the border cells detected during step I, are further processed at the pixel level. Suppose, k number of rough clusters have been obtained in the first phase of clustering. The pixels only in the border cells are checked for their re-assignment to clusters for quality cluster detection. The k rough clusters will have one seed pixel each. Now, let x

Fig. 1. a. Original image with grid structure; b. The four rough clusters and c. The final four clusters after smoothening the cluster borders

be a pixel in a border cell. The distance of x with each of the k seeds is calculated and x will be assigned to that cluster with which it has the least distance w.r.t. the seed. This process is repeated for all pixels belonging to border cells. The final clustering obtained for the image of Fig. 1a. is shown in Fig. 1c.

The cluster expansion based on the grid cells detects the rough cluster structures since after expansion of a cluster the algorithm searches for the next candidate cell which reflects a variation in the hue value in the dataset. The process starts expanding the new region till there is again a hue value variation. This process iterates till all the cells have been classified. The partitioning based process of smoothening the cluster borders gives a finer clustering result since the cluster expansion based on cells may sometimes misclassify the border points. This process tries to reassign the border points to the most relevant clusters which may be misclassified during the cell based expansion. It improves the quality of the clusters to a great extent.

3   The Proposed *DisClus*

The method is divided into three phases. In the first phase, the satellite image is partitioned into regions with marked overlappings at an initiator node and sent to each of the nodes available for clustering. The second phase is executed in each of the participating nodes. In this phase, the clustering of the data on the partitions is performed using *SCLUST* at each node. Then, in the third phase, the nodes transmit the cluster results back to the initiator node where the result are merged to get the final result.

The proposed architecture adopts a shared nothing architecture. It considers a system having k-nodes where the whole image D is located in any of the nodes (say *node* 1, also referred here as *initiator node*). It executes a fast partitioning technique to generate the k initial overlapped partitions. The partitions are then distributed among $k - 1$ nodes and one partition is kept at the initiator for cluster detection. Finally, the local cluster results are received from the nodes at this node (*node* 1) and a merger module is used to obtain the final cluster results. Next, each of the phases is explained in brief. **Phase I:** In the *initiator node*, the dataset is spatially divided into $n \times n$ non-overlapping square grid cells, where n is a user input, and maps the data points to each cell. It then calculates the density of each cell. The grid mesh is then partitioned with some overlap between adjacent partitions and distributed over k available computers (nodes). No subsequent movement of data between partitions will take place. An overlap of single grid cell width occurs between two adjacent partitions. The grid cells in the overlapped regions are locally clustered in both the adjacent partitions. Thus, they provide the information for merging together the local clustering results of two adjacent partitions.

Load Balancing: Partition D_i is sent to processor P_i, $i=1,\cdots, k$ for concurrent clustering. Since no data movement takes place after the partitions are created, care has been taken so that each processor receives nearly equal number of data objects for processing. We assume that the speed of all the processors are equal. The range of a_s is divided into intervals of width of one *cell_width* and the frequencies of data in each interval is counted. The load balancing is done in a manner similar to [23] which ensures that each partition gets number of objects nearly equal to N/k.

Phase II: In this phase, SCLUST is executed in each of the k nodes over the partition of data received from the *initiator node*. For the partition D_i in node i, the grid cells in it will be assigned *cluster_id* according to the clusters formed in that partition.

The cluster expansion based on grid cells reduces the computation time as data points are not considered for cluster expansion, only the density information of each cell is used. Moreover, the information of the marked cells used during merging process of Phase III saves the cost of merging to a great extent. Finally, Phase II transmits the cluster objects to the *initiator node* along with the *cluster_ids*.

Phase III: Here, the cluster results received from the k nodes undergo a simplified, yet faster merging procedure to obtain the final clusters. The Merger module first joins the partitions received from the k nodes according to their overlapping marked cells. It considers the marked grid cells (overlapping cells) of the candidate partitions. If any of the marked grid cells is identified by different *cluster_ids* by different partitions (say l, m), then the smallest of the *cluster_ids* (say l) is assigned to that cell. Finally, all those cells having the same *cluster_id* as that of the replaced *cluster_id* (m) is assigned with *cluster_id* l.

The following lemma provides the theoretical basis for the merging process.

Lemma 1. *Let m be a marked cell in the overlapping region of two adjacent partitions p_i and p_{i+1} and C_i and C_j are two clusters belonging to p_i and p_{i+1} respectively. If $m \in C_i$ and $m \in C_j$, then C_i and C_j are merged.*

Proof. Suppose, m be a marked cell and cell $x \in C_i$ in p_i and cell $y \in C_j$ in p_{i+1}. If $m \in C_i$ and $m \in C_j$, then x and y are reachable from m and $m \in C_i \cap C_j$. So,

x is connected to y and cells x and y should be in the same cluster. Therefore, clusters C_i and C_j should be merged.

3.1 Complexity Analysis

Since the proposed technique is executed in three phases and each phase is independent of each other, therefore, the total complexity will be the sum of the complexities due to these three phases. The first phase, divides the dataset of N points into $n \times n$ cells which are patitioned into k overlapped partitions with a total of $((k - 1) \times n)$ overlapped cells. Therefore, this phase results in a complexity of $O(n \times n)$ approximately, where $n << N$. After partitioning, $(N + (k - 1) \times t)$ points will be transmitted to k nodes, where t is the average number of points present in an overlapped region, results in a complexity of $O((N + (k - 1) \times t)$. The second phase results in a complexity of $O(((n \times n)/k + n) + (C \times b))$ [22], where C is the number of clusters detected locally and b is the number of border points obtained in a partition in a node. The clustered points are re-transmitted to the initiator node with a transmission cost of $O((N + (k - 1) \times t)$. The third phase is responsible for merging of the clusters resulting in almost $O(N + k \times t)$ time. Thus, the overall time complexity of $DisClus$ will be $O(n \times n) + O(N + (k - 1) \times t) + O(((n \times n)/k + n) + (C \times b)) + O(N + (k - 1) \times t) + O(N + k \times t)$. Therefore, the time complexity becomes $O(N)$, since $N >> (n \times n)$ and $N >> ((k - 1) \times t)$.

4 Performance Evaluation

The algorithm was implemented using Java in Windows environment with Pentium IV processor with 1 GHz speed and 256 MB RAM. To smooth out any variation, each experiment was carried out for several times and the average result was taken. The algorithm was tested over several real-life satellite images as shown in Table 1. The Dataset 1 is shown in figure 2 (a). The clusters obtained from the image of Fig. 2 are shown in Fig. 2b. Figure 3 (a) shows Dataset 2. There is a prominent black stretch across the image which is the river *Hoogly*. The prominent light patch at the bottom right corner is the *Salt Lake stadium* and the black patches nearby are the fisheries. Two parallel lines at

Table 1. Results of the clustering algorithm over several multi-spectral satellite images

Serial No.	Dataset	Spectral Bands	Resolution	Clusters Detected
1	Landsat MSS	4	79 m	4 clusters
2	IRS LISS II image of Kolkata, West Bengal	4	36.25 m	4 clusters
3	Cartosat-I image of Sonari, Assam	4	2.5 m	5 clusters
4	IRS P6 LISS IV image of Borapani, Meghalaya	4	5.8 m	5 clusters

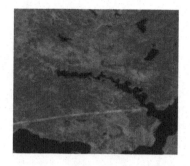
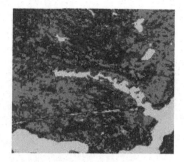

Fig. 2. a) Landsat-MSS. b) *DisClus* Output of 2 (a).

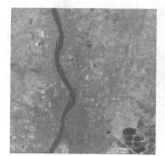

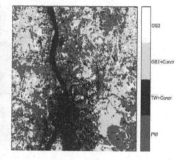

Fig. 3. a) IRS Kolkata. b) *DisClus* output. c) FCM output.

the upper right hand side of the image correspond to the airport runway in the *Dumdum* airport. Other than these there are several water bodies, roads, open spaces, etc. in the image. *DisClus* automatically detects four clusters for this data as observed in Fig. 3b. From our ground knowledge, we can infer that these four clusters correspond to the classes: Water Bodies (black color), Habitation and City area (deep grey color), Open space (light grey color) and Vegetation (white color). The river *Hoogly*, stadium, fisheries, city area as well as the airport runway is distinctly discernible in the output image. The predominance of city area on both sides of the river, particularly at the bottom part of the image is also correctly classified which corresponds to the central part of Kolkata city. Figure 3c shows the Kolkata image partitioned using FCM algorithm. It can be seen from the result that the river Hoogly and the city area has not been properly classified. These two objects have been classified as belonging to the same class. Similarly, the whole Salt Lake city as a whole has been put into one class. However, some portions such as canals, the Dumdum airport runway, fisheries, etc. have been classified properly.

The experiments on the images presented next is aimed to handle two different types of terrains (plain and hilly) in order to see the variation of classification accuracy. Dataset 3 shows the plain built up area of Sonari in Sibsagar district of Assam (Fig. 4a). Some characteristic regions in the image are the river

Fig. 4. a) Cartosat-1 of Sonari. b) *DisClus* output of 4 (a).

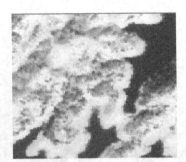 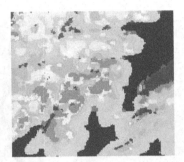

Fig. 5. a) IRS of Borapani. b) *DisClus* output of (a).

Brahmaputra shown in black color and spirally cutting across the middle of the image, roads, agricultural land, human settlements, etc. The *DisClus* clustering algorithm automatically detects 5 clusters (Fig. 4b corresponding to river, road, agricultural land, water bodies and human settlements.

The fourth dataset used in this work shows a view of the Borapani area of the state of Meghalaya (Figure 5 (a)). The characteristic regions in this image are the Deep water (Deep Blue color), Wetlands (light blue color), Vegetation (Red and Pink colors) and Open spaces (White color). *DisClus* clustered the image into five classes as shown in Fig. 5b. The resulting image classified the regions as: deep water (dark blue), wetland (sky blue), vegetation (pink), open spaces (white) and pond water (black). It can be seen that the water body at the left hand top corner of the image has been detected which corresponds well to the ground information available.

From the experimental results given above, we can conclude that the technique is highly capable of detecting clusters of all shapes.

4.1   Performance and Scalability Analysis

In our implementation environment, there is no inter-processor communication except for a singleprocessor communicating with each of the remaining processors. Each processor has the same specification i.e. PIV with 1 GHz speed

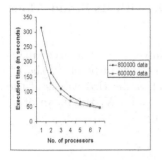 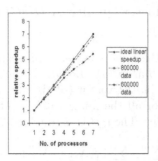 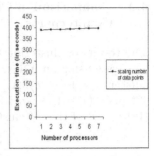

Fig. 6. a) Execution time. b) Relative Speedup curves. c) Scale-up curve.

and 128 MB RAM and the processors are connected through Ethernet LAN of speed 10/100 Mbps. To smooth out any variation, each experiment was carried out for five times and the average results were taken and each reported data point is to be interpreted as an average over five measurements. Our algorithm was implemented in JAVA in Linux environment in a HP xw8600 WS.

i. Parallel Execution Time: $T(k)$, the parallel execution time of a program is the time required to run the program on k nodes in parallel. When $k = 1$, $T(1)$ denotes the sequential run time of a program on a single processor. Figure 6a reveals that the execution time decreases significantly with the increase in the number of processors.

ii. Speedup: Speedup is a measure of relative performance between a multi-processor system and a single processor system, defined as, $S(k) = T(1)/T(k)$. On experimenting it has been found that the speedup factor increases with the increase in the number of processors. Figure 6b shows relative speedup curves for two data sets with points $N = 8 \times 10^5$ and 6×10^5. The number of dimensions and the number of clusters are fixed for both the data sets. The solid line represents "ideal" linear relative speedup. For each data set, a dotted line connects observed relative speedups, which is a sublinear type.

iii. Efficiency: The efficiency of a program on n processors, i.e. $E(k)$ is defined as the ratio of speedup achieved and the number of processors used to achieve it. $E(k) = S(k)/k = T(1)/k.T(k)$. In case of the proposed technique we observed that too many processors does not ensure the efficiency.

iv. Scale-up: The scale-up characteristic of the proposed technique has been found to be satisfactory with the increase in the number of processors as can be seen from Fig. 6c. Here the number of data points is scaled by the number of processors while dimensions and number of clusters are held constant.

While comparing to DBSCAN, OPTICS, EnDBSCAN, GDLC and Density-isoline, the proposed *DisClus* requires only two parameters i.e. the number of grid cells, i.e. n and threshold α. However, from our experiments it has been observed that the threshold α does not vary significantly with different datasets.

4.2 Comparison of Cluster Quality of *DisClus* with Its Stand-Alone Counterparts

The results of clustering the remote sensing images have been evaluated quantitatively using an index, β as in [24]. Let n_i be the number of pixels in the ith cluster ($i = 1, \cdots, c$), X_{ij} be the vector (of size 3×1) of the HSI values of the jth pixel ($j = 1, \cdots, n_i$) for all the images in cluster i, and $\bar{X}_i$ the mean of n_i HSI values of the ith cluster. Then, β is defined as [24]:

$$\beta = \frac{\sum_{i=1}^{c} \sum_{j=1}^{n_i} (X_{ij} - \bar{X})^T (X_{ij} - \bar{X})}{\sum_{i=1}^{c} \sum_{j=1}^{n_i} (X_{ij} - \bar{X}_i)^T (X_{ij} - \bar{X}_i)}$$

where n is the size of the image and $\bar{X}$ is the mean HSI value of the image. It may be noted that X_{ij}, $\bar{X}$, and $\bar{X}_i$ are all 3×1 vectors.

The above measure is the ratio of the total variation and within-cluster variation and is widely used for feature selection and cluster analysis [5]. For a given image and c (number of clusters) value, the higher the homogeneity within the segmented regions, the higher the β value. The proposed DisClus has the highest β as can be seen in Table 2. *DisClus* was also compared with its other stand-alone and density based counterparts in terms of general parameters and the result is shown in Table 3.

Table 2. Comparison of β values for different clustering algorithms

Method	k-means [14]	Astrahan's [4]	Mitra's [5]	DisClus
β	5.30	7.02	9.88	15.31

Table 3. Comparison of DisClus with its counterparts

Algorithms	No. of parameters	Structure	Complexity (Approximate)
k-means	1 (N)	Spherical	$O(N)$
FCM	1 (N)	Non-Convex	$O(N)$
DBSCAN	2 ($MinPts, \varepsilon$)	Arbitrary	$O(NlogN)$ using $R*$ tree
OPTICS	3 ($MinPts, \varepsilon, \varepsilon\prime$)	Arbitrary	$O(NlogN)$ using $R*$ tree
DisClus	2 (n, α)	Arbitrary	$O(N)$

5   Conclusions

A distributed grid-density based clustering with a partitioning approach for smoothening the cluster borders has been presented. The technique has been extended to be capable of detecting clusters of varying shapes, sizes and densities qualitatively. Experimental results are reported to establish the superiority of the algorithm in terms of scale-up and speedup.

Acknowledgement

The authors are grateful to ISRO for supporting this work under RESPOND scheme. The authors also convey thanks to Dr. B. Gopala Krishna of SAC (Ahmedabad) and Mr. D. Chutia of NESAC for providing critical comments and some test images.

References

1. Han, J., Kamber, M.: Data Mining: Concepts and Techniques. Morgan Kaufmann Publishers, San Fransisco (2004)
2. Ester, M., Kriegel, H.P., Sander, J., Xu, X.: A density-based algorithm for discovering clusters in large spatial databases with noise. In: Proceedings of KDD 1996, pp. 226–231 (1996)
3. Ankerst, M., Breuing, M.M., Kriegel, H.P., Sander, J.: Optics: Ordering points to identify the clustering structure. In: Proceedings of ACM-SIGMOD 1999, pp. 49–60 (1999)
4. Astrahan, M.M.: Speech analysis by clustering, or the hyper-phoneme method. Stanford A. I. Project Memo (1970)
5. Mitra, P., Murthy, C.A., Pal, S.K.: Density-based multiscale data condensation. IEEE Transactions on Pattern Analysis and Machine intelligence 24(6) (June 2002)
6. Wang, W., Yang, J., Muntz, R.R.: Sting: A statistical information grid approach to spatial data mining. In: Proceedings of VLDB 1997, Athens, Greece, pp. 186–195 (1997)
7. Agrawal, R., Gehrke, J., Gunopulos, D., Raghavan, P.: Automatic subspace clustering of high dimensional data for data mining applications. In: Proceedings of SIGMOD 1998, Seattle, pp. 94–105 (1998)
8. Nagesh, H.S., Goil, S., Choudhary, A.N.: A scalable parallel subspace clustering algorithm for massive data sets. In: Proceedings of International Conference on Parallel Processing, p. 477 (2000)
9. Sarmah, S., Das, R., Bhattacharyya, D.K.: A distributed algorithm for intrinsic cluster detection over large spatial data. International Journal of Computer Science 3(4), 246–256 (2008)
10. Dhillon, I., Modha, D.: A data clustering algorithm or distributed memory multiprocessors. In: Workshop on Large-scale Parallel Knowledge Discovery in Databases (1999)
11. Xu, X., Jager, J., Kriegel, H.-P.: A fast parallel clustering algorithm for large spatial databases. Data Mining and Knowledge Discovery 3(3), 263–290 (1999)
12. Januzaj, E., et al.: Towards effective and efficient distributed clustering. In: Proceedings of the ICDM 2003 (2003)

13. Pizzuti, C., Talia, D.: P-autoclass: Scalable parallel clustering for mining large data sets. IEEE Transactions on Knowledge and Data Engineering 15(3), 629–641 (2003)
14. McQueen, J.B.: Some methods for classification and analysis of multivariate observations. In: Proceedings of the Fifth Berkeley Symp. Math. Statistics and Probability, vol. 1, pp. 281–297 (1967)
15. Ball, G.H., Hall, D.J.: A clustering technique for summarizing multivariate data. Behavioural Science 12, 153–155 (1967)
16. Yamazaki, T.: A robust clustering technique for multi-spectral satellite images. In: Proceedings of the International Symposium on Noise Reduction for Imaging and Communication Systems, ISNIC (1998)
17. Pal, P., Chanda, B.: A symmetry based clustering technique for multi-spectral satellite imagery, http://www.ee.iitb.ac.in/~icvgip/PAPERS/252.pdf
18. Ameri, F., Zoej, M.J.V., Mokhtarzade, M.: Satellite image segmentation based on fuzzy c-means clustering,
    http://www.gisdevelopment.net/technology/ip/ma06_121abs.htm
19. Bandyopadhyay, S., Pal, S.K.: Pixel classification using variable string genetic algorithms with chromosomal differentiation. IEEE Transactions on Geoscience and Remote Sensing 39(2), 303–308 (2001)
20. Maulik, U., Bandyopadhyay, S.: Fuzzy partitioning using a real-coded variable-length genetic algorithm for pixel classification. IEEE Transactions on Geoscience and Remote Sensing 41(5), 1075–1081 (2003)
21. Bandyopadhyay, S., Maulik, U., Mukhopadhyay, A.: Multiobjective genetic clustering for pixel classification in remote sensing imagery. IEEE Transactions on Geoscience and Remote Sensing 45(2), 1506–1511 (2007)
22. Sarmah, S., Bhattacharyya, D.K.: A grid-density based technique for clustering satellite image. ISPRS Journal of Photogrammetry and Remote Sensing (Communicated) (2009)
23. Borah, B., Bhattacharyya, D.K., Das, R.K.: A parallel density-based data clustering technique on distributed memory multicomputers. In: Proceedings of the ADCOM (2004)
24. Pal, S.K., Ghosh, A., Shankar, B.U.: Segmentation with remotely sensed images with fuzzy thresholding and quantitative evaluation. International Journal of Remote Sensing 21(11), 2269–2300 (2000)

Performance Evaluation of a Wormhole-Routed Algorithm for Irregular Mesh NoC Interconnect

Arshin Rezazadeh[1], Ladan Momeni[2], and Mahmood Fathy[1]

[1] Department of Computer Engineering
Iran University of Science and Technology
University Road, Narmak, Tehran, Iran 16846-13114
[2] Department of Computer Engineering
Science and Research Branch – Azad University of Ahvaz
rezazadeh@comp.iust.ac.ir, momeni@iau-asrc.ac.ir,
mahfathy@iust.ac.ir

Abstract. Irregular routing algorithms are based on fault-tolerant algorithms. They are capable of use with some modifications for irregular networks, and conventionally use several virtual channels (VCs) to pass faults and irregular nodes. A well-known wormhole-switched routing algorithm named f-cube3 employs three virtual channels to overtake faulty blocks. We have estimated an irregular routing algorithm derived from f-cube3 as a solution to increase the utilization of links with a higher saturation point which uses fewer numbers of VCs in comparison to f-cube3 by reducing desired virtual channels to two supporting irregular network. Moreover, simulation of both algorithms, for the same setting has been presented. Over and above, as the simulation results show, our algorithm has a higher performance in comparison with f-cube3 even with one less VC. As well, the results show that our algorithm has less blocked messages in the network with higher switched and routed messages in Network-on-Chip (NoC).

Keywords: Network-on-Chip, utilization, irregular mesh, wormhole switching, virtual channel.

1 Introduction

A possible approach for getting over the limiting factor in future system-on-a-chip designs is to use an on-chip interconnection network instead of a global wiring [6]. On-chip networks relate closely to interconnection networks for parallel computers, in which each processor is an individual chip [15]. The tile-based network-on-chip architecture is known as a suitable solution for overcoming communication problems in future VLSI circuits [6] [10] [11]. Such chips are composed of many tiles regularly positioned in a grid where each tile can be, for example, an embedded memory, or processor, connected to its adjacent tiles through routers [6][12]. Each tile has two segments to operate in communication and computation modes separately [9].

This enables us to use packets for transferring information between tiles without requiring dedicated wirings. A NoC is a regular or irregular set of routers that are connected to each other on a point to point link in order to provide a communication

K. Kant et al. (Eds.): ICDCN 2010, LNCS 5935, pp. 365–375, 2010.

backbone to the cores of a SoC. The most common template for NoC is a 2-D mesh where each resource or set of resources is connected with a router [1]. In brief, NoCs present the scalable performance needed by systems which grow with each new generation [2].

Routing is the process of transmitting data from one node to another in a given system. Most past interconnection networks have implemented deterministic routing where messages with the same source and destination addresses always take the same network path. This form of routing has been popular because it requires a simple deadlock-avoidance algorithm, resulting in a simple router implementation [6]. Wormhole routing [5] requires the least buffering (flits instead of packets) and also allows low-latency communication. To avoid deadlocks among messages, multiple virtual channels (VC) are simulated on each physical channel [3].

All routers have five ports, where one is used for its core and the other four ports are used for communication channel between neighbor switches. As a consequence of insensitivity to distance, pipelined flow of messages, and small buffer requirements, we have used wormhole technique for the switching [3]. After receiving the packet header, first the routing unit determines which output should be used for routing this packet according to its destination and then the arbiter requests for a grant to inject the packet to a proper output using the crossbar switch.

This paper evaluates a fault-tolerant routing algorithm based on Sui-Wang's [16] algorithm. In this paper we show enhancements of the use of virtual channels in a physical link when a message is not blocked. In this method, a message uses only two VCs, in normal conditions. Our simulation results show that performance of f-cube3 algorithm is worse than the improved one, if-cube2 (improved/irregular f-cube2). We simulate the algorithms for two modes with different irregular blocks. Results for all of situations show that our algorithm has better (1) utilization, (2) average of switched messages, (3) average of routed messages, and (4) average of blocked messages compared to base algorithm. Also, it can work in higher message injection rates, with higher saturation point.

The rest of paper is structured as follows. In section 2 the irregular routing algorithms used in NoC with a comparison of f-cube3 fault-tolerant routing algorithm and the enhanced irregular routing algorithm are described followed by section 3 which presents how we have simulated these two algorithms and defines performance parameters that are considered. Finally, section 4 summarizes and concludes the results given in this paper.

2   Irregular Routing

Currently, most of the proposed algorithms for routing in NoCs are based upon deterministic routing algorithms which in the case of link failures, cannot route packets. Since adaptive algorithms are very complex for NoCs, a flexible deterministic algorithm is a suitable one [7]. Deterministic routing algorithms establish the path as a function of the destination address, always applying the same path between every pair of nodes. This routing algorithm is known as dimension-order routing. This routing algorithm routes packets by crossing dimensions in strictly increasing (or decreasing) order, reducing to zero the offset in one dimension before routing in the next one [8].

Fault tolerance is the ability of the network to function in the presence of component failures. The presence of faults renders existing routing algorithms to deadlock- and livelock-free routing ineffective. The fault-tolerant routing has been proposed as an efficient routing algorithm to preserve both performance and fault-tolerant demands in Network-on-Chips. As faulty network is similar to irregular network, we use fault-tolerant algorithms with some modifications to deal with irregular algorithms. Many algorithms have been suggested to operate in faulty conditions without deadlock and livelock. Some of these algorithms like [3] [13] [14] [16] are based on deterministic algorithms. In [16], Sui and Wang have improved the Boppana and Chalasani's [3] deterministic algorithm using less VCs. This improved algorithm uses three VCs to pass the both single and block faults. Since our evaluated fault-tolerant routing algorithm is based on this algorithm, in the reminder of this section we are going to describe how Sui and Wang's deterministic algorithm works by three VCs with our modification that reduces the number of required VCs to two.

As adaptive routing requires many resources, if cyclic dependencies between channels are to be avoided, deterministic based fault-tolerant routing algorithms are more useful for NoCs because of simple implementation, simple structure of routers and more speed, low power consumption and lower space used by routers. The e-cube algorithm is the most commonly implemented wormhole routing algorithm. Boppana and Chalasani's deterministic algorithm [3] has used e-cube technique. E-cube is an deterministic algorithm for n-cube meshes.

2.1 f-cube3 Algorithm

The algorithm presented by Sui and Wang [16], f-cube3, uses one less VC in comparison with the algorithm is discussed in [3]. Since each node in this algorithm needs fewer buffers, the area used by buffers of a chip would be reduced. Such an algorithm is able to pass f-ring and f-chain even with overlapped faulty regions (f-regions) [16]. Each message is injected into the network as a row message and its direction is set to null. Row message is a message that uses a horizontal link when injected to a network. Messages are routed along their e-cube hop if they are blocked by faults. When faults are encountered, depending on the message type and the relative position of the destination nodes to the source nodes, the direction of messages are set to clockwise or counter-clockwise. To do this, f-cube3 uses Set-Direction(M) procedure as given in [16]. Messages are routed on f-rings or f-chains according to the specified directions. The direction of a message which is passed the f-region would be set to null again. When an end point of f-chain is reached, messages take a u-turn and their directions are reversed. Figure 1 shows an example of f-ring and f-chain.

Sui and Wang used four types of messages; WE, EW, NS, and SN. In their method, all messages use virtual channel number 0, if not blocked by faults; otherwise number 1 and 2. With this channel assignment, three virtual channels per physical channel are needed. It is noted that WE, EW, NS, and SN messages use disjoint sets of virtual channels. An entire column fault disconnects meshes and is not considered in this algorithm. Finally, they proved deadlock and livelock freeness of their algorithm. In the next section we will explain our improved fault-tolerant routing algorithm, if-cube2.

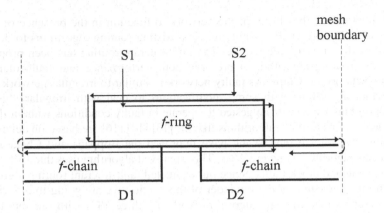

Fig. 1. An example of f-ring and f-chain and deadlock [16]

2.2 if-cube2 Algorithm

First, we show how to enhance the well-known f-cube3 routing algorithm. This algorithm is based on f-cube3, and able to pass f-ring or f-chain. Like [16] each message is injected into the network as a row message and its direction is set to null and e-cube routes a message in a row until the message reaches a node that is in the same column as its destination, and then routes it in the column. Then it would be changed as a column message to reach the destination. At each point during the routing of a message, the e-cube specifies the next hop to be taken by the message. A column message could not change its path as a row message, unless it encounters with an irregular node. The message is said to be blocked, if its e-cube hop is on an irregular block. In such a situation, a column message could change its direction into clockwise or counter-clockwise.

In if-cube2, at first, each message should be checked if it has reached to destination node. Else, if this message is a row message and has just reached to the column of the destination node, it would be changed as a column message. Next, if a message blocked, the Set-Direction(M) procedure would be called to set the direction of the message. The role of this procedure is to pass f-region by setting the direction of the message to clockwise or counter-clockwise. Again, the direction of the message will be set to null when the message passed a f-region. While the direction of a message is null, we use only two VCs for routing process by using every two VCs and no need to any extra virtual channels for routing. A message encountered with a f-region, uses predefined virtual channels as given in [16].

In [16], it is explained that how virtual channels would be used when a message is passing irregular region. With this channel assignment only two virtual channels per physical channel are needed in our method. It is noted that WE, EW, NS, and SN messages use disjoint sets of virtual channels. Note that in this algorithm a message which passed an irregular region or not encountered any irregular region, can use all VCs while only one extra VC is used in primitive algorithm except that two VCs to pass the irregular region. Since WE messages can travel from west to east but not from east to west, there can't be a deadlock among WE messages waiting in different columns.

if-cube2 algorithm
begin
/* the current host of message M is (sx, sy) and its
destination is (dx, dy). */

set message type (EW, WE, NS, or SN) based on the
address of the destination
route message M as follows:

> **if** sx = dx and sy = dy, deliver the message
> and **return**
> **if** the message M has reached the destination
> column **then** set the message type to NS or SN
> according to destination node
> **if** exist free path **then** the message M is
> forwarded along the e-cube path and use both
> 2 virtual channels
> **if** the message has encountered a irregular
> region **then**
> the message M picks a direction to follow
> along the irregular ring according to [16] and
> the relative location of the destination

end.

Deadlock and Live lock Freeness: A WE message can travel from north to south or south to north, if its next e-cube hop is an irregular node. A north-to-south (south-to-north) WE message can take south-to-north (north-to-south) hops only if it encounters an end node and takes an u-turn at the end node. No deadlock occurs among EW messages can be assured by similar statements. NS messages can travel from north to south but not from south to north; there can't be a deadlock among NS messages waiting in different rows. NS messages are designed to get around the irregular components in a counterclockwise direction. An NS message can take a u-turn at an end node located on the WEST boundary of 2-D meshes and change its direction to be clockwise, but can't take a u-turn at the EAST boundary of 2-D meshes, since no entire row of out of order components is allowed. Thus, no deadlock can occur among NS messages waiting on the same row. No deadlock can occur among SN messages that are assured by similar statements. Since the number of broken links and nodes is finite and message never visits an irregular node more than once, our routing scheme is also live lock-free [16]. Also *if*-cube2 uses 2 VCs in normal mode and uses one special VC when encounter with irregular region given in figure 2.

The technique evaluated in this paper has one primary advantage over the one presented in the previous work. According to [16], a flit always uses one of three virtual channels. However, in the current paper, a flit is allowed to use all virtual channels instead of just one fixed virtual channel, while does not encounter any irregular region. Using this modification, simulations are performed to evaluate the performance of the enhanced algorithms in comparison to the algorithm proposed in prior work. Simulation results indicate an improvement in some parameters described in the next section. This modification allows us to use only two virtual channels instead of three

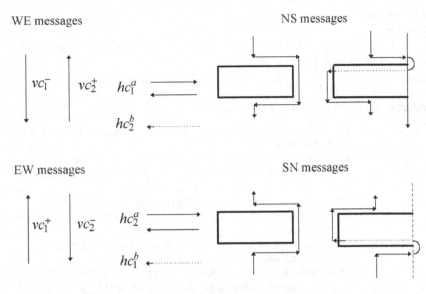

WE messages

NS messages

EW messages

SN messages

Fig. 2. Usage of Virtual Channels (VCs)

because when message routes on an irregular node, it uses one of the predefined virtual channels mentioned in [16], and while routed in non-irregular hops, it uses that two virtual channels. *If*-cube2 algorithm has been shown as follows.

3 Performance Evaluation with Simulation

In this section, we describe how we perform the simulation and acquire results from the simulator. The more blocking packets in the network during one period of time, consumed more buffers. One of the parameters we have considered as a performance metric of our algorithm, related to free buffer space, is the average number of blocked messages (ANBM) in the network. The less blocking packets, the freer buffers will be available. Network utilization can be increased by organizing the flit buffers associated with each physical channel into several virtual channels. A virtual channel consists of a buffer, together with associated state information, capable of holding one or more flits of a message [4]. We consider every buffer hold one flit for each cycle in the rest of this paper.

Some parameters we have considered are an average number of switched messages (ANSM) and average number of routed messages (ANRM) in each period of time. Another examined parameters in this paper is the utilization of the network which is using our routing algorithm, if-cube2. Utilization illustrates the number of flits in each cycle, which passed from one node to another, in any link over bandwidth. Bandwidth is defined as the maximum number of flits could be transferred across the normal links in a cycle of the network. We have examined utilization over message injection rate (MIR) and average message delay (AMD) over utilization for all sets of cases.

3.1 Simulation Methodology

We have simulated a flit-level 16 × 16 mesh with 32 and 48 flit packets for the uniform traffic pattern – the source node sends messages to any other node with equal probability. This simulator can be used for wormhole routing in meshes. The virtual channels on a physical channel are demand time-multiplexed, and it takes one cycle to transfer a flit on a physical channel. We record statistics measured in the network with the time unit equal to the transmission time of a single flit, i.e. a clock cycle. Our generation interval has exponential distribution, which leads to Poisson distribution of a number of generated messages per a specified interval.

In this simulation, we have considered 5% and 10% of the total network links' breakdown to make an irregular network. The network includes 480 links. Specifically, for the 10% case, we have set 12 nodes to make three blocks for irregular network. For the 5% case, we have set six nodes to make two blocks for irregular network. A node, in which its all links are faulty or places at the middle of the irregular region, never sets as a destination of messages.

The number of messages generated for each simulation result is 1,000,000 messages. The simulator has two phases: start-up, steady-state. The start-up phase is used to ensure the network is in steady-state before measuring parameters. For this reason, we do not gather the statistics for the first 10% of generated messages. All measures are obtained from the remaining of messages generated in steady-state phase.

Finally, in the remaining of this section, we study the effect of using two VCs on the performance of if-cube2. We perform this analysis under a different traffic distribution pattern, i.e. hotspot and matrix transpose. It is noted that only parts of simulation results are presented in this paper.

3.2 Comparison of f-cube3 and if-cube2

We defined utilization as the major performance metric. For an interconnect network, the system designer will specify a utilization requirement. Figures 3 to 7 show the

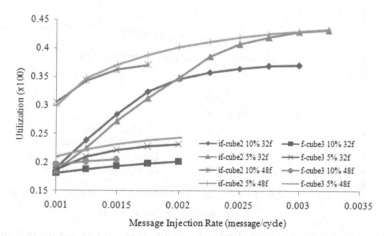

Fig. 3. Utilization of f-cube3 and if-cube2 in uniform traffic for 5% and 10% mode by 32 and 48 flits packets

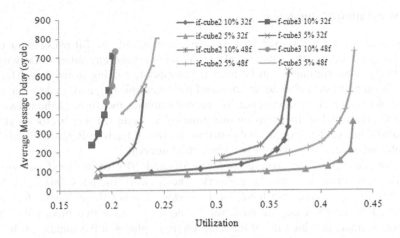

Fig. 4. Performance of f-cube3 and if-cube2 in uniform traffic for 5% and 10% mode by 32 and 48 flits packets

simulation results for two different cases, 5 and 10 percent with 32 and 48 flits on 16 × 16 mesh. Figure 3 shows the utilization over the message injection rate for two cases of irregular regions with two different message lengths, 32 and 48 flits.

As we can see, the utilization of the network channels which uses the *f*-cube3 algorithm is lower while the if-cube2 algorithm has been higher utilization. As an example in the 10% mode of f-cube3 with 32 flit packets, the utilization for 0.002 MIR is 20.18% at 100% traffic load; however, the other algorithm, if-cube2, could achieve 37% utilization in 0.003 MIR at high traffic load – more than 80% improvement in this case. In fact, our irregular routing algorithm has been higher utilization for higher MIRs. Additionally, improvement can be found in other cases.

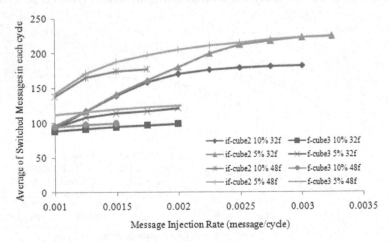

Fig. 5. Average number of switched messages (ANSM) of f-cube3 and if-cube2 in uniform traffic for 5% and 10% mode by 32 and 48 flits packets

The most valuable comparison we have done between these two algorithms is the rate of average message delay over utilization. Comparative performance across different cases in figure 4 is specific to the several irregular region sets used. For each case, we have simulated previous sets for 100% traffic load. The injection control helps us here; otherwise, we would have to perform the tedious task of determining the saturation point for each set.

As an example in this figure, we can look at the amount of average message delay for both algorithms with 23.15% utilization for 5% mode and 32 flit packets. In this point of utilization, the network which is using *f*-cube3 has more than 555 AMD at 100% traffic load while the other network, using *if*-cube2, has less than 85 AMD, and it has not been saturated. Comparing the utilization of these algorithms for 100% traffic load, it is obvious the network using *if*-cube2 has 43.14% utilization, whereas the other one has just 23.18% utilization. We have improved utilization of network more than 85% by our proposed algorithm at 100% traffic load for this case. Other cases are also considerable.

We have also shown that the average of switched messages in each cycle has been increased by our algorithm. This parameter shows the average number of flits switched from the input buffer to the output buffer of each node in one cycle. Figure 5 shows the ANSM per MIR. As an illustration, we can see at 0.0015 MIR, the ANSM of *if*-cube2 is 174.04 with 10% mode and 48 flit packets, where this value is 98.74 for *f*-cube3 – a great enhancement.

The ANRM is the third parameter simulated for comparing the power of the *if*-cube3 algorithm and *f*-cube3 algorithm. As figure 6 illustrates, the *f*-cube3 algorithm cannot be route messages as well as the *if*-cube3 algorithm. As seen in this figure, *f*-cube3 has 2.4 ANRM at 0.002 MIR while *if*-cube3 has more than 4.0 ANRM at the same MIR for 5% mode and 48 flit packets.

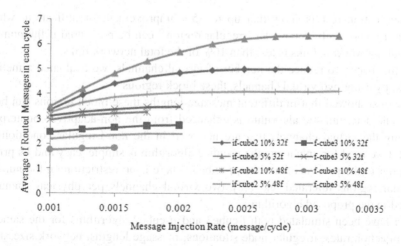

Fig. 6. Average number of routed messages (ANRM) of f-cube3 and if-cube2 in uniform traffic for 5% and 10% mode by 32 and 48 flits packets

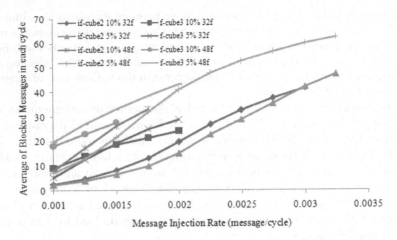

Fig. 7. Average number of blocked messages (ANBM) of f-cube3 and if-cube2 in uniform traffic for 5% and 10% mode by 32 and 48 flits packets

The last figure we use is ANBM. If nodes of a communication system have more free buffers, messages may deliver simply across the interconnection network. As shown in figure 7, the ANBM of the *if*-cube3 algorithm is less than *f*-cube3. For instance, in 0.002 MIR for 10% mode and 32 flit packets, we can see the 28.5 ANBM for *f*-cube3 while this value for *if*-cube3 is 14.9 ANBM. Besides, we can find this modification for other cases similar to this case.

4   Conclusion

The simulation results show that up to 85% improvement of utilization, which is needed to work with rectangular irregular regions, can be recovered if the number of original not working links is less than 10% of the total network links.

In this paper, to reduce the number of virtual channels, we evaluated a method to shrink, by using two virtual channels, these block regions.

We also showed that in different message lengths these block regions can be handled. The deterministic algorithm is enhanced from the non-adaptive counterpart by utilizing the virtual channels that are not used in the non-irregular conditions. The method we used for enhancing the *if*-cube2 algorithm is simple, easy and its principle is similar to the previous algorithm, *f*-cube3. There is no restriction on the number of irregular regions tolerated and only two virtual channels per physical channel are needed in the proposed algorithm.

We have been simulated both *f*-cube3 and *if*-cube2 algorithms for the same message injection rates, irregular node situations, message lengths, network size, and the percentage of irregular nodes. All of parameters we have examined show better results for *if*-cube2 in comparison with the *f*-cube3 algorithm.

References

1. Ali, M., Welzl, M., Zwicknagl, M., Hellebrand, S.: Considerations for fault-tolerant network on chips. In: The 17th International Conference on Microelectronics, December 13-15, pp. 178–182 (2005)
2. Benini, L., De Micheli, G.: Networks on chips: A new SoC paradigm. IEEE Computer, 70–78 (January 2002)
3. Boppana, R.V., Chalasani, S.: Fault-tolerant wormhole routing algorithms for mesh networks. IEEE Trans. Computers 44(7), 848–864 (1995)
4. National Dally, W.J.: Virtual channel flow control. IEEE TPDS 3(2), 194–205 (1992)
5. Dally, W.J., Seitz, C.L.: Deadlock-free message routing in multiprocessor interconnection networks. IEEE Trans. Computers 36(5), 547–553 (1987)
6. Dally, W.J., Towles, B.: Principles and practices of interconnection networks. Morgan Kaufman Publishers, San Francisco (2004)
7. Dally, W.J., Towles, B.: Route packets, not wires: On-chip interconnection networks. In: Proceedings of Design Automation Conference, Las Vegas, NV, USA, June 18-21, pp. 684–689 (2001)
8. Duato, J., Yalamanchili, S., Ni, L.: Interconnection networks: An engineering approach. Morgan Kaufmann, San Francisco (2003)
9. Guerrier, P., Greiner, A.: A generic architecture for on-chip packet-switched interconnections. In: Proceedings of Design Automation and Test in Europe Conference and Exhibition, Paris, France, March 27-30, pp. 250–256 (2000)
10. Hemani, A., Jantsch, A., Kumar, S., Postula, A., Oberg, J., Millberg, M., Lindqvist, D.: Network on chip: an architecture for billion transistor era. In: IEEE NorChip Conf., November 2000, pp. 120–124 (2000)
11. Kumar, S., Jantsch, A., Millberg, M., Oberg, J., Soininen, J., Forsell, M., Tiensyrj, K., Hemani, A.: A network on chip architecture and design methodology. In: Symposium on VLSI, April 2002, pp. 117–124 (2002)
12. Matsutani, H., Koibuchi, M., Yamada, Y., Jouraku, A., Amano, H.: Non-minimal routing strategy for application-specific networks-on-chips. In: ICPP 2005, International Conference Workshops on Parallel Processing, June 14-17, 2005, pp. 273–280 (2005)
13. Rezazadeh, A., Fathy, M., Hassanzadeh, A.: If-cube3: an improved fault-tolerant routing algorithm to achieve less latency in NoCs. In: IACC 2009, IEEE International Advanced Computing Conference, March 6-7, 2009, pp. 278–283 (2009)
14. Rezazadeh, A., Fathy, M.: Throughput Considerations of Fault-Tolerant Routing in Network-on-Chip. In: Second International Conference on Contemporary Computing (IC3 2009), Communications in Computer and Information Science (CCIS), August 17-19, vol. 40, pp. 81–92. Springer, Heidelberg (2009)
15. Srinivasan, K., Chatha, K.S.: A technique for low energy mapping and routing in network-on-chip architectures. In: ISLPED'05, pp. 387-392, San Diego, California, USA, August 8-10 (2005)
16. Sui, P.H., Wang, S.D.: An improved algorithm for fault-tolerant wormhole routing in meshes. IEEE Trans. on Computers 46(9), 1040–1042 (1997)

Dynamic Multipath Bandwidth Provisioning with Jitter, Throughput, SLA Constraints in MPLS over WDM Network

Palash Dey[1], Arkadeep Kundu[1], Mrinal K. Naskar[2], Amitava Mukherjee[3], and Mita Nasipuri[1,*]

[1] Dept. of CSE, Jadavpur University, Kolkata 700 032, India
palash1988dey@gmail.com, arkadeep_ju@yahoo.com,
mitanasipuri@yahoo.com
[2] Dept. of ETCE, Jadavpur University, Kolkata 700 032, India
mrinalnaskar@yahoo.co.in
[3] IBM India Pvt. Ltd., Salt Lake, Kolkata 700091, India
amitava.mukherjee@in.ibm.com

Abstract. Multipath bandwidth provisioning is one of the prime interest of next generation optical networks. It is a policy to distribute the requested bandwidth in multiple link disjoint paths on the basis of some optimization function. It also helps to increase network throughput. By using backup path provisioning, we can meet availability requirement of service level agreement (SLA). But multipath bandwidth provisioning leads to problem like jitter which is the difference of delay between two paths. In this paper, we propose a dynamic multipath bandwidth provisioning scheme in telecom mesh network which takes both throughput and jitter into account. It also meets SLA requirement of incoming requests. Our provisioning scheme is dynamic in the sense that it allocates bandwidth for service requests that arrive periodically with no knowledge of future requests and hence requiring an online algorithm. Our algorithm uses 1:N protection scheme against restoration since only protection can guarantee connection availability which is very important to meet SLA. Simulation studies show that efficient multipath bandwidth provisioning using our proposed algorithm can result in total network throughput to be 70% to 90% as well as keeping the effect of jitter that is buffer space overhead to a substantial of 8% to 10% of total load. We will show the simulation result with mean down time 400 second/year and 500 second/year.

Keywords: Availability, optical network, WDM, protection, throughput, jitter, SLA, dynamic.

1 Introduction

With continuously increasing demand of high speed services, only optical wavelength division multiplexing (WDM) promises increased bandwidth based on SONET or

---

[*] Corresponding author.

K. Kant et al. (Eds.): ICDCN 2010, LNCS 5935, pp. 376–391, 2010.

Gigabit Ethernet. Also to spread the total load over the entire network to achieve both improved network throughput and congestion control, we need multipath bandwidth provisioning. Backup path provisioning is a sheer overhead while the network is operating normally. Resource redundancy needs to be minimized to reduce total network cost. Hence we need dynamic multipath bandwidth provisioning scheme.

Multipath bandwidth provisioning scheme arises the problem of jitter which is especially an important issue in high speed optical networks. Even small difference in delay between two paths results in the need of huge buffer space at destination.

A single optical fiber may carry enormous amount of information, due to the rapid development of WDM technology under which 160 or 320 wavelength channels may be carried by a fiber link [1]. Currently, the fastest wavelength channel supports a data rate of 40 Gbps, which means more than seven CDROMs' worth of data can be transferred within a second. Therefore, fiber cuts (which are major contributors of network outages) caused by natural disaster, wildlife, or construction, may lead to huge data loss and service disruption [2]. So survivability issue is gaining increasing attention in modern network design. As we do not have any prior information of any future bandwidth request we need dynamic bandwidth provisioning. (Though our study uses MPLS over WDM mesh networks for illustration purpose the approach has broader applicability in other networks). Also studies show that fiber links are much more prone to failure than node. So we will consider only link failure.

Connection availability is one of many important metrics to measure Quality of Service (QoS) in a survivable network. It is the probability that the connection will be found in the operating state at a random time in the future. Meeting SLA is much required from service provider's point of view. Any violation of SLA may draw penalty from service provider to customer. So meeting SLA is also a stringent requirement from designer's point of view.

Hence requirements for this two layer model are:

1. dynamic multipath bandwidth provisioning
2. jitter based bandwidth provisioning
3. availability against link failures
4. meeting SLA

Differential delay in MPLS over WDM is an active field of research. In [3], the authors presented an analysis of the effect of differential delay can have potential effect on bandwidth blocking ratio. Backup path provisioning in MPLS over WDM network is another active field of research. In [4], the authors discussed efficiency issues of backup provisioning in WDM network. Availability issues in MPLS over WDM network is another field of active research. In [5], the authors analyzed multiple backups and primary backup link shearing for dynamic service provisioning in survivable WDM mesh network. In [6], the authors proposed dynamic bandwidth provisioning and survivability. In this paper we propose a dynamic multipath bandwidth provisioning scheme which considers both jitter and throughput along with meeting SLA requirement.

The paper is organized as follows. In section 2, we discuss analytical model and formulate the problem. In section 3 our algorithms have been proposed. In section 4, we have shown the working principle of our algorithm with a small example network. Section 5 consists of simulation studies of our algorithm on a practical subnet. Finally the paper is concluded in section 6.

2 Analytical Model and Problem Statement

We assume the following conditions while investigating connection availabilities in a telecom mesh network, e.g., an MPLS over WDM mesh network:

1. Network components i.e. nodes and links can be only in either available or unavailable state.
2. For each link, the percent mean down time, bandwidth and propagation delay are independent of each other and known in advance.
3. We assume only links can fail since failure rate of links are multiple of failure rate of nodes.
4. We only consider propagation delay and not the delay incurred for waiting in queues in routers along the lightpath.
5. We assume that at most one link can be in fail state at any instant of time.

In this section, we first state the problem and next we introduce a dynamic multipath bandwidth provisioning scheme. We state the problem as follows:

Given: A telecom mesh network is represented as a weighted directed graph G (V, E, Bw, MDT, Del). Bw is a mapping function, Bw: E$\rightarrow$ Z$^+$ (where Z$^+$ denotes the set of positive integers) which maps each link with its bandwidth. MDT is a mapping function MDT: E$\rightarrow$Z$^+$ which maps each link with its corresponding percent mean down time. Del is another mapping function, Del: E$\rightarrow$Z$^+$ which maps each link with its delay. A connection request is represented as R(s, d, bw, ad), where s and d are source and destination nodes respectively. bw is the requested bandwidth. ad is the maximum allowable down time per year. We assume a global parameter percent bs which is defined as the amount of buffer space with respect to bandwidth request which can be allocated at destination router for each request.

Find: Optimal dynamic multipath availability based service provisioning scheme with bandwidth request bw between s and d subject to jitter and network throughput along with meeting service level agreement. Given the current network state, which includes the network topology as a weighted graph G, which holds residual bandwidth, delay and mean down time of each link, route each connection request with respect to jitter, network throughput and availability of connection.

2.1 Jitter Based Approach

In this section we propose a jitter aware multi-path bandwidth provisioning scheme. Suppose there are n disjoint paths from s to d. Path i has delay d_i and has been allocated x_i bandwidth for this particular request. Hence the request is acceptable when total requested bandwidth $b=\sum x_i$. Also without loss of generality we can assume $d_1 \leq d_2 \leq \ldots d_i \leq d_{i+1} \leq \ldots \leq d_n$.

Now we will calculate buffer space in terms of bits required at the receiver's end to cop up with jitter.

$$\begin{aligned}
\text{Buffer space (B)} &= x_1(d_n - d_1) + x_2(d_n - d_2) + \ldots + x_{n-1}(d_n - d_{n-1}) \\
&= d_n \sum_{i=1}^{n-1} x_i - \sum_{i=1}^{n-1} x_i d_i \\
&= d_n(b - x_n) - \sum_{i=1}^{n-1} x_i d_i \\
&= d_n b - \sum_{i=1}^{n} x_i d_i
\end{aligned}$$

$d_n b$ is a constant. Hence to reduce buffer space we maximize $\sum_{i=1}^{n} x_i d_i$. This is maximized if we can allocate total requested bandwidth in a single path resulting in no buffer space requirement at receiver. But this may not be possible because there may be no path to carry total bandwidth hence necessitating multipath bandwidth provisioning scheme. Here we provide an algorithm MIN_JITTER that finds out the combination of paths if exists, which is capable of offering requested bandwidth and at the same time meeting buffer space constraint.

The jitter based load distribution problem can be formulated as follows:

$$\text{Minimize} \quad d_n b - \sum_{i=1}^{n} x_i d_i$$
$$\text{subject to } \sum_{i=1}^{n} x_i = b$$
$$\text{and } x_i^* \geq 0 \text{ for } i = 1, 2,.., n$$

First consider the case of single path provisioning. In single path provisioning, jitter is zero. So to minimize buffer space requirement at destination we minimize multipath provisioning as much as possible. Hence we find minimum number of paths required to provide the requested bandwidth and distribute the load into those paths only. The necessary algorithm for implementing this scheme is described in section 3.

2.2 Residual Capacity Based Approach

A path from vertex u to vertex v is denoted by $p_{u,v}$. Physical and logical topologies can be represented by graphs $G^P = (V^P, E^P)$ and $G^L = (V^L, E^L)$ where V^P, V^L are the set of vertices in the physical and logical layer respectively. E^P, E^L is the set of edges in the physical and logical layer respectively. It is obvious that $V^L \subseteq V^P$.

Here, we define function called cost function for each traffic flow passed from source to destination as

$$D(x) = D_1(x_1) + D_2(x_2) + \ldots + D_n(x_n)$$

$$= \sum_{\text{all paths}} (\text{traffic in the path/residual capacity of the path})$$

that are used to

send r to destination

$$= \sum_{i=1}^{n} (x_i^*/C_i - x_i^*) \tag{1}$$

where x_i^* is the traffic passed through path x_i and C_i is the residual capacity of path x_i, n is the number of paths which are used to send the traffic b from source to destination. The cost functions will help us to allocate more bandwidth to the path which has more spare capacity and keep up links with sparse capacity as much as possible. Cost function is dependant on two factors, (a) Traffic Load and (b) sparse capacity of the path. As x increases, D increases and reverse for C. Minimizing x/(c-x) is maximizing residual bandwidth i.e.,(c-x) and that implies minimizing x, so x is kept in the numerator to minimize it and (c-x) in the denominator to maximize it.

The load distribution problem can be formulated as follows

$$\text{Minimize} \quad \sum_{i=1}^{n} (x_i^*/C_i - x_i^*)$$
$$\text{subject to } \sum_{i=1}^{n} x_i^* = b$$
$$\text{and } x_i^* \geq 0 \text{ for } i = 1, 2,.., n$$

Let there be two paths x_1 and x_2 between a pair of source and destination, which are used to send traffic flow b from source to destination. Two are two possibilities:

1: The entire traffic will be sent through x_1
2: The traffic will be divided into x_1^* and x_2^* and then sent through x_1 and x_2.

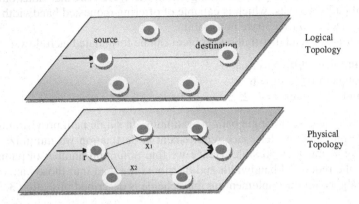

Fig. 1. Distribute traffic r in two paths x_1 and x_2

Case 1: the entire traffic is passed through x_1 (say $C_1 > C_2$) upto which the cost function will be minimum. So we have to find out upper bound for b passed through x_1. Then b passes through x_1 if

$D_1(b) + D_2(0) \leq D_1(b-\delta h) + D_2(\delta h)$ for very small δh

$\rightarrow D_1(b) - D_1(b-\delta h) \leq D_2(\delta h) - D_2(0)$

$\rightarrow \dfrac{[D_1(b-\delta h) - D_1(b)]}{(-\delta h)} \leq \dfrac{D_2(\delta h) - D_2(0)}{(\delta h)}$

$\rightarrow \lim_{(-\delta h) \to 0} \dfrac{[D_1(b-\delta h) - D_1(b)]}{(-\delta h)} \leq \lim_{(-\delta h) \to 0} \dfrac{D_2(\delta h) - D_2(0)}{(\delta h)}$

$\rightarrow \partial D_1(b)/\partial x_1 \leq \partial D_2(0)/\partial x_2$
$\rightarrow C_1/(C_1-b)^2 \leq 1/C_2$
$\rightarrow b \leq C_1 - \sqrt{C_1 C_2}$ (2a)

So, if $b \leq C_1 - \sqrt{C_1 C_2}$ then the traffic passes through x_1.

Case 2: $b > C_1 - \sqrt{C_1 C_2}$ i.e., when the traffic passes through x_1 and x_2 ($x_1^* > 0$ and $x_2^* > 0$) then

$\partial D_1(x_1^*)/\partial x_1 = \partial D_2(x_2^*)/\partial x_2$
$\rightarrow C_1/(C_1-x_1^*)^2 = C_2/(C_2-x_2^*)^2$
$\rightarrow \sqrt{C_1}/(C_1-x_1^*) = \sqrt{C_2}/(C_2-x_2^*)$
$\rightarrow x_1^* = \sqrt{C_1}[b-(C_2-\sqrt{C_1 C_2})]/[\sqrt{C_1}+\sqrt{C_2}]$ and
$\quad x_2^* = \sqrt{C_2}[b-(C_1-\sqrt{C_1 C_2})]/[\sqrt{C_1}+\sqrt{C_2}]$ (2b)

Let there be three paths x_1, x_2, x_3. So, if $b \leq C_1 - \sqrt{C_1 C_2}$ then the traffic will pass through x_1. If $b > C_1 - \sqrt{C_1 C_2}$ and $b \leq C_{12} - \sqrt{C_{12} C_3}$ (where $C_{12} = C_1 + C_2$) then the traffic will be passed through x_1 and x_2 ($x_1^* > 0$ and $x_2^* > 0$) and

$x_1^* = \sqrt{C_1}[\ b - (C_2 - \sqrt{C_1 C_2})]/[\sqrt{C_1} + \sqrt{C_2}]$ and
$x_2^* = \sqrt{C_2}[\ b - (C_1 - \sqrt{C_1 C_2})]/[\sqrt{C_1} + \sqrt{C_2}]$

If $b > C_{12} - \sqrt{C_{12} C_3}$ (where $C_{12} = C_1 + C_2$) then the traffic will be passed through x_1, x_2 and x_3 ($x_1^* > 0$ $x_2^* > 0$ and $x_3^* > 0$) and

$x_{12}^* = \sqrt{C_{12}}[\ b - (C_3 - \sqrt{C_3 C_{12}})]/[\sqrt{C_{12}} + \sqrt{C_3}]$ and
$x_3^* = \sqrt{C_3}[\ b - (C_{12} - \sqrt{C_3 C_{12}})]/[\sqrt{C_{12}} + \sqrt{C_3}]$ $\hspace{2cm}$ (3)

where $x_{12}^* = x_1^* + x_2^*$.

In general if there are n+1 paths between the source and destination then if $b \leq C_{1n} - \sqrt{C_{1n} C_{n+1}}$ (where, $C_{1n} = C_1 + C_2 + .. + C_n$) then the traffic passes through x_1, $x_2, .., x_n$ and if $b > C_{1n} - \sqrt{C_{1n} C_{n+1}}$ then the traffic passes through x_1, x_2, $x_{3,.....} x_n$ and x_{n+1} and

$x_{1n}^* = \sqrt{C_{1n}}[b - (C_{n+1} - \sqrt{C_{n+1} C_{1n}})]/[\sqrt{C_{1n}} + \sqrt{C_{n+1}}]$ and
$x_{n+1}^* = \sqrt{C_{n+1}}[b - (C_{1n} - \sqrt{C_{n+1} C_{1n}})]/[\sqrt{C_{1n}} + \sqrt{C_{n+1}}]$ $\hspace{2cm}$ (4)

where $x_{1n}^* = x_1^* + x_2^* + x_3^* + .. + x_n^*$.

Tradeoff between load balancing and JITTER:

Suppose we have found n paths from source and destination. Here we discuss TRADEOFF algorithm to balance the load as a tradeoff between buffer space and bandwidth. We call this paths $p_1, p_2, ..., p_n$. Suppose jitter based multipath bandwidth provisioning algorithm allocates bj_i bandwidth for corresponding path p_i. Suppose MIN_COST algorithm tells us to allocate bt_i bandwidth for corresponding path p_i. We introduce a parameter $p \in [0, 1]$ which finds optimal load distribution scheme. We allocate bandwidth b_i for path p_i.

$$b_i = p * bj_i + (1-p) * bt_i .$$

Hence p=0 implies bandwidth distribution is according to MIN_COST algorithm and p=1 implies bandwidth distribution is according to jitter based multipath bandwidth provisioning algorithm. Here we will propose an algorithm for finding optimal value of p meeting jitter constraint. Description of TRADEOFF algorithm is given in section.

2.3 Availability Based Approach

In this subsection, we find out the expression for path availability. Suppose a particular path consists of n links with percentage mean down time $m_1, m_2, ..., m_n$. Let m be the mean down time of the path. Since at worst case all links can be down for non overlapping intervals then $m = \sum_{i=1}^{n} m_i$.

Finding out paths: We first find out the shortest path from the source and destination using any existing routing algorithm like OSPF. After finding a path we will delete all logical links from network layer mapping and find out another one similarly. We continue until there does not exist any path from that source and destination. At this point we have a link-disjoint set of paths from the source and destination. We just described a simple link disjoint path finding algorithm but in general any link disjoint path finding algorithm can be used. Now we calculate mean down time for each path and choose only those whose mean down time is less than maximum allowable down time.

After choosing each path we test its availability from its %MDT metric and compared it with maximum allowable down time of bandwidth request. Hence this provisioning scheme satisfies SLA requirement with high probability. But there exists small but nonzero probability that one of multipath may be unavailable for more than maximum allowable down time. For this reason we keep one link disjoint path as backup path such that that backup path can carry maximum load of other paths. When a link fails, we will switch all bandwidth to the backup paths until the failed link is active. Basically we are using N:1 backup path provisioning scheme.

3 Algorithm

MIN_JITTER Algorithm:
The description of the algorithm MIN_JITTER is given below.

Input: Graph G(V, E, Bw, Del), Request : R(s, d, bw).
Output: Link-disjoint paths to provide bandwidth B in such a way that the effect of jitter i.e. the required buffer space is minimum.

1. Sort the paths on effective bandwidth in descending order
2. Find minimum i such that $\sum_{j=1}^{i} bw_j \geq bw$
3. Find the path say p_k with least delay among the chosen ones
4. Assign total effective bandwidth in all chosen paths except p_k
5. Assign the residual load to p_k

Number of link disjoint paths between source and destination is $O(|E|)$. Now step 1 can be done in $O(|E|)$ time complexity if we use bucket sort since we know the range of bandwidth of a path. Each step 2, 3 and 4 requires $O(|E|)$ time complexity. So given all link disjoint paths have been found, our algorithm runs in $O(|E|)$ time complexity.

MIN_COST Algorithm:
The description of the algorithm MIN_COST is given below.

Input : Graph G(V, E, Bw, Del), Request : R(s, d, bw).
Output : Link-disjoint paths to provide bandwidth B in such a way that the cost function described in equation (1) is minimized.

1. Begin with G^P and G^L and take $M=\varnothing$.
2. For each $e^L \in E^L$, find out mapping M placed onto the physical layer.
3. Divide traffic through all links $e^P \in E^P$ ($e^P = M(e^L)$) from each source to destination so that cost function will be minimum.
4. If any $e^P \in E^P$ gets disrupted then assign the capacity of e^P to zero again call the MIN-COST algorithm.

Computational complexity of min-cost algorithm is $O(|E|)$.

TRADEOFF Algorithm:
The description of the algorithm TRADEOFF is given below.

Input: Bandwidth distribution as per MIN_COST algorithm and MIN_JITTER algorithm.

Output: Bandwidth distribution as a tradeoff between MIN_COST and MIN_JITTER algorithm with an effort to keep the buffer space requirement less than some predefined buffer space.

1. $p_{max} = 1$, $p_{min} = 0$, $\in = 0.0001$ // $\in$ is some predefined error term
2. while $(p_{max} - p_{min} > \in)$ {
3.   mid$=(p_{max} + p_{min})/2$
4.   if (p=mid satisfies buffer space constraint)
5. $p_{max} =$ mid
6.   else
7. $p_{min} =$ mid
8. }
    return p_{max} as optimal value of p

Total number of iteration required for convergence of above algorithm is $\ln (1/\in)$.

JTSPLIT Algorithm:
The description of the algorithm JTSPLIT is given below.

Input: Graph G(V, E, Bw, MDT, Del), Request : R(s, d, bw, ad) and maximum allowable buffer space.

Output: Link-disjoint paths to provide bandwidth B and backup path and buffer space required is less than maximum allowable buffer space.

1. Find all link disjoint paths between the pair of source and destination.
2. Calculate MDT of each path by adding the MDT of each link constituting the path.
3. Take only those paths whose MDT is less than maximum allowable down time for the request.
4. Separately keep the path with maximum bandwidth.
5. Find cumulative bandwidth of the rest of the selected paths. If the cumulative bandwidth is less than the bandwidth requested, then we block the request.
6. Apply MIN_COST algorithm on selected paths and find the bandwidth assignments. Let it be vector b_t.
7. Apply MIN_JITTER algorithm on selected paths and find the bandwidth assignments. Let it be vector b_j.
8. Apply Modified MIN_COST algorithm to find final bandwidth assignments of the paths.
9. Now we allocate the maximum assigned bandwidth to the previously separated path as back up path

Time complexity of the algorithm described above is O (|E|).

4 An Example

In JTSPLIT, we find total number of link disjoint paths from the given source and destination. Now we calculate MDT of each path which is just the sum of the MDTs of each
link. We choose those paths which satisfy the availability constraint of the request.

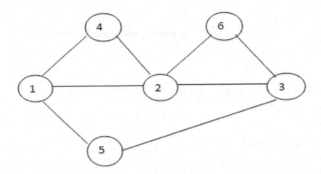

Fig. 2. Example network

Consider the example network shown in fig.2 with source be node1 and destination
be node3.

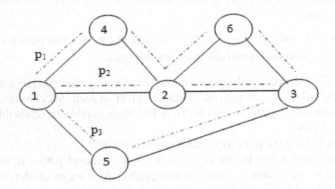

Fig. 3. Finding out link disjoint paths

Suppose three link disjoint paths have been found between node1 and node3. They
are $p_1(1\text{-}4\text{-}2\text{-}6\text{-}3)$, $p_2(1\text{-}2\text{-}3)$, $p_3(1\text{-}5\text{-}3)$.

Consider each path satisfies availability criteria. We calculate effective bandwidth
of each path. Bandwidth of a path is the minimum of residual bandwidths of each link
constituting the path. Let path p_3 be the path with highest bandwidth. We use p_3 as
backup path.

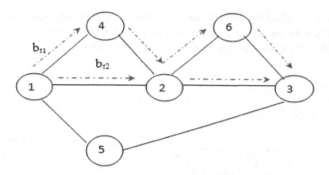

Fig. 4. After applying MIN_COST algorithm

Now we apply MIN_COST algorithm on the paths p_1 and p_2.

Suppose MIN_COST algorithm assigns bandwidth bt_i to path p_i. This bandwidth assignment is a temporary assignment and not the final outcome.

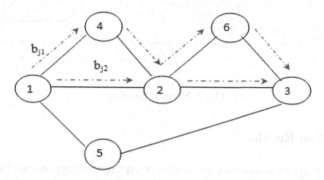

Fig. 5. After applying MIN_JITTER algorithm

Now we apply jitter based approach on paths p_1 and p_2. Suppose jitter based algorithm assigns bandwidth bj_i to path p_i. This bandwidth assignment is also temporary and not the final one.

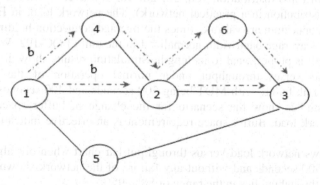

Fig. 6. After applying TRADEOFF algorithm

We run the TRADEOFF algorithm and find the appropriate value of 'p' using this algorithm. Then the bandwidth b_i assigned to path p_i is $p*bj_i + (1-p)*bt_i$. We will find $b_{max} = \max\{b_i\}$. Now we allocate bandwidth b_{max} to path p_3.

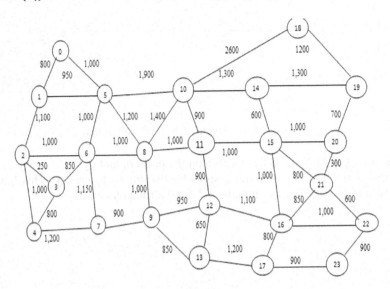

Fig. 7. Network topology

5   Simulation Results

We simulate a dynamic network environment on the topology shown in Fig. 7, with 16 wavelengths per link. The link label indicates its distance in *km*. We assume that the connection arrival processes are independent at all nodes and the connection holding time follows a negative exponential distribution. Connection requests are uniformly distributed among all node pairs. The capacity of each wavelength is OC-192, as per today's practical channel speeds. The number of connection requests follows the bandwidth (bps) distribution 100: 50: 20: 10: 10: 4: 2: 1 (which is close to the bandwidth distribution in a practical network). The network load, in Erlangs, is defined as the connection arrival rate, times the average connection holding time, times a connection's average bandwidth normalized in the unit of OC-192. We assume that MDT of a link is proportional to its length. Simulation results show different scenarios like load versus throughput under normal operation of the network and under single link failure with MDT being 500 seconds and 400 seconds respectively. Simulation studies show the scenario for the change of buffer space requirement against network load. Buffer space requirement is an effective indication of jitter of the network.

Fig 8 shows network load versus throughput bar chart when our algorithm is run with MDT=500 seconds and without any failure of the network shown in Fig 7. We observe that throughput lies in the range of 88%-95%.

5.1 No Link Failure

a) MDT=500 seconds

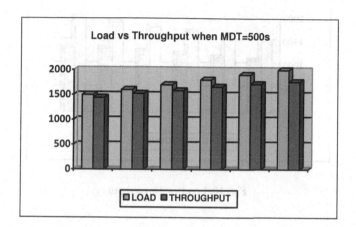

Fig. 8. Load vs Throughput

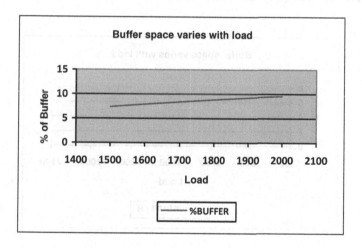

Fig. 9. Buffer space vs network load

Fig 9 shows buffer space versus network load graph when our algorithm is run with MDT=500 seconds and without any failure of the network in Fig 7. We observe that buffer space overhead lies in the range 7.4%-9.6%.

b) MDT = 400 seconds

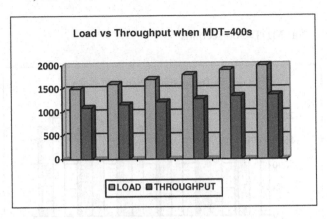

Fig. 10. Load vs Throughput

Fig 10 shows network load versus throughput bar chart when our algorithm is run with MDT=400 seconds and without any failure of the network in Fig 7. We observe that throughput lies in the range of 68%-73%.

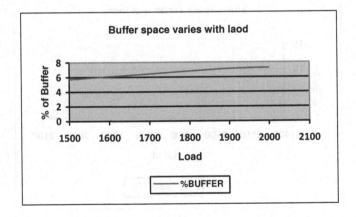

Fig. 11. Buffer space vs network load

Fig 11 shows buffer space versus network load graph when our algorithm is run with MDT=400 seconds and without any failure of the network in Fig 7. We observe that buffer space overhead lies in the range 5.7%-7.3%.

5.2 Single Link Failure

a) MDT=500 seconds

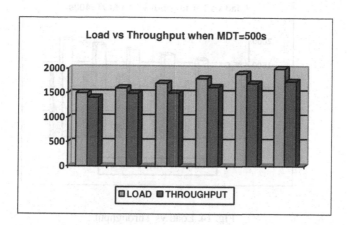

Fig. 12. Load vs Throughput

Fig 12 shows network load versus throughput bar chart when our algorithm is run with MDT=500 seconds and with single link failure of the network in Fig 7. We observe that throughput lies in the range of 86%-93%.

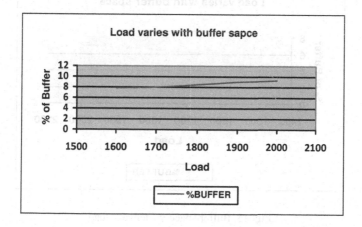

Fig. 13. Buffer space vs network load

Fig 13 shows buffer space versus network load graph when our algorithm is run with MDT=500 seconds and with single link failure of the network in Fig 7. We observe that buffer space overhead lies in the range 7.3%-9.3%.

b) MDT=400 seconds

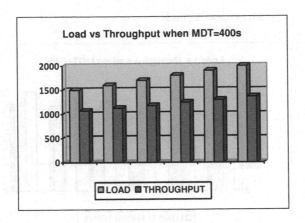

Fig. 14. Load vs Throughput

Fig 14 shows network load versus throughput bar chart when our algorithm is run with MDT=400 seconds and with single link failure of the network in Fig 7. We observe that throughput lies in the range of 66%-71%.

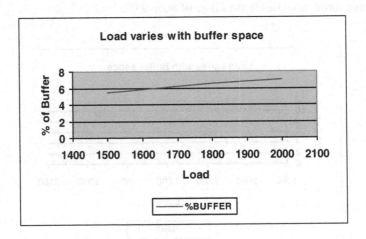

Fig. 15. Buffer space vs network load

Fig 15 shows buffer space versus network load graph when our algorithm is run with MDT=500 seconds and with single link failure of the network in Fig 7. We observe that buffer space overhead lies in the range 5.5%-7.1%.

6 Conclusion

In this paper we have proposed the scheme to fulfill the jitter and SLA aware dynamic bandwidth provisioning of spare bandwidth. We have also presented the concept of availability to ensure that even after failure of some link flow of traffic is maintained. To conclude the differential delay aware dynamic provisioning of spare capacity and the backup path provisioning give us efficient solution for designing, diagnosing and upgrading the topologies in MPLS-over-WDM network.

References

[1] Mukherjee, B.: Optical WDM Networks. Springer, Heidelberg (2006)
[2] Grover, W.D., Tipper, D.: Design and operation of survivable networks. J. Network and Systems Management 13(1), 7–11 (2005)
[3] Mukherjee, B., Martel, C.: Survivable Multipath Provisioning with Differential Delay Constraint in Telecom Mesh Networks. In: IEEE INFOCOM 2008 proceedings, April 13-18, pp. 191–195 (2008)
[4] Tornatore, M., Lucerna, D., Pattavina, A.: Improving Efficiency of Backup Reprovisioning in WDM Networks. In: IEEE INFOCOM 2008 proceedings, April 13-18, pp. 196–200 (2008)
[5] Song, L., Mukherjee, B.: On The Study of Multiple Backups and Primary-Backup Link Sharing for Dynamic Service Provisioning in Survivable WDM Mesh Networks. IEEE Journal on selected areas in communications 26(6) (August 2008)
[6] Pal, A., Dey, P., Kundu, A., Mukherjee, A., Naskar, M.K.: Dynamic Bandwidth Provisioning and Survivability in IP over WDM Network. In: ANTS 2007, December 15-17 (2007)

Path Protection in Translucent WDM Optical Networks*

Q. Rahman, S. Bandyopadhyay, A. Bari, A. Jaekel, and Y.P. Aneja

University of Windsor, Windsor, ON, N9B 3P4, Canada
{rahmanq,subir,bari1,arunita,aneja}@uwindsor.ca

Abstract. Translucent WDM networks are receiving attention as long-haul back bone networks. One important aspect of such networks that has not received attention is the possibility of cycles in the path of a translucent network. This is the first work on implementing path protection in translucent networks, considering the possibility of cycles. Two formulations have been proposed here for dynamic lightpath allocation. The first is more comprehensive but may take an unacceptably long time. The second formulation is very fast but, in general, has slightly worse performance. We have studied the performances of these formulations using a number of well-known networks.

1 Introduction

Optical noise, chromatic dispersion, nonlinear effects, polarization mode dispersion (PMD) and cross-talk cause the quality of an optical signal to degrade as it propagates through the fibers in a wavelength division multiplexed (WDM) optical network[9,10,12,13]. The distance an optical signal can propagate before its quality degrades to a level that necessitates 3R regeneration (*reamplify, reshape* and *retime*)[10] is called the *optical reach*[13]. In a translucent WDM network, a lightpath, henceforth called a *translucent lightpath*, starts from a source node, say S, uses a path $S \rightarrow x_1 \rightarrow x_2 \rightarrow \cdots \rightarrow x_p \rightarrow R_k \rightarrow \cdots \rightarrow R_p \rightarrow \cdots \rightarrow R_q \rightarrow \cdots \rightarrow D$ and ends at the destination node D. Each of the paths $S \rightarrow \cdots \rightarrow R_k$, $R_k \rightarrow \cdots \rightarrow R_p$, ..., $R_q \rightarrow \cdots \rightarrow D$ has a total length less than the optical reach r and $R_k, R_p, \cdots, R_q$ are regenerator nodes where the incoming signal undergoes 3R regeneration. It is convenient to view a translucent lightpath as a concatenation of transparent lightpath components and we will call each transparent lightpath component a *segment*. A translucent lightpath from S to D, using two regenerators R_1 and R_2, and three segments are shown in Fig. 1. In general, in a translucent lightpath from S to D, the first segment is from S to some regenerator (R_1 in Fig. 1), the last segment is from a regenerator (R_2 in Fig. 1) to D and the remaining segments are from one regenerator to another (in Fig. 1, there is only one such segment, from R_1 to R_2). We

---

* S. Bandyopadhyay, A. Jaekel and Y. P. Aneja have been supported by discovery grants from the Natural Sciences and Engineering Research Council of Canada.

K. Kant et al. (Eds.): ICDCN 2010, LNCS 5935, pp. 392–403, 2010.

assume that all-optical wavelength converters are not available, so that the wavelength continuity constraint[3] must be satisfied for each segment. In designing wide area translucent networks, two problems have received significant attention. The Regenerator Placement Problem (RPP) identifies a minimum number of nodes in a given network topology which should have 3R regenerating capacity [5,6,9,10,11,12,13,17,19]. Given a network topology with certain nodes having 3R regenerating capability, and a number of lightpaths already in existence, the Routing with Regenerator Problem (RRP) is to optimally route a new request for communication using a minimum number of 3R regenerators [4,16,18].

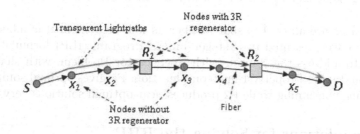

Fig. 1. A translucent lightpath through a physical topology

An example of a long haul network (taken from [4]) with distances between the nodes in kilometers is shown in Fig. 2. If the optical reach is $r = 2000$ kilometers, an optical signal from node A cannot reach node H without regeneration. For communication between A and H, if there is a regenerator at D, a translucent lightpath $(P = A \rightarrow B \rightarrow C \rightarrow D \rightarrow F \rightarrow G \rightarrow B \rightarrow C \rightarrow H)$ with two segments $(S_1 = A \rightarrow B \rightarrow C \rightarrow D)$ and $(S_2 = D \rightarrow F \rightarrow G \rightarrow B \rightarrow C \rightarrow H)$ can be established.

Property 1: *If a translucent lightpath has two segments, S_a and S_b sharing common fiber(s), the same channel cannot be used for both S_a and S_b [8].*

For instance, in Fig. 2, the segments S_1 and S_2 of the translucent lightpath P have the common fiber $B \rightarrow C$. If channel c_1 is available on all the fibers in the network, when processing a request for communication from A to H, channel c_1 cannot be used for both segments S_1 and S_2. This important restriction has not been taken into account in previous work on routing [5,6,9,10,11,12,13,16,17,18,19]. Clearly, if two segments of a translucent lightpath P share a common fiber, the route used by P must have a cycle. Such cycles do not appear in transparent lightpaths.

Schemes to handle faults in optical networks[7,14,15,20] have received a lot of attention. *Shared path protection* is a popular scheme due to its efficient use of resources and relatively fast recovery time. In dynamic lightpath allocation using shared path protection, in response to a request for communication, two lightpaths have to be set up - a primary lightpath and a backup lightpath which are mutually fiber-disjoint. If two primary paths are edge-disjoint, the corresponding

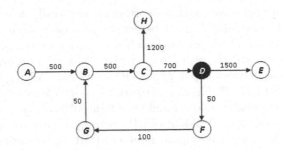

Fig. 2. Long haul optical network with distances between the nodes in kms

backup paths are allowed to share a fiber as well as a channel number. In this paper we have presented two Integer Linear Program (ILP) formulations (P1 and P2) to address the Routing with Regenerator Problem, with shared path protection, taking Property 1 into consideration. P1 gives optimal solutions but can be time consuming while P2 produces near-optimal solutions very fast.

2   Formulations for Solving the RRP

In both formulations P1 and P2, we assume that a number of requests for communication have been already processed. Each successful request for communication results in i) a route and wavelength assignment for a primary and a backup translucent lightpath, ii) the deployment of the primary lightpath and iii) the reservation of the resources for the backup lightpath, to be used if there is a fault affecting the primary lightpath. When a communication is over, all resources for the corresponding primary and the backup lightpath will be released for use in future requests for communication. There is a database containing, for each ongoing communication, information about the primary lightpath and the resources reserved for the backup lightpath. This database is used by both formulations P1 and P2 when processing a new request for a communication, say, from S to D. The objective of both P1 and P2 is to determine, if possible, the route of the primary (backup) translucent lightpath from S to D, and the channel number allocated to each segment of the primary (backup) lightpath. The total number of 3R regenerators used by the primary and the backup translucent lightpath should be as small as possible. Formulation P1 given below considers all possible paths from S to D and will succeed if it is possible to set up a primary and a backup translucent lightpath from S to D. For fast processing, in formulation P2, the search space has been restricted to some extent, so that it may occasionally fail, even if a valid primary and a backup translucent lightpath from S to D exists.

2.1   P1: An Optimal ILP Formulation for Path Protection

The constants in P1 describe the network and the lightpaths that have been deployed already to support existing requests for communication. The network has n nodes, with set $\mathcal{E}$ of edges, with each edge $e \in \mathcal{E}$ representing a fiber, capable of carrying n_{ch} channels. M denotes a large positive number. The maximum possible number of segments in the translucent lightpath from S to D will be a specified constant s, determined by the upper limit of acceptable Bit Error Rate (BER) and the communication delay. The distance of edge $e \in \mathcal{E}$ will be d_e. $\mathcal{L}$ denotes the total number of communication currently in progress. The channel number allocated to the kth segment of the lth existing backup lightpath $(1 \leq l \leq \mathcal{L})$ will be f_l^k. The originating (terminating) node of the fiber representing directed edge e will be denoted by $o(e)$ $(t(e))$. δ_i, w_e^q, z_e^q, a_e^l, $b_e^{l,h}$ denote constants. If node i is a 3R regenerator, $\delta_i = 1$; otherwise $\delta_i = 0$. If an existing primary (backup) lightpath uses channel q on edge e, $w_e^q(z_e^q) = 1$; otherwise $w_e^q(z_e^q) = 0$. If the lth existing primary lightpath, $(1 \leq l \leq \mathcal{L})$, uses edge e, $a_e^l = 1$; otherwise $a_e^l = 0$. If segment h of the lth backup lightpath, $(1 \leq l \leq \mathcal{L})$, uses edge e, $b_e^{l,h} = 1$; otherwise $b_e^{l,h} = 0$. W_q^k, Z_q^k, X_e^k, Y_e^k are binary variables. If segment k of the new primary (backup) lightpath uses channel q, $W_q^k(Z_q^k) = 1$; otherwise $W_q^k(Z_q^k) = 0$. If segment k of the new primary (backup) lightpath uses edge e, $X_e^k(Y_e^k) = 1$; otherwise $X_e^k(Y_e^k) = 0$. $\gamma_{l,h}^k$ denotes a non-negative continuous variable for the new backup path whose values are restricted by the constraints, such that $\gamma_{l,h}^k = 1$, if segment k of the new backup path shares an edge and a channel number used by segment h of the lth existing backup path; otherwise $\gamma_{l,h}^k = 0$.

The objective of P1 is to minimize a composite function involving the total number of regenerators in the new primary and the new backup lightpaths, and the total number of channels in the new primary and the new backup lightpaths. By making M sufficiently large, in equation (1), we ensure that the first priority is to minimize the number of regenerators and the second priority is to minimize the total number of physical links used in the new primary and the new backup lightpaths.

Objective function:

$$\text{minimize} \ \ M \cdot \sum_{k=1}^{s} \sum_{e:o(e)=i} (\delta_i \cdot X_e^k + \delta_i \cdot Y_e^k) + \sum_{k=1}^{s} (X_e^k + Y_e^k) \tag{1}$$

subject to:

1. Satisfy the flow balance equations for both the new primary lightpath and the new backup lightpath and ensure that the segment number following a regenerator node is 1 more than the segment number preceding the regenerator node.

$$\sum_{e:o(e)=S} X_e^1 = 1; \quad \sum_{k=1}^{s} \sum_{e:t(e)=S} X_e^k = 0 \tag{2}$$

$$\sum_{e:o(e)=S} Y_e^1 = 1; \quad \sum_{k=1}^{s} \sum_{e:t(e)=S} Y_e^k = 0 \tag{3}$$

$$\sum_{k=1}^{s} \sum_{e:o(e)=D} X_e^k = 0; \quad \sum_{k=1}^{s} \sum_{e:t(e)=D} X_e^k = 1 \tag{4}$$

$$\sum_{k=1}^{s} \sum_{e:o(e)=D} Y_e^k = 0; \quad \sum_{k=1}^{s} \sum_{e:t(e)=D} Y_e^k = 1 \tag{5}$$

$$\sum_{e:o(e)=i} X_e^k - \sum_{e:t(e)=i} X_e^k = 0: \quad \delta_i = 0, \forall k, 1 \le k \le s, \forall i, 1 \le i \le n, \quad i \ne S, i \ne D \tag{6}$$

$$\sum_{e:o(e)=i} X_e^{k+1} - \sum_{e:t(e)=i} X_e^k = 0: \quad \delta_i = 1, \forall k, 1 \le k \le s, \forall i, 1 \le i \le n, \quad i \ne S, i \ne D \tag{7}$$

$$\sum_{e:o(e)=i} Y_e^k - \sum_{e:t(e)=i} Y_e^k = 0: \quad \delta_i = 0, \forall k, 1 \le k \le s, \forall i, 1 \le i \le n, \quad i \ne S, i \ne D \tag{8}$$

$$\sum_{e:o(e)=i} Y_e^{k+1} - \sum_{e:t(e)=i} Y_e^k = 0: \quad \delta_i = 1, \forall k, 1 \le k \le s, \forall i, 1 \le i \le n, \quad i \ne S, i \ne D \tag{9}$$

2. The length of any segment of the new primary lightpath or the new backup lightpath cannot exceed the optical reach r.

$$\sum_{e \in \mathcal{E}} X_e^k \cdot d_e \le r: \quad \forall k, 1 \le k \le s \tag{10}$$

$$\sum_{e \in \mathcal{E}} Y_e^k \cdot d_e \le r: \quad \forall k, 1 \le k \le s \tag{11}$$

3. Each segment of the new primary lightpath or the new backup lightpath must have exactly one channel number assigned to it.

$$\sum_{q=1}^{n_{ch}} W_q^k = 1: \quad \forall k, 1 \le k \le s \tag{12}$$

$$\sum_{q=1}^{n_{ch}} Z_q^k = 1: \quad \forall k, 1 \le k \le s \tag{13}$$

4. The new primary lightpath must not share an edge with the new backup lightpath.

$$X_e^k + Y_e^h \le 1: \quad \forall e \in \mathcal{E}, \forall k, h, 1 \le k, h \le s \tag{14}$$

5. The channel number assigned to each segment of the new primary lightpath must be unused on each fiber used by the segment.

$$w_e^q \cdot X_e^k + W_q^k \le 1: \quad \forall e \in \mathcal{E}, \forall k, 1 \le k \le s, \forall q, 1 \le q \le n_{ch} \tag{15}$$

$$z_e^q \cdot X_e^k + W_q^k \le 1: \quad \forall e \in \mathcal{E}, \forall k, 1 \le k \le s, \forall q, 1 \le q \le n_{ch} \tag{16}$$

6. No segment of the new backup lightpath can share both the channel number and the fiber used by any other existing primary lightpath.

$$w_e^q \cdot Y_e^k + Z_q^k \leq 1: \quad \forall e \in \mathcal{E}, \forall k, 1 \leq k \leq s, \forall q, 1 \leq q \leq n_{ch} \qquad (17)$$

7. The new backup lightpath may share a channel number with another existing backup lightpath only if the corresponding primary lightpaths are edge-disjoint. Equations (18), (19) and (20) ensure that, for all $k, h, 1 \leq k, h \leq s$ and for all $l, 1 \leq l \leq \mathcal{L}$, the continuous variable $\gamma_{l,h}^k$ has a value 1 if and only if the kth segment of the new backup lightpath shares some edge e as well as the channel number with the hth segment of the lth existing backup lightpath; otherwise $\gamma_{l,h}^k$ has a value 0.

$$Z_{f_l^h}^k + Y_e^k - \gamma_{l,h}^k \leq 1: \quad \forall e \in \mathcal{E} : b_e^{l,h} = 1, \qquad (18)$$
$$\forall k, h, 1 \leq k, h \leq s, \forall l, 1 \leq l \leq \mathcal{L}$$

$$\gamma_{l,h}^k - Z_{f_l^h}^k \leq 0: \quad \forall k, h, 1 \leq k, h \leq s, \forall l, 1 \leq l \leq \mathcal{L} \qquad (19)$$

$$\gamma_{l,h}^k - \sum_{e:b_e^{l,h}=1} Y_e^k \leq 0: \quad \forall e \in \mathcal{E}, \forall k, h, 1 \leq k, h \leq s, \forall l, 1 \leq l \leq \mathcal{L} \qquad (20)$$

$$X_e^k + a_e^l + \gamma_{l,g}^h \leq 2: \quad \forall e \in \mathcal{E}, \forall k, h, g, 1 \leq k, h, g \leq s, \forall l, 1 \leq l \leq \mathcal{L}, \quad (21)$$

8. If two segments of the new lightpath (primary or backup) share a fiber, they must be assigned distinct channel numbers. As shown in Fig. 2, a translucent lightpath may have cycles and this constraint ensures that, whenever two segments of a lightpath share a fiber, they must be assigned distinct channel numbers. Equations (22) and (23) enforce this restriction for the primary lightpath and the backup lightpath respectively.

$$X_e^k + X_e^h + W_q^k + W_q^h \leq 3: \quad \forall e \in \mathcal{E}, \forall k, h, 1 \leq k, h \leq s, k \neq h, \qquad (22)$$
$$\forall q, 1 \leq q \leq n_{ch}$$

$$Y_e^k + Y_e^h + Z_q^k + Z_q^h \leq 3: \quad \forall e \in \mathcal{E}, \forall k, h, 1 \leq k, h \leq s, k \neq h, \qquad (23)$$
$$\forall q, 1 \leq q \leq n_{ch}$$

Equations (18) through (21) need some explanations. If, in segment k, the new backup lightpath uses a channel number that has been already used by segment h of the existing l^{th} backup path, $Z_{f_l^h}^k = 1$. Then (19) indicates that $\gamma_{l,h}^k \leq 1$. Now, if an edge e that has been used by segment h of the lth existing backup lightpath (i.e., $b_e^{l,h} = 1$) is also shared by the new backup lightpath in some segment k, then $Y_e^k = 1$. The purpose of (18) is to state that, in this situation, $\gamma_{l,h}^k \geq 1$, so that the only value of $\gamma_{l,h}^k$ that satisfies both (18) and (19) is $\gamma_{l,h}^k = 1$.
    If segment k of the new backup lightpath does not share any edge used by segment h of the existing l^{th} backup lightpath, equation (20) states that $\gamma_{l,h}^k \leq 0$.

Since all variables must be greater than or equal to 0, $\gamma_{l,h}^k$ must be 0. Now if the same segment k of the new backup lightpath also does not share the same channel number as used by segment h of the lth backup path, $Z_k^{f_l^h} = 0$. In this situation, (18) states that $\gamma_{l,h}^k \geq 0$. Since (20) states that $\gamma_{l,h}^k \leq 0$, the only solution that satisfies both (18) and (20), in this situation, is $\gamma_{l,h}^k = 0$.

It is important to note that our objective is to use a minimum number of regenerators in the new primary and backup lightpaths. If a translucent lightpath enters a node with 3R regenerator capability, it does not necessarily mean that we have to use 3R regeneration at that node. To achieve this, each node with 3R regeneration capability should be viewed as a virtual pair of nodes - one with 3R regeneration facility and one without. Both nodes in this virtual pair shares the same input and output fibers. It may be verified that if a lightpath enters a node with 3R regenerator capability and does not need 3R regeneration, in the solution computed by our formulation, the lightpath will enter the node in the virtual pair with no facility for 3R regeneration.

2.2 P2: An Efficient ILP Formulation for Path Protection

In P2 the idea is to limit the search for the routes for any segment of the primary (backup) lightpath to pre-determined edge-disjoint paths. For every pair (x, y) of nodes, such that it is possible to go from x to y without exceeding the optical reach r, using at least 2 edge-disjoint paths, we pre-compute, if possible, m edge-disjoint paths from x to y. Here m is a small number, fixed in advance. If m edge-disjoint paths from x to y do not exist, we pre-compute as many edge-disjoint paths from x to y as possible. We will use $\mathcal{R}$ to denote the set of all pre-computed paths. Both the new translucent primary lightpath and the new backup lightpath from S to D uses the same path $S \Rightarrow R_k \Rightarrow R_p \Rightarrow \ldots \Rightarrow R_q \Rightarrow D$, involving the same regenerators $R_k, R_p, \ldots, R_q$. Here an edge $x \Rightarrow y$ means that there are pre-computed routes to set up a transparent lightpath from x to y. Once this path is determined, each edge $x \Rightarrow y$ in the path will correspond to a segment in the primary as well as a segment in the backup lightpath. P2 will select two of the m pre-computed paths from x to y - one for the primary transparent lightpath and another for the backup transparent lightpath. Following the observations in Section 1, the only nodes of interest are the source S, the destination D and the regenerators. The only pre-computed routes of interest consist of routes in $\mathcal{R}$ are those which are a) from S to a regenerator, b) from a regenerator to another, and c) from a regenerator to D. We will use $\mathcal{P}$ to denote these routes of interest.

In P2, in addition to the symbols used in P1, we will use n_p^j to denote the number of fibers in the jth route of the source-destination pair p. The source(destination) node of the source-destination pair p will be specified by $s(p)(d(p))$. Here $A_p, \mathbb{W}_p^{j,q}, \mathbb{Z}_p^{j,q}, \mathbb{X}_p^j, \mathbb{Y}_p^j$ denote binary variables. If the source-destination pair p is selected to handle the new request for communication, $A_p = 1$; otherwise $A_p = 0$. If the jth pre-computed route is selected to realize the segment of the new primary (backup) lightpath corresponding to the source-destination pair $p \in \mathcal{P}$, $\mathbb{X}_p^j(\mathbb{Y}_p^j) = 1$; otherwise $\mathbb{X}_p^j(\mathbb{Y}_p^j) = 0$. If the new primary(backup) lightpath uses channel q in the jth route of the source-destination pair p, $\mathbb{W}_p^{j,q}(\mathbb{Z}_p^{j,q}) = 1$; otherwise $\mathbb{W}_p^{j,q}(\mathbb{Z}_p^{j,q}) = 0$. In formulation P2, $\alpha_{p,e}^j$, $\kappa_{y,j}^{x,i}$, β_p^j, θ_p^j, $b_e^{l,h}$ are constants. If the jth route of the source-destination pair p includes physical edge e, $\alpha_{p,e}^j = 1$; otherwise $\alpha_{p,e}^j = 0$. If the ith route of the source-destination pair p and the jth route of the source-destination pair q share some edge(s), $\kappa_{y,j}^{x,i} = 1$; otherwise $\kappa_{y,j}^{x,i} = 0$. The set of available channel numbers that can be used to set up a new primary lightpath using the route j of the source-destination pair p is β_p^j. The set of channel numbers used by the existing primary lightpaths using one or more edges in route j of the source-destination pair p will be denoted by θ_p^j. The channel number used by the lth existing backup lightpath in source-destination pair p will be specified as ω_p^l. Here $\lambda_{p,h}^{j,l}$ denotes a non-negative continuous variable for the new backup path, whose values are restricted by the constraints, such that $\lambda_{p,h}^{j,l} = 1$ if the jth route for the source-destination pair p shares an edge with the segment h of the lth backup lightpath, and the channel number $Z_p^{j,q}$ matches ω_p^l; otherwise $\lambda_{p,h}^{j,l} = 0$. If the segment h of the lth existing backup lightpath uses edge e, $b_e^{l,h} = 1$; otherwise $b_e^{l,h} = 0$.

The formulation for P2 is given below. The objective function of P2 denotes the same function used in P1 but uses a slightly different formula due to the way we have formulated P2.

Objective function:

$$\text{minimize } M \cdot \sum_{p \in \mathcal{P}} A_p + \sum_{p \in \mathcal{P}} \left(\sum_{j1=1}^{m} n_p^{j1} \cdot \mathbb{X}_p^{j1} + \sum_{j2=1}^{m} n_p^{j2} \cdot \mathbb{Y}_p^{j2} \right) \quad (24)$$

subject to:

1. Each selected source-destination pair, selected to handle the new request for communication, must satisfy the flow balance equations.

$$\sum_{p:s(p)=i} A_p - \sum_{p:d(p)=i} A_p = \begin{cases} 1 \text{ if } i = S, \\ -1 \text{ if } i = D, \\ 0 \text{ otherwise.} \end{cases} \quad (25)$$

2. For each source-destination pair, selected to handle the new request for communication, there must exist one route, through the physical topology, for the corresponding segment of the primary (backup) lightpath.

$$\sum_{j=1}^{m} \mathbb{X}_p^j = A_p : \quad \forall p \in \mathcal{P}. \quad (26)$$

$$\sum_{j=1}^{m} \mathbb{Y}_p^j = A_p : \quad \forall p \in \mathcal{P}. \quad (27)$$

3. The primary lightpath segment, corresponding to each selected source-destination pair, must be assigned exactly one channel number, not used

by any existing primary or backup lightpath that shares any fiber in the path used by the new segment.

$$\sum_{q:q\in\beta_p^j} \mathbb{W}_p^{j,q} = \mathbb{X}_p^j: \quad \forall p \in \mathcal{P}, \forall j, 1 \le j \le m. \tag{28}$$

4. The backup lightpath segment, corresponding to each selected source-destination pair, must not use a channel number assigned to an existing primary lightpath that shares any fiber in the path used by the new segment.

$$\sum_{q:q\notin\theta_p^j} \mathbb{Z}_p^{j,q} = \mathbb{Y}_p^j: \quad \forall p \in \mathcal{P}, \forall j, 1 \le j \le m. \tag{29}$$

5. The route used by each segment of the new primary lightpath must be edge-disjoint with respect to the route used by each segment of the new backup lightpath.

$$\mathbb{X}_{p1}^{j1} + \mathbb{Y}_{p2}^{j2} \le 1: \quad \kappa_{p2,j2}^{p1,j1} = 1, \forall p1, p2 \in \mathcal{P}, \forall j1, j2, 1 \le j1, j2 \le m. \tag{30}$$

6. A segment of the new backup lightpath may share a channel as well as a fiber with a segment of an existing backup lightpath, only if the new primary lightpath is edge-disjoint with respect to the primary lightpath corresponding to that existing backup lightpath. In a way very similar to equations (18) - (20) of formulation P1, equations (31) - (33) ensure that the continuous variable $\lambda_{p,h}^{j,l}$ has a value 1, if and only if the jth pre-computed route for segment p of the new backup lightpath shares some edge e as well as the channel number that are also used by segment h of the lth existing backup lightpath; otherwise, $\lambda_{p,h}^{j,l}$ has a value 0. Whenever $\lambda_{p,h}^{j,l} = 1$, equation (34) ensures that the new primary lightpath does not share any edge in the physical topology with the lth existing primary lightpath.

$$\mathbb{Z}_p^{j,\omega_h^l} + b_e^{l,h} \cdot \alpha_{p,e}^j \cdot \mathbb{Y}_p^j - \lambda_{p,h}^{j,l} \le 1: \quad \forall j, 1 \le j \le m, \tag{31}$$
$$\forall p, h \in \mathcal{P}, \forall l, 1 \le l \le \mathcal{L}.$$

$$\lambda_{p,h}^{j,l} - \mathbb{Z}_p^{j,\omega_h^l} \le 0: \quad \forall j, 1 \le j \le m, \forall p, h \in \mathcal{P}, \forall l, 1 \le l \le \mathcal{L}. \tag{32}$$

$$\lambda_{p,h}^{j,l} - \sum_{e:b_e^{l,h}=1} \alpha_{p,e}^j \cdot \mathbb{Y}_p^j \le 0: \quad \forall j, 1 \le j \le m, \forall p, h \in \mathcal{P}, \forall l, 1 \le l \le \mathcal{L}. \tag{33}$$

$$\alpha_{p,e}^j \cdot \mathbb{X}_p^j + a_e^l + \lambda_{t,h}^{k,l} \le 2: \quad \alpha_p^{j,e} = 1, \forall p, t, h \in \mathcal{P}, \tag{34}$$
$$\forall j, k, 1 \le j, k \le m, \forall l, 1 \le l \le \mathcal{L}.$$

7. If the routes used by any pair of segments of the new primary (backup) share a fiber, the pair of primary (backup) segments must be assigned distinct channel numbers.

$$\mathbb{W}_{p1}^{j1,q} + \mathbb{W}_{p2}^{j2,q} \le 1: \quad \forall q, 1 \le q \le n_{ch}, \kappa_{p2,j2}^{p1,j1} = 1, \tag{35}$$
$$\forall p1, p2 \in \mathcal{P}, \forall j1, j2, 1 \le j1, j2 \le m.$$

$$\mathbb{Z}_{p1}^{j1,q} + \mathbb{Z}_{p2}^{j2,q} \le 1: \quad \forall q, 1 \le q \le n_{ch}, \kappa_{p2,j2}^{p1,j1} = 1, \tag{36}$$
$$\forall p1, p2 \in \mathcal{P}, \forall j1, j2, 1 \le j1, j2 \le m.$$

3   Experimental Results

For experiments, we have considered three well-known networks, the 14 node
NSFNET backbone network, the 21 node ARPA-2 network and the 24 node
USANET backbone network [9]. We have used the same inter-node distances
as given in [9] for all these networks, and the optical reach, r, was set to 474,

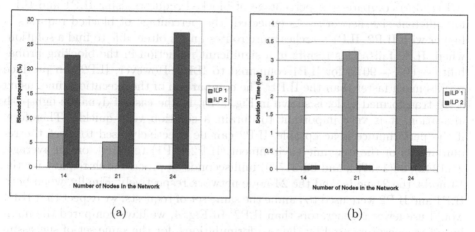

(a)   (b)

Fig. 3. Comparison of (a) blocking probabilities (b) program execution time, while
using the ILP1 and the ILP2 on different size networks

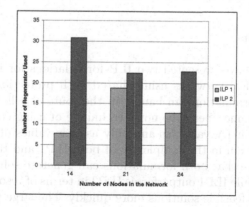

Fig. 4. Comparison of the number of regenerator required by the ILP1 and the ILP2
on different size networks

300, and 400 (as suggested in [9]) for the 14-node, the 21-node, and the 24-node network respectively. Also, the average number of traffic requests were set to 84, 100 and 172, and the number of channels were set to 8, 16 and 16, for the 14, 21 and 24 nodes network, respectively. For each size of the number of traffic requests, 10 sets of requests were randomly generated. The results presented in this section represent the average values of the 10 sets of experiments.

For the simulations with ILP2, we pre-computed three edge-disjoint shortest paths, if possible, through the physical topology between each pair of nodes that does not require a regenerator node. For any given pair of such nodes, if three edge-disjoint paths could not be found, we selected two edge-disjoint shortest paths between the pair, i.e., $2 \leq m \leq 3$. The experiments were carried out on a Sun Fire X2200 M2 Server [1], using ILOG CPLEX version 11.1 [2].

Fig. 3(a) compares the percentage of blocked requests using ILP1 and ILP2 for different size networks. As expected, the percentage of blocked requests is higher with ILP2. ILP1 searches more routes and is often able to find a solution, where ILP2 fails. This results in a significant reduction in the blocking probabilities (60% - 90%) for ILP1 compared to ILP2. However, ILP2 can produce results much faster than the ILP1. The comparison of the execution time, using a log-transformed scale, is shown in Fig. 3(b). In the case of dynamic lightpath allocation, it is very important to obtain a solution very quickly. Therefore, if the performance is acceptable, ILP2 can be effectively used to meet the requirements of the dynamic environment. ILP2(ILP1) required, on an average, 25(1242), 26(18373), and 36(31780) milliseconds to process each request for the 14-node, the 21-node, and the 24-node network respectively. Finally, when both ILP1 and ILP2 were used to handle the same set of requests, we expect that ILP1 would use fewer regenerators than ILP2. In Fig. 4, we have compared the number of regenerators used by the two formulations, for the same set of successful requests. The amount of improvement, in terms of the number of regenerators needed, varied with the network topology and the set of requests. However, as shown in Fig. 4, ILP1 requires less regenerators than ILP2 in all cases.

4   Conclusions

In this paper, we have presented two ILP formulations for resource allocation in translucent optical networks using shared path protection. Unlike previous approaches, our formulation can handle in the route of a lightpath, where two segments use the same fiber. The novel technique of using continuous variables (that behave like binary variables and only assume values of 0 or 1), results in a significant reduction in the complexity of both ILP1 and ILP2. Experimental results demonstrate that both formulations can generate solutions for practical sized networks. While ILP1 outperforms ILP2 in terms of resource requirements, ILP2 can generate feasible solutions more quickly. The large reduction of search space allows ILP2 to be much more faster making it more suitable for dynamic lightpath allocation.

References

1. http://www.sun.com/servers/x64/x2200/
2. http://www.ilog.com/products/cplex/
3. Bandyopadhyay, S.: Dissemination of Information in Optical Networks. Springer, Heidelberg (2008)
4. Bandyopadhyay, S., Rahman, Q., Banerjee, S., Murthy, S., Sen, A.: Dynamic lightpath allocation in translucent wdm optical networks. In: IEEE International Conference on Communications, IEEE/ICC 2009 (2009)
5. Carpentar, T., Shallcross, D., Gannet, J., Jackal, J., Lehman, A.V.: Method and system for design and routing in transparent optical networks. U. S. Patent Number 7286480 B2 (October 2007)
6. Chatelain, B., Mannor, S., Gagnon, F., Plant, D.V.: Non-cooperative design of translucent networks. In: Global Telecommunications Conference, GLOBECOM 2007 (2007)
7. Huo, W., Guang, L., Assi, C., Shami, A.: Survivable traffic grooming in optical networks with multiple failures. In: Canadian Conference on Electrical and Computer Engineering (2005)
8. Sen, A., Murthy, S., Bandyopadhyay, S.: On sparse placement of regenerator nodes in translucent optical networks. In: Globecom (2008)
9. Shen, G., Grover, W.D., Cheng, T.H., Bose, S.K.: Sparse placement of electronic switchoing nodes for low blocking in translucent optical networks. OSA Journal of Optical Networking 1(12) (2002)
10. Shen, G., Tucker, R.S.: Translucent optical networks: the way forward. IEEE Communications Magazine 45 (2007)
11. Shinomiya, N., Hoshida, T., Akiyama, Y., Nakashima, H., Terahara, T.: Hybrid link/path-based design for translucent photonic network dimensioning. Journal of Lightwave Technology 5(10), 2931–2941 (2007)
12. Simmons, J.: On determining the optimal optical reach for a long-haul network. Journal of Lightwave Technology 23 (March 2005)
13. Simmons, J.: Network design in realistic all-optical backbone networks. IEEE Communications Magazine 44 (2006)
14. Somani, A.K.: Survivability and traffic grooming in WDM mesh networks. Cambridge University Press, Cambridge (2006)
15. Thiagarajan, S., Somani, A.K.: Traffic grooming for survivable wdm mesh networks. In: Proceedings of SPIE Optical Networking and Communications (2001)
16. Yang, X., Ramamurthy, B.: Dynamic routing in translucent wdm optical networks: The intradomain case. Journal of Lightwave Technology 23(3), 955–971 (2005)
17. Yang, X., Ramamurthy, B.: Sparse regeneration in translucent wavelength routed optical networks: architecture, network design and wavelength routing. Photonic network communications 10 (2005)
18. Yang, X., Ramamurthy, B.: Dynamic routing in translucent wdm optical networks: the interdomanin case. Journal of Lightwave Technology 23 (March 2005)
19. Zhou, B., Pramod, S.R., Mouftah, H.T.: Adaptive ber-assured routing in translucent optical networks. In: Workshop on High Performance Switching and Routing (HPSR 2004), pp. 209–213 (2004)
20. Zhou, D., Subramaniam, S.: Survivability in optical networks. In: IEEE Network, pp. 16–23 (November-December 2000)

Post Deployment Planning of 3G Cellular Networks through Dual Homing of NodeBs

Samir K. Sadhukhan[1], Swarup Mandal[2], Partha Bhaumik[3], and Debashis Saha[1]

[1] Indian Institute of Management, Calcutta
{samir,ds}@iimcal.ac.in
[2] Wipro Technologies, Kolkata, India
swarup.mandal@wipro.com
[3] Department of Computer Science and Engineering, Jadavpur University, Kolkata, India
partha.b@ieee.org

Abstract. 3G Cellular networks typically consist of a group of NodeBs connected to a Radio Network Controller (RNC), and a group of RNCs to a Serving GPRS Support Node (SGSNs) as well as to a Mobile Switching Centre (MSCs). Post deployment planning of such network is to re-plan the connectivity among the above mentioned network elements with an objective to minimize the cost of operation of the network. This planning problem is traditionally solved under single homing consideration (i.e., one NodeB is homed with only one RNC). However, a single homing solution becomes ineffective when the subscriber distribution changes over time and groups of subscribers begin to show a specific diurnal pattern of their inter-MSC/SGSN mobility. One of the solutions for this problem is dual-homing where some selected NodeBs are connected to two RNCs to reduce the complex handoffs involving two different RNCs as well as two different MSCs/SGSNs. In this paper, we have mapped the dual-homing problem into a search problem and used Simulated Annealing (SA) and Tabu Search (TS) techniques to optimally select the NodeBs and RNCs to be connected. A comparison of the performances of the two meta-heuristic techniques reveals that, though both are efficient enough to produce good solutions, TS is found to be better than SA throughout.

Keywords: Network planning, Cellular network, 3G, dual-homing, NodeB, RNC, MSC, SGSN, Tabu Search, Simulated Annealing.

1 Introduction

3G Cellular network planning is typically carried out in two phases, namely pre-deployment planning and post-deployment planning [1]-[2]. Here, we consider the post-deployment planning, as this is a more dominant case now-a-days for operators who are already in cellular business for about a decade. In this phase, an operator usually faces a substantial increase in subscriber base vis-à-vis gradual change in mobility pattern of the existing subscriber base [6]. This change in the mobility pattern is supplemented by the change of pattern of diurnal movement of the subscribers which is very common due to evolution of settlement pattern. A part of the problem arising out

K. Kant et al. (Eds.): ICDCN 2010, LNCS 5935, pp. 404–419, 2010.
© Springer-Verlag Berlin Heidelberg 2010

of the changes in mobility pattern can be addressed by regrouping NodeBs into new clusters (i.e., by changing the connectivity of NodeBs to RNCs) [3]-[7], which requires a major overhauling of network connectivity. But the change of diurnal mobility pattern cannot be addressed by single homing approach. Hence, selective dual-homing of NodeBs (where one NodeB may be connected to at most two RNCs (Fig. 1) unlike single homing where one NodeB is connected to one RNC only) is a viable option to try during post-deployment planning stage. In this paper, we have considered this dual homing problem where some of the NodeBs will be connected to two RNCs in an optimal manner to reduce handoff cost.

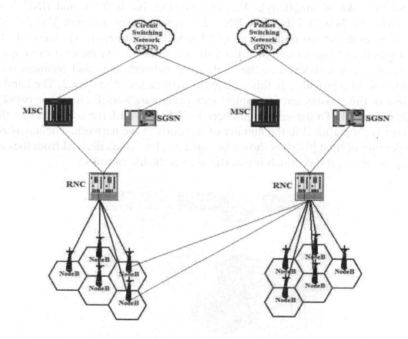

Fig. 1. Dual-homing of NodeBs

In single-homing case, researchers have usually viewed this planning problem as NodeB-RNC assignment problem and solved it using either a meta-heuristic [1]-[2] or a domain-specific heuristic [4]-[6]. But the literature survey does not show any work involving post-deployment dual-homing of NodeBs in 3G cellular networks. The closest match to the concept that we promote here can be found in [1] which, however, deals with Asynchronous Transfer Mode (ATM) networks (not cellular networks). There authors have used a meta-heuristic technique, namely genetic algorithm (GA), to solve the problem. Following their steps, in this work, we have considered 3G networks for dual homing of NodeBs, and mapped the dual-homing optimization problem into a combinatorial optimization problem and solved it with two different meta-heuristic techniques, namely Simulated Annealing (SA) and Tabu Search (TS)

To explain the problem further, let us define three types of handoff, namely simplest, simple and complex. We call a handoff simplest when no MSC/SGSN is involved in the handoff process. In this case, subscriber will move from one NodeB to another NodeB connected to same RNC. Hence, in the case of simplest handoff, one RNC handles the whole handoff process. On the contrary, a simple handoff involves two different RNCs connected to same MSC/SGSN, whereas a complex handoff involves two RNCs which are connected to two different MSCs/SGSNs. Here, simplest handoff cost is lower than that of a simple handoff and cost of simple handoff is lower than that of a complex handoff. The goal of dual-homing of NodeBs is to reduce the total handoff cost of the network.

Let us explain the problem with a small toy problem. Fig. 2 shows an existing 3G network (conceptual diagram) of three RNCs and five NodeBs (MSCs/SGSNs are omitted for the sake of simplicity). We are assuming that RNC 1, and RNC 3 are connected to same MSC/SGSN while RNC 2 is connected to different MSC/SGSN. Let us also assume that the cost of a simple handoff is μ times ($\mu >1$) the cost of a simplest handoff and cost of complex handoff is λ times ($\lambda >1$) the cost of simplest handoff. Here, μ and λ depends on the load on the network and other business parameters of the service provider. In this case let us assume $\mu=1.5$ and $\lambda= 2$. The handoff cost per unit of time arising out of simplest handoff among NodeBs for the network is indicated in Table 1. To derive the numbers in Table 1, we have used the fact that handoff cost is proportional to the number of handoffs in the network. The amortized link cost per unit of time [9-10] is shown in Table 2. This cost is derived from the cost of creating the physical link which is amortized over the life of links.

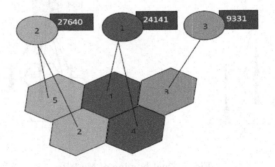

Fig. 2. Single-home Network

The spare call handling capacities of RNCs are shown in square boxes in Fig. 2. The call handling capacities for the NodeBs are indicated in Table 3.

Table 1. Handoff Cost

NodeB \ NodeB	1	2	3	4	5
1	0	24	21	18	9
2	24	0	0	15	11
3	21	0	0	15	0
4	18	15	15	0	0
5	9	11	0	0	0

Table 2. Link Cost

NodeB \ RNC	1	2	3
1	-	170	125
2	105	89	185
3	75	242	-
4	34	178	99
5	178	-	269

Table 3. NodeB Capacity

NodeB	1	2	3	4	5
Capacity	12342	13722	4848	7776	9312

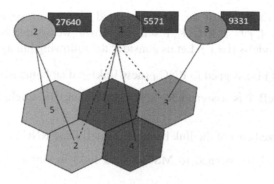

Fig. 3. Dual-home Network

The total complex handoff cost of the single home network is given by 2 * (h_{15} + h_{12} + h_{24}) = 2 * (9+24+15) = 96, total simple handoff is given by 2 * (h_{13}+ h_{34}) = 2 * (21 + 15) = 72 and total simplest handoff cost is 2 * (h_{52} + h_{14}) = 2 * (11 + 18) = 78. The total link cost per unit time is given by 123. So the total cost is 96 * 2.0 + 72 * 1.5 + 78 + 123 = 501. Now to reduce the handoff cost, a dual-homed network as shown in Fig. 3 may be formed from the single homed network (Fig. 2). In this case, the complex handoff cost is 2 * h_{15} = 2 * 9 = 18, simple handoff cost is 0 and simplest handoff cost is 2 * (h_{12} + h_{14} + h_{13} + h_{42} + h_{41} + h_{43} + h_{52}) = 2 * (24 + 18 + 21 + 15 + 18 + 15 + 11) = 122 and additional link cost is 105 + 75 = 180. So the total cost is 18 * 2.0 + 0 * 1.5 + 122 + 123 + 180 = 461. So the reduction will be 501 – 461 = 40 unit of cost.

For post deployment planning, the configuration of the single homed network is taken as input and planning is done with an objective to reduce the handoff cost of the network making NodeBs dual-homed. A set of rules are followed for deciding a NodeB's dual homing. As for example, a NodeB can be connected to an RNC (for dual homing), if the call handling capacity of the NodeB is not greater than the spare call handling capacity of the RNC (capacity constraint) and the amortized link cost between the NodeB and the RNC is less than the handoff cost reduction that arises due to dual homing of the NodeB (cost constraint).

This paper is organized in five sections. Following introduction (Section 1), mathematical formulation is presented in Section 2. Section 3 describes SA and TS based solution methodologies. Section 4 contains the experiential results with discussion. Section 5 concludes the paper.

2 Mathematical Formulation

Let us consider that, in the 3G network of a mobile telecom service provider (MTSP), there are n NodeBs, r RNCs, m MSCs and s SGSNs, whose locations are known. Let I ={1,2, ... n} denote the set of NodeBs, J= {1,2, ... r} denote the set of RNCs, K={1,2, ...m} denote the set of MSCs and L={1,2, ... s} denote the set of SGSNs. From the existing single-home network, the initial assignments of NodeBs to RNCs to MSCs and SGSNs are known a priori. Throughout this formulation, we use a small letter to denote a member of the set represented by the corresponding capital letter; for example, $i \in I, j \in J, k \in K, l \in L$. Moreover, we assume NodeB i and NodeB i′ are different NodeBs ($i \neq i′$). Let us consider the following binary variables:

$x_{ij} = 1$, if NodeB i is assigned to RNC j (new link) in dual home network, 0, otherwise

$d_{ij} = 1$, if NodeB i is assigned to RNC j (old link) in single home network, 0, otherwise

c_{ij} is the amortized cost of the link between NodeB i and RNC j

$d'_{jk} = 1$, if RNC j is assigned to MSC k (old link) in single   home network, 0, otherwise

$d''_{jl} = 1$, if RNC j is assigned to SGSN l (old link) in single home network, 0, otherwise

Cap_i and Cap'_i	are the capacity in circuit switching (number of calls per unit of time) and capacity in packet switching (bits per second) of NodeB i.
Cap''_j and Cap'''_j	are the capacity in circuit switching (number of calls per unit of time) and capacity in packet switching (bits per second) of RNC j.
f_{ij}^{voice}	is the amount of voice traffic produced by NodeB i destined to RNC j
f_{ij}^{data}	is the amount of data traffic produced by NodeB i destined to RNC j
$H_{ii'}^{msc}$	is the cost per unit of time for simple handoff between NodeB i and NodeB i′ involving only one MSC
$H_{ii'}^{'msc}$	is the cost per unit of time for complex handoff between NodeB i and NodeB i′ involving two MSCs
$H_{ii'}^{sgsn}$	is the cost per unit of time for simple handoff between NodeB i and NodeB i′ involving only one SGSN
$H_{ii'}^{'sgsn}$	is the cost per unit of time for complex handoff between NodeB i and NodeB i′ involving two SGSNs

Let us assume the following:
The cost of a simple voice handoff is μ_1 times the cost of a simplest voice handoff.
The cost of a complex voice handoff is λ_1 times the cost of a simplest voice handoff.
The cost of a simple data handoff is μ_2 times the cost of a simplest data handoff.
The cost of a complex data handoff is λ_2 times the cost of a simplest data handoff.

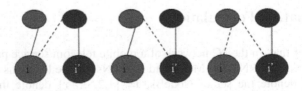

Fig. 4. Dual-homing of NodeB converts complex/simple handoff to simplest handoff

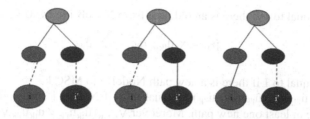

Fig. 5. Dual-homing of NodeB converts complex handoff to simple handoff

In Fig. 4, NodeBs that are connected to different RNCs in single homing, are connected to one RNC using at least one new link. Thus, the new link between NodeB-RNC converts complex or simple handoffs into simplest handoff. In Fig. 5, NodeBs are connected different RNCs which are connected to same MSC/SGSN. Thus the new link between NodeB-RNC converts complex handoffs into simple handoffs.

Following Fig. 4, let us define the following variables:

$$t_{ii'j} = d_{ij}x_{i'j}, \; w_{ii'} = \sum_{j \in J} t_{ii'j}$$

Then $(w_{ii'} \lor w_{i'i})$ is equal to 1 if NodeB i and NodeB i' are under same RNC using one old link and one new link. The operator $\lor$ stands for logical OR.

$$\hat{t}_{ii'j} = x_{ij}x_{i'j}, \; \hat{w}_{ii'} = \sum_{j \in J} \hat{t}_{ii'j}$$

Then $\hat{w}_{ii'}$ is equal to 1 if NodeB i and NodeB i' are under same RNC using new links only.

Then $(w_{ii'} \lor w_{i'i} \lor \hat{w}_{ii'})$ is equal to 1 if NodeB i and NodeB i' are under one RNC using at least one new link. Therefore, the reduction of simple handoff and complex handoff to simplest handoff in the dual-home network for voice will be:

$$\sum_{i \in I} \sum_{i' \in I} (w_{ii'} \lor w_{i'i} \lor \hat{w}_{ii'}) \left((1 - 1/\mu_1)H_{ii'}^{msc} + (1-1/\lambda_1)H_{ii'}^{'msc} \right)$$

It is to be noted that, between two given NodeBs, there will be only one type of handoff in the single home network.

Similarly, the reduction of simple handoff and complex handoff to simplest handoff in the dual-home network for data will be:

$$\sum_{i \in I} \sum_{i' \in I} (w_{ii'} \lor w_{i'i} \lor \hat{w}_{ii'}) \left((1-1/\mu_2)H_{ii'}^{sgsn} + (1-1/\lambda_2)H_{ii'}^{'sgsn} \right)$$

Following Fig. 5 and considering the connectivity from RNC to MSC, let us define the following composite variables:

$$p_{ijk} = d_{ij}d_{jk}', \; u_{ik} = \sum_{j \in J} p_{ijk}$$

Then u_{ik} is equal to 1 if there is an old path from NodeB i to MSC k.

$$\hat{p}_{ijk} = x_{ij}d'_{jk}, \; \hat{u}_{ik} = \sum_{j \in J} \hat{p}_{ijk}$$

Then $\hat{u}_{ik}$ is equal to 1 if there is a new path NodeB i to MSC k.

Then $(\hat{u}_{ik}\hat{u}_{i'k} \vee u_{ik}\hat{u}_{i'k} \vee \hat{u}_{ik}u_{i'k})$ is equal to 1 if NodeB i and NodeB i′ are under MSC k using at least one new path. Moreover $\vee_{k \in K}(\hat{u}_{ik}\hat{u}_{i'k} \vee u_{ik}\hat{u}_{i'k} \vee \hat{u}_{ik}u_{i'k})$ is equal to 1 if *NodeB i* and *NodeB i′* are under one *MSC* using at least one new path.

Following Fig. 5 and considering the connectivity from RNC to SGSN, let us define the following variables:

$$q_{ijl} = d_{ij}d''_{jl}, \; v_{il} = \sum_{j \in J} q_{ijl}$$

Then as v_{il} is equal to 1 if there is an old path from NodeB i to SGSN l.

$$\hat{q}_{ijl} = x_{ij}d''_{jl}, \; \hat{v}_{il} = \sum_{j \in J} \hat{q}_{ijl}$$

Then $\hat{v}_{il}$ is equal to 1 if there is a new path NodeB i to SGSN l.

Then $(\hat{v}_{il}\hat{v}_{i'l} \vee v_{il}\hat{v}_{i'l} \vee \hat{v}_{il}v_{i'l})$ is equal to 1 if NodeB i and NodeB i′ are under SGSN l using at least one new path. Moreover $\vee_{l \in L}(\hat{v}_{il}\hat{v}_{i'l} \vee v_{il}\hat{v}_{i'l} \vee \hat{v}_{il}v_{i'l})$ is equal to 1 if *NodeB i* and *NodeB i′* are under one *SGSN* using at least one new path.

Therefore the reduction of complex handoff to simple handoff in the dual-home network will be

$$\sum_{i \in I}\sum_{i' \in I}\{\bigvee_{k \in K}(\hat{u}_{ik}\hat{u}_{i'k} \vee u_{ik}\hat{u}_{i'k} \vee \hat{u}_{ik}u_{i'k})(1 - \mu_1/\lambda_1)H_{ii'}^{'msc} + \bigvee_{l \in L}(\hat{v}_{il}\hat{v}_{i'l} \vee v_{il}\hat{v}_{i'l} \vee \hat{v}_{il}v_{i'l})(1 - \mu_2/\lambda_2)H_{ii'}^{'sgsn}\}$$

Therefore, the total reduction of handoff will be

$$HC = \sum_{i \in I}\sum_{i' \in I}\left\{\bigvee_{k \in K}(\hat{u}_{ik}\hat{u}_{i'k} \vee u_{ik}\hat{u}_{i'k} \vee \hat{u}_{ik}u_{i'k})(1 - \mu_1/\lambda_1)H_{ii'}^{'msc} + \bigvee_{l \in L}(\hat{v}_{il}\hat{v}_{i'l} \vee v_{il}\hat{v}_{i'l} \vee \hat{v}_{il}v_{i'l})(1 - \mu_2/\lambda_2 H_{ii'}^{'sgsn}\right\}$$

$$\left\{1 - \sum_{i \in I}\sum_{i' \in I}(w_{ii'} \vee w_{i'i} \vee \hat{w}_{ii'})\right\}$$

$$+ \sum_{i \in I}\sum_{i' \in I}(w_{ii'} \vee w_{i'i} \vee \hat{w}_{ii'})((1-1/\mu_1)H_{ii'}^{msc} + (1-1/\lambda_1)H_{ii'}^{'msc} + (1-1/\mu_2)H_{ii'}^{sgsn} + (1-1/\lambda_2)H_{ii'}^{'sgsn})$$

(A)

The term $\{1 - \sum_{i \in I}\sum_{i' \in I}(w_{ii'} \vee w_{i'i} \vee \hat{w}_{ii'})\}$ is multiplied in equation (A) to add either the handoff reduction from complex handoff to simple handoff or the handoff reduction from complex handoff to simplest handoff between two NodeBs.

The total cost of the new links in the dual-home network will be

$$LC = \sum_{i \in I}\sum_{j \in J} x_{ij}c_{ij}$$

(B)

The link constraints are

$$x_{ij} + d_{ij} \leq 1$$

The link constraint signifies that there could be at most one link (either an old link or a new link or no link) between *NodeB i* and *RNC j*.

$$\sum_{j \in J} x_{ij} \leq 1$$

The above constraint signifies that *NodeB i* can be assigned to at most one *RNC* using a new link. The capacity constraints can be considered in two ways:

i. Worst case capacity constraints (when the capacity of NodeBs are considered) are

$$\sum_{i \in I} cap_i (x_{ij} + d_{ij}) \leq cap_j''$$

$$\sum_{i \in I} cap_i' (x_{ij} + d_{ij}) \leq cap_j'''$$

ii. Best case capacity constraints (when the capacity utilization of NodeBs are considered) are

$$\sum_{i \in I} f_{ij}^{voice} (x_{ij} + d_{ij}) \leq cap_j''$$

$$\sum_{i \in I} f_{ij}^{data} (x_{ij} + d_{ij}) \leq cap_j'''$$

Therefore the dual-homing problem can be formulated as:

Maximize

$$HC - LC \tag{C}$$

Where

$$t_{ii'j} = d_{ij} x_{i'j} \qquad\qquad i, i' \in I, j \in J, (i \neq i') \tag{1}$$

$$w_{ii'} = \sum_{j \in J} t_{ii'j} \qquad\qquad i \in I, i' \in I \ (i \neq i') \tag{2}$$

$$\hat{t}_{ii'j} = x_{ij} x_{i'j} \qquad\qquad i \in I, i' \in I, j \in J \ (i \neq i') \tag{3}$$

$$\hat{w}_{ii'} = \sum_{j \in J} \hat{t}_{ii'j} \qquad\qquad i \in I, i' \in I \ (i \neq i') \tag{4}$$

$$p_{ijk} = d_{ij} d_{jk}' \qquad\qquad i \in I, j \in J, k \in K \tag{5}$$

$$u_{ik} = \sum_{j \in J} p_{ijk} \qquad\qquad i \in I, k \in K \qquad (6)$$

$$\hat{p}_{ijk} = x_{ij} d'_{jk} \qquad\qquad i \in I, j \in J, k \in K \qquad (7)$$

$$\hat{u}_{ik} = \sum_{j \in J} \hat{p}_{ijk} \qquad\qquad i \in I, k \in K \qquad (8)$$

$$q_{ijl} = d_{ij} d''_{jl} \qquad\qquad i \in I, j \in J, l \in L \qquad (9)$$

$$v_{il} = \sum_{j \in J} q_{ijl} \qquad\qquad i \in I, l \in L \qquad (10)$$

$$\hat{q}_{ijl} = x_{ij} d''_{jl} \qquad\qquad i \in I, j \in J, l \in L \qquad (11)$$

$$\hat{v}_{il} = \sum_{j \in J} \hat{q}_{ijl} \qquad\qquad i \in I, l \in L \qquad (12)$$

Subject to

$$x_{ij} + d_{ij} \leq 1 \qquad\qquad i \in I, j \in J \qquad (1)$$

$$\sum_{j \in J} x_{ij} \leq 1 \qquad\qquad i \in I \qquad (2)$$

$$\sum_{i \in I} cap_i(x_{ij} + d_{ij}) \leq cap''_j \qquad\qquad j \in J \qquad (3)$$

$$\sum_{i \in I} cap'_i(x_{ij} + d_{ij}) \leq cap'''_j \qquad\qquad j \in J \qquad (4)$$

So, here problem is to find the dual homing assignment matrix, $[x_{ij}]_{nxr}$, while maximizing the reduction of total cost given by the expression, (C) subject to the constraints indicated in the equations (1) – (4).

The objective function, formulated above, is not linear and contains boolean operator 'OR' and product of binary variables. The boolean operator 'OR' can be converted to arithmetic addition as follows:

$$X \vee Y = X + Y - XY, \text{ where X and Y are binary variable.}$$

The nonlinear term XY (i.e., the product of two binary variables) can be converted to linear form using additional variable $Z = XY$ (Z is binary too) and by adding the following type of constraints in the above formulation.

$$Z \leq X$$

$$Z \leq Y$$

$$Z \geq X + Y - 1$$

Similarly, product of more than two binary variables can be converted to linear form using additional binary variables and constraints. Thus, the above formulation of the problem can be converted to a 0-1 integer linear programming (ILP) problem. It is obvious from the formulation that an exhaustive enumeration technique for assigning NodeBs in dual homing problem requires checking r^n combinations. So, when the problem size is large, heuristic techniques are suitable to solve such problems [3].

3 Simulated Annealing and Tabu Search Techniques

To solve the NodeB to RNC assignment problem, we have used two meta-heuristic techniques – Simulated Annealing and Tabu Search.

The connectivity between NodeBs and RNCs of the single home network (Fig. 2) and the dual home network (Fig. 3) can be represented as matrices (states) shown in Fig. 6. Each row corresponds to one NodeB and each column corresponds to one RNC. 'x' denotes an old link from NodeB to RNC, '1' denotes a new link from NodeB to RNC.

x	o	o		x	o	o
o	x	o		1	x	o
o	o	x		1	o	x
x	o	o		x	o	o
o	x	o		o	x	o

(a)   (b)

Fig. 6. (a) Single home state (b) Dual home state

Simulated Annealing. In SA we start with an initial solution which is found randomly and is made the current state (say S). Then, in every iteration, a neighbour of the current state is randomly selected. If the acceptance probability of the selected state is greater than some threshold (depending on the costs of the two states and the temperature of the system), the selected state is accepted for further exploration and is made the current state. If the selected state is not accepted, another neighbour is selected randomly. In this way the search continues. All possible combinations of NodeB-to-RNC assignments are generated in this search space. Hence every state can be reached from every other state and the reachability criterion is satisfied.

If the cost C' of the randomly chosen neighbour S' of current state S is less than the cost C of current state S, then the neighbour is selected as the current state for the next iteration. Otherwise, a random number R (0, 1) between 0 and 1 is chosen from a uniform distribution.   If P(C, C', T) > R (0, 1) the neighbour is selected as the next current state. Otherwise, the present current state is propagated to the next iteration as the new state. The acceptance P(C,C',T) is defined by the Boltzmann probability factor as follows:

$$P(C,C',T) = 1 \qquad\qquad\qquad , \text{if } C' < C$$

$$= \exp(-\Delta C/T) \quad \text{where } \Delta C = C' - C , \text{otherwise}$$

The temperate T is updated by using the relation $T = T * \alpha$ after every M iterations, starting with the initial temperature $T = T_0$. The cooling rate is α. the rate at which the temperature decreases $(0 < \alpha < 1)$ and T_0, the initial temperature.

Algorithm SA:

Step 1: (initialization) *iteration_count* = 0, 0<α<1 (cooling_rate), *max_iteration_count*, T, M
Step 2: Find an initial feasible solution S. C = cost of S. Set *best_state* = S, *best_cost* = C.
Step 3: Set S as the current state.
Step 4: (termination) If *iteration_count* > *max_iteration_count* then exit with output node *best_state* and cost *best_cost*.
Step 5: Randomly select a neighbour of state S.
Step 6: Call the selected neighbor state S'. C' = cost of S'.
Step 7: Check if S' is the best solution found so far; if yes, store it as *best_state* and its cost C' as *best_cost*.
Step 8: Generate a random number R between 0 and 1. Compute the acceptance probability as follows:
        P(C,C',T) = 1 if C' < C
                  = exp ((C-C')/T) otherwise
Step 9: if P(C,C',T) > R, select S' to be the next state S and C = cost of S.
Step 10: *iteration_count* = *iteration_count* + 1
Step 11: if *iteration_count* mod M = 0 then T = T * α
Step 12: Goto Step 4.

Tabu Search. This process is somewhat similar to SA. We start with an initial solution which is found randomly. In every iteration of the TS mechanism, we have to find a new solution by making local movements on this current solution. The neighbourhood function is used to find all neighbours of the current state S i.e. the neighbourhood set of S. The next solution state is the best solution among all the possible neighbours of S not in the tabu list.

Algorithm TS:

Step 1: (initialization) *iteration_count* = 0, *max_iteration_count*, N (size of tabu_list)
Step 2: Find an initial feasible solution S from the state space. C=cost of S. Set *best_state* = S, *best_cost* = C.
Step 3: Set S as the current state.
Step 4: (termination) If *iteration_count* > *max_iteration_count* then exit with output node *best_state* and cost *best_cost*.
Step 5: Generate the feasible neighbour set N(S) of the state S.
Step 6: Select the best state from N(S) which is not in the tabu_list. Call this state S'. C' = cost of S'.
Step 7: Check if S' is the best solution found so far; if yes, store it as *best_state* and its cost C' as *best_cost*.
Step 8: Add S' to the tabu_list.
Step 9: Select S' to be the next state S and C= cost of S.
Step 10: *iteration_count* = *iteration_count* + 1
Step 11: Goto Step 4.

Initial Feasible Solution. To generate an initial feasible solution, we take a greedy approach. A NodeB-to-RNC connection is only made if the handoff reduction achieved is greater than the link cost (cost constraint), if the capacity of RNC is sufficient to accommodate the capacity of the NodeB (capacity constraint) and the NodeB is not already dual-homed (link constraint). Since we are designing a dual-homing approach, a NodeB cannot have more than 2 links i.e. a NodeB cannot be connected to more than two RNCs. After connecting a NodeB to a RNC, the capacity of the

RNC is reduced by an amount equal to the capacity of the NodeB. We simply try to connect NodeBs to RNCs one after another in this fashion provided the capacity constraint, cost constraint and link constraint are satisfied for each new connection. This ultimately results in a complete solution after which no more connections are possible. Then the main algorithm sets about improving this initial solution.

For generating the initial solution to our example problem, connections are attempted one after another in a directed manner i.e. in the order 1-to-1, 2-to-1, 3-to-1, 4-to-1, 5-to-1, 6-to-1, 1-to-2, 2-to-2, 3-to-2 and so on. For simplicity and clarity, for solving this problem we consider $\mu_1=\lambda_1=\mu_2=\lambda_2=1$. The initial solution thus generated and the NodeB-NodeB handoff cost after the generation are:

Node B \ RNC	1	2	3
1	X	0	0
2	1	X	0
3	1	0	X
4	X	0	0
5	0	X	0

NodeB \ NodeB	1	2	3	4	5
1	-	-	-	-	9
2	-	-	-	-	-
3	-	-	-	-	-
4	-	-	-	-	-
5	9	-	-	-	-

Total cost of this solution = Single home link cost + Dual home link cost + Handoff cost = (34 + 89) + (105 + 75) + (9 + 9) = 321. Hence cost reduction = Single home cost − dual home cost = 561 − 321 = 240.

Neighbourhood Function. We use the same neighbourhood function for SA and TS. Neighbours of a state S are generated by changing one connection of the state S at a time, thus generating all permutations which differ from S in exactly one NodeB. Neighbourhood generation of one state is shown.

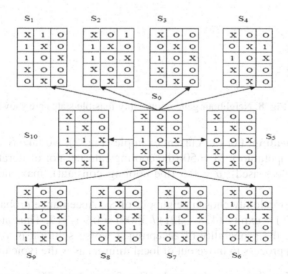

Fig. 7. Neighbour states of S_0

In the example shown in Fig. 7, S_0 is the initial solution which we generated in the previous step. $S_1, S_2 \ldots S_{10}$ are neighbours of the state S_0. Here S_1 and S_2 differ from the parent S_0 at NodeB 1, S_3 and S_4 differ from the parent at NodeB 2 and so on. Hence all pairs of states that differ from each other in exactly one NodeB are neighbours of each other.

All neighbours of a state may not be feasible. Only feasible neighbours of a state at the next level without repetitions are its neighbour. In the context of the current example, referring to Fig. 7, S_3 and S_5 are the only feasible neighbours of S_0. All other neighbours are not feasible.

Example. The initial state (S_0) and its feasible neighbours (S_3, S_5) are shown in Fig. 8.

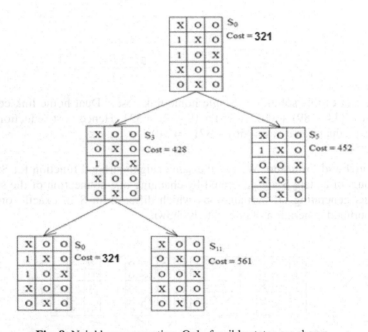

Fig. 8. Neighbour generation. Only feasible states are shown

Simulated Annealing. For our current example (Fig. 2), we take SA parameters $T_0 = 3000$ (initial temperature), $M = 50$ (the cooling rate i.e. no. of iterations after which temperature is decreased), $\alpha = 0.5$ (the cooling constant), max. no. of iterations = 1000.

Let S_3 be the randomly chosen neighbour of S_0. Acceptance probability of the state $S_3 = \exp(-\Delta C/T) = \exp(-(428 - 321)/3000) = 0.964319$. Thus at initial high temperature we see the probability of accepting a worse solution is very high and this helps the search process to move out of local minima as is the typicality of SA.

Tabu Search. For the current example (Fig. 2), we take TS parameters max no. of iterations = 3, $N = 2$ (size of tabu list).

In TS, the initial solution (S_0) is first put into the tabu list.

Of the two feasible neighbours of S_0, the costs are 428 for S_3 and 452 for S_5. Hence the best neighbour of S_0 is S_3, and it is not in the tabu list. It is accepted, made the current state (to be explored next) and entered into the tabu list. The list now contains S_0 and S_3.

S_3	S_0

For the next iteration, there are two feasible neighbours of S_3 viz. S_0 and S_{11}. The costs are 321 for S_0 and 561 for S_{11}. Of these two neighbours, S_0 is already in the tabu list. So the best neighbour not in the tabu list is S_{11}. So S_{11} is put into the list and S_0 is expelled from the list. So the tabu list now contains S_3 and S_{11}.

S_{11}	S_3

S_{11} is then made the current state and search continues in this way.

4 Results and Discussion

We divide a rectangular area into multiple hexagonal NodeBs created using a non orthogonal Cartesian system inclined at 60^0. Each NodeB has exactly six neighbouring NodeBs except the boundary NodeBs that have less than six neighbouring NodeBs. A specified set of RNCs and MSCs are placed randomly in some NodeBs such that an MSC is co-located with an RNC. Subsequently, NodeBs are assigned to RNCs, and RNCs are assigned to MSCs using nearest neighbour distance.

After the creation of the above synthetic 3G single home network architecture, a set of MTs (mobile terminals) are randomly placed inside the NodeBs. From the random movement of the MTs, the number of handoffs for neighbouring NodeBs and the handoff types are recorded. The handoff costs for neighbouring NodeBs are generated by multiplying the number of handoffs obtained from the movement of MTs and cost per handoff depending on the type of handoff. Amortized costs for links from NodeB to RNC and RNC to MSC are taken proportional to the physical distances. Spare capacities of RNCs and capacities of NodeBs of the network are generated from a uniform distribution.

Algorithms SA and TS are run on 100 instances of single home network, and average solution cost is recorded against the RNC-NodeB pair (RNCs, NodeBs). Fig. 9 compares the algorithms with respect to average solution costs. For each dual-homed architecture solution, the reduction in simple/complex handoff cost for the network is calculated, considering the cost of amortized link (NodeB to RNC), subject to the capacity constraints of the RNCs. Average solution costs obtained by SA and TS as percentage of initial cost (the cost of single home network) is indicated in Fig. 9. Fig. 10 shows that the saving is more when the network size increases.

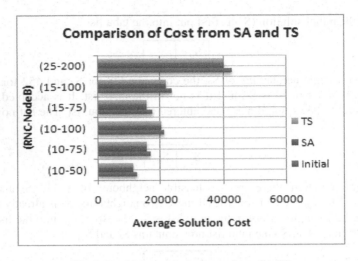

Fig. 9. Dual-home solution costs from SA,TS

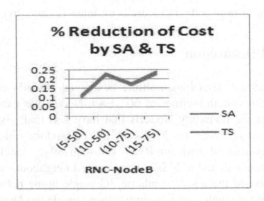

Fig. 10. Percentage Reduction of Cost from SA & TS

5 Conclusion

Dual-homing of NodeBs reduces the handoff cost but additional capacities are required in RNCs. We have formulated the problem as a combinatorial optimization problem. We have generated the handoff cost using random walk model. The dual homing problems are solved using SA and TS meta-heuristic search techniques. It is found that TS technique is capable of finding better solution in this domain.

References

1. Din, D.-R., Tseng, S.S.: A genetic algorithm for solving dual-homing cell assignment problem of the two-level wireless ATM network. Computer Communications 25, 1536–1547 (2005)

2. Demrikol, I., Ersoy, C., Caglayan, M.U., Delic, H.: Location Area Planning in Cellular Networks Using Simulated Annealing. In: Proc. IEEE INFOCOM (2001)
3. Pearl, J.: Heuristics: Intelligent search strategies for computer problem solving. Addison-Wesley, Reading (1984)
4. Saha, D., Mukherjee, A., Bhattacharya, P.S.: A Simple Heuristic for Assignment of Cells to Switches in a PCS Network. In: Proc. Wireless Personal Communications, pp. 209–224 (2000)
5. Bhattacharjee, P.S., Saha, D., Mukherjee, A.: An Approach for Location Area Planning in a Personal Communication Services Network (PCSN). IEEE Trans. on Wireless Communication (2004)
6. Mandal, S., Saha, D., Mahanti, A.: Heuristic Search Techniques for Cell to Switch Assignment in Location Area Planning for Cellular Networks. In: Proc. IEEE International Conference on Communications (ICC), pp. 4307–4311 (2004)
7. Transl. J. Magn. Japan, vol. 2, pp. 740–741 (August 1987); [Digests 9th Annual Conf. Magnetics Japan, p. 301, 1982]
8. Young, M.: The Technical Writer's Handbook. University Science, Mill Valley (1989)
9. Sadhukhan, S.K., Mandal, S., Saha, D.: A Heuristic Techneque for Solving Dual-homing Assignment Problem of 2.5G Cellular Networks. In: Proc. IEEE ICCTA, Kolkata, India, pp. 66–71 (2007)
10. Sadhukhan, S.K., Mandal, S., Biswas, S.R., Bhaumik, P., Saha, D.: Post-deployment Tuning of UMTS Cellular Networks through Dual-homing of RNCs. In: Proc. IEEE COMS-NETS 2009, Bangalore, India (January 2009)

K-Directory Community: Reliable Service Discovery in MANET

Vaskar Raychoudhury[1], Jiannong Cao[1], Weigang Wu[2], Yi Lai[1], Canfeng Chen[3], and Jian Ma[3]

[1] Department of Computing, The Hong Kong Polytechnic University, Kowloon, Hong Kong
[2] Department of Computer Science, Sun Yat-sen University, Guangzhou, 510275, China
[3] Nokia Research Center, Beijing, China
{csvray,csjcao,csylai}@comp.polyu.edu.hk,
wuweig@mail.sysu.edu.cn,
Canfeng-david.chen@nokia.com, Jian.j.ma@nokia.com

Abstract. Service discovery in MANET suffers from frequent service un-availability due to failures of service providers or directory nodes. Ensuring network-wide service availability by replication requires minimizing costs associated with storage, update and discovery. Existing works in MANET have not addressed these challenging issues adequately. In this paper, we propose a distributed directory-based service discovery protocol (SDP) for MANET. Our protocol works by electing top K nodes with rich resources as directories, which are then divided into multiple quorums. Services registered with a directory are replicated among its quorum members. This approach reduces replication and update costs, and guarantees network-wide service availability using the quorum intersection property. An incremental election policy is adopted to cope with directory failures. We have carried out extensive simulations and also developed a prototype system. Our performance evaluation results show that, compared with similar work, our protocol significantly reduces message cost and improves system robustness.

1 Introduction

Service discovery in MANET has remained an interesting research problem for years. Existing service discovery solutions for MANET adopt either directory-based [1, 2, 3, 4] or directory-less [5, 6, 7] methods. Current research works address several challenging issues, such as, building proper infrastructure to reduce discovery delay and boost discovery success, and providing support for enhancing scalability [3]. But the service availability issue has been largely ignored.

Service unavailability can arise out of many possible failure situations. Simple service failure is easy to address by requiring users to discover new services. But, directory failures are rather complicated to handle as it renders all services registered with the failed directory unavailable. So, services registered with a failed directory must re-register with other available directories in order to publish themselves. Service availability is also hampered by limitation of discovery scopes. All the above problems

K. Kant et al. (Eds.): ICDCN 2010, LNCS 5935, pp. 420–433, 2010.

become more challenging due to the dynamic and resource-constrained nature of MANET and the existing solutions do not cope well.

In order to ensure network-wide service availability, a directory based solution appears to be more suitable than a directory-less one, as the later uses expensive message broadcast and lacks robustness. Also, to enhance availability, we need to replicate service information among multiple directory nodes. Wide-spread replication can waste scarce system resources and increase update cost. So, it is crucial to arrive at a message-efficient solution which can support availability at minimum extra cost.

To address the above challenges, we propose a distributed directory-based service discovery protocol for MANET. Our proposed protocol is fault tolerant and message-efficient. We select top K nodes, among all the nodes in the network, as directories, considering relatively higher resource content. Together, we call the K directory nodes as *directory community*, as they work collaboratively to enhance robustness by increasing service availability in the system. The directory nodes then form quorums among themselves. We replicate a service with the quorum members of a directory, which ensures network-wide service availability with minimal replication. Following the quorum intersection property, we can guarantee that if a service matching user request is available, the user can certainly find the service by forwarding a request only to its quorum members. This reduces service discovery cost. The message overhead is further checked by dividing the network into one or more tree-structured domains, thereby eliminating loops, and also by restricting broadcast and flooding. We also consider directory failure, where, a failed directory is one which either crashes or becomes unfit of hosting services due to resource dissipation. We handle directory failure by an incremental directory election approach. The primary contributions of this paper are:

- We have presented a fault tolerant SDP for mobile ad hoc networks which operates using a community of K directory nodes. Our protocol ensures service availability by replicating services among directory quorums formed by the members of the directory community.
- We have carried out extensive simulations to evaluate the performance of our proposed protocol, and we present our results with in-depth analysis. Our results show that our protocol is scalable and fault-tolerant. Also, it can guarantee service availability with low message overhead.
- We have also implemented our protocol on a wireless testbed system. The experimental results obtained are found to be in congruence with the simulation results.

The rest of the paper is organized as follows. Section 2 reviews existing service discovery protocols for MANET and how they address the availability issue. In Section 3, we present the system model and some preliminary operations required for our protocol, including directory election and quorum construction methods. We describe our proposed protocol in Section 4, which covers mechanisms for infrastructure maintenance and detailed service discovery operations. We report simulation results in Section 5 and describe our testbed system and testing results in Section 6. Finally, Section 7 concludes this paper with directions of our future works.

2 Related Work

Existing service discovery protocols for MANET can be classified into directory-less and directory based SDPs.

Directory-less SDPs adopts mainly three different approaches. The first approach is service information flooding which is costly and hence unsuitable for resource-poor MANET environments. The second approach works by building DHT-based P2P overlay for MANET. There are several MANET-oriented DHT systems, such as, Ekta [5], MADPastry [6], and CrossROAD [7]. However, DHT-based systems for service discovery fail to ensure availability in MANET as they construct a DHT substrate without taking into account the actual physical distance between nodes. This can cause undesirably long search latency and deterioration of success ratio of service discovery with the growing network scale. The third and final approach for directory-less service discovery works by generating service hierarchy [8, 9] which is quite costly.

To cope with the problems of directory-less solutions, directory based SDPs have been proposed for MANET [1, 2, 3, 4]. The general approach is to develop a virtual backbone and to disseminate service advertisements and discovery requests using the backbone. The protocol in [1] forms a backbone of directory nodes in the network layer in order to use the same backbone for both service discovery and routing. But this protocol is very costly as they require maintaining two different overlay structures. Tyan et al. [2] improved the protocol in [1] by making use of a location-aware routing protocol, where the network is divided into hexagonal grids, each having a gateway. The connected overlay of gateways forms a virtual backbone. However, tracking and handling gateway mobility proves to be very costly. Another similar approach has been proposed by Sailhan et. al. [3]. Their objective is to achieve scalability in a hybrid network by minimizing traffic and compressing directory profile. The authors did not consider resource-constrain or node failure during service discovery, and hence, can not guarantee service availability. Kim et. al. [4] proposed a volunteer node based SDP for MANET where volunteers are relatively stable and resource rich nodes and form an overlay structure. The volunteers in fact act as directory nodes. This approach, though similar to our work, has a couple of limitations. Firstly, the overlay may develop loops and cycles, which may increase service discovery cost. Secondly, the volunteer advertisement broadcast can significantly increase the traffic.

3 System Model and Preliminaries

In this section we introduce our system model and the assumptions and describe some preliminary tasks that are required for our service discovery protocol to work on.

3.1 System Model

We consider service discovery in a MANET that consists of a set of n (n>1) mobile nodes, each of which has a unique ID. Each node provides one or more services to others and can seek for services from others. Whether two nodes are neighbors, i.e. they are directly connected, is determined by the signal coverage range and the distance between the nodes. A node may fail by crashing, but it acts correctly until it possibly crashes. Nodes that exit the environment are also considered as failed. A node only knows the IDs of its neighboring nodes. Each node has a weight associated with it. The weight of a node indicates its ability to serve as a directory node and can be any performance related attribute such as the node's battery power, computational capabilities etc. Two nodes may have the same weight value in which case the node with higher id is selected over the other.

3.2 Preliminaries

As mentioned previously, our service discovery protocol works using a quorum of directory nodes carefully chosen considering their available resources. To realize this objective, we first select directory nodes using a K directory election algorithm for MANET. The elected K directories then execute a quorum generation algorithm to form directory quorums. Below we briefly describe the related mechanisms.

- **K Directory Election:** Mobile wireless networks consist of limited-resource devices. In order to ensure higher life time and processing capability of the elected directory nodes we focus on electing top K nodes based on weight which is an abstract property and can be used to refer to any required attribute of a node, e.g. remaining battery life, memory size, processing capacity, etc. To achieve this objective, we make use of our previously proposed weighted top K leader election algorithm [10] to select K directory nodes with higher resource and lower mobility. The algorithm operates in three phases. We first select some coordinator nodes (named RED nodes) with highest weight among their 2-hop neighbors. Those RED nodes then start diffusing computations [11] to collaboratively collect the weight values of all the nodes in the environment to choose top K weighted nodes as K directories. Each directory then executes a quorum generation algorithm described below and constructs its own quorum.

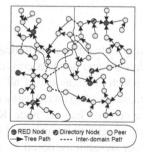

RED Node ● Directory Node ○ Peer
→ Tree Path ---- Inter-domain Path

K0: {0, 1, 2, 3, 6, 9, 12},	K12: {12, 13, 14, 15, 18, 21, 24},
K1: {1, 2, 3, 4, 7, 10, 13},	K13: {13, 14, 15, 16, 19, 22, 0},
K2: {2, 3, 4, 5, 8, 11, 14},	K14: {14, 15, 16, 17, 20, 23, 1},
K3: {3, 4, 5, 6, 9, 12, 15},	K15: {15, 16, 17, 18, 21, 24, 2},
K4: {4, 5, 6, 7, 10, 13, 16},	K16: {16, 17, 18, 19, 22, 0, 3},
K5: {5, 6, 7, 8, 11, 14, 17},	K17: {17, 18, 19, 20, 23, 1, 4},
K6: {6, 7, 8, 9, 12, 15, 18},	K18: {18, 19, 20, 21, 24, 2, 5},
K7: {7, 8, 9, 10, 13, 16, 19},	K19: {19, 20, 21, 22, 0, 3, 6},
K8: {8, 9, 10, 11, 14, 17, 20},	K20: {20, 21, 22, 23, 1, 4, 7},
K9: {9, 10, 11, 12, 15, 18, 21},	K21: {21, 22, 23, 24, 2, 5, 8},
K10: {10, 11, 12, 13, 16, 19, 22},	K22: {22, 23, 24, 0, 3, 6, 9},
K11: {11, 12, 13, 14, 17, 20, 23},	K23: {23, 24, 0, 1, 4, 7, 10},
K24: {24, 0, 1, 2, 5, 8, 11}.	

Fig. 1. Service Discovery Architecture   **Fig. 2.** An Example Directory Quorum

- **Construction of Directory Quorum:** In our protocol, the quorum is constructed following the method proposed by Lin et al. [12]. We choose their method because of several advantages. Firstly, the quorums are symmetric, i.e. each node is included in the same number of quorums and all the quorums have the same number of nodes. This will ensure even load distribution among the directory nodes. Secondly, this method allows flexibility in quorum size with respect to the number of directories. Finally, the method allows generation of multiple quorums for each node (based on multiple generating sets) to enhance the availability of the quorum system. Fig. 3 presents the pseudo code of the quorum generation algorithm given by [12]. From equation (i) in the Q_Gen $Algorithm$ in Fig. 3, there can be more than one quorum generation set for a given m. Lin et. al. [12] has proved that the size of quorums can be smallest when m equals $\sqrt{[(K+1)/2]}$. Let us consider an example with 25 directory nodes $\{K_0, K_1,..., K_{24}\}$, so that, $K = 25$, $m = 4$, $c = 7$ and $\tau = 4$. Some of the possible quorum generation sets formed with the given values are: $\{\{0, 1, 2, 3, 4, 8, 12\}, \{0, 1, 2, 3, 5, 9, 12\}, \{0, 1, 2, 3, 6, 9, 12\}, \{0, 1, 2, 3, 6, 9, 13\},...\}$. We construct the quorums with the quorum generation set $\{0, 1, 2, 3, 5, 9, 12\}$ as shown in Fig. 2. One can see that any two quorums have a nonempty intersection. If the number of directories $K = n^2$ for some n, the size of quorums generated by the above described quorum construction method is $\approx (3n)/2$, for $m = n$. This quorum size is comparatively smaller than many other available schemes and that is why we chose this method for quorum generation over the others. For every directory node we generate a quorum of smallest size.

/******************Q_Gen $Algorithm$*****************************/
(2A) Var: c, τ, m, w, i, K
(2B) $c \leftarrow \lceil \frac{K}{m} \rceil, \tau \leftarrow \lceil \frac{K+1}{2m} \rceil, 1 \leq m \leq K;$

(2C) Quorum generation set
$Q_g = \{0, 1, ..., m-1, w_1, w_2, ..., w_{\tau-1}\}$ .... (i)
where, $m-1 \leq w_1 \leq 2m-1$, $0 < w_{i+1} - w_i \leq m$ for all $1 \leq i \leq \tau-2$, and $w_{\tau-1} \geq (K-1)/2$

Fig. 3. Pseudo code for the Construction of Directory Quorums

4   The Proposed Service Discovery Protocol

After the preliminary operations have been completed, every domain root periodically collects information about the directories present in its domain and sends a common directory advertisement message (ADV_{dd}) to other nodes which contains list of all the domain directories. To avoid broadcast, directory advertisements are distributed using the domain tree. A node receiving ADV_{dd} caches it and finds the nearest directory node. Key to the efficient functioning of our protocol is the proper and timely maintenance of the domain trees and the directory quorums in the face of sheer dynamicity posed by the mobile ad hoc networks. In this section we shall describe our protocol in detail. Initially in sub-section 4.1, we give a brief description of the data structures and message types used in our protocol. Sub-section 4.2, describes our policies for maintaining directory quorums and domain trees together known as infrastructure maintenance. Sub-section 4.3, elaborates methods for service registration and service information replication followed by sub-section 4.4, which presents the mechanisms for service request and reply.

4.1 Data Structures and Message Types

While executing our protocol, each node i maintains necessary information about its state in the data structures listed in Table 1 and exchange messages listed in Table 2.

Table 1. Data Structures

Variable	Meaning
id_i	Identifier of node i
wt_i	Weight of node i
wt_sent_i	Binary variable indicating whether node i has informed its weight to the elector or not
$root$	Identifier of domain root node
$pred_i$	Predecessor of i in the diffusion tree
$succ_i$	Successors of i in the diffusion tree
new_wt	Set of new nodes joining the network and their weights maintained by the domain root
Dir_List	Set of domain directories known to the domain root
LDR	Set of K directories and their weights maintained by the elector

Table 2. Message types

Message	Purpose
ADV_{dd} (root, pred, Dir_List, new_wt)	Domain directory advertisement by domain root to its successors and the elector. Parameter new_wt is optional. Only when a new node joins the network, its weight is sent to elector.
Dom_Dir_HB (wt_i)	Heart-beat message by a domain directory to the domain root upon receiving an ADV_{dd}. The weight value is sent to check whether the directory node is still capable of hosting services.
ATTACH_REQ	A disconnected or newly joined node broadcasts a request to join a domain tree
REP	A node replies upon receiving an ATTACH_REQ
ATTACH(i)	Node i requests to attach to the node which first sends a REP
ACK(i,wt_i)	A newly joined node sends its weight to the domain root, upon receiving a ADV_{dd}
LEADER (LDR)	For the elector to announce the new set of K leaders to all other nodes

4.2 Maintenance of Service Discovery Infrastructure

Maintenance of service discovery infrastructure is crucial for our service discovery protocol. Below we discuss separately the procedures of maintaining domain tree structures and the directory quorums in presence of node mobility and arbitrary topological changes.

Domain Tree Maintenance. To maintain the domain tree structure we need to handle the following events that may happen mainly due to the node mobility:

1. **A node leaves current domain:** When a node leaves the domain the domain tree gets disconnected and the successors of the departing node have no parent. To avoid this condition, it is important to detect such a scenario and handle it, in order to keep the domain tree connected. In our protocol, every node periodically checks its connectivity with its parent (*pred*) in the tree. If node i loses connection with parent j, node i broadcasts an *ATTACH_REQ* to all nodes within its wireless transmission range. Any node n receiving an *ATTACH_REQ* replies with a *REP* and starts a timer. When node i receives the first REP, it sends an *ATTACH* to the sender and ignores the other *REP*s. When node n receives an *ATTACH* from node i, it adds i in the successor set and forwards the next incoming ADV_{dd} to it along with other successors.

2. **A node joins a new domain:** A node can join a domain either as a node which freshly joins the network or as a node which migrates from another domain. In either case, the node assumes that it has no parent and it follows the steps mentioned in (1) in order to join a domain tree.

3. **A directory node leaves current domain:** Directory nodes periodically send *Dom_Dir_HB* to the domain root. When the domain root receives *Dom_Dir_HB* messages it updates the list of available domain directories in order to reflect joining of new directories to the domain and leaving of old directories from the domain. In case, the weight of a directory falls below some threshold, the domain root informs the elector to replace it considering failed. Also the domain tree is updated to keep it connected when a directory node leaves the current domain. When a directory node joins a different domain following step (2) it will send the heart-beat message to the new domain root upon receiving the ADV_{dd}.

4. **A domain root leaves current domain:** This problem is tackled by using a backup node for the domain root. Every root node selects a comparatively high resource node as the backup root. The backup root node will monitor the root node and in case the later fails or migrates out of the current domain, the backup node can take over as the root node. If the domain root joins a different domain, it follows step (2).

Directory Quorum Maintenance. Maintaining the directory quorum structure is critical to satisfy the quorum intersection property which assumes that quorum nodes are stable and always available. Unless a failed quorum node is replaced readily, service lookup may fail. In order to ensure higher availability of quorum members, we propose an incremental directory election approach.

After a newly joined node attaches to some domain, it receives a ADV_{dd} from the domain root, and sends an *ACK(id, wt)* message to the root informing its id and weight value. Domain roots periodically update the elector about the newly joined nodes, so that, the elector always maintains a list of all the nodes currently available in the network. Once a node has sent its weight value to the elector, it does not need to do such operation any more even if it migrates across domains. But, a node must update its weight to the domain root if its weight changes from the initial value. In case, the existing directories become unavailable, the elector chooses from other suitable nodes to replace for unavailable directories and sends *LEADER* messages to each directories informing about the changes. After a new directory takes charge for an old directory, it will contact its quorum members and register services maintained by them. It will also send heart beat to its current domain root, so that the domain root includes it as a domain directory in the next ADV_{dd} message.

4.3 Service Registration

Service providers register only with functional information. Detailed service context (Fig. 4) is forwarded to the user on request. When a service provider ($\mathcal{P}$) wants to register a service (S), he registers with the nearest directory, called the *publishing host* (*PH*). Similarly, for a user looking for a service, the nearest directory with which he may register is called the *lookup host* (*LH*).

Service Identification: *Type (generic service class), Name, Description, Alias, Version number*
Service Functionality: *Specific functionalities provided by a service instance*
Service Attributes: *Cost, Time (time of service availability or validity), Security features, Provider's address (IP, URL, etc.), Make, Special attributes (color or B&W for a printer)*
Service Requirements: *Computational (CPU power), Storage (Memory size), Energy (remaining battery life), Display (screen size), Others (e.g., audio, input/output, software, etc.)*

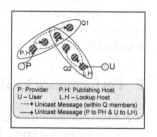

P: Provider   P.H: Publishing Host
U – User   L.H – Lookup Host
---→ Unicast Message (within Q members)
——→ Unicast Message (P to PH & U to LH)

Fig. 4. Service Context Information

Fig. 5. Quorum-based Service Matching Process

After receiving the registration request from $\mathcal{P}$, the *PH* registers the service locally and forwards the request to its quorum members. After the service has been registered at all the quorum members, *PH* receives an acknowledgement from each of them and then it sends an acknowledgement back to $\mathcal{P}$ informing $\mathcal{P}$ about the other directory nodes to which service S has been registered.

The service registration is updated using a lease-based approach. Each registration is associated with a lease. The service provider $\mathcal{P}$ needs to renew its lease with the *PH* before timeout. Failing to do so, due to unavailability of either $\mathcal{P}$ or *PH*, will prompt the *PH* to delete the service information and to inform its quorum members to follow suit. In case of any change made to S, $\mathcal{P}$ informs the *PH* about the new version number. *PH* makes the change and updates its quorum members in order to maintain consistency. If the *PH* is unavailable, $\mathcal{P}$ can try to contact other quorum members of *PH* - nearest to it - with whom it can renew the lease. This ensures the availability of S even if the *PH* fails. If S is updated in the mean time, to a higher version, its replicas will not be updated accordingly. So, if a user discovers S, he will ask $\mathcal{P}$ for the copy with the highest version number. When *PH* fails, $\mathcal{P}$ registers with a new *PH*, either from its cache, or by sending a directory request, to the neighboring domain.

4.4 Service Request/Reply

When a user (U) is interested to discover a particular service S, he sends a discovery request to its lookup host (*LH*). After *LH* receives a user request, it checks its own registration information for a matching service and if available, it replies the user with the identity of the service provider, $\mathcal{P}$. LH also forwards the discovery request to its quorum members which can directly reply to U if a matching service is found. After U receives a reply, it checks the functional information and contacts the provider to receive complete service context information. Unused service replies are cached for possible future needs.

To illustrate the quorum based service discovery approach, we use the following example. Let us consider that, the service provider $\mathcal{P}$ has registered the service S with its publishing host, say $\mathcal{K}_{11}$, (Figure 2) which has replicated the service to its quorum (Q_{11}), i.e., $\{\mathcal{K}_{12}, \mathcal{K}_{13}, \mathcal{K}_{14}, \mathcal{K}_{17}, \mathcal{K}_{20}, \mathcal{K}_{23}\}$. Now when U sends a service discovery request to its lookup host, say $\mathcal{K}_{23}$, it then forwards the request to its quorum Q_{23}, i.e. $\{\mathcal{K}_{24}, \mathcal{K}_{0}, \mathcal{K}_{1}, \mathcal{K}_{4}, \mathcal{K}_{7}, \mathcal{K}_{10}\}$. Since, $Q_{11} \cap Q_{23} = \{\mathcal{K}_{23}\}$, $\mathcal{K}_{23}$ can match U's discovery request with $\mathcal{P}$'s advertisement.

Following the quorum intersection property, we can guarantee that, using our service discovery approach, if a service requested by a user is available, it must be matched by the user's lookup host or its quorum members.

5 Performance Evaluation

We have carried out extensive simulations to evaluate the performance of our proposed protocol. To prove the efficiency of our protocol, we have chosen to compare with the volunteer node based service discovery protocol presented in [4]. We generally follow the simulation settings from [4] for easy comparison. The time to live (TTL) values for the volunteer advertisement (TTL_{max_a}) and the service request (TTL_r) messages are fixed at 3 and 2, respectively to obtain the best performance of their protocol. Moreover, for the optimal performance, every client belongs to a maximum of 2 volunteer regions and each volunteer advertises themselves once every simulation minute. Rest of the simulation parameters are same for both the protocols and are listed in Table 3.

Table 3. Simulation Parameters

Parameters	Values			
Number of nodes, (N)	50	100	150	200
Territory scale (m^2)	700	1000	1200	1400
Number of service types (n_s)	20	40	60	80
K/n	25%			
Transmission radius	250 m			
Routing-protocol	Least hops			
Node failure rate (F_R)	10%, 20%, 30%, 40%, 50%			
Mobility Model	Random Waypoint			
Max. node speed (V_{max})	5m/s, 10m/s, 20m/s			
Min. node speed (V_{min})	5 m/s			
Pause time (milli-seconds)	10			

5.1 Simulation Setup and Metrics

The simulation system consists of two modules: the network backbone consisting of domain trees and directory quorums and the service discovery protocol. The network nodes are randomly scattered in a square territory. The total number of nodes is varied to examine the effect of system scale on the performance. To make the performance results in different scenarios comparable, we also scale the territory size according to the total number of nodes. For message routing, we have implemented a simple protocol based on the "least hops" policy. A routing table is proactively maintained at each node. Directory advertisement and service request intervals are set at once and twice, respectively, at every simulation minute.

The directory election and quorum formation are carried out prior to the service discovery operations. Later, directory nodes are incrementally added to replace failed directories. The weight values of the nodes are assigned randomly. In case of node failures, the faulty nodes are randomly selected and a faulty node crashes in a randomly chosen time. The failure detection part is simulated based on the heartbeat-like approach.

In the simulations, we measure the performance of both the protocols using the following metrics:

- *NM (Number of Messages):* The total number of "end-to-end" messages exchanged in our protocol for directory election, quorum formation and backbone maintenance. Such a message may be forwarded by several intermediate nodes in the network level.
- *NH (Number of Hops):* The total number of hops corresponding to the messages exchanged where one "hop" means one network layer message. Compared with NM, NH can reflect the message cost more precisely.
- *HR (Hit Ratio):* The ratio of the total number of successful discovery requests to the total number of discovery requests.
- *TD (Time Delay):* This is the average delay between the time any successful request is sent from a client and the time corresponding reply is received by the same client.

We assume that, every node is a service provider that provides a service of a certain type. A service type is assigned to each node in a round robin fashion. Therefore, with high n_s, service density ($d_s = N/n_s$ average number of service providers providing a same type of service) is low and vice versa.

5.2 Simulation Results and Analysis

Below we present our simulation results with analysis. We have simulated our protocol, labeled as "Q-SDP" and the volunteer-based SDP [4] labeled as "V-SDP". We run each simulation for 20 simulation minutes and each point is obtained by averaging over 10 different runs. We first report the performance with varied node mobility and then we discuss the effect node failure rates on the performance.

Effect of Node Mobility

In Fig. 6(a)-(d), we present the performance results of our protocol by varying V_{max} from 5m/s to 20m/s and keeping the node departure rate at 20%. We plot the results for V_{max} at 5 and 20m/s and omit the results for 10m/s which follow the same trends.

From Fig. 6(a) and (b) we observe that NM and NH increases with N for both "V-SDP" and "Q-SDP" where "V-SDP" always incurs more messages than "Q-SDP". This is because, while "Q-SDP" disseminates messages using a tree, "V-SDP" broadcasts volunteer advertisements. Moreover, at higher node speeds and with node failures, volunteer nodes in "V-SDP" may fail or can migrate away, in which case, the service requesters may not have any volunteer in range and they search for volunteer nodes using broadcast. This further increases NM and NH for "V-SDP".

From Fig. 6(c) we can see that increase in TD with N is faster for "V-SDP" than "Q-SDP". This is due to the fact that with node mobility and node departure or failure, volunteer nodes are scarce and the delay in discovering service becomes higher as the volunteer nodes decrease in number. Searching for new volunteer nodes significantly increases TD for "V-SDP". We, on the other hand, reduce much of TD by choosing nearest directory as *LH* or *PH* and forwarding discovery requests using the domain tree.

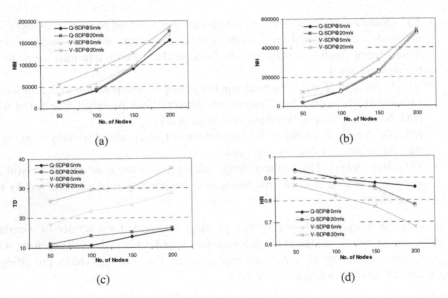

Fig. 6. (a). NM versus N. (b). NH versus N. (c). TD versus N. (d). HR versus N.

From Fig. 6(d) we observe that HR decreases with N more for "V-SDP" than "Q-SDP". This is because, with a failure rate (F_R) of 20%, the service density (d_s) in the network decreases rapidly, so the HR for "V-SDP" also decreases quickly in absence of matching services. "Q-SDP", however, can guarantee service availability as long as a single matching service exists in the network.

Effect of Node Failure

In Fig. 7(a)-(d), we present the performance results of our protocol by varying the node failure rate (F_R) from 10% to 50% for 100 nodes and keeping the V_{max} at 20m/s.

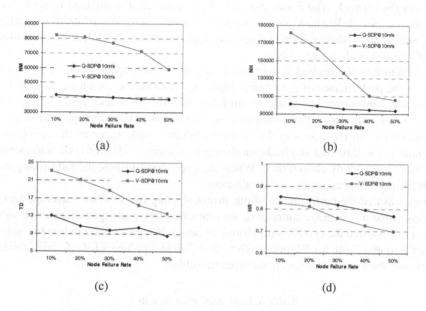

Fig. 7. (a). NM versus F_R (b). NH versus F_R (c). TD versus F_R (d). HR versus F_R

From the performance graphs we can observe that all the performance metrics decreases with increased F_R. This is straightforward, because with increase in F_R, N decreases, so NM, NH and TD also decrease. With high F_R, service density in the system decreases rapidly, so the HR also decreases as matching services may not be found. We can see that our protocol performs better than "V-SDP" under different failure rates. So, our protocol proves to be more robust under high node failure rates and higher node mobility.

6 Implementation of a Prototype System

To further demonstrate the feasibility of our protocol in real applications, we implement it on a sensor network testbed. The testbed contains 20 MicaZ [13] sensor nodes running TinyOS and a MIB600 gateway and is distributed over a single floor of the Mong Man Wai building, The Hong Kong Polytechnic University.

In order to make our system more flexible, we implement three major components. On the bottom, we have an end-to-end routing layer which is responsible for message delivery between nodes in the network. Above the routing layer, we have a quorum layer. It uses the send/receive interface provided by the routing layer to exchange messages between the quorum members. On the top layer, we have the service module.

It uses the update and read interface provided by the quorum layer to allow the clients to register services. We assign random numbers to different sensor nodes as weights. Total number of directories is K where we choose K as $\lceil N/4 \rceil$, N being total number of nodes in the network. The nodes are considered static as it is difficult to make them mobile in a testbed. We have also implemented node failure. We arbitrarily switch off some sensor nodes during service discovery and consider them failed. We considered maximum node failure rate of 10%.

In addition to the testbed system itself, we also have a special node employed to monitor the performance of the system. Initially, when the execution starts, each node undergoes a bootstrapping phase to initialize the variables and chooses a random weight value. After that, the monitoring node broadcasts the topology and directory information to all the nodes in the network. When a node receives the topology, it populates its neighbor list and finds out the nearest directory. Then a node starts service discovery at randomly chosen time. When the execution finishes, the monitoring node sends the performance results to the computer.

We measured the performance of our protocol using two metrics – average service response time and average number of service discovery messages transmitted in the network. We tested the system with 10 and 20 nodes. We generated random topologies. The experiment is run for 10 times each with different topologies for a fixed number of nodes, and the average values are reported in Table 4.

Table 4. Implementation Results

Performance Metrics	Values (N=10)	Values (N=20)
Average hit ratio	100%	96.5%
Average service response time (ms)	12	37
Average number of messages sent for each sensor node	1	1

The results are in congruence with our simulation results and show that the success rate of service discovery is very high and the discovery time is low. Since the average number of service discovery messages sent by each node is 1 at most, we can logically conclude that our protocol can minimize the energy spent by sensor nodes.

7   Conclusion and Future Work

In this paper, we propose a distributed directory-based fault tolerant service discovery protocol for mobile ad hoc networks. Initially, nodes with higher resource and lower mobility are elected as directories. The directory nodes then form quorums and replicate services among the quorum members in order to enhance service availability. Quorum intersection property is used for network-wide service availability with low message overhead. To tolerate the failure of directory nodes, an incremental directory election approach has been adopted. Besides extensive simulations we also have implemented our protocol on a testbed of wireless sensor nodes. The simulation and experiment results show that our protocol increases service availability and system robustness even with a high rate of node failure. In future we want to carry out more experiments on a testbed consisting of handheld devices to evaluate the applicability of our protocol in a dynamic mobility environment.

Acknowledgments. This work is partially supported by Hong Kong RGC under GRF PolyU 5102/06E, Nokia University Collaboration Grant H-ZG19, and China National 973 program under the grant 2009CB320702.

References

1. Kozat, U.C., Tassiulas, L.: Service discovery in mobile ad hoc networks: an overall perspective on architectural choices and network layer support issues. Ad Hoc Networks 2(1), 23–44 (2004)
2. Tyan, J., Mahmoud, Q.H.: A Comprehensive Service Discovery Solution for Mobile Ad Hoc Networks. ACM/Kluwer Journal of Mobile Networks and Applications (MONET) 10(8), 423–434 (2005)
3. Sailhan, F., Issarny, V.: Scalable Service Discovery for MANET. In: Proc. IEEE PerCom, pp. 235–246 (2005)
4. Kim, M.J., Kumar, M., Shirazi, B.A.: Service Discovery Using Volunteer Nodes in Heterogeneous Pervasive Computing Environments. J. Pervasive and Mobile Computing 2, 313–343 (2006)
5. Pucha, H., Das, S., Hu, Y.: Ekta: An efficient DHT substrate for distributed applications in mobile ad hoc networks. In: Proc. 6th IEEE Workshop on Mobile Computing Systems and Applications, WMCSA (2004)
6. Zahn, T., Schiller, J.: MADPastry: A DHT substrate for practically sized MANETs. In: Proc. 5th Workshop on Applications and Services in Wireless Networks, ASWN (2005)
7. Delmastro, F.: From Pastry to CrossROAD: Cross-layer ring overlay for ad hoc networks. In: Proc. 3rd IEEE International Conference on Pervasive Computing and Communications Workshops, pp. 60–64 (2005)
8. Helal, S., Desai, N., Verma, V., Lee, C.: Konark—A Service Discovery and Delivery Protocol for Ad Hoc Networks. In: Proc. IEEE WCNC, pp. 2107–2113 (2003)
9. Chakraborty, D., Joshi, A., Finin, T., Yesha, Y.: Towards Distributed Service Discovery in Pervasive Computing Environments. IEEE Transactions on Mobile Computing (July 2004)
10. Raychoudhury, V., Cao, J., Wu, W.: Top K-leader Election in Wireless Ad Hoc Networks. In: ICCCN 2008 (2008)
11. Dijkstra, E.W., Scholten, C.S.: Termination Detection for Diffusing Computations. Info. Proc. Lett 11(1) (1980)
12. Lin, C.M., Chiu, G.M., Cho, C.H.: A New Quorum-Based Scheme for Managing Replicated Data in Distributed Systems. IEEE Trans. Computers 51(12), 1442–1447 (2002)
13. Crossbow Technology, http://www.xbow.com/

An Online, Derivative-Free Optimization Approach to Auto-tuning of Computing Systems

Sudheer Poojary, Ramya Raghavendra, and D. Manjunath

Dept of Electrical Engineering, IIT Bombay, Mumbai India
{sudheer,ramyarag}@iitb.ac.in, dmanju@ee.iitb.ac.in

Abstract. We develop an online optimisation framework for self tuning of computer systems. Towards this, we first discuss suitable objective functions. We then develop an iterative technique that is robust to noisy measurements of objective function and also requires fewer perturbations on the configuration. We essentially adapt the Nelder-Mead algorithm to work with constrained variables and also allow noisy measurements. Extensive experimental results on a queueing model and on an actual system illustrate the performance of our scheme.

1 Introduction

In a typical large scale computing environment the computing cluster supports a number of applications. Each of these applications will have a 'quality of service' (QoS) requirement so that a service level agreement (SLA) may be met. The QoS requirement can be specified in a number of ways, typically as a function of response time and throughput. For the computing system to be able to satisfy these QoS requirements, each of the applications should be allocated resources, e.g., CPU capacity, memory size (main memory and/or cache), I/O rate and network bandwidth. Thus for a workload, i.e., the set of concurrent applications, the resource requirement is the vector of each of the resources that are needed to satisfy their QoS requirement. In this scenario, two issues immediately come to mind—(1) identify the workload profile, i.e., the resource requirements of each application, and (2) if the resource requirement can be identified, then manage instances of overload, i.e., when the requirement on one or more of the resources exceeds capacity, perform an equitable distribution. As has been extensively pointed out in literature, the first of these is not an easy task. Even if one could identify the requirements of each of the applications, an equitable allocation is an even trickier problem. Thus, to perform both these tasks manually demands extensive experience and expertise on the workload profile and on the computing system. Further, the timescales over which the changes in the workload profile occur may not allow manual intervention. Hence, it is now well established that both the above tasks are best performed autonomically. In this paper, we consider an optimisation based approach to auto-tuning and resource allocation.

K. Kant et al. (Eds.): ICDCN 2010, LNCS 5935, pp. 434–445, 2010.

1.1   Application Performance Measures

Developing an optimisation based autonomic tuning mechanism requires that we first define the notion of the performance of an application. Toward this, in this paper we model the computer system to be a queue and assume that each application generates a class of customers. This is reasonable for most applications where the load can be described as jobs or transactions.

With a queueing system view, the most obvious measure of the performance for an application is the 'response time' for its jobs, i.e., the delay experienced by the corresponding customer class in the queueing system abstraction. If the queue depth is finite and arriving jobs can be dropped then the blocking probability is a performance measure. Alternatively, we could measure throughput (or goodput) for the application. While these are obvious measures, some more measures have been developed that are of use in systems where the resources are to be shared among a number of users. We will consider two such measures.

Power (P) of a queue is the ratio of the throughput (λ) to the response time (R), i.e., $P := \frac{\lambda}{R}$ [1]. For a fixed service rate, as we increase the load of a user (or equivalently as we decrease the allocated capacity for a fixed offered load) the delay increases. It has been argued that Power is a natural characterisation of resource usage for real time traffic in networks and can hence also be applied to characterise a workload in a computer system where it is natural for each user to demand high capacity and low latency. For an M/M/1 queue, the power is maximum for a utilisation of 0.5. This corresponds to, on the average, having one job in the system. The peak value of the power function can be shifted through the following generalisation.

$$P = \frac{\lambda^\alpha}{R} .\qquad(1)$$

Jain's Fairness Index (JFI) [2] is a measure of how fairly the resources are allocated among competing users. If x_i is the fraction of resource allocated to user i, when n users are sharing a resource, then

$$JFI := \frac{\left(\sum_i x_i\right)^2}{n \sum_i x_i^2} .\qquad(2)$$

It is easy to see that $\frac{1}{n} \leq JFI \leq 1$ with the system being perfectly fair when $JFI = 1$ and perfectly unfair when $JFI = \frac{1}{n}$.

The objective function and the constraints that we design for the optimisation needs to address all possible overload situations by being able to identify it and also move towards the best resource allocation during those times. We propose that the optimisation method should use an objective function based on an absolute performance measure like the delay and throughput or even power and use JFI as a constraint to permit a fair sharing of the resources.

1.2   Workload Profiles and Resource Allocation Issues

A straightforward classification of workloads would be to identify the 'limiting resource(s)' for the application, i.e., the resource that determines the performance of the application. For example, decision support systems are CPU and memory intensive and require comparatively little I/O or network bandwidth. On the other hand, an online transaction processing system requires significantly higher I/O (and possibly network) bandwidth and is not CPU intensive. Thus these types of applications can coexist in a system and utilise the resources efficiently.

The resource requirement of a workload describes the workload profile. The workload profile varies with time. When the total resource requirement presented to the system is within the total capacity, all the jobs receive adequate amount of resource. However, there are times when the total resource requirement is greater than the system capacity. Under such conditions, the system needs to allocate the resources suitably. To tune the performance of the system a number of configuration parameters are available that can be tuned for optimal performance. These will be the variables in our optimisation problem.

1.3   Approaches to Self-tuning in Literature

A large body of the literature on self-tuning is based on discrete time control theoretic formulations. Fig. 1 illustrates these approaches. The tunables, u, and the performance function, Y, are first identified. $Y(t)$ is the output from the system. The reference output Y_{ref} is also identified. The objective of the control system will be to operate the system such that the output is close to Y_{ref}. A series of measurements are then performed to build a model that relates the tunables u to the output Y. The workload input to the system is $W(t)$. The noise in the measurement process due to short term fluctuations in the workload is $N(t)$.

Feedback control has been used to tune system performance in [3, 4, 5] using some form of admission control as the control input. Resource utilisation (e.g., CPU and memory utilization) [4], queue length [3] and response time [5] are used as system output. Adaptive controllers, where the model parameters are load-dependent have been used in [5] to deal with workload changes.

Control theoretic techniques require building a model, that relates the control input to the system output. The model is obtained using measurement data for a 'representative' test workload. The actual workload however varies over time and the system behavior would vary as the workload changes. This would require re-building of the model, which may not be straightforward. Also, a suitable

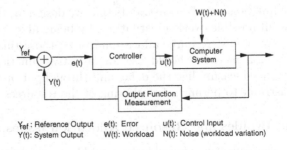

Fig. 1. Tuning using feedback control system

controller needs to be designed. The reference output for a given workload profile also needs to be identified. Furthermore control theoretic formulations assume that the system is indeed controllable.

Optimisation-based methods do not require model-building which serves as the principal advantage over control theoretic methods. The techniques based on optimisation work with little knowledge of where the optimum lies in the configuration space. This is another benefit of adopting the optimisation-based approach to self-tuning.

Optimisation based self tuning has been used to minimise the response time for a TPC-W setup by varying the buffer pool sizes on a DB2 Universal database server in [6]. The Nelder-Mead algorithm is used as the optimisation technique.

1.4 Problem Statement and Contribution

We describe a derivative-free optimisation method for self-tuning, or auto re-source allocation, in a computer system. The Nelder-Mead method is modified to work in a real system where the allowable values for the tunables is constrained. Further, we modify the algorithm to ensure that the optimum is tracked even when the workload profile is time-varying. The technique is first tested on a the-oretical model where the functional relation between the objective function and the variables is known. Here, we explore different objective functions. The tech-nique is then applied to allocate CPU capacity to different virtual machines on a single physical machine. Extensive numerical results illustrate the performance of the algorithm.

2   Optimisation Based Self Tuning

Optimization algorithms can be derivative based or derivative free. Derivative-based algorithms find the optimum point by iteratively selecting the next point along the gradient. Let X be the set of variables and $f(X)$ the function that is to be minimised. Let the gradient of $f(X)$ at X^k be $\nabla f(X^k)$. An iterative, derivative based optimisation would choose the next point $X^{(k+1)}$ by

$$X^{(k+1)} = X^{(k)} + \alpha * (-\nabla f(X^{(k)})) . \qquad (3)$$

where α is the step size and $(-\nabla f(X^{(k)}))$ is the direction. In a computing system, $X = (x_1, x_2 ... x_n)$ is the set of tunables, the quantity of each of the resource that is allocated and $f(X)$ is the objective function that captures the performance. Equation (3) is useful when the form of $f(X)$ is known. In a computer system this is difficult to know a priori because the exact relationship between the tun-ables and the performance is not easy to characterise. Hence, the value of the function can be known only by making measurements on the system with $X^{(k)}$ as its configuration setting. The gradient $(\nabla f(X^{(k)}))$ can be evaluated by taking the difference in the measurements at different configuration settings. We need two measurements per variable and hence $2n$ measurements per iteration. Thus for each iteration, the system is perturbed $2n$ times. Function evaluations by

measurement are subject to noise and would slow the convergence of the optimisation algorithm. Also, if the noise is significant, the algorithm might wander and
never get close to the optimum. Derivative-free optimization techniques would
offer lesser perturbations and are more immune to noisy evaluations of $f(X)$.

We consider a derivative-free optimisation algorithm for self tuning. Derivative-
free optimization techniques are also called direct search methods. A class of direct search techniques are 'simplex techniques'. In this method, a non-degenerate
simplex is generated in each iteration of the algorithm. The simplex is used to
search the configuration space for an optimum. We use the Nelder-Mead (NM)
simplex technique [7]. In this technique, we need a maximum of 2 measurements
per iteration. We adapt it for use in a real system where there are constraints
on the allowable values of the variables and the load is time varying.

We use the basic NM algorithm on a simple queueing model of web server
system. We also explore objective functions based on power and Fairness Index.

2.1   The NM Technique on a Queueing Model

A web server with two bottleneck resources of the CPU and the I/O node is
modeled as a closed queuing network (see Fig. 2). Two applications are running
on this web server and they form two classes of customers. Each application
is allowed a thread pool of fixed size. Class 1 is CPU intensive and Class 2 is
I/O intensive. The CPU is modeled as a processor sharing queue with service
rates α_1 and α_2 for the two customer classes. The I/O subsystem is modeled as
FIFO queue with service rates β_1 and β_2 for the two classes. Node 1 is the idling
queue and represents the inactive threads in the system and is modeled as an
$M/M/\infty$ queue. New jobs arrive for inactive threads at rates λ_1 and λ_2. On the
completion of a CPU schedule, a class i thread requires I/O access with a fixed
probability p_{d_i} and retires to the idling queue with probability $(1 - p_{d_i})$. The
thread pool sizes for the two applications are, respectively, K_1 and K_2.

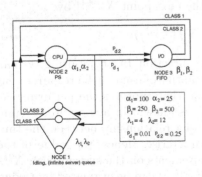

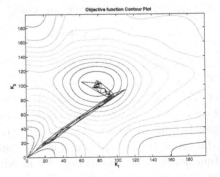

Fig. 2. The closed queueing network
model with two applications

Fig. 3. Convergence of Nelder-Mead
simplex technique on the queueing
model

The thread pool sizes K_1, K_2 are the variables and the objective function is

$$F(K_1, K_2) = a_1 P_{1n} + a_2 P_{2n} + a_3 JFI(P_{1n}, P_{2n}) . \qquad (4)$$

Here, P_{in} is the normalized power for customers of class i as given by (1). The normalisation is done using the maximum value of the power function attained by customers of the class. a_i are the weights associated with each term. We need to normalise because the magnitudes of the achievable powers of the two classes are significantly different. JFI is the Jain's fairness index as described in (2).

Figure 3 shows the convergence path for model parameters given in Fig. 2. The algorithm converges to the optimum in less than twenty steps. This is encouraging for use in online optimisation of a real system. The objective function though, poses some problems. Note that we need to normalise the power. This is not possible in a real system without exploring the whole configuration space. Hence, we will demonstrate the NM based self tuning using a simple objective function. We are investigating other objective functions that use JFI and power.

2.2 Issues and Fixes for Use of NM in a System

There are two important issues which need to be addressed when the NM technique is used for optimising behaviour of a real computer system. Firstly, we are concerned about the simplex becoming large. The Nelder-Mead technique moves towards the optimum point by moving away from the worst point in the simplex. The new simplex is computed by reflecting the worst point of the current simplex. On a computing system, this amounts to changing the system configuration to the reflected point and measuring the system performance at this point. If this point is far away from the present system setting, the system is perturbed significantly. This is undesirable as we do not know if the performance of the system would get better by moving to this new system configuration. A similar concern arises when we deal with the extended point in the algorithm. A further concern here is that the reflected or the extended point may be outside the feasible region for the parameters. Secondly, we have an issue with the simplex becoming too small. In the presence of noisy measurements, the difference between the values of the objective function at two points on the simplex might be lesser in magnitude than the value of noise. This can mislead the algorithm to move to a point that is away from the optimum. Also, the small size of simplex might restrict its movement. This might make the simplex get stuck at a region that is away from the optimum especially when the workload varies dynamically.

Restricting the maximum size that a simplex grows into can address the first issue. This would keep a check on the amount of perturbation introduced while we move the system configuration setting from the worst point in the simplex to a new point. The second issue can be handled by ensuring that any two points in the simplex that is obtained at the end of an iteration are at a distance greater than a minimum threshold. This is to ensure that the noise in the system does not affect the ordering of the points in the simplex. Thus we modify the basic NM method to ensure that after each iteration the size of the simplex is within a upper and lower bound. We also ensure that the new simplex is in the feasible region. We use [8] when the size of the simplex exceeds the upper and lower bounds. Here, the size of the simplex remains constant in every iteration. We describe this method for function minimization below.

Given an initial simplex, the worst point in the simplex is reflected through the centroid across the other points to obtain the second simplex. Next, the second-worst point in the first simplex is reflected across the centroid of the second simplex to obtain a third simplex. This is repeated M times while retaining the best point of the original simplex. At each iteration, the sum of the cost function values at each point of the simplex is computed. The minimum of all the sum values is found. The simplex that corresponds to this minimum sum is used as the simplex for the next iteration. The sum of the function values is used as a judging criterion because it corresponds to the simplex that has the minimum average function value. We call this the *MSimplex* method.

The MSimplex method is described in Algorithm 1 and illustrated in Fig. 4 for a two-dimensional configuration space with $M = 3$ with initial simplex, $S_0 = (A_1, B_1, C_1)$ and A_1 the worst point in the simplex. R_1, R_2 and R_3 are the reflected points obtained.

Algorithm 1. The MSimplex algorithm in n dimensions

Algorithm MSimplex
INPUT: Simplex $S^0 = (X_1, \ldots, X_{n+1})$
OUTPUT: Simplex S^1
Sort and rename vertices of S^i such that $f(X_1) \geq f(X_2) \geq \cdots \geq f(X_{n+1})$
Obtain G^0 as centroid of S^0.
for $i = 1 \ldots M$ **do**
    Reflect X_i through G_{i-1} to get R_i
    Simplex $S^i = (X_1, \ldots, R_i, X_{i+1}, \ldots, X_{n+1})$
    Obtain G^i as centroid of S^i.
    if all vertices of S^i are feasible, **then**
        $sum_i = $ sum of $f(\cdot)$ at vertices of S^i.
    else
        $sum_i = \infty$
    end if
end for
$S^1 = S_{\arg \min_j \{sum_j\}}$

Let $A_{\max}$ be the maximum allowable area of the simplex and $S_{\min}$ be the minimum length of a side of the simplex. When these two conditions are violated in the 'basic' algorithm, we invoke the MSimplex method described above.

The amount of reflection, extension and contraction is controlled by three scalar quantities—r, e and c, respectively, the coefficients of reflection, expansion, and contraction. These quantities satisfy $r > 0$, $e > 1$, $0 < c < 1$. These are used as follows. Let X_k^i be the k-th point in the i-th iteration. These points are assumed ordered such that $f(X_1^i) > f(X_2^i) > f(X_3^i) > \cdots > f(X_{n+1}^i)$. The centroid G of the n best points is calculated from the relation $G^i = \frac{\sum_{i=1}^{(n)} x_i}{n}$.

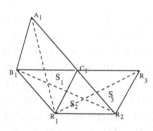

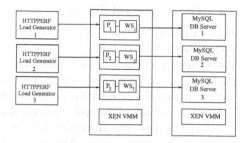

Fig. 4. Illustrating the MSimplex method for two dimensions. The three simplexes for $M = 3$ are shown.

Fig. 5. Experimental setup (P: Muffin proxy server, VMM: Virtual machine monitor)

The reflected, extended and the contracted points are obtained using (5). We assume $r = 1$, $e = 2$ and $c = 0.5$.

$$R^i = (1 + r)G^i - rX_{n+1}, \quad E^i = (1 + re)G^i - reX_{n+1},$$
$$M_1^i = (1 - c)G^i + cX_{n+1}, \quad M_2^i = (1 + rc)G^i - rcX_{n+1} . \qquad (5)$$

The Online NM method [1] that we propose here is the basic NM-method in which the MSimplex is invoked whenever the new simplex meets the conditions described in Section 2.2— the size of the simplex is outside the specified bounds or a point in the simplex is outside the feasible region for the tuning variable. We re-measure the best point of the simplex in every iteration to ensure that the ordering of the vertices of the simplex is appropriate. [9] also considers modifications to the Nelder-Mead algorithm but is motivated by different reasons and also takes a different approach than that presented here.

3 Experimental Evaluation of NM-MSimplex Algorithm

We evaluate the Online-NM algorithm experimentally, using the following objective function.

$$F(c_1, c_2, \ldots, c_m) = \sum_{i=1}^{m} \left(\frac{\lambda_i}{\sum_{i=1}^{m} \lambda_i}\right) R_i . \qquad (6)$$

where $(c_1, c_2, \ldots, c_m)$ is the amount of resource allocated to each of the m workloads, λ_i is the throughput of workload i and R_i is the response time experienced by workload i. An example of such a situation is when multiple applications share the same physical CPU and the CPU share assigned to each of these applications is a variable. Such a scenario is seen when we have virtual machines on a single physical machine. Our experimental testbed consists of three virtual machines that run on a single physical machine with XEN as the hypervisor.

---

[1] An elaborate explanation of the algorithm can be found at
http://www.ee.iitb.ac.in/~dmanju/poojary-raghavendra-icdcn2010.pdf

3.1   Experimental Setup

The details of the experimental testbed are as shown in Fig. 5. We have a two-tier system with Apache being the web server and MySql being the database server. WebCalendar application is deployed on the Apache web server. httperf is used for load generation on three client machines. The requests issued by httperf can have exponential or uniform or fixed inter-arrival times. One client machine is connected to one of the web servers, the web server is connected to one of the database servers. The three web servers are hosted on three virtual machines on the same physical machine. The same is true with the database servers. We have used Xen as the hypervisor. The values of the response times for the requests at the web server are logged into a file by Muffin proxy server. These values are communicated to the host machine through socket programs for calculating the value of the objective function.

As the rate at which requests arrive at the web-server increases, its CPU consumption increases. The resource consumption of each virtual machine is governed and guided by the rate and the pattern of arrival of requests into the web-server the VM is hosting. Hence, we can say that the demand for CPU is dependent on the workload on virtual machine.

Specifically, we determine CAP that needs to be allocated to the VMs VM_1 and VM_2. The remaining CAP is allocated to VM_3. Note that CAP is just an upper bound on the CPU cycles that will be allocated to the VM.

3.2   Parameter Setting

We need to set two parameters in the algorithm, the smallest side of the simplex (S_{min}) and the maximum allowable area (A_{max}) of the simplex cautiously. The value of A_{max} can be set to a value such that the maximum deviation in the system setting does not cause a very pronounced perturbation. However, a low value of A_{max} might lead to slower convergence of the algorithm by getting to the MSimplex method more often leading to an increased number of perturbations. It needs to be noted that a higher value of S_{min} will undoubtedly provide better noise immunity, but it will also increase the distance between the actual optimum and the convergent point. An infeasible point is encountered when the sum of the CAP values exceeds 100 or when either CAP_1 or CAP_2 or both are negative. The MSimplex method is invoked when the infeasible points are encountered.

4   Experimental Results and Conclusion

We conducted experiments with different workload profiles. In the first experiment, the load profile was kept constant. For this static workload scenario, we had exponential inter-arrival times between the requests to the web-server on each virtual machine. The arrival rate of requests (expressed per second) into VM_1, VM_2 and VM_3 were 0.25, 1 and 3 respectively. Fig. 6 illustrates the convergence path of the simplex to the optimum. The initial simplex expands in size and later contracts while it is close to the optimum. The algorithm converges close to the region where the optimum is situated. The axes show CAP_1 and CAP_2.

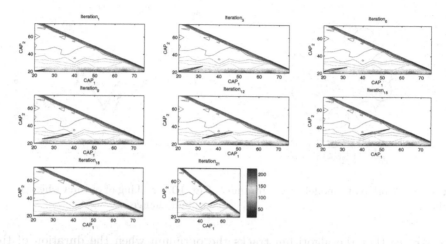

Fig. 6. Simplex movement on the function contour

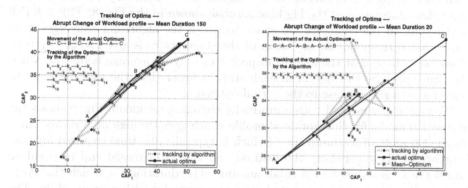

Fig. 7. Results for dynamic workload; three state Markov chain model; mean duration of 150 units in each state

Fig. 8. Results for dynamic workload; three state Markov chain model; mean duration of 20 units in each state

In the next experiment we choose a dynamic workload profile for the three virtual machines.

A three state Markov chain was used to model the workload profile. The three states A, B and C represent different arrival rates into the three virtual machines. In state A, B and C the arrival rates into VM_1, VM_2 and VM_3 are 0.5, 1, 4; 4, 4, 4; and 4, 1, 0.5 respectively. The transition rates are assumed to be identical and is denoted by μ. We used 150, and 20 for the values of $\frac{1}{\mu}$. The results for each of these cases is presented in the Figs. 7 and 8. The big green dots denoted by A, B and C represent the points in the configuration space where the algorithm would converge to, if the system was input with a load represented by the states A, B and C respectively.

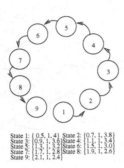

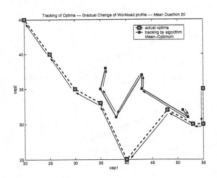

Fig. 9. Workload model for gradual change

Fig. 10. Tracking of optima when there is gradual change

We see that the algorithm tracks the optimum when the duration of time spent in each state is large (150), Fig. 7. When the mean duration spent in each state is 20, the behaviour of the algorithm is oscillatory. Notice that the algorithm moves around the big blue asterisk shown in the Fig. 8. This asterisk is the point in the configuration space to which the algorithm converges if an input that corresponds to the mean of the three states is given to the system. Thus, we believe that the algorithm perceives only an average behaviour when the time spent by the system in each state is lower than the time required to converge to a region close to the actual optimum.

We next experimented with a gradually changing workload. Fig. 9 shows the generation model for this workload profile which goes through nine states. After about 200 units of warm-up time (which is typically the time required for convergence by the algorithm), the load on one VM is increased and the load on another VM is reduced by a small amount. The duration for which the workload profile remains same is distributed exponentially with a mean of 20. The vector corresponding to the mean inter-arrival times for each VM for each state is shown in Fig. 9. We see that the algorithm tracks the optimum reasonably well and is as shown in Fig. 10.

We adapted the Nelder-Mead direct search method to develop an online optimisation based self-tuning mechanism. For our experimental results, we considered a rather straightforward objective function. Variants of this objective function are being tried. More variables can make the problem more interesting.

Acknowledgments. We thank Dinkar Sitaram and Ganesh Handige for many early discussions and of Hewlett Packard (India) for support of this work.

References

1. Kleinrock, L.: Power and deterministic rules of thumb for probabilistic problems in computer communications. In: Proceedings of the International Conference on Communications (June 1979)

2. Jain, R., Chiu, D.M., Hawe, W.: A quantitative measure of fairness and discrimination for resource allocation in shared systems. Technical Report DEC TR-301, Digital Equipment Corporation, Littleton, MA (1984)
3. Gandhi, N., Tilbury, D.M., Parekh, S., Hellerstein, J.: Feedback control of a lotus notes server: Modeling and control design. In: Proceedings of the American Control Conference, pp. 3000–3005 (2001)
4. Diao, Y., Hellerstein, J.L., Parekh, S.: MIMO control of an Apache web server: Modelling and controller design. In: Proceedings of the American Control Conference, pp. 4922–4927 (2002)
5. Kamra, A., Misra, V., Nahum, E.M.: Yaksha: A self-tuning controller for managing the performance of 3-tiered web sites. In: Proceedings of IEEE International Workshop on Quality of Service (IWQOS), June 2004, pp. 47–56 (2004)
6. Diao, Y., Eskesen, F., Froehlich, S., Hellerstein, J.L., Spainhower, L.F., Surendra, M.: Generic online optimization
of multiple configuration parameters
with application to a database server. In: Brunner, M., Keller, A. (eds.) DSOM 2003. LNCS, vol. 2867, pp. 3–15. Springer, Heidelberg (2003)
7. Olsson, D.M., Nelson, L.S.: The nelder-mead simplex procedure for function minimization. Technometrics 17(1), 45–51 (1975)
8. Xiong, Q., Jutan, A.: Continuous optimization using a dynamic simplex method. Chemical Engineering Science 58(16), 3817–3828 (2003)
9. Bagchi, S., Das, R., Diao, Y., Kaplan, M.A., Kephart, J.O.: Dynamic online multi-parameter optimization system and method for autonomic computing systems, US Patent Application 20080221858

Consistency-Driven Probabilistic Quorum System Construction for Improving Operation Availability*

Kinga Kiss Iakab**, Christian Storm, and Oliver Theel

Carl von Ossietzky University of Oldenburg
Department of Computer Science, D-26111 Oldenburg, Germany

Abstract. Pessimistic quorum-based data replication strategies generally strive for maximizing operation availabilities while adhering to a strict consistency notion. Unfortunately, their operation availabilities are strictly upper-bounded. Probabilistically relaxing the consistency notion permits to overcome this bound, introducing probabilistic data replication strategies that allow for a data consistency vs. operation availabilities trade-off. We present two construction algorithms transforming strict quorum systems into probabilistic ones and compare them in terms of operation availabilities and degree of data consistency.

1 Introduction

Managing data via replication is a well-known technique for improving operation availabilities in distributed systems. A distributed system consists of several connected processes, each managing a copy of the data object. A replication strategy provides two operations on a replicated data object: writing new data and reading data. Strict pessimistic replication strategies ensure that no operation execution results in an inconsistent replicated data object according to a strict consistency notion such as, e.g., sequential consistency [1]. Unfortunately, the operation availabilities provided by these strict strategies are bounded [2]. Allowing operation execution to sacrifice a certain degree of consistency by enforcing the strict consistency notion only probabilistically, improves on the operation availabilities: operation executions are allowed even in cases where strict pessimistic replication strategies must hinder them. Hence, at a particular point in time, probabilistic operations are more likely to be available than pessimistic ones. The class of strict pessimistic replication strategies forks a new subclass, namely the probabilistic strategies relaxing strictly pessimistic consistency notions. In contrast to correctness-critical systems such as, e.g., power plant control systems, for which strict pessimistic strategies qualify and are mandatory, the application domain of probabilistic strategies is availability- and timeliness-oriented systems which are "instant reaction"-critical: A slightly inconsistent but "orientative"

---

* This work is supported by the German Research Foundation, grant GRK 1076/1.
** Also affiliated with the Transilvania University of Braşov, Romania.

K. Kant et al. (Eds.): ICDCN 2010, LNCS 5935, pp. 446–458, 2010.

answer helps performing the task better than waiting for the correct answer, possibly violating timing constraints. In particular, probabilistic strategies are suitable for managing data with small variations in time for which probabilistic read results deviate only slightly from strictly consistent ones.

Generally, strict pessimistic replication strategies employ the concept of quorum systems for maintaining consistency by guaranteeing the mutual exclusion of consistency-endangering concurrent operations. A quorum system is a tuple of a read and a write quorum set. Quorum sets are sets of subsets of the set of processes s.t. every two write quorums and every read and write quorum intersect while two read quorums need not to intersect. Prior to executing an operation, the unanimous agreement and shared-exclusive read-read, write-read locking of quorums – selected according to some strategy – must be reached or the operation cannot be performed and is unavailable. If a quorum is found and a write operation is being performed, then the new data value is written to each replica of the quorum's processes and their version number is set to a new maximum. A read operation returns the value of a replica with the highest version number among the replicas in the read quorum. In contrast to strict pessimistic quorum systems, for probabilistic quorum systems the quorum sets' non-empty intersection in at least one process is guaranteed only with high probability, thereby trading-off (strict) data consistency for higher operation availabilities.

In this paper, we present and analyze two new probabilistic quorum construction algorithms that allow to balance the data consistency vs. availabilities trade-off for the read and the write operation. The algorithms transform a given strict quorum system into a probabilistic quorum system that imposes an order on the quorums of a quorum set in which they must be probed. The basic idea is to first select and try executing an operation with strict quorums and to use probabilistic quorums only in case no strict one is available, then accepting relaxed consistency constraints. If neither a strict nor a probabilistic quorum is available, then the respective operation is unavailable. Analysis results are presented for probabilistic strategies obtained by applying the algorithms on three well-known pessimistic replication strategies. The results illustrate the trade-off and show the increase in availability compared to schemes from related work.

The remainder of this paper is structured as follows. The next section relates previous work to our approach. In Section 3, the system model as well as strict and probabilistic quorum systems are formally introduced. The two algorithms for constructing probabilistic quorum systems are presented in Section 4. Section 5 illustrates the evaluation of the data consistency vs. operation availabilities trade-off and a compares our results with previous approaches. Section 6 discusses and analyzes the general behavior of the constructions by the means of a well-suited application scenario. Finally, Section 7 concludes the paper.

2   Related Work

Previous research on constructing probabilistic quorum systems has traded-off various quality-of-service measures for a relaxed (strict) consistency notion. [6]

focus on a probabilistic quorum construction whose major concern is communication efficiency in terms of small-sized messages. [7] introduced a subclass of quorums that are able to cope with message delays in large-scale dynamic systems. Being the motivation for employing data replication using quorum systems, the primary quality measure is high operation availability. The operation availability provided by a specific quorum construction depends on the data consistency notion to be guaranteed: the higher (lower) the consistency requirements, the lower (higher) is the operation availability. [8] introduced specific probabilistic quorums which achieve optimal operation availability with respect to their construction method under varying load and probe complexity values, a measure due to [9]. [10] used proper subsets of strict read quorums for performing probabilistic read operations, thereby trading an increased read operation availability for probabilistic data consistency guarantees on the value delivered.

While these approaches consider only one type of operation or address other quality measures, our approach focuses on increasing the read operation *as well as* the write operation availability by using probabilistic replication for enabling a more balanced data consistency vs. operation availabilities trade-off.

3   System Model

Let $\mathcal{P} = \{1, 2, ..., N\}$ be the set of processes in a distributed system. Let processes be fully connected by perfect communication links. Processes may crash-fail and recover independently with a uniform process availability $a \in [0, 1]$.[1]

Definitions (Strict System). A *quorum set* $\mathcal{Q}$ over universe $\mathcal{P}$ is a set of subsets of $\mathcal{P}$. A *minimal quorum set* $\mathcal{Q}$ over $\mathcal{P}$ is a quorum set over $\mathcal{P}$ s.t.: $\forall Q_1, Q_2 \in \mathcal{Q} : Q_1 \nsubseteq Q_2$. A *(strict) intersecting quorum set* $\mathcal{Q}$ over $\mathcal{P}$ is a quorum set s.t.: $\forall Q_1, Q_2 \in \mathcal{Q} : Q_1 \cap Q_2 \neq \emptyset$. A *strict quorum system* (SQS) QS over $\mathcal{P}$ is a tuple $\left(\mathcal{Q}_\mathcal{R}^S, \mathcal{Q}_\mathcal{W}^S\right)$ s.t.: (1) $\mathcal{Q}_\mathcal{R}^S$ is a quorum set, (2) $\mathcal{Q}_\mathcal{W}^S$ is an intersecting quorum set and (3) $\forall Q_1 \in \mathcal{Q}_\mathcal{R}^S, Q_2 \in \mathcal{Q}_\mathcal{W}^S : Q_1 \cap Q_2 \neq \emptyset$. $\mathcal{Q}_\mathcal{R}^S \left(\mathcal{Q}_\mathcal{W}^S\right)$ is called *strict read (write) quorum set*. An element Q of $\mathcal{Q}_\mathcal{R}^S$ $\left(\mathcal{Q}_\mathcal{W}^S\right)$ is called *strict read (write) quorum*. A *partially ordered strict quorum system* QS is a 4-tuple $\left(\mathcal{Q}_\mathcal{R}^S, \mathcal{Q}_\mathcal{W}^S, \leq_\mathcal{R}^S, \leq_W^S\right)$ s.t.: (1) $\mathcal{Q}_\mathcal{R}^S$ is a strict read quorum set, (2) $\mathcal{Q}_\mathcal{W}^S$ is a strict write quorum set, (3) $\leq_\mathcal{R}^S \subseteq \mathcal{Q}_\mathcal{R}^S \times \mathcal{Q}_\mathcal{R}^S$ is a partial order relation for read quorums, and (4) $\leq_W^S \subseteq \mathcal{Q}_\mathcal{W}^S \times \mathcal{Q}_\mathcal{W}^S$ is a partial order relation for write quorums.

In the following, for ease of presentation, partially ordered quorum sets will be considered as sequences of quorum sets with decreasing priority on the ordered elements. Some replication strategies, e.g., the Tree Quorum Protocol (TQP) [4], require a partial order on the set of (read) quorums.

As mentioned earlier, the need for relaxing the consistency requirement arises if there is no other method to ensure high operation availabilities. This relaxation is directly related to the intersection property of quorums. Consequently, the

---

[1] For ease of presentation. The approach can easily be generalized for non-uniform process availabilities.

concept of *probabilistic quorum systems* [11] has been introduced. The concepts of probabilistic intersecting quorum sets and probabilistic quorum systems are defined as follows:

Definitions (Probabilistic System). A *probabilistic intersecting quorum set* $\mathcal{Q}$ over universe $\mathcal{P}$ is a quorum set s.t.: $\forall Q_1, Q_2 \in \mathcal{Q} : P(Q_1 \cap Q_2 \neq \emptyset) \leq 1 - \epsilon$, where $\epsilon \in (0,1)$ is a constant. A *probabilistic quorum system* (PQS) $\mathcal{QS}$ over $\mathcal{P}$ is a tuple $(\mathcal{Q}_\mathcal{R}^\mathcal{P}, \mathcal{Q}_\mathcal{W}^\mathcal{P})$ s.t.: (1) $\mathcal{Q}_\mathcal{R}^\mathcal{P}$ is a quorum set, (2) $\mathcal{Q}_\mathcal{W}^\mathcal{P}$ is a probabilistic intersecting quorum set with $\epsilon_w \in (0,1)$ and (3) $\forall Q_1 \in \mathcal{Q}_\mathcal{R}^\mathcal{P}, Q_2 \in \mathcal{Q}_\mathcal{W}^\mathcal{P} :$ $P(Q_1 \cap Q_2 \neq \emptyset) \leq 1 - \epsilon_{rw}$, where $\epsilon_{rw} \in (0,1)$. $\mathcal{Q}_\mathcal{R}^\mathcal{P}$ $(\mathcal{Q}_\mathcal{W}^\mathcal{P})$ is called *probabilistic read (write) quorum set*. An element Q of $\mathcal{Q}_\mathcal{R}^\mathcal{P}$ $(\mathcal{Q}_\mathcal{W}^\mathcal{P})$ is called *probabilistic read (write) quorum*.

Informally, this definition states that (1) every two write quorums, and (2) every read and every write quorum intersect only with very high probability if ϵ_w and ϵ_{rw} are close to 0. Thus, it is possible that some pairs of quorums (apart from read quorum pairs) do not intersect. The potential intersection of read and write quorums implies the violation of strict consistency with some small probability. This relaxation of the intersection property grants a *gain in availability* and a *loss of consistency* for PQS.

Similarly to strict systems, the concept of a partially ordered probabilistic quorum system is defined. Having one SQS and one PQS over the same universe $\mathcal{P}$, a union quorum system (UQS) $(\mathcal{Q}_\mathcal{R}^\mathcal{U}, \mathcal{Q}_\mathcal{W}^\mathcal{U}) := (\mathcal{Q}_\mathcal{R}^\mathcal{S} \cup \mathcal{Q}_\mathcal{R}^\mathcal{P}, \mathcal{Q}_\mathcal{W}^\mathcal{S} \cup \mathcal{Q}_\mathcal{W}^\mathcal{P})$ can be constructed for increasing the availability of the original SQS. Note that a UQS is also a PQS.

Definitions (Parameters). The *probabilistic read (write) quorum rate* r_r $(r_w) \in [0,1]$ of a PQS is the rate reflecting the percentage of non-strict read (non-strict write) quorums with respect to the number of all read (write) quorums in the PQS. The *probabilistic extension size* (d_r, d_w) of a PQS is the pair of the numbers of non-strict read and non-strict write quorums in the PQS. The *read probability* of a distributed system $x \in [0,1]$ is the probability that if an operation is executed, then this operation is a read operation. In a complementary manner, $1 - x$ is the *write probability* of a distributed system.

Thus, the probabilistic read and write quorum rate of a UQS is $r_r = |\mathcal{Q}_\mathcal{R}^\mathcal{P}| /$ $(|\mathcal{Q}_\mathcal{R}^\mathcal{S}| + |\mathcal{Q}_\mathcal{R}^\mathcal{P}|)$ and $r_w = |\mathcal{Q}_\mathcal{W}^\mathcal{P}| / (|\mathcal{Q}_\mathcal{W}^\mathcal{S}| + |\mathcal{Q}_\mathcal{W}^\mathcal{P}|)$. For ease of the construction algorithms' presentation in Section 4, we subsequently assume that $r = r_r = r_w$. The probabilistic extension size of a UQS is $(d_r, d_w) = (|\mathcal{Q}_\mathcal{R}^\mathcal{P}|, |\mathcal{Q}_\mathcal{W}^\mathcal{P}|) =$ $(|\mathcal{Q}_\mathcal{R}^\mathcal{S}| \cdot r / (1-r), |\mathcal{Q}_\mathcal{W}^\mathcal{S}| \cdot r / (1-r))$.

Note the importance of the probabilistic quorum rate r as it influences the data consistency of a PQS. If increasing r, two cases arise. (1) The probability of quorum intersections can decrease implying increasing data inconsistency. (2) More probabilistic quorums intersect and, thereby, the overall intersection probability of quorums can be higher than for smaller values of r. The probabilistic extension size (d_r, d_w) can be regarded as a "measure" of operation availability for PQSs. If (d_r, d_w) "increases", then the total number of read and write quorums increases, i.e., the probability of selecting one available read and write quorum monotonically increases, resulting in monotonically increased operation availabilities. Thus, the relation between (d_r, d_w) and r illustrates the trade-off between consistency and availabilities when using PQSs.

4   Probabilistic Quorum Construction

This section presents two probabilistic quorum construction algorithms, both with an emphasis on data consistency. They each construct a PQS with d_r read and d_w write quorums based on a given SQS serving as input to the algorithms. If the constructed probabilistic quorums are small in cardinality, they can lead to high operation availability but only low data consistency. Contrarily, if the quorums are large, they can lead to consistent operations but only with low availability. The general criteria for constructing a PQS are: (1) quorum sizes in the PQS must be smaller than quorum sizes in the SQS, (2) quorums in the PQS must be large enough to ensure a high intersection probability. Consequently, the final aim is to construct a union quorum system of the input SQS and the output PQS, in which strict quorums have priority over probabilistic ones.

4.1   Minimal Quorums-Based Construction

The *Minimal Quorums-Based Construction Algorithm* (MQA) pursues the following idea: The algorithm takes every read and write quorum Q from the input SQS and generates all $(|Q| - 1)$-combinations from Q, that have one element less than Q. All different combinations are added to the PQS. After the generation, three cases are possible. (1) Exactly d_r or d_w quorums are generated complying to the input probabilistic quorum rate r. (2) Less quorums are generated, so the algorithm must double-insert some of them to satisfy the input probabilistic quorum rate r. Clearly, the availability of operations will not increase by the latter. The objective is only to meet the probabilistic quorum rate r and to compare the results of the construction algorithms later in a fair manner. In order to formally allow repeating quorums in the PQS, henceforth, we consider the definition of PQS adapted to multisets. (3) More quorums are generated than needed, so the algorithm has to delete some of them. In all cases, it has to be decided which quorums should be added or removed. Depending on the sequence of two consecutive operations chosen from the set of possible operations being strict read, strict write, probabilistic read, probabilistic write, the generated quorum set for the previous operation and the generated quorum set for the current operation are used to construct an *intersection operation table* of the quorums: for every quorum, the total number of intersections with the previous operation's quorum set is calculated. In case of partially ordered quorum sets, the intersections are weighted according to the priority classes of sets of the quorum sets. Then, if required, quorums are added to the PQS in decreasing order of the number of non-empty intersections. Similarly, if required, quorums are removed from PQS in increasing order of the number of non-empty intersections with quorums from the previous operation's quorum set. Probabilistic quorums generated from some original SQS priority class will be added (removed) to (from) the corresponding priority class in the PQS. The following algorithm formalizes these steps.

Input: $(\mathcal{Q}_{\mathcal{R}}^{\mathcal{S}}, \mathcal{Q}_{\mathcal{W}}^{\mathcal{S}})$, r

$\mathcal{Q}_{\mathcal{R}}^{\mathcal{P}} := \text{generatePQS}(\mathcal{Q}_{\mathcal{R}}^{\mathcal{S}}); \quad \mathcal{Q}_{\mathcal{W}}^{\mathcal{P}} := \text{generatePQS}(\mathcal{Q}_{\mathcal{W}}^{\mathcal{S}})$

$d_r := |\mathcal{Q}_{\mathcal{R}}^{\mathcal{S}}| \cdot r / (1 - r); \quad d_w := |\mathcal{Q}_{\mathcal{W}}^{\mathcal{S}}| \cdot r / (1 - r)$

$$(\mathcal{Q}_{\mathcal{R}}^{\mathcal{P}}, \ \mathcal{Q}_{\mathcal{W}}^{\mathcal{P}}) := \begin{cases} (\text{computePQS}(\mathcal{Q}_{\mathcal{R}}^{\mathcal{P}}, \mathcal{Q}_{\mathcal{R}}^{\mathcal{S}}, d_r), \mathcal{Q}_{\mathcal{W}}^{\mathcal{S}}) & \text{if PRoSR in the operation sequence,} \\ (\text{computePQS}(\mathcal{Q}_{\mathcal{R}}^{\mathcal{P}}, \mathcal{Q}_{\mathcal{W}}^{\mathcal{S}}, d_r), \mathcal{Q}_{\mathcal{W}}^{\mathcal{S}}) & \text{if PRoSW in the operation sequence,} \\ (\mathcal{Q}_{\mathcal{R}}^{\mathcal{S}}, \text{computePQS}(\mathcal{Q}_{\mathcal{W}}^{\mathcal{P}}, \mathcal{Q}_{\mathcal{R}}^{\mathcal{S}}, d_w)) & \text{if PWoSR in the operation sequence,} \\ (\mathcal{Q}_{\mathcal{R}}^{\mathcal{S}}, \text{computePQS}(\mathcal{Q}_{\mathcal{W}}^{\mathcal{P}}, \mathcal{Q}_{\mathcal{W}}^{\mathcal{S}}, d_w)) & \text{if PWoSW in the operation sequence,} \\ (\text{computePQS}(\mathcal{Q}_{\mathcal{R}}^{\mathcal{P}}, \mathcal{Q}_{\mathcal{R}}^{\mathcal{S}}, d_r), \mathcal{Q}_{\mathcal{W}}^{\mathcal{S}}) & \text{if PRoPR in the operation sequence,} \\ (\mathcal{Q}_{\mathcal{R}}^{\mathcal{S}}, \text{computePQS}(\mathcal{Q}_{\mathcal{W}}^{\mathcal{P}}, \mathcal{Q}_{\mathcal{W}}^{\mathcal{P}}, d_w)) & \text{if PWoPW in the operation sequence,} \\ \text{selectPQS}(\mathcal{Q}_{\mathcal{R}}^{\mathcal{P}}, \mathcal{Q}_{\mathcal{W}}^{\mathcal{P}}, d_r, d_w) & \text{if PRoPW in the operation sequence} \end{cases}$$

Output: $(\mathcal{Q}_{\mathcal{R}}^{\mathcal{P}}, \mathcal{Q}_{\mathcal{W}}^{\mathcal{P}})$

```
function generatePQS(Q^S)
  Q^P := <{},...,{}>, |Q^P| = |Q^S|
  for i := 1 to |Q^S|
    for j := 1 to |Q_i^S|
      X := combinations(Q_{i,j}^S, |Q_{i,j}^S| - 1)
      Q_i^P := Q_i^P ∪ X_l : X_l ∉ Q_r^P, r < i
        for l = 1...|X|
  remove all Q_i^P with Q_i^P = ∅ from Q^P
  return Q^P   function sort(Q^A, Q^B)
  for k := 1 to |Q^A|
    for i := 1 to |Q_k^A|
      a_{k,i} := 0  /*consistency indicators*/
      for l := 1 to |Q^B|
        a_{k,i} := a_{k,i} + (|Q^B| - l + 1)·
          nrOfInters(Q_{k,i}^A, Q_l^B)
    L_k := sort Q_k^A decreasingly according to
      the values from a_k
  return L   function computePQS(Q_1, Q_2, d)
  Q^P := Q_1
  L := sort(Q_1, Q_2)
```

```
  k := 1;  i := 1
  while (|Q^P| < d)  /*less quorums, repeat*/
    Q_k^P := Q_k^P ∪ L_{k,i};  i := i + 1
    if i > |L_k| then k := k + 1
    if k > |L| then k := 1
      i := 1
  k := |L|;  i := |L_k|
  while (|Q^P| > d)  /*more quorums, delete*/
    Q_k^P := Q_k^P \ L_{k,i};  i := i - 1
    if i < 1 then k := k - 1
    if k < 1 then k := |L|
      i := |L_k|
  remove all Q_i^P with Q_i^P = ∅ from Q^P
  return Q^P   function selectPQS(Q_R^P,
    Q_W^P, d_r, d_w)
  Q_{R1}^P := computePQS(Q_R^P, Q_W^P, d_r)
  Q_{W1}^P := computePQS(Q_W^P, Q_{R1}^P, d_w)
  Q_{W2}^P := computePQS(Q_W^P, Q_R^P, d_w)
  Q_{R2}^P := computePQS(Q_R^P, Q_{W2}^P, d_r)
  (Q_{Rn}^P, Q_{Wn}^P) := highestInterProb((Q_{R1}^P,
    Q_{W1}^P), (Q_{R2}^P, Q_{W2}^P))
  return (Q_{Rn}^P, Q_{Wn}^P)
```

For example, if $N = 4$ and the replication strategy used is the Grid Protocol (GP) [3] where the processes are arranged in a 2-rows and 2-columns logical grid, then the input of MQA is $(\langle\{\{1, 2\}, \{1, 4\}, \{2, 3\}, \{3, 4\}\}\rangle, \langle\{\{1, 2, 3\}, \{1, 2, 4\}, \{1, 3, 4\}, \{2, 3, 4\}\}\rangle)$ and $r = 0.5$. The output of the construction algorithm is the PQS $(\langle\{\{1\}, \{2\}, \{3\}, \{4\}\}\rangle, \langle\{\{1, 2\}, \{1, 3\}, \{1, 4\}, \{2, 3\}\}\rangle)$. According to this input and output, the following partially ordered UQS is constructed: $(\langle\{\{1, 2\}, \{1, 4\}, \{2, 3\}, \{3, 4\}\}, \{\{1\}, \{2\}, \{3\}, \{4\}\}\rangle, \langle\{\{1, 2, 3\}, \{1, 2, 4\}, \{1, 3, 4\}, \{2, 3, 4\}\}, \{\{1, 2\}, \{1, 3\}, \{1, 4\}, \{2, 3\}\}\rangle)$.

The input SQS of MQA can also be a partially ordered SQS. The quorum selection in the resulting UQS is as follows: The quorum selection inside a priority class is done randomly. Strict quorums preserve their partial order and they have priority over probabilistic ones.

4.2 All Quorums-Based Construction

The objective of the *All Quorums-Based Construction Algorithm* (AQA) is to increase strict operation availability while at the same time decreasing the data consistency less than using MQA. With this aim, the construction is adapted in a "more" consistency-oriented manner. Revisiting the GP example, the quorums from the MQA approach can be represented by a 4×4 Karnaugh-Veitch map as in Fig. 1(a). The strict read quorum set input part is $\mathcal{Q}_{\mathcal{R}}^{S} = \{\{1,2\}, \{1,4\}, \{2,3\}, \{3,4\}\}$. According to MQA, for reading, four probabilistic quorums $\{1\}$, $\{2\}$, $\{3\}$, $\{4\}$ are generated. In the Karnaugh-Veitch map, these quorums are vertical and horizontal neighbors of the minimal strict quorums. Not only these can be considered as probabilistic quorums, but also neighbors of non-minimal strict quorums like $\{1, 2, 3\}$, $\{1, 2, 4\}$, $\{1, 2, 4\}$, and $\{1, 2, 3, 4\}$. With this method, two additional neighbors $\{1, 3\}$ and $\{2, 4\}$ are found as indicated in Fig. 1(b). As these quorums do not respect the strict GP quorum construction rules, they are probabilistic quorums and their size is greater than the size of

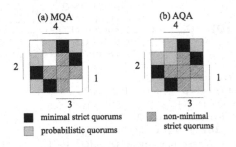

Fig. 1. Basic idea of AQA

probabilistic quorums generated using MQA. By this means, the intersection probability of the quorums is higher, thereby potentially guaranteeing higher data consistency. In the following, the generatePQS function is presented, which is the only differing part of the formalized version of AQA.

If the quorum system is partially ordered, then the algorithm proceeds as MQA. Returning to the previous GP example, the input strict quorum system is the same as in the previous subsection. The output PQS is $(\langle\{\{1,3\}, \{2,4\}, \{1\}, \{2\}\}\rangle, \langle\{\{1,2\}, \{1,3\}, \{1,4\}, \{2,3\}\}\rangle)$. After the union of the strict and probabilistic quorum systems, the final result is $(\langle\{\{1,2\}, \{1,4\}, \{2,3\}, \{3,4\}\}, \{\{1,3\}, \{2,4\}, \{1,2\}\}\rangle, \langle\{\{1,2,3\}, \{1,2,4\}, \{1,3,4\}, \{2,3,4\}\}, \{\{1,2\}, \{1,3\}, \{1,4\}, \{2,3\}\}\rangle)$.

```
function generatePQS(Q^S, P)
  Q^P := ⟨{}, ..., {}⟩, |Q^P| = |Q^S|
  for i := 1 to |Q^S|
    for j := 1 to |Q_i^S|
      X := combinations(Q_{i,j}^S, |Q_{i,j}^S| − 1)
      for p :∈ P
        X' := X ∪ {p}
        if X' ∉ Q^S
          Q_i^P := Q_i^P ∪ X'_l : X'_l ∉ Q_r^P, r < i
          for l = 1...|X'|
      Q_i^P := Q_i^P ∪ X_l : X_l ∉ Q_r^P, r < i
      for l = 1...|X|
  remove all Q_i^P with Q_i^P = ∅ from Q^P
  return Q^P
```

5   Evaluation

Our approach allows probabilistic read and write operations for increasing their availability for classes of applications that favor availability over consistency. Data consistency depends on the probability that two consecutive read and write operations' quorums have processes in common. In this context, the intersection probabilities for strict read quorums, probabilistic read quorums, strict write quorums and probabilistic write quorums have to be considered.

5.1   Markov Chain Analysis

We used a discrete-time Markov chain to analyse the consistency vs. availabilities trade-off of the derived UQSs. For this, the Markov chain from Fig. 2 was used, with eight states, every two of them related to the four different types of operations: strict write (SW), probabilistic write (PW), strict read (SR), probabilistic read (PR). The set of states is $\mathcal{S} = \{\text{SW}, \text{PW}, \text{SR}, \text{PR}, \text{SW'}, \text{PW'}, \text{SR'}, \text{PR'}\}$. The former four represent states, for which the last available and therefore successfully executed operation was one of these four operations. The latter four represent states, for which the last operation was unavailable and therefore unsuccessful, but the previous available and therefore successful operation was one of the former four. A read (write) operation is executed with probability x $(1 - x)$. Additionally, we use the following availability notations: A_{Op} for operation Op, $A_{Op_2}^{Op_1}$ for operation Op_2 if the previous operation was Op_1. $I_{Op_1 Op_2}$ is the intersection probability for the quorum sets of two consecutive operations Op_1 and Op_2. These values can be easily calculated during the constructions and are therefore omitted. The transition probabilities of the Markov chain are calculated using the read probability of the distributed system and the strict and probabilistic availabilities of quorum sets, which are constructed depending on the previous operation. For example, the transition probability A from state SW to itself is the probability that a write operation is executed multiplied by the availability of the quorum set for strict write operations. P is the transition matrix of the Markov chain; some of its transition probabilities are: $A = (1 - x) \cdot A_{SW}$, $B = (1 - x) \cdot (1 - A_{SW}) \cdot A_{PW}^{SW}$, $C = x \cdot A_{SR}$, $D = x \cdot (1 - A_{SR}) \cdot A_{PR}^{SW}$, $E = 1 - x \cdot A_{SR} - x \cdot (1 - A_{SR}) \cdot A_{PR}^{SW} - (1 - x) \cdot A_{SW} - (1 - x) \cdot (1 - A_{SW}) \cdot A_{PW}^{SW}$. The remaining transition

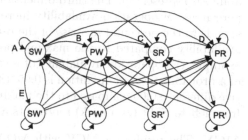

Fig. 2. Markov chain used for the analysis

probabilities are calculated similarly. The aim of the Markov chain analysis is to determine the operation availabilities and data consistency values in steady state. Let π be the steady state vector. The read (write) operation availability A (R) (A (W)) is the sum of all probabilities of transitions, which lead to a strict or probabilistic read (write) state in the Markov chain, multiplied by the steady state probability of the source state: $A(R) := \sum_{Op \in \mathcal{S}} \pi(Op) \cdot x \cdot (A_{SR} + (1 - A_{SR}) \cdot A_{PR}^{Op})$, $A(W) := \sum_{Op \in \mathcal{S}} \pi(Op) \cdot (1 - x) \cdot (A_{SW} + (1 - A_{SW}) \cdot A_{PW}^{Op})$. The data consistency is calculated using the intersection probabilities of two possible consecutive operations: $C = \pi \cdot CM$, where CM is a consistency vector containing the sum of the products of transition probabilities between two states in the Markov chain and the intersection probabilities between the previous and all possible current operations. Formally, $CM(Op_1) := \sum_{Op_2 \in \mathcal{S}} P(Op_1, Op_2) \cdot I_{Op_1 Op_2}$ for $Op_1 \in \mathcal{S}$.

5.2   Results

The overall motivation is to understand the qualitative relation between the degree of consistency and operation availabilities. For this purpose, we applied our approaches to classic replication strategies. Both, MQA and AQA were analyzed for $N = 13$ processes. For constructing the SQS, three replication strategies were considered: the Majority Consensus Voting (MCV)[5], the Grid Protocol and the Tree Quorum Protocol. GP is structure-based replication strategy. TQP is structure-based and partially ordered. The probabilistic quorum rate r is varied between 0.0 and 0.9. This variation is non-regular because of our initial assumption $r = r_r = r_w$. In this case, depending on the strategy and the number of strict quorums, only specific r-values can be considered. The uniform process availability a in the system was varied between 0.0 and 1.0 by step size 0.05 with an exception in the $[0.05, 0.6]$ interval, where the step size was set to 0.025 for highlighting the relevant interval for our approach. As read probability of the distributed system, we chose $x = 0.8$. The trade-off between the *percentage* of availability *increase* and the degree of consistency was analyzed, with r and a varied as mentioned above. The analysis results are represented as three-dimensional maps. On the x-axis, the degree of data consistency is represented in decreasing order from left to right. On the y-axis, the uniform process availability is represented. The third dimension represented by the color scale[2] is the percentage of operation availability increase. This operation availability corresponds to the percental increase of the relative difference of the strict operation availability compared to the maximal possible availability of 1.0. Thus, if, for example, the operation availability of a strict read operation is 0.9 and the one of a probabilistic read operation is 0.95, then the percentage increase of the relative difference 0.05 compared to the maximal increase of 0.1 is 50%. Every curve from left to right (and back) represents a particular value of r.

MCV. The results for MCV with MQA and AQA for read and write availabilities are shown in Fig. 3. The results are identical, because if $N = 13$, the read and write quorum sets are the same and there is no quantitative difference between MQA and AQA for MCV. All neighbors of strict minimal and non-minimal quorums are already determined with MQA, so AQA is not able to further increase the data consistency. The availability increase in percentage is not very high. For $r = 0.75$ and $a = 0.45$, it is ap-

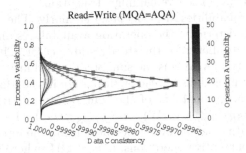

Fig. 3. MCV availability percentage increase

prox. 21.69% for both, read and write operations. The corresponding data consistency value is 99.97%. MCV is a strategy with large quorum sizes,

---

[2] More detailed colored maps can be obtained from the authors' home page.

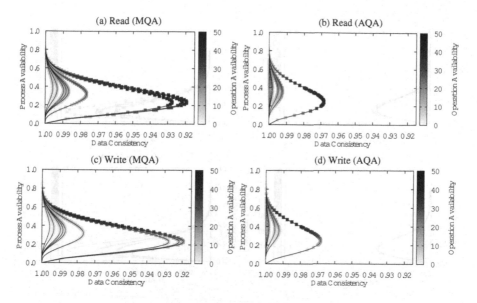

Fig. 4. GP availability percentage increase

so a slight consistency relaxation does not result in a high availability increase.

GP. The results for GP with MQA and AQA are given in Fig. 4. For the GP with $N = 13$ processes, a 3-rows and 5-columns grid was used where positions 4 and 5 in row 3 are empty. With MQA and for $r = 0.9$ and $a = 0.3$, an 44.41% availability increase can be reached for the read operation and an 29.24% increase for the write operation. This availability is gained at the cost of approx. 7.32% of data consistency. For $r = 0.9$ and $a = 0.45$, the read availability increase is 34.68% and the write availability increase is 42.59% traded-off for 3.21% data consistency. Using AQA, a high availability increase of 44.41% (29.24%) occurs if $r = 0.9$ and $a = 0.3$ for read (write) operations and the lost consistency is 2.99%. For $r = 0.9$ and $a = 0.45$, the read (write) availability increase is 34.68% (42.59%) with loosing 1.48% of data consistency. The AQA approach is thus more "consistency-oriented" than the MQA approach with the increase being at most the same as for MQA, but the consistency loss is smaller.

TQP. The results of TQP for MQA and AQA are illustrated in Fig. 5. For TQP with $N = 13$ processes, a tree with three levels is used in which every node has three children. This tree structure and also the partial order of the (read) quorum system has a non-typical effect on the construction algorithms: with MQA, there is a high availability increase of 34.92% for the read operation if $r = 0.5$ and $a = 0.2$. The corresponding increase for the write operation is 0.10% with 88.94% of data consistency. If $r = 0.9$ and $a = 0.65$, the increase is 0.92% (40.18%) for the read (write) operation if the data consistency is 99.57%. Strict read quorums are already highly available by the TQP construction, but strict

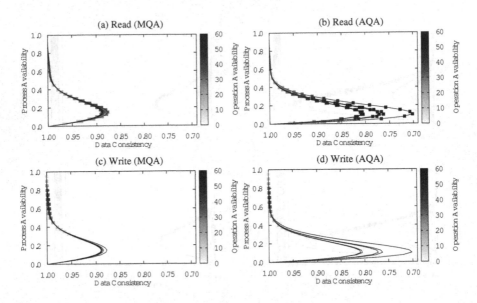

Fig. 5. TQP availability percentage increase

write quorums are not. This explains why the availability increase for the write operation is higher if processes are not highly available but also not extremely unavailable. On the other side, with AQA, the availability increases are 58.88% and 0.017% if $r = 0.5$ and $a = 0.2$ corresponding to 79.13% data consistency. If $r = 0.9$ and $a = 0.65$, the availability increases are 0.95% and 22.07% for the read and write operation with a data consistency of 99.86%. The data consistency for AQA is not always higher than for MQA, as one expects. This is due to the role of the tree structure and the high priorities of the small-sized read quorums. In case of MQA, the tree structure is partially preserved while AQA generates many quorums which do not resemble the logical tree structure of TQP.

6   Discussion

Availability increase corresponding to some data consistency loss depends on many factors: the original replication strategy, the processes' availability, the probabilistic replication degree, and the system's read probability. For the latter, we used a value intended to represent a read-dominated system.

There are some general characteristics which are uncovered by our analyses. If the value of a is in the $[0.8, 1.0]$ interval, then strict quorums are already highly available, and, because of their priority over probabilistic quorums, the availability increase is very small. Below $a = 0.8$, there is a significant availability increase. The availability increase for high r values is reached depending on the replication strategy around $r = 0.4$ for the read operation and around $r = 0.5$ for the write operation. If a is in the $[0.0, 0.2]$ interval, the availability increase is again non-significant, because not even the probabilistic quorums are available anymore. Another characteristic is related to the fact that the write availability increases in terms of the graphical representation from the top to the bottom "earlier" than the read availability. Write quorums have usually higher quorum sizes than read quorums. Therefore, strict write quorums are from the top to the bottom of the graph "earlier" unavailable than read quorums. In this case, probabilistic write quorums are used "before" probabilistic read quorums, explaining that the high write availability increase occurs "before" the high read availability increase when observing the graph from the top to the bottom.

As said, high availability increase occurs if the uniform process availability is relatively low. The relevant interval for real-life systems in normal conditions is often in the interval $[0.65, 1.0]$ [12]. Thus, to exploit the characteristics uncovered by our approach, one can use PQSs generated by the presented algorithms in application scenarios where a "last alternative" is desirable for executing read and write operations with a small loss in data consistency. This may be the case in systems, in which at some point in time processes are starting to crash and the processes' availability decreases below 0.65. If the processes' availability is greater than 0.65, our approach incurs no cost, because strict operations have priority over probabilistic ones. If the process availability is less than 0.65, then our approach is well-suited for executing "last minute" highly available operations (i.e., a "last pull-out" option) with a probabilistic consistency guarantee.

7 Conclusions

We presented two probabilistic quorum system construction algorithms which relaxes consistency for the benefit of increased operation availabilities. We analyzed these constructions and identified the one offering a more balanced consistency vs. availabilities trade-off. Contrary to previous approaches, our approaches consider both, probabilistic read *and* write operations. Operations are executed in a consistency-driven manner, i.e., strict quorums have priority over probabilistic ones. Both constructions were successfully applied to the three replication strategies MCV, GP, and TQP. They show an increase in the read operation availability and a significant increase of the write operation availability.

References

1. Lamport, L.: How to Make a Multiprocessor Computer That Correctly Executes Multiprocess Programs. IEEE Transactions on Computers 28(9), 690–691 (1979)
2. Theel, O., Pagnia, H.: Optimal Replica Control Protocols Exhibit Symmetric Operation Availabilities. In: Proc. of the 28th International Symposium on Fault-Tolerant Computing (FTCS-28), pp. 252–261. IEEE, Washington (1998)
3. Cheung, S.Y., Ammar, M.H., Ahamad, M.: The Grid Protocol: A High Performance Scheme for Maintaining Replicated Data. IEEE Transactions on Knowledge and Data Engineering 4(6), 582–592 (1992)
4. Agrawal, D., El Abbadi, A.: The Tree Quorum Protocol: An Efficient Approach for Managing Replicated Data. In: Proc. of the 16th International Conference on Very Large Database, pp. 243–254. Morgan Kaufmann, San Francisco (1990)

5. Thomas, R.H.: A Majority Consensus Approach to Concurrency Control for Multiple Copy Databases. ACM Transactions on Database Systems 4(2), 180–209 (1979)
6. Chockler, G., Gilbert, S., Patt-Shamir, B.: Communication-Efficient Probabilistic Quorum Systems for Sensor Networks. In: Proc. of the 4th International Conference on Pervasive Computing and Communications Workshops, pp. 111–117. IEEE, Washington (2006)
7. Gramoli, V., Raynal, M.: Timed Quorum Systems for Large-Scale and Dynamic Environments. In: Tovar, E., Tsigas, P., Fouchal, H. (eds.) OPODIS 2007. LNCS, vol. 4878, pp. 429–442. Springer, Heidelberg (2007)
8. Yu, H.: Signed Quorum Systems. In: Proc. of the 23rd Symposium on Principles of Distributed Computing, 246–255. ACM, New York (2004)
9. Peleg, D., Wool, A.: How to Be an Efficient Snoop, or the Probe Complexity of Quorum Systems. SIAM Journal on Discrete Mathematics 15(3), 416–433 (2002)
10. Liebig, C., Pagnia, H., Schwappacher, F., Theel, O.: A Quality-of-Service Approach for Mobile Users of Replicated Data in Distributed Systems. In: Proc. of the 10th European Simulation Multiconference, pp. 842–851. SCS (1996)
11. Malkhi, D., Reiter, M.K., Wright, R.N.: Probabilistic Quorum Systems. In: Proc. of the 16th Symposium on Principles of Distributed Computing, pp. 267–273. ACM, New York (1997)
12. Warns, T., Storm, C., Hasselbring, W.: Availability of Globally Distributed Nodes: An Empirical Evaluation. In: Proc. of the 27th International Symposium on Reliable Distributed Systems, pp. 279–284. IEEE, Washington (2008)

Hamiltonicity of a General OTIS Network

(Short Paper)

Nagendra Kumar[1], Rajeev Kumar[2], Dheeresh K. Mallick[3], and Prasanta K. Jana[4]

[1,2,4] Department of Computer Science and Engineering,
Indian School of Mines University, Dhanbad 826 004, India
[3] Birla Institute of Technology, Mesra 835 215, India
{nagendraism,ra_cse_ism}@yahoo.co.in, dkmallick@gmail.com,
prasantajana@yahoo.com

Abstract. In this paper, we present a novel method to construct a Hamiltonian cycle for an $n \times n$ general OTIS network. Our method is common for both odd and even value of n in contrast to two separate schemes for odd and even n as described in [1]. We also provide an algorithm that generates a Hamiltonian cycle of a general $(n + 2k) \times (n + 2k)$ OTIS network directly from a basic Hamiltonian cycle of an $n \times n$ OTIS network.

Keywords: Hamiltonian Cycle, OTIS network, optoelectronic parallel computer, Durand-Kerner method.

1 Introduction

Optical Transpose Interconnection System (OTIS) proposed by Marsden [2] is an optoelectronic interconnection system that exploits full advantages of both the electronic and optical links. An $n \times n$ OTIS network consists of n^2 processors that are divided into n groups (also called clusters) in the form of an $n \times n$ lattice. The processors within the same group are interconnected by usual electronic links and the processors of two different groups are by optical links. The interconnectivity among the processors within a group usually follows some popular network (called basis network) such as mesh, hypercube etc. and accordingly the OTIS network is called as OTIS-Mesh, OTIS-Hypercube and so on. The interconnectivity among the different groups follows the OTIS rule, i.e., p^{th} processor of the gth group is connected to the gth processor of the pth group. In the recent years, an extensive study has been made on several issues of OTIS network. For example, topological properties have been discussed in [3], [4], [5], [6], [7]. Parallel algorithms for various operations have been developed such as image processing [8], matrix multiplication [9], basic operations [10], polynomial interpolation and polynomial root finding [11], prefix computation [12], sorting [13].

Hamiltonicity is an useful property of an interconnection network that supports fault tolerance, emulation of linear array, ring algorithms and many others. A cycle in an interconnection network N is called a Hamiltonian cycle (H-cycle) if it contains every node of N exactly once. If there exists a Hamiltonian cycle in N, then N is called Hamiltonian. Hamiltonicity for various interconnection networks such as star

K. Kant et al. (Eds.): ICDCN 2010, LNCS 5935, pp. 459–465, 2010.
© Springer-Verlag Berlin Heidelberg 2010

graphs, crossed cubes, complete graph, WK-recursive network have been studied in [14], [15], [16], and [17] respectively. The problem of Hamiltonicity for OTIS network was originally proposed by Day et al. [3] with the following open problem: If there exists an L-length H-cycle in every basis network G (Group), then there exists an L^2-length H-cycle in the whole OTIS network (OTIS-G). Hamiltonicity for OTIS k-ary n-cube has been reported in [4]. An initial work on Hamlitonicity of a general OTIS network is done by Parhami [5]. In his detailed work [1] later, he has shown that an $n \times n$ OTIS network is Hamiltonian if its basis network is Hamiltonian. However, he has presented two different methods for the construction of H-cycle by treating n separately for odd and even cases. As a result, their method yields two dissimilar H-cycles for odd and even values of n.

In this paper, we further study Hamiltonicity of a general OTIS Network and present a common proof for the existence of a H-cycle for both the odd and even value of n. We also show that given any basic H-cycle in an $n \times n$ OTIS network, we can directly generate a H-cycle for $(n + 2k) \times (n + 2k)$ OTIS network assuming $n \geq 6$ and $k \geq 1$.

2 Proposed Algorithm

We first present here, some basic terminologies that help in understanding our proposed method.

***Definition* 1** (open/closed link): In a H-cycle, a link (x, y) between any two nodes x and y is said to be open if it is not a part of the H-cycle; otherwise it is said to be closed. For example, the links $(3, 4)$ and $(0, 1)$ in cluster 0 of Fig. 1(a) are open and closed respectively. The H-cycle is shown in bold line in this figure. We denote these links by $x \xrightarrow{\text{open}} y$ and $x \xrightarrow{\text{closed}} y$ respectively.

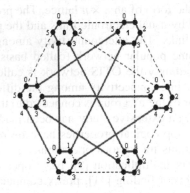
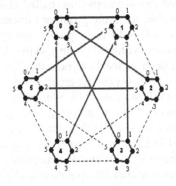

(a) 3 and 4 are consecutive clusters with the link (0, 5) open

(b) 1 and 2 are the consecutive clusters with the link (0, 5) open

Fig. 1. Two different basic Hamiltonian cycles for $n = 6$

Definition 2 (basic Hamiltonian cycle): A H-cycle in an $n \times n$ OTIS network (for $n \geq$ 6) is said to be basic if it has exactly two consecutive clusters (in ascending index) in each of which the electronic link $(0, n - 1)$ is open but closed in the remaining clusters. Two such different basic H-cycles for $n = 6$ are shown in Fig. 1.

As per the definition, the clusters (i.e., groups) in a basic H-cycle may have the open links other than $(0, n - 1)$. There may exist more than one basic H-cycle for any value of n as illustrated in Fig. 1. Our method is given by the following theorem.

Theorem 1. Given a basic H-cycle H_n ($n \geq 6$ and n is odd or even) in an $n \times n$ OTIS network, there exists at least one H-cycle H_{n+2} in the $(n + 2) \times (n + 2)$ OTIS network and H_{n+2} is also basic.

Proof (by construction):

Step 1. Let α, β ($= \alpha + 1$) be two consecutive clusters in the basic H-cycle H_n in which the link $(0, n - 1)$ is open. Choose any other two consecutive clusters from the remaining $n-2$ clusters of H_n and name them as γ and δ ($=\gamma + 1$) respectively. For example, in the basic H-cycle H_6 of Fig. 1(a), choose $\alpha = 3$ and $\beta = 4$; $\gamma = 1$ and $\delta = 2$.

We now map H_n on $(n + 2) \times (n + 2)$ OTIS network. As an example, mapping of H_6 (Fig. 1(a)) on to 8×8 OTIS network is shown in Fig. 2. While mapping H_n onto the $(n + 2) \times (n + 2)$ OTIS network, we use some logical links, which should not be the part of the final H-cycle H_{n+2}. However, this will be taken care in the final construction of H_{n+2}.

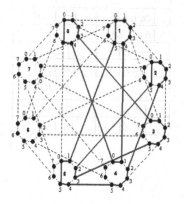

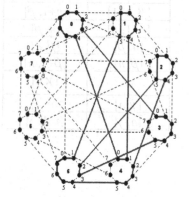

Fig. 2. Hamiltonian cycle H_6 (Bold line)   **Fig. 3.** Exploring the nodes of the clusters 0 and 5 of the 2nd group

Step 2. We now divide the $n + 2$ clusters of the $(n + 2) \times (n + 2)$ OTIS network into two groups. The clusters α, β, γ, δ, n, $n + 1$ are kept in the 1st group and the remaining ones in the 2nd group. H_n is then extend into $(n + 2) \times (n + 2)$ OTIS network to construct H_{n+2} as follows.

2.1. In each cluster of the 2nd group, there is a logical link $(0, n - 1)$ and the nodes n and $n + 1$ are unexplored. We remove the logical link, i.e., $(0, n - 1)$ by visiting the nodes n and $n + 1$ via the path $n - 1 \rightarrow n \rightarrow n + 1 \rightarrow 0$ as shown in Fig. 3.

For exploring the nodes of the 1st group, we have the following observations.

i)   In each of the clusters α and β, the nodes n and $n + 1$ are unexplored.
ii) In each of the clusters γ and δ there is a logical link $(0, n - 1)$ and the nodes n and $n + 1$ are unexplored.
iii) All the nodes of the clusters n and $n + 1$ are unexplored.

2.2. We now visit all the unexplored nodes of the 1st group via the path starting from the clusters γ and δ as separately shown in Table 1 and Table 2 respectively in which $[x, y]$ indicates the xth node of the cluster y and any increment or decrement operation on x and y is modulo $n + 2$. The result after this step is shown in Fig. 4 in which the traversed path is shown by shadow line. Note that both the paths generated by Table 1 and Table 2 are symmetrical.

Table 1. Path traversal from γ

From	To
$[0, \gamma]$	$[n+1, \gamma]$
$[n+1, \gamma]$	$[\gamma, n+1]$
$[\gamma, n+1]$	$[\gamma-1, n+1]$
$\vdots$	$[\beta, n+1]$
$[\beta, n+1]$	$[n+1, \beta]$
$[n+1, \beta]$	$[n, \beta]$
$[n, \beta]$	$[\beta, n]$
$[\beta, n]$	$[\beta+1, n]$
$\vdots$	$[\gamma, n]$
$[\gamma, n]$	$[n, \gamma]$
$[n, \gamma]$	$[n-1, \gamma]$

Table 2. Path traversal from δ

From	To
$[0, \delta]$	$[n+1, \delta]$
$[n+1, \delta]$	$[\delta, n+1]$
$[\delta, n+1]$	$[\delta+1, n+1]$
$\vdots$	$[\alpha, n+1]$
$[\alpha, n+1]$	$[n+1, \alpha]$
$[n+1, \alpha]$	$[n, \alpha]$
$[n, \alpha]$	$[\alpha, n]$
$[\alpha, n]$	$[\alpha-1, n]$
$\vdots$	$[\delta, n]$
$[\delta, n]$	$[n, \delta]$
$[n, \delta]$	$[n-1, \delta]$

Step 3. Merge the paths resulted from steps 2.1 and 2.2 to obtain the final H-cycle H_{n+2}. The final Hamiltonian cycle after this step is shown in Fig. 5, which is obtained from Fig. 3 and Fig. 4.

The above method can generate a different H-cycle for a different set of γ and δ (e.g., $\gamma = 0$ and $\delta = 1$ in Fig. 1(a) keeping the same value of α and β. This can be noted that in the final H-cycle α and β are the only clusters in which link $(0, n+1)$ is open. Therefore the resultant Hamiltonian is also basic.

3 Method for Generating Hamiltonian Cycle

We now describe the method to generate H-cycle H_{n+x} directly from a basic H-cycle H_n. However, without any loss of generality, we assume here $x = 2k$, $k \geq 1$. We first represent H_n by a matrix as follows:

$$a_{i,j} = \begin{cases} 1, \text{ if the electronic link } (j, (j+1) \bmod n) \text{ exists in the } i^{th} \text{ cluster} \\ 0, \text{ otherwise} \end{cases}$$

$$\text{for } 0 \leq i, j < n.$$

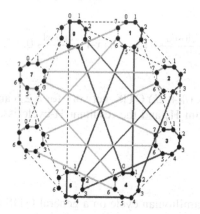 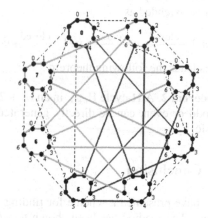

Fig. 4. Visiting remaining unexplored nodes of the 1ˢᵗ group for $n = 6$

Fig. 5. Final Hamiltonian cycle

The basic motivation of this representation is to generate the matrix that represents higher size H-cycle directly from a given basic H-cycle. As per the construction method of H_{n+2} from H_n described in section 2, we note the following observations for certain edges of the clusters belonging to the first group as defined in step 2 of the proof of Theorem 1 in section 2.

1) $n\text{-}1 \xrightarrow{\text{open}} n$, $\ n \xrightarrow{\text{closed}} n+1$, $\ n+1 \xrightarrow{\text{open}} 0$, for α and β (alternatively open and closed)

2) $n\text{-}1 \xrightarrow{\text{closed}} n$, $\ n \xrightarrow{\text{open}} n+1$, $\ n+1 \xrightarrow{\text{closed}} 0$, for γ and δ (alternatively closed and open)

3) $\alpha \xrightarrow{\text{open}} \beta$ and $\gamma \xrightarrow{\text{open}} \delta$ and remaining edges are closed for the clusters n and $n+1$

Therefore, we can generate H_{n+x}, $(x = 2k, k \geq 1)$ directly from H_n by extending the above observations as follows:

1) $n\text{-}1 \xrightarrow{\text{open}} n,\ n \xrightarrow{\text{closed}} n\text{+}1,\ n\text{+}1 \xrightarrow{\text{open}} n\text{+}2,\ n\text{+}2 \xrightarrow{\text{closed}} n\text{+}3,\ \dots,\ n\text{+}x\text{-}$
$1 \xrightarrow{\text{open}} 0$, for α and β

2) $n\text{-}1 \xrightarrow{\text{closed}} n,\ n \xrightarrow{\text{open}} n\text{+}1,\ n\text{+}1 \xrightarrow{\text{closed}} n\text{+}2,\ n\text{+}2 \xrightarrow{\text{open}} n\text{+}3,\ \dots,$
$n\text{+}x\text{-}1 \xrightarrow{\text{closed}} 0$, for γ and δ

3) $\alpha \xrightarrow{\text{open}} \beta$ and $\gamma \xrightarrow{\text{open}} \delta$ for all the clusters $n, n\text{+}1, \dots, n\text{+}x\text{-}1$

Similarly the paths $n\text{-}1 \xrightarrow{\text{closed}} n \xrightarrow{\text{closed}} n\text{+}1 \xrightarrow{\text{closed}} 0$ of the 2nd group clusters can be extended as

$$n\text{-}1 \xrightarrow{\text{closed}} n \xrightarrow{\text{closed}} n\text{+}1 \xrightarrow{\text{closed}} n\text{+}2 \xrightarrow{\text{closed}} n\text{+}3 \dots n\text{+}x\text{-}1 \xrightarrow{\text{closed}} 0.$$

This leads the following theorem.

Theorem 2. A H-cycle H_{n+2k} in an $(n + 2k) \times (n + 2k)$ OTIS network for $n \geq 6$ and n is odd or even, can be directly generated from H_n and the resultant H-cycle is also basic.

4 Conclusion

We have presented a scheme for finding a Hamiltonian cycle on a general OTIS network. The method has been shown to work for both the odd and even value of n in contrast to [1]. It has been shown that given a basic Hamiltonian cycle, multiple Hamiltonian cycles of higher size can be directly generated. As in [1], our result also supersedes the proofs for the Hamiltonicity of many networks, as they are the special cases of the general OTIS network.

References

1. Parhami, B.: The Hamlitonicity of swapped (OTIS) networks built of Hamiltonian component networks. Information Processing Letters 95, 441–445 (2005)
2. Marsden, G., Marchand, P., Harvey, P., Esener, S.: Optical transpose interconnection system architectures. Optics Letters 18, 1083–1085 (1993)
3. Day, K.: Topological properties of OTIS networks. IEEE Trans. Parallel and Distributed Systems 13, 359–366 (2002)
4. Day, K.: Optical transpose k-ary n-cube networks. J. of Systems Architecture. 50, 697–705 (2004)
5. Parhami, B.: Swapped interconnection networks: Topological, performance, and robustness attributes. J. of Parallel and Distributed Computing 65, 1443–1452 (2005)
6. Sahni, S.: Models and algorithms for optical and optoelectronic parallel computers. Intl. J. of Foundations of Computer Science 12, 249–264 (2001)
7. Zane, F., Marchand, P., Paturi, R., Esener, S.: Scalable network architectures using the optical transpose interconnection system (OTIS). J. of Parallel and Distributed Computing 60, 521–538 (2000)

8. Wang, C.F., Sahni, S.: Image processing on the OTIS-Mesh optoelectronic computer. IEEE Trans. Parallel and Distributed Systems 11, 9–109 (2000)
9. Wang, C.F., Sahni, S.: Matrix multiplication on the OTIS-Mesh optoelectronic computer. IEEE Trans. Computers 50, 635–646 (2001)
10. Wang, C.F., Sahni, S.: Basic operations on the OTIS-Mesh optoelectronic computer. IEEE Trans. Parallel and Distributed Systems 9, 1226–1236 (1998)
11. Jana, P.K.: Polynomial interpolation and polynomial root finding on OTIS-mesh. Parallel Computing 32, 301–312 (2006)
12. Jana, P.K., Sinha, B.P.: An Improved parallel prefix algorithm on OTIS-Mesh. Parallel Processing Letters 16, 429–440 (2006)
13. Osterloh, A.: Sorting on the OTIS–Mesh. In: 14th Intl. Parallel and Distributed Processing Symp (IPDPS 2000), pp. 269–274 (2000)
14. Fu, J.-S.: Conditional fault-tolerant Hamiltonicity of star graphs. Parallel Computing 33, 488–496 (2007)
15. Huang, H., Fu, J., Chen, G.: Fault-free Hamiltonian cycles in crossed cubes with conditional link faults. Information Sciences 177, 5590–5597 (2007)
16. Fu, J.S.: Conditional fault Hamiltonicity of the complete graph. Information Processing Letter 107, 110–113 (2008)
17. Fu, J.S.: Hamiltonicity of WK-Recursive network with and without Faulty nodes. IEEE Trans. on Parallel and Distributed Systems 16, 853–865 (2005)

Specifying Fault-Tolerance Using Split Precondition Logic

(Short Paper)

Awadhesh Kumar Singh[1] and Anup Kumar Bandyopadhyay[2]

[1] Department of Computer Engineering, National Institute of Technology,
Kurukshetra, India 136119
aksinreck@rediffmail.com
[2] Department of Electronics and Telecommunication Engineering,
Jadavpur University, Kolkata, India 700032
anupbandyopadhyay@hotmail.com

Abstract. The focus of the paper is to provide a formal logic, for specifying fault-tolerant systems, using a state and transition based approach. Another goal is to reason, formally, about the possible behaviors of a system consisting of some malicious nodes. The Byzantine agreement protocol serves as an illustration for the notation. The contribution is the development of a style of modeling and reasoning that allows for a straightforward and thorough analysis of fault-tolerant systems.

Keywords: Byzantine agreement, State transition rule, Weakest self-precondition, Weakest cooperation requirement, Correctness.

1 Introduction

The Split Precondition Logic (SPL) is motivated by Dijkstra's *wp*-logic for sequential systems [1]. It was introduced to verify statically structured distributed systems [2]. The underlying system was assumed fault free. Hence, the present article is to demonstrate the power of SPL in the environment where nodes may be faulty. We propose to extend the proof technology into the realm of most insidious faults, namely Byzantine, where processes may be unreliable and may depict unpredictable behavior. Therefore, the article is not simply, a case study or, about re-presenting a known approach; it also aims to demonstrate that the SPL is suitable for modeling and reasoning about the fault-tolerant systems. Although, SPL may not sound as a well-developed methodology, the concepts presented here are not introduced casually. Therefore, the Byzantine agreement protocol has been chosen for the illustration. Our approach could successfully handle it through the abstractions of inter-process communication.

2 The Split Precondition Logic (SPL)

Like every formal language, the split precondition logic also has a well-defined syntax and semantics. A brief description of the mathematical model is being given in the following paragraphs. The readers may refer [2] for the details of formulation.

K. Kant et al. (Eds.): ICDCN 2010, LNCS 5935, pp. 466–472, 2010.

A set $P.X$ of states and a set $P.R$ of state transition rules define a process P. On the similar lines a set $S.P$ of processes interacting through message transactions define a system S. The expression $in(P.x)$ represents that a process P is in state $P.x$. The initial state of process, which is predefined, is denoted by the expression $initial(P.x_0)$. The collection of states of all the processes belonging to set $S.P$ is termed as state SX of the system S.

A state transition rule represents the movement of process from one state to other. In order to fire any transition rule $P.r$ and eventual establishment of post condition Q, there exists a corresponding weakest precondition $wp(P.r, Q)$. We postulate the value of wp for a specific post condition Q and for a specific transition $P.r$. In our logic, weakest precondition has been splitted into two entities.

(i) $wsp(P.r, Q)$, termed as weakest self precondition and is related to the process P itself.
(ii) $wcr(P.r, Q)$, termed as weakest cooperation requirements and includes the cooperation requirements from other processes.

Thus, the total weakest precondition would be given by the following expression:

$$wp(P.r, Q) = wsp(P.r, Q) \wedge wcr(P.r, Q)$$

The above expression justifies the appropriateness of the name Split Precondition Logic. Since, the cooperation requirements have already been included in the wp in our approach, separate proof of cooperation is not necessary. Any transition rule $P.r$ is described jointly by weakest precondition $wp(P.r, Q)$ and post condition Q.

3 The Byzantine Agreement

We consider the Byzantine agreement protocol given in [3]. However, it is specified, there, in UNITY. We present it in SPL below.

3.1 The Informal Specification

Each process is either Reliable or Unreliable. Each Reliable process reaches one of two decisions, *false* or *true*. One process g is distinguished and has associated with it a Boolean value B. It is required that:

(1) If g is Reliable, the decision value of each Reliable process is B.
(2) All Reliable processes reach the same decision.

Faults may make Reliable processes Unreliable.

3.2 The Formal Specification

We assume authenticated communication: messages sent by Reliable processes are correctly received by Reliable processes, and Unreliable processes cannot forge messages on behalf of Reliable processes.

The agreement is reached within $N+1$ rounds of communication, where N is the maximum number of processes that can be Unreliable. In each round r, where $r \leq N$, every Reliable process j that has not yet reached a decision of *true* checks whether g

and at least $r-1$ other processes have reached a decision of *true*. If the check is successful, j reaches a decision of *true*. If j does not reach a decision of *true* in the first N rounds, it reaches a decision of *false* in round $N+1$. For formal description we define following states of the processes in the system.

Sr.	STATE	SEMANTICS
1.	$(P_j.rel = 1)$	State denoting that process j is Reliable
2.	$(P_j.rel = 0)$	State denoting that process j is Unreliable
3.	$(P_j.d^r = 1)$	State denoting process j's tentative decision up to round r is *true*
4.	$(P_j.d^r = 0)$	State denoting process j's tentative decision up to round r is *false*
5.	$(P_j.d^r = ?)$	State denoting process j's tentative decision up to round r is unknown
6.	$(P_j.c_k^r = 1)$	State denoting that in round r process j knows that process k has reached a decision of *true*
7.	$(P_j.c_k^r = 0)$	State denoting that in round r process j knows that process k has reached a decision of *false*
8.	$(P_j.c_k^r = ?)$	State denoting that in round r process j does not know whether process k has reached a decision

The byzantine agreement algorithm is described by the following transition rules, along with the fault it tolerates.

Main Routine
j, k, l: arbitrary processes, initially, assumed to be reliable.
while $r < N+1$ (Starting from $r = 0$ we need $N+1$ iterations)

   begin
   $\langle Transition\ Rules \rangle$

   end
do $r = r + 1$

Transition Rules:
$P_j.r_0 ::\%$ we assume authenticated communication, hence, an Unreliable j cannot for

Reliable k set $in(P_j.c_k^r = 1)$ to *true* unless $in(P_k.d^{r-1} = 1)$ is *true*. %

$wsp((P_j.r_0, in(P_j.c_k^r = 1)) = in(P_j.rel = 0)$; $wcr((P_j.r_0, in(P_j.c_k^r = 1)) = in(P_k.d^{r-1} = 1)$
End of $P_j.r_0$;
$P_j.r_1 ::\%$ A reliable process j gets prepared to pass the information contained in

$in(P_k.d^{r-1} = 1)$ to other processes. Process j can know process k's decision in round r if either it knows process k's tentative decision in round $r-1$ or there exist some other process l that knows process k's decision in round $r-1$. %

$P_j.r_1$::

$$Q_1 = [in(P_j.c_k^r = 1) = \{in(P_k.d^{r-1} = 1) \vee in(P_l.c_k^{r-1} = 1)\}]$$

$$Q_2 = [in(P_j.c_k^r = 0)]; Q_3 = [in(P_j.c_k^r = ?)]$$

$$Q = Q_1 \vee Q_2 \vee Q_3$$

$$B_1 = true; B_2 = [in(P_j.rel = 0) \wedge in(P_k.rel = 1)]; B_3 = [in(P_j.rel = 0) \wedge in(P_k.rel = 0)]$$

$$B = B_1 \vee B_2 \vee B_3$$

$$wp(P_j.r_1, Q) = B \wedge \{B_1 \Rightarrow wr(select, in(P_j.r_1.s_1))\} \wedge$$

$$\{B_2 \Rightarrow wr(select, in(P_j.r_1.s_2))\} \wedge \{B_3 \Rightarrow wr(select, in(P_j.r_1.s_3))\} \wedge$$

$$\{in(P_j.r_1.s_1) \Rightarrow wp(P_j.r_1^1, Q_1)\} \wedge \{in(P_j.r_1.s_2) \Rightarrow wp(P_j.r_1^2, Q_2)\} \wedge$$

$$\{in(P_j.r_1.s_3) \Rightarrow wp(P_j.r_1^3, Q_3)\}$$

End of $P_j.r_1$;

Let, *Pred* be some predicate and *Sum(Pred, r)* be the number of times the predicate *Pred* becomes *true* for a fixed r. Formally, it is specified below:

$$Sum(Pred, r) = \sum_{\forall k} \chi(Pred(k, r)), \text{ where } \chi \text{ is an integer function defined as follows:}$$

$$\chi(Pred(k,r)) = 1 \quad \text{for } Pred(k,r) = true$$
$$\qquad\qquad = 0 \quad \text{otherwise}$$

Now, for the sake of brevity, we further define another variable *sum* as follows:

$$sum = Sum(in(P_j.c_k^r = 1))$$

We assume authenticated communication: messages sent by Reliable processes are correctly received by Reliable processes, and Unreliable processes do not forge messages on behalf of Reliable processes. Hence, each process j knows, in round r, the decision of that k arbitrary processes with whom it has any communication. Informally, *sum* is merely a local counter at the site of each process j that counts the number of such processes k, iff in round r process j knows that process k has reached a decision of *true*.

$P_j.r_2$:: % in each round r, the tentative decision of each Reliable process j is set to *true* iff its previous tentative decision is *true* or $\{in(P_j.c_g^r = 1) \wedge (sum \geq r)\}$ holds. %

$$Q_1 = [in(P_j.d^r = 1) = \{in(P_j.d^{r-1} = 1) \vee \{in(P_j.c_g^r = 1) \wedge sum \geq r\}\}]; Q_2 = [in(P_j.d^r = ?)]$$

$$Q = Q_1 \vee Q_2$$

$$B_1 = true; B_2 = [in(P_j.rel = 0)]$$

$$B = B_1 \vee B_2$$

$$wp(P_j.r_2, Q) = B \wedge \{B_1 \Rightarrow wr(select, in(P_j.r_2.s_1))\} \wedge \{B_2 \Rightarrow wr(select, in(P_j.r_2.s_2))\} \wedge$$

$$\{in(P_j.r_2.s_1) \Rightarrow wp(P_j.r_2^1, Q_1)\} \wedge \{in(P_j.r_2.s_2) \Rightarrow wp(P_j.r_2^2, Q_2)\}$$

End of $P_j.r_2$;

Byzantine Fault (B_f)

N is the maximum number of processes that can be Unreliable.

Let, $C = [Sum(in(P_k.rel = 0)) < N]$

The following transition rule represents the occurrence of Byzantine Fault.

B_f :: % Faults may make Reliable processes Unreliable.%

$$wsp(B_f, in(P_j.rel = 0)) = in(P_j.rel = 1)$$

$$wcr(B_f, in(P_j.rel = 0)) = C$$

End of B_f;

3.3 The Predicate for Byzantine Fault Tolerance

Property 1 and 2 of the specification can easily be proved by induction. However, the agreement algorithm would be B_f–tolerant if the following predicate P remains satisfied throughout the life time of the system.

$P = A \wedge [B \wedge C \wedge D \wedge E]$

Informally, P states that the domain of execution of the agreement algorithm satisfies the following four conditions. (A) The number of Unreliable processes is at most N. (B) Before the first round, the tentative decision of each Reliable process j is *false*, and each $in(P_j.c=1)$ state is *false*. (C) In each round r, the tentative decision of each Reliable process j is set to *true* iff its previous tentative decision is *true* or $\{in(P_j.c_g^r = 1) \wedge (sum \geq r)\}$ holds (D) $in(P_k.c_j^r = 1)$ of each other process j is set to *true* only if $in(P_j.d^r = 1)$ is *true*. (E) In each round r, for all Reliable processes j and k, if the current tentative decision of j is *false* then $in(P_j.c_k^r = 1)$ is *true* iff $\{in(P_k.d^{r-1} = 1) \vee in(P_l.c_k^{r-1} = 1)\}$ is *true*.

(A)   System invariant $Inv = [Sum(in(P_k.rel = 0)) \leq N]$

(B)   Initial state $I \triangleq \exists j : \{in(P_j.rel = 1) \Rightarrow \neg in(P_j.d^0 = 1) \wedge \neg in(P_j.c_k^0 = 1)\}$

(C) $in(P_j.d^r = 1) \Rightarrow in(P_j.d^{r-1} = 1) \vee \{in(P_j.c_g^r = 1) \wedge (sum \geq r)\}$

(D) $in(P_k.c_j^r = 1) \xrightarrow{\;P\;} in(P_j.d^r = 1)$

(E) $\neg in(P_j.d^{r-1} = 1) \Rightarrow [in(P_j.c_k^r = 1) \Rightarrow \{in(P_k.d^{r-1} = 1) \vee in(P_l.c_k^{r-1} = 1)\}]$

4 The Proof of Correctness

Upon execution of transition rules,

(A)   The first conjunct of P is trivially preserved since no transition rules update any *rel* value.

(B)   The first clause of the second conjunct is preserved since no transition rules update any d^0 or c^0 value.

(C)   The second clause of the second conjunct is preserved from post condition Q_1 of transition rule $P_j.r_2$ as there is no precondition required.

(D)   The third clause of the second conjunct can be proved by considering the representation of a transition rule as a cause and effect relation [4]. According to this scheme a transition rule $P.r$ may be represented as $Q \xrightarrow{P} wp(P.r, Q)$, and reads "the post condition Q of a transition rule $P.r$ *implies in the past* the corresponding weakest precondition $wp(P.r, Q)$". Using this we can write the following equation from the transition rule $P_k.r_0$.

$$in(P_k.c_j^r = 1) \xrightarrow{P} [in(P_k.rel = 0) \land in(P_j.d^{r-1} = 1)]$$

$\Rightarrow$ { predicate calculus }

$$in(P_k.c_j^r = 1) \xrightarrow{P} in(P_j.d^{r-1} = 1) \tag{1}$$

Also, from the post condition Q_1 of the transition rule $P_j.r_2$

$$in(P_j.d^r = 1) \Rightarrow in(P_j.d^{r-1} = 1) \tag{2}$$

Hence, from equation 1 and 2, we can write as follows.

$$in(P_k.c_j^r = 1) \xrightarrow{P} in(P_j.d^r = 1)$$

Therefore, predicate (D) holds.

(E)   The last clause of the second conjunct is preserved from post condition Q_1 of transition rule $P_j.r_1$ as there is no precondition required.

5 Conclusion

In SPL, the system specifications use notations such as state-transition diagrams. The cooperation requirements have already been included, in the *wp*, in SPL. Thus, the separate proof of cooperation is not necessary [5]. Hence, our proof is simple and straightforward. We have chosen to manifest its strength through specification of the Byzantine agreement protocol, because sometimes good examples are more instructive than formal theories. Moreover, the SPL uses logical reasoning, which is still the only way to prove correctness in the case of larger systems [6].

References

1. Dijkstra, E.W.: A Discipline of Programming. Prentice Hall, Englewood Cliffs (1976)
2. Singh, A.K., Bandyopadhyay, A.K.: Verifying Mutual Exclusion and Liveness Properties with Split Preconditions. J. Comp. Sc. & Tech. 19(6), 795–802 (2004)

472   A.K. Singh and A.K. Bandyopadhyay

3. Arora, A., Gouda, M.: Closure and Convergence: A Foundation of Fault-Tolerant Computing. IEEE Trans. Soft. Engg. 19(11), 1015–1027 (1993)
4. Banerjee, J., Bandyopadhyay, A.K., Mandal, A.K.: Ordering of Events in Two-Process Concurrent System. ACM SIGSOFT Soft. Engg. Notes 32(4), 1–7 (2007)
5. Chandi, K.M., Sanders, B.A.: Predicate Transformers for Reasoning about Concurrent Computation. Sc. Comp. Prog. 24, 129–148 (1995)
6. Dierks, H.: Comparing Model Checking and Logical Reasoning for Real-Time Systems. Formal Aspects of Computing 16(2), 104–120 (2004)

Fast BGP Convergence Following Link/Router Failure

Swapan Kumar Ray and Susmit Shannigrahi

Computer Science and Engineering Department, Jadavpur University, Kolkata, 700032, India
skray@ieee.org, susmit@fedoraproject.org

Abstract. A Modified Border Gateway Protocol (MBGP) has been proposed towards achieving faster BGP convergence in the Internet following link/router/ network failures. MBGP adopts the overall strategy of distributed fault detection-cum-identification, fault notification and rediscovery-cum-readvertisement of valid routes. In the assumed simplified model of the Internet, the sole MBGP router in each autonomous system (AS) identifies any failed component using the novel concept of special neighbors and notifies the identity of the failed component to all the MBGP routers in the Internet. Six new messages, including a query-response message pair and four permanent withdrawal messages, have been proposed in MBGP, without changing the BGP message format. The path exploration problem is significantly reduced because some failures cause no path exploration, the others do but only in a small number of nearby routers and, finally, no invalid messages are ever exchanged. Simulation studies have demonstrated significantly faster convergence of MBGP over BGP.

Keywords: BGP Convergence, Slow Convergence in BGP, Fast BGP Convergence, Link or Router Failure in Internet, Path Exploration in BGP, Modified BGP, Special Neighbors.

1 Introduction

The Border Gateway Protocol (BGP) [1] is the de-facto standard for the inter-domain or inter-autonomous system (AS) routing protocol in the Internet. Unfortunately, BGP suffers from the problem of unstable routing and slow convergence following events like the failure of a link or a router, change of AS policies, failure or resetting of the underlying TCP connections, etc. [2]-[4]. This slow convergence of BGP is considered a serious problem for the growth of the Internet because of reasons like excessive loss/delay of packets which hamper the performance of applications like VoIP, streaming video, etc., and cause severe congestion and router overloads in the Internet.

The main reason behind the delayed protocol convergence in BGP is the so-called path exploration phenomenon that is present in all path vector protocols like BGP because they are inherently associated with path dependencies which refers to a recursive path learning phenomenon. The path selected by a router depends on paths learnt by its neighbors; the latter, in turn, depends on what the neighbors have learnt from their neighbors; and so on. Thus, in BGP, following a failure event, some of the paths become invalid so that routers go through a cycle of selecting and propagating invalid paths till all routers in the Internet have learnt valid paths after all obsolete paths have been explored and invalidated. Solving the path exploration problem in BGP is hard and

K. Kant et al. (Eds.): ICDCN 2010, LNCS 5935, pp. 473–484, 2010.
© Springer-Verlag Berlin Heidelberg 2010

it is made even harder because BGP allows arbitrary choice of import, export and route selection policies[2]. However, the policy aspects of BGP have not been considered in this paper.

In this paper, we have proposed a method called Modified BGP (MBGP) where each router periodically monitors its immediate neighborhood to detect any failure occurring in any of its neighboring routers, connecting links, or its own internal network. In case a router or a link or a network is found to have failed, the monitoring router first broadcasts, through flooding over the entire Internet, "Permanent Withdrawal (till repair) of the failed component. Immediately, thereafter, it discovers locally optimum alternative valid routes (these replace all invalidated routes and, obviously, avoid the failed component) and advertises them to its neighbors. Upon receipt of the Permanent Withdrawal message from the monitoring node, all routers in the Internet remove, from their routing tables, all routes that pass through the failed component and immediately choose the next best available path vectors from their backup routing tables. Some of the chosen routes may, of course, be later replaced by better routes that might be received from the neighbors. Although the monitoring router announces locally optimum replacement routes for the possible benefit of its neighbors, the latter (as well as their neighbors, and so on) are obviously free to choose some, all or none of them.

It should be noted from the above that because the failure is detected by a router locally and reliably, and no invalid routes are propagated by any router in the Internet, the path exploration will be drastically reduced and the BGP will achieve a fast convergence. Detection of a failed component has been achieved by the novel concept of "special neighbors of a router in the network. This was initially developed in connection with studies on the count-to-infinity and slow convergence problem in distance vector (DV) routing [16][17] and was later applied in some preliminary work on BGP convergence [18][19]. Finally, 6 new routing control messages have been proposed to be incorporated in BGP, without, however, changing any of the existing message formats.

The paper has been organized into seven sections. Following this introductory section, we briefly review some related works in Section 2. Section 3 is devoted to discussing the MBGP basics. The simplified model of the BGP and of an AS network that have been assumed for the present study is presented in Section 4. Section 5 describes the detailed working of the MBGP. Description of the simulation procedure and comparative results of BGP and MBGP have been provided in Section 6. Finally, some concluding remarks have been made in Section 7.

2   Related Works

In their pioneering work, Labovitz and others [2] - [4] showed, through experimental measurements, that the Internet may take a large time, even on the order of tens of minutes, to get back to its stable state operation after a fault has occurred. They observed that the BGP path selection process on the Internet backbone routers mainly caused this delay and the end-to-end internal paths suffered intermittent loss of connectivity, increased packet loss and large latency during this delayed convergence of BGP. Vendor-specific router implementation decisions and ambiguities in BGP specifications[1] were demonstrated as the main reasons for convergence delay [3],[5],[6],[9]. Some studies on BGP convergence problem and its solution were made in [7] - [9] but the suggested ideas were not much practical. An important new direction towards solving the route instability and delayed convergence problem in BGP emerged with the realization that the best way to reduce path exploration is to determine its root cause and then notify the affected routers about it [10]-[12]. However, two unwelcome features in [10]-[12] are the need for modification of the BGP update message format and the considerable processing and memory overhead of the notified routers. Finally, a few papers like [13]-[15] have concentrated on only identifying the root cause of route changes. Unfortunately, the proposed methods are fairly complex and do not appear to be much practicable.

In the remaining portion of this paper, we shall describe the various aspects of our proposed MBGP algorithm including the broad philosophy, the fault sensing mechanism, the various simplifications, assumptions and modifications related to the BGP and the simulation procedure with results for BGP and MBGP. The overall strategy adopted in our method may be broadly described as "distributed fault detection, notification, and rediscovery-cum-readvertisement of alternative valid routes" and it incorporates some insights gained from published research.

3   MBGP Philosophy and Background

3.1   Broad Philosophy of MBGP

A philosophical thought that lies behind our proposed approach towards reducing path exploration in the Internet can be explained with an analogy. We imagine the Internet in its "stable condition" as a vast pool of "calm water". Occurrence of a "component failure" in the Internet which can occur at any time and anywhere is analogous to a "random stone throw" into the vast pool of "calm water". The resultant disturbance in the body of water generates ripples moving in all directions from the "point of disturbance" which is analogous to the "physical location of the failed component". The resultant (radial) movement of ripples may be likened to the "path exploration" phenomenon in the Internet. At the end of the path exploration process, the BGP finally "converges", i.e., the pool of water "again becomes calm". Obviously, a small ripple would die down quickly, disturbing only a small area, whereas a big ripple would remain active for a long time and would disturb a large area. In a similar manner, in the present Internet, some faults cause the path exploration process to last a short duration and result in the exchange of a small number of invalid messages; other faults cause long path exploration, resulting in the exchange of large number of invalid and valid messages before the BGP converges.

Continuing with our above analogy, we endeavor, in the proposed method, to sense any incidence of "random stone throw" as close to its point of occurrence (both in time and in place) as possible and, thereafter, take remedial measures to control the the resultant ripple movement. This would make the disturbed pool of water become calm again with a minimum delay and (as a consequence) with minimum spread of the ripple movement. In order to realize, in practice, this goal of having reduced path exploration, we endow each router in the Internet with some additional intelligence. This allows the router to periodically monitor its neighborhood for sensing the failure of any neighboring component, locate or identify the failed component, notify the neighboring routers about the failed component determine (if possible) an alternative valid route that avoids

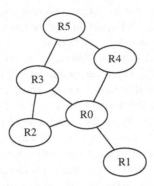

Fig. 1. A network graph to illustrate the four special neighbors

the failed component and, finally, advertise the alternative valid routes to its neighbors. Of course, the BGP neighbors receiving these updates are free to ignore them if they have better routes available. However, it is most important to note that only valid routes are propagated in the Internet to ensure that BGP convergence is achieved much faster.

3.2   Special Neighbors and Their Utilization

Concept of several types of special neighbors (SN) of a router were introduced and utilized in [16]-[19] in connection with studies on DV routing protocol and BGP. In this subsection, we describe four types of SNs which have enabled a BGP router to detect a faulty component in its immediate neighborhood and take appropriate measures towards reducing path exploration in MBGP. We shall use the simple network graph of Fig. 1 to illustrate these SNs neighbors.

1. Singly-Connected Neighbor (SCN): A neighboring router R_y is a SCN of the router R_x if R_x is the sole neighbor of R_y so that R_y can communicate with all other routers in the network only via R_x . In Fig. 1, R1 is a SCN of R0 and is a pendant node in the network. It is obvious that in case of failure of the router R_y or link R_x R_y, R_x can declare R_y to be a Lost Destination(LD) to all routers in the network.
2. Multi-Connected Neighbor (MCN): If a neighboring router R_y of the router R_x is not its SCN, then R_y is a MCN of R_x. In Fig. 1, all neighbors of R_0, except R_1 are its MCNs. It is obvious that in case a router R_x loses its communication with its MCN R_y, because of the failure of the connecting link $R_x R_y$, then R_x can still communicate with R_y, although in an indirect manner.
3. Co-Neighbor(CN) or Triangle Neighbor (TN): If the MCN neighbor R_y of the router R_x is also a neighbor of another MCN neighbor R_z of R_x, i.e., if R_x, R_y and R_z form a triangle in the network graph and are all mutual neighbors of one another, then R_y is a CN of R_x for R_z and similarly, R_z is a CN of R_x for R_y. In Fig. 1, R_2 and R_3 are CNs of R_0 for R_3 and R_2, respectively. It is obvious that in case the router R_x loses its communication with a neighbor R_y (R_z), where $R_y(R_z)$ is a CN of R_x for $R_z(R_y)$, then R_x can utilize $R_z(R_y)$ for easily ascertaining whether the link $R_x R_y(R_x R_z)$ or the router $R_y(R_z)$ has failed.

4. Quadrilateral Neighbor (QN): If a router R_x has two MCN neighbors R_y and R_z who have a common neighbor R_w, who is not a neighbour of R_x, i.e, the four routers R_x, R_y, R_z and R_w together form a quadrilateral, then R_y is a QN of R_x for R_z and, similarly, R_z is a QN of R_x for R_y. In Figure 1, R_0, R_3, R_5 and R_4 form a quadrilateral and $R_3(R_4)$ is a QN of R_0 for $R_4(R_3)$. It may be observed that in case the router R_x loses its communication with the QN $R_y(R_z)$, it can still send a message to $R_y(R_z)$ via $R_z(R_y)$ to ascertain whether the link $R_xR_y(R_xR_z)$ or the router $R_y(R_z)$ has failed. One important point that needs to be noted regarding the utilization of a CN and a QN in BGP is that the policies of the concerned routers should not stand in the way of utilizing these special neighbors. MBGP utilizes the above four categories of special neighbors to great advantage as will be described in section 5.

4 Simplified Model of BGP and Some Assumptions

Both the BGP and the Internet architecture are highly complex. In order to study the proposed modification in the BGP, we have assumed a simplified view of the global Internet as an Interconnection of N ASes where each AS has a single BGP speaking router connected to multiple independent IP internetworks, each via a dedicated link to a non-BGP gateway router connected to the internal network. A BGP router within each AS thus peers with one or more BGP speaking routers in other ASes and several non-BGP routers within its own AS, as shown in Figure 2. The nine ASes, AS_0 through AS_8, have their respective BGP routers R_0 through R_8 and their respective pairs of non-BGP internal routers (R_{00}, R_{01}) through (R_{80}, R_{81}). Only two representative internal networks have been shown within AS_8.

Some of the ASes have been assumed to be stub ASes while the others have been assumed to be transit ASes, there being no multihoming. There is only one stub AS, namely, AS_7, in Figure 2. For simplicity, we have assumed that the transit ASes do not provide geographical store-forwarding of packets but provide store-forward of packets for remote ASes via only e-BGP links.

We assume that the following component failures can occur in the simplified model of the Internet.

– An e-BGP link connecting two neighboring BGP routers
– A BGP router
– A link connecting a BGP router to one of its gateway routers
– A gateway router
– An internal network to the link connecting a gateway router to it.

However, in the context of the above possible faults, we shall make the fairly reasonable assumption that only one fault can occur at a time.

Next, we assume that the two BGP routers sharing each e-BGP link maintain a reliable TCP connection over the link and periodically exchange KEEPALIVE messages. Similarly, within each AS, the BGP router and the gateway router communicate using an intra-AS protocol like RIP-2 and exchange periodic updates of their routing tables. Thus in case either a neighboring BGP router or a gateway router fails or the connecting

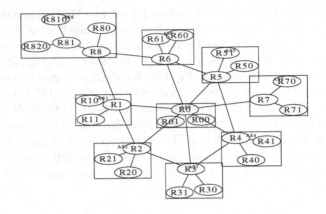

Fig. 2. Simplified model of the Internet adopted for our study

link fails, a BGP router will detect the failure within a limited delay by the absence of the expected KEEPALIVE or periodic update message. However, if a link connecting a gateway router to its internal network fails, the gateway router will let the BGP router within the AS know about the failure, again within a limited delay.

Finally, we make the following two assumptions regarding the tables that each BGP router maintains.

1. We assume that each router, after joining the Internet, receives the Path Vector Advertisement Table (PVAT) of each of its neighbors and stores them in a Composite Path Vector Table (CMP_PVT) which thus contains multiple routes to reach each destination network. From its CMP_PVT, each router selects its best route to reach each destination, stores all these best routes in its own PVAT and advertises them to all its neighbors. In the absence of policies, each BGP router chooses its best route to each destination as the one that has the minimum number of hops in its AS-PATH vectors.

2. In order to keep itself prepared to deal with any link or router failure that may occur any time in its immediate neighborhood, each BGP router maintains two neighbor-related tables. The first one is a Neighbor Particulars Table (NPT) in which are stored particulars like AS#, IP address, prefixed advertised, etc. The second one is a Special Neighbor Status Table (SNST) in which are stored information about each neighboring router like whether it is a SCN or MCN and who are its CNs and QNs, etc. Each BGP router builds up its NPT and SNST from its CMP-PVT.

5   Modifications Incorporated in BGP

In this section, we shall outline the steps followed by the MBGP router R_x to achieve greatly reduced path exploration following the detection of failure of any of the five components listed in section 4.

5.1   Failure of a BGP Router

1. If a neighboring BGP router R_y fails, R_x does not receive the KEEPALIVE message from R_y before the hold timer for R_y times out and hence it detects the failure of either R_y or the link $R_x R_y$.
2. R_x now checks whether its TCP connection with R_y has been broken or reset by attempting to open a TCP connection with R_y afresh. Obviously, the attempt fails in this case.
3. R_x then consults its SNST to know whether R_y is its SCN or MCN. If R_y is found to be a SCN, then R_x simply announces a "permanent withdrawal" of the router R_y to all BGP routers in the Internet by broadcasting (through flooding), a PERMANENT SCN-ROUTER WITHDRAWAL (R_y) message over the entire Internet. On receipt of this message, all BGP routers just delete all routes advertised by R_y from their respective CMP_PVTs and PVTs; no alternative routes need be discovered.
4. In step 3 above, if R_y is found to be a MCN, then R_x needs to ascertain whether R_y itself or the connecting link $R_x R_y$ has failed. Towards this, R_x checks its SNST to know whether it has one or more CNs or QNs or both for R_y. If yes, then R_x sends one or more ROUTER-FAIL CHECK messages to R_y via these CNs and QNs. However, since no ROUTER-OK (R_y) response comes back, R_x learns that the router R_y has failed. Then R_x first broadcasts a PERMANENT MCN-ROUTER WITHDRAWAL (R_y) message to declare the MCN R_y an LD. This results in (i) permanent removal of all routes stored in all BGP routers in the Internet that were originated by R_y and (ii) temporary withdrawal of those routes which only passed by R_y.
5. Immediately thereafter, R_x (as well as other routers which had temporarily withdrawn all routes which passes by R_y) tries to discover alternative routes and advertises them to their neighbors. This initiates some amount of path exploration, but best alternative routes are soon found out for the temporary withdrawn destinations. The following points may be noted in the present context.
    (a) In case R_x finds from its SNST that no CN or QN exists for R_y, it searches its CMP_PVT for knowing if any neighbor of it had advertised to it any path originating from R_y and then sends a ROUTER-FAIL CHECK message to R_y via this path. Actually, the SNST only provides some shorter paths and that too readily.
    (b) Sending multiple ROUTER-FAIL CHECK messages via possibly independent paths, if available, increases the reliability of the router/link failure checking process.
    (c) Each neighbor of R_x, after receiving the updated (new) routes from R_x, are free to accept or ignore them in case they themselves have better (shortr) routes stored in their CMP_PVTs.

5.2   Failure of an e-BGP Link

Let us assume that in step 4 in section 5.1, R_x receives a ROUTER-OK response from R_y against ROUTER-FAIL CHECK probe message sent by it. As a result, R_x learns that the link $R_x R_y$ has failed and, consequently, R_y is no longer its neighbor. So, R_x

first removes the entry of R_y from its NPT and SNST and then broadcasts a PERMA-NENT LINK WITHDRAWAL (link-id) message over the entire Internet. Next R_x removes the set of routes, that were advertised by R_y as well as the subset of these routes that R_x had thereafter propagated to its other neighbors, from its CMP_PVT and its PVT, respectively. Then R_x discovers alternative routes to those destinations(avoiding the failed link) and advertises them. Thus each BGP router in the Internet receives the PERMANENT LINK WITHDRAWAL (link-id) message from R_x, immediately followed by the BGP UPDATE message(s) sent by R_x. In between the two messages, each BGP router discovers and uses alternative routes, although these routes may soon be replaced by better routes.

5.3   Failure of Components within an AS

From the simplified model of the Internet shown in Figure 2, it is evident that, within an AS, three types of components may fail, namely, a gateway router, the link connecting it to the BGP router and, finally, an internal network or the link connecting it to the gateway router. The BGP router can detect the failure of the gateway router or the connecting link by the non-receipt of the DV table from the gateway router and the failure of the network from the content of the DV table received from the gateway router. In case of any failure within its AS, the BGP router thus simply uses the concept of a SCN and broadcasts a PERMANENT NETWORK WITHDRAWAL (network prefix) message.

5.4   New Messages Use the Existing BGP Message Format

BGP uses only 4 types of messages, namely, OPEN, UPDATE, NOTIFICATION and KEEPALIVE [1]. All BGP messages have a common 19-byte header followed by separate or special format for each message type, with the exception of KEEPALIVE which is just the 19-byte header containing no information. The header has a 16-byte MARKER field, a 2-byte LENGTH field and a 1-byte TYPE field. Presently, only 4 values, viz, 1,2,3 and 4 have been assigned to the TYPE field to identify the OPEN, UPDATE, NOTIFICATION and KEEPALIVE messages, respectively. Thus, it is possible to use the TYPE field in the BGP header to create the new routing control messages needed by MBGP. MBGP needs 6 additional messages, namely, PERMANENT SCN-ROUTER WITHDRAWAL (router-id), PERMANENT MCN-ROUTER WITH-DRAWAL (router-id), PERMANENT LINK WITHDRAWAL (link-id),PERMANENT NETWORK WITHDRAWAL (network prefix(es)), ROUTER-FAIL CHECK (router-id) and ROUTER OK (router-id). The value of the TYPE field and the format of the respective attributes may be assigned following the convention used in the design of the BGP message format.

6   Simulation Procedure and Results

Though RFC 4271 [1] describes the BGP in details, it does not contain much idea about its implementation. As a result, most router vendors have come up with their own

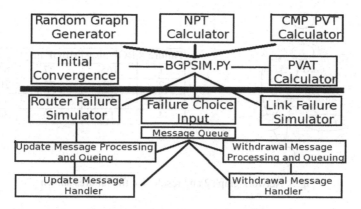

Fig. 3. Simulation Model of BGP 4.0

implementations details of which are, unfortunately, not available in the public domain. So, for simulating the process of convergence in BGP and MBGP, we have employed the simplified model of BGP described in section IV and simulated it, leaving out the internal networks within the ASes, using the simulator module shown in figure 3.

The main routine or the simulator program bgpsim.py in Fig 3, in association with the different subroutines, first builds the various tables from a given graph of ASes (in the absence of internal networks, an AS is reduced to just a BGP or MBGP router) which is fed as its input, either manually or from a random graph generation subroutine. It exchanges the initial messages, on behalf of the nodes, till the BGP converges into a steady state, thereby simulating the nodes in the graph booting up and exchanging messages till the network stabilizes. The simulator then injects a random failure of a link or router in accordance with the user's choice and simulates and prints the exchange of messages between the ASes till the network stabilizes again.The different subroutines that have been used in the simulation of the BGP are shown in Fig 3. Similarity in the basic design and the method of simulation has allowed reuse of codes and flowcharts of BGP while simulating MBGP. Only two new subroutines, namely, Router and Link Failure Simulator and the Permanent Withdrawal Message Handler, needed to be written for the MBGP.

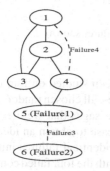

Failure #	BGP msgs	MBGP msgs	% impr
1	90	33	63 %
2	63	18	71 %
3	68	18	74 %
4	12	9	25 %

Fig. 4. Network graph 1 and results for the failures shown

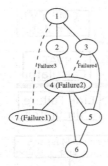

Failure #	BGP msgs	MBGP msgs	% impr
1	165	27	84 %
2	90	72	20 %
3	17	10	41 %
4	13	10	30 %

Fig. 5. Network graph 2 and results for the failures shown

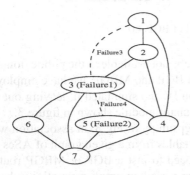

Failure #	BGP msgs	MBGP msgs	% impr
1	325	114	65 %
2	662	29	95.6 %
3	28	9	68 %

Fig. 6. Network graph 3 and results for the failures shown

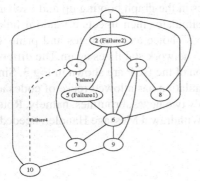

Failure #	BGP msgs	MBGP msgs	% impr
1	3256	41	98.7 %
2	63	18	71 %
3	68	18	74 %
4	12	9	25 %

Fig. 7. Network graph 4 and results for the failures shown

The process of convergence in BGP and MBGP has been studied on four different network graphs with two router failures and two link failures, all chosen randomly, being successively injected in each network. The number of messages that were exchanged during the process of convergence were counted in each case to obtain an idea of how fast the MBGP converges relative to the BGP, following identical failures injected on identical network graphs. The four network graphs, along with the four failed components in each graph are shown in Fig. 4 through Fig. 7, each figure being accompanied by the number of messages exchanged till the BGP and the MBGP converge. The results clearly demonstrate that the MBGP has a significantly reduced path exploration compared to BGP and, as a consequence, it converges much faster.

7 Concluding Remarks

Some modifications have been proposed to BGP, in the form of a Modified BGP (MBGP), to enable it to converge much faster following a link, router or internal network failure. This will reduce packet losses, router congestion, increased packet delay and other deleterious effects that occur in the Internet during the delayed convergence of BGP. The MBGP adopts the overall strategy of "distributed fault detection, fault notification and rediscovery-cum-readvertisement of alternative valid routes". A novel concept of special neighbors in conjunction with a new query-response message pair, enable each MBGP router to detect a component failure and identify the failed component locally, quickly, reliably and with negligible overhead. All MBGP routers in the Internet are immediately notified by the fault-detecting router, through flooded broadcast of one of four new permanent withdrawal messages, about the identity of the failed component. Two of these messages which broadcast the permanent withdrawal of a singly connected router and of a singly connected network, result in immediate MBGP convergence with no path exploration. The other two messages, which broadcast the permanent withdrawal of a link and of a multiconnected router, start a path exploration which, however, dies down quickly because no invalid routes are ever generated in MBGP and very few downstream routers actually switch routes and fewer still do it multiple times. Simulation studies have demonstrated a significantly faster convergence of MBGP over BGP. With its distributed fault identification and concomitant fast converging capabilities, the MBGP as well as similar future algorithms will have the potentiality to make the global Internet "the largest self-regulating engineering system in the world".

References

1. RFC4271, http://www.ietf.org/rfc/rfc4271.txt
2. Labovitz, C., Ahuja, A., Bose, A., Jahanian, F.: Delayed Internet Routing Convergence. In: SIGCOMM 2000 (2000)
3. Labovitz, C., Wattenhofer, R., Venkatachary, S., Ahuja, A.: The Impact of Internet Policy and Topology On Delayed Routing Convergence. In: INFOCOM (April 2001)
4. Labovitz, C., Ahuja, A., Bose, A., Jahanian, F.: Delayed Internet Routing Convergence. IEEE/ACM Trans. Network, 293–306 (2001)
5. Griffin, T., Presmore, B.: An Experimental Analysis of BGP Convergence Time. IEEE ICNP (November 2001)
6. Mao, Z.M., Govindan, R., Varghese, G., Katz, R.: Route Flap Damping Exacerbates Internet Routing Convergence. ACM SIGCOMM (2002)
7. Griffin, T., Shepherd, F.: The Stable Path Problem and the Interdomain Routing. IEEE ICNP (November 2001)
8. Pei, D., Zhao, X., Wang, L., Massey, D.M., Su, A., Lixia Zhang, S.F.: Improving Bgp Convergence Through Consistency Assertions. In: INFOCOM 2002 (2002)

9. Bremler-Barr, A., Afek, Y., Schwarz, S.: Improved BGP Convergence via Ghost Flushing. In: IEEE INFOCOM (2003)
10. Pei, D., Azuma, M., Massey, D., Zhang, L.: BGP-RCN: Improving BGP Convergence Through Root Cause Notification. Computer Networks 48(2), 175–194 (2005)
11. Zhang, H., Arora, A., Liu, Z.: A Stability-Oriented Approach to Improving BGP Convergence. In: IEEE International Symposium on Reliable Distributed Systems (2004)
12. Chandrashekar, Z., Duan, Z.-L.: Zhang, and J. Krasky: Limiting Path Exploration in Bgp. In: INFCOM, Miami, USA (2005)
13. Feldmann, A., Maennel, O., Mao, Z.M., Berger, A., Maggs, B.: Locating Internet Routing Instabilities. ACM SIGCOMM Computer Communication Review archive 34(4) (October 2004)
14. Lad, M., Nanavati, A., Massey, D., Zhang, L.: An Algorithmic Approach to Identifying Link Failures. In: IEEE PISPDC, pp. 25–34 (2004)
15. Teixeira, R., Rexford, J.: A Measurement Framework for Pin-pointing Routing Changes. In: IEEE SIGCOMM 2004 workshop (2004)
16. Ray, S.K., Paira, S.K., Sen, S.K.: Modified Distance Vector Routing Avoids the Count-to-Infinity Problem. In: Proc. Intl. Conf. on Commun. devices and Intell. Systems (CODIS 2004), Calcutta, January 8-10, pp. 31–34 (2004)
17. Sen, S.K.: An Improved Network Routing Scheme Based on Distance Vector Routing. Ph.D (Engg.) Thesis of Jadavpur University (January 2008)
18. Ray, S.K., Ghosh, P., Sen, S.: Modified BGP has Faster Convergence. In: Proc. NCC 2006, I.I.T Delhi, January 27-29, pp. 404–408 (2006)
19. Shannigrahi, S.: Reducing path Exploration in BGP. M.C.S.E Thesis of Jadavpur University (June 2009)

On Using Network Tomography for Overlay Availability

Umesh Bellur and Mahak Patidar

Department of Computer Science and Engineering
Indian Institute of Technology, Bombay

Abstract. Overlay networks are logical abstraction on a physical network (underlay) where each overlay node corresponds to a specific underlay node and overlay links correspond to paths on the underlay. The use of network layer information for constructing overlay networks can greatly improve their performance. Knowledge of underlay properties such as available bandwidths, loss rates and topology can help in efficient construction, maintenance and optimization of overlays which have to provide service guarantees. In absence of any support from the network core, it becomes necessary to infer those properties by performing end-to-end measurements on the network. We develop probing techniques which infer information about the structure of the underlay and use it for construction of fault-tolerant overlay networks. Algorithms and measurement techniques for the same are presented together with the experimental findings.

1   Introduction

Overlay networks free the application designer from having to understand the intricacies and variations of the underlying physical network. They provide a logical abstraction over the underlay. Traditionally, overlay nodes do not require or use information about the nodes and links in the physical path. Overlay links correspond to physical paths (involving several physical nodes) and a message sent from one overlay node to another traverses one of potentially many physical paths depending on how routing is done at the IP level.

Awareness of the underlay is important from a QoS perspective. Such "'aware'" networks include a partial knowledge of the physical nodes and links corresponding to the paths between overlay nodes, and/or mechanisms for extracting knowledge from the underlying network layers to provide better services. In spite of existing work in the area, understanding dynamically changing network characteristics is extremely difficult - network parameters are hard to obtain as the routers provide very little support to collect such information. Even services like *traceroute* are blocked by many routers. Hence, explicit measurements have to be performed by the end hosts by either sending special probes or by studying various flows passively. Researchers in the field of network tomography have devised methods which can greatly improve the effectiveness of overlay networks. Network tomography deals with estimating network performance parameters like delays and loss rates based on special probing and traffic measurements at a limited subset of the nodes. The network behavior is inferred using carefully designed measurements and without the support from network core. Network tomography techniques can infer link level delays, available network bandwidth, loss distributions

K. Kant et al. (Eds.): ICDCN 2010, LNCS 5935, pp. 485–496, 2010.

and origin destination traffic metrics. Each of these dynamic parameters can help in providing QoS based routing for overlay networks. For example, the loss distributions can help in routing critical application data through paths with minimum loss rates; available bandwidth information can be used for admission control in the flows; estimates of origin-destination traffic can help in balancing the load on the overlay and link level delays can be used to find best paths for delay tolerant applications like voice and video conferencing. It is worth re-emphasizing that the power of tomography techniques comes from the fact that they do not assume any support from the network core.

In our work, we focus on ensuring high availability in the overlay. Loosely speaking, availability is the ability of the network to be impervious to (in terms of providing redundancy) a node or link failure. Simply having redundant paths at the overlay level is insufficient to ensure this property. Redundancy at the overlay level needs to be backed by redundancy at the underlay for true fault tolerance. We have developed network tomography methods which help us deduce certain underlay properties like the amount of overlap (at underlay level) between two overlay paths and bottleneck bandwidth of a path. These properties are then used in selecting redundant paths between a pair of communicating overlay nodes in such a way that the joint probability of failure of a path and the redundant paths is minimized. This ensures that if a path fails, there is a backup path available with a high probability. We have conducted extensive simulations to show the effectiveness of our methods. We have also identified additional applications of other methods like topology discovery, etc and have done simulations to test the applicability.

2   Motivation and Problem Definition

There are many methods in literature which construct failure resilient overlays by providing path redundancy at the overlay layer [1][2]. All of them, focus on providing multiple overlay paths between the communicating nodes. These paths are chosen with little regard to the actual network topology. The apparent failure resilience obtained by having multiple redundant overlay paths does not necessarily ensure true redundancy. A large portion of those paths may share the same set of network links. This means that failure of a shared network link may affect more than one overlay path. Consider figure 1 for example. Although $P2$ and $P3$ look completely separate on overlay layer, they have many common links at the network layer. In fact, each link of $P2$ is a link of $P3$. Failure of $P2$ will automatically imply failure of $P3$. Hence choosing $P3$ as a redundant alternate path for $P2$(or vice-versa) will not really give us failure resilience. However if we choose $P1$ as an alternate path for $P2$, we have very good failure resilience since they share no underlay links.

It is clear from the preceding discussion that network topology should be taken into account for choosing alternate overlay paths. However, topology information is not easy to obtain. Hence we need a technique to infer the topology information without any support from the network elements.

A closer look at figure 1 reveals that the entire topology is not required. The reason why $P2$ and $P3$ should not be chosen simultaneously is that they have high failure correlation. Hence, we just need a measure of failure correlation between paths. Detailed discussion on modeling of failure correlation between paths can be found at [1][3][4].

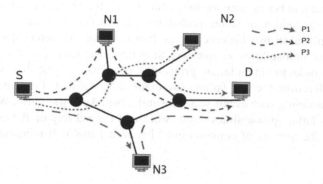

Fig. 1. Overlay Network: Paths with common network links

In this work, we propose that the number of common network links between two paths is a good measure of the failure correlation between them. Based on this, we then devise algorithms which attempt to find this number for any two paths between a source-destination pair. The methods we propose do not require time synchronization between the end hosts. This is very attractive as there is no overhead of clock synchronization. Besides, network clock synchronization lacks precision [5].

2.1 Problem Formulation

The underlay property we are most interested in is the number of common network links between two overlay paths between a source-destination pair. We call this the *degree of overlap* between two overlay paths. Between a source-destination pair, we can select multiple overlay paths. This ensures that if one path fails, we have fallback paths. For the purpose of discussion, we only consider two paths. The findings can be easily generalized to more than two paths.

The degree of overlap is an important parameter for ensuring resilience to path failures because intuitively, fewer the number of common links between two paths, lower the chances of both the paths failing simultaneously(due to a failure in the underlay). While selecting two paths (out of the many available) between a source destination pair, we should ensure that the paths with minimum degree of overlap are selected in order to maintain high fault-tolerance.

Assuming that each of the underlay links fail independently, the probability that two paths P_1 and P_2 between source-destination pair (S, D) fail due to failure of a common link(assuming non-common links do not fail) can be given by

$$J(S, D, P_1, P_2) = 1 - (1 - p_1)(1 - p_2) \ldots (1 - p_k) \qquad (1)$$

where $p_1, p_2, \ldots, p_k$ are the failure probabilities of the k common links $l_1, l_2, \ldots, l_k$.

Clearly, J is controlled by the number of common links (each of $(1 - p_i)$ is less than 1). Hence, we focus on finding the degree of overlap between any two paths. This is achieved by devising intelligent probing strategies (discussed later) on the network. Once overlap information is known, fault tolerance can be ensured by choosing those paths that have minimum overlap from the available set. In reality, J will not only depend on the number of common links, but also on the probability of failure of those links. Also, the total joint failure probability (due to failure of any set of links) will include additional terms which account for failure of non-common links.

The failure probabilities are not easy to obtain. One reason is that links fail very rarely, so in order to obtain failure probability of a link, historic data has to be made available. Moreover, the link failures are many times attributed to maintenance work and hence modeling such events with probabilities makes little sense. We therefore do not quantify failure probabilities in this work and instead rely on the assumption that minimizing the number of common links between paths will minimize their failure correlation.

2.2   Assumptions

There are some basic assumptions about the network which we require for our methods to work. These assumptions, which are common to most probing studies [6] [7] [8] [9] are enumerated below.

1. Routers are store-and-forward and use FIFO queuing.
2. The paths do not change during the measurement period.
3. Host clock resolution is granular enough to enable accurate timing measurements.
4. Probing hosts can inject back to back packets into the network.

Assumption 1 is needed to ensure that orderings of probe packets are preserved. Assumption 2 is required for consistency across different measurements. If a path change occurs during measurements, we cannot combine the results from measurements before and after the change. Assumptions 3 and 4 can be easily followed by using proper operating system kernel. While many analytical methods assume environments free of cross traffic while the probing is in progress, we discard this to establish the robustness of the methods in realistic settings.

2.3   Existing Probing Strategies

Here we describe some of the probing methods which are useful for finding number of common links between two paths. The results are stated without proof. The proofs and many other interesting properties can be found in [10][8] from which we have also borrowed standard terminology for *Probe, Interarrival time, Interdeparture time, back-to-back packets & base-bandwidth*.

1. Packet-Pair Property: Consider a path of n physical links $L_1, L_2, \ldots, L_n$ with base bandwidths $b_1, b_2, \ldots, b_n$ respectively. If a probe of the form $[pp]$ is injected at L_1, with $D(p) = L_n$, then the interarrival time of the two packets at L_n is $\frac{s(p)}{min_k b_k}$. This result can be used to estimate the bottleneck base bandwidth of a path between two end hosts.

2. Tailgating Property: Consider a path of n physical links $L_1, L_2, \ldots, L_n$ with base bandwidths $b_1, b_2, \ldots, b_n$ respectively. If a probe of the form $[pq]$ is injected at L_1, with $D(p) = D(q) = L_n$ and if $\forall k \leq n, \frac{s(p)}{s(q)} \geq \frac{b_{k+1}}{b_k}$, then $[pq]$ will remain back-to-back along the entire path. This property is used in choosing the size of the probe packets.

3. Packet Queuing Property: Consider a probe of the form $[pX]$ where $s(p)$ is very large and $s(q)$ is very small. X will queue behind p at every intermediate router until p reaches its destination. This probing scheme is referred as *paced probe*. The packet p is called *pacer packet*. A variant of paced probe will be used in many of the techniques described later.

4. Preservation of Spacing: Consider a path of n physical links $L_1, L_2, \ldots, L_n$ with base bandwidths $b_1, b_2, \ldots, b_n$ respectively. If a probe of the form $[p][p]$ is injected at L_1, with $D(p) = L_n$ and an inter-departure time of $\triangle$, then $\triangle$ will be preserved over all links L_i if and only if $\frac{s(p)}{\triangle} \leq min_{1 \leq k \leq n} b_k$. This property is used to find the bottleneck bandwidth of prefix of a path.

3 Our Approach

Consider Figure [2] with source S and destination D. We aim to find the number of common network links between the two overlay paths shown. Note that the links in the figure denote logical links corresponding to one or more physical links. The physical links(and routers) which belong to exactly one path are not shown. Also, the intermediate overlay nodes have not been drawn for clarity.

Two overlay paths can overlap in any arbitrary fashion at the physical layer. However, we can break the overlapping regions into three cases each representing an overlay sub-path:

A. One sender overlay node and two receiver overlay nodes
B. Two sender overlay nodes and one receiver overlay node
C. Two sender overlay nodes and two receiver overlay nodes

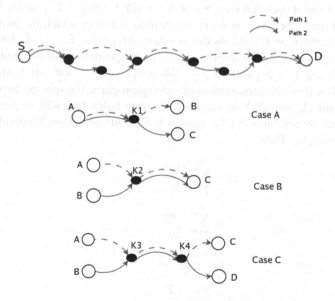

Fig. 2. Different Cases of Overlapping Paths

Cases B and C occur very rarely on the Internet. Once two paths diverge, it is very unlikely that they will meet again (except at receiver)[11]. Moreover, it has been argued for long that overlay paths with only one intermediate overlay node are sufficient to provide any QoS constraint which is achievable by paths with more than one intermediate overlay node [12] [13]. Hence, we do not study cases B and C . Our focus then becomes to find the number of common prefix links between two overlay paths. Based on the above argument, we claim that the number of common prefix links gives a reasonable measure of failure correlation between two paths.

3.1   The Solution

Case A is the most frequently occurring situation on the Internet. Any two paths with the same source will have some overlap initially. Some authors propose to have minimum initial overlap by making the two paths diverge from each other (at the overlay layer) as early as possible [11]. While this is a good strategy, it assumes that topology information is known which is not always the case.

Here, we give two methods to find the number of common links for case A. This is essentially same as finding the length of prefix of the sub-path which is common to the two paths. The first method gives a lower bound on the number of common links, whereas the second gives an exact number. Both the methods use the transmission delays of the links constituting the paths. The amount of probing required is less for the first method but it is not as accurate as the second one. The second algorithm uses $log_2 N$ number of probes where N is the minimum of length of the two paths. This can be further reduced by combining the two methods.

Lower Bound Method. Here, we find a lower bound on the number of links on sub-path $AK1$ (figure 3). We use the packet queuing property described in section 2.3. A probe $[XpY]$ is sent from A such that $s(p) >> s(X) = s(Y)$, $D(p) = C$, and $D(X) = D(Y) = B$. Y will queue behind p at every router until $K1$ after which the paths of p and Y diverge. Let there be n links on the sub-path $AK_1 : L_1, L_2, \ldots, L_n$ (in that order) and corresponding base bandwidths $b_1, b_2, \ldots, b_n$ respectively. The difference in the arrival time of X and Y at K_1 will be $\Delta = \frac{s(p)}{b_1} + \frac{s(p)}{b_2} + \ldots + \frac{s(p)}{b_n}$ (as Y always queue behind p). Also, from the preservation of spacing property, the spacing between X and Y will remain Δ, provided the required property holds (we will discuss the situation when it does not hold shortly). Let us denote the bottleneck base bandwidth of path AK_1 as $b_0 = min_k b_k$. Then,

$$\Delta = \sum_{i=1}^{n} \frac{s(p)}{b_i} \tag{2}$$

$$\leq \sum_{i=1}^{n} \frac{s(p)}{b_0}$$

$$\leq \frac{n \times s(p)}{b_0}$$

$$\Rightarrow n \geq \frac{b_0 \times \Delta}{s(p)} \tag{3}$$

Hence, we obtain a lower bound on n. We still need to ensure that the spacing between the packets X and Y is preserved. For this, we use the preservation of spacing property described earlier. We send a probe of form $[X][pY]$, i.e introduce a known delay(say d) between X and p. Then, from preservation of spacing property we require

$$\frac{s(p)}{\Delta + d} \le Min_{n+1 \le k \le m} b_k \tag{4}$$

where $b_{n+1}, \ldots, b_m$ denote the base bandwidths of links $L_{n+1}, \ldots, \L_m$ along the sub-path $K_1 B$. We can control the value of d, so the spacing Δ will be preserved. Another way is to send probes of the form $[Xp^rY]$, i.e. sending r large sized packets instead of just one. This will increase the value of Δ. Similar techniques are used in [10][14] to increase the Δ value.

To obtain the bottleneck bandwidth b_0 of AK_1, we use the method described in [10]. It is an application of the packet pair property. To summarize:

Step 1: Calculate Δ by sending a probe $[XpY]$ (or its variant described above)
Step 2: Calculate b_0(bottleneck bandwidth of path AK_1
Step 3: Use Equation 3 to find a lower bound on n

This method gives a lower bound on the value of n, giving us a measure of minimum failure correlation of the two paths. It is particularly useful when the base bandwidths along the shared path are close to the bottleneck bandwidth. In this case, approximating b_i by b_0 will not create much difference in in equation 3 and the lower bound on n will be close to actual value. However, it underestimates n when the base bandwidths along the shared path are very much larger than the bottleneck bandwidth. This and other analysis is presented later in the experimental results section. The method is efficient since just one probe is required once we know the bottleneck bandwidth. Finding bottleneck bandwidth also requires just one probe as discussed in section 2.3.

The Exact Path Length Method. We now describe a method which gives an exact value of the length of AK_1. Probes similar to that used in the Lower Bound Method ($[XpY]$) are used with some modifications. We first make an important observation about our earlier method which guides our solution. Note that we were able to obtain Δ corresponding to AK_1 because the large packet(p) was destined to B. More precisely, we were able to find the Δ corresponding to a sub-path on which the second small packet(Y) queued behind p. In order to find Δ value for a sub-path of choice, we need to force the queuing of Y behind p for that sub-path. We can do this by exploiting the properties of TTL field in the IP header. TTL is generally set to a large number(typically 32 or 64) at the source and is decremented(by one) by every router along the path. A packet is discarded by a router if its TTL value reaches zero. To obtain Δ corresponding to a sub-path of length R, we set the TTL value of p to R. Now, Y will queue behind p only for R links.

The TTL field can also be used to find the path lengths of AB and AC. These are obtained by subtracting the TTL value of a packet at the receiver end from that set by sender(Initial TTL - Final TTL). Without loss of generality, assume that $Length$ $(AK_1) = n < L = length(AB) \le length(AC)$.

Having got the maximum value of n(i.e. L), we send a probe of form $[XpY]$ from A such that $s(p) >> s(X) = s(Y)$, $D(p) = C$, and $D(X) = D(Y) = B$. This will give the value of Δ for path $AK1$. Call this Δ_0. Now, we send a series of probes $[XpY]$ with packet sizes same as above, but in each iteration, we set the TTL value of p such that the Δ value approach Δ_0. When a TTL value results in a Δ which is close enough to Δ_0, we know that that TTL value is the value of n. At the start of each iteration, we know the range to which n belongs(for the first iteration, the minimum value is 1 and maximum value is L). For the first iteration, we set TTL to average of minimum and maximum. This will give a Δ value corresponding to path of Length $\frac{L}{2}$. If the Δ value is more than Δ_0, we reduce the TTL for the next iteration (set it to average of current minimum and current TTL) else we increase the TTL (set it to average of current TTL and current maximum).

The above procedure does a binary search on the possible value of n and hence will complete in $log_2 L$ probes. To summarize:

Step 1: Calculate Δ_0 by sending a probe $[XpY]$ with $D(X) = D(Y) = B$ and $D(p) = C$
Initialize: $min \leftarrow 1$; $max \leftarrow L$;
Repeat:
    Step 2: $ttl \leftarrow \frac{min+max}{2}$
    Step 3: send probe [XpY] with TTL value for p as ttl
    Step 4: calculate Δ
    Step 5: if($\Delta < \Delta_0$) $min \leftarrow ttl$ else $max \leftarrow ttl$

Until: $\Delta \approx \Delta_0$

This method attempts to find an exact value for n. The procedure completes in $O(log_2 L)$ probes. The maximum value of TTL set by most operating systems is 32. Hence, we have to make only 5 probes to arrive at the final result. It should be noted that the source needs feedback from the destination node about the value of Δ, so this will take additional messages(equal to number of iterations). If there is cross traffic in the network, delay measurements can vary. Thus, we may have to send the same probes many times and average the results. An important point is that we make our decisions based on the delay introduced by the links. A high speed link will introduce very small delay, and hence it would be very difficult to detect. This problem is more severe if there are many high speed links towards the end of the common path. The method will terminate if Δ is sufficiently close to Δ_0, but we may still have some undetected high speed links. To detect such links, additional probes will be required to ascertain the value of n. This can be improved using the lower bound on n obtained by the earlier method. This can be used to initialize the value of minimum length of AK_1 in the initialization step, thus saving some probes. This can be very effective when the link speeds are close to the bottleneck bandwidth of path AK_1.

3.2 Application: Deducing Topology Tree

We now demonstrate an application of the methodology developed in the previous section to the case of topology tree detection. Topology identification is central to many applications like isolation of network congestion and detection of network performance degradation [15]. Given a source node S and destination nodes $D_1, D_2, \ldots, D_n$, the aim is to find the topology tree rooted at S. We make the assumptions described earlier. Here, only one sender node is present, hence only case A of figure [2] applies. For each pair of destinations, we find the degree of overlap of their corresponding paths from source using the methods from the previous section. Once the degree of overlap is known, we know the distance from source at which two paths diverge. Also, the distance between sender and receiver nodes can be known by subtracting the TTL value at the receiver from that at the sender. Hence, we can construct the topology tree completely. The cost of topology detection using this method and other experimental findings are presented in the next section.

4   Experimental Results

We discuss the findings of experiments conducted using $ns2$ network simulator.

4.1   Deducing Topology Tree

In this section, we explain experiments on the method for topology detection as discussed in Section 3.2. The topology being considered is shown in Figure 3 The topology has nine receivers (denoted $D1$ to $D9$) and link bandwidths ranging from 0.5 to 10 Mbps. The maximum overlap is 7 and minimum overlap is 1. We conducted simulations in low, moderate and high cross-traffic scenarios using the Exact Path Length Method. For low cross-traffic case, the average utilization of all the links was 15 % and varied from 5-25 %. For moderate traffic, the average link utilization was 25 % and varied from 5-50 %. For high cross-traffic case, the average was 45 % and varied from 5-90 %. We also varied the TTL until Δ was close to Δ_0 within .25ms. We sent between 40 and 70 probes per pair and observed the total number of correctly identified prefix lengths.

The second part of Figure 3 shows the effects on accuracy as the number of probes are increased. Accuracy is the difference between the actual number of overlapping links and those detected by our algorithms relative to the actual number of overlapping

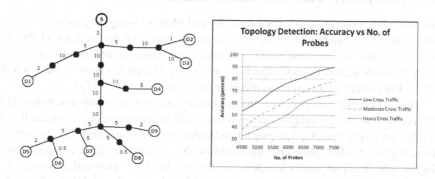

Fig. 3. The Topology Used for Tree Detection and Accuracy as a function of Probes

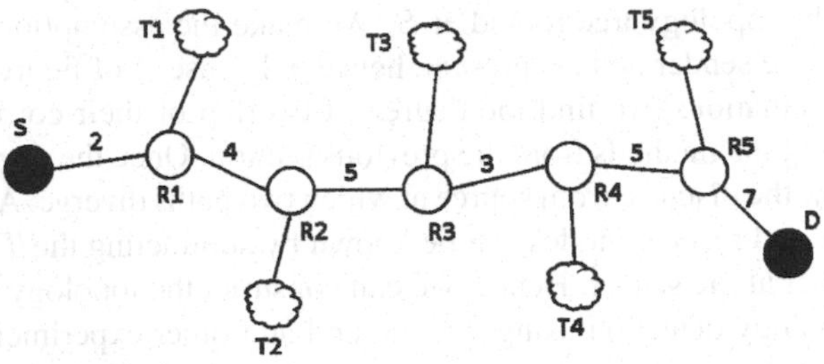

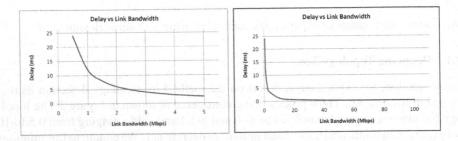

Fig. 4. Topology Used to Test Effect of Cross Traffic

Fig. 5. Transmission delay with high and low bandwidth links

links. Three scenarios are shown with different cross-traffic conditions. As shown in the graph, as the total number of probes are increased, the accuracy increases for all the three scenarios. Even under heavy traffic conditions, the accuracy is more than 60 % with total 6000 probes which average to 58 probes per destination pair. This is roughly equal to 100KB. We conclude that our method is fairly accurate over a wide range of traffic conditions and at the same time is very communication efficient.

4.2 Experiments on the Lower Bound Method

We did a few experiments on the Lower Bound Method using the topology of Figure 4. We changed the bandwidths of the links to see the effect on the accuracy of the method. We found that for low cross-traffic scenario, even when the link bandwidths are more than the bottleneck bandwidth(fixed at 3 Mbps) by 4Mbps, the accuracy drops to below 40 %. For further details of cross traffic results, we refer you to [16].

This is because n depends on the summation of inverse of the link bandwidths on the paths. This inverse relation causes a sharp fall in accuracy even when the link bandwidths are larger than the bottleneck bandwidth by a small amount. This becomes clear form Figures 5 which shows the transmission delay caused by links to a packet of 1000 Bytes. The first part shows the delay as the bandwidth is changed and second graph shows the delay specifically for low bandwidth links(less than 5 Mbps). From the two figures, it is clear that the delay decreases sharply as the bandwidths are increased. Also, in presence of cross-traffic, low delays are hard to detect. Hence, the method produces poor results when the bandwidths are large. We conclude that this method is not practical and can only be used in limited settings where the links bandwidths are very small (less than 3 Mbps) and are close to the bottleneck bandwidth.

5 Conclusions

Overlay networks require knowledge of underlay characteristics in order to provide good fault-tolerant services. Since the network elements do not cooperate to provide such information, special measurement techniques are required to infer underlay properties.

Our approach to construct fault tolerant overlays require underlay topology information, specifically the amount of overlap between overlay paths at the underlay layer. We use special end-to-end probing techniques to infer the overlap information. We have devised two such techniques and have demonstrated their applicability through extensive simulations. The results indicate that one of our Methods (Accurate Path Length Method) is very accurate under a wide range of network load conditions. The other method (Lower Bound Method) is applicable under very limited conditions. We have also identified an application of our methods to the case of topology detection. The experimental results for topology detection show that we can get very accurate results with modest communication overheads.

References

1. Cui, W., Stoica, I., Katz, R.: Backup path allocation based on a correlated link failure probability model in overlay networks. In: Proceedings of 10th IEEE International Conference on Network Protocols, 2002, pp. 236–245 (2002)
2. Ratnasamy, S., Handley, M., Karp, R., Shenker, S.: Topologically-aware overlay construction and server selection. In: INFOCOM (2002)
3. Han, J., Watson, D., Jahanian, F.: Topology aware overlay networks. IEEE INFOCOM (2005)
4. Wang, L., Griffioen, J., Calvert, K., Shi, S.: Passive inference of path correlation. In: Proceedings of the 14th international workshop on Network and operating systems support for digital audio and video, pp. 36–41 (2004)
5. Mills, D.: Internet Time Synchronization: The Network Time Protocol. In: Yang, Z., Anthony Marsland, T. (eds.) Global States and Time in Distributed Systems. IEEE Computer Society Press, Los Alamitos (1994)
6. Bolot, J.: End-to-end packet delay and loss behavior in the internet. ACM SIGCOMM Computer Communication Review 23, 289–298 (1993)
7. Carter, R., Crovella, M.: Measuring bottleneck link speed in packet-switched networks. Performance evaluation 27, 297–318 (1996)
8. Lai, K., Baker, M.: Measuring link bandwidths using a deterministic model of packet delay. SIGCOMM, 283–294 (2000)
9. Mah, B.: Estimating bandwidth and other network properties. Internet Statistics and Metrics Analysis (2000)
10. Harfoush, K., Bestavros, A., Byers, J.: Measuring bottleneck bandwidth of targeted path segments. In: INFOCOM (2003)

11. Fei, T., Tao, S., Gao, L., Guerin, R.: How to select a good alternate path in large peer-to-peer systems. IEEE INFOCOM (2001)
12. Andersen, D., Balakrishnan, H., Kaashoek, F., Morris, R.: Resilient overlay networks. ACM Press, New York (2001)
13. Andersen, D.G., Snoeren, A.C., Balakrishnan, H.: Best-path vs. multi-path overlay routing. In: Proceedings of the 3rd ACM SIGCOMM conference on Internet measurement. ACM, New York (2003)
14. Coates, M., Castro, R., Nowak, R., Gadhiok, M., King, R., Tsang, Y.: Maximum likelihood network topology identification from edge-based unicast measurements. In: Proceedings of the 2002 ACM SIGMETRICS international conference on Measurement and modeling of computer systems, pp. 11–20 (2002)
15. Chen, Y., Bindel, D., Song, H., Katz, R.: An algebraic approach to practical and scalable overlay network monitoring. ACM SIGCOMM Computer Communication Review 34, 55–66 (2004)
16. Patidar, M.: Constructing underlay-aware fault tolerant overlay networks. In: Dual Degree Dissertation Department of Computer Science And Engineering IIT Bombay (2008)

QoSBR: A Quality Based Routing Protocol for Wireless Mesh Networks

Amitangshu Pal, Sandeep Adimadhyam, and Asis Nasipuri

Electrical & Computer Engineering,
The University of North Carolina at Charlotte, NC 28223-0001
{apal,sadimadh,anasipur}@uncc.edu

Abstract. In this paper we present a QoS based routing protocol for wireless mesh networks that tries to maximize the probability of successful transmissions while minimizing the end-to-end delay. The proposed routing protocol uses reactive route discoveries to collect key parameters from candidate routes to estimate the probability of success and delay of data packets transmitted over them. To make sure that it estimates these quantities for the flow of data packets and not control packets, we propose a new route quality metric that uses performance models of data packet transmissions that are obtained from offline experiments. We present simulation based performance evaluations of the proposed QoS based routing protocol and show its benefits in comparison to some other known routing protocols.

Keywords: Wireless mesh networks, on-demand routing, QoS.

1 Introduction

Wireless mesh networks (*WMNs*) consist of mesh routers and mesh clients, where the mesh routers have minimal mobility and form the backbone of the network using multi-hop transmissions. *WMNs* are dynamically self-organized and self-configured, enabling the nodes to automatically establish and maintain mesh connectivity among themselves [2]. These networks have low installation and maintenance costs, and provide reliable service. They can also be scaled up easily by installing additional routers to increase geographical coverage and service, if required.

A number of multimedia applications such as voice over IP (*VoIP*) and video on demand (*VOD*) are becoming increasingly popular in mobile wireless devices. But unlike traditional data applications, these applications require *QoS* guarantees to support user service requirements. In this paper, we present a *QoS* based routing protocol that tries to optimize the end-to-end throughput and delay by using an interference based routing metric. Although a lot of work has been reported on *QoS* based routing for multi-hop wireless networks, most of the proposed approaches rely on the usage of control packets to estimate route quality. But control (broadcast) packets differ from actual data packets as they are smaller in size and are sent at a lower transmission rate than data packets. This

K. Kant et al. (Eds.): ICDCN 2010, LNCS 5935, pp. 497–508, 2010.
© Springer-Verlag Berlin Heidelberg 2010

leads to unexpected problems, such as the communication *"gray zone problem"* [8], and consequently, the data transmission performance may be poorer than expected. To address this issue, we propose a scheme that tries to obtain *predicted route quality* by developing appropriate interference models using off-line measurements. Our predictions are based on actual data packet transmissions, thus eliminating the gray zone problem.

The rest of the paper is organized as follows. In section 2, we discuss previous works on routing and *QoS* support in mesh networks. In section 3, we discuss the network model that is assumed in this work. In section 4, we describe our quality metric based on probability of success (*POS*) and delay. Section 5 describes our proposed *QoS* based routing protocol (*QoSBR*). In section 6, we present performance evaluations of *QoSBR* and its comparison with a popular shortest-path based routing protocol (*AODV*) and another QoS based routing protocol *MARIA* [4]. Conclusions are presented in section 7.

2   Related Work

Several routing protocols have been proposed that try to improve QoS by estimating parameters related to wireless interference. In [4], the authors use conflict graphs to characterize interference. They propose an interference aware *QoS* routing protocol *MARIA*, where nodes involved in a route discovery estimate the residual bandwidth in its neighborhood and forwards the information over the route request packet (*RREQ*). The destination selects the route based on the highest minimum residual bandwidth, i.e. the least interference. An algorithm that chooses the route that has minimum commitment period of the bottleneck node is presented in [6]. Commitment period is defined as the sum of the time the node spends in transmission/reception and the time a node has to reserve to be idle for enabling the flow of interfering traffic. Thus reducing the commitment period results in reduced interference. In the *DARE* protocol [3], all nodes in a path reserve time slots for a flow and all nodes near the reserved path abstain from transmissions during the reserved time slots, thus minimizing the possibility of interference. In [9], the authors propose an algorithm where each mesh router periodically measures the *RSSI*, average *SINR*, average number of transmission rounds, average residual block error rate and the actual spectral efficiency of the transport channel. For any path, the algorithm uses this information to meet minimum tolerable levels of a set of metrics.

Other approaches to *QoS* routing have also been proposed. In [5], a *Genetic Algorithm (GA)* for *QoS* multicast routing has been defined. Every route has to guarantee the bandwidth and delay requirements. Among all the routes satisfying the *QoS* requirements, the algorithm chooses the route that has the minimum hop count. *QUORUM* [7] estimates the end-to-end delay by sending *DUMMY-RREP* packets, which have the same size, priority and data rate as the actual data packets. The source selects the route for which the average delay of the *DUMMY* packets is within acceptable bounds and starts transmitting data traffic. In *Wireless Mesh Routing (WMR)* [10] the required bandwidth and delay constraints are embedded in the route discovery message. This information is used by nodes propagating the route discovery packets to help in determining the shortest-path route to mesh router.

All the above approaches mainly use control packets for estimating the link quality. Our scheme is different from the perspective that we use heuristics to measure data transmission quality metrics of a route.

3 Network Model

We consider a mesh network that consists of mesh clients representing end users, mesh routers that communicate with the clients, and a single Internet Gateway that communicates with the mesh routers and the Internet. In this paper, we focus on routing within the mesh routers only. We consider that clients are interested to establish communication with the gateway, for accessing the Internet. It is assumed that the gateway is aware of the locations of the mesh routers, and keeps track of all active nodes and neighborhood information. Although not addressed in this paper, such neighborhood information can be obtained in a static network by employing appropriate channel probing techniques. For this work, we make use of this information to enable the gateway to play the central role in all routing decisions. Although mesh routers may have multiple radios that can be configured to operate on multiple orthogonal channels to increase throughput, in this work each mesh router is assumed to have only one radio to communicate with the peer mesh routers.

4 Development of a QoS Metric Based on Simulation

With these assumptions, we present our approach for developing a routing metric that tries to capture the QoS of routes from clients to the gateway in terms of the end-to-end POS and delay. We show that the primary factors influencing the throughput and delay in a link can be effectively captured by two measurable quantities: (a) the number of active neighbors of the sender, and (b) the number of interfering nodes of the receiver. Another key idea obtained from these studies is the notion of *dependent* interferers that do not affect the performance of a receiver in the traditional sense. We develop mathematical models to represent the POS and delay under these factors, which are extended to the development of an end-to-end route quality metric.

For a given test link, we term those neighbors of the transmitter of the test link that are currently transmitting on the same channel as the transmitter and fall within its carrier sensing range as its *active neighbors*. These are the nodes with which the transmitter has to compete to gain access to the channel. The channel access ratio (CAR), defined as the fraction of the offered load that gets access to the channel, depends on its number of active neighbors. All the transmitting nodes that fall outside the carrier sensing range of the transmitter of the test link interfere with the reception of the receiver. The interference power from these nodes get added at the receiver. As the number of interferers increase, the probability that a transmitted packet on the test link will be successfully received reduces. The probability of success at the receiver also depends on the frequency of occurence of interfering transmissions, which increase with transmitted load of the interfering nodes. Consequently, the quality of a link depends on the number of active neighbors of the transmitter and the number of interferers of the receiver along with a number of other parameters such as transmitted load, locations and interplay of neighboring nodes etc. Since these relationships are complex, we use simulations to carefully evaluate the important effects and then develop simple mathematical models to describe them.

4.1   Simulation Environment

We use the *network simulator–2 (ns2)* [1] to perform these link quality assessments for developing models that can be used to estimate the quality of a link. The parameters used in the simulations are listed in Table 1. We consider *CSMA/CA* without *RTS/CTS*, and hence, we blocked the *RTS/CTS*. To measure the exact characteristics of the channel, we also block the *ACK* packets.

Table 1. Simulation environment

Parameter	Values used	Parameter	Values used
Max node queue length	200	Data packets size	1000 bytes
Propagation Model	Two Ray Ground	Transmitter antenna gain	0 dB
Receiver antenna gain	0 dB	Transmit power	20 dBm
Noise floor	-101 dBm	SINRDatacapture	10 dB
SINRPreamblecapture	4 dB	PowerMonitor Threshold	-86.77 dBm
Modulation scheme	BPSK	Traffic Generation	Exponential

4.2   CAR vs. Number of Active Neighbors

The transmission range with the chosen simulation parameters is found to be 155 meters. We first study the variation of the CAR in a test link with respect to the distance between an active neighbor and the transmitter for different loads of the active neighbor. This is plotted in Fig. 1, which shows that the carrier sensing range (CSR) is also 155 meters. As expected, as long as the interferer is within the CSR, the CAR is independent of the distance from the interferer and depends on the load.

We next determine the effect of the number of active neighbors on CAR by varying the number of active neighbors and the result is depicted in Fig. 2. It is observed that the CAR is not noticably affected by the active neighbors for loads lower than 150 kbps, but it drops significantly and non-linearly at higher loads, especially for higher number of active neighbors.

4.3   Queuing and Access Delay at the Test Link

The queuing delay Q_d is the property of the transmitting router, which is the time that a packet has to wait in its transmission queue before it actually reaches

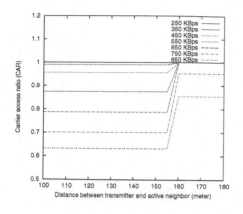

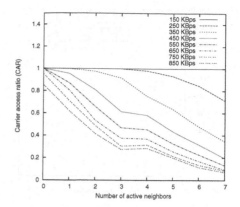

Fig. 1. Variation of CAR with respect to distance from an active neighbor

Fig. 2. Variation of CAR with the number of active neighbors

the head of the queue and starts contending for the channel. Q_d is directly related to the length of the queue and the arrival rate of the packets entering in the queue. On the other hand, the access delay Q_a is the time that a packet at the head of the transmission queue has to wait before the contention in the channel is resolved by $CSMA/CA$ and the packet gets access to the channel and starts transmission. The sum of the average queuing and access delays, referred to as total delay t_d, can give a good estimate of the amount of contention in the channel for the test link. We performed simulations with different number of active neighbors. It was found that a quadratic polynomial closely describes the variation of the delay with respect to the number of active neighbors n_a as follows:

$$T_d(n_a) = An_a^2 + Bn_a + C \tag{1}$$

where A, B and C are the best fit coefficients that depend on the offered load. These coefficients were found to be $A = -3.57 \times 10^{-7}$, $B = 4.814 \times 10^{-6}$ and $C = 0.001443$ for 5 KBps; $A = 1.88 \times 10^{-6}$, $B = 9.54 \times 10^{-6}$, $C = 0.00146$ for 35 KBps; and $A = -7.023 \times 10^{-7}$, $B = 5.25 \times 10^{-5}$ and $C = 0.001425$ for 65 KBps. Delays obtained from simulations and the best fit curves described above are shown in Fig. 3, which validates the quadratic approximation.

4.4 POS at the Receiver

The variation of a test link with respect to the distance from an interfering node from the receiver for different transmission loads is depicted in Fig. 4. It is observed that the interfering range is 235m. When an interferer is within this range, its interference power causes the SINR at the receiver of the test link to drop below the minimum SINR threshold. Consequently, within this range, the *POS* is constant and depends on the load. For the rest of the paper we assume the grid spacing to be 150 meters, with which a receiver can have up to 5 interferers.

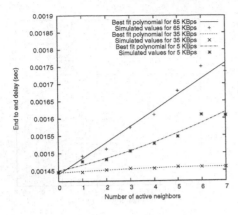

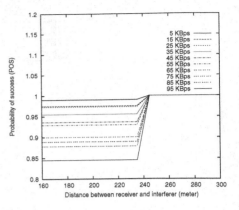

Fig. 3. Experimentally obtained model of delay versus number of active neighbors

Fig. 4. Variation of POS with respect to distance from an interferer

Generally, a link in a wireless network comes under the influence of a number of interferers whose transmission may be dependent or independent of other transmitters. Independent interferers are those whose transmissions are not in any way affected by one another, i.e. each node's transmissions occur independent of those from the others. So, if S is the transmitter and D is the receiver in a test link, then the POS of the link $S \to D$ in the presense of a set of N independent interferers I with transmitted load L (L is given by $CAR \times$ offered load) can be written as:

$$P_S(I) = \prod_{k=1}^{N} P_S(i_k) \tag{2}$$

where $I = \{i_1, i_2, \ldots, i_N\}$ is the set of N interferers of D and $P_S(i_k)$ is the probability of success of the test link when i_k is transmitting. Note that $P_S(i_k) = 1 - P_t(i_k)$, where $P_t(i_k)$ is the probability that a transmission from interferer i_k overlaps with the test packet from S and depends on the transmitted load L. We use simulations to determine the effect of L on $P_S(i_k)$, which is found to fit a quadratic curve as follows:

$$P_S(i_k) = Q.L^2 + R.L + T \tag{3}$$

where $Q = -1.49184 \times 10^{-6}$, $R = -0.00128499$ and $T = 0.998588$. The simulation results and the best fit curve are shown in Fig. 5.

It must be noted that although the set I can be estimated by the set of nodes that are located within the interfering range of the receiver, some additional factors affect the accuracy of equation (2). Firstly, wireless propagation can be highly non-isotropic because of shadowing, multipath reflections, and other long term fading effects. This can make it difficult to estimate the actual interference from a source from its distance from the receiver. However, because of the

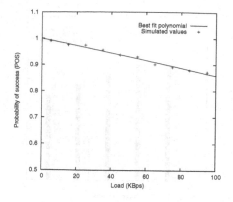

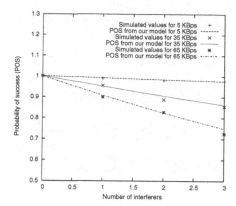

Fig. 5. Experimentally obtained model of POS versus load in the presence of one interferer

Fig. 6. POS versus number of interferers: model and simulation results

threshold effect of the interference from any source, we find that using the interfering range to identify interferers is generally acceptable. Secondly, equation (2) is based on the assumption that the set of interferers in I transmit independently of one another. The number of interferers whose transmissions are independent of each other is often hard to obtain. We discuss this issue in more detail in the next section. The above two factors need additional considerations if RTS/CTS and ACK packets are assumed, which is not discussed in this paper. Thirdly, this approximation disregards the effect of the aggregate interference of nodes that are located outside the interfering range of the receiver. This effect may cause inaccurate results in dense and highly active networks.

Fig. 6 depicts the comparison of results obtained from the approximate model in equation (2), where all the nodes have the same load, and hence, the same $P_S(i_k)$ for all i_k. The actual POS values obtained from simulations closely match the values obtained from the model, as shown in Fig. 6. So we conclude that the POS of a test link for a given load can be approximately estimated from the number of active neighbors of the transmitter and the number of interferers of the receiver using the models developed above.

4.5 Dependent Interferers and Dependencies

We now address the issue of independence of transmissions from interferers in the set I. We show with an example that not all nodes located within the interference range of a test receiver can transmit independently. For example, let us consider the scenario shown in Fig. 7, where the test link 20→21 has 3 active interferers: 16, 22, 27. However, since nodes 16 and 22 are active neighbors of each other, they cannot transmit at the same time. So, when all these nodes are active, at any point of time either 16 or 22 will transmit after resolving contention with each other, and 27 transmit can transmit independently of 16 and 22. Hence, we call 16 and 22 to be dependent interferers, whereas 27 is independent of 16 and 22.

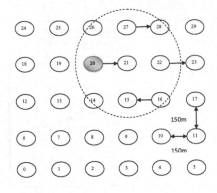

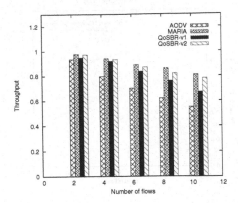

Fig. 7. 20→21 has 3 interferers and at most 2 can transmit at the same time, so dependency of D(3,2). Interference range = 235 meter is shown by dotted.

Fig. 8. Comparison of Throughput

Given a set of N_t nodes within the interfering range of a receiver, let N_a be the maximum number of interferers that can gain access to the channel simultaneously (i.e. independently). For any test link, we define the combination of N_t and N_a as a "dependency" $D(N_t, N_a)$. So, as evident from the discussion above, the dependency in Fig. 7 is $D(3,2)$. To obtain the effect of dependent and independent interferers on the POS, we evaluated the POS under different dependencies with varying loads, as shown in Table 2. It can be observed that the POS only depends on the effective number of interferers N_a, since the values of POS for $D(1,1)$, $D(2,1)$, $D(3,1)$ are similar, and so are those for $D(2,2)$, $D(3,2)$. So, for dependent interferers, we express the POS as

$$P_S(I) = \prod_{k=1}^{N_a} (P_S(i_k)) = \prod_{k=1}^{N_a} (1 - P_t(i_k)) \tag{4}$$

4.6   Route Quality Metric for Multi Hop Mesh Networks

We now extend the above models of the estimated POS and delay of a test link to define an end-to-end route quality metric. This is based on the objective of maximizing the end-to-end POS and minimizing the end-to-end delay in the route. The net POS is taken as the product of the POS of every individual link on the route and the total delay is taken as the sum of the link delays. Consequently, we define the route quality $QOS\_R(r)$ metric for route r of length v operating at load L as follows:

$$QOS\_R(r) = (\prod_{f=1}^{v} P_S(I_f)) / \sum_{f=1}^{v} T_d(n_{af}) \tag{5}$$

Table 2. POS with different dependencies

Load(KBps)	D(1,1)	D(2,1)	D(2,2)	D(3,1)	D(3,2)	D(3,3)
5	0.99	0.99	0.98	0.99	0.98	0.9776
15	0.975	0.976	0.96	0.98	0.951	0.943
25	0.973	0.953	0.915	0.953	0.9169	0.9164
35	0.955	0.938	0.888	0.9521	0.896	0.854
45	0.936	0.935	0.8886	0.94	0.878	0.829
55	0.929	0.92	0.849	0.9138	0.8522	0.794
65	0.9	0.909	0.828	0.907	0.848	0.7044
75	0.889	0.9	0.7912	0.903	0.79	0.716
85	0.878	0.879	0.752	0.869	0.785	0.685
95	0.871	0.86	0.773	0.86	0.779	0.685

Here, f is a link on the route from source to destination, $P_S(I_f)$ is the *POS* of link f, I_f is the set of interferers, and $T_d(n_{af})$ is the delay experienced by a packet with n_{af} active neighbors.

5   QoSBR Routing Protocol

In this section we describe the proposed QoS based routing protocol *QoSBR* that uses the quality metric derived in the previous section. *QoSBR* is a reactive routing protocol that tries to select routes with the highest ratio of the end-to-end *POS* and delay based on parameters collected and conveyed by *RREQ* packets. We present two versions of *QoSBR*, which differ in the contents of the propagating *RREQ* packets and how the quality metric is calculated. These are described in detail below.

When the source does not have a route to the destination, it broadcasts a route request packet (*RREQ*) to its neighbors. The *RREQ* packet contains four fields: the number of active neighbors of the sender (A), the accumulated *POS* on the current route (P_S), the accumulated delay in the current route (T_d), and a timestamp. These quantities are initialized at the source to the number of active neighbors of the source, $P_S = 1$, $T_d = 0$, and timestamp = the time when the *RREQ* packet was generated. Every intermediate node updates the accumulated *POS* and delay based on the number of active neighbors of the previous node and its active interferers before forwarding it. All intermediate nodes do the same thing until the *RREQ* reaches the destination where the destination calculates the quality metric $QOS\_R = P_S/T_d$. The timestamp is used to reduce unnecessary flooding of *RREQ* packets throughout the network. The destination waits for the first ten packets and forwards a route reply packet (*RREP*) back on the route that has the highest QOS_R value. The source then starts sending the data packets via this route. In this version, the intermediate nodes are required to calculate the *POS* and delay, for which the nodes must know its active neighbors and interferers. One way to achieve this is for the gateway to forward this information to all nodes at periodic intervals, which causes additional overhead.

In order to avoid the overhead problem mentioned above, we propose another version of the *QoSBR* routing protocol, where the *RREQ* packet simply carries the sequence of nodes that it has traversed, and the destination (gateway) uses the node location and neighborhood information to calculate the end-to-end *POS* and delay, and hence the *QOS_R* for each route. In addition to solving the problem of providing all nodes with node location information, *QoSBR_v2* can also calculate the route quality more accurately because it can use global location information to determine dependent and independent interferers based on the information conveyed by each *RREQ* packet. But the disadvantage of this scheme is that as the intermediate routers have to append its own IDs, the size of the *RREQ* packet gets larger as it propagates along the network, which can be a problem for large networks.

6 Performance Evaluation of QoSBR

We present the performance of the proposed *QoSBR* routing protocol in comparison to *AODV* and *MARIA* [4] in a general simulation scenario. We consider the same network scenario as shown in Fig. 7, which consists of 30 nodes placed in a grid. The channel bandwidth is assumed to be 2 Mbps. We have choosen 29 as the destination (Internet gateway) and all sources send packets to the gateway. The sources are selected randomly. Each flow runs *UDP* with a transmission rate of 35 KBps. Each flow is alive for 200 seconds. We have averaged the results over 10 such simulations.

We vary the number of flows and measure the average throughput, delay and jitter of the data flows using the three different routing protocols. The results are shown in Fig. 8–10. It is observed that *QoSBR_v2* performs better than *QoSBR_v1*, as *QoSBR_v2* requires the destination to measure the quality of a route after getting all the intermediate nodes in the route, while in *QoSBR_v1* the quality is calculated in the intermediate routers which only know the *existing*

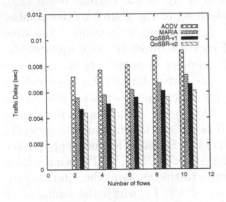

Fig. 9. Comparison of Delay

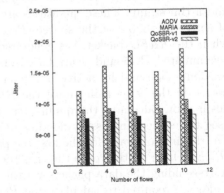

Fig. 10. Comparison of Jitter

active nodes and query packet information. But both *QoSBR_v1* and *QoSBR_v2* provide significantly better performance than *AODV* in terms of throughput, delay, and jitter. This is because the shortest path does not necessarily provide the best quality. It is observed that *MARIA* also gives better performance than *AODV*, in terms of throughput, delay and jitter. While *MARIA* gives a little higher throughput than *QoSBR-v2*, *QoSBR_v2* provides a significant improvement in delay and jitter over *MARIA*. The reason is that *MARIA* only chooses the route based on higher residual bandwidth i.e. lesser interference, without considering the delay. But the delay is an important parameter for determining a good route in many applications. While calculating the throughput, *QoSBR_v2* considers the effect of dependent and independent interferers where *MARIA* chooses routes based on only residual bandwidth without considering the dependencies among the interferers. Hence, there would be many scenarios where *MARIA* will give inferior performance than *QoSBR_v2* as *QoSBR_v2* considers both *POS* and delay. Such an example is shown in Fig. 11, where route chosen by *MARIA* for the flow $5 \rightarrow 29$ is much longer than *QoSBR_v2* in presence of background traffic $16 \rightarrow 22 \rightarrow 28 \rightarrow 29$. The performance of these two routes have been shown in Table 3 and Table 4 in presence of background traffic. From Table 3, we can see that the route chosen by *MARIA* gives almost same throughput compared to *QoSBR_v2*. But the traffic delay for *MARIA* is much larger than *QoSBR_v2*, as seen from Table 4.

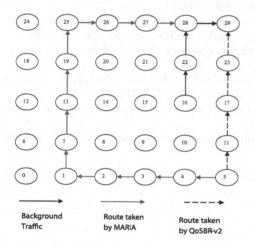

Fig. 11. Routes chosen by MARIA and QoSBR-v2 when the source-destination pair is 5→29 and 16→22→8→29 is the background traffic

Table 3. Comparison of throughput

Load (KBps)	MARIA	QoSBR_v2
5	0.988	0.9799
15	0.969	0.96
25	0.945	0.936
35	0.923	0.917

Table 4. Comparison of delay (sec)

Load (KBps)	MARIA	QoSBR_v2
5	0.0176	0.0058
15	0.0176	0.0058
25	0.01765	0.0058
35	0.01769	0.0058

7   Conclusion and Future Work

Mesh networks are a promising approach to wireless Internet connectivity for mobile users and routing remains a major concern in multi-hop wireless mesh networks. In this paper, we have developed $QoSBR$, a novel QoS aware routing protocol for wireless mesh networks. Specifically, $QoSBR$ takes two QoS metrics into account: POS and end to end delay. Our QoS based routing scheme achieves encouraging results with the help of proposed quality metric for link.

There are a number of grounds to do future work on this topic. Firstly, we plan to work on the presented scheme under more general assumptions, such as usage of RTS/CTS and ACK packets. We also intend to apply this to multiple gateway nodes using anycasting. In addition, we will extend this QoS-based routing approach to incorporate multiple channels with multiple radios for each mesh routers to reduce co-channel interference.

References

1. The network simulator - ns-2 webpage, http://www.isi.edu/nsnam/ns/
2. Akyildiz, I.F., Wang, X., Wang, W.: Wireless mesh networks: a survey. Computer Networks 47(4), 445–487 (2005)
3. Carlson, E., Karl, H., Wolisz, A., Prehofer, C.: Distributed allocation of time slots for real-time traffic in a wireless multi-hop network (2004)
4. Cheng, X., Mohapatra, P., Lee, S., Banerjee, S.: Maria: Interference-aware admission control and qos routing in wireless mesh networks. In: ICC (2008)
5. Ke, Z., Li, L., Sun, Q., Chen, N.: A qos multicast routing algorithm for wireless mesh networks. In: SNPD (1), pp. 835–840 (2007)
6. Kolar, V., Abu-Ghazaleh, N.B.: A multi-commodity flow approach for globally aware routing in multi-hop wireless networks. In: PerCom, pp. 308–317 (2006)
7. Kone, V., Das, S., Zhao, B.Y., Zheng, H.: Quorum - quality of service in wireless mesh networks. MONET 12(5-6), 358–369 (2007)
8. Lundgren, H., Nordström, E., Tschudin, C.F.: The gray zone problem in ieee 802.11b based ad hoc networks. MC2R 6(3), 104–105 (2002)
9. Romdhani, L., Bonnet, C.: Cross-layer qos routing framework for wireless mesh networks. ICWMC, 382–388 (2008)
10. Xue, Q., Ganz, A.: Qos routing for mesh-based wireless lans. IJWIN 9(3), 179–190 (2002)

An ACO Based Approach for Detection of an Optimal Attack Path in a Dynamic Environment

Nirnay Ghosh, Saurav Nanda, and S.K. Ghosh

School of Information Technology
Indian Institute of Technology, Kharagpur 721302, India
nirnay.ghosh@gmail.com, sauravsit@gmail.com, skg@iitkgp.ac.in

Abstract. *Attack graph* is a tool to analyze multi-stage, multi-host attack scenarios in a network. Each attack scenario is depicted by an *attack path* which is essentially a series of *exploits* with a severity score that presents a comparative desirability of a particular network service. In an *attack graph* with a large number of *attack paths*, it may not be feasible for the administrator to plug all the vulnerabilities. Moreover, in a dynamic environment where the severity of an *exploit* changes with time, a framework is required that detects an *optimal attack path* or *most favored path* from a given *attack graph* in an environment. This paper proposes a framework for finding out an *optimal attack path* using *Ant Colony Optimization (ACO)* technique under a dynamic environment. Given an *attack graph* and the severity scores of the *exploits*, an *optimal attack path* is detected using customized *ACO* algorithms. A case study has been presented to demonstrate the efficacy of the proposed methodology.

1 Introduction

Today's enterprise networks have become vulnerable to intrusions, and correlated multi-stage, multi-host attacks. Moreover, the present day network security scanners viz. Nmap[1], Nessus[2], Cybercop[3] are efficient as far as detecting vulnerabilities local to a system. One such tool that gives description about the correlated attacks is *attack graph*. An *attack graph* consists of a number of *attack paths* each of which is a series of *exploits* that an attacker uses at different stages of an attack to break into a network. Each *exploit* in the series satisfies the pre-conditions for subsequent *exploits* and makes a casual relationship among them.

Majority of the previously reported works deal with *complete attack graphs*, where all possible scenarios are depicted [8] [9] [10]. *Complete attack graph* has inherent scalability problems and requires exponential time for generation. Moreover, such an *attack graph* has redundant nodes and edges and has problems related to understandability and visual representation. These problems have been

---

[1] http://www.insecure.org/nmap/index.html
[2] http://www.nesssus.org
[3] http://www.nai.com

K. Kant et al. (Eds.): ICDCN 2010, LNCS 5935, pp. 509–520, 2010.

addressed in [2] [6] [7], where the authors have proposed the concept of *minimal attack graph* based on explicit assumption of *monotonicity* i.e. once the attacker has gained a certain level of privileges he does not have to relinquish them. A *minimal attack graph* contains only successful paths that terminate to a desired node termed as the *goal* that an attacker aims to compromise. In the present work, *minimal attack graph* has been used for computing an *optimal attack path*.

One method of quantitatively analyzing *attack graph* is to assign severity scores to the *exploits* obtained from some well-known public domain databases viz. NVD[4], Nessus, Bugtraq[5] in which an *exploit* is assigned a *Base Score (BS)*, a *Temporal Score (TS)*, and an *Environmental Score (ES)*(details are given in section 2). Combination of these three *scores* provides the *conditional probability* of an *exploit* when all of its preconditions in the *attack graph* are already satisfied [1]. This *score* may enable the administrator to determine the degree of severity relative to an exploitable vulnerable service in the network and also compute the most severe *attack path*. However, the evolving nature of a vulnerability with time is largely ignored [1]. The degree of threat posed by an *exploit* varies as new patches for the corresponding vulnerability are released or more technical detail for that vulnerability becomes available. Therefore, the *scores* related to an *exploit* changes in a dynamic environment.

In this work, a methodology has been proposed to conceive a dynamic environment where the severity related to a vulnerability may change over time. A novel approach based on one of the *soft computing technique*, called, *Ant Colony Optimization (ACO)* has been presented which accepts an *attack graph* and the *individual scores* of the *exploits* as input to generate an *optimal attack path* under dynamic environment.

The organization of the rest of the paper is as follows. Section 2 presents a notion of severity scores. Section 3 describes *Ant Colony Optimization* technique with related formulae. Section 4 presents the proposed framework. Section 5 demonstrates the proposed framework with a concrete case study. Section 6 discusses the results and section 7 concludes the paper.

2   CVSS-Based Severity Scores

In this section, CVSS[6] concept for quantifying an *exploit* or a *vulnerability* has been presented. Some well-acknowledged public domain repositories viz. NVD, Nessus, and Bugtraq contain *CVSS scores* of more than 37,000 published *vulnerabilities*. The *CVSS* assessment for any vulnerability measures three areas of concern [5] viz. *Base Score (BS)*, *Temporal Score (TS)*, and *Environmental Score (ES)*.

TS has *three* temporal metrics used in *CVSS score* which are: *Exploitability (E)*, *Remediation Level (RL)*, and *Report Confidence (RC)*. The *Temporal*

---

[4] http://nvd.nist.gov/
[5] http://www.securityfocus.com/archive/
[6] http://www.first.org/cvss/

Group Score (TGS) is calculated as $TGS = (E \times RL \times RC)$ [1]. The value of TGS lies within the range 0.67 to 1.0.

The *Temporal Score (TS)* is given by:

$$TS = BS \times TGS \tag{1}$$

Application of both *Temporal Score* and *Environmental Score* are optional [5]. But in real-world scenario, the administrator always intends at plugging the detected vulnerabilities from time to time with vendor-specific patches. These patches are released periodically and therefore, the threat posed by an exploit also varies over time. Hence, the effect of the *Temporal Score* needs to be integrated with *CVSS Base Score* for modeling various temporal aspects of a vulnerability/exploit. The *CVSS Temporal Score* for each exploit obtained from equation (1) is converted to *probability scores (p(e))* following a simple approach [1].

$$p(e) = TemporalScore/10 = TS/10 \tag{2}$$

This probability obtained from the *CVSS score* is interpreted as the *conditional probability* of an *exploit* when all its pre-conditions depicted in the *attack graph* are already satisfied [1].

3   Ant Colony Optimization (ACO)

Ant Colony Optimization (ACO), a well-known soft computing technique [4], is inspired by the behavior of ants in finding the most optimal path to food. The ants (initially) wander randomly, and upon finding food return to their colony while laying down *pheromone* trails. If other ants find such a path, they are likely to follow the trail, returning and reinforcing it if they eventually find food. Over time, however, the *pheromone* trail starts to evaporate, thus reducing its attractive strength. The *pheromone* trail on a shorter path takes more time to evaporate. *Pheromone* evaporation has also the advantage of avoiding the convergence to a locally optimal solution. If there were no evaporation at all, the paths chosen by the first ants would tend to be excessively attractive to successive ones and positive feedback eventually leads all the ants following a single path. *Ant colony optimization* algorithms have been used to produce *near-optimal solutions* to a large number of problems and the *Traveling Salesman Problem* being the most popular of them all [11]. In this work, *ACO* has been chosen for detection of *optimal attack path* from a given *attack graph* as it is itself an *optimization algorithm*. Therefore, *two* important functions in *ACO* are:

Edge Selection: The probability with which an ant selects the path from node i to node j is calculated based on the formula given below:

$$P_{i,j} = \frac{(\tau_{i,j})^{\alpha}.(\eta_{i,j})^{\beta}}{\sum (\tau_{i,j})^{\alpha}.(\eta_{i,j})^{\beta}} \tag{3}$$

where, $\tau_{i,j}$ is the amount of pheromone on arc $\{i,j\}$, α is a parameter to control the influence of $\tau_{i,j}$, $\eta_{i,j}$ is the desirability of arc i,j, β is a parameter to control the influence of $\eta_{i,j}$.

Pheromone Update: The *pheromone* update is an important phase of this process as the ants increase the *pheromone* deposition on some paths from where they are traveling to reach the food and on the same time the *pheromone* evaporates from the other paths with time. The formula for pheromone evaporation is given as:

$$\tau_{i,j} = (1 - \rho).\tau_{i,j} + \Delta\tau_{i,j} \tag{4}$$

where, $\tau_{i,j}$ is the amount of pheromone on a given arc i,j, ρ is the rate of pheromone evaporation, $\Delta\tau_{i,j}$ is the amount of pheromone deposited, typically given by,

$$\Delta\tau_{i,j}^k = \begin{cases} 1/L_k & \text{if ant } k \text{ travels on edge } i,j \\ 0 & \text{Otherwise} \end{cases}$$

where, L_k is the cost of the kth ant's tour.

4   ACO-Based Optimal Attack Path Detection

For a particular network configuration, an *attack graph* depicts an exhaustive set of multi-stage, multi-host attack scenarios which are represented by *attack paths*. In a real-world scenario, all *attack paths* may not be evenly severe from attackers' perspective. Some *attack paths* may be exploited with relatively less effort while the others may not. But any *attack path* that gets successfully exploited by a *colony of attackers*[7], observed over a period of time, influences subsequent attackers to follow that path until some preventive measures are adopted by the network administrator. Therefore, from an exhaustive set of *attack paths*, a subset (may be one) of which will be preferred by subsequent *colony of attackers*. This subset of *attack paths* that gets frequently exploited is termed as *optimal attack path(s)*.

The above mentioned scenario has similarity with *Ant Colony Optimization (ACO)* technique where variation in the concentration of *pheromone deposit* with time is similar to situations in dynamic network environment where the threats posed by *exploits* (constituting an *attack path*) varies as new technical details become available or corresponding vendor-specific patches are released.

ACO technique, therefore, enables detection of an *optimal attack path* from a given *attack graph*. The notion of *optimal attack path* in the context of this work is the *attack path* which attracts largest number of attackers from a *colony of attackers* and finally the *probability of selecting that path* converges to one. The proof of convergence for *ACO* has been reported in some literatures [11] [3].

Therefore, two main reasons for selecting *ACO*, which generates *near-optimal solutions*, as the basis of the proposed framework are as follows:

---

[7] In this work, it has been assumed that the attackers belonging to a particular *colony* are well coordinated by means of some *social engineering* techniques.

1. Detection of an *optimal attack path* from an *attack graph* depending upon the preference shown by a *colony of attackers* over a period of time.
2. Realization of a real-world network environment where the threat associated with each *exploit/vulnerability* dynamically changes and eventually influences the selection of *optimal attack path*.

4.1   Mapping of ACO Formulae with CVSS-Based Severity Score

The formula for selection of a particular edge by a *colony of ants* (refer eqn.(3)) may be observed to have two distinct parts viz. *amount of pheromone on the arc* $(\tau_{i,j})$ (variable part), and *desirability of the arc* $(\eta_{i,j})$ (constant part)

Likewise, the formula for *Temporal Score (TS)* related to an *exploit* (refer eqn. (1)) consists of two entities viz. *Base Score (BS)* (constant part), and *Temporal Group Score (TGS)* (variable part)

Temporal Group Score (TGS) for an *exploit* allows the administrator to model time variant factors in determining the severity of a vulnerability. It consists of *Exploitability (E)*, *Remediation Level (RL)*, and *Report Confidence (RC)* whose scores fluctuate among a set of annotated values over a period of time. Similarly, in the context of *ACO*, the concentration of *pheromone* trail alters with time, depending upon whether or not a particular path has been selected by the *colony of ants*. This fluctuation in *TGS* with time is bounded by a *threshold* which corresponds to a lower-bound for *pheromone* trail below which the concentration becomes insignificant i.e. the existing *pheromone* trail cannot be used by the *colony of ants* to find the *shortest path*. Likewise, in this work, the *threshold* marks the minimum value for *TGS* which a *colony of attackers* needs to qualify before successfully executing an *exploit*.

On contrary, the *Base Score (BS)* relevant to an *exploit* remains constant over time, drawing a resemblance with the *desirability of an arc* $(\eta_{i,j})$ in case of *ACO*.

4.2   Optimal Path Detection Algorithm

This section describes customized *ACO* algorithm that have been used to find an *optimal attack path* from a given *attack graph*. The algorithm consists of two processes viz. *Process*1 (refer to Algorithm 1) and *Process*2 (refer to Algorithm 2) which use a shared memory. *Process*1 declares a data structure, which includes BS, E, RL, RC, TGS, and a matrix containing the *probability values* $(P_{i,j})$ in the shared memory. The integrity of the data, when the processes enter into the critical section, is maintained by semaphores. After a particular node has been traversed, *Process*1 selects a neighboring node by comparing the *TGS* values with the *threshold*.

With every iteration, *Process*1 finds an *attack path* and this continues till the entire *colony of attackers* gets exhausted. It may be observed, after a fair number of iterations, all subsequent iterations converge to a single path. *Process*2 involves the continuous decay of *TGS* values for each node with increasing time. A decay in the *TGS* value may be attributed to a decrease in the value of

Input: Attack Graph with initial configuration
Output: Optimal Attack Path
foreach *attacker k of colony* **do**
   | $AttackPath = NULL$;
   | **for** $i=0$ *to nodes* **do**
   | | color[i]=$White$;
   | **end**
   | $start=0$;
   | Append($start$);
   | color[$start$]=$Black$;
   | **while** $start! = goal$ **do**
   | | $wait(semid1)$;
   | | Read the values of E, RL, RC from shared memory;
   | | Calculate the current TGS value;
   | | Calculate the *probability* of selecting the neighboring nodes;
   | | **foreach** *neighbor j of currentnode* **do**
   | | | **if** $heus[j].TGS > threshold$ **then**
   | | | | $flag = 1$;
   | | | **end**
   | | **end**
   | | **if** $flag = 1$ **then**
   | | | Find next node based on highest TGS value;
   | | **end**
   | | **else**
   | | | find next node using $RandomWalkAlgorithm$;
   | | **end**
   | | color[$start$]=$Black$;
   | | Append($start$);
   | | Update TGS ;
   | | $signal(semid2)$;
   | **end**
   | Display $AttackPath$;
end

Algorithm 1. Process 1

Input: Previous TGS value
Output: Updated TGS value
Settimer (*timeslice*)
while *true* **do**
   | **if** $CheckTimer(timeslice) = 1$ **then**
   | | $wait(semid2)$
   | | Decay TGS values
   | | $signal(semid1)$
   | **end**
end

Algorithm 2. Process 2

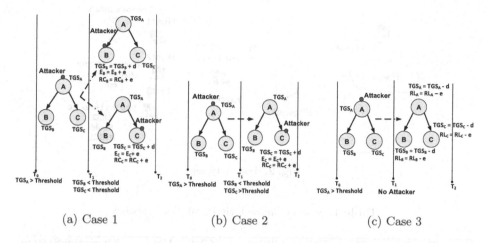

Fig. 1. Variation of E, RL, RC with time

(a) Case 1   (b) Case 2   (c) Case 3

$RemediationLevel(RL)$, as new patches for a particular vulnerability are released periodically.

The change in values for different attributes of TGS (i.e. E, RL, and RC) under dynamic environment may be described by a simple three node *attack graph* given by figure 1. Figure 1 shows the variation in the values of E, RL, and RC with time by depicting three different scenarios. The *attack graph* consists of three *exploits* A, B, and C which constitute its nodes. In figure 1(a), during time slice T_0, the TGS value for A is higher than the *Threshold*. Therefore, the attacker (shown by small circle), executes the *exploit* A during time slice T_0 and has options to execute either of B or C. The TGS values for B and C, TGS_B and TGS_C, are less than the *threshold*. The selection of the next node will be done based on $RandomWalkAlgorithm$. Hence, in the next time slice, T_1, the next *exploit* that the attacker may execute is either B or C. In both cases, TGS_B or TGS_C will have a δ increment following increments in corresponding E and RC values by some ϵ amount.

Figure 1(b) depicts a scenario where the TGS value for *exploit* C exceeds the *Threshold*. Therefore, node C will be selected as the next node in time slice T_1 by the subsequent attackers. This further increments the TGS_C value by δ amount.

In figure 1(c), a scenario is shown where no attacker has arrived during time slice T_1. As a result, there is a decrement in TGS_A, TGS_B, and TGS_C values by δ amount as the corresponding RL values get reduced by some ϵ.

5   Case Study

A Test network similar to [10] has been considered (refer to Figure 2). $Host3$ is taken as the target machine or *goal* and the MySQL[8] database running on

---

[8] http://www.mysql.com

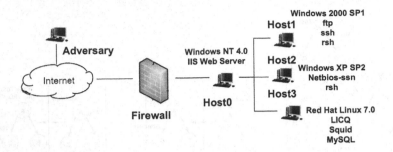

Fig. 2. Test network

Table 1. System Characteristics of Test Network

Host	Services	Ports	Vulnerabilities	CVE – IDs	OperatingSystem
H0	IIS Web Service	80	IIS buffer overflow	CVE-2002-0364	Windows NT 4.0
H1	ftp	21	ftp rhost overwrite	CVE-2008-1396	
	ssh	22	ssh buffer overflow	CVE-1999-1455	Windows 2000 SP1
	rsh	514	rsh login	CVE-1999-0180	
H2	Netbios-ssn	139	Netbios-ssn nullsession	CVE-2003-0661	Windows XP SP2
	rsh	514	rsh login	CVE-1999-0180	
H3	LICQ	5190	LICQ-remote-to-user	CVE-2001-0439	
	Squid Proxy	80	squid-port-scan	CVE-2001-1030	Red Hat Linux 7.0
	Mysql DB	3306	local-setuid-bof	CVE-2006-3368	

that machine is the critical resource. The attacker's aim is to compromise $H3$ and gain *root* privilege on that host. The system characteristics of the hosts in the network including their operating system type, services running in them, number of open ports, and existing *generic* vulnerabilities, are composed in the Table 1. These data are obtained from some vulnerability scanners viz. Nessus and some public websites viz. NVD, Bugtraq.

5.1   Attack Graph and Exploit-Specific CVSS Scores for Test Network

The exploits presented in the Test network (refer to Figure 2) may be combined in appropriate way based on their *preconditions* and *effect* to generate different attack scenarios [10]. These attack scenarios are realized by *attack paths*. Several such *attack paths* are collapsed to form an *attack graph*. The *attack graph* for the given network configuration is shown in Figure 3. Each node in the *attack graph* (shown by circles) represents *exploit* and an edge represents either a *condition* or an *available exploit* or the *privilege* gained after the application of the *exploit*. The *attack graph* consists of 16 nodes which have been numbered from 0 to 15. *Node 0* represents the *starting node* from where all the attack scenarios generate and *node 15* is the *goal* node where all the attacks terminate.

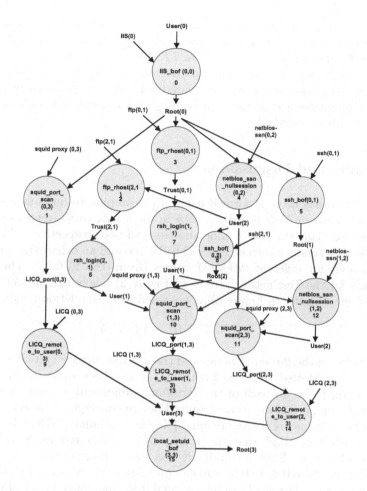

Fig. 3. Attack Graph for Test network

Table 2. CVSS-based Scores of the Exploits

Exploits	BS	E	RL	RC	TGS	TS	p(e)
IIS buffer overflow	7.5	0.9	0.87	1.0	0.783	5.8725	0.587
ftp rhost overwrite	4.3	0.85	0.95	1.0	0.8075	3.4723	0.347
rsh login	7.5	1.0	1.0	1.0	1.0	7.5	0.75
ssh buffer overflow	7.5	0.85	1.0	1.0	0.85	6.375	0.637
netbios-ssn-nullsession	5.0	0.95	0.95	0.95	0.8574	4.2868	0.428
LICQ-remote-to-user	7.5	1.0	0.95	1.0	0.95	7.125	0.713
squid-port-scan	7.5	0.95	0.87	0.95	0.7852	5.8889	0.589
local-setuid-buffer overflow	5.0	0.95	1.0	1.0	0.95	4.75	0.475

An *exploit* available from the *attack graph* (refer to Figure 3) has individual CVSS-based scores. The *Base Score (BS)*, *Temporal Group Score (TGS)* (comprising of *E, RL, RC*), *Temporal Score (TS)*, and the *probability value (p(e))* relevant to each *exploit* have been summarized in Table 2 . The data used for computing the *probability scores* are available in some well-known public sites. This score quantifies a *conditional probability* of an *exploit* when all its preconditions are already satisfied.

6   Results and Discussions

The simulation has been performed using gcc^9 compiler to find out an optimal attack path between *Node 0* and *Node 15* in the *attack graph* (refer to Figure 3) which are essentially the *source* node and the *goal* node respectively. The colony size of the attackers has been considered to be 100 and an exhaustive simulation has been done for different *threshold* values (from 0.85 to 0.95). The *optimal attack path* for the Test network (refer to Figure 2) involving different nodes of the *attack graph* (refer to Figure 3) as obtained from simulation result is:

$$0 \rightarrow 4 \rightarrow 8 \rightarrow 10 \rightarrow 13 \rightarrow 15$$

A graph between the *threshold* values and the *average number of iterations before convergence*, is plotted (refer to Figure 4). It has been done by running the simulation six times for each of the *threshold* values and an average has been taken for the number of iterations required before convergence for each of them. The *threshold* value (refer Algorithm 1) is the minimum *TGS* value for any node in the *attack graph* that the *colony of attackers* require to achieve for further exploitation. Experimentally it has been observed that the *threshold* value is varying from 0.85 to 0.95 and can go up to a maximum of 1.0. Therefore, lower-bound of the *threshold* can be assigned 0.85 since the number of iterations

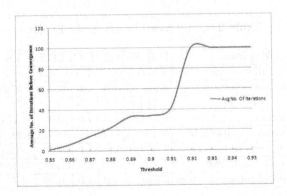

Fig. 4. Threshold Vs Average Number of Iterations before Convergence

---
[9] http://gcc.gnu.org

required to find out the optimal attack path below it is only 1. The upper-bound for TGS is taken as 1.0 since it is the maximum value which TGS may attain. Also from Figure 4, it may be observed that after the *threshold* reaches 0.92, the average number of iterations required before convergence is more than 100 and it is same for further values of *threshold*. Therefore, given a colony size of 100, for any *threshold* above 0.92, prediction of an *optimal attack path* is not possible.

This unpredictable behavior is contributed by the *dynamic environment* which has been conceived in this work. If the *threshold* is set to a lower value, it will take relatively less time to attain it rather than if it is at some higher value. This is because the both increment as well decrement in TGS value is taken into consideration following the principle that the *severity* related to an *exploit* varies over a period of time. Therefore, the *colony of attackers* will require comparatively less number of iterations to converge to a particular path if the *threshold* is set at a lower value rather than a higher value. The plot in Figure 4 shows that the *threshold* value till which a convergence occurs before the *colony of attacker* gets exhausted is 0.91. It may be observed that this value is the *mean* of the lower and the upper-bound of the TGS value. Therefore, empirically it may be concluded that *ideal threshold* $(\overline{Th})$ for the given network configuration (refer to Figure 2) is given by the following relationship:

$$\overline{Th} = \frac{Th_{lower} + Th_{upper}}{2}$$

Another inference may be drawn from the detection of *optimal attack path* from a given *attack graph*. If a static environment is perceived, the TGS values for an *exploit* remains constant. Under this situation, the *attack path* (refer to Figure 3) that majority of the attackers from a given colony size will prefer is:

$$0 \rightarrow 5 \rightarrow 10 \rightarrow 13 \rightarrow 15$$

However, simulation result yields a different *attack path* as this work considers a dynamic environment where the severity of an *exploit* changes with time. Therefore, if an administrator uses *attack graph* to analyze security strength of a network, he needs to take the effect of dynamic environment into account. Hence, analyzing *attack graph* from theoretical perspective (i.e. static environment) may not detect a correct *optimal attack path* as in real-world networks, severity associated with an *exploit* does not remain constant.

7   Conclusion

In this paper, a novel approach based on *Ant Colony Optimization* (ACO) technique is presented to detect an *optimal attack path* from a given *attack graph* for a particular network configuration. The novelty of the work lies in perceiving a dynamic network scenario where the severities of *exploits* changes over a period of time. The most preferred *attack path* (by the *attacker's colony*) is considered here as *optimal attack path*. In the present work *attack scenarios* are generated, for a given *attack graph*, with a *colony size* of hundred attackers. The *Temporal Group Score (TGS)* of an *exploit* is mapped to the *pheromone* update phenomenon of *ACO*. Since, *ACO* provides a near-optimal solution, the mapping helps in detection of an *optimal attack path*.

References

1. Measuring network security using dynamic bayesian network (2008), http://csrc.nist.gov/staff/Singhal/qop2008_DBN_paper.pdf (accessed on June 2009)
2. Ammann, P., Wijesekera, D., Kaushik, S.: Scalable, graph-based network vulnerability analysis. In: Proceedings of CCS 2002: 9th ACM Conference on Computer and Communications Security, pp. 217–224. ACM Press, New York (2002)
3. Gutjahr, W.J.: Aco algorithms with guaranteed convergence to the optimal solution. Information Processing Letters 82(3), 145–153 (2002)
4. Maniezzo, V., Gambardella, L.M., Luigi, F.D.: Ant colony optimization (2004), http://citeseer.ist.psu.edu/644427.html;http://www.idsia.ch/~luca/aco2004.pdf
5. Mell, P., Scarfone, K., Romanosky, S.: Common vulnerability scoring system. IEEE Security & Privacy Magazine 4(6), 85–89 (2006)
6. Noel, S., Jajodia, S., O'Berry, B., Jacobs, M.: Efficient minimum-cost network hardening via exploit dependency graph. In: Omondi, A.R., Sedukhin, S.G. (eds.) ACSAC 2003. LNCS, vol. 2823. Springer, Heidelberg (2003)
7. Pamula, J., Jajodia, S., Ammann, P., Swarup, V.: A weakest-adversary security metric for network configuration secuirty analysis. In: Proceedings of 2nd ACM Workshop on Quality of Protection, pp. 31–38. ACM Press, New York (2006)
8. Ritchey, R., O'Berry, B., Noel, S.: Representing tcp/ip connectivity for topological analysis of network security. In: Proceedings of the 18th Annual Computer Security Applications Conference, ACSAC 2002 (2002)
9. Ritchey, R.W., Ammann, P.: Using model checking to analyze network vulnerabilities. In: Proceedings of the 2000 IEEE Symposium on Security and Privacy, May 2000, pp. 156–165 (2000)
10. Sheynar, O.: Scenario Graphs and Attack Graphs. PhD thesis, Carnegei Mellon University, USA (April 2004)
11. Stutzle, T., Dorigo, M.: A short convergence proof for a class of ant colony optimization algorithms. IEEE Transactions on Evolutionary Computation 2002, 358–365 (2002)

Author Index

Acharya, H.B.   184
Adimadhyam, Sandeep   497
Ammari, Habib M.   92
Aneja, Y.P.   392

Bandyopadhyay, Anup Kumar   466
Bandyopadhyay, Subir   116, 392
Banerjee, Prith   1
Banerjee, Satyajit   341
Bansal, Piyush   79
Bari, Ataul   116, 392
Bellur, Umesh   485
Bernard, Samuel   167
Bhandari, Vartika   6
Bhattacharyya, Dhruba Kumar   353
Bhattacherjee, Souvik   231
Bhaumik, Partha   404
Biswas, Subir   128
Borran, Fatemeh   67

Cangussu, João   18
Cao, Jiannong   420
Cera, Márcia C.   242
Chen, Canfeng   420
Chen, Ying   116
Choudhary, Ashish   42
Chowdhury, Atish Datta   341
Cobb, Jorge A.   30

Dantu, Ram   18
Das, Abhijit   231
Das, Sajal K.   92
Derbel, Bilel   155
Devismes, Stéphane   167
Dey, Palash   376
Dhar, Subhankar   283
Dubey, Abhishek Kumar   219
Dutta, Aveek   271

Fathy, Mahmood   365

Ganguly, Niloy   219
Geetha, V.   258
Georgiou, Yiannis   242
Ghose, Sujoy   219

Ghosh, Nirnay   509
Ghosh, S.K.   509
Ghosh, Subhas Kumar   341
Gopal, Prasant   79
Gouda, M.G.   184
Grunwald, Dirk   271
Gu, Yi   142
Gupta, Anuj   54, 79
Gupta, Manish   4

Hans, Sandeep   54

Jaekel, Arunita   116, 392
Jamadagni, H.S.   104
Jana, Prasanta K.   459
Jhunjhunwala, Ashok   5

Kasiviswanathan, Shiva   295
Kiss Iakab, Kinga   446
Kumar, Nagendra   459
Kumar, Rajeev   459
Kundu, Arkadeep   376

Lai, Yi   420
Locher, Thomas   195

Ma, Jian   420
Maillard, Nicolas   242
Mallick, Dheeresh K.   459
Mandal, Swarup   404
Manjunath, D.   434
Mitra, Bivas   219
Momeni, Ladan   365
Mukherjee, Amitava   376
Mysicka, David   195

Nanda, Saurav   509
Nandi, Subrata   207
Nasipuri, Asis   497
Nasipuri, Mita   376
Naskar, Mrinal K.   376
Navaux, Philippe O.A.   242

Pal, Ajit   207
Pal, Amitangshu   497

Pandu Rangan, C.   42, 54
Paroux, Katy   167
Patidar, Mahak   485
Patra, Arpita   42
Paul, Himadri Sekhar   265
Paul, Suman   207
Phithakkitnukoon, Santi   18
Poojary, Sudheer   434
Potop-Butucaru, Maria   167
Prabhakar, T.V.   104

Raghavan, Prabhakar   2
Raghavendra, Ramya   434
Rahman, Q.   392
Ramachandran, Umakishore   323
Rao, Jayanthi   128
Ray, Swapan Kumar   473
Raychoudhury, Vaskar   420
Rezazadeh, Arshin   365
Richard, Olivier   242
Rieck, Michael Q.   283

Sadhukhan, Samir K.   404
Saha, Debashis   307, 404
Saha, Dola   271
Sahni, Sartaj   3
Sahu, Amar   104
Sardar, Bhaskar   307
Sarmah, Sauravjyoti   353

Schiper, André   67
Schmid, Stefan   195
Shannigrahi, Susmit   473
Sicker, Douglas   271
Singh, Awadhesh Kumar   178, 466
Sircar, Ansuman   307
Sreenath, Niladhuri   258
Srinathan, Kannan   54, 79
Sroufe, Paul   18
Storm, Christian   446
Swaroop, Abhishek   178

Talbi, El-Ghazali   155
Theel, Oliver   446
Tixeuil, Sébastien   167

Urgaonkar, Bhuvan   295

Vaidya, Nitin H.   6
Vasudevan, Sudarshan   295
Venkatesha Prasad, R.   104

Wattenhofer, Roger   195
Wu, Qishi   142
Wu, Weigang   420

Yusuf, Lateef   323

Zhao, Bo   295